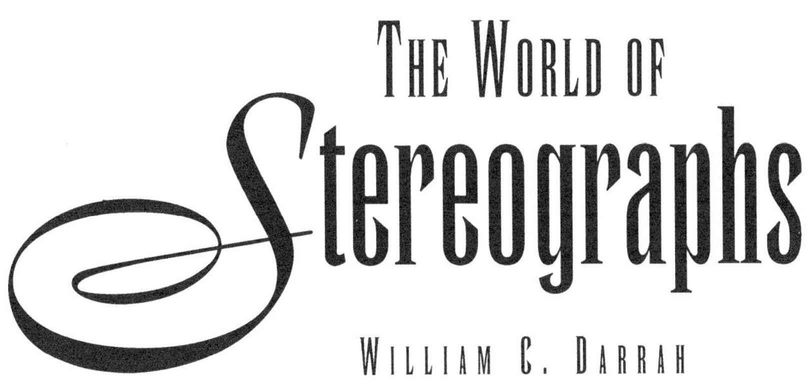

Land Yacht Press
Nashville

Published by
Land Yacht Press
Nashville, Tennessee

Copyright © 1997 the Heirs of William C. Darrah
All Rights Reserved.

Copyright © 1977 William C. Darrah

No part of this book may be reproduced or used in any form by any means, electronic or mechanical, including photocopying and recording, without the express written permission of the copyright owner and the publisher.

Printed on acid-free paper in the United States of America
Reprint edition published July 1997

Cover design: Go Design, LLC
Cover Photograph: © Karina McDaniel
Text: *Caledonia* typeface

Illustrations in the original 1977 edition copied from stereographs in the
William C. Darrah Collection
and other photographic work by Joseph H. Dubbs

ISBN 0-9650513-1-5

Land Yacht Press is an imprint of the
Richiuso Publishing Group

Publisher's note: The stereographs reproduced on pages 27 through 42 were originally reproduced in color in the original edition. In order to keep the price of the present edition as low as possible these stereographs have been reproduced in black and white.

To order multiple copies of *The World of Stereographs* write or fax:

Land Yacht Press
P.O. Box 210262
Nashville, TN 37221-0262
FAX: 615-646-2086

TO HELEN

PREFACE TO THE NEW EDITION

I'm delighted that this book, Darrah's second and definitive work on stereophotography is available again; for years it was the standard reference and now can continue to be so. Indeed, Darrah's books were one of two factors that led to the resurgence of interest in stereophotography during the sixties and seventies. The second factor? In 1974 Rick Russack was considering forming a club of stereoview collectors to be called *The National Stereoscopic Association.* We met to discuss the matter; the main question was whether there were enough interested people in the country to justify such a society. Russack had a mailing list of about 150, and we reacted skeptically to Darrah's guess that there might be twice or three times that number. With this encouragement Russack plunged ahead; he invited Darrah to be an officer of the organization but he declined since he was already hard at work on his second volume. Certainly this combination of a solid reference book and a national organization with a fine magazine combined to spark new interest in an old branch of photography.

Those familiar with the field are already aware of this book's few shortcomings. Most troubling for purists, perhaps, Darrah regarded photographs as historical documents, not as works of art, so you must look elsewhere for pretentious pontifications on aesthetics, or the hidden meanings in an image. Second, being practically blind in one eye he couldn't really see in stereo, and therefore didn't have full appreciation of the depth factor. Finally, and to my mind the only serious flaw, he cut off his history of stereography with the end of production of card-mounted views, so the later formats such as Viewmaster are not covered. But even given these few faults, it remains the place where one starts when dealing with stereoscopic photography.

Begun in 1966, this book finally appeared a decade later, long delayed as Darrah continued to expand it and search out new information. There's been a good bit of research done on photography during the last twenty years, and it's really remarkable that the great majority of Darrah's data and opinions have stood the test of time. This book is still a tribute to the energy and thoroughness of a scholarly man, all the more impressive since it was created entirely by hand, without the aid of computers and word processors. I'm sure that a new generation of readers will find it as useful and enjoyable as I did when I first opened it.

T. K. Treadwell
Past-President, National Stereoscopic Association

PREFACE

This book is a survey of and guide to stereographs which were popular from 1851 to 1935. The illustrations have been selected to supplement the narrative, not to produce a picture book.

I have considered stereographs from four points of view: historical, geographical, topical, and by the photographers who produced them. *The World of Stereographs* has been written primarily for collectors and curators. Were it not for them, stereographs would still be the neglected step-child of photographic history. At the same time I have tried to summarize information gathered over thirty-five years to present sufficient background to be helpful to historians of photography and, hopefully, to share my enjoyment of stereo views more generally.

I have wrestled with two dilemmas that cannot be solved satisfactorily. The first involves documentation. Ideally every statement should be so annotated that an interested reader can verify it for himself. I have specifically cited nearly 5000 stereographs, more than 4000 photographers and referred to 1200 specific series of views. Footnotes are given for only a few comments. To document every comment would require several thousand footnotes—an utterly impractical situation. To provide some assistance to scholars, however, I am fully annotating two copies, one to be deposited in the library of the International Museum of Photography at George Eastman House, and the other in the library of the American Stereoscopic Association.

The other dilemma concerns the selection of photographers mentioned in the book. Barely half of those known to me are included. Certainly many of those who have not been cited are more deserving than some who are mentioned. The checklists had to be kept to workable size and I wished to suggest the broadest feasible geographic distribution. Thus the selection boils down to personal choice and prejudice.

I have avoided criticism of specific stereographs as works of art, primarily because I have disciplined myself to accept each image in terms of the purpose for which it was originally intended. If the photographer achieved what he set out to do, credit is properly due him. If one adopts such an attitude, the conflicting philosophies of photography as an art, which have plagued photography since its inception, have minimal relevance to the vast majority of stereographs.

General information about collecting stereographs has not been included in this book. Readers interested in beginning a collection are referred to my STEREO VIEWS: A HISTORY OF STEREOGRAPHS IN AMERICA AND THEIR COLLECTION (1964) and two useful recent books, COLLECTOR'S GUIDE TO NINETEENTH CENTURY PHOTOGRAPHS by William Welling (1976) and COLLECTING PHOTOGRAPHICA by George Gilbert (1976).

This project would have been impossible without the help of many friends and institutions. During the early stages of my collecting and research Roy Mabie, Dr. G. L. Howe and Mrs. Lorraine Dexter set me on the right path, an appreciation for the dual attributes of stereographs, beauty and history. Over many years Frederick C. Lightfoot and Earl Moore have generously shared their knowledge and experience. In more recent years T. K. Treadwell, Mason Philip Smith, Ronald and Vivian Lowden, Richard Russack, Mrs. Janet Lehr and Russell Norton have been similarly helpful.

Many librarians have rendered assistance but none more frequently and graciously than Miss Anna Jane Moyer of the Gettysburg College Library.

Special thanks are due to Tom and Elinor Burnside (Daguerrean Era, Pawlet, Vermont). Without even telling me in advance, they shipped their personal file of *Photographic News* (1859-1873), "for as long as needed," to spare me hundreds of hours reading microfilm. Their thoughtfulness has brightened life's way.

Miss Ann Harnsberger has assisted with editing the narrative. The Times and News Publishing Company has again catered to whims but tempered them with valued counsel. The colophon at the end of this book more fully expresses my appreciation to the staff.

Above all others, my wife, Helen Hilsman Darrah has had a loving hand in my books. For a life-time she has encouraged my researches and served unselfishly as collaborator and critic.

William C. Darrah

Gettysburg, Pennsylvania
June, 1977

TABLE OF CONTENTS

CHAPTER ONE

EARLY HISTORY OF STEREOGRAPHS

The stereograph, also known as the stereogram and commonly simply as a stereo view, is a double photograph or printed image paired in such a manner that, when viewed with a stereoscope, it appears as a three-dimensional or solid image. It was conceived in the infant years of photography and perfected between 1850 and 1854.

The art of photography dates from the discoveries of Niepce, Daguerre and Talbot between 1826 and 1837 and publication of methods by Daguerre, Bayard and Talbot in 1839. Two very different processes were involved, photosensitized metal and photosensitized paper. The method of Niepce and Daguerre gained immediate success and overshadowed, for a time, those of Hippolyte Bayard and Fox Talbot.

The daguerreotype process records a photographic image on a sensitized silver-plated sheet of copper. At first the exposure time to record an image was very slow, but the use of bromine fuming shortened the time considerably. The method, especially suited to portraiture, became enormously popular and practitioners plied their skill in many parts of the world.

The daguerreotype had two inherent limitations: (1) each picture was unique, i.e., one of a kind, although copies could, of course, be made; (2) the lustrous surface reflected light so that viewing was sometimes difficult. Despite these limitations, the minute detail recorded by the daguerreotype could be examined with a magnifying glass. Viewers amused themselves identifying features not visible to the unaided eye. The earliest stereographs were daguerreotypes. Many were produced experimentally during the later 1840's and commercially in the 1850's.

Simultaneously and independently, Bayard and Talbot photographed with sensitized paper. A paper negative could be used to produce multiple positive copies. Bayard called his prints "calotypes," while in England paper prints were usually designated "talbotypes." Removal of all traces of residual chemicals from the paper required skill and patience. Incomplete "fixing" and removal of salts resulted in gradual fading, a problem that plagued many photographers. Nevertheless, some surviving calotypes are among the finest photographic images ever produced.

Many attempts were made to photosensitize the surfaces of other materials, including glass, porcelain, stone, iron, zinc and wood. Practical methods were developed successfully for each of these materials, and all of them found applications in the printing and illustrating trades.

Glass proved to have special advantages in photography. It was transparent, non-porous and could be coated evenly with a vehicle to hold the sensitive chemical salts. Egg albumen and gelatin were the earliest coating materials. Later, collodion (a solution of nitrocellulose in a mixture of ether and alcohol) provided a more reliable coating to receive the light-sensitive chemicals.

By 1851, barely twelve years after the introduction of photography, there were three major ways by which images could be produced: daguerreotype, calotype and glass-collodion. Both calotype and collodion permitted printing multiple copies. The positive print required a very high quality linen paper showing no grain or watermark. Positives on glass enjoyed popularity until the early 1870's.

There were two principal processing methods for finishing paper prints, salt and albumen. The true calotype was a positive print from a paper negative, being printed on paper prepared with common salt. The result was a beautiful soft texture seldom achieved by any other process. Not all salt prints are true calotypes, however. Many were printed from glass negatives coated with either albumen or collodion and thus show sharper definition even though the print surface is similar.

The collodion process, invented and announced by Scott Archer in 1851, involved wet collodion on glass. The negative image was sharp, with precise rendition of fine detail. Combined with albumenized paper, invented by Louis-Desiré Blanquart-Evrard, the glossy albumen positive print dominated photography until 1890. The development of stereography falls largely within this period.

Both the salt print and the albumen print involved "printing out" by exposure to direct light (sunlight or artificial) until the desired intensity and contrast of the image were obtained. At this point the image was "fixed" by pyrogallic acid or hyposulfite.

The process of "developing" a latent image by chemical agents independent of light, although already known in the 1840's, did not come into general use until the perfection of bromide papers in the early 1880's.

During the decade between 1851 and 1862 photographers were exploring and exploiting daguerreotypy, which declined rapidly after 1856, paper and waxed paper negatives, which were seldom used after 1857, and a wide range of methods for toning albumen prints from collodion negatives.

Briefly, 1854-1860, the ambrotype, variously called glass daguerreotype and glass-collodion positive, flourished as a cheap competitor of the daguerreotype. The negative was treated with mercuric chloride (which whitened the image) and then mounted in front of a black surface. The image thus appeared as a positive. A few stereo ambrotypes were produced.

Some historians of photography draw a distinction between daguerreotypy and photography, restricting the latter term to processes that are used to produce multiple copies from a single negative. Inasmuch as ideas and experiences were exchanged freely in continuing experimentation in all aspects of heliography, no such distinction seems warranted.

The evolving technology for transforming fleeting moments into permanent records enabled the photographer to reach a vast viewing audience and exert a profound influence upon society. The stereograph, although but one type of photograph, was the first visual mass medium.

An essential ingredient in the success of the stereograph was the availability of viewing instruments. In 1850 Sir William Brewster invented the lenticular stereoscope. Some years earlier (1838) Charles Wheatstone, in conjunction with studies on bifocal human vision had devised a reflecting stereoscope, but this was an experimental laboratory instrument unsuited for viewing a photograph. Even so, several photographers exhibited large stereoscopic pictures with the Wheatstone apparatus.

tracted the particular attention of the Queen, and before the closing of the Crystal Palace, executed a beautiful stereoscope, which I presented to Her Majesty, in his name. In consequence of this public exhibition of the instrument, M. Dubosq received several orders from England, and a large number of stereoscopes were thus introduced to this country. The demand, however, became so great, that opticians of all kinds devoted themselves to the manufacture of the instrument, and photographers both in Daguerreotype and Talbotype, found it a most lucrative branch of their profession to take binocular portraits of views to be thrown into relief by the stereoscope."

Dubosq recognized the viewing limitations of the stereo-daguerreotype and proposed modification of the

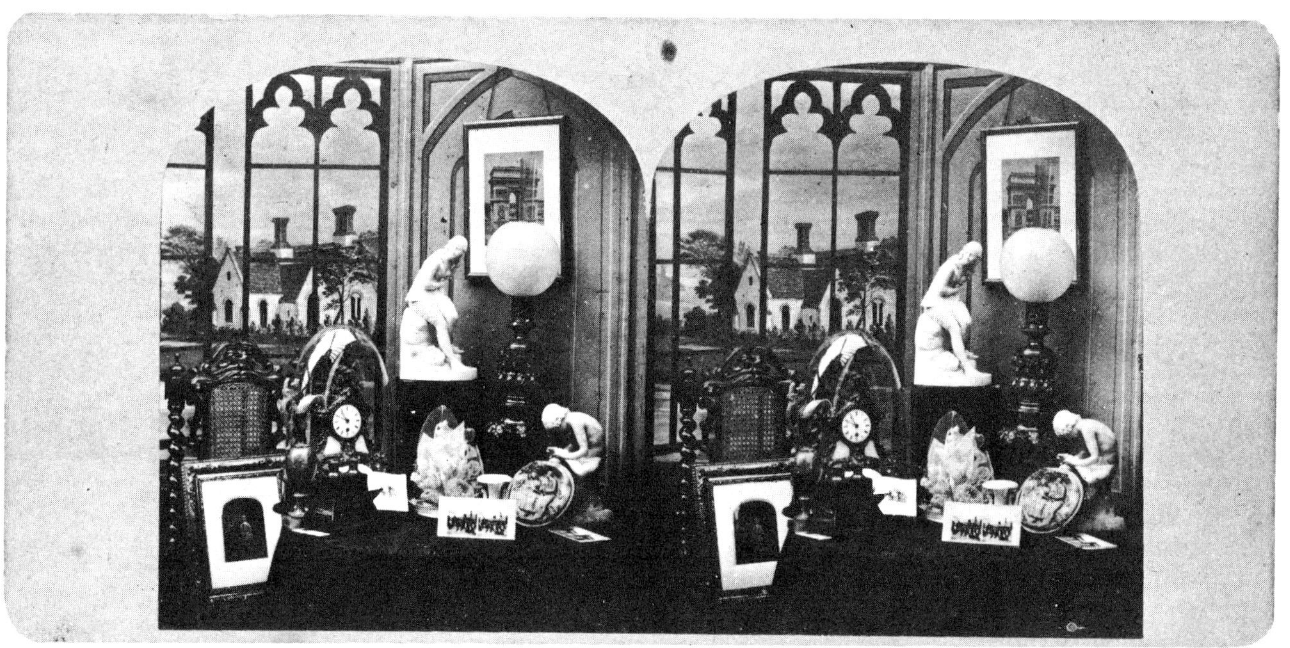

1. "Artistic Arrangement." Note Brewster stereoscope and various photographs placed to show the capabilities of the camera. The background window with a manorial building is a painted studio prop. English, 1856.

Brewster solved the viewing problem by using a closed box that could be opened on one or two sides to admit light. Two adjustable lenses, placed on the top, permitted the viewer to look at a daguerreotype resting on the floor of the box. Light entering from the sides was sufficient to illuminate the picture. Brewster took a model instrument, constructed by Louden of Dundee, Scotland, to Paris, where Jules Dubosq began to manufacture beautiful lenticular stereoscopes for sale. Brewster's own words relate the story (*The Stereoscope*, 1870, p. 31):

> "While the lenticular stereoscope was thus exciting much interest in Paris, not a single instrument had been made in London, and it was not till a year after its introduction into France that it was exhibited in England. In the fine collection of philosophical instruments which M. Dubosq contributed to the Great Exhibition of 1851 . . . he placed a lenticular stereoscope with a beautiful set of binocular Daguerreotypes. The instrument at-

stereoscope to accommodate translucent paper and glass positive images. Accordingly, a ground glass base was provided so that the viewer could hold the instrument toward the souce of light. The Brewster type stereoscope monopolized the British market until 1875.[1]

The invention of the familiar hand stereoscope is attributed to Oliver Wendell Holmes, medical doctor, Harvard professor, poet and essayist. In 1859 his friend and fellow Bostonian, Joseph L. Bates, constructed several instruments and about a year later improved the design by adding a sliding card holder and a hood to shield the eyes from extraneous light. The Holmes stereoscope not only met with immediate enthusiastic success but it shifted the center of stereo activity to America, where it remained unchallenged for eighty years. Holmes did not

[1] For an excellent comparison of types of stereoscopes 1850-1930, see the colored plate in Jones, John, *Wonders of the Stereoscope*, pp. 22-23, 1976, Alfred A. Knopf.

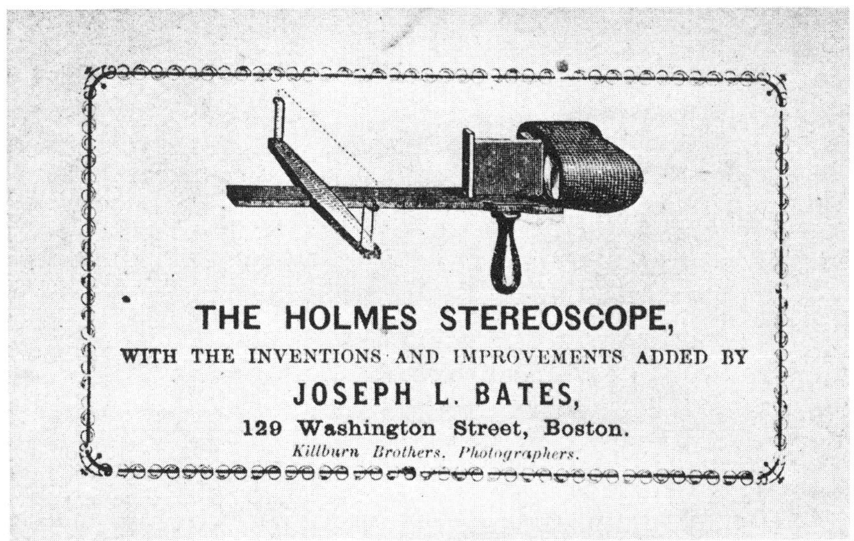

2. The famous Holmes-Bates stereoscope logo used by several New England stereo publishers. This is one of the Kilburn Brothers formats. 1866.

apply for a patent, and within a few months similar instruments were being made by many opticians throughout eastern United States.

Another line of development involved the cameras employed in taking negatives for stereoscopic photographs: At first, the photographer simply made two exposures, moving his camera to a new position for the second exposure. The same result could be obtained by carefully positioning two cameras. Photographers experimented with angles and distances. Professional periodicals carried lively debates on the "ideal" angle and the ability to exaggerate the illusion of depth ("hyperspace"). Many stereographs printed from negatives taken with a single camera show the intrusion of a horse and wagon or a shift in the positions of people on one of the paired prints.

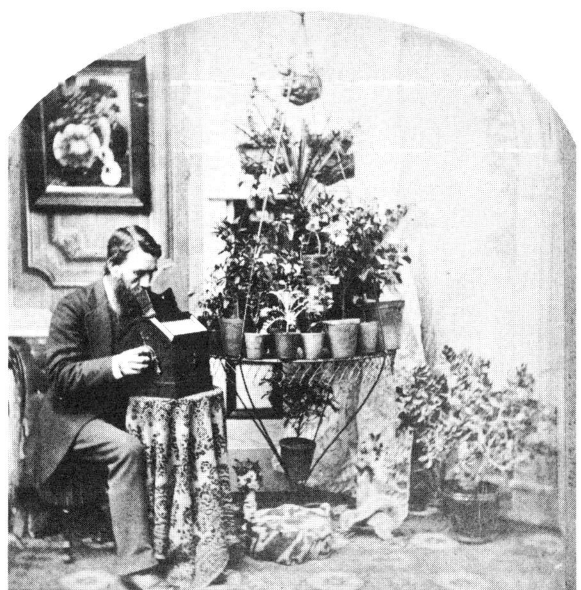

3. Alexander Beckers' revolving stereoscope (patented April, 1857), constructed to hold 100 or 200 views on an endless belt. The model shown is ca. 1865. J.A. French photo 1868.

Stereoscopic cameras were manufactured commercially in 1854, but individual models had been constructed before 1850. Disderi's famous four-lens cameras (ca. 1860) were designed to take simultaneously, two stereoscopic pairs or four single carte-de-visite negatives. A repeating back enabled the photographer to take four stereo pairs or eight singles before reloading the camera.

With versatile cameras, varied glass and paper images and convenient viewing instruments, all of the appurtenances for producing and enjoying stereographs were at hand.

We must not overlook the human factors that go into the making of a "photograph." To do so would miss the whole spirit of photography. The technology involves materials, processes, instruments and machines. The camera by itself does not take the picture. Only in the hands or control of an operator can it perform that which it has been set to do. The subject, lighting and focus are choices made by the photographer according to his personal skill. These technical details are only the beginning of his eventual contribution. Indeed, the motives, feelings, artistry and ingenuity—whether romantic or naturalistic—expressed through his total craftsmanship can be appreciated only by a careful examination of his finished work.

Stereographs thus provide a virtually inexhaustible reservoir of information concerning the life and times of yesteryear through the eyes of its cameramen.

Paper stereographs, usually called card views, were commercially produced before 1853, and by that year brisk international trade had begun. Shops in London, Paris, Rome, and in many other cities catered to tourist as well as local demand.

The London Stereoscopic Company was organized in 1854 by George Swann Nottage. Through mass production and highly organized merchandising methods, the company quickly became prominent. Within two years, half a million Brewster stereoscopes had been sold (the Company boasted "A stereoscope for every home") and

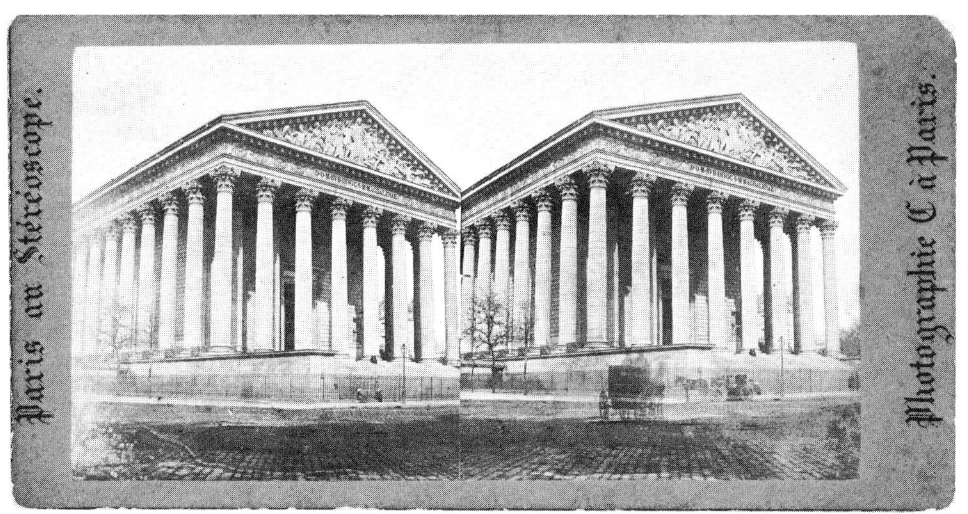

4. Stereograph made from two negatives. Note the "ghosts" of two carriages that have moved into view. Ste. Madeleine, Paris. Negative ca. 1856.

there was a trade-list of more than 10,000 different stereographs. By 1858 the trade list had increased to more than 100,000 titles.

The two most important competitors of the London Stereoscopic Company during the mid-1850's were Negretti & Zambra and Gladwell's City Stereoscopic Depot. Hundreds of shops of many kinds in the cities of Europe were retailing stereo views. There were even lending shops that rented stereoscopes and views "in great variety for the day or evening" at moderate cost. John C. May, Aylesbury Photographic Establishment, advertised his service extensively (1855-56).

Brewster stereoscopes and European stereographs, purchased by American tourists in London, Paris and Rome, began to appear in the parlors and libraries of their mansions in Boston and New York.

No later than 1852, probably earlier, D. Appleton Company of New York offered for sale a variety of European views, and a short time later Langenheim offered Negretti and Zambra card views for sale in Philadelphia. Brewster stereoscopes were prominently displayed in the shops of optical instrument dealers in the larger American cities from 1853 until the introduction of the Holmes stereoscope. Many of these were manufactured in the United States.

By 1860 every country in the world touched by Western culture had its own stereo photographers (hereafter called stereographers) or had been visited by energetic practitioners, amateur and professional.

The ensuing popularity of stereographs and the demand for low-priced views led many photographers and profit-seeking publishers, especially in England, to pro-

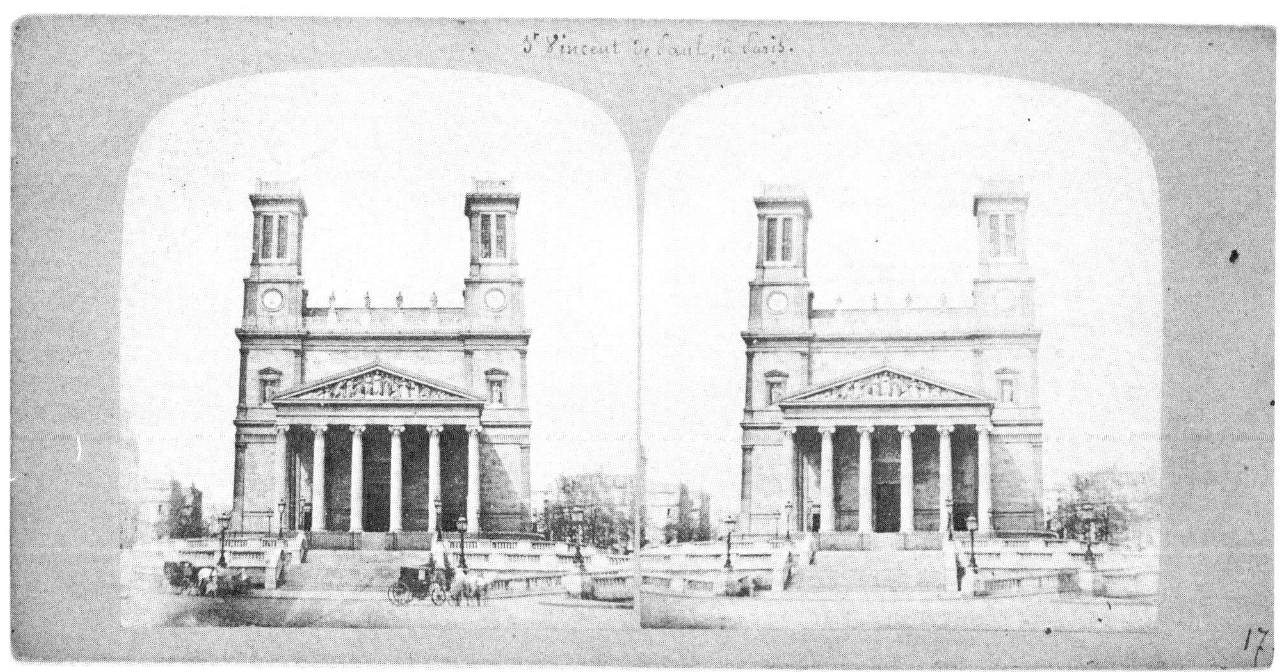

5. Stereograph made from two negatives. Note parked carriage in left image. Paris 1857.

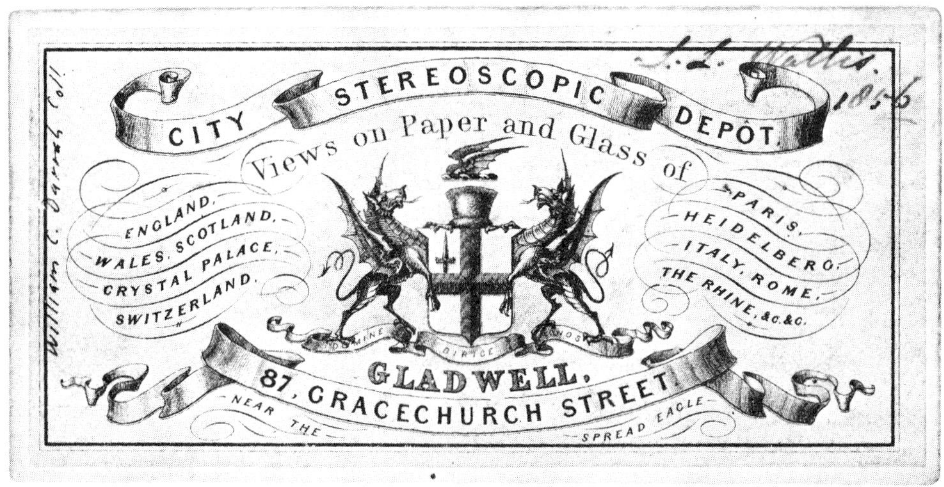

6. Imprint of Gladwell's City Stereoscopic Depot, London (1854-1858). Note that no American views were available. See also Figure 87.

duce trivial and vulgar views. More and more photographers critized the poor taste reflected by the kinds of views being sold and expressed disgust for stereography.

These criticisms had little influence on the overall output of publishing companies, many of which continued to produce fine views, largely for export, well into the 1870's.

In France, Germany and the United States professional disdain did not impede development of the stereograph. While a much smaller proportion of photographers worked with stereo in France and particularly in Germany than in England, a majority of the first-rate American photographers applied their skills to the stereograph, even though many of them did not develop a commercial line of these views.

Oliver Wendell Holmes did much more to encourage interest in stereographs than invent a hand viewer. In two essays published in *Atlantic Monthly*, "The Stereoscope and Stereograph" (June, 1859) and "Sun Painting and Sun Sculpture" (May, 1861), Holmes wrote enthusiastically about them. He coined the term "stereograph," proposed the creation of stereographic libraries, and called attention to their educational possibilities.

The name stereograph was immediately adopted in the United States, although many photographers preferred to call them stereoscopic views. In Great Britain all of the major publishers, including London Stereoscopic Company, Wilson, Bedford and William England accepted stereograph. Historically, there is little basis for the term stereogram because, prior to 1860, photography was commonly called "sun writing" or "heliography." However we may wish to name them, Holmes was eloquent:

> "The stereograph . . . is to be the card of introduction to make all mankind acquaintances."

Again,

> "Of infinite volumes of poems that I treasure in this small library of glass and pasteboard . . . "

And finally,

> "The time will come when a man wishes to see any object natural or artificial, he will go to the Imperial, National, or City Stereographic Library."

Not all writers shared Holmes' enthusiasm for stereo photography. Charles Dickens declared:

> "The application of photography to the stereoscope produces an extremely pretty toy that is of no use except as an elegant and valuable illustration of a train of scientific reasoning."

Dickens' verdict, like Holmes' prediction, was mistaken. Only now has the lapse of time provided the perspective of history which gives new meaning to the cameramen's records. Continuing that history, modern technology, combining electronics with photography has proliferated three or four instruments into a thousand. Images compete with words for the mind of man.

CHAPTER TWO

THE DIVERSITY OF STEREOGRAPHS

THE PHOTOGRAPHER AND HIS BUSINESS

Almost from the outset, stereography was a publishing business, selling photographic images. This cannot be over-emphasized. Negatives were bought, resold, multiplied, copied legitimately and pirated illegitimately. Many of the most famous photographers purchased negatives and advertised them as their own. The indispensable work of assistants was seldom properly credited.

A person desiring to become a photographer during the period 1855-1890, much as today, had three options: to attend classes for formal instruction, to take employment as an assistant to an established photographer, or to teach himself through published manuals and trial and error. Great photographers emerged from each approach, but the second alternative, learning from an experienced operator, was the most frequent.

Between 1850 and 1860 for an investment of only forty or fifty dollars, an individual could obtain ten lessons, a camera, and materials sufficient to make two dozen daguerreotypes or glass negatives. The expectation of quick financial reward lured many persons of limited abilities to take up photography as a profession.

A few examples will demonstrate common patterns for gaining experience. William Henry Jackson began as a colorist in the studio of A. S. Holmes, Troy, New York, and as an assistant to A. F. Styles of Rutland, Vermont. John A. Mather, in the late 1850's, earned five dollars a week to assist an itinerant photographer traveling through West Virginia, Ohio, and western Pennsylvania. William H. Tipton, at the age of twelve, went to work for the Tyson Brothers of Gettysburg, Pennsylvania, and subsequently purchased the establishment, which he operated for fifty years.

Practical experience came through another direct approach. Wives learned the trade from their husbands, sons and daughters from their fathers, and brothers from brothers. Some establishments like those of Levi Mumper (Gettysburg), H. H. Bennett (Kilbourn City) and David Bachrach (Baltimore) continued in the family for several generations.

Most photographers experimented with every aspect of photography and advertised expertise in several branches: daguerreotype, ambrotype and paper photograph; portrait and landscape; stereoscopic views and cartes de visite; enlarging and copying; indoor and outdoor work. Although a few photographers became successful as specialists in one or two types, the large majority depended upon diversification for their incomes. As in any business, the problems of earning a living transcended all other considerations. Few photographers could afford to ignore public taste or popular demand.

THE NUMBERS OF STEREOGRAPHERS

Compilation of a complete check list of photographers who produced stereographs will probably never be achieved. Over a period of thirty years I have indexed 6150 American and Canadian stereographers, derived entirely from actual examination of their card views. Yet, this list is far from complete, probably representing between 50% and 60%. How complete can be estimated by comparing the numbers of photographers who produced both cartes de visite and stereographs. Since, for all practical purposes, every photographer between 1860 and 1880 made cartes de visite, a large random sampling should provide some fairly reliable data (see Appendix).

A comparison of 3135 American and Canadian carte de visite photographers discloses that only 35.5% of them produced stereo views commercially between 1855 and 1890. If this figure is valid, an inference may be drawn from the numbers of photographers reported by the U. S. Censuses of 1860, 1870 and 1880. The inferred total of stereophotographers would thus approximate 12,000.

My index of non-North American stereographers now includes a few more than 1800 names, more than 80% of whom are from Great Britain, France, Italy, Switzerland and Germany.

THE NUMBER OF STEREOGRAPHS

Any attempt to estimate the total number of different stereo views is little more than educated guesswork. The trade list of a single photographer ranged from a few dozen to many thousands of titles. In *Stereo Views* (1964) the total was estimated to be between three-and-a-half to five million in the United States alone. Now it would appear that the total probably exceeds five million: fifty publishers produced more than 10,000 each, one hundred produced 5,000 views, approximately eight hundred publishers issued 1000 each, at least 2500 produced more than 500 each. No reliable numerical data for the remaining 3000 photographers are available.

Assuming an average trade list of 500 titles for 12,000 stereographers, the total comes to six million, which may be too great but is wholly reasonable.

The number of European stereographs certainly exceeds a million, possibly two million.

Many publishers remained in business for twenty years or more, while others operated for very brief periods.

One example will show the rapid accumulation of a stereo negative file. H. S. Fifield from 1868-1883 operated a summer studio at Lincoln, New Hampshire, near the Flume. With a single background—the poised boulder in the flume—he photographed tourists who wished to have a memento of their visit. Fifield averaged more than a thousand negatives a season for fifteen years, each year beginning a new series starting with negative number one. It is almost impossible now to assemble a long run of Fifield's stereos because each title, essentially personal, was sold in very limited quantity.

Many photographers took two or three hundred negatives a year for ten or fifteen years, gradually building an extensive trade list. Many of the individual titles may have been published in small quantities for brief periods, while other, more appealing subjects might have been "in print" for ten years or more. It was a common practice to reuse a glass plate if the negative proved to be defective, inferior or obsolete. The emulsion and image were simply removed. In consequence, no additional prints could be prepared.

THE MANUFACTURE OF STEREOGRAPHS

Five steps were involved in the manufacture of a card stereograph:

(1) making positive prints from the negative, including washing and drying them (usually overnight);
(2) trimming the prints with a scissors or die;
(3) pasting prints on the card;
(4) drying under gentle pressure;
(5) applying labels and imprints.

The entire operation extended over three days and two nights, although some large establishments were able to speed the process by using drying ovens or warming tables. A single skilled workman could produce 50 to 60 card mounts a day, or up to 350 per week. If the process was carried out, with a division of labor, five operators could produce more than 3,000 per week.

Manufacture of stereo views in quantity involved more working space and labor than most photographers could afford. M. A. Kleckner, with two helpers, made his own views and worked throughout slack winter months to have 20,000 to 30,000 cards ready for the summer tourist trade at Mauch Chunk, Pennsylvania.

To meet the needs of the operators of small studios, there originated a service called "photoprinting," or today, "photofinishing." Although the photoprinter became a key partner in the stereo view trade, he remained virtually anonymous. In many studios only negatives were taken (although the photographer probably made proofs), the photoprinting being done on other premises.

Photoprinting businesses were in existence before 1854. Enterprising individuals advertised such service for amateurs in England and the United States.

By the latter 1860's every large city in the United States had one or more photoprinters. For instance, New York and Philadelphia each had five or more, Boston, four, at least two each in Chicago, Saint Louis, Minneapolis, Cleveland, San Francisco and Washington, D. C. Pittsburgh, Detroit, Rochester and Baltimore had a least one well-patronized establishment. These companies, owned and operated by able photographers, printed huge quantities of cartes de visite, stereo views and larger photographs as desired.

The photoprinter offered a convenient, money-saving service. The photographer could select a suitable card format from a wide variety of styles, colors and qualities. He could order prints untrimmed, trimmed for mounting, mounted with labels, or mounts completely finished with his own imprint and titles printed with type selected from a variety of fonts. (Gummed labels on card mounts were usually applied by the photographer, who either printed them with a small hand press or had them done by a local printer.)

Collectors are sometimes puzzled by the identical or similar mounts and printing styles issued by different photographers. Some have concluded that these represent business combinations organized to promote sales, whereas such card similarities mean nothing more than patronage of the same photoprinter.

The importance of photoprinters will be considered further in connection with mass production of stereo views.

THE PUBLISHER

The issuance of stereographs has always been considered to be *publishing* in the true sense of the word, namely, to bring before the public. As early as 1854 many stereo views bore imprints such as "William Woodward, Photographer and Publisher" or "Philip Delamotte, photographer, published by London Stereoscopic Company." This was general practice until 1900. When the photographer was himself the publisher, marketing was relatively simple. Views were sold at his studio and by agents or outlets, such as opticians' and art shops. Many photographer-publishers were also able to engage in extensive mail order business.

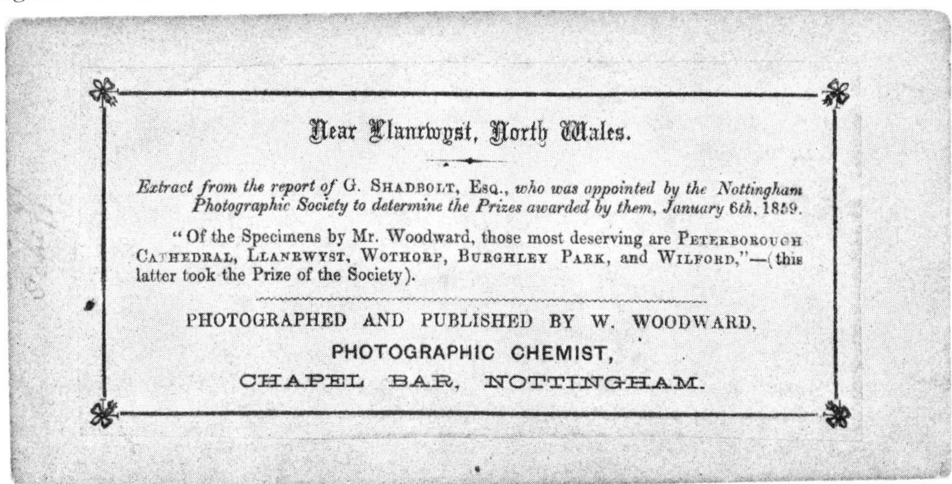

Near Llanrwyst, North Wales.

Extract from the report of G. Shadbolt, Esq., *who was appointed by the Nottingham Photographic Society to determine the Prizes awarded by them, January 6th*, 1859.

"Of the Specimens by Mr. Woodward, those most deserving are Peterborough Cathedral, Llanrwyst, Wothorp, Burghley Park, and Wilford,"—(this latter took the Prize of the Society).

PHOTOGRAPHED AND PUBLISHED BY W. WOODWARD,
PHOTOGRAPHIC CHEMIST,
CHAPEL BAR, NOTTINGHAM.

7. Photographer and publisher imprint. William Woodward. Negative 1858, card issued 1859.

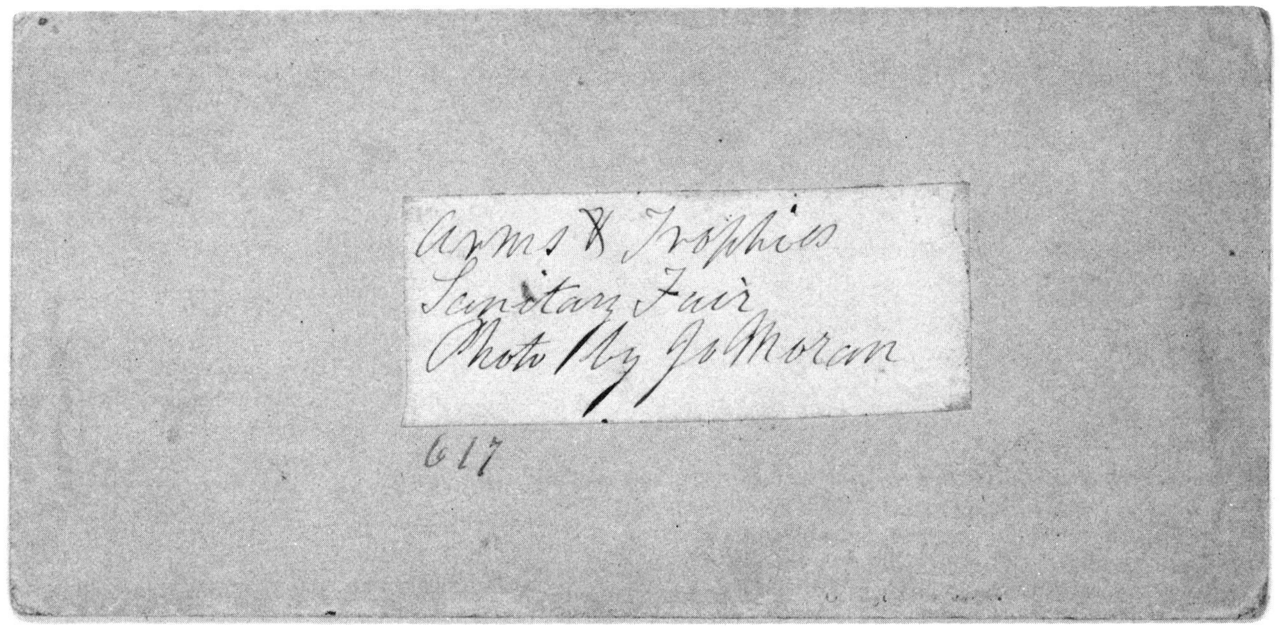

8. A signed autographed label. John Moran, "Arms & Trophies" exhibit, Sanitary Fair, Philadelphia, June, 1864.

Nevertheless, a large share of the stereo trade was carried out by a relatively few publishers like London Stereoscopic Company, Ferrier, J. Andrieu ("JA", Paris) and E. & H. T. Anthony. These companies employed photographers who took thousands of negatives, purchased negatives from many sources, and paid for the use of others. These publishers generally did their own photoprinting, but many publishers contracted for all photoprinting work.

The large publishing houses of stereographs reached their culmination in the period 1902-1935 with the world-wide enterprises of Underwood & Underwood, Keystone View Company and H. C. White Company.

The interrelationships between photographer and publishers were sometimes complicated. Many collectors misunderstand the circumstances that were involved.

Nearly every collector has been confronted with identical stereo images on cards of different publishers. In many cases it is not possible to identify the original issue. Generally this situation arises from the widespread buying and selling negatives, not only the original but often copy-negatives. The simplest case is the "successor."

Upon discontinuing business, due to his retirement, bankruptcy or death, a photographer's file of negatives and all rights pertaining to them usually passed to a new owner. Copyrighted or not, prints could be issued without crediting either the original photographer or previous owner. There are many examples; for instance, C. E. Watkins purchased the Central Pacific Railroad negatives of A. A. Hart. I. W. Taber seized them from Watkins for non-payment of bills. Neither owner credited Hart.

Another difficulty stems from a complicated practice of "shopping around" for additional negatives for the publisher's trade list. Photographic periodicals carried many advertisements seeking good stereo negatives. A publisher might purchase a single choice negative or a series of a hundred. When the cards were issued, the name of the photographer was not given. Prints from the same negative—or, more likely, from copy negatives—might appear under several imprints and formats, with no clue to their common origin.

To make matters worse, there was the slick trick of selling identical copy negatives to several publishers and neglecting to inform each purchaser that he was not securing "sole rights."

The importance of copy negatives, especially to the original photographer for regular production of stereographs, is seldom appreciated. It was a simple procedure to make a sharp positive print on glass and then use this positive as a "negative" to print an unlimited number of additional copy negatives. Nearly all highly-prized or irreplaceable negatives were so handled in printing operations. In fact, this procedure was recommended by editors of photographic periodicals in the 1850's. The great publishers printed entirely from copy negatives.

It was a slight step from the copy negative as a safeguard against damage or loss during production to copying a print without permission. Although dishonest, this was not necessarily illegal. Many views had never been copyrighted, and for many others copyrights had expired. The flood of cheap copy issues in the late 1870's and early 1880's included every type of appropriation of other peoples' work.

We are seldom in possession of the contractual agreements between photographer and publisher or between seller and successor. It is, therefore, impossible to state categorically that a particular copy issue was illegally pirated.

During the period 1875-1890 there were many publishers whose entire production was based on copy negatives made from old stereographs. There were even copies of copies. The cheaper the line, the poorer the quality of the images. Earlier piracies, even among highly reputable photographers and publishers, are often of such

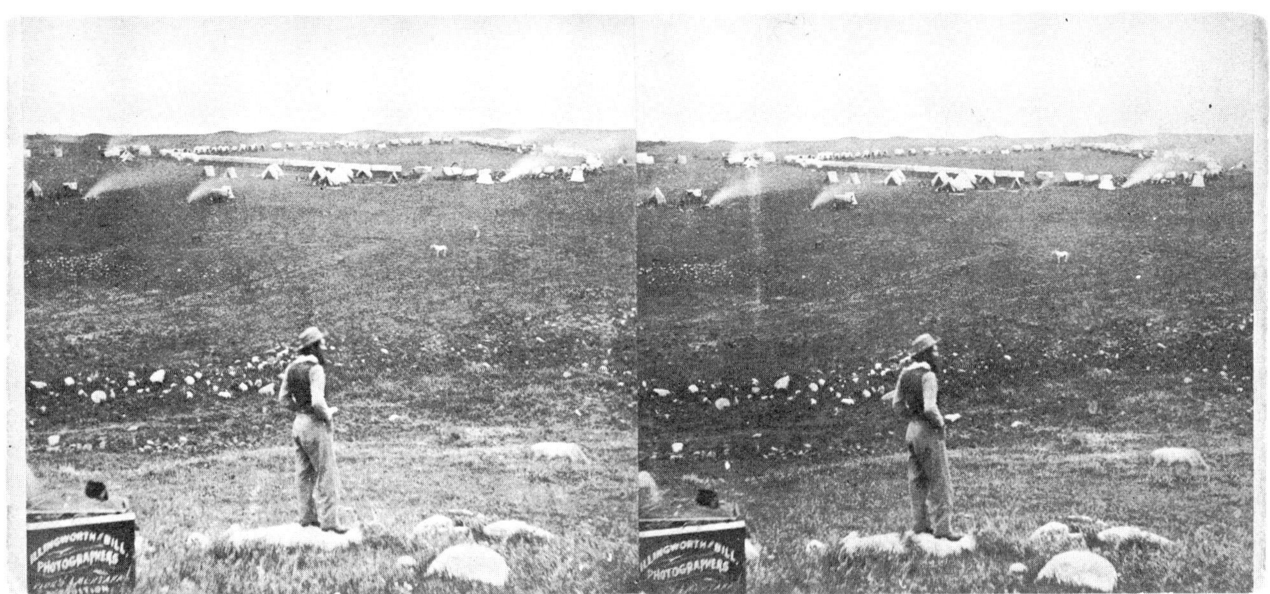

9. Illingworth and Bill, "Corral at South Bend of Cheyenne River." Fisk Expedition, 1866. Carbutt cropped the banner with the photographers' names when he published this series of views in 1866-1867.

excellent quality that one is frustrated by the difficulties in identifying or authenticating the origin of the card or negative.

A succeeding owner often removed all marks that might reveal the identity of the original photographer. This could be done by cropping the print, making a new negative slightly enlarged to avoid the unwanted mark, or by retouching to remove numbers or initials. When Carbutt published a series of views of the Fisk Expedition to Montana (1866), he cropped the banner displaying the names of Illingworth and Bill, the photographers of the expedition.

IDENTIFICATION AND DOCUMENTATION OF STEREOGRAPHS

A novice who has before him an assortment of stereo views may be bewildered by the miscellany: cards of many colors, some flat, others warped; some on thick card stock, others thin; some with labels pasted on them, others with printed or handwritten titles or other information; some mounted photographs, others printed halftone images. What do these varieties mean?

Since stereographs were produced continuously from 1851 to 1940, we can anticipate that there was some chronologic sequence in the types of formats used for mounting the prints. Improved manufacturing methods, new ideas and new fashions resulted in changing formats. In fact, the different formats represent well-defined periods of stereo history. Each has characteristics that serve to identify it with considerable accuracy.

An overview can be appreciated by "keying" the types of views and indicating the periods to which they belong. When keying a card, a series of choices (either/or) must be made until there is no alternate. Begin by comparing the set of number ones; then proceed to the next set of numbers and so on.

Attention is called to the footnotes, which qualify or amplify statements in the keys.

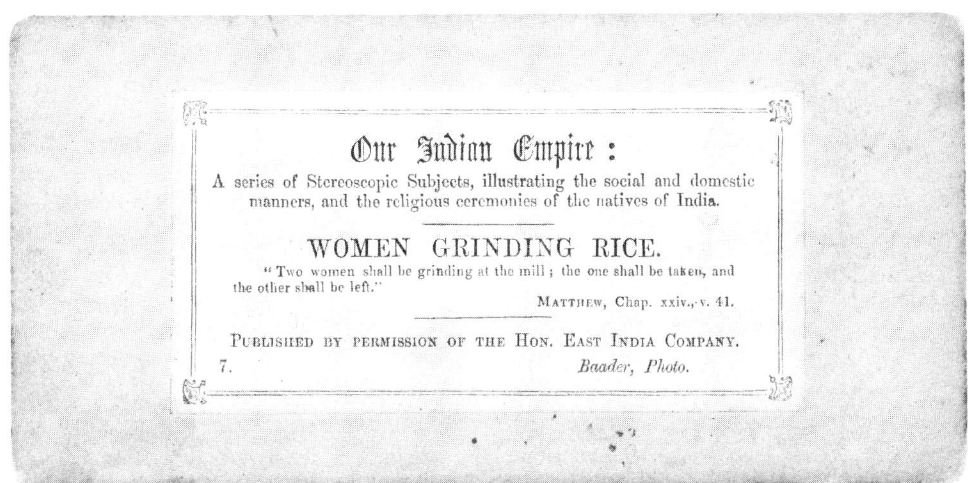

Our Indian Empire :

A series of Stereoscopic Subjects, illustrating the social and domestic manners, and the religious ceremonies of the natives of India.

WOMEN GRINDING RICE.

"Two women shall be grinding at the mill; the one shall be taken, and the other shall be left."

MATTHEW, Chap. xxiv., v. 41.

PUBLISHED BY PERMISSION OF THE HON. EAST INDIA COMPANY.

7. *Baader, Photo.*

10. A well documented view which includes series title, subject title, photographer's name and notation. Negretti & Zambra, publishers. 1859.

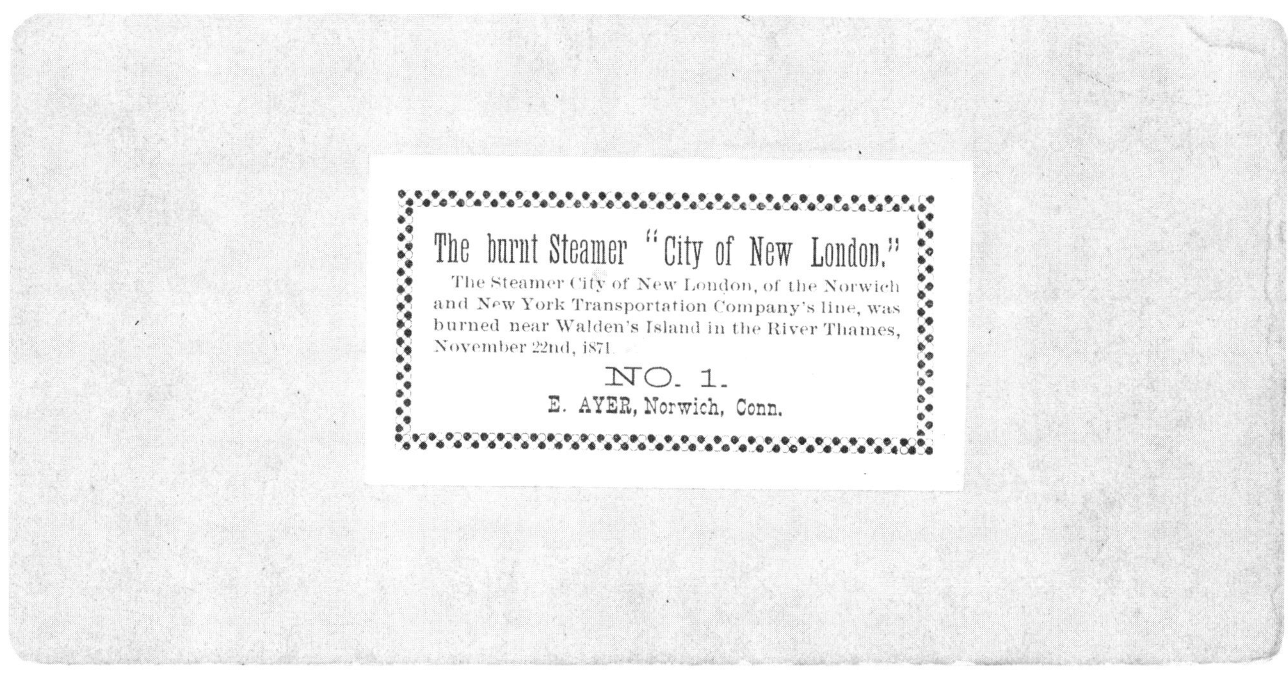

11. A fine example of a documentary view accompanied by detailed information. E. Ayer photo. 1871.

TYPES OF STEREOGRAPHS

1. Images actual photographs
   2. Images on metal
      3. on copper, image rich black *daguerreotype* 1849—60
      3. on iron, image with poor contrast *ferrotype* ("tintype") 1860-75[1]
   2. Images not on metal
      4. on glass
         5. image white, on black background *ambrotype* 1854-1860
         5. transparency, glass mount 1850—75[2]
      4. on paper
         6. mounted on flat cards 1852-90
         6. on curved cards 1879-1940
1. Images printed, not photographs mounted
   7. impression continuous lithograph, offset, etc. 1853-90
   7. impression consisting of small dots "half-tone," 1898-1930

There are several rare formats not included in the above key. Porcelain views (image blue, gray or pink) were produced for a brief period (ca. 1855) by Langenheim Brothers. Since more than 99% of all stereographs are card-mounted or printed on card, a detailed key to them follows.

Small views 4-5 cm x 11-13 cm produced between 1902 and 1938 are not included in the keys.

KEY TO CARD (PAPER) STEREOGRAPHS

1. Images actual photographs mounted
   2. on thin card, of various colors, 1851-58
      3. surface of print not lustrous, salt print, calotype 1851-58
      3. surface lustrous, albumen print 1852-58
   2. on thick card, various colors
      4. card mount flat 1857-90[3]
         5. corners cut square 1857-70[4]
            6. card white, gray or cream 1857-63
            6. card yellow, many shades progressively darker 1861-70
            6. card red, lavender, green or blue 1866-70
         5. corners cut rounded, cards of many colors 1868-90
            7. standard size 1868-90
            7. larger sizes 1873-90[5]
      4. card mount enclosing a thin tissue transparency 1857-80[6]
      4. card mount not flat, "warped" 1879-1940
            8. buff mount 1879-1910, rarely to 1920
            8. gray mount 1892-1940
            8. black mount 1902-1910[7]
   2. unmounted, issued as glossy prints on heavy photographic paper 1898-1935[8]

[1] Ferrotype stereo views only until 1875, for small portraits until 1912, rarely later.

[2] A few standard size glass mounts were produced in 1900. Small sizes approximately 4.5-6.0 cms x 11.5-13.0 cms were produced between 1904 and 1920.

[3] Mostly 1857-1883.

[4] Some square-cornered mounts occur in later issues, especially in larger formats. In Europe to 1900.

[5] Several sizes: 4" x 7", 4½" x 7", 5" x 7" and occasional intermediate sizes.

[6] Mostly 1865-1875, a few produced 1898-1904 in the United States.

[7] Keystone View Co. produced views intended for eye exercises on black mounts between 1928 and 1960 but not for regular issues.

[8] Commercial issues almost exclusively of European manufacture; some amateur views distributed in the United States.

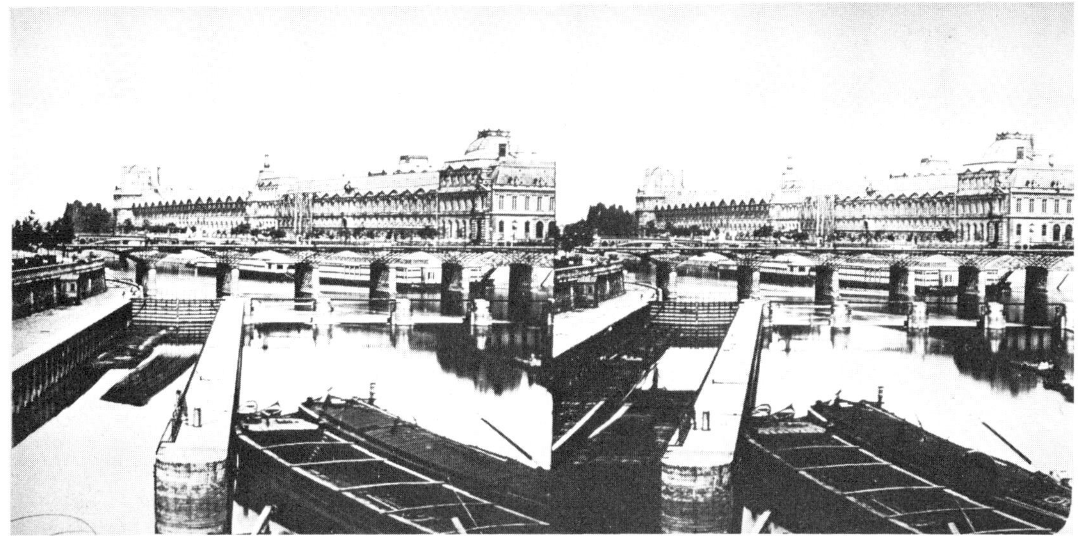

12. Claude-Marie Ferrier. Glass transparency. The Seine River Paris. 1858. C.M. Ferrier was the master of the positive print on glass.

1. Images printed, not actual photographs
   9. printed image more or less continuous
      10. Impression coarse, often color-printed
          xylograph 1853-1859
      10. Impression more or less fine
          lithograph, collotype, etc. 1856-1910[9]
   9. Printed image half-tone, consisting of small dots 1898-1930
      11. monochrome (gray, black, sepia, rarely red or blue)
      11. polychrome, multicolored

The dates indicating the period during which the format was produced must be used with some caution. A photographer with old card stock would use it until the supply was exhausted. A village photographer who produced his own stereos might not own a corner cutter (patented 1868) and, therefore, continue to produce square cornered cards long after the new style was popular. A combination of features, however, would probably reveal the period of manufacture.

The first key is applicable to stereographs of worldwide origin, with a few exceptions. For example, about 1900-1910 a fine series of Japanese cards were issued on large, very thick, black card stock, unlike any other used in the manufacture of stereographs.

The second key is specifically applicable to cards of American origin. In Europe the familiar 1870 type of card remained in use, essentially unchanged until 1900, but by that time a heavy high gloss enamel finish is usual on cards of British and German manufacture. Gilt printing was used in many high quality issues between 1885 and 1900. About 1900 the curved mount popular in America was adopted by several British publishers, no doubt encouraged by the vigorous marketing by agents of American stereo publishers.

[9] Many types and processes, including lithographs on stone, xylographs (wood engravings), photogelatine methods: collotypes, heliotypes, albertypes, etc. Some of the finest albertypes and heliotypes are almost indistinguishable from actual photographs. Early printed stereographs are rare.

TISSUE STEREOGRAPHS

J. L. Tardieu (1853) demonstrated that a positive print on thin translucent paper could be mounted between two glass plates or on a card which had been cut out to make a frame. The image could be tinted and viewed against a source of light as a transparency. The tissue format, with improvements, was available commercially in 1855. The most important addition was a second translucent paper used as a protective backing. A card backing frame was also added.

The outline of the image was traced upon the albuminized surface of the backing tissue and then tinted in blending colors. The two colored sides were pasted together and mounted in the card frame. Various devices were used to heighten the effect. The image paper was sometimes waxed to increase translucency. Such features as candle flames, chandeliers, and windows could be pierced to admit light through one or both papers. Some publishers used sturdy card mounts that were embossed with elaborate frames and vignettes.

Large numbers of tissue stereos were published between 1858 and 1875 and small numbers occasionally thereafter, until 1905. They are commonly called "French tissues." Although the majority were manufactured in France, photographers in other countries also produced them.

The publishers of most French tissues remain unidentified. The views that have an imprint usually bear only initials (JA = J. Andrieu; LL = Leon & Levy; EL = E. Lamy; BK = B. Kuhn; JQ = J. Queval; etc.). The early English photographers who produced tissue views are J. Elliott, Charles Goodman, Philip Delamotte, and William Woodward. Many English tissues bear only the blindstamp or strip labels of the London Stereoscopic Company.

A few tissues were produced in Germany, Italy and the United States. The fine tissue views of Netherlands, Greece, Palestine, Egypt and Russia seem to have been manufactured in France.

The two best-known American series are those by

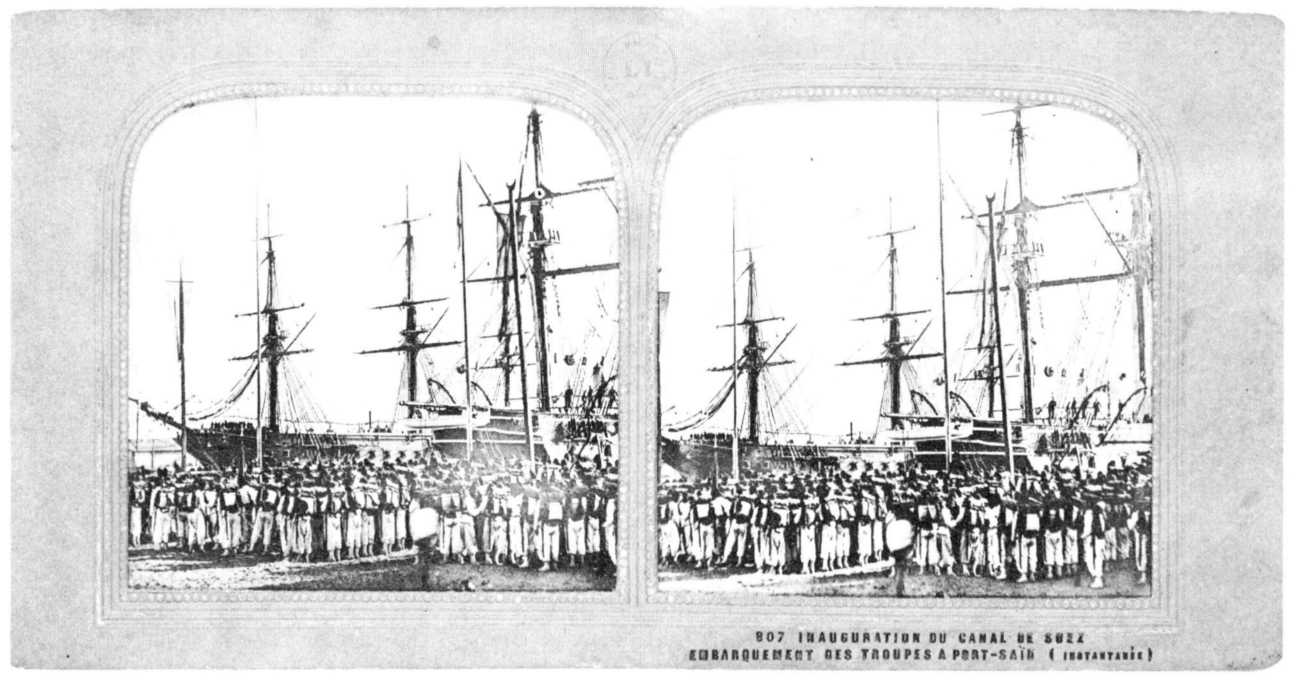

13. A Tissue stereograph. "Opening of the Suez Canal, Embarkation of troops at Port Said." November, 1869. Ch. D. photo. Leon & Levy publishers. Note blind imprint at top center.

Charles Pollock, beautifully tinted interior views of the White House (1873) and an extensive line of almost 500 numbers by R. Y. Young (1898-1904), including various celebrations in California and Texas cities.

Lamy published a small number of views of the Union and Central Pacific Railroads, with strip labels in French or English. The source of his negatives is not known.

The format was used for every type of subject: wars, architectural, scenic, documentary, exhibitions, comics and, rarely, portraits. The most celebrated tissue stereos are the "Diables"—"A Journey in Hell." See page 64.

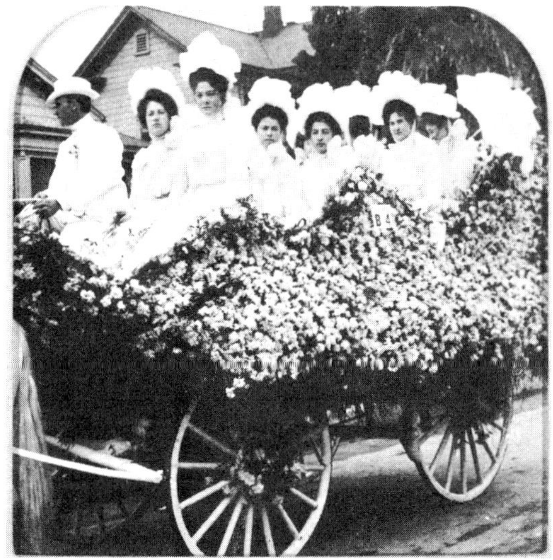

14. A Tissue stereograph. Floral Float, Los Angeles California. R. Y. Young photo. 1901.

CARD STOCK AND SIZES

It has been noted that the earliest paper stereographs were mounted on thin cards measuring approximately 3½ x 7 inches. This standard size was determined by the stereoscopic instrument devised by Brewster, which, in turn, was based upon the distance between the centers of the human eyes. Various devices, such as adjustable lenses and movable slide holders, were applied to the various types of stereoscopes to accommodate individual variations in eye distance and vision. Early cards are frequently slightly smaller in one or both dimensions.

In 1873 larger card sizes were introduced in the United States. It was believed that this would accentuate the illusion of depth in scenic views. Moreover, this new option offered for sale more expensive deluxe stereographs. Demand for larger cards lasted about ten years.

The 4" x 7" size was designated "artistic" or "cabinet," the 4½" x 7" size was "deluxe," and the 5" x 7" size was "imperial." Between 1874 and 1877 a 4¾" x 7" card was also marketed. Unfortunately, many photographers ignored the generally accepted distinctions and simply advertised all their larger cards as "deluxe" or "imperial."

THICKNESS OF CARD STOCK

The card stock used for mounting paper stereographs during the period 1852-1857 ranges from .014"-.020" in thickness (an ordinary playing card has a thickness of .010"-.012"). The card was often calendered to give a smoother front surface. The stock was white or colored, with blue, green, lavender, gray or brown, the more common hues. Yellow card was rarely used before 1858.

,Card thickness was increased gradually during the years 1858-59, when the typical .040" was almost universally adopted. Notable exceptions are the cheap French yellow mounts produced during the 1860's.

The thick card was pasteboard, made of layers of matte or sheets of paper glued together and compressed under rollers or heavy weights. This card stock was of excellent quality and durability. The corners were strong and resistant to bending or breaking. About 1870 single matte heavy cardboard made from straw or wood pulp became available. This stock was more porous, less dense and structurally weaker than pasteboard. The corners were prone to rapid wear and fraying and frequent breaking. Less expensive grades, slightly thinner than the usual stock used especially for cheap copy issues, did not withstand much handling. During the 1870's many fine views were mounted on poor card stock, very probably without the realization that these lacked durability and permanence.

Microscopic examination reveals identifiable characteristics of more than thirty distinct types of card stock used between 1852-1885. The various issues of most stereographs can be dated within an accuracy of two or three years by card stock alone.

COLOR OF CARD STOCK

The earliest known paper stereographs are mounted on white card, but these were quickly followed by stock of blue or green hue and then by lavender ("pink") or gray. Occasionally, brown mounts also were used. The blue and green mounts were most common from 1855-1857.

White and gray stock predominated in the period 1858-1862. By 1858 enameling on one or both sides had become popular. The enamel finish was resistant to soiling under normal handling of the card and repellent to water if wiped quickly. In the 1870's some fine issues were given a thin wax coating to "waterproof" them. The enameled card was used, except for cheap issues in France, almost universally throughout the 1860's.

In the 1870's, following the depression of 1873 and increasing use of cardboard made from wood pulp, enameling was limited to one side or omitted altogether. In the cheap reprint series, a thin yellow layer of paper or coating was substituted for the durable enamel finish found on earlier cards.

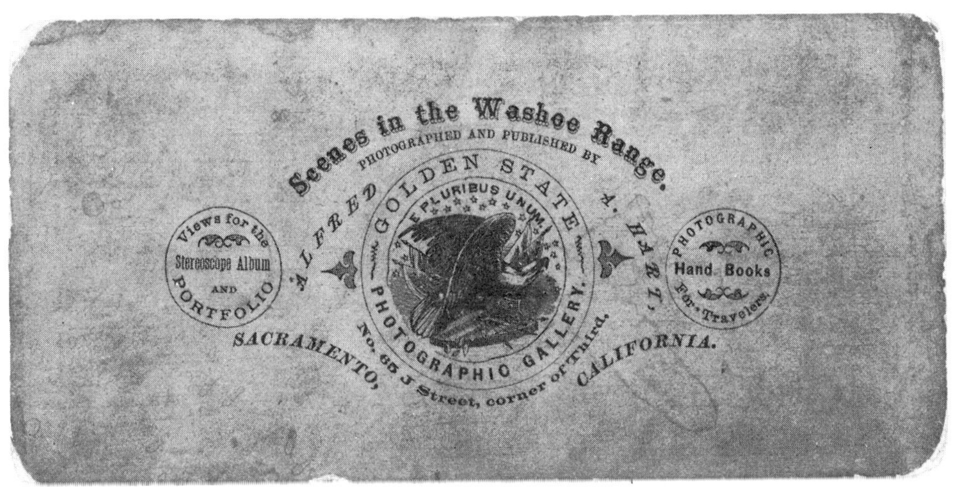

15. A photographer's imprint. Alfred A. Hart, 1865. ("Scenes on the Washoe Range—Reno, Nevada in the distance.")

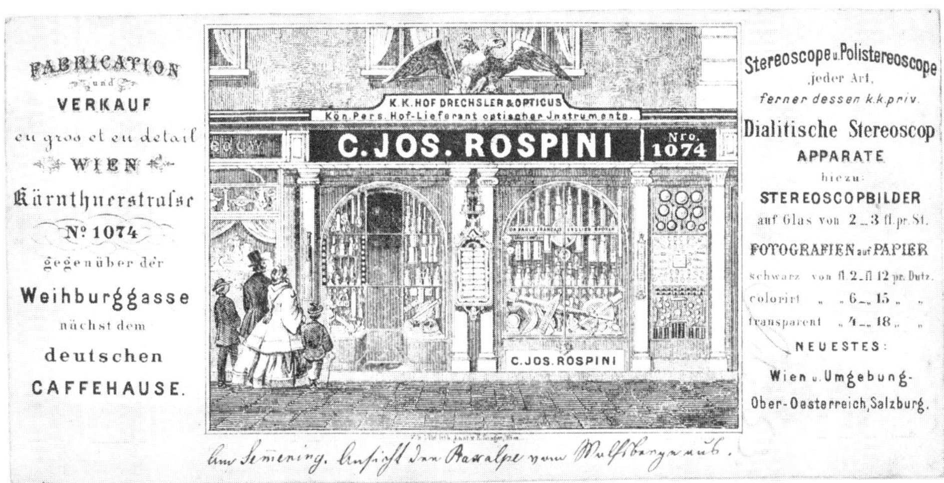

16. An unusual photographer-publisher imprint. C.J. Rospini, Vienna Austria. (Stereos ca. 1857-1872). Card ca. 1862. Note prices for various types of photographs.

With the tremendous popularity of stereo views in the mid-1870's, spreading among rich and poor alike, demand for inexpensive cards in addition to the high quality issues led to the use of a wide range of card stocks. Publishers of views could select from eight basic qualities, enameling in any combination of twelve colors, four card sizes with optional gilding of edges, moresque backs or waterproofing. Wilson, Hood & Co. (Philadelphia) between 1872 and 1878 cut cards from four qualities of stock and maintained an inventory of more than eighty kinds of cards for immediate delivery.

Although card stock and photographic papers were manufactured in Germany, France and the United States, international trade was so extensive and imitation so immediate that at any given time the most commonly used mounts were uniform throughout the world. A. M. Collins (Philadelphia), manufacturer of photographic cardboard, between 1868 and 1880 sold seventy percent of the stock used in the United States.

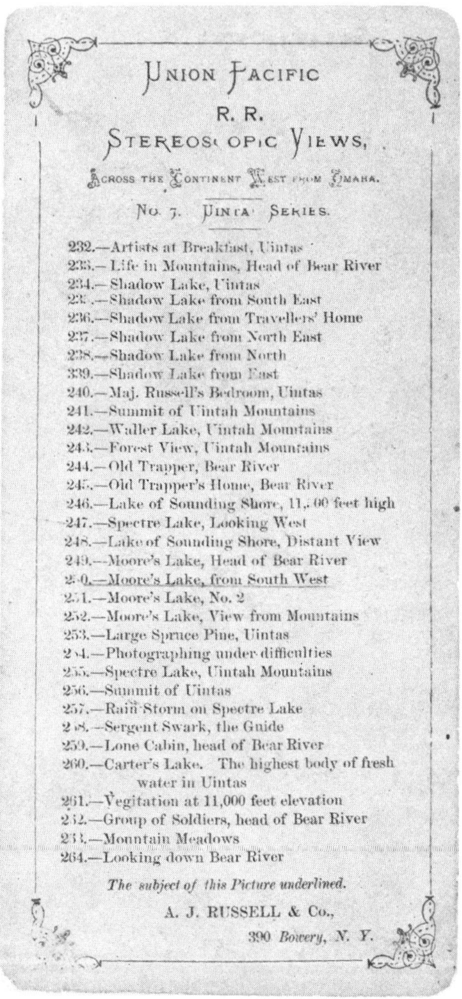

UNION PACIFIC
R. R.
STEREOSCOPIC VIEWS,
ACROSS THE CONTINENT WEST FROM OMAHA.

NO. 7. UINTA SERIES.

232.—Artists at Breakfast, Uintas
233.—Life in Mountains, Head of Bear River
234.—Shadow Lake, Uintas
235.—Shadow Lake from South East
236.—Shadow Lake from Travellers' Home
237.—Shadow Lake from North East
238.—Shadow Lake from North
339.—Shadow Lake from East
240.—Maj. Russell's Bedroom, Uintas
241.—Summit of Uintah Mountains
242.—Waller Lake, Uintah Mountains
243.—Forest View, Uintah Mountains
244.—Old Trapper, Bear River
245.—Old Trapper's Home, Bear River
246.—Lake of Sounding Shore, 11,000 feet high
247.—Spectre Lake, Looking West
248.—Lake of Sounding Shore, Distant View
249.—Moore's Lake, Head of Bear River
250.—Moore's Lake, from South West
251.—Moore's Lake, No. 2
252.—Moore's Lake, View from Mountains
253.—Large Spruce Pine, Uintas
254.—Photographing under difficulties
255.—Spectre Lake, Uintah Mountains
256.—Summit of Uintas
257.—Rain Storm on Spectre Lake
258.—Sergent Swark, the Guide
259.—Lone Cabin, head of Bear River
260.—Carter's Lake. The highest body of fresh water in Uintas
261.—Vegitation at 11,000 feet elevation
262.—Group of Soldiers, head of Bear River
263.—Mountain Meadows
264.—Looking down Bear River

The subject of this Picture underlined.

A. J. RUSSELL & Co.,
390 *Bowery, N. Y.*

17. A typical series list of titles printed either on the card back or on a label applied to it. A.J. Russell, "Union Pacific Rail Road" series. Fourteen sub-series such as this No. 7 comprised the total. 1869-1870 issue.

CURVED OR "WARPED" MOUNTS

In the late 1870's B. W. Kilburn began to use a card mount that was given slight curvature to increase the illusion of depth. So far as can be determined, no patent was applied for. In 1882 he introduced a thicker buff card with greater curvature that became the Kilburn hallmark for a quarter century. Within a few years the entire American stereoscopic industry converted to the warped card mount.

IMPRINTS AND LABELS

Prior to 1855 a stereograph seldom bore a photographer's or publisher's name or imprint. A title if given appears in manuscript. Many beautiful classic views bear no data whatsoever. Among these incunabula are artistic gems of great merit. We can be certain that all were issued in limited numbers.

By 1856, the photographer and/or publisher imprint came into wide use. Many photographers, however, used only one or two initials, either printing them on the card or marking them on the negative. There are scores of combinations of initials found on early stereographs that thus far have not been identified.

With the adoption of publishers' imprints, related views were issued in series with appropriate titles and subtitles. Classes and categories of subjects were listed in trade catalogues. More and more information was provided in printed legends on the backs.

SUMMARY

A stereograph shows much of its origin and history. The card format and stock, together with the image mounted upon it, are typical of the period during which it was produced. The labels, imprints and titles make it possible to relate the individual card to others produced by the same photographer or publisher.

Like books and printed ephemera, stereographs are subject to critical "bibliographic" documentation and from careful examination provide a wealth of information supplementing the photographic image.

CHAPTER THREE

THE FIRST DECADE 1851-1860

Photography was the wonder of the age. The excitement of innovation and accomplishment attracted painters, sculptors, chemists, physicists and amateurs of every background. Two aspects vied with each other for attention, the technical which dealt with methods and the artistic which concerned pictures. Throughout the late 1840's and 1850's the technical approach dominated photography in England, France, Germany and the United States. Probably the scientific and academic backgrounds of most experimenters were the primary reasons for this emphasis.

There were many practitioners who were more interested in photography as a fine art, but it was inevitable that their outlook would be determined by their experience as painters. These two competing but not necessarily antagonistic approaches resulted in two distinct traditions in photography, artistic and utilitarian.

With the commercialization of photography, particularly of stereographs, enjoyment was no longer limited to the professional few. Daguerreotype stereoscopic views of the Crystal Palace were exchanged as gifts among friends, kings and princes.

The calotype was already popular in France and making headway in England. Introduction of the collodion negative-albumen print further stimulated an ever-expanding range of exploration with stereography, but almost always within the context of painting: portraiture, still life, pastoral scenes and allegory.

The photograph can capture more perfect detail than is possible with the human hand and record in an instant an event or a scene that will be forever past. The realism of the photograph was, paradoxically, both the strength and the weakness of the medium. This caused great concern among painters, especially those who were dependent upon painting miniatures for a living. More fundamentally, to what extent dare the photographer manipulate effects to produce his picture?

Three trends were set in motion when commercial production of stereographs began: (1) the shift from artist-photographer to professional merchant-photographer; (2) a movement away from the artist's unique creativity toward catering to popular taste—that which would sell; and, most important, (3) the application of photography, especially stereographs, to many practical uses. Photography had many important applications in science, commerce and industry and subtle influences on leisure and learning. In short, a new industry had been born.

DAGUERREOTYPES

We have already noted the excitement caused by the display of Brewster's stereoscope at the Great Exhibition and the stereo daguerreotypes by Claudet, Mayall, Negretti and others. As stereoscopes rapidly gained popularity, demand for stereographic pictures kept pace. Many of the best known daguerreotypists contributed their skills to the creation of beautiful images.

Daguerreotypy was especially suited to portraiture. The soft, rich tones produced a pleasing likeness. Limited space also tended to keep daguerreotypy in the studio, although many wonderful outdoor daguerreotypes were produced. Surviving stereo daguerreotypes are of three main categories: portraits (individuals, husband and wife, less frequently, groups of people), nudes and statuary.

As in painting, the nude was a favorite subject and many beautiful French and English examples have been preserved. Photographs of the dead, frequently a child, represent a curious example of sentimental appeal.

Sculpture, a passionate interest of the Victorian age, was another popular field for the photographer. A considerable proportion of known stereo daguerreotypes depict statuary, many with skillful use of light and shadow.

Outdoor stereo daguerreotypes, much rarer than studio images and other interior views, present a wide field for the collector.

Since a given daguerreotype view was either unique or issued in relatively small numbers (individually copied), no enumeration of titles or photographers will be given here.

In 1853 (March 8) J. F. Mascher of Philadelphia patented a small case (93 mm x 118 mm, 3⅝ x 4¾ inches) provided with stereoscopic lenses to hold a stereo portrait. For five or six years, this format was popular in America. Many photographers purchased cases, bearing the Mascher name, for their trade. Imitations were manufactured by several unidentified persons.

By strange coincidence, at the same time in England, apparently entirely independently, William E. Kilburn registered (Jan. 12, 1853) a similar folding stereo viewing case, approximately 120 mm. wide, holding a stereo daguerreotype portrait.

The Mascher viewer was applied to book format, with a pair of lenses inserted in the front cover. Usually this format was a cloth covered folder holding twelve, eighteen or twenty-four paper prints.

The high cost of stereo daguerreotypes compared with other types of photographs and the difficulty in examining them combined to limit demand for them. They were rapidly supplanted by the paper print mounted on card and, briefly, by the ambrotype. Most stereo daguerreotypes were produced before 1855, although a few were made as late as 1860.

AMBROTYPES

For a brief period, 1854-56, the ambrotype stereo view competed with the daguerreotype. The ambrotype was a collodion negative, treated and mounted so that it could be viewed as a positive. They were simply cheap imita-

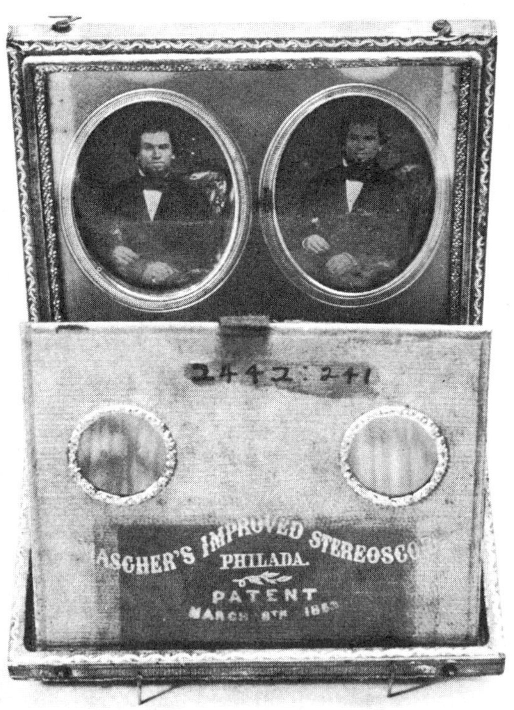

18. Mascher's folding stereoscope used for portraiture, 1853-1860.

tions of daguerreotypes, not only in their images and style of mounting but also in the range of subjects. There are ambrotypes of the Crystal Palace. Portraits, including death portraits, predominate. They were never important in stereography.

FERROTYPE OR TINTYPE

The ferrotype, also known as the melainotype or tintype, was patented in the United States by H. L. Smith in 1856. Later, in December of the same year a similar patent was granted in England to William Kloen and Daniel Jones. The process was essentially similar to that for the ambrotype. The negative image on a blackened (japanned) surface of a thin sheet of iron appears as a reversed positive.

The tintype was enormously popular as a cheap portrait photograph, especially of school children and at amusement parks, from 1858 to 1910. Only a few stereo ferrotypes were produced, mostly in the late 1860's and early 1870's. The ferrotype is the rarest form of stereograph.

CARD STEREOGRAPHS

Mounted paper prints

With the advent of paper prints mounted as card views, stereoscopic photography came into its golden age. Unlike daguerreotypy, the collodion wet-plate method, for all its difficulties, allowed the cameraman to venture into field, forest and seashore and to range the world. By selling copies of his work, he could support further field work and extend the scope of his artistry.

At first, paper-print photographers imitated the daguerreotypist and painter in every possible manner: portrait, still life, sculpture; but the potential of the albumen print was quickly recognized.

Five major subjects attracted great interest: the still life, sculpture, architecture, natural scenery and the group.

Still life stereographs

The ability of the photograph to record faithfully the minutest detail challenged the artist to pursue its limits.

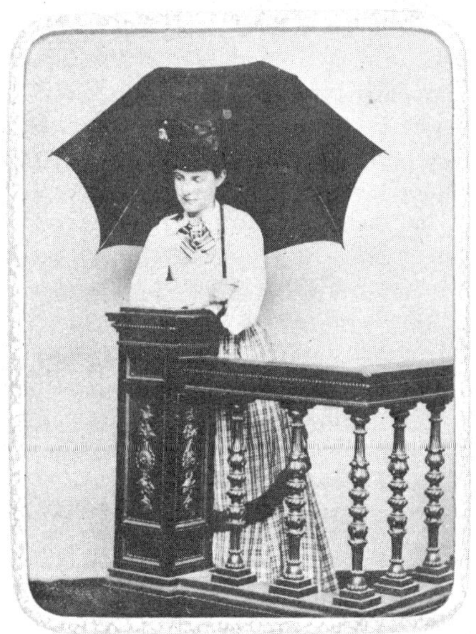

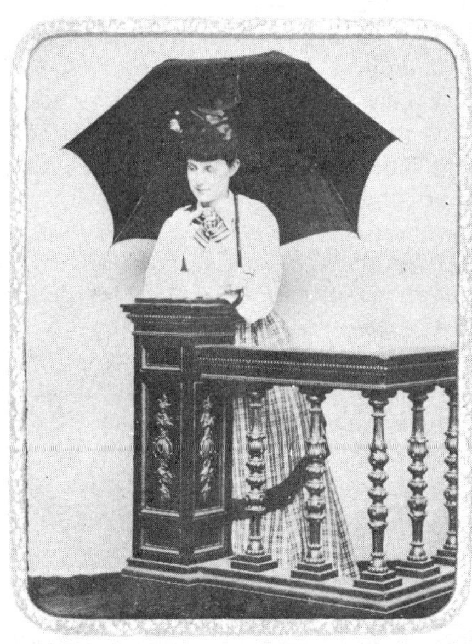

19. Tintype (Ferrotype) stereograph. The rarest form of stereo views. Unknown photographer, New England. ca. 1867.

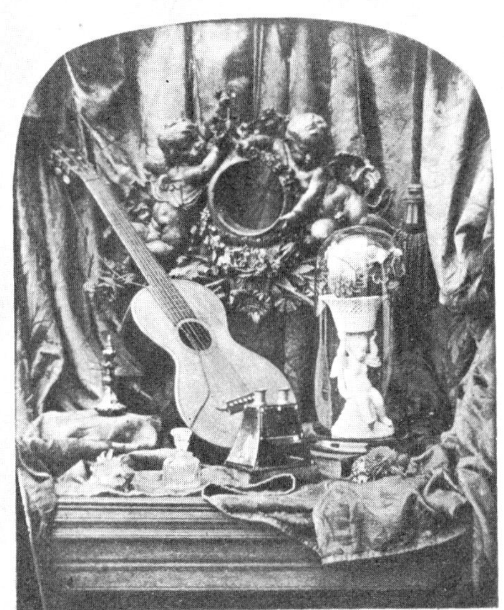
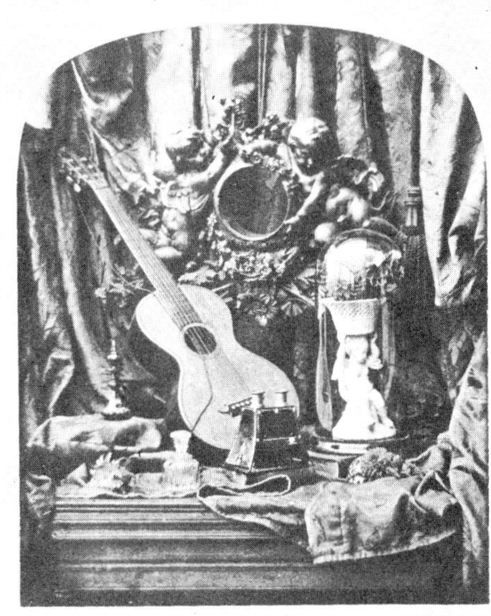

20. T.R.Williams still life arrangement. Note Brewster stereoscope in foreground. This view is known both as daguerreotype and calotype. ca. 1854.

Ingenious arrangements were devised to exploit detail, create graceful spacial parameters and achieve artistic appeal.

T. R. Williams, Roger Fenton and Lake Price produced striking still lifes. Williams, an associate of Claudet and a daguerreotypist since 1849, excelled in compact composition, striking contrast and intriguing selection of objects. Some of his views were issued as both daguerreotypes and paper prints. Most of his negatives have the initials "TRW" inscribed near the lower left margin or worked into the background.

Roger Fenton was attracted to arrangements of fruits and table miscellany. The complicated, almost cluttered, table arrangements usually include several photographs carefully placed at varying distances from the camera to test the "truthfulness" of the stereograph. Under magnification it is actually possible to identify the subject of and objects in the stereograph in the arrangement.

Lake Price, a well-known painter, produced many still lifes, including game birds hung with garlands of vegetables. Price tinted his still life stereographs, whereas Williams and Fenton generally did not.

Although many English photographers produced still-life stereographs in the 1850's and early 1860's, relatively few photographers in other countries issued them. Adolphe Braun of Dornach was renowned for his still lifes, but only a few early examples are known to have been issued as stereos.

In the United States Soule, Meinerth and Kilburn produced arrangements of cut flowers, sea shells and various other materials. None of their work compares with the best European stereos.

Sculpture

Sculpture had a special appeal, not only to photographers but also to the cultured generally. Virtually every well-known statue, classical and contemporary, was photographed again and again. The museum collections of the Louvre, Vatican, British Museum, as well as those in private ownership were reproduced in beautiful stereographs. Sculptures displayed at exhibitions were promptly photographed so that views could be offered for sale as mementos of the occasion.

Literally thousands of such subjects were produced. The works of Canova, Danneker, Thorwaldsen, Baily and Foley are but a few of the sculptors whose works became the subjects of popular household pictures in the 1850's and early 1860's.

Philip H. Delamotte in 1857 photographed "The Art Treasures of the Manchester Exhibition." The views were published on ornate gilded card mounts by the London Stereoscopic Company.

William England, Roger Fenton and Charles Goodman were among the outstanding sculpture photographers. William England was especially active in this category well into the mid-1870's. See Sculpture, page 188.

Architecture

John Ruskin's widely read *Seven Lamps of Architecture* (first ed. 1849) had much influence on Victorian tastes. The book was at the height of acclaim when photography was rapidly developing as an art form. Enthusiasm for formal gardens, topiary and architecture knew few bounds. Moreover, Victorian pride in the past further contributed to this interest in architecture. The many castles and abbeys, some barely recognizable as overgrown heaps of rubble, were visited by photographers who recorded them in infinite detail.

A steady stream of stereo views depicting the classic antiquities of Rome, Naples, Athens, Egypt and the Holy Land, together with those of the cathedrals, public buildings and palaces of the tourist centers of Europe provided mementos of the journey and vicarious adventure for those who had to remain at home.

Architectural photography posed a number of technical problems not encountered in studio or scenic work. Perspective, height of towers or parapets in limited space often resulted in badly distorted, unreal or awkward pictures. Some amusing, even ugly views indicate how troublesome it was to photograph a cathedral at close range in a town square.

In many stereographs the structure to be portrayed is poorly centered or is so isolated from its surroundings that the image, though technically good, is not pleasing. The sense of loftiness is usually missing. Nevertheless, there were many magnificent views. Details of arches, doorways and windows—again, the influence of Ruskin—were recorded beautifully. Castles and bridges in striking settings demonstrated the wonderful potential of the scenic and topographic view.

Among the most attractive architectural views made between 1855 and 1870 are the interiors of cathedrals and other great buildings, all of which had to be photographed with natural light at exposure times ranging from a few minutes to an entire week. The problems of illumination were such that we can only marvel at the achievements of George W. Wilson, William England, V. A. Prout, J. Elliott, William Woodward, W. R. Sedgfield and Francis Bedford, to name only a few of the best.

To prepare for photographing the interior of a dimly lighted cathedral, it was necessary to study for several days the shifting light from morning to sundown. When ready, the photographer carefully positioned his camera and exposed the plate from two to seven days. The shifting direction of sunlight gradually unmasked the recesses of the hall. Many of these incredibly beautiful English interiors show a wealth of detail that normally would escape the eyes of a visitor who remained in the hall for only a half-hour. The stone floor minimized vibration so that no movement of the camera occurred.

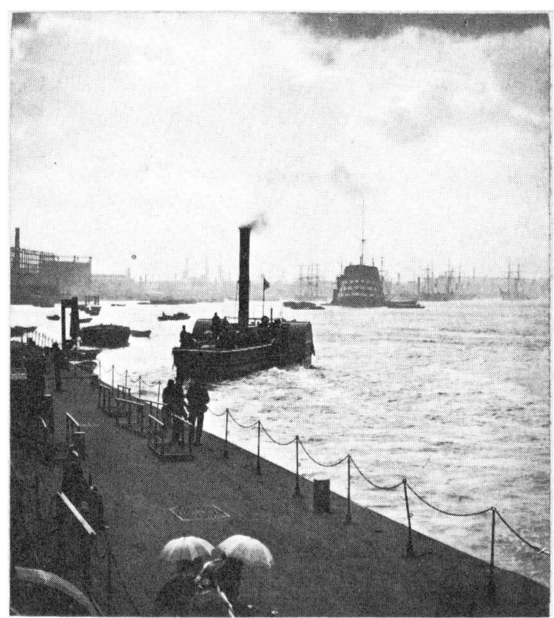

21. George W. Wilson. "On the Thames at Greenwich—Departure of the Boat" "Instantaneous." 1857.

Scenic stereographs

Little need be said here about scenic views because they constitute the majority of card views. The earliest examples are pastoral scenes or rugged landscapes, wholly imitative of the painter. Both naturalistic and romantic, they show rural life, cattle, lakes, glens and mountains. By 1855-65 however, the touring photographer had grasped the capabilities of the sweeping panorama. Francis Frith produced a magnificent series of Egypt and the Near East. William England's Swiss scenery for the Alpine Club, George Wilson's Scottish scen-

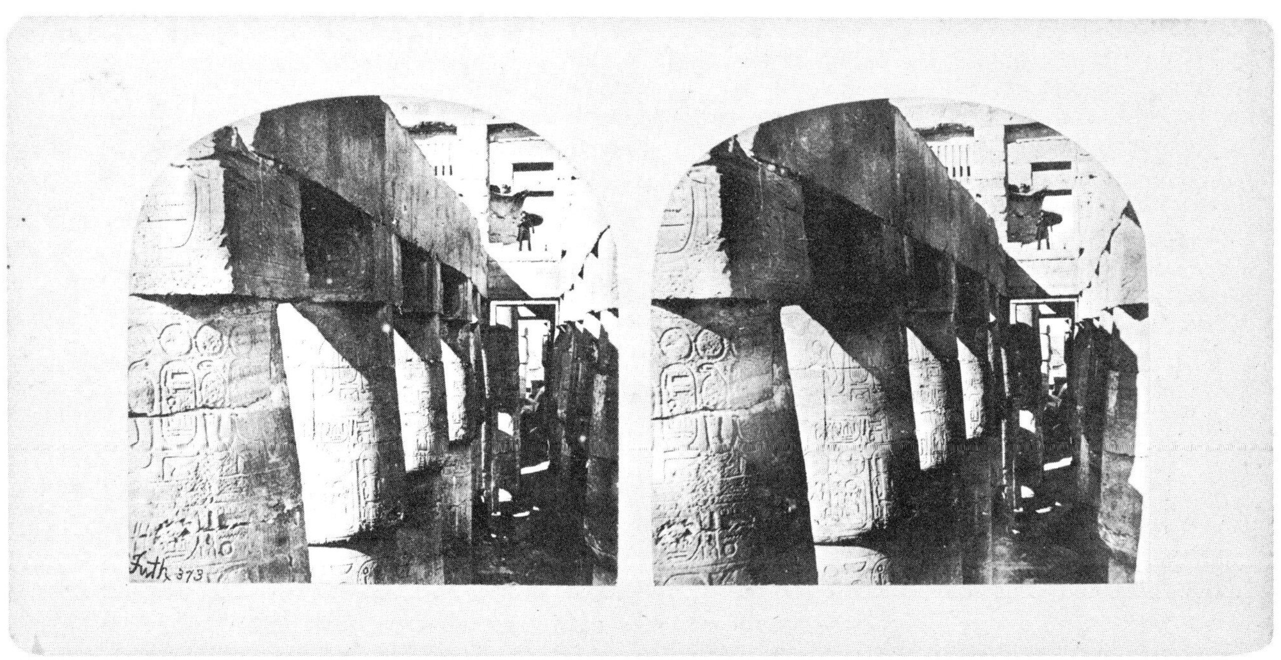

22. Francis Frith, "Views in Egypt and Nubia, Great Hall of Columns at Karnac." Note contrasting light and shadow. Negretti & Zambra, publishers. 1858.

ery, and Adolphe Braun's views of the Upper Rhine and Alps, set standards equaled by few photographers.

In 1857, Wilson introduced the so-called instantaneous photograph, by which he was able to capture the breaking wave or the wake of a boat and, thereby, increase the illusion of motion and action. The exposure shutter time was approximately one-fifth of a second. By focusing on a fairly distant point and avoiding a ninety degree approach, it was possible to record excellent sharpness.

Le Gray in France produced fine seascapes, a few known in stereo. In the United States (1859-1865) several photographers, among them E. Anthony, John Soule and John Heywood, advertised seascapes and harbor scenes as "instantaneous." The term, however, refers only to short exposure time and does not mean high speed in the modern sense.

Frith's Near East views, mentioned above, are remarkable in several respects. From September 1856 to July 1857, he traveled to Egypt and the Holy Land to take a series of the fabled monuments of antiquity. Upon his return to England, Negretti and Zambra published one hundred titles, on gray cards with printed descriptions on the backs. The views were so enthusiastically received that Frith made two more excursions, the first, November 1857 to May 1858 (Palestine, Syria and Jerusalem), and again in the summer of 1859 (a 1500-mile expedition up the Nile River). Negretti and Zambra published approximately 500 titles. Beginning in 1860 the views were published on glass and paper by Frith's photograph company newly established at Reigate.

Frith produced fine stereographs of English scenery in the 1850's. He invariably scratched his name on the negative and usually also the negative number. Some mounted prints lack the signature because of cropping.

Groups

Probably no other aspect of stereography allowed greater freedom or more opportunity for ingenuity than did the group. Simply defined, a "group" portrays two or more persons in a pose other than portrait. In the hands of a clever photographer, however, this device could be sentimental, moralistic, allegorical, comic, risque or erotic. And the earliest stereographers exploited all of them!

Thousands of titles were produced between 1852 and 1862. A selection of a few representative types will suggest the range of possibilities. These "compositions" will be described more fully in Chapter Seven.

The objective of the group was essentially pictorial, the effect being achieved by staging and enhanced by a wide variety of painted backgrounds and stage properties. In fact, the technical perfection of many stereo views of trivial scenes seemed to many critics to be worthy of much better subjects.

Among the typical serious views, the following may be cited:

J. Elliott, "Mary Queen of Scots—Compelled to Sign Her Abdication"

J. Reynolds, "The Old Curiosity Shop, Little Nell and Her Grandfather" Figure 58.

Gebhardt and Rottman, "Hamlet, Prince of Denmark, Act V, Scene I, 'Alas Poor Yorick' " Figure 59.

Phiz (Hablot Knight), "The Mother's Grave"

Lake Price produced scenes from *Robinson Crusoe* and *Don Quixote*. Figure 62.

Among the humorous groups, one finds the comic "Mr. Bottomly" series that depicts a gentleman with an enormous *derriere* (grotesque stuffing in his trousers), usually in the ball room dancing with Miss Longshanks or an overweight partner.

"Crinoline troubles," hoopskirts, were a favorite subject for Victorian jokes. They were shown as embarrassing unmanageables or as a convenient hiding place for the lover surprised by the intrusion of the young lady's mother. Figure 73.

Courtship, children at play, mother and child and bereavement are among the more common themes for sentimental views.

Risque groups seem mild or harmless to the present age. Indeed, the captions are often more suggestive than the photograph itself. Stereos of partially dressed women and inadequately covered bosoms shocked many.

Erotic and some pornographic views were produced in London and Paris in the 1850's. Street peddlers sold them to school boys, soldiers and college students. Offenders

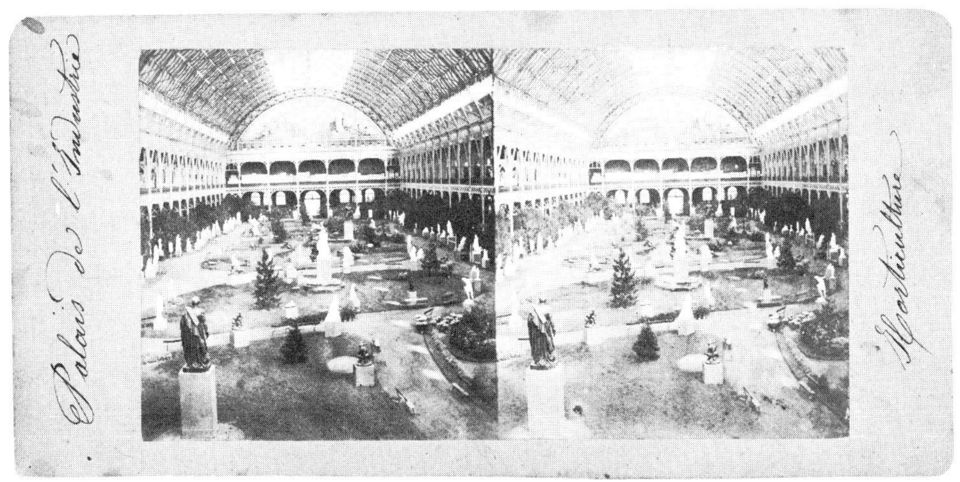

23. International Exhibition, Paris 1855. Horticultural exhibit in the Palace of Industry. Unknown photographer.

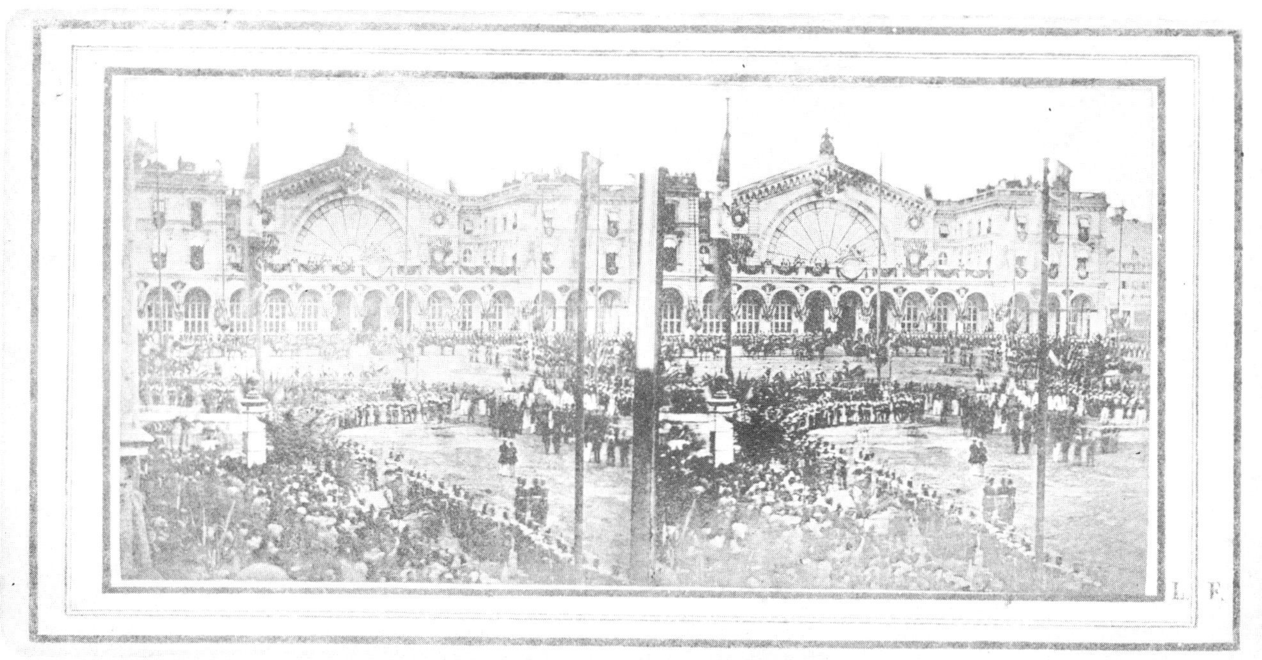

24. Arrival of the Queen of England in Paris to attend the International Exhibition. 1855. "L.F." photo.

were arrested, complaints were published in the press, but the nuisance persisted. The publishers, who were nameless, merely moved to a new location and resumed business. (It may be of passing interest to note that no pornographic stereographs were produced commercially in the United States until the period 1900-1925.)

Documentary Views

Photographic recording of an event at a particular time documents the incident to a degree not possible by any other medium. The stereographs of the Crystal Palace are documentary inasmuch as they record the building, the exhibits and the visitors in 1851. The reconstruction and reopening of the Crystal Palace at Sydenham in 1853 were documentary. "The Arrival of the Queen of England in Paris" to attend the International Exposition (1855) is a fine example.

The tremendous potential of documentary views became apparent during the Crimean War, when Roger Fenton and no fewer than twenty other photographers recorded the aftermath of battle.

Just what stereographs—if any—were taken during the Crimean War is still a mystery. In 1948 I examined two stereographs in the possession of Roy Mabie, one showing two seated very young wounded soldiers and the other only gabions and weapons at close range. These poorly preserved, faded calotypes were not identified in any way, although Mabie thought them to be "by Fenton." It is now believed that Fenton did not issue any Crimean stereographs. There is, however, a stereo war view displayed in the foreground of one of his still arrangements.

There are a number of surviving 1855 stereographs of British troops, with equipage and in various military formations. They were probably photographed in England.

The Austro-Italian war in 1859 was well covered by a dozen French and Italian stereographers. The events depicted range from mobilization and embarkation of troops, battlefield dead, to the return of the victorious armies.

Major historical events were not the only attractions for photographers. Countless lesser occasions were interesting enough to have been captured in a negative, from which replicated prints were then distributed. The construction, maiden voyage and subsequent damage from a boiler explosion on board the *Great Eastern* steamship were nicely stereographed. The "official" series was published by the London Stereoscopic Company (1858-59).

The Henley Regatta in 1858 was won by the Trinity team from Cambridge. Poulton issued a tinted stereograph of the team with the names printed on the reverse.

The most remarkable accomplishment in stereo in the 1850's, however, was the photographing of almost every city in Europe and the seaports bordering the Mediterranean Sea in the Near East and Africa. The glass views of France, Holland, Italy, and Algiers are exquisite. Although many of these were manufactured by the well-known photographic publishers Ferrier, Ferrier and Soulier, Dubosq & Soleil, Negretti & Zambra, the vast majority of these early glass views bear no photographer's name. What is more frustrating, many have no title or other identification.

It will be noted that most of the examples referred to in this chapter are English. It was in England and Scotland that the scope of stereography as a medium in itself was first fully explored. This is not to imply that novelties and beautiful examples of the various types of views were not produced elsewhere. Certainly in France and Italy there was great stereographic activity during the 1850's, but most of the innovative work was being done in England.

At any rate, photographers during this first decade discovered the wide range of artistic, documentary and recreational possibilities of stereography.

CHAPTER FOUR

DEVELOPMENT OF STEREOGRAPHS IN AMERICA

European stereographs were introduced in the United States in 1851, and by 1853 foreign card views were being sold commercially by the D. Appleton Company. Mascher patented his folding stereo case in March 1853, indicating that already there was significant interest and some knowledge of stereography in America.

We do not know how many photographers experimented with stereographs in the early 1850's, but the Langenheim Brothers are credited with the commercial publication of the first American stereographs. Frederick and William Langenheim, born in Brunswick, Germany, settled in Philadelphia in 1840. Throughout the 1840's Frederick practiced daguerreotypy, and during this period he was granted an American patent for photographing on transparent substances, such as glass. Langenheim called these transparencies "hyalographs."

Frederick next traveled to Paris (1850), where he became familiar with the stereographs. In 1854 the Langenheims began commercial production of glass and paper stereographs. During the next seven years they developed a large trade list of American and foreign views.

In 1854 Langenheim solicited subscriptions from patrons to finance a photographic junket from Philadelphia to Niagara Falls by way of the southern anthracite coal field, Catawissa and Williamsport. Among the great rarities of the Langenheims' early work are the twelve views on glass in the series "The Coal Region near Pottsville." No complete set is known—not even the list of titles. Fewer than a score of surviving copies are known.

Langenheim glass views were sold tinted and untinted. The coloring was beautifully done but generally has deteriorated. Representative series on glass include:

"Philadelphia and Environs"
"The City of Washington"
"Baltimore"
"Pittsburgh"
"Mount Vernon"
"Niagara Falls"
"The White Mountains"
"Beauties of the Hudson River"

In the mid-1850's Langenheim produced a few stereo images on porcelain, a format that never gained popularity.

Card views were also produced in 1854, the earliest issue having small square images framed in gold. Although many Langenheim titles are known only as glass transparencies and others only as paper prints, it is probable that all titles regularly offered in the trade list were available in both formats.

Most of the stereographs issued between 1854 and 1858 bear a copyright dated 1854 or 1855 and the glass views an 1850 date—which refers only to the hyalograph patent and has nothing to do with the date of the image.

In addition to transparencies and card-mounted paper images, the Langenheims issued several folders of ten or twelve views, or double that number, printed back to back. The front cover had a pair of lenses inserted so that the viewer could appreciate the stereo effect. The design was basically that of Mascher, who had obtained a patent

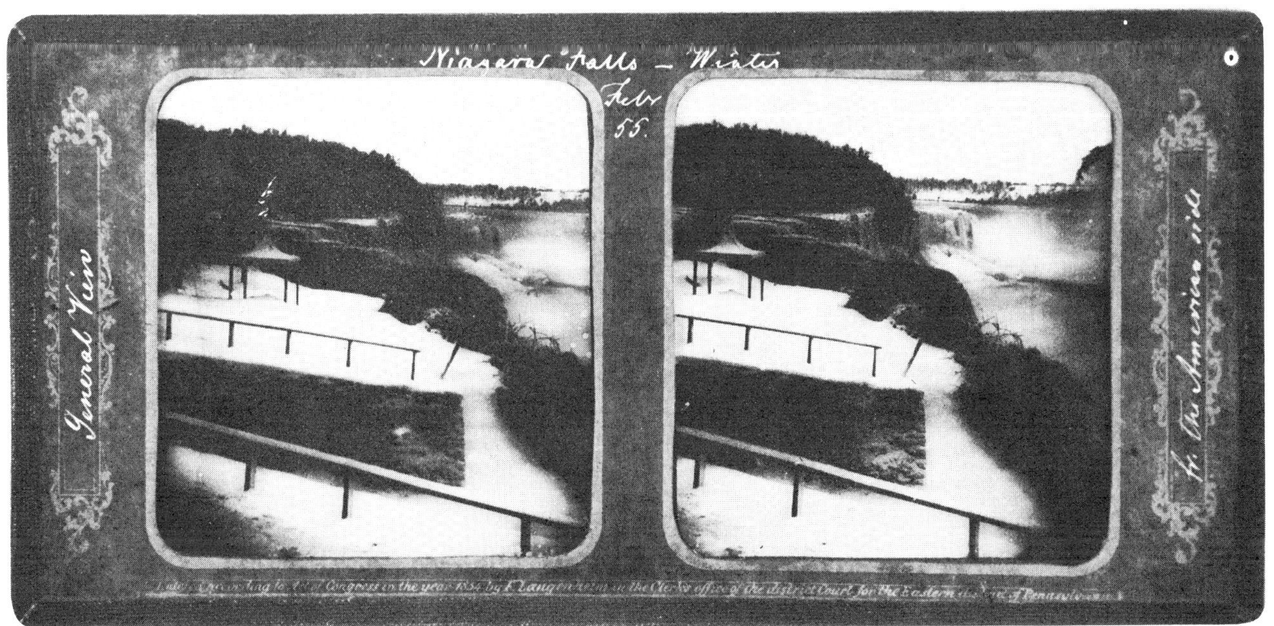

25. Langenheim Brothers. Glass transparency. "Niagara Falls, Winter. Feb. '55." Note cut-out paper frame placed between image and the cover glass.

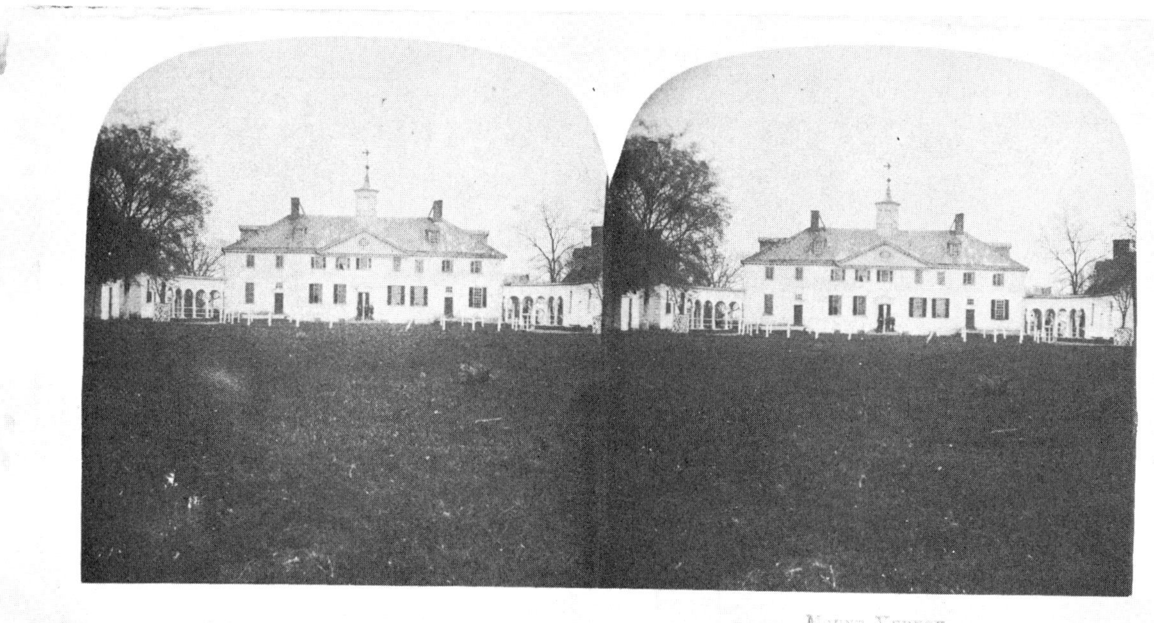

26. Langenheim Brothers. View of Mount Vernon. Negative 1856, 1859 issue. Langenheim blind imprint on right margin.

for the pocket folder. The images are chromolithographs, possibly printed in France. All of the sets I have examined were copyrighted in 1856 and 1858.

Langenheim glass views enjoyed an excellent reception. A reasonably complete check-list of them has not yet been compiled, but there were certainly more than 800 titles. Among the stereos are scores of portraits of prominent Americans. Those depicting the person at his home or estate are true stereo. Some of the portraits are copied from earlier Langenheim daguerreotypes, and so the paired images are non-stereo.

In addition to the fine variety of American views, the Langenheims maintained a large trade list of foreign stereographs. Some were printed from negatives taken by Frederick Langenheim, but the large majority were manufactured by Negretti & Zambra. There is substantial evidence that some of the gray mount Langenheim European and Egyptian (Frith) views were manufactured in Philadelphia from copy negatives.

The Langenheims, in 1848, licensed from Fox Talbot, for the sum of $6000, exclusive American rights to the calotype process, expecting to sell licenses to other photographers. They were unable to sell a single license but used the calotype process themselves.

For several years the card views bore a small strip label, "Langenheim's American Stereoscopic Views, Entered according to Act of Congress, 1858." For a brief period, 1859-60, they also applied a blind stamp to the side margin of the card face.

By 1860 the Langenheim magic lantern slide business, begun several years earlier, had increased to the extent that the production of stereos was curtailed. "The American Stereoscopic Company" was separated from the parent company, with William Langenheim retaining financial management and A. Watson, an old employee, in charge of photographic activities.

The magic lantern slide, 3¼ x 3¼ inches in size, was usually one-half of a stereo pair. Between 1854 and 1862 the Langenheim lantern slides were printed from the negatives in the regular trade list.

Few new stereo titles were added during the 1860's. The Great Sanitary Fair (1864), however, provided the impetus for the last stereo venture. About twenty titles comprised the series, "published by the American Stereoscopic Company, W. Langenheim General Agent, Negatives taken by A. Watson."

In the winter of 1864-65, the Langenheims severed all connections with the American Stereoscopic Company and sold the business, but not the Langenheim negatives, to Watson and his associates, who moved to 16 Maiden Lane, New York City.

OTHER EARLY AMERICAN PUBLISHERS

Although Langenheim was the undisputed pioneer stereographic publisher in the United States, there were others who were experimenting with stereo during the early 1850's. Most important of these was J. E. McClees, also a Philadelphian.

McClees had been working with paper prints, using collodion negatives, in 1852. He produced paper stereographs in 1853 but did not offer them for sale. Between 1855 and 1860, perhaps earlier, McClees issued stereographs of Philadelphia, Wissahickon Creek and a tinted series, "Washington City, 1859." McClees' stereos are very rare, suggesting that small quantities were produced commercially.

The house of D. Appleton has previously been recognized as the first to sell stereographs in America. After acting for several years as importer and distributor of European views, D. Appleton Company, in 1856, followed the Langenheims and began the publication of stereographs and printed stereo views in book and folder formats. They issued a number of Mascher-type pocket folders with lenses, each containing a dozen views, such as Niagara Falls, Paris, the Tuilleries, American scenery, etc. The views are usually xylographs and photogelatin prints, made in the United States, a circumstance that deserves investigation.

Edward Anthony, Delos Barnum, George Stacy, Franklin Gage, John Heywood and William Notman issued stereographs commercially before 1859. By the end of 1860, no fewer than two hundred American photographers were producing them on glass and paper.

This sudden expansion of stereography was encouraged by a remarkable venture by the London Stereoscopic Company. In 1859 they dispatched William England, chief photographer, to the United States and Canada to take an extensive sequence of negatives, from which a fine series of card stereos could be published. To augment coverage, some additional negatives were purchased from American photographers. Figures 43 and 44.

The stereographs were issued on enameled ivory mounts, beautifully tinted or untinted and with full descriptive legends on the ornate backs. The United States series had a flying eagle vignette, while the Canada series had the coat of arms. A handsome selection of one hundred of the approximately 400 titles was sold as a set in 1859 with the remaining numbers being issued in 1860. They were sold until 1866, but in diminishing quantity after 1863. The Canada series was mounted on blue as well as on ivory enameled cards.

During 1860 the London Stereoscopic Company exhibited their American series, along with other select views, in all of the principal cities of the United States from Boston to New Orleans, westward from Chicago and St. Paul to San Francisco. Many of the displays were at local mechanical and industrial fairs.

Similar mounts with attractive ornate back with appropriate vignette and descriptive legend were widely imitated by American photographers. Barnum used it for his historical series of Boston (1859), as did Stacy, Notman and several unidentified photographers, who failed to include their names in their individual designs.

Anthony (E. Anthony; E. & H. T. Anthony)

The Anthony firm rose rapidly to a position of preeminence among American stereopublishers. During the late summer of 1859, Edward Anthony issued a series of approximately 175 views of New York scenery, including a fine group of the Fourth of July regatta in New York Harbor. The following line was printed at the bottom of the face of each card: "Entered according to the Act of Congress in the year 1859 in the clerk's office of the District Court of the United States for the Southern District of New York." On the reverse, a printed label bears the title, negative number and the note, "Published by E. Anthony, Broadway, New York, Copyright secured."

This was not the first Anthony issue. There were at least three earlier issues, although probably all were within 1859.

Chronologic sequence of early Anthony labels:

1. Manuscript, "Anthony's Instantaneous Views" on ivory cards. Example: "No. 12, New York from Brooklyn Heights"
2. Large white label
   As 1 above but printed, not manuscript; on ivory cards.
3. As 2 above, but "copyright secured" added at bottom of label; on ivory cards.
4. Large white label; number at top, title at center, "published by E. Anthony; Broadway, New York" at bottom. Ivory cards.
5. Similar to 4 but bottom line reads: "Published by E. Anthony, 308 Broadway, N. Y." Ivory cards.
6. Similar to 5 but address changed to 501 Broadway. Ivory cards.
7. Narrow strip label, otherwise similar to 6.

In 1860, E. Anthony moved to larger quarters at 501 Broadway and remained there until 1871, when even larger facilities were needed. In 1862 Edward took his

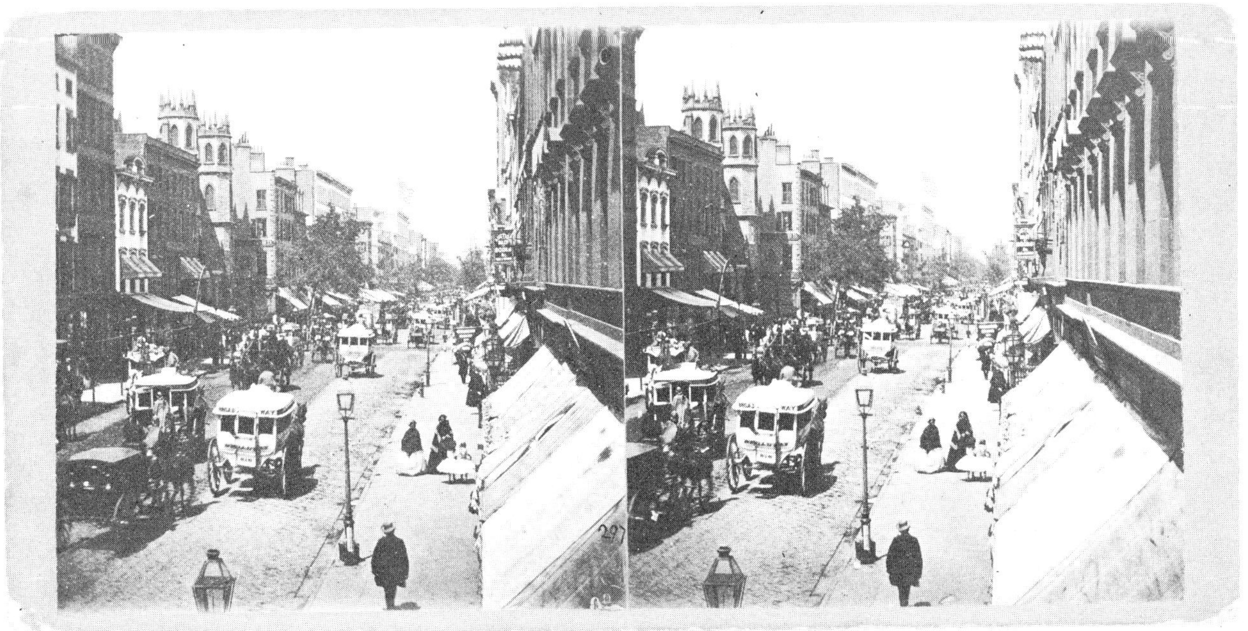

27. E. Anthony. New York City. "Broadway looking north from the balcony of the Metropolitan Hotel." 1859.

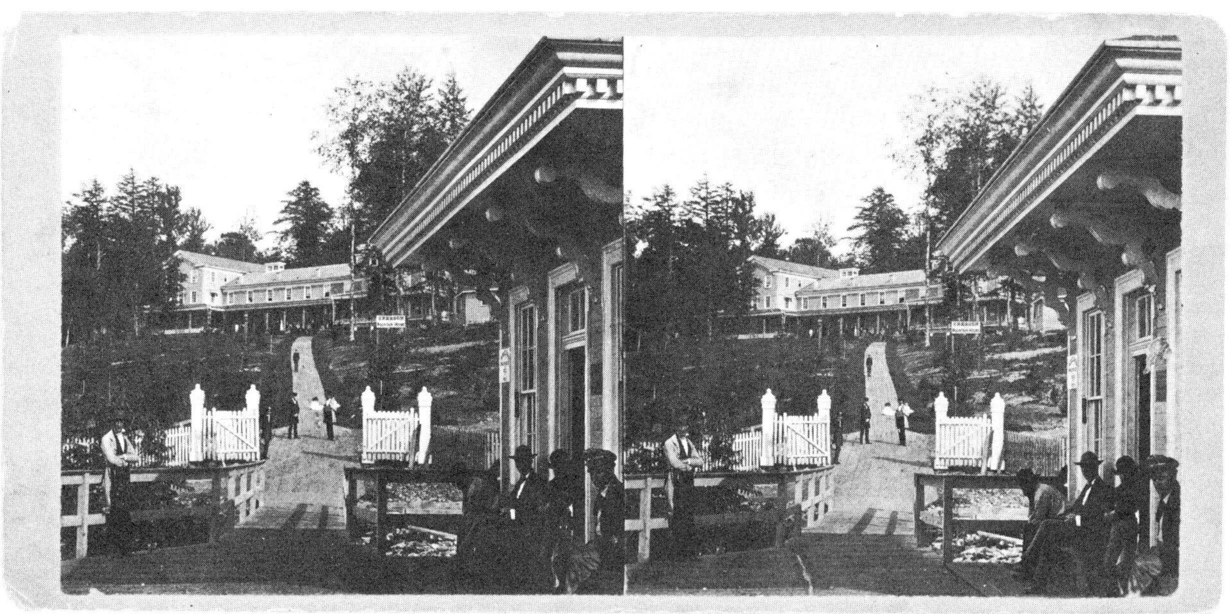

28. E. Anthony. "The Picturesque of the Pennsylvania Central Rail Road." The Cresson Mountain House. 1860.

brother, Henry T. Anthony, into partnership, but the company name was not changed until 1863.

For more than fifteen years, the Anthony firm produced a huge volume of stereo views and by 1873 had a trade list of more than 11,300 titles. As new titles were added, many old numbers were discontinued. Figures 27, 28, 37 and 45.

E. & H. T. Anthony had become the largest supplier of photographic materials in America, not only papers, glass and chemical reagents but also cameras, enlargers, apparatus, studio props and publications. When, in 1874, popularity of stereo views declined sharply—but only temporarily—Anthony discontinued issuing stereo views under their own imprint.

For another eighteen years, however, at least until 1892 Anthony manufactured large quantities of stereographs, mostly from their old negatives, but sold them exclusively wholesale without an Anthony imprint or clue to Anthony manufacture. Yet, in 1889 E. & H. T. Anthony received a grand prize gold medal for stereographs at the Paris exhibition.

Among the fine Anthony series were the following:

- Public Buildings of New York City
- Glens of the Catskills
- Beauties of the Hudson
- Majesty and Beauties of Niagara
- Niagara in Winter
- A visit to Central Park in 1863
- The Picturesque on the Pennsylvania Central Railroad
- The Picturesque on the Erie Railroad
- Views in and about Saratoga Springs
- Yosemite Valley, California
- Newport and its Villas

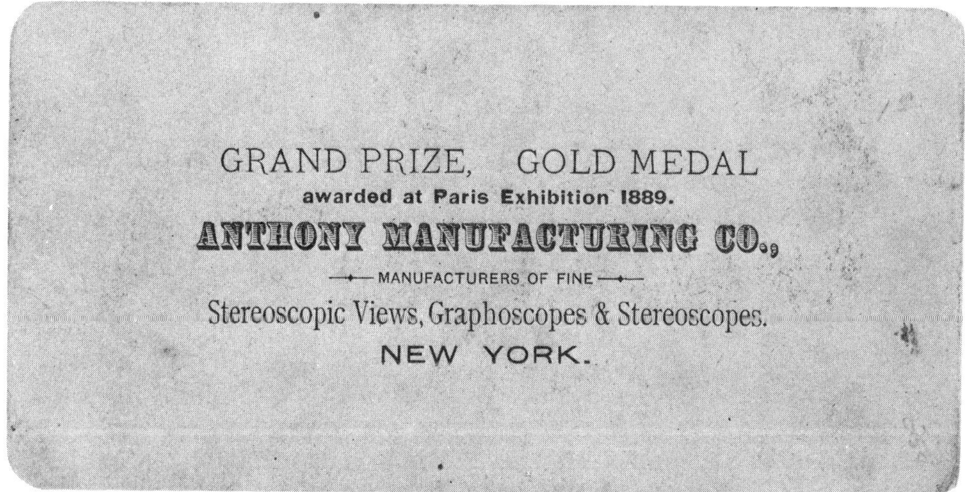

29. E. & H.T. Anthony advertising imprint, 1890. Although Anthonys discontinued publishing stereographs under their own name in 1874, they continued to manufacture them until 1892.

Glimpses of the Great West
White Mountain Views
Hills and Dales of New England
Southern Scenes

There were many smaller series illustrating various cities, including Washington, Philadelphia, Baltimore, Ithaca, Cincinnati, Montreal and Quebec.

In addition to these series printed from Anthony negatives (taken by Anthony's photographers or purchased), the Company published many series under an Anthony label but without Anthony numbers. Typical are Gardner's views of the Civil War (not to be confused with the "War for the Union" series), the Mammoth Cave series (Waldack negatives), and Swiss Scenery (Braun negatives).

Anthony numbers are generally, but not consistently, in chronologic sequence. However, there are gaps in the numbering that, so far, have not been adequately explained. Many numbers were assigned to more than one negative. When a negative was damaged, a new one replaced it. The scene was usually similar, perhaps a second negative taken at the same time as the original. But it may have been taken years later. Less likely, but occasionally, an entirely different subject was inserted. There are at least five Anthony numbers, for each of which there are five distinct negatives.

Anthony prints are characterized by a rich black tone that was envied by many contemporary photographers. With a little experience, an Anthony image can be recognized from a distance. From 1862 to 1869, the prints were mounted on enameled yellow cards of several shades, progressively darker until 1864. From 1870 to 1874, a mount with red face and white back was used. Briefly in the late 1860's a few enameled cards with red face and lavender ("pink") backs were used.

In the early 1860's Anthony produced a variety of small custom made sets, usually eight, ten or twelve cards, for churches, schools, fraternal and social organizations, and family celebrations. Generally, these were beautifully tinted and very well made. The negatives were neither assigned Anthony numbers nor listed in trade catalogues. All are rare, owing to the small numbers issued for private distribution.

One other venture deserves mention. In 1880 E. & H. T. Anthony issued a small series (about thirty-six numbers), "Views of New York and Vicinity by the New Gelatine-Bromide Process," primarily to promote their new dry plate. The prints lack contrast and in all respects are inferior to their earlier stereographs. Nevertheless, the series is important in the history of photography.

Delos Barnum published a few stereographs of Boston as early as 1857, but his first important project, prompted, no doubt, by William England's fine views, was the "American Historical Series of Stereoscopic Pictures" (copyright 1859) on enameled ivory mounts with ornate bordered backs and descriptive legends. How many titles were included in the series is not known, but there were more than fifty. Most of the scenes depict landmarks of the American Revolution in Boston, Lexington and Concord, including the dwellings of Paul Revere, John Adams and other patriots. The familiar small blindstamp Barnum imprint was sometimes used on cards of this issue. Over the period 1857 to 1875, Barnum published well over two thousand titles, with those of Boston, Saratoga and Niagara predominating.

George Stacy began operating in 1859 and quickly became a major producer of stereo views. He remained in business only a few years, returning to England about 1864. Among the excellent series published by Stacy are *The Great Eastern* in New York Harbor, The Civil War (Fortress Monroe), Central Park, and public buildings of New York City and Washington, D. C. About 1863, Stacy used yellow card mounts, on the back of which were handstamped in blue ink negative numbers and titles, together with the initials, "G. S."

The negatives passed to other hands, possibly to a photoprinter who secured them for indebtedness, in 1865. The views were in continuous production until 1873.

The D. Appleton Company followed the fashion and adopted the enameled ivory card mount in 1859 for fine views of New York, Boston and Washington, D. C. Among

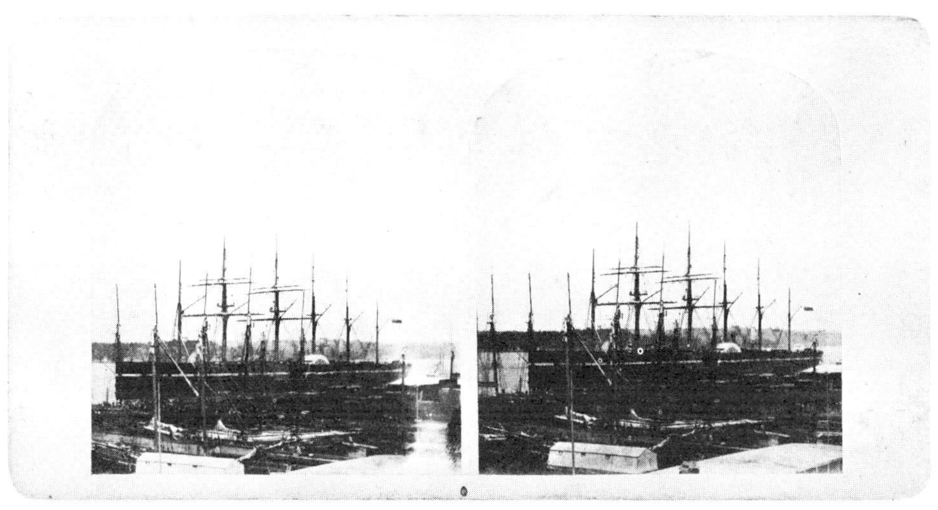

30. George Stacy. "The Great Eastern Steam ship" New York Harbor. 1860.

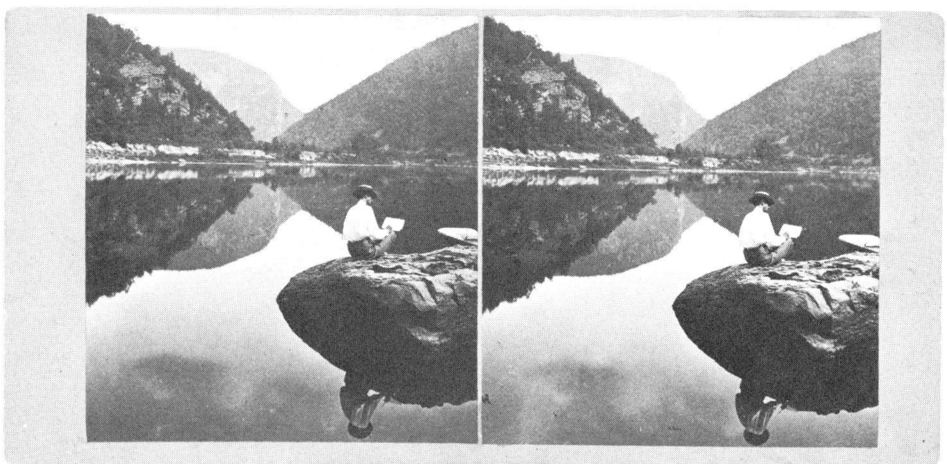

31. John Moran. Delaware Water Gap. 1865.

the documentary stereographs is a small series of the visit of the Prince of Wales in 1860.

In 1860 the Appleton cards bear a white label that names the New York Stereoscopic Company as co-publisher. The photographic department of Appleton was merged with the New York Stereoscopic Company. The Appleton imprint appears on a large series of fine views mounted on enameled gray cards.

The New York Stereoscopic Company began issuing views early in 1859 on ivory mounts. In 1860 gray mounts, not enameled, were used. The boxed imprint and title were printed on the reverse. More than six hundred titles are known, about one-third of which are European, including Moscow and St. Petersburg, and Constantinople. The New York Stereoscopic Company dissolved in 1864.

The Appleton views on enameled gray cards were distributed under the imprint of the American Stereoscopic Company in 1863-64 and without any publisher's imprint 1864-66.

As previously mentioned, the American Stereoscopic Company formed by the Langenheim Brothers had been purchased by Watson and associates, who moved to New York. The company began to purchase files of negatives from many sources until 1868, at which time the trade list included approximately 2200 numbers. The trade list was organized in small series of 30 to 50 related titles. A large blue or pink label, pasted on the back of the cards, lists the numbers and titles in each series. The American Stereoscopic Company was among the first (1866) to use this device extensively in the United States. Although the American Stereoscopic Company ceased operations in 1871, the many titles in their series were published by unknown parties until 1876. At first, the company name is simply clipped from the large series label, but later issues have new labels, none with a publisher's imprint. Charles Pollock of Boston was the publisher of many of these views from 1873-75.

The name "American Stereoscopic Company" was used by two publishers between 1895 and 1908, but neither had any relationship to the Langenheim and Watson companies or to each other. The more important of these later firms was that of R. Y. Young, 725-727 Broadway, ca. 1895-1905.

By 1862, hundreds of American photographers were issuing stereographs. Most of their work was scenic, architectural and documentary. Their trade was largely local or regional. Relatively few found means to distribute views nationally. The large publishers and wholesalers, like Anthony, handled huge quantities of foreign views but were not interested in promoting those of their American competitors.

(Continued on Page 44)

ILLUSTRATIONS OF COLORED STEREOGRAPHS

The thirty two hand tinted stereographs which are reproduced on the following pages present a cross-section of popular artistic views published between 1853 and 1865. One American view, figure 50, by J. F. Jarvis was issued in 1873.

Relatively few American stereographs were tinted, although Anthony, Appleton, McClees and the New York Stereoscopic Company produced them in the late 1850's and early 1860's. In the 1870's Griswold, Kilburn and Weller issued nicely colored compositions. The finest tinted views were produced in England and France during the period 1855-1865.

This exquisite tinting was done with transparent water colors which did not obscure detail in the photographic image. The skilled colorists sometimes worked in teams, each member applying only one or two colors.

All stereographs that were available tinted were also sold uncolored at a lesser price, usually five or ten cents less.

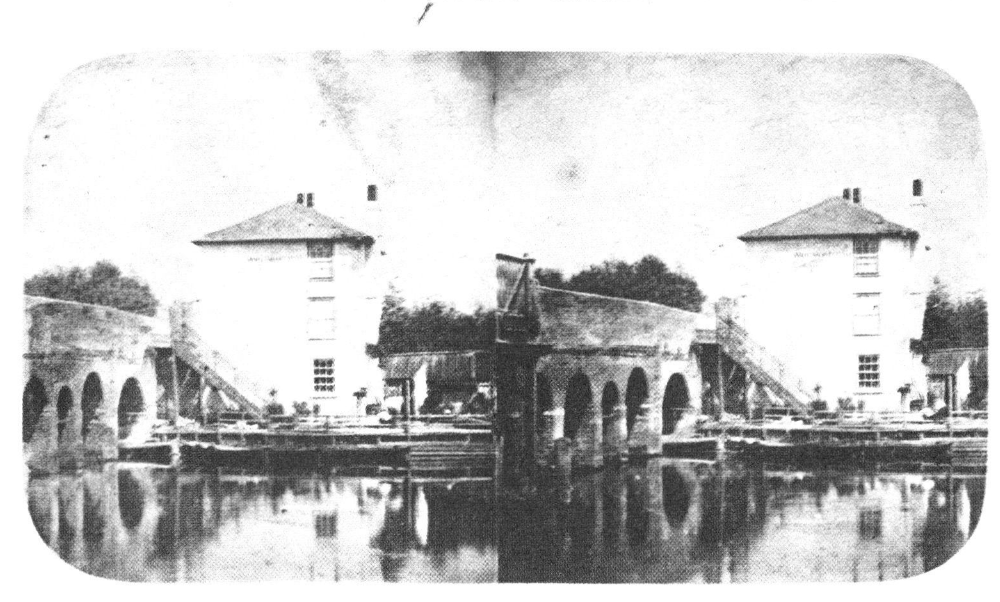

32. "Waterman's Cottage" Early English view, ca. 1853. Unknown photographer.

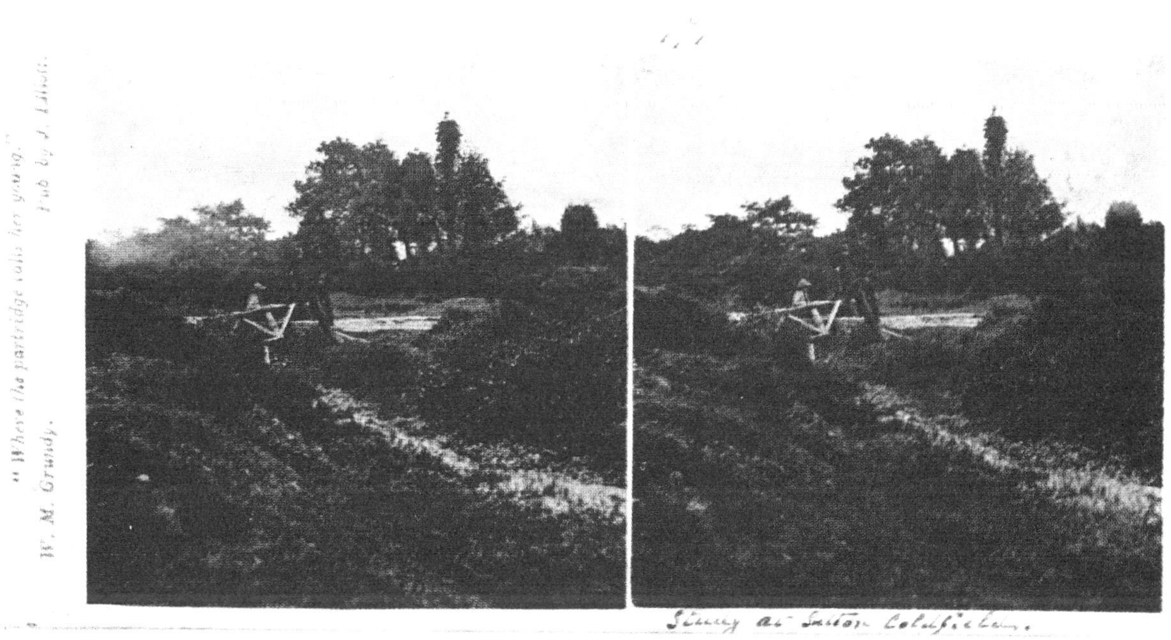

33. William Grundy. "A Study at Sutton Coldfield." 1857.

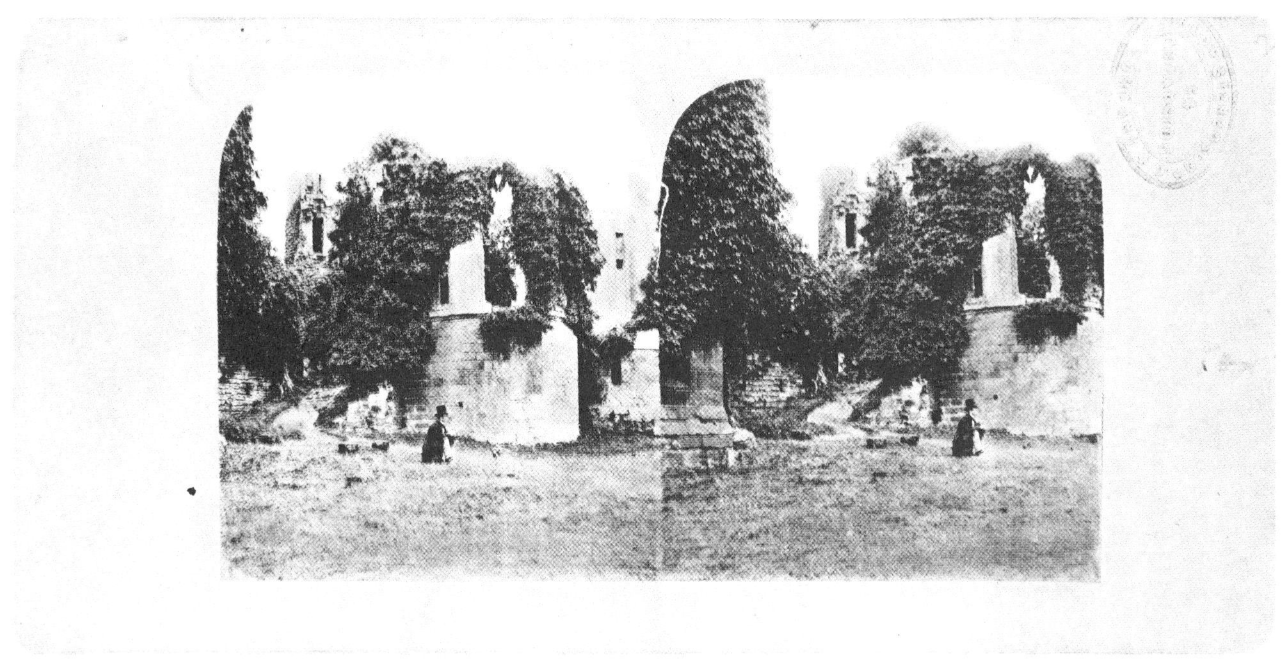

34. William Woodward, "Kenilworth Castle, The Banquet Hall." 1855. London Stereoscopic Company, publisher.

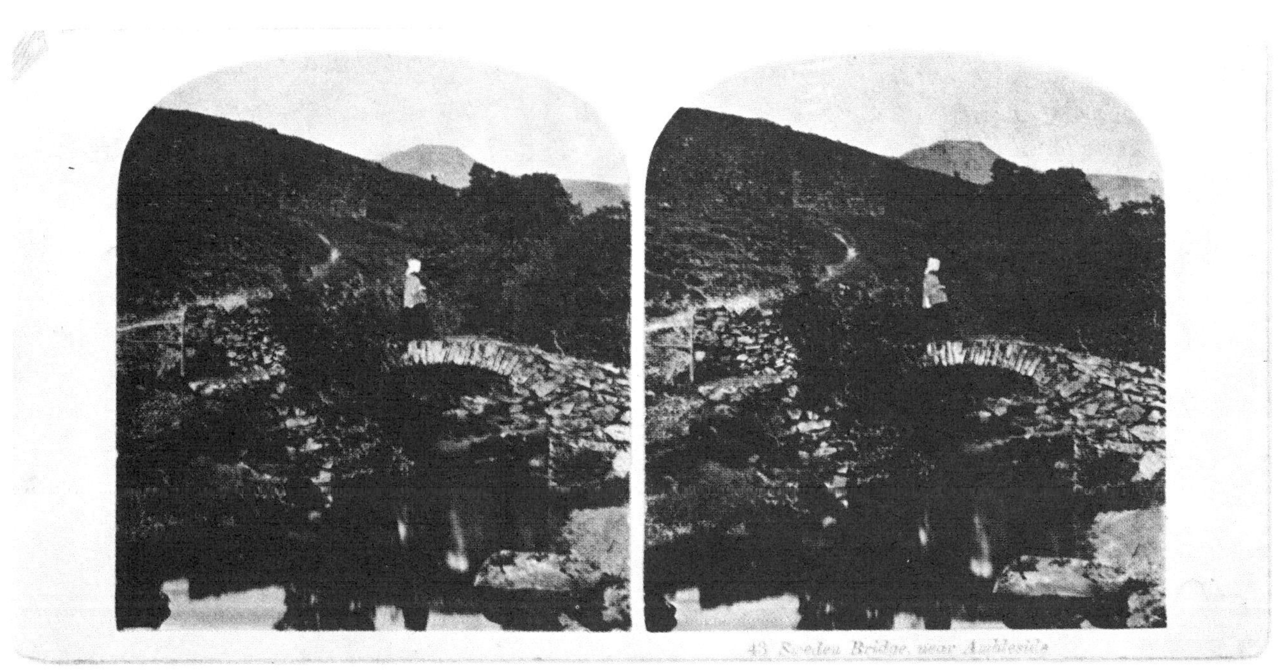

35. T. Ogle and T. Edge "Sweden Bridge near Ambleside." ca. 1858.

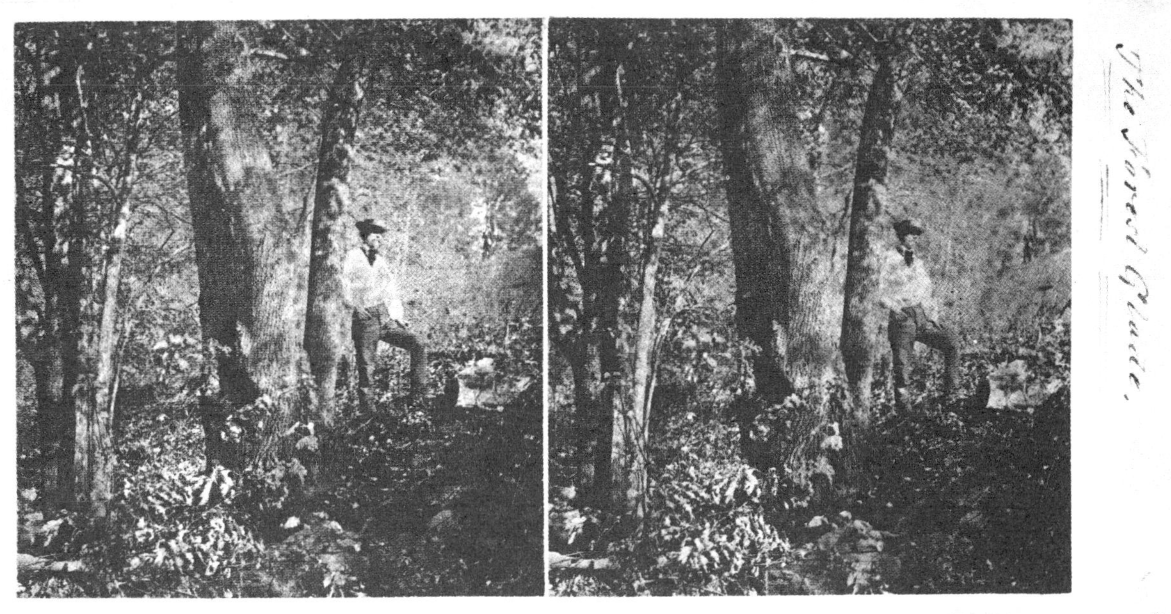

36. John Moran. "Autumn Studies; The Forest Glen." 1860.

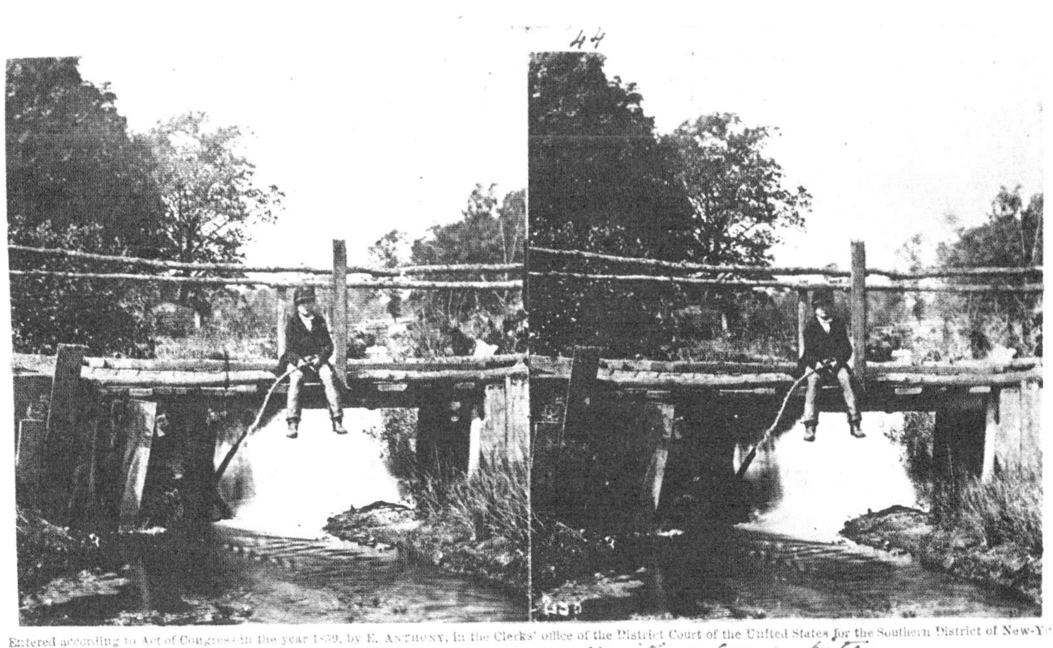

37. E. Anthony. "The Rustic Fisherman—Waiting for a bite." 1859.

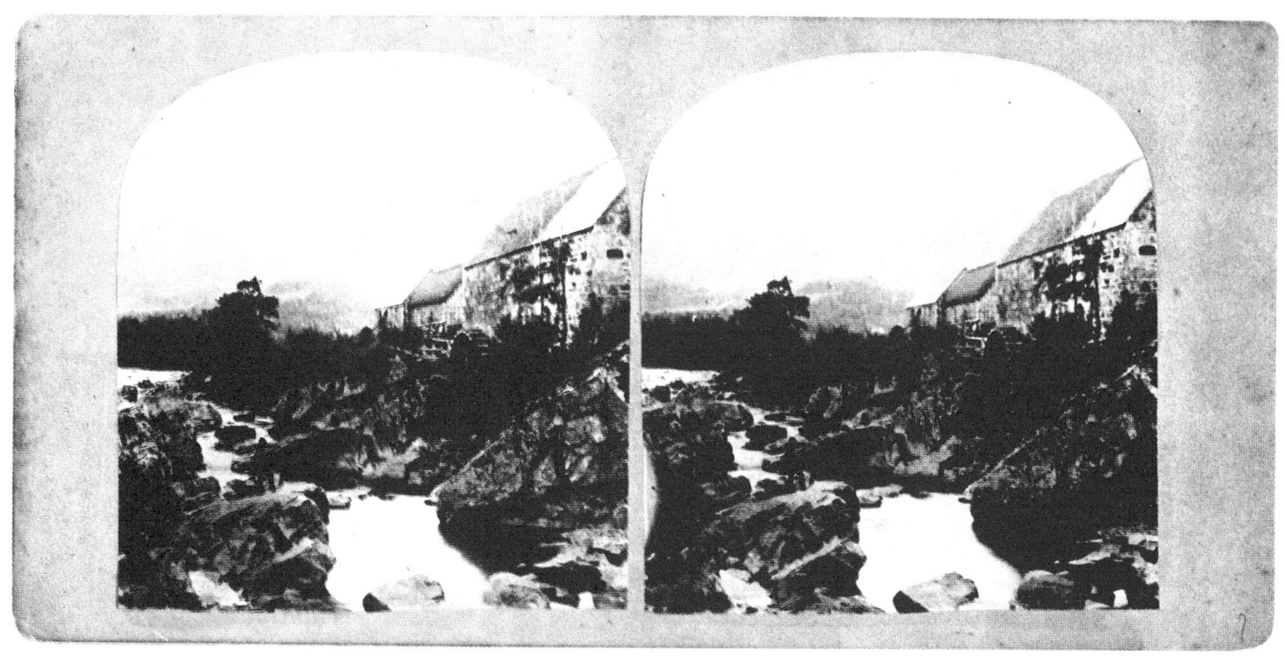

38. Roger Fenton. "Old Mill, Castleton Braemer, Scotland." 1857.

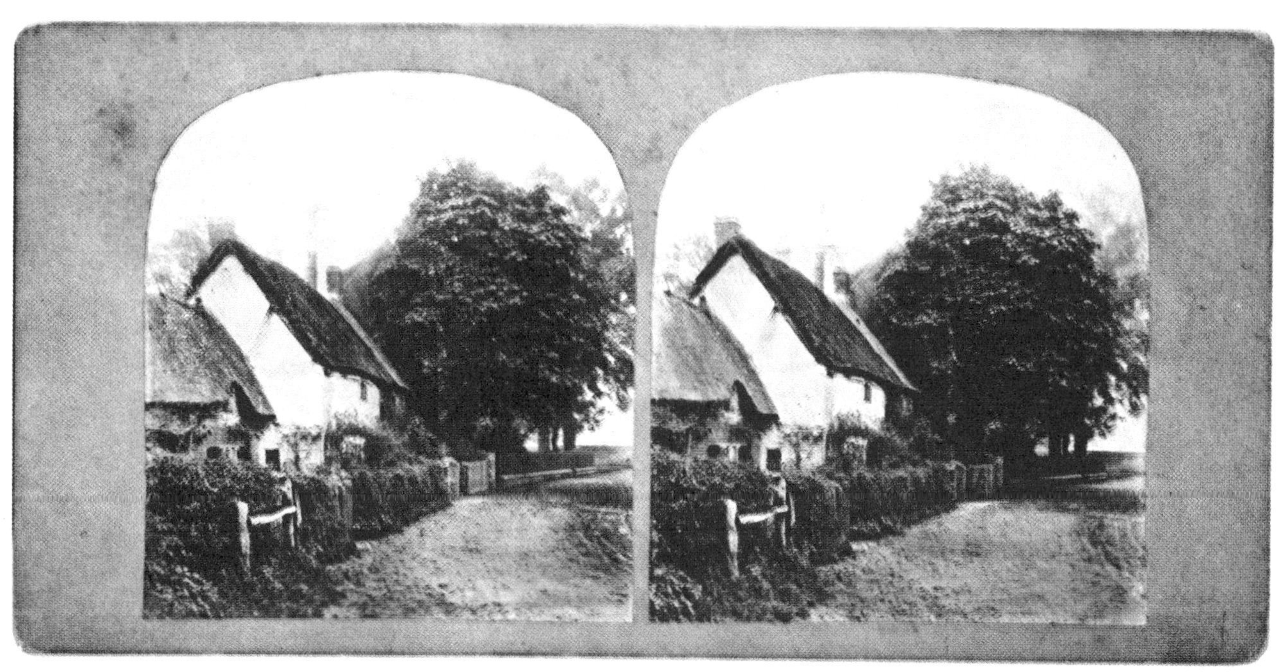

39. William Woodward. Wilford, Nottinghamshire. 1858.

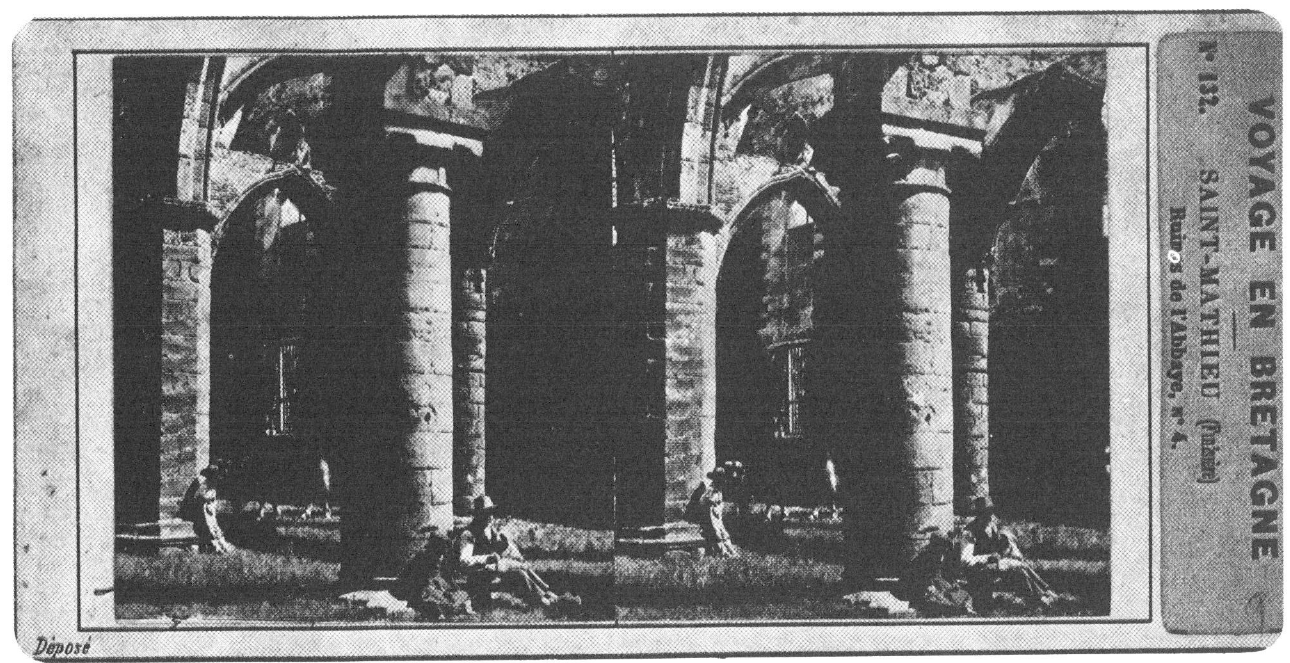

40. Jouvin. Ruins of the Abbey of St. Mathieu, Brittany, France. ca. 1860.

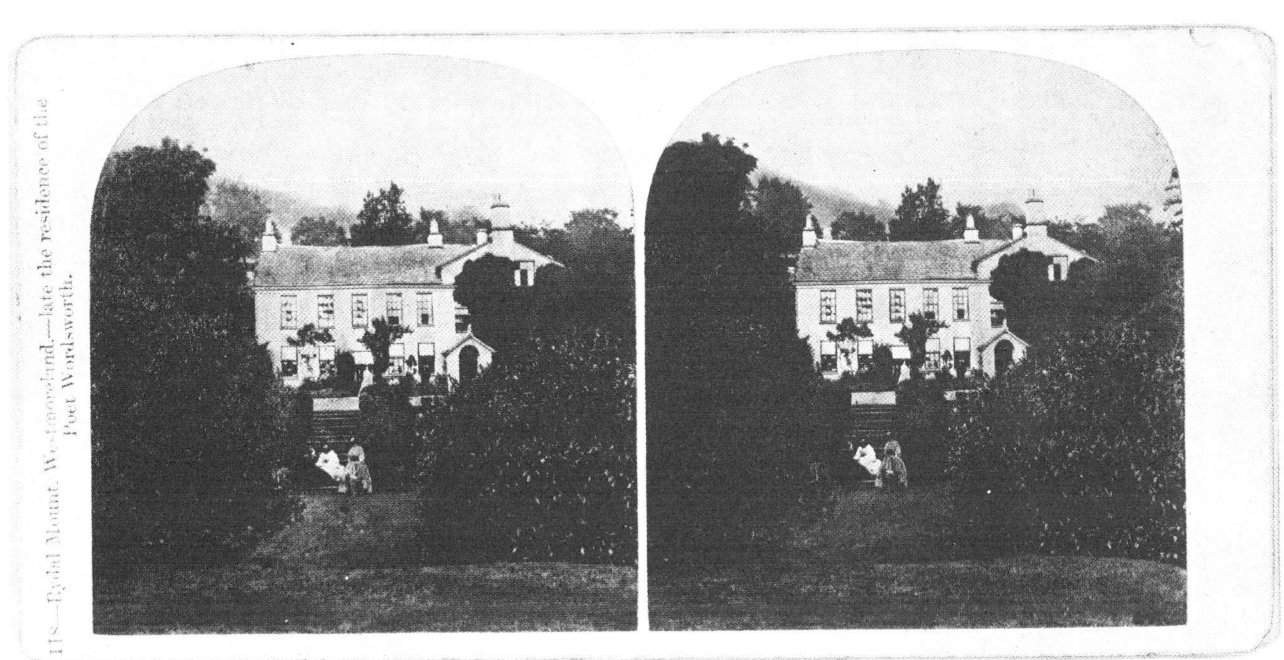

41. Rydal Mount, Westmoreland, Residence of Wordsworth. ca. 1860. J. Elliott, publisher.

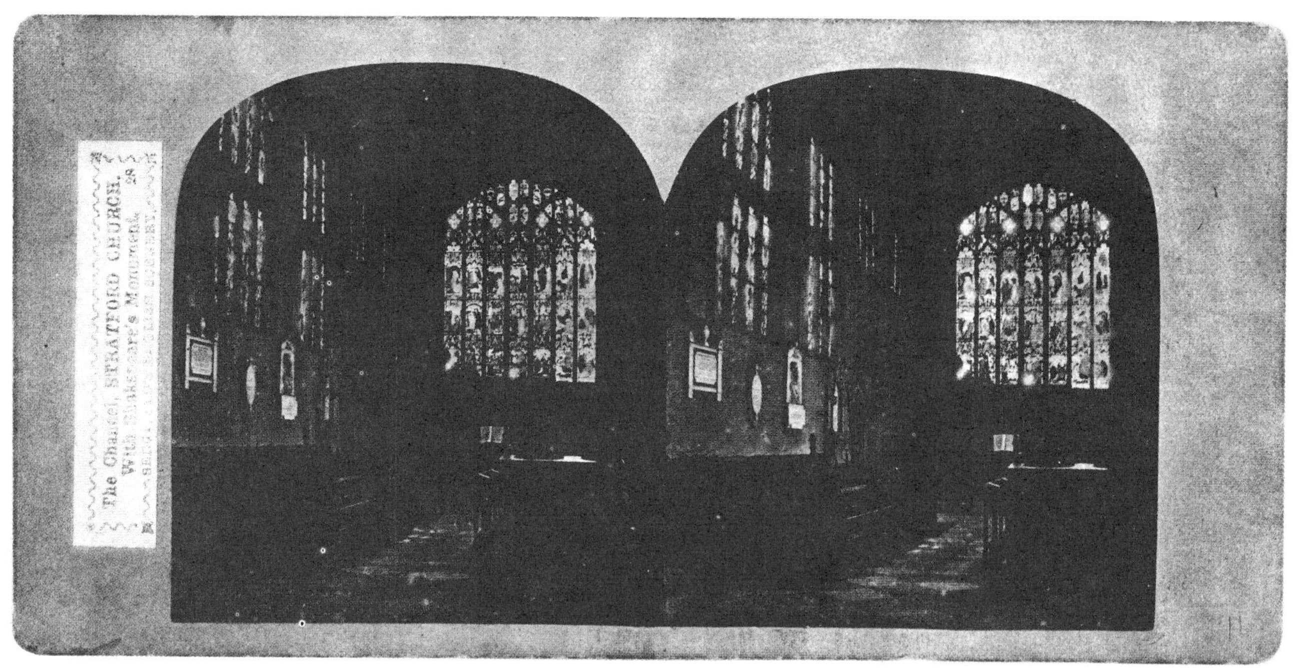

42. William Sedgfield. Stratford Church, with Shakespeare Monument. Typical Sedgfield interior view. 1859.

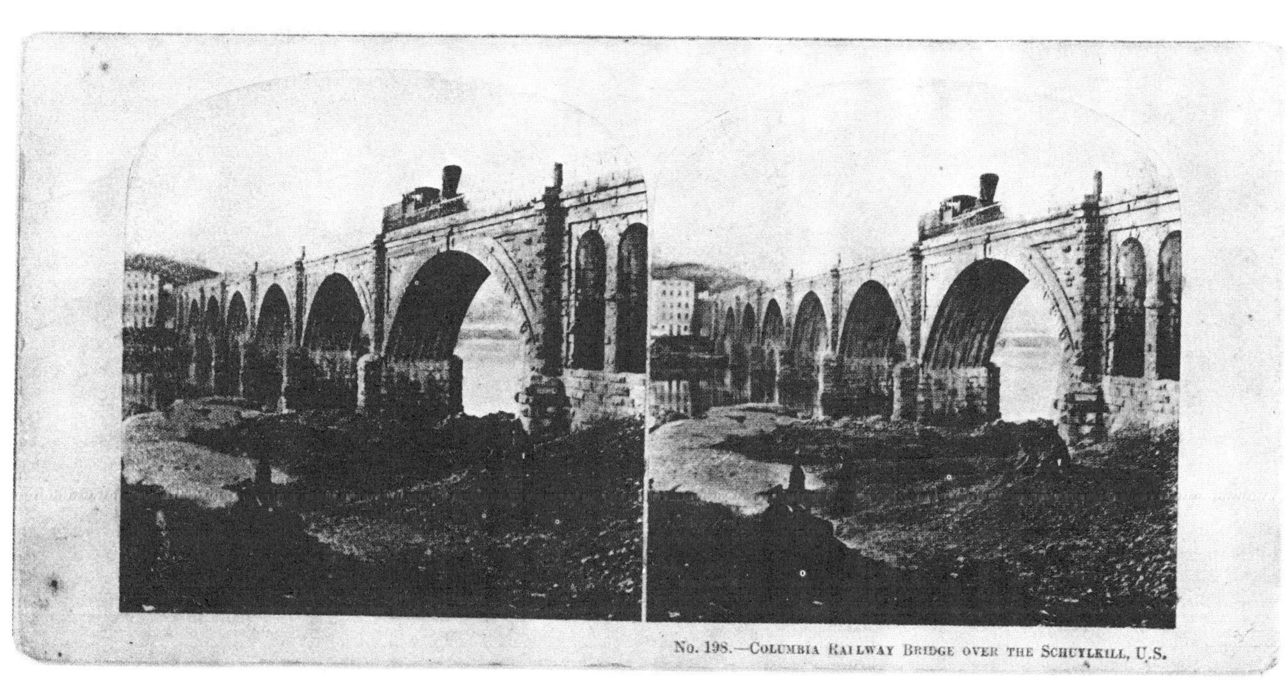

43. William England. Columbia Railway Bridge over the Schuylkill River, Philadelphia. London Stereoscopic Company, publisher. 1859.

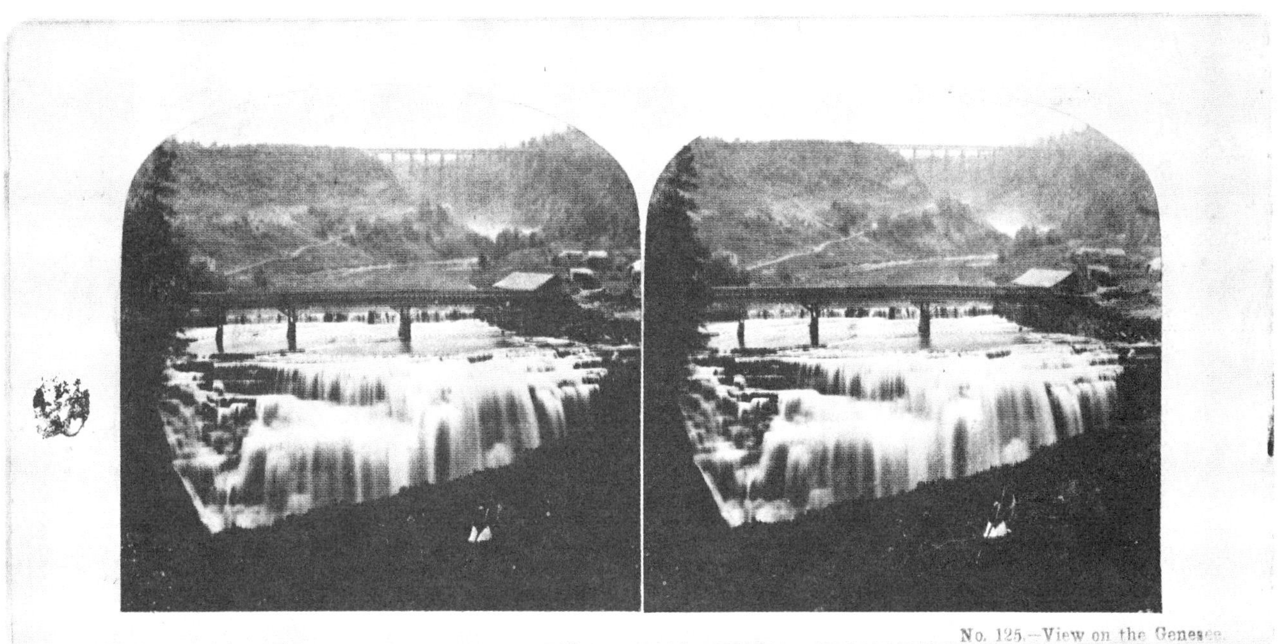

44. William England. "View on the Genesee River, Portage, New York." 1859. London Stereoscopic Company, publisher.

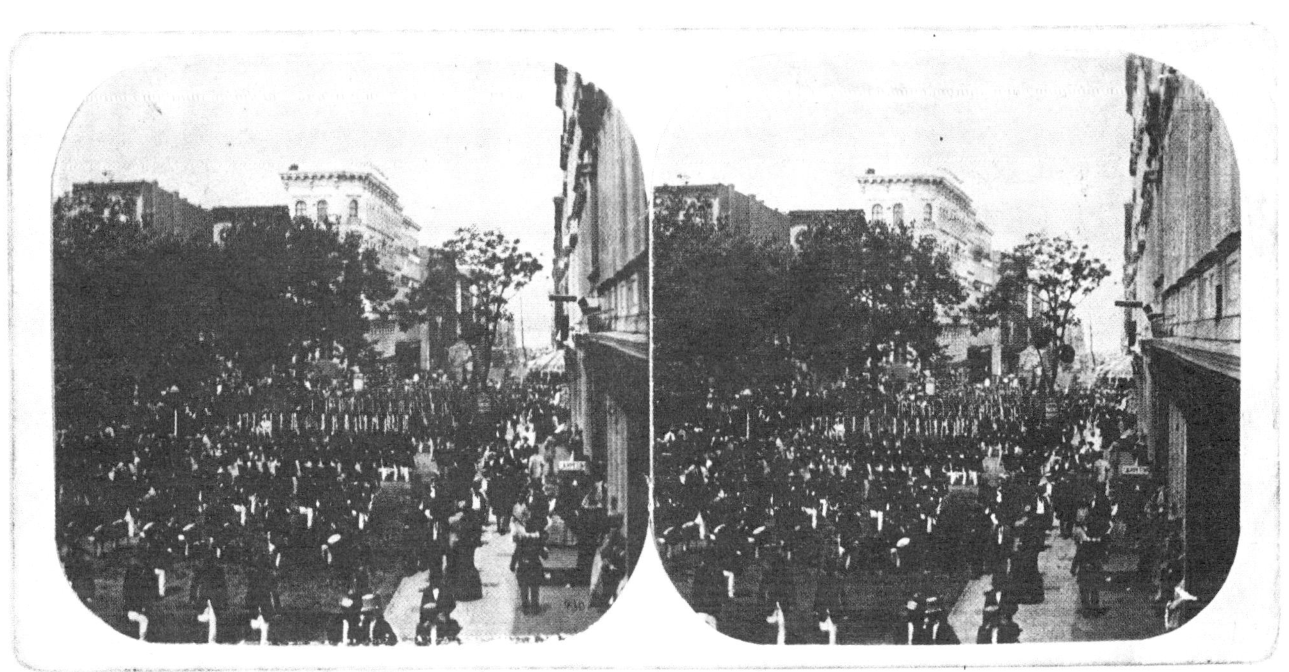

45. E. Anthony. "New York City, Fourth of July Parade, a company of infantry on Chambers Street." 1860.

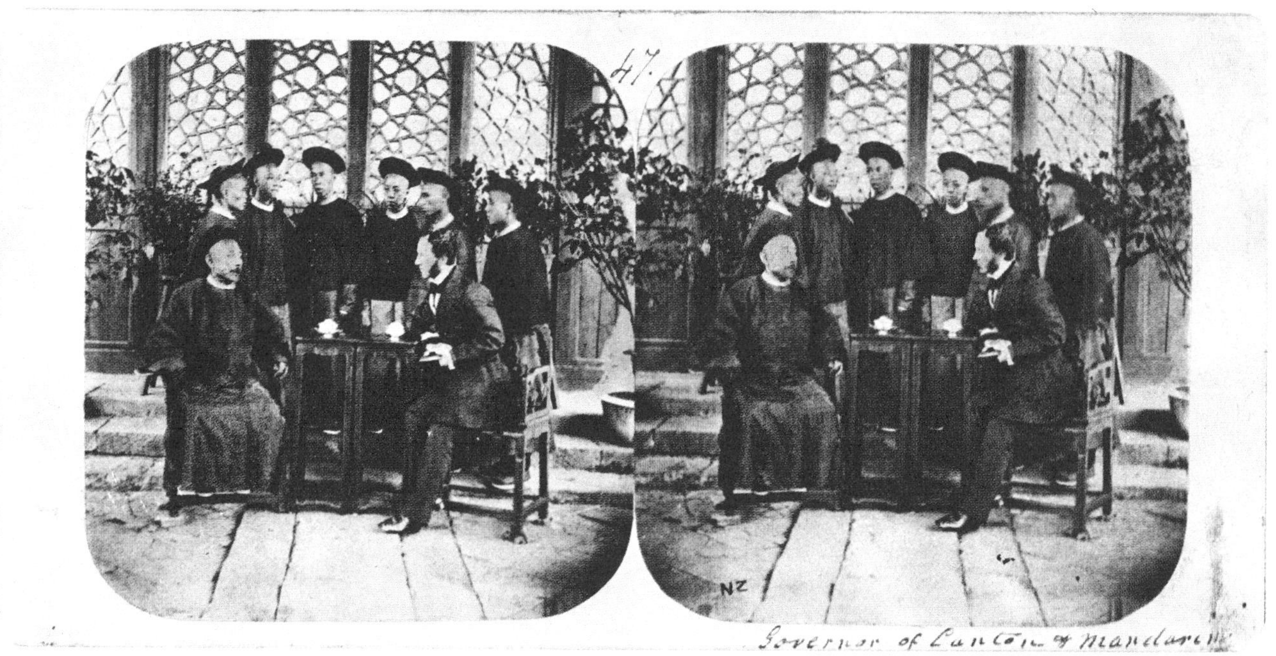

46. F. Beato. "Pey Kwei, the Governor of Canton, with Commissioner Parkes and attendants." Negretti & Zambra, publishers. 1860.

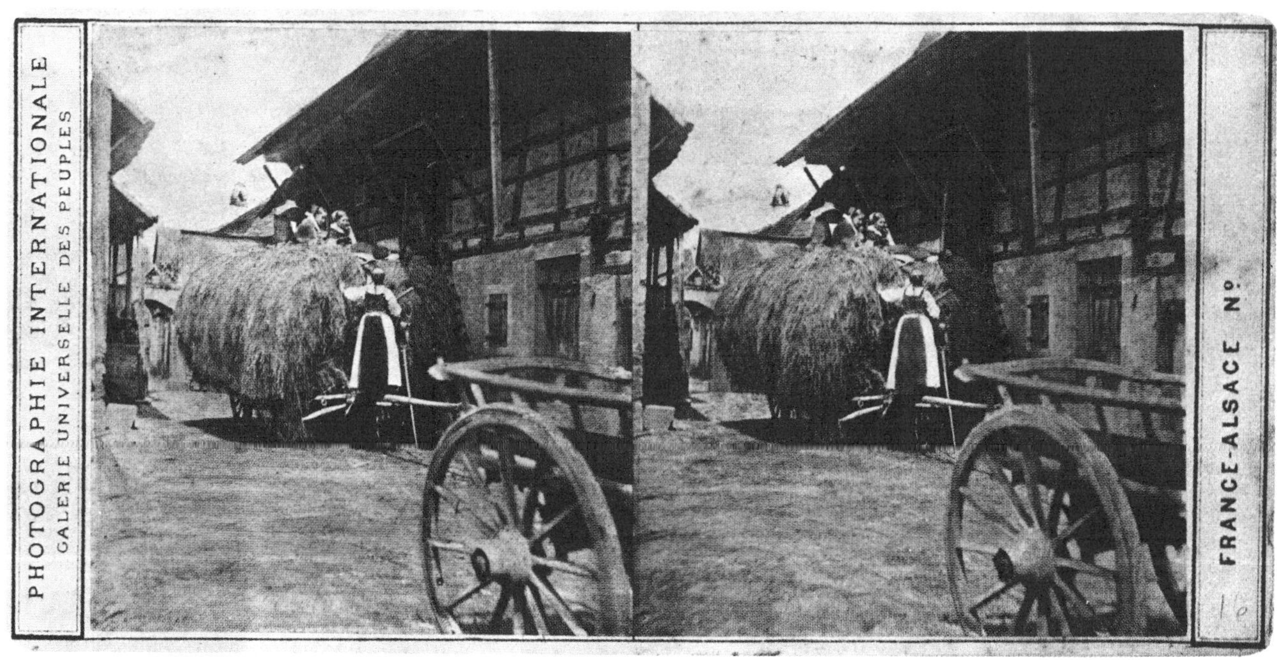

47. Lallemond & Hart. "Universal Gallery of Peoples." Alsace, France. 1864.

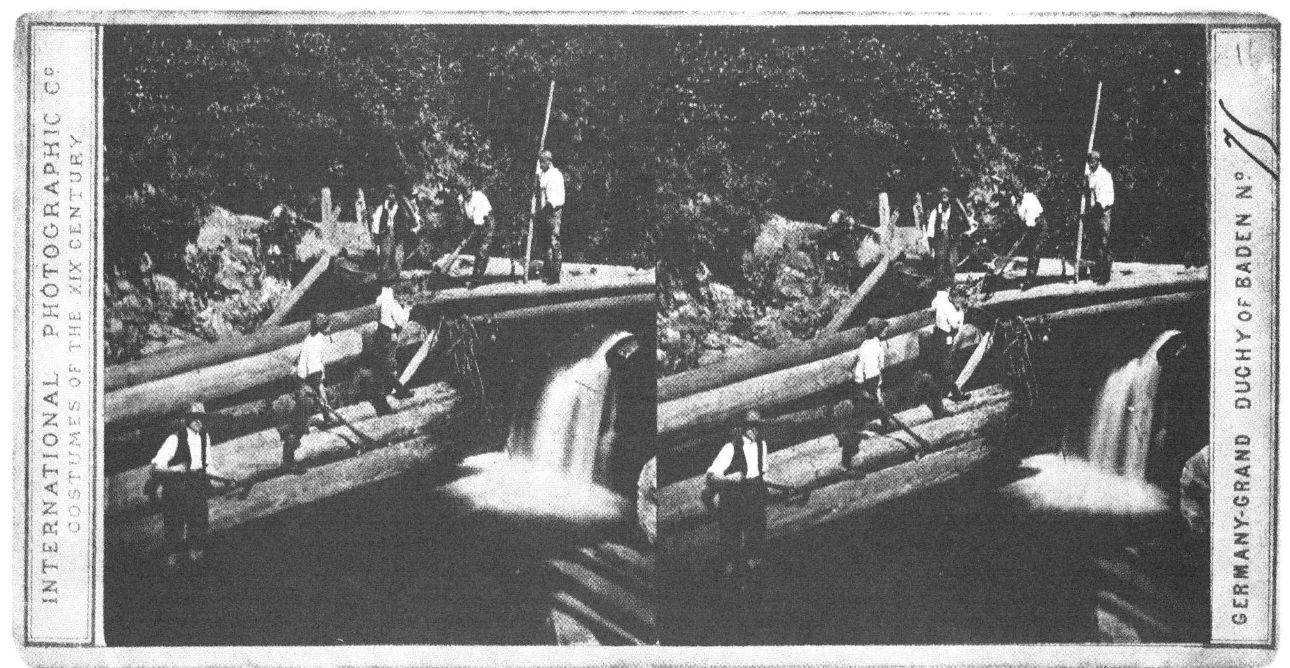

48. Lallemond & Hart. "Costumes of the XIX Century." Lumbermen, Baden, Germany. ca. 1865.

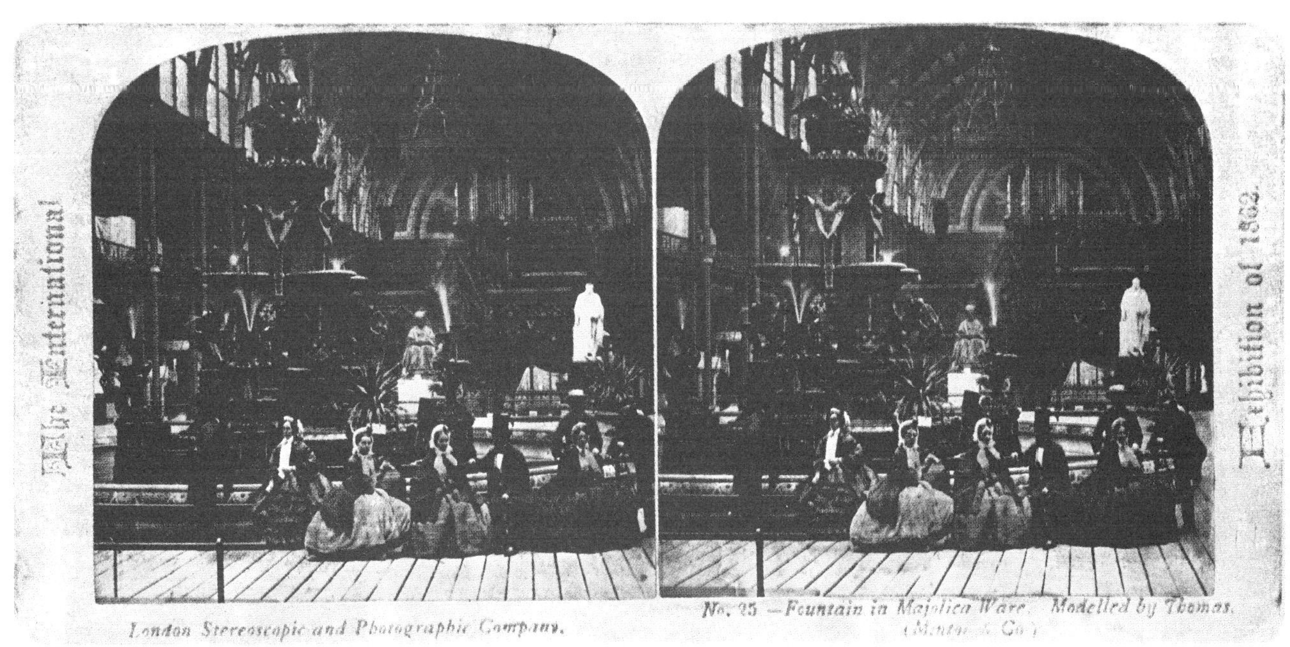

49. William England. International Exhibition, London, 1862. "Fountain in Majolica Ware." London Stereoscopic Company, publisher.

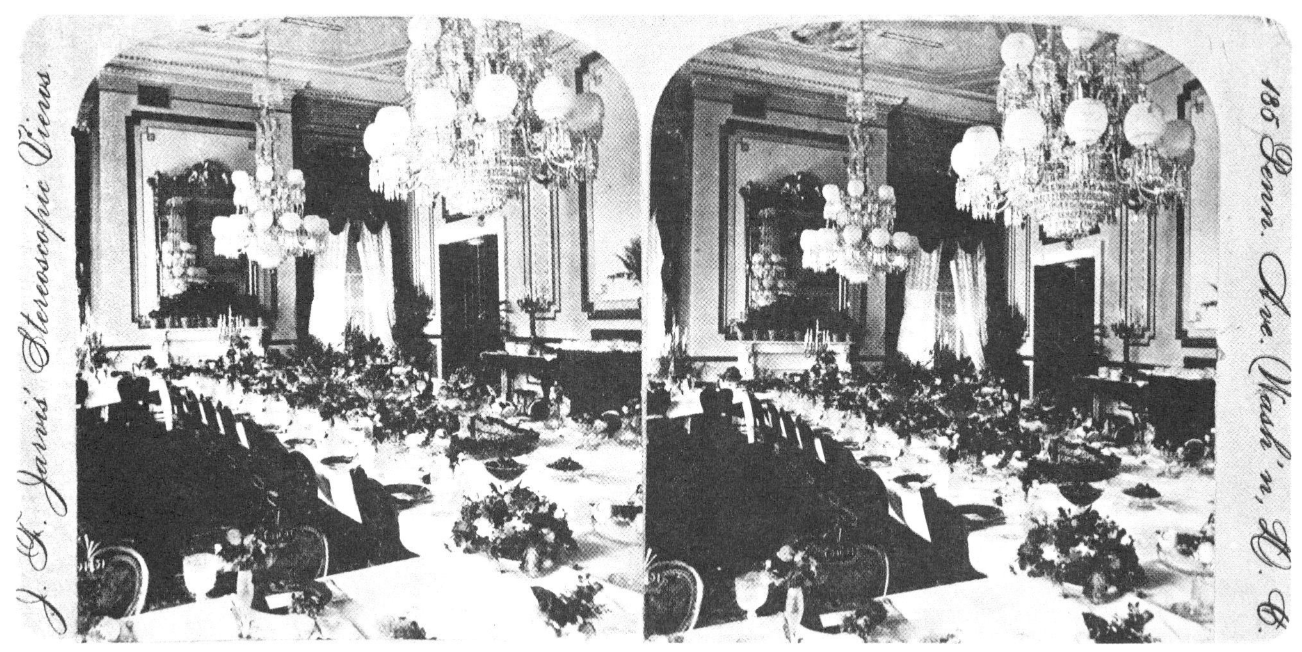

50. J.F. Jarvis, White House Series. "State Dining Room." 1873.

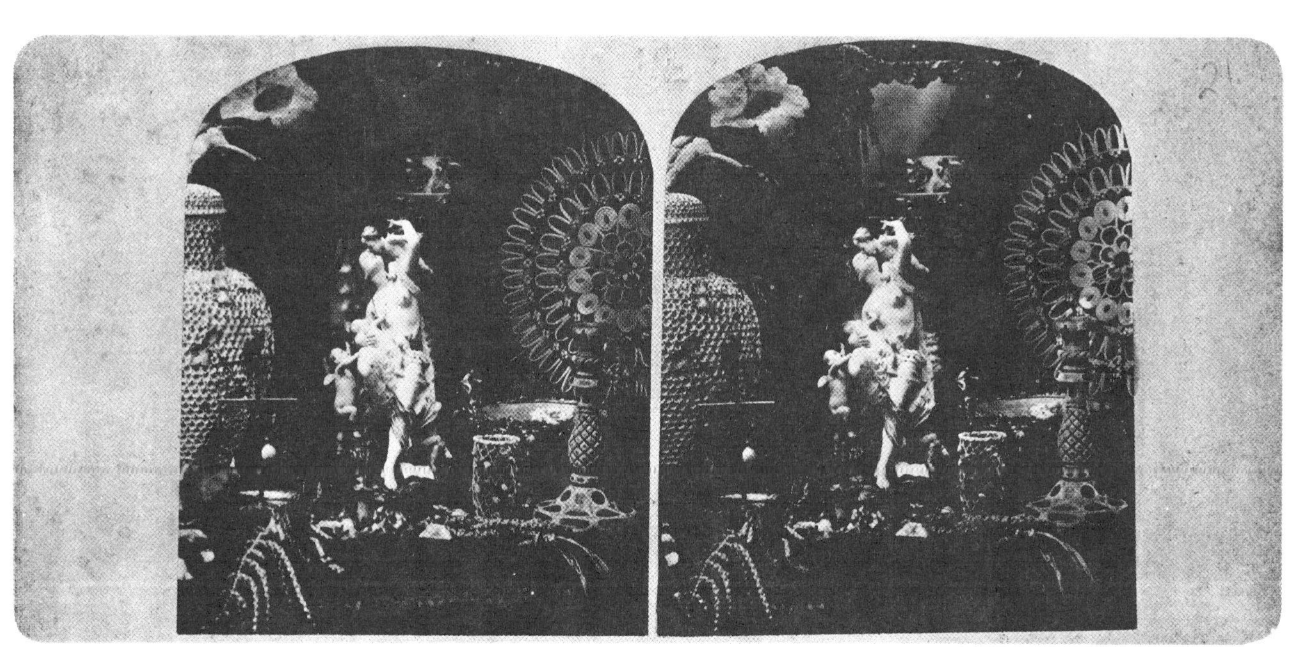

51. J. Elliott. "Artistic Arrangement." 1856.

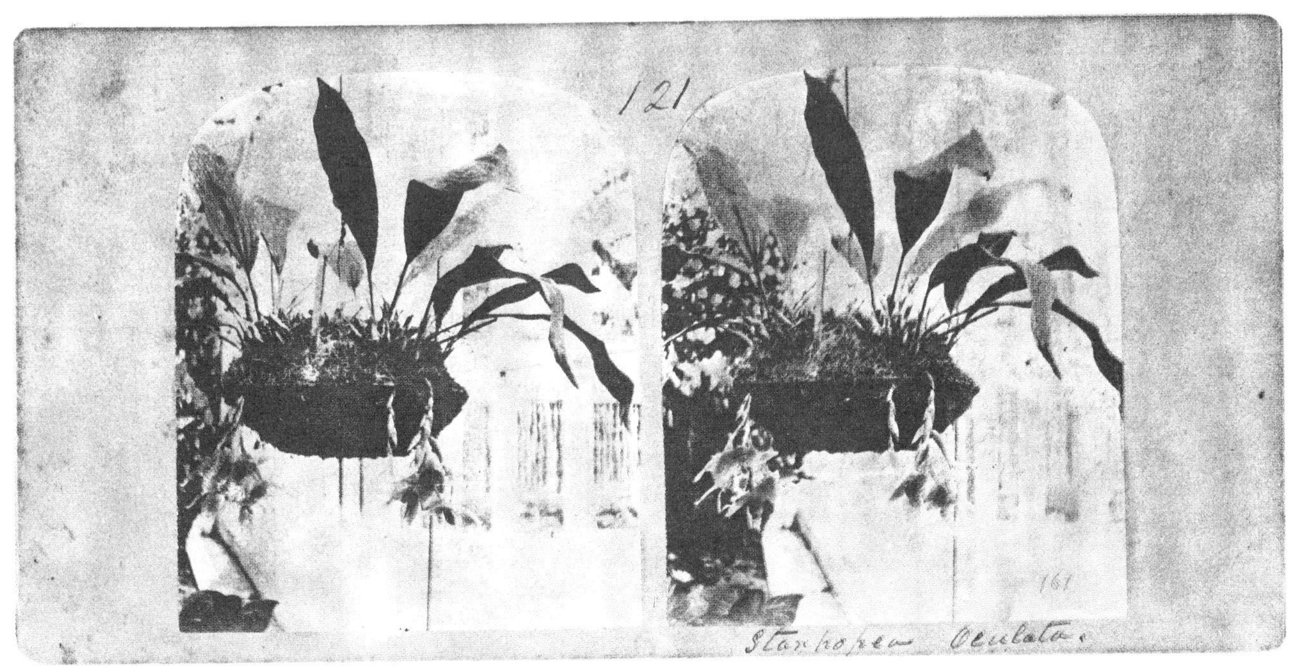

52. Poulton and Son. Chatsworth Series. "*Stanhopea oculata*, native to Brazil to Mexico. Named in honor of the Earl of Stanhope. Introduced into England in 1829." 1858.

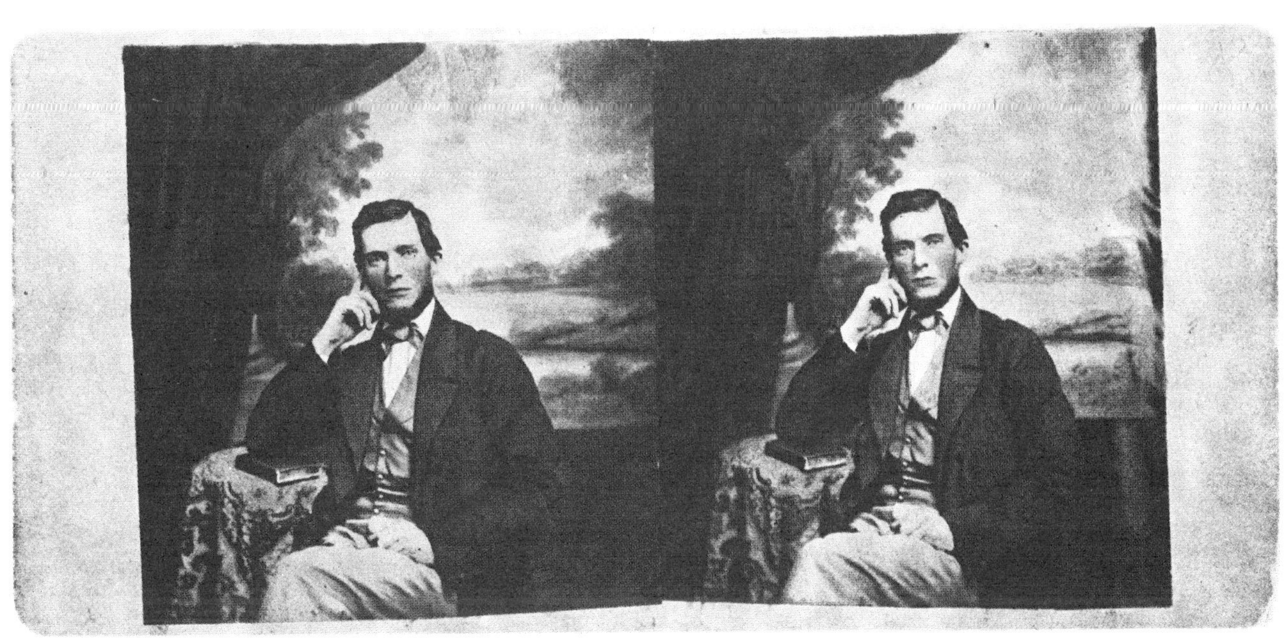

53. Portrait of an American gentleman. Stereo portraits against a painted background are very rare. Unknown photographer, probably from Philadelphia. ca. 1862.

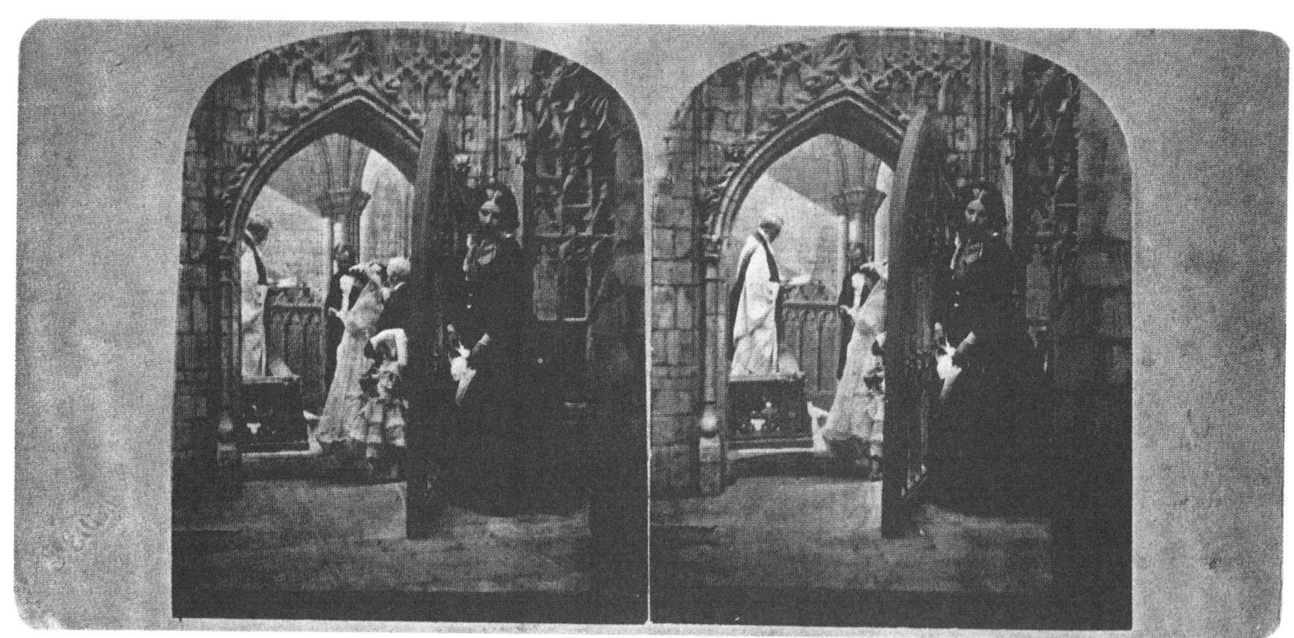

54. J. Elliott. "Broken Vows." A typical sentimental view. ca 1856.

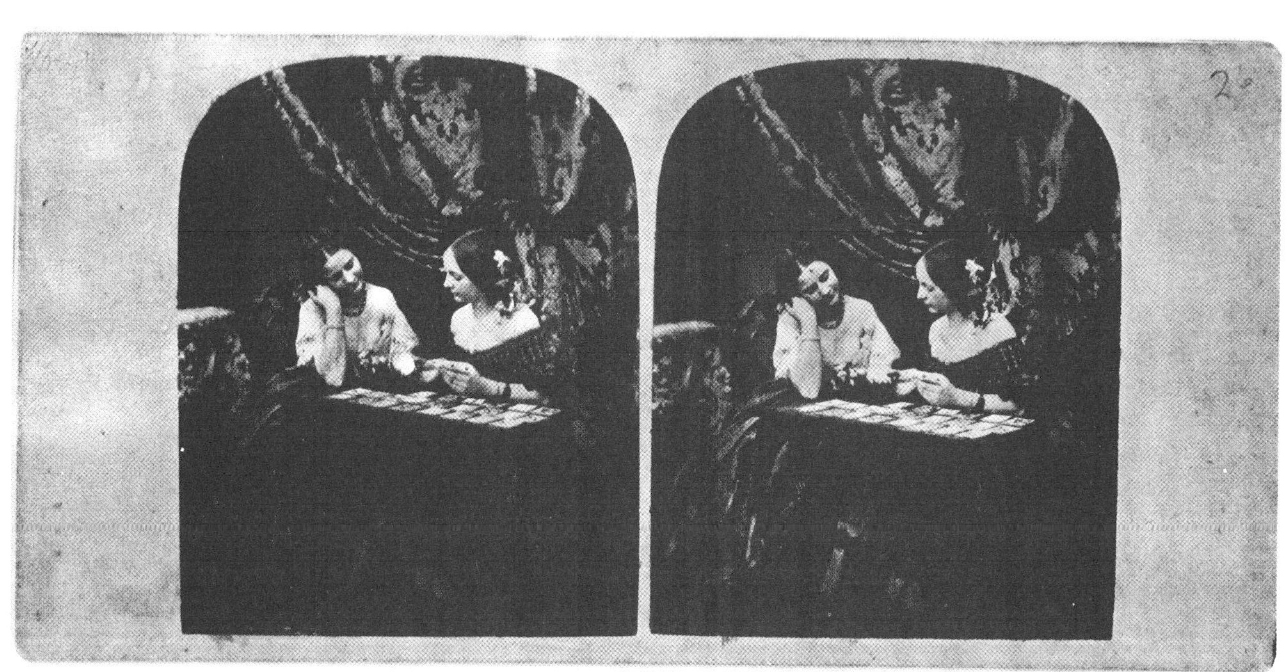

55. J. Elliott. "Fortune Telling." ca. 1856.

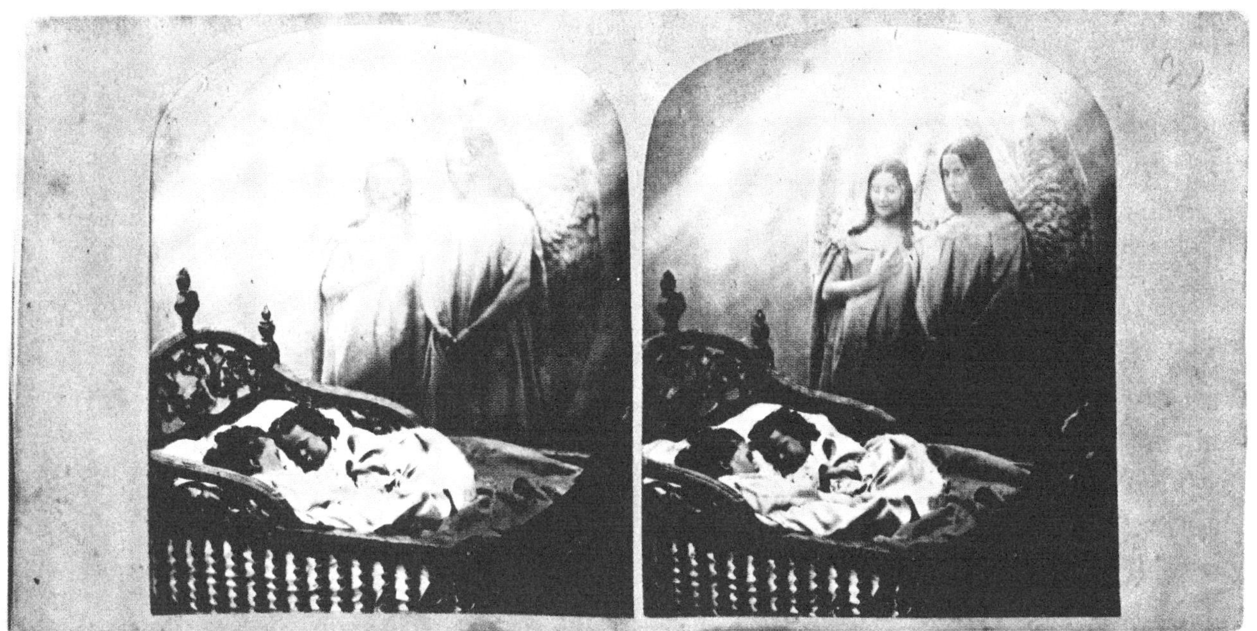

56. Alfred Silvester. "Guardian Angels." Note use of ghost figures. ca. 1856.

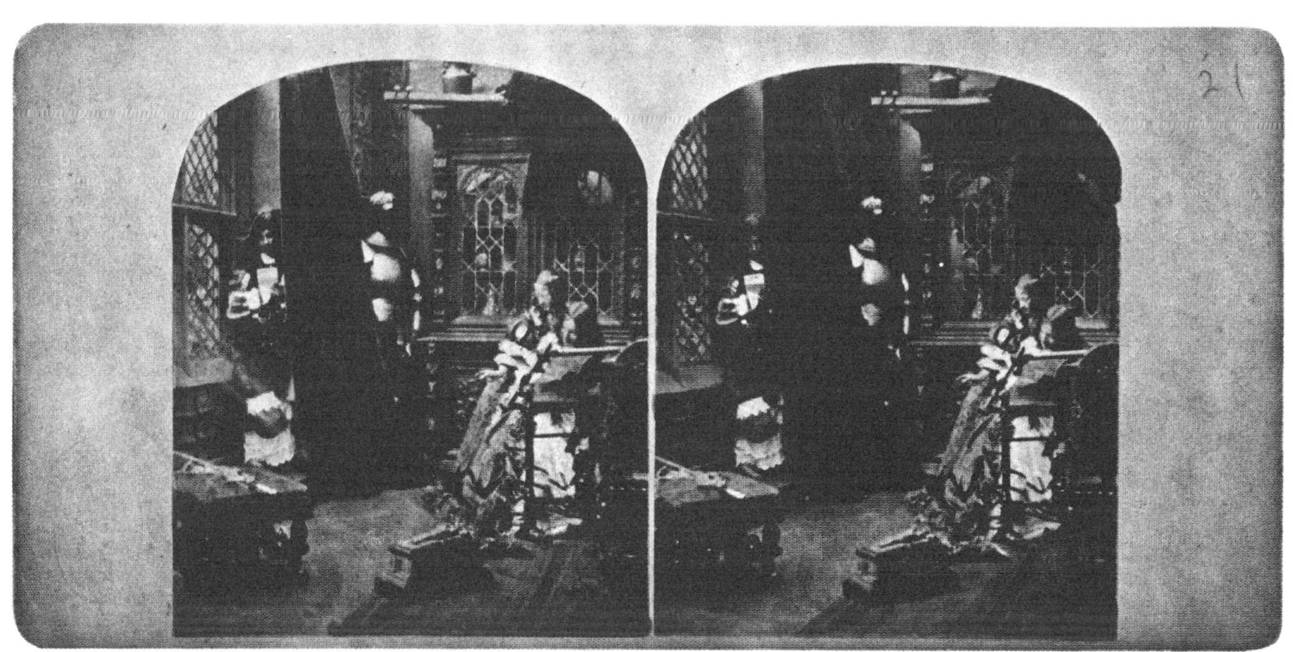

57. J. Elliott. "The First Love Letter." An elaborate studio setting. ca. 1856.

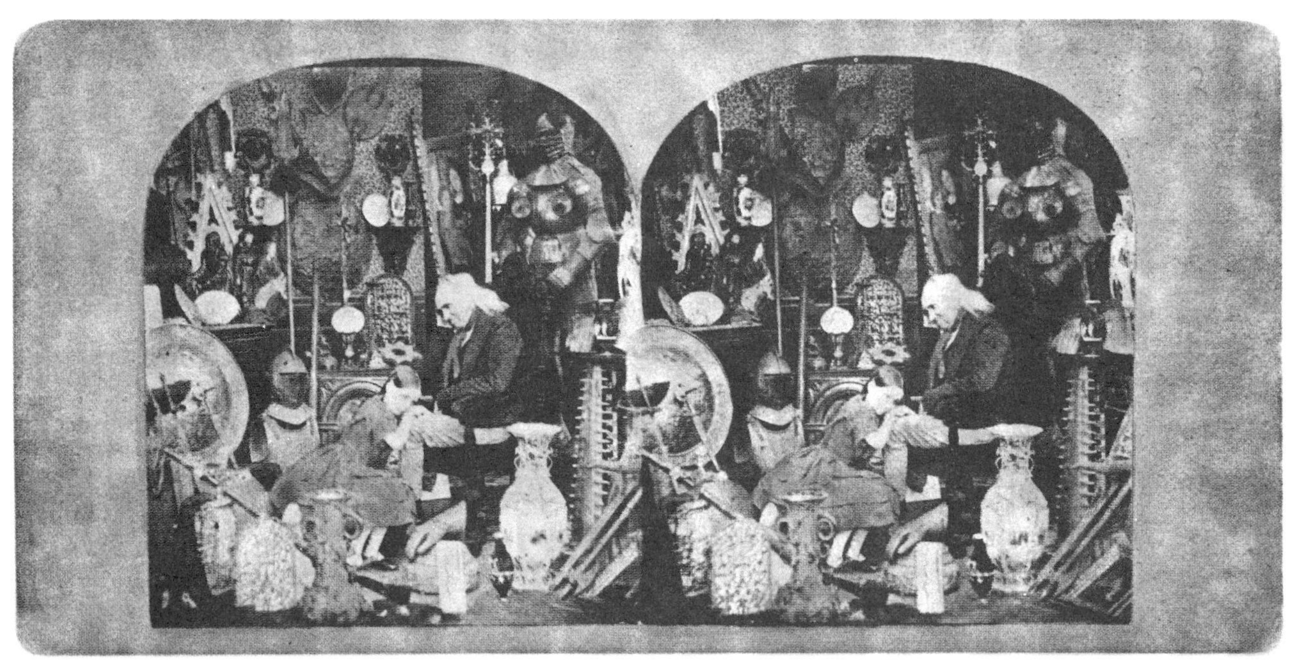

58. James Robertson. "Little Nell and Her Grandfather," *The Old Curiosity Shop*, by Charles Dickens." ca. 1858.

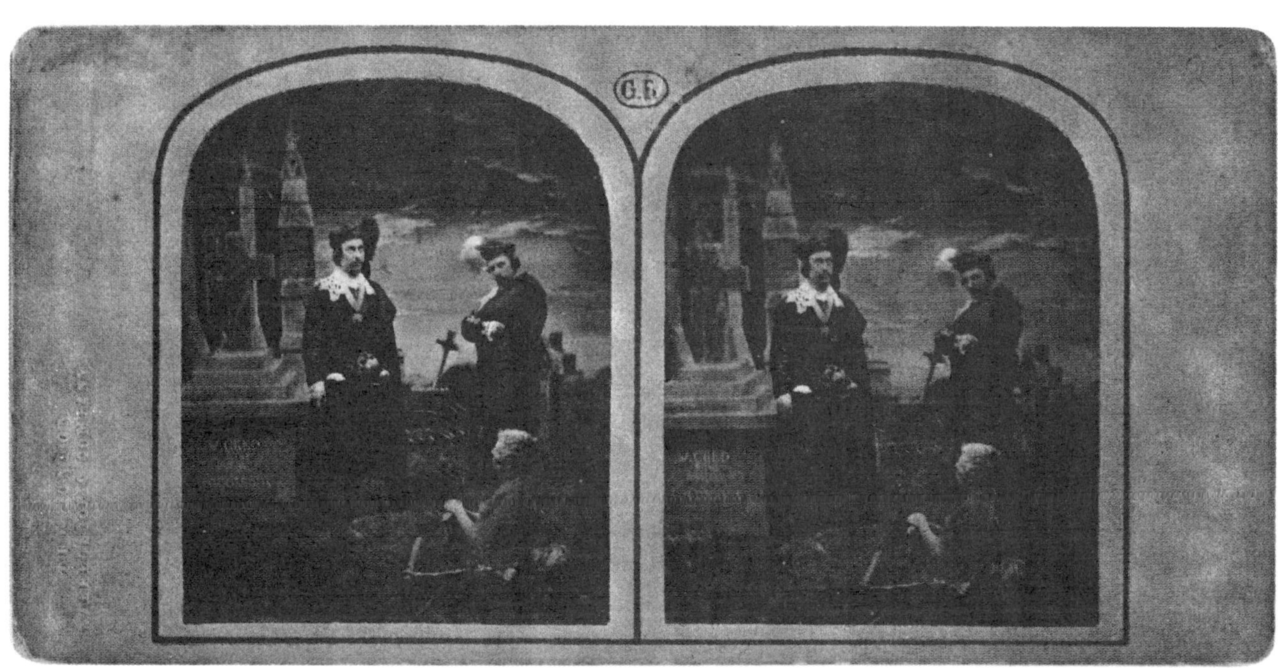

59. Hablot Knight ("Phiz".) " 'Alas, poor Yorick', Hamlet, Prince of Denmark, Act V. Scene I. " Gebhardt & Rottman, publishers. 1857.

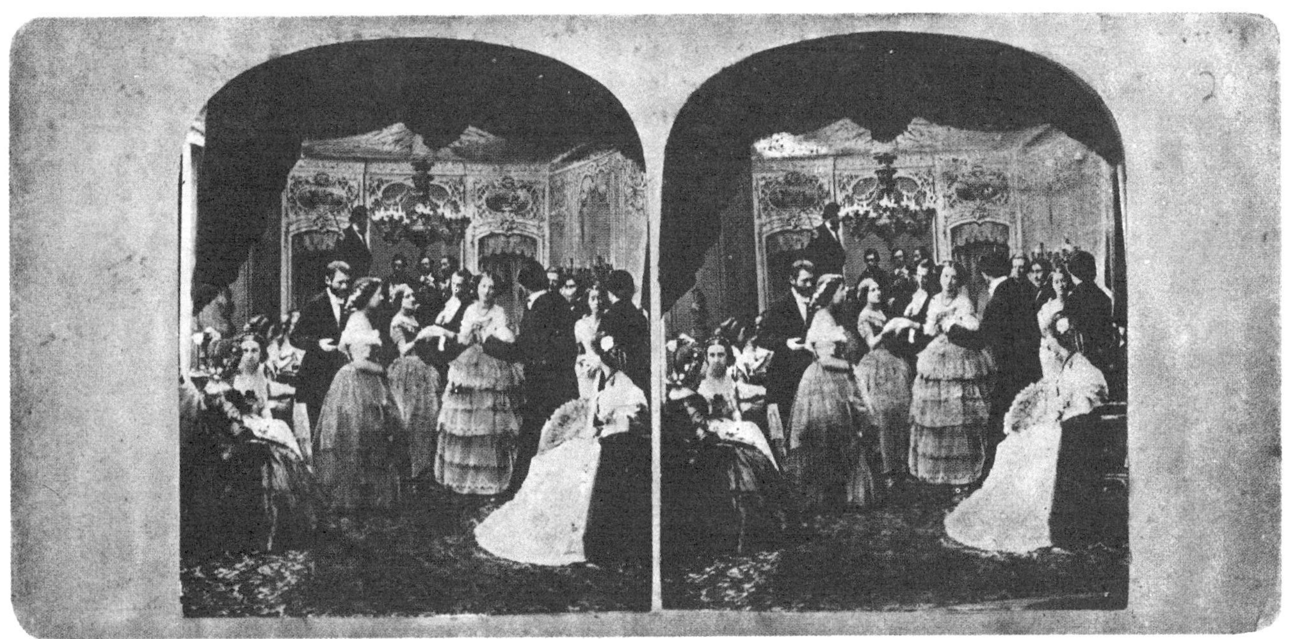

60. Montage, composed from several photographs. Note sizes of heads of the groups of dancers and musicians. J. Elliott, publisher. ca. 1858.

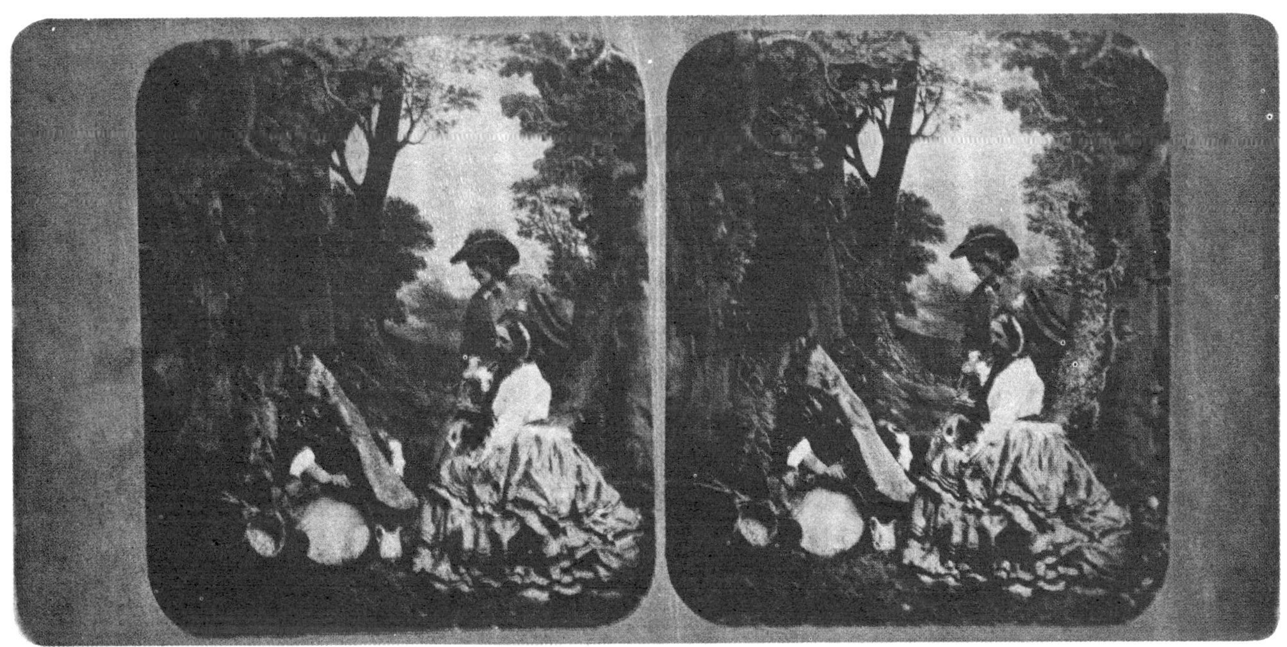

61. Rustic Scene. This studio set and backdrop were used for a dozen similar groups. English, ca. 1856.

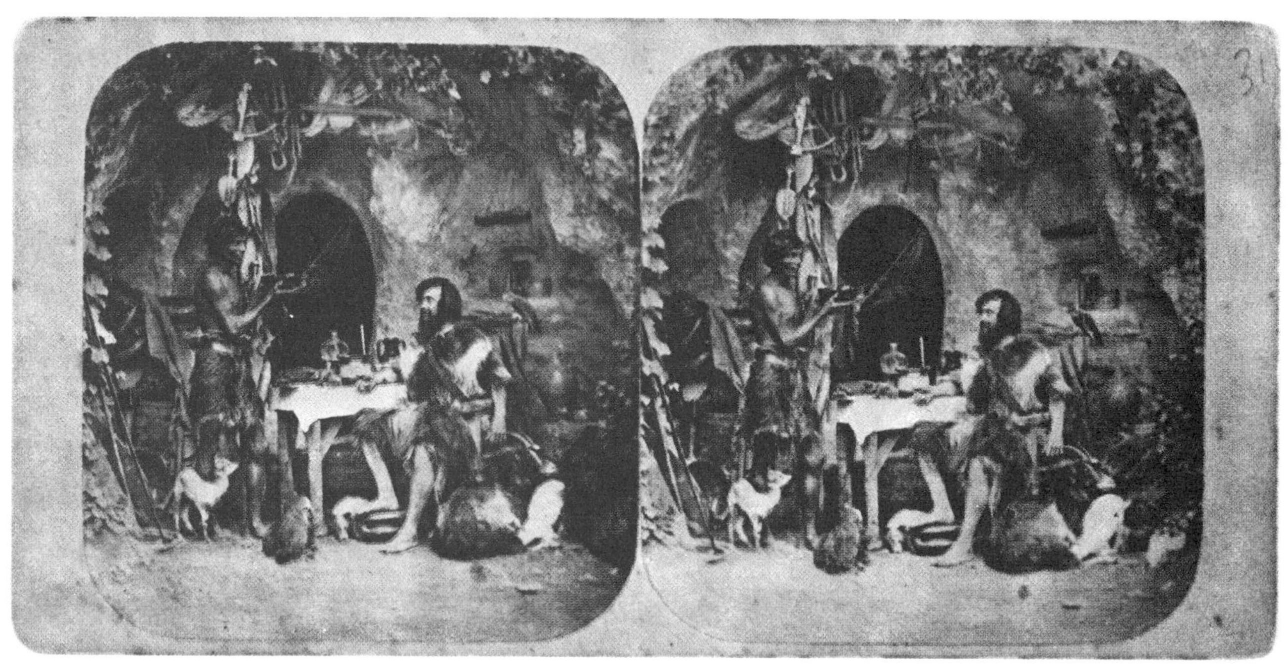

62. Lake Price. "Robinson Crusoe and Friday." Negative 1855, Card ca. 1857.

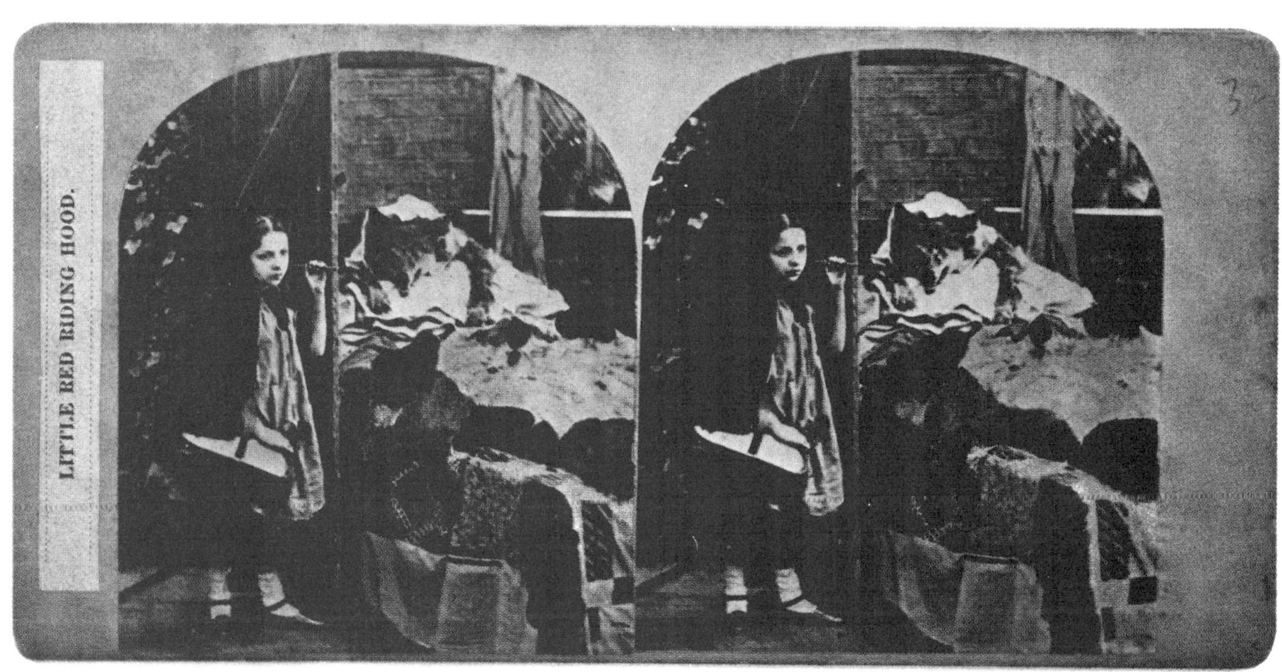

63. "Little Red Riding Hood." One of a set of four scenes. 1856. Unknown photographer. The London Stereoscopic Company produced this set continuously until 1870. There were also many copy issues.

SOME NOTES ON TINTED VIEWS

The popularity of tinted stereographs, as noted earlier, was confined largely to the period 1854-1875. A plain photograph, particularly a portrait, could be given warmth and more life-like appearance by coloring. Furthermore, miniature painters had accustomed European and American society to colored portraits. The tinting of scenic views was really an extension of the desire to achieve natural effects which were beyond the capability of photography.

As early as July 1839, John Herschel obtained a photograph of the spectrum but was unable to fix the color image. He predicted, however, that at some future time methods for photographing natural color would be discovered. Not until a century later was his prediction fully realized.

Meanwhile the mid nineteenth century demand for colored photographs had to be met by painters. In fact, hundreds of miniaturists who found themselves unemployed as a result of photography, banded into associations and advertised their skills in photographic periodicals and by handbills distributed among urban photographers.

We can distinguish between three different objectives in tinting stereographs: artistic, technical accuracy and effect.

The scenes by Grundy (figure 33) and Fenton (figure 38) were tinted to enhance natural beauty, with faithful attention to the landscape, although the coloring of sky, water and rocks may have been idealized. Stereographs showing flags, military uniforms or specimen plants, such as Poulton's *Stanhopea* (figure 52) were usually accurately colored. Minute detail, another aspect of accuracy, is illustrated by William England's view of the Majolica fountain at the International Exhibition (figure 49).

In contrast, sentimental and comic views were often harshly painted to heighten ridiculous effect. Sometimes this coarseness escapes notice because it contributes to the scene. Note for example Little Red Riding Hood (figure 63).

Categorically, all tinted stereographs produced before 1863 were colored with transparent water colors. Beginning about 1863-64, the newly discovered synthetic liquid aniline colors became available.

The photograph colorist used as many as ninety colors. Root, for instance, lists more than eighty "essential colors, the same as are employed by miniature painters" (1864, page 276). Towler (1864, page 225) gives a smaller number, emphasizing "the twenty-two most used." He commented, "it is remarkable, however, to see with how few colors the *real artist* can execute the most finished work." (Today a brilliant palette will have only eight colors). Both Root and Towler indicate the uses of specific colors such as for red hair, drapery, imitation of mother of pearl, wrought iron, etc.

Liquid aniline colors, developed consequent to William Perkin's discovery (1856) of the synthetic dye known as mauve, were enthusiastically applied to albumin prints. The albumin surface did not require preparation and the aniline colors flowed freely and controllably over it. Towler "highly recommended them for the ordinary practitioner in card pictures."

English and American photographic supply houses carried full lines of Chinese and Prussian water colors in sets and as individual cakes and aniline colors, listing them in their trade catalogues into the late 1870's.

Readers desiring to learn more about this aspect of stereographs are referred to *How to Paint Photographs in Water Colors* by George B. Ayres (1st ed. 1870) and the less accessible but more influential earlier articles by Alfred H. Hall, published serially in *Humphrey's Journal* (vols. 11, 12, 1859, 1860).

Tinted stereographs hold a notable place in the history of photography. On one hand they point out some limitations of photography at a time when the interpretation of the photograph and the philosophy of photography itself was controversial. On the other hand they are a link with the tradition of miniature painting, despite the fact that the painter is now a colorist rather than the artist. Even so, the tinted stereograph has an added quality, an added dimension which compounds its impact.

(Continued from Page 26)

Resident photographers before 1870 had established studios in virtually every town and village in the United States and Canada.

These local operators were of four main types, each characterized by the stereo work produced.

(1) The photographer who specialized in the production of stereographs but confined his practice to local subjects. If operations were continued for a decade or more, the trade list would range from several hundreds to several thousands of titles.

(2) The resort photographer (there were hundreds of them at Niagara Falls, Saratoga, the White Mountains, Catskills, etc.) who virtually limited his work to the tourist trade. Many produced negatives numbered in the thousands.

(3) The studio photographer who, as a side line, occasionally produced stereoscopic portraits, poses, interiors of churches and public buildings, commonly including a small series of local town views.

(4) The opportunist who produced a few views when some unusual event—flood, fire, train-wreck, parade, or such—created a transitory market for souvenirs. In some instances the negatives, or rights to them, were sold to large-volume publishers.

Nearly every photographer who did his own publishing developed his individual fashion of mounting and labeling, his own style and artistry, and even his peculiar methods of merchandising. Many energetic photographers maintained highly profitable nation-wide mail order business.

There were other photographers who remained artists at heart and paid little attention to the commercial pressures, even though they relied upon photography for a livelihood. While many names deserve recognition, only two can be cited here, Carl Meinerth and John Moran.

Carl Meinerth, artist-musician-photographer, operated in Portsmouth, New Hampshire, prior to 1860 and moved to Newburyport about 1866. He became a partner of R. E. Mosely, whom he succeeded about 1867. Meinerth produced beautiful still lifes, child portraits, and many true-life sentimental views in addition to town and harbor views of Portsmouth and Newburyport. He also experimented with scientific photography. Meinerth worked in the spirit of English and German artist-photographers of the 1850's, yet with a style all his own.

John Moran, a fine, versatile photographer, was the unsung member of renowned Philadelphia family of artists that included his brothers Edward and Thomas. His earliest known stereographs date from 1859 or 1860. In the tradition of Grundy he produced beautiful rural scenes along Wissahickon Creek. Later scenic work, including the Allegheny and White Mountains, displays the trained eye of the painter. Moran also produced beautiful architectural views, mostly of Philadelphia buildings and institutions nearby. John Moran continued photography into the 1870's, serving with the Selfridge Expedition to Darien and the astronomical team that photographed the transit of Venus in Tasmania. Figures 31 and 36.

Stereographic Exchange Clubs

During the early burst of stereo enthusiasm, 1859-1862, several groups of interested individuals met to exchange ideas and share experience. Effective professional societies had not yet been organized in the United States.

One of the most remarkable associations was the Amateur Photographic Exchange Club, organized in 1861 by John Towler of Hobart College and Coleman Sellers of Philadelphia. About twenty members, including scientists, artists, college professors and businessmen, agreed to exchange stereographs, with technical data on the methods used in making them. Each member was obligated to "exchange with every other member, six times a year, at least one stereographic print, mounted and finished." The Exchange Club survived only three years, largely because several of its most active members were involved in the Civil War, but also because the growing number of skilled professionals diminished need for such an experimenting club.

Stereographs by members of the Amateur Photographic Exchange Club are very rare. Some of the members failed to meet their exchange obligations and others were active for only a few months, unavoidably because they had entered military service. The total number of cards produced did not exceed 2000, and many titles are known today from single surviving copies.

This American club was actually inspired by "The Stereoscopic Exchange Club," organized in England in April 1859. This Club had forty charter members and ultimately a total of more than 150, including two colonials, Alex Henderson of Montreal and S. Clifford of Hobart, Australia. Correspondents of the British club complained bitterly about the poor and trivial photographs being exchanged by some of the members. Officers of the British club urged adoption of the American requirement that technical data should be given on the label with each stereograph.

Some historians of photography have confused the American Stereoscopic Exchange Club (1867-1870) with the earlier Amateur Photographic Exchange Club. There was no connection whatsoever. The American Stereoscopic Exchange Club was organized by professional photographers to share their experience in producing stereo views. The prime movers were Hanson E. Weaver and Mrs. Weaver, recently moved to Washington from Hanover, Pennsylvania; J. W. Love of Portage, Wisconsin; and C. Kneeland of Pittsburgh. Among the twenty other members were S. Hall Morris of Auburn, New York; E. M. VanAken of Lowville, New York; J. Loeffler, Staten Island; J. H. Lakin, Montgomery, Alabama; W. G. Smith, Cooperstown; H. P. McIntosh, Newburyport; and W. E. Bowman, Ottawa, Illinois.

Much of the information concerning this club has been derived through the stereograph collection of Mrs. Weaver, who preserved in pristine condition the exchanges received by her husband.

From 1863 to 1939, the arbitrary date marking the end of commercial manufacture of stereographs, the center of stereographic activity was in the United States. Innovation, novelties, automated mass production, new applications of stereographs—all had origins in America. The most important of these was mechanized mass production.

CHAPTER FIVE

MASS PRODUCTION OF STEREOGRAPHS

The demand for stereographs and, by 1860, for cartes de visite increased so rapidly that several photographic establishments organized production facilities on a grand scale. By dividing the different steps of manufacture into a production line and employing many hands, the capacity was almost unlimited. Soon after its founding, the London Stereoscopic Company was manufacturing more than a thousand stereographs per day. In 1862 the firm sold more than three hundred thousand views of the International Exhibition within six months. Such volume, in addition to the regular issues, demonstrates a remarkable production capacity.

By the mid 1860's at least a score of stereo publishers were manufacturing more than two thousand views per day. E. & H. T. Anthony, Ferrier (Paris), Adolphe Braun (Dornach) and J. Andrieu (Paris) are but four examples. In the early 1870's simple mechanization techniques accelerated production to three thousand with the same number of helpers. Braun had one hundred employees in his factory, but they were engaged in manufacturing all types of photographs.

Kilburn Brothers (Littleton, New Hampshire) erected a large three-story factory with special rooms for printing, toning, washing, drying and mounting. The division of labor was in no way different from already-established practice. Improvements resulted from greater efficiency in passing from one operation to another. The only mechanization was an endless-belt exposure machine which, by eliminating handling of each exposure, doubled the rate of production of prints. Employing fifty-two persons, some of whom were maintenance men and clerks, the Kilburns produced, on an average, three thousand finished stereographs per day. In other words, the Kilburn factory could easily publish a million cards per year.

Contributing to the huge volume of stereographs were many photoprinters with facilities equal to or greater than those of Kilburn or Anthony. The work of one of the most important of these, Charles Pollock of Boston, may be taken as a typical example. Pollock's main trade was custom printing for independent photographers. He was an accomplished photographer, maintained a spacious retail emporium in Boston and operated, at Foxboro, Massachusetts, one of the largest photoprinting establishments in the world. The factory was set up to print many jobs simultaneously, i.e., by separate production lines. Pollock claimed that his factory made more than four thousand stereographs per day between 1872 and 1874, in addition to the production of cartes de visite and cabinet views. He was one of the first American publishers to issue the same stereo view in several formats of different quality. (The French were doing this ten years earlier.) Some of Pollock's titles were published on as many as six different types of mounts, ranging from very cheap to fine.

Pollock's high quality work met the most demanding standards of his clients. Scores of New England's best-known photographers depended upon Pollock for manufacturing their stereographs. Many of the fine views by photographers of Boston, Lynn, Lowell and Lawrence were printed and mounted by Pollock. Examples of his less-expensive work may be found in the large trade lists of such resort photographers as G. W. Tirrell, II (East Weymouth, Mass.) and A. P. Munger (Hampton Village, N. H.).

Although Pollock's major output was custom work, he acted as publisher of several cheap lines, which were sold wholesale without any publisher's imprint. A few of these cards bear the initials CP printed on the margin of the card face. These were sold at his Boston emporium.

Pollock also published a number of series of excellent views bearing a Pollock imprint. The most unusual is a set of tinted tissues of the White House (1872), one of the very few tissue formats produced in the United States. It was Pollock who produced the "Florida Club" series for a group of Boston photographers and their friends, the first issue of which (1868) was initially sold by subscription for the Christmas trade.

It is probable that Charles Pollock was related to G. & W. E. Pollock, who operated a similar, but somewhat smaller, photoprinting facility in New York City. They, too, produced a huge volume of stereographs (1864-74) along with cartes de visite and cabinet photographs.

The photoprinters were important in the mass production of stereo views and in reducing the retail price of cards. Yet, they contributed very little to the advancement of photography. They merely provided an essential service, freeing the photographer from the onerous and costly routine of printing and mounting quantities of his own images.

Shortly before 1880 a new dimension was introduced to the stereograph business. The mass producer was not only the publisher but also became the retailer. Retailing by door-to-door canvassers became organized, first on a national and then quickly on an international scale.

B. W. Kilburn, successor to Kilburn Brothers

When, in 1877, Edward Kilburn retired from business, B. W. Kilburn reorganized the company. He shifted emphasis from White Mountain scenery to world-wide subjects and a fully diversified trade list, including comic and sentimental views of appeal to both children and adults. Recognizing the differences in education, culture and social status of potential clientele and, at the same time, the growing interest in world affairs, Ben Kilburn cautiously developed his idea. Between 1877 and 1879 he published a fine series of views of the British Isles on both

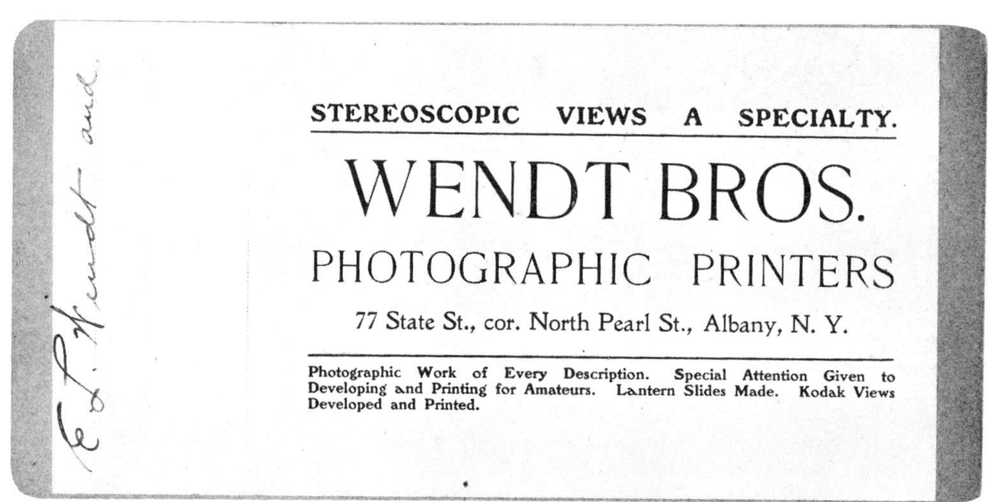

64. A photoprinter's service. Wendt Brothers (Julius and L.E.), Albany New York, ca. 1900-1915. Wendt autograph.

standard and cabinet mounts. Historical buildings and landmarks in England, Scotland and Ireland made up the larger part of the series. The project was an immediate success. During the next few years a trade list of about a thousand numbers was in active production, with approximately three hundred White Mountain scenes among them.

Kilburn's real innovation, however, was in merchandising. In 1879 canvassers were sent to several selected New England town to demonstrate a variety of views, take orders, and a week later, deliver the stereo views and collect the money due. Working on a straight commission basis, these young men proved the feasibility of selling stereo views door-to-door. By 1883 several hundred canvassers were engaged, mostly during the summer and fall, in the northeastern United States and in the Midwest. An agency had been set up in Chicago to stock the stereo views and better control their distribution.

With this encouragement Kilburn began expansion of the file of negatives. B. W. Kilburn, himself, took thousands of views throughout the United States, Europe and the Near East and, beginning in 1890, employed photographers to tour the world.

Meanwhile, late in 1881 the bromide-gelatin dry plate became available. Kilburn switched to its use and adopted the buff curved mount. The prints from the dry plates had some coarseness and lacked the sharp contrast for which the earlier Kilburn views were noted. At the same time, production methods were more fully mechanized. Faster printing, automatic developing (instead of printing out with light) and automatic washing eliminated human control. As a result, many Kilburn views published between 1882 and 1894 have faded and many others seem to us to have been poorly made. Not until the late 1890's did Kilburn again produce prints consistently with sharp contrast.

The B. W. Kilburn trade list (new series, no. 1, 1877) ultimately exceeded 16,000 numbers. Among the most notable series are:

The Johnstown Flood 1889
Columbian Exposition 1892, 1893
Coronation of Czar Nicholas II 1894
Queen Victoria Jubilee 1897
Spanish-American War 1898
William McKinley 1898-1901
Alaska Gold Rush 1898-1902
Boer War 1898-1902
International Exposition, Paris 1900
Pan American Exposition 1901
Russo-Japanese War 1904
Louisiana Purchase Exposition 1904

Scattered through the trade list are thousands of scenic views from every part of the world, from Japan to New Zealand, from Finland to Orange River Colony.

The several thousand comic and sentimental views were usually sold as "singles," but many were in sequential sets of two, three, four, to a dozen views relating a picture story (such as "Courtship and Marriage"). Among the great diversity are to be found photographs of the presidential candidates and their running-mates, race horses, prize-winning dogs, floral arrangements and allegorical subjects. The patriotic, moralistic or fanciful captions for these views were, in most cases, written by Ben Kilburn himself.

The Kilburn Company ceased production in 1909, having been in continuous operation since 1865.

Underwood & Underwood

This great publishing company began humbly in 1882 as a distributing and house-to-house canvassing business. Elmer Underwood, aged twenty, and his brother Bert, eighteen, who had set up a book selling agency, opened a small office in Ottawa, Kansas, to distribute west of the Mississippi River the stereographs of Charles Bierstadt (Niagara Falls), J. F. Jarvis (Washington, D. C.) and the Littleton View Co., a competitor of B. W. Kilburn. Within two years Underwood and Underwood had expanded their exclusive franchises to all of North America, excepting Bierstadt's views sold at his shops in Niagara Falls and Jarvis' outlets in Washington.

The combined trade lists gave the Underwoods a great range of views, including Yosemite Valley (Bierstadt), the Holy Land (Bierstadt), British Isles (Jarvis) and a splendid variety of the humorous and sentimental (mostly from Weller's negatives owned by Littleton).

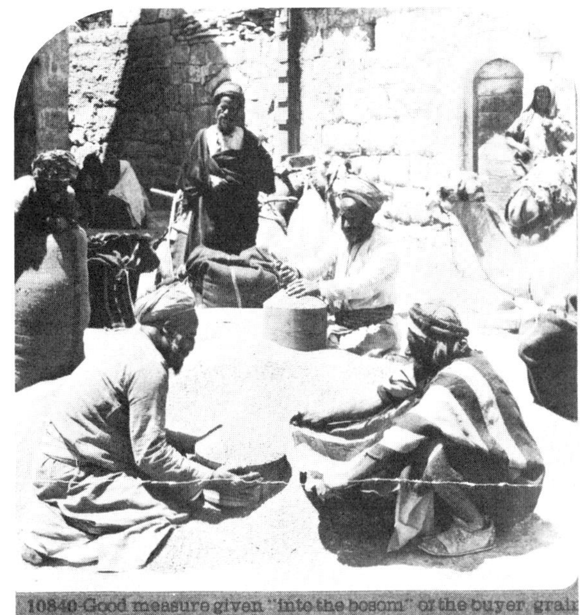

65. Bert Underwood. Grain Market, Bethlehem, Palestine. 1897. Underwood & Underwood, publishers.

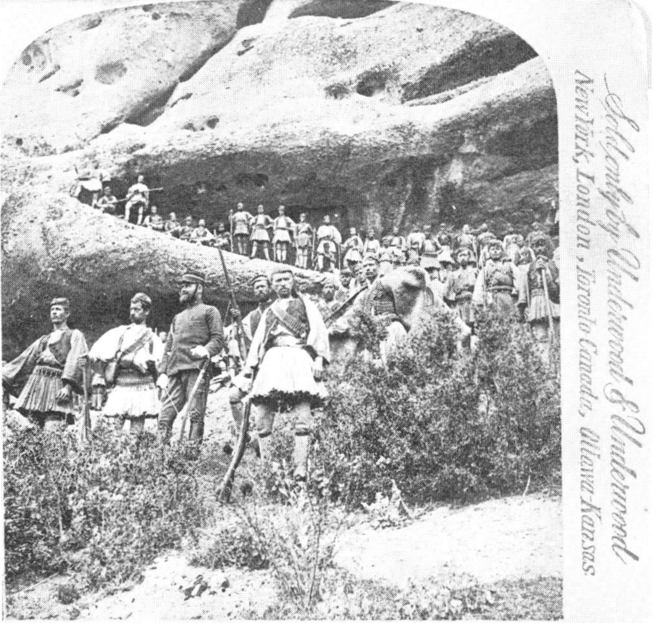

66. Bert Underwood. Davelis and his band of insurgents. Graeco-Turkish War. Macedonia. 1897. Underwood & Underwood, publishers.

The Underwoods opened branches in Baltimore (1887) and New York (1891), relocating the main office there. Gradually the firm began to publish original views to supplement their trade list.

After nine years merchandizing stereo views with his brother, Bert Underwood took a few hurried lessons in photography from M. Abel in Mentone, France (1891). Prior to that time he "had never held a camera in his hands." Perhaps long experience in what kinds of pictures would sell led him to a theory and practice in photography which became the standards which all future photographers employed by Underwood were expected to follow. In essence, the photograph must show action and novelty. If the subject is a person, it must suggest personality. Ideally, the viewer should be able to experience the action or experience vicariously. Popular interest, he believed, "can always be measured in terms of the personal equation." "The able photographer sees all the possible pictures before he used his plate for the *best* one. The best one must get at the heart of the subject, the hub around which all the action revolves."[1]

The splendid travel views of Italy, Greece, the Holy Land and Egypt published by Underwood were produced from Bert's negatives.

Beginning in 1897, the company employed full-time staff photographers and free lance operators for specific assignments. Regrettably, we know the names of only a few of these men.

By 1901 the Underwoods were publishing twenty-five thousand stereographs a day and three hundred thousand stereoscopes a year. The firm had become the greatest publisher in the industry, far outstripping any previous or contemporary company.

The techniques for canvassing were refined and systematized. "Territories" were carefully drawn and salesmen provided with specific instruction for soliciting in each community. The initial contacts were made with the school superintendent, the public librarian and the town banker. Paydays for workmen were carefully noted in advance. The salesmen, mostly between the ages of 18 and 25, were chosen for appearance, manners, culture and character. The Underwood sales organization relied heavily on college and seminary students seeking summer employment. These seasonal workers augmented a corps of year-round canvassers in the cities and larger towns, where transportation in winter was less difficult.

In 1897 Underwood & Underwood purchased the photoprinting facilities of Jarvis and Bierstadt and, shortly thereafter, those of William H. Rau of Philadelphia. For some time all of these plants were kept in operation as the trade list steadily increased.

After Underwood gained complete control of these manufacturing facilities (1897-1898), greater attention was given to photographic skill. Many stereographs deserve careful study. The photographer placed his camera at various ingenious vantage points, such as roof tops, to capture expansive vistas with striking effects. In other instances, the photographer placed himself in a crowd of people and caught their expressions in conversation, prayer or at work.

The growth of the Underwood company is recorded in the many Underwood imprints. The earliest imprint is a simple rubber hand stamp, "Sold by Underwood and Underwood, Ottawa, Kansas" (some cards *dated* 1882). Beginning in 1887 the imprints can be dated approximately by the branch offices named in the imprint. The design of the imprint was finalized in 1901 and,

[1] Bert Underwood, unpublished reminiscences. Courtesy of Mrs. E. Roy Underwood and Mrs. Robert S. Underwood.

thereafter, was used with only minor variants.

At the turn of century, Underwood introduced the "boxed set" and the "stereographic library." The boxed set was a selection of a series of cards, usually one hundred, arranged in a sequence that would simulate a tour to the country depicted. Thus, a set of views of England, France or Italy would closely parallel a typical guided tour familiar to many Americans.

Captions for these collections were printed in six languages—English, French, German, Spanish, Russian, Swedish. Some of the earlier issues had titles in only three or four languages (English, French, Spanish; English, French, Spanish, German).

A descriptive guide-book was prepared to accompany each card set, although its purchase was optional. An ingenious copyrighted map system showed the exact position of the camera when each photograph was taken, and a line on the map indicated the exact location and boundaries of the photograph.

The basic idea of a travel set was, of course, recognized by Negretti and Zambra in 1858, when they issued Frith's renowned series of Egyptian views. But the idea of Underwood & Underwood went much further. The Underwood set was not merely a series of views of a particular region, it was a carefully integrated sequence of views that would show cities, government buildings, industry, topography, natural resources, agriculture and people—all peoples in a mixed population. Nothing like it had appeared in stereo before.

The first sets, entitled "Italian," "Russian," "Holy Land," etc., had one hundred cards each. The "Paris Exposition" had sixty and "Niagara Falls," thirty. Others, made to order, included "United States Scenery," "South African War," "France," "Germany," and "Scandinavia." This venture was an immediate success, and for the next fifteen years the bulk of Underwood's stereo production went into boxed sets. New tours were assembled, the most popular among them being "China," "Japan," "India," "Ceylon" and "Egypt."

In addition to the larger sets, many smaller selections were issued in uniform book-like slip cases: "A Spanish Bull Fight" (twelve cards), "A Visit to Pope Pius X" (twelve), "The Grand Canyon" (eighteen).

Between 1902 and 1910 more than 300 different sets were assembled into the "Underwood Stereographic Library." The large majority, however, were assembled only to order. It should be noted that the same view might be included in different sets. A given view might be used in such sets as "World Tour," "United States," "National Parks," "California" and "Physical Geography." The duplication, however, is not as frequent as many collectors believe.

In addition to their regular trade sets, Underwood occasionally produced small sets for private organizations, such as churches, schools and fraternities. Although these are seldom seen because of their limited distribution, some have considerable interest. The forty-two card set "Lyndhurst" (Tarrytown, N.Y., 1905) includes fine views of children playing football and baseball, cooking and sewing classes, flying balloons and kites, and watching a magician, an organ grinder and his monkey, together creating an unusually complete picture.

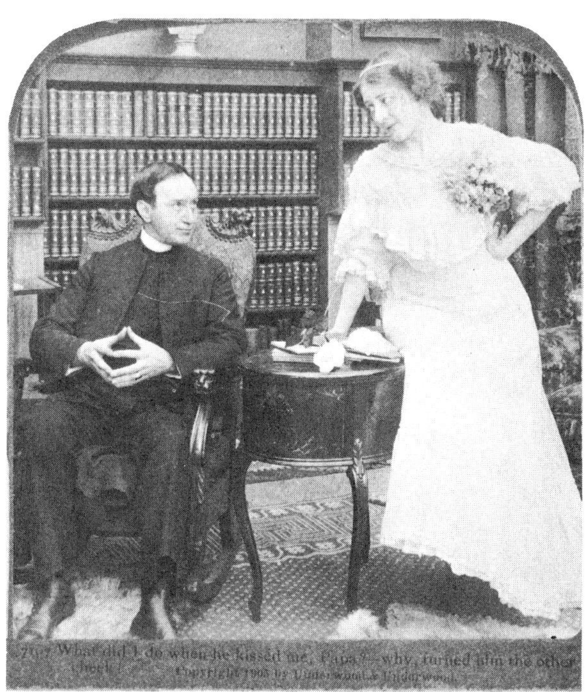

67. The "Underwood Stereographic Library" in the background of a humorous scene. "What did I do when he kissed me, Papa?—Why I turned the other cheek." Underwood & Underwood, publishers, 1905.

About 1910 the Underwood and Underwood Company had expanded into a number of activities, notably in news photography. News services had become the chief concern and most profitable division of the company. From this time on, their stereographic publishing decreased steadily. Few new stereo negatives were added to the files after 1912, the major exception being a flurry of activity during the early war years 1914-1916.

Some new boxed sets were assembled for educational purposes: "Art Series" (sixty cards), "Mathematical Diagrams" (twenty-five), "Panama Canal" (forty-five). A few other sets were revised, such as "Animal Series" (184; one hundred wild animals, eighty-four domesticated animals), "Bird Series" (ninety-two), and the various technology sets: "Textiles" (116), "Iron and Steel" (sixty), "Ceramics" (forty-four), etc.

The total number of titles published by Underwood & Underwood exceeds 30,000 and possibly reached 40,000. As with most publishers, some earlier numbers have been assigned to more than one negative. After 1902 the firm did not consistently indicate the negative number on the stereo card.

Production of stereographs was discontinued in 1920. As early as 1912, Underwood had sold some of its negatives to the educational division of Keystone View Company. Subsequently, between 1921 and 1923, it conveyed all remaining stereo stock and rights to Keystone.

Keystone View Company

In the early summer of 1892, B. L. Singley, an enthusiastic amateur photographer in Meadville, Pennsylvania, issued a small series of approximately thirty views recording damage caused by the flooding of French Creek

(June 5 and 6). The images were mounted on thick curved ivory cards. The modest success of this local issue launched the Keystone View Company, which was to become the most important stereopublisher in the twentieth century.

The trade list at the end of 1892 consisted of only a hundred titles, but the French Creek flood views were not among them, the series beginning with a new number 1. The negative file increased rapidly. By the end of 1893 there were 535 numbers, and at the close of 1894 the numbers had reached 900. In 1900 the list had grown to approximately 8000 titles, some being given numbers in the 12000's. By 1940, more than 40,000 titles had been produced commercially. Between the years 1896 and 1899, numbering was not strictly chronologic; rather, blocks of numbers were assigned to specific categories. Some of these categories were not filled, i.e., some of the numbers were probably never used.

There are many annoying problems for the collector of early Keystone views. Often there are as many as eight or ten different negatives with the same number. Some of these are given to several negatives made at the same time. Others are for replacement negatives of the same scene, taken as much as eight years later. Still others bear no relation whatsoever to the original subject. Many trivial subjects included in the first thousand numbers were discontinued, and other subjects were inserted to fill these numbers.

Furthermore, Singley "shopped around" for card stock. Between 1892 and 1896 he issued views on at least ten different types of cards. Some of these were used for only a few months, others, for two years. It must always be remembered that the card dates only the mounted print, and the given number may not be a reliable guide to the date of the negative.

For example, No. 615, "Innocents Abroad," a child with bulldog, had two 1894 negatives, two 1896, and three 1898, each with its copyright date correctly noted. The 1896 negatives show the same child and dog, with the child obviously more than a year older.

Among the first thousand Keystone numbers there was a wide variety of subjects, heavily weighted with humorous and sentimental views. Singley, an avid hunter, posed with friends and neighbors for many hunting and outdoor scenes. Like Ben Kilburn, he composed the captions for his views, reflecting his personal patriotic, religious and moral values.

There were also some scenes of seldom-photographed Pennsylvania towns. Singley, as a typical American tourist, visited the British Isles, France and Italy and returned home with about a hundred negatives which he added to his trade list. He visited the Columbian Exposition and likewise added a small series of titles. These early Keystone views are of minor interest.

Singley, himself, took all Keystone negatives prior to 1897. The quality of the prints is generally mediocre to very poor. The subjects are often trivial, the documentary ones matter-of-fact. The poor prints did not result from poor negatives, however, because vastly superior images were made from them after 1898. By this time Singley had become the administrator and manager, leaving technical production to a highly skilled staff. Processing techniques improved steadily, and by 1900 the Keystone views were among the best.

The Keystone View Company expanded its operation rapidly. The manufacturing facilities were enlarged, door-to-door canvassers were employed and professional photographers were dispatched throughout the world. Branch offices were established in many countries, the largest foreign branch being located in London.

Singley did not use the Keystone name for the views sold in Great Britain. Instead, he distributed them under the imprint, "The Fine-Art Photographers' Publishers Co." from 1897 to 1908. Generally, the card bears the phrase "made in the USA" and a B. L. Singley copyright date. There are two formats, light gray card with red-brown imprint and dark gray card with silver imprint.

The marked increase in popularity of stereographs between 1898 and 1906 was stimulated by several events of historic importance. The expansion of Underwood, Kilburn, Keystone and other companies rode the crest of this wave of enthusiasm. The Columbian Exposition of 1892-1893 had been thoroughly stereographed. Huge quantities of these views were distributed. The presidency of William McKinley was accompanied by a show of patriotism that was further encouraged by the Spanish-American War (1898). The Alaskan Gold Rush caused great excitement. In rapid succession the Boer War, the Pan-American Exposition, assassination of McKinley, the Boxer Rebellion, and Russo-Japanese War kept photographers and publishers busy.

Keystone cautiously entered the boxed set market, imitating the book-like slip case used by Underwood. There was no attempt to issue guide books. Instead, Keystone returned to the early practice of printing descriptive legends on the backs of the cards.

The most successful branch of Keystone's activity was its Educational Department, organized in 1898. The application of stereographs to visual education was ingeniously exploited. A number of sets of views illustrating geography, commerce, technology, history and nature study were assembled for school instruction. Some of the sets were available with legends appropriate to different grade levels (i.e., primary, secondary, etc.). Teachers' manuals were prepared to accompany the educational sets. One of the boxed sets, "Costume" (copyright 1906), included one hundred views, beautifully hand tinted and illustrating native costumes throughout the world.

Singley personally contacted an impressive editorial board to select a "Keystone 600" set. Fifty-eight prominent professional educators agreed to serve, among them: Charles W. Eliot, President Emeritus of Harvard; Alfred Bushnell Hart, historian; J. M. Coulter, botanist; Alma B. Comstock naturalist; C. V. Kirby, art educator; Anna M. Cooley and Edith P. Chace, professors of household arts, Columbia; Alfred Vivian, Dean of the College of Agriculture, Ohio State University; and Frank M. McMurry, professor of elementary education at Columbia.

These experts selected prints that would illustrate their special fields of interest, wrote and edited legends to accompany the views and suggested references to books and articles that would provide supplementary information. By combining subjects, a single view could serve multiple purposes. For instance, No. 556, "The Date

Palm," would illustrate the plant (botany), deserts, nomads and Africa. Again, No. 409, "Carding and Spinning Wool, Telemarken, Norway," would illustrate textiles, wool, spinning, Norway and native costume. In this way six hundred views could cover the world and man.

A carefully classified and thoroughly cross-indexed guide book, *Stereoscopic Encyclopedia* (1st ed. 1906, 10th ed. 1923), with thousands of references, accompanied the Keystone 600 set. There were, for instance, 72 stereo views with 188 references to "hygiene and health"; 225 views and 448 references to "literary subjects and settings"; 137 views and 178 references to "vocational guidance"; and 153 views and 154 references to "racial geography, peoples of all lands."

The set was revised frequently, especially after 1918. There was increased sophistication along with necessary corrections in geographic names to correspond to boundary changes after World War I. One category prominent in the post-war issues is "community civics," involving 299 stereographs—of the 600—with 806 references, prepared by Arthur W. Dunn. Dunn, author of several textbooks, including *The Community and the Citizen* (D. C. Heath & Co., 1916), served in the United States Bureau of Education.

A second manual, more pedagogically oriented, *Visual Education–Teacher's Guide to the Keystone "600" Set* was first issued in 1907 (10th ed., 1927).

In 1924 Keystone produced a "1000" educational set with an accompanying handbook. Earlier (1920) a "Primary Set" with 200 cards had been issued.

It is difficult for us to evaluate the influence or effectiveness of these visual aids. Millions of children were taught by them. In 1922 Keystone boasted that every American city with a population of 50,000 or more had adopted the "Keystone System" for its public schools.

As noted previously, the Keystone View Company in 1912 had purchased rights to several series of Underwood negatives for use in educational sets. Keystone had already begun to purchase negative files from other publishers. The entire Kilburn file passed to Keystone in 1909. Between 1911 and 1915 those of Berry, Kelley & Chadwick and H. C. White Company were secured. There were other purchases from Underwood before 1920, and in 1922 the remaining stereo negatives, prints, guide books and all rights to them were obtained by Keystone. Manufacturing facilities were modernized to incorporate the latest photoprinting and related equipment.

After 1920, for all practical purposes, Keystone View Company was the only major publisher of stereographs in the world. From this position of leadership, Keystone promoted its views from large offices in London, Paris, Sidney, Capetown, Rio de Janeiro and Tokyo, and from dozens of smaller scattered agencies, with unprecedented success.

Considerable impetus to this trade derived from the sale of World War I sets. Keystone had been frustrated in its efforts to have an on-the-spot battlefield photographer. Red-tape and bureaucratic stalling blocked every attempt to secure permission. In the closing months of 1918, just before the Armistice, Andrew S. Iddings, photographer for Keystone, finally received permission to photograph the battlefields and military operations. He returned in 1919 with several thousand stereo negatives, the majority of which were taken in 1919. The Underwood file included about six hundred war negatives made mostly in 1914-1916 in England, Flanders and Germany and of the preparedness and mobilization activities in the United States.

By selecting and combining titles from the two sources, Keystone published many versions of their World War I sets. Best known is the 100-200-300 set (first issue 1923), although thirty-six, sixty and seventy-two card sets were available in 1918 and 1919, and a one-hundred card set in 1921. The common 100- and 200-card sets were simply selections from the 300 set. A 400-card set was stocked briefly (1928-1930) and a 1000-card set was assembled for several customers. The guide books are generally issues for the 100-200-300 set, but one was also prepared for the 100-200-300-400 set.

In 1923 Keystone undertook its most ambitious project, the assembling of a "World Tour" or 600 stereographs. A 300-card version was issued in 1924 and a 400 set (100-200-300-400) in 1925 (guidebook copyrighted January, 1930). It was followed by a 1000-card set (1930) and a 1200 set in 1931. Considering the world-wide depression of this period, the venture was daring, indeed.

As with their educational sets, Keystone View Company sought an advisory editorial board, this time with thirteen members instead of fifty-five. Among them were Carl Sandburg and Ernest Thompson Seton.

To make the actual selection of negatives and to take additional photographs, wherever desirable, to complete an outstanding series, Keystone engaged the popular travel lecturer, Burton Holmes. Holmes also wrote the excellent guidebook. The set was advertised as "the cream of a million negatives," a literal truth because in 1936 the company held more than two million negatives, only a fraction of which had been used for commercial production.

These travel sets, especially those sold without a guide book, show many variations. There are frequent substitutions, such as up-dated views to replace old city scenes.

In addition to the regularly produced sets, there are deluxe boxed sets, morocco-covered and lined with red or purple velvet, with cards gilt edged. These were custom made for wealthy clients; never regularly issued.

The Keystone numbering system is essentially chronologic and complete after 1898. The order, however, is in sequence of date of issue, not date of negative. A trade list number was not assigned until it was selected for publication. When an old negative purchased from another company was activated, a new Keystone number was assigned to it in regular sequence. So far as I am aware, the original source is always given (V = Underwood, W = White, etc.). Very few of the vast number of purchased negatives were used by Keystone. One cannot but wonder if the purchases were made primarily to prevent the negatives from falling into the hands of competitors, who might reissue them in cheap formats. Many publishers, between 1905 and 1915, were dumping cheap views on the market. A considerable share of these were distributed as free premiums by metropolitan newspapers.

Many Keystone views have supplementary numbers, such as H235, P103, or a number preceded by a small diamond, asterisk or star. These refer to positions in a set and should not be confused with negative numbers.

Throughout its later history, i.e., after 1905, Keystone published fine views. Only briefly during the depression year of 1933 was there an attempt to cheapen the quality of card stock in order to lower the retail price of views.

With the passing of years has come a growing recognition of the invaluable record provided by Underwood and Keystone View Company, perhaps unwittingly, as they documented the modernization of the world. The automobile, air craft, steel and concrete construction, power engineering—these are but a few of the technological aspects of society that fall almost wholly within the span of Keystone's stereographic production.

Keystone View Company ceased regular production in 1939 but continued to manufacture views for optometric purposes. Individual orders for stereographs were filled until 1970. The commercial trade list exceeded 43,000 numbers.

H. C. White Company, North Bennington, Vermont

This company began publishing stereographs in 1899. Hawley C. White had a spectacle lens grinding business in New York City in 1870. Four years later he moved to Vermont, where he established a factory and became the principal manufacturer of Holmes type stereoscopes in the world.

Taking advantage of the resurgent demand for views and their applications in classroom instruction, White produced prints of high quality. Several patents, of doubtful validity, were obtained for his "Perfec Stereographs" on the basis of extravagant claims.

In 1907 White erected a three-story factory of brick and reinforced concrete, which, for a short period, was the finest and most mechanized stereo publishing facility in the world. The entire photoprinting process was automated. The glass negatives were clamped in front of a lamp under which an endless belt carried the printing paper, stopped for the set time and then advanced the paper for the next exposure. Such machines had been in use since 1866. The White operations, however, mechanized developing, fixing and washing machines with which it was possible to maintain uniform standards of quality. Prints were trimmed with a high-speed die-cutter. Titles were printed automatically at the rate of 10,000 per hour. There were three washing machines, each with a capacity of 5000 prints per 10-hour day. Automatic driers, utilizing piped steam, had a capacity of 15,000 prints a day. A special machine gilded the printed titles and imprint on the deluxe format of White stereographs.

The H. C. White Company continued large-scale production of three models of hand stereoscopes, wood, wood and metal and all metal.

An instructive series of twenty-four views illustrating the manufacture of stereographs and stereoscopes was published by H. C. White Company in 1908, primarily for the use of their salesmen, but they were sold to the general public as well.

The trade list was developed through the efforts of staff photographers. The company boasted that in seven years its chief photographer had traveled 140,000 miles and had visited all the continents.

Twenty-two boxed sets of one hundred cards, closely imitating those of Underwood, were issued beginning in 1904. In addition to these, H. C. White published approximately three dozen small sets comprised of twelve to thirty-six views.

Ultimately, the trade list of individual titles exceeded 12,800 numbers. Among the remarkable groups are the following:

Coney Island 490-513
The U. S. Navy 7400-7441
General Slocum Disaster 8400-8405
The Baltimore Fire 10381-10395

About 1910 the H. C. White Company, which by this time had offices in New York, Chicago, San Francisco and London, made arrangements with Doubleday-Page Company to act as sole distributor of their line of stereographs. Business had declined drastically, especially in the educational field, where Keystone's superiority had proved to be secure. Some time before 1915 the entire White file of negatives was purchased by Keystone View Company.

The H. C. White stereographs, particularly their deluxe "Aladdin" format, mounted on black cards, are, photographically, among the best produced in the twentieth century. A small percentage of them were sold beautifully hand tinted.

Smaller Publishing Companies

Three additional publishers, briefly successful between 1910 and 1915, deserve mention.

Stereo Travel Company, Corona (Long Island), N. Y.

This company, organized about 1904, specialized in the publication of boxed sets and, by 1913, had assembled twenty-six tours, of one hundred cards each. While the usual countries, France, England, Italy, Japan, etc., were included there were several of outstanding interest: "New York City," Sicily, Panama, Jamaica and Cuba.

The New York City set includes many views with people at work, such as peddlers, street-cleaners, firemen at a burning building and many more. The photographer was not interested in skyscrapers and harbor scenes; he caught with his camera the tempo of the city. The negatives were taken between 1909 and 1911.

The Sicily set—the photographer is not credited—likewise concentrated on people. Even when the view depicts Greek, Roman and Saracen ruins, shepherds and townspeople are going about their business, seemingly oblivious to both the photographer and the ancient ruins. Among the views in this set are two touching scenes of emigrants leaving for America.

In addition to the regular trade listings, Stereo Travel did some custom publishing for private organizations. Perhaps the most unusual of these is the set simply titled "Motor" (1909), composed of sixty views, recording the first "Indianapolis 500" automobile race and the races at Lowell, Massachusetts. There is a dazzling array of identified racing cars and their drivers.

Stereo Travel Company reached its zenith in 1913 and discontinued business in 1916.

Griffith & Griffith, Philadelphia, Pa.

George W. Griffith, a photographer since his youth, had been a canvasser for Underwood & Underwood. About 1896 he teamed with his brother and organized a distributing company patterned after that of Underwood. The Griffiths marketed the views of H. L. Roberts (successor to Roberts & Fellows, in turn successors to Edward L. Wilson) and William H. Rau. In 1897 they added the line of M. H. Zahner of Niagara Falls.

In 1899 G. W. Griffith began photographing various attractions in the United States, Europe and Asia to build a file of original negatives. In 1900 the company issued a variety of humorous groups, including several small sets of four to twelve cards.

Like its competitors, Griffith and Griffith sought world-wide business. In 1908 offices were opened in St. Louis and Liverpool; but two years later these were moved to Chicago and London, and additional offices were established in Hamburg, Milan and St. Petersburg.

The Griffith trade list reached 10,000 titles in 1910. Although the company continued operations until 1917, few titles were added after 1912. Its business was carried out entirely by canvassers.

Carlton H. Graves (Universal Photo Art Company)

Carlton H. Graves, who was associated with his father, Jesse A. Graves, in the 1870's, was active from 1880 to 1910. His first notable series was the Johnstown Flood (1889). For a time his views were distributed by the Globe Photo Art Company. Between 1896 and 1904, Graves published under the imprint "Universal Photo Art Company," and thereafter as "Graves Stereal-Graphs."

The Globe Photo Art Company, located in Bettsville, Ohio (circa 1892-1898), was essentially a cooperative photoprinting facility doing the work for C. H. Graves, L. M. Melander and Brothers (Chicago), Gates Brothers (Chicago), Wm. Chase (Baltimore) and R. K. Bonine (Tyrone, Pa.). All of these photographers, who had been operating since the 1870's, were simply not equipped to compete with the aggressive marketing methods of Kilburn and Underwood. The Globe cooperative, which was not very successful, ceased business shortly after Graves withdrew in 1897.

Approximately twenty other publishers produced stereographs in some quantity for brief periods. None of them is of particular significance, although each distributed notable titles not duplicated by any other company. Only five American and one English companies will be mentioned here.

The American companies, in order of importance:

American Stereoscopic Company (R. Y. Young), New York, N. Y., ca. 1896-1906.

Alfred S. Campbell, Elizabeth, N. J., ca. 1893-1904.

Berry, Kelley & Chadwick, Chicago, Dallas & Atlanta, ca. 1900-1910

Whiting View Company, Cincinnati, Ohio ca. 1901-1912.

American View Company, New York, N. Y., ca. 1900-1906.

Several English publishers adopted the American canvassing methods on a world-wide scale. Since their stereographs are seldom seen in the United States, they will be cited under The British Isles (page 102). Most successful was H. D. Girdwood ("Realistic Travels"), ca. 1908-1916, who opened branch offices in Toronto, New York, Bombay and Capetown. The quality of his line was very good, and many geographic views are of interest. Like his American contemporaries, Girdwood shows people in most of the stereographs.

SUMMARY

The large volume publishers were more concerned with selling their sets or series than single cards. A company that issued fifty sets would have four or five thousand different negatives in production. Yet the canvassers were instructed to take orders for single cards, no matter how small the sale. Publishers like Underwood, White and Keystone had more than ten thousand titles in print at any given time.

Between 1885 and 1935 the stereographic record of major events and the peoples of the world were more systematically stereographed than had been possible during the preceding fifty years. Travel was easier. The techniques for assembling a picture story were better developed.

The primitive systems of agriculture and transportation still prevalent in many countries were recorded with no less fidelity than the achievements of the latest engineering technology.

Unfortunately, we know the names of only a few of the excellent photographers who toured the world in the employ of these great publishers. Rarely were they given credit or recognition. The skill and artistry of many of these twentieth century images equal the best of the early classics. The very nature of mass production, however, tends to obscure fine workmanship and to lessen our appreciation of their artistic and historic merits.

CHAPTER SIX

HALF-TONE STEREOGRAPHS—"LITHOPRINTS"

The unprecedented demand for stereo views at the turn of this century encouraged publishers to reach out for a still wider market by producing inexpensive card views. The development of photomechanical processes, especially those adapted to press printing, provided the opportunity.

Underwood, Keystone and Kilburn, by mass production, were able to retail their fine views at a price of six cards for one dollar for purchases of twelve or more cards. The price was still too expensive for families of low income. By printing methods, a card could be sold for three cents or less.

Inexpensive printed stereo pictures were, by no means, new. Appleton was selling colored xylographs (wood engravings) in 1856-59. These views did not compare favorably with photograph views and never gained popular appeal.

Basically any method adapted to a printing press requires the transfer of a photographic image to a sensitized surface in such manner that it will accept ink and then transfer the ink to paper. The idea is as old as photography itself. A daguerreotype could be etched with nitric acid and used as an intaglio plate from which a number of positive prints could be pulled.

Many methods for photosensitizing the surfaces of stone, metal, wood blocks for engraving and other materials were devised before 1865.

Alphonse Poitevin (1855) used bichromated gelatin which hardened under light to sensitize a variety of surfaces. J. A. Cutting and L. H. Bradford (Boston, 1858) patented a similar process in the United States. These "collotype" methods were improved in many ways so that by 1870 a dozen variants were used for printing pictures and illustrations for books.[1]

Between 1856 and 1878 many different kinds of mechanically inkprinted stereo views were published. All but the cheap copy issues of the latter 1870's are very rare. Early printed views were experimental in the sense that they did not compete with photographic images.

The possibility of breaking up a photographic image into small dots to achieve half tone with printing inks was realized by Talbot in 1852. Not until the early 1880's, however, did the method become practical. Patents were granted to several inventors in Germany, France, England and the United States between 1878-82. All of the schemes involved the use of a grid screen of crossed lines placed between the camera and the subject being photographed.

The screen method developed by F. E. Ives (Philadelphia, 1881, 86) and improved by Max Levy (Philadelphia, 1890) became known as the half tone block or screen process.

The term half tone has two meanings. In its original sense, it refers to an intermediate tone which is neither very dark nor very light. In the printing industry, it is a photographic image reproduced as a printed image composed of small dots.

The detail recorded in a printed half tone depends upon the fineness of the screen grid. Coarser impressions were made with 85 to 100 line screens. Better stereo prints were made with screens of 120 to 133 lines. Finer screens were not used for the printing of stereo views.

Human color vision is essentially three color perception. If many small yellow dots are printed among many red dots, the mind will perceive orange. Combination of three colors of dots—yellow, red and blue—can produce all shades and colors. The impressionist painters were well aware of the practical aspects of color perception.

Color printing by half tone was perfected in the 1890's. This was accomplished by color separation using color-sensitive negatives. When three "printers"—one for yellow, one for red, and one for blue—are used to print images superposed in that order, a richly colored impression can be produced. In modern practice a fourth printer, black, is used to sharpen the outline and increase shading effects.

In preparing the "printers" color filters are required. A blue-violet filter is used for the yellow printer, a green filter for the red printer, and an orange-red filter for the blue printer. A light yellow filter is used to make the black printer. By 1898 highly reliable color-sensitive negatives were being manufactured by J. Carbutt (Philadelphia), Lumiere (France), Sanger, Shepherd & Company (England), E. Albert (Germany) and several others. Natural light proved to be a troublesome factor in color photography. It was too variable being correlated with time of day, weather, season and city smog. Improvements in electrical illumination solved the major problem.

Color printed half tone stereo views were introduced in 1898 and by 1900 had become common. By 1904 no less than twenty multicolored issues were being produced in the United States.

Underwood and Keystone did not enter into the half tone business, instead they pushed their travel and educational lines. On the other hand, H. C. White and Griffith & Griffith, after some hesitation, published their more popular views both as photo and half tone stereos.

About 1903 Sears Roebuck Company and Montgomery Ward Company, the two largest mail order retailers in the United States, offered multicolored lithoprints to their customers. The two lines were very similar, including many identical scenes. The cards were printed in Chicago, the chief center of three-color printing at that time. Millions of copies of these lithoprints were sold over

[1] For a concise description of photomechanical printing methods see H. Gernsheim, *History of Photography*, pp. 357-372, 1955.

many years at eighty-five cents per hundred. Even today, the most commonly encountered colored half tone stereos are the green bordered Sears Roebuck and the gray bordered Montgomery Ward cards.

Griffith & Griffith and H. C. White, both retailing views by door to door canvassing, sought to garner the cheap trade in addition to their regular sales. Agents were carefully instructed to demonstrate the colored half tones to a prospective buyer *only* if the sale of mounted photo views seemed unlikely.

Companies that published only lithoprints did not engage in door to door selling. The low value of individual cards did not warrant this kind of merchandising. Instead, the cards were printed in great volume, sold to jobbers and "publishers." Ultimately most of these cards were retailed in shops of great variety: drug stores, novelty stores, stationers, book stores, etc.

Great quantities were distributed as premiums by cereal and tea companies, department stores, newspapers, and so on. These premiums were distributed in two main ways: one card for each purchase of a packaged article, or a dozen cards in exchange for a coupon or proof of purchase (such as a "box top"). Some department stores gave a number of cards in proportion to the amount of a sale, such as, six for a three dollar purchase, a dozen for a five dollar purchase, etc. As an extra bonus, the customer could purchase a first-rate stereoscope for ten or fifteen cents, a fraction of its value. Ownership of a good viewer increased the desire for more views and, hence increased the purchases of the cereal (Pettijohns, Quaker Oats.)

Another frequent scheme permitted a customer to purchase at a minimal price a set of twenty-five or a hundred cards if the order was accompanied by a coupon or clipped advertisement. A. C. Cook (seedsman, Hyde Park, N. Y., 1908-1910) offered his customers nearly 2000 titles from which to choose.

The use of lithoprint stereos for sales promotion extended from about 1904 to 1928 but had declined considerably after 1916. In the 1920's and 30's, there was another cycle of premium stereo issues, throughout the world but especially in Australia and New Zealand. The cards distributed during this latter period, however, were of small format, mostly 1¾ x 4½ inches (4.5 x 12.5 cms), for so-called junior folding stereoscopes. The subjects were generally of natural history (birds, mammals, insects, fish, wild flowers, mushrooms, etc.) in sets of sixteen, twenty, or twenty-five views.

Lithoprints were occasionally given as souvenirs or rewards. The John B. Stetson Mission Sunday School (Philadelphia, 1910) each Sunday presented the pupil with a Holy Land scene on the back of which was printed a Bible verse. The date of attendance is also printed on the card (e.g., May 22, 1910).

A variant was used by a Methodist Episcopal organization, active in the Philadelphia area about 1912. Each pupil was given a sheet on which were printed three stereo images illustrating the Holy Land. The child was expected to cut out the views and mount them on card board at home.

Souvenir half tone stereographs are of great variety. All are very scarce. Search for a particular subject or a specific card would require considerable effort. Most souvenir stereos are monochromes but some excellent multicolored views are known. W. M. Benninger's Stock Farm (Northampton County, Pa., 1908-13) distributed a stereograph of their exhibit of Holstein milk cows at the Atlanta Exposition. The Benninger lithoprinted cards are known multicolored and in monochrome red or black.

We are more concerned here, however, with lithoprints as a category rather than as novelties.

The major publishers and distributors of color printed half tone stereo views were:

American Colortype Company	New York and Chicago
American Stereoscopic Company	New York
Atlas View Company	New York
Barnes & Crosby Company	Chicago
Griffith & Griffith	New York
T. W. Ingersoll	St. Paul
Kawin & Company	Chicago
Montgomery Ward Company	Chicago
Sears Roebuck Company	Chicago
H. C. White Company	New York
World Wide View Company	Chicago

A full line of lithoprints included world travel, sentimental, comic, and religious views, requiring a mininum trade list of 900 to 1200 titles. Several publishers offered more than 2000 titles.

Griffith & Griffith and White emphasized comics and sentimentals which did not compete with their better scenic photograph views. T. W. Ingersoll produced several hundred serious and humorous views of hunting and fishing in his list of more than 2500 titles.

The finest multicolored lithoprints were photographed and published by Hans Hildenbrand (Stuttgart, Germany) about 1902-08 under the registered name "Chromoplast." The cards are slightly larger than standard size with the images boxed in heavy black borders. No lithoprints manufactured in the United States attained a comparable degree of excellence. The three printing companies that came closest were Barnes & Crosby, Kawin & Company and American Colortype. Many American Colortype issues, however, were very cheaply and poorly done.

Probably the best color half tone stereos printed in the United States are to be found in the medical series, "Diseases of the Skin," published by S. I. Rainforth, M.D. (New York, 128 cards, 1910).

There are other features of some issues that show the publisher's desire to improve the durability and appeal of his card views.

Several manufacturers sized the cards with talc so that a soiled image could be wiped clean with a damp cloth. Other series were given a gloss finish. Some of these high gloss views were advertised as "oleographs," a designation that was probably a registered trade name. The permanence and durability of the finish was determined by the substance used to produce the gloss (dextrin, gelatin, drying oil, varnish, or wax).

Another device, the extended legend, used by several publishers deserves mention. Most stereo views are accompanied by a brief title or explanation. In 1897 Underwood began to print a fuller explanation on the reverse of its stereographs. Keystone adopted the descriptive note for its views about 1902.

The idea was carried much further in many lithoprints. The extended legend frequently ran to 350, even 450 words. Views intended to amuse children would have a complete fairy tale or short story printed on the card. If three or four sequential views were issued, the story was divided into as many parts. The same method was used for serious travel cards, such as the Holy Land. The descriptions are carefully composed to meet a somewhat lower level of education than completed high school. There is no condescension however—the vocabulary is essentially familiar. The publisher obviously intended his views to be educational as well as entertaining.

Notable series of Multicolored Lithoprints

The Holy Land 200 cards
T. W. Ingersoll series
Sears Roebuck series

The Russo Japanese War 100 cards
Sears Roebuck

Louisiana Purchase Exposition, 1904 100 cards
Sears Roebuck, also identical views on white cards without publishers imprint

Louisiana Purchase Exposition, 1904 25 cards
World's Series

San Francisco Earthquake, 1906 25 cards
W. B. Smith

The Great White Fleet, 1908-09 25 cards

The United States Navy, 1918 25 cards
E. Muller, Jr.

American Indians, 1904 45 cards including a selected set of 25
Sears Roebuck

The Grand Canyon—The Cataract Canyon of Arizona 1908 25 cards
T. S. Baldwin

There are other distinct series illustrating each of the subjects listed above, mostly without a publisher's imprint.

Among the many rare small series of colored half tone views there are some unusual subjects not known in other stereo formats:

The Balkan War, 1912-14 20 (?) cards
J. Hollinger, Jr., New York
Titles in Slavic and English

Italian-Turkish War, 1911-12 12 cards
Scenes in Tripoli
Unknown American publisher
Titles in English and Italian

World War (I) 1914-15 24 cards
Olivetti, Folimarino & Co., New York
Printed by Aste & Co.
Titles in Italian and English

Mexican Border Incident, 1915-16 about 25 cards
Mostly scenes in Chihuahua, Mexico
Unknown publisher

Less rare but seldom found in good condition are the six-card slapstick comic sets published by Herman Knutzen (Chicago, 1906).

"The Industrious Painter and the Idle Apprentice"
"The Artist"
"Hans and Looey Putting Powder in Fader's Pipe"
"The Magician With an Egg"
"The Dentist"
"The Cello Player"
"The Sleeping Drunks"

Monochrome Half Tone Stereos

Monochrome half tones can, of course, be printed in ink of any color. Generally the printing was done in black on white card, but olive brown or olive gray ink was used frequently. Sepia is uncommon. Red and blue were occasionally used for printing souvenir novelties.

The largest series of black and white half-tones appeared about 1904 and was in continuous production until 1911 or 1912. The cards, which have images on both sides, bear no publisher's imprint. There were several one hundred card sets, i.e., two hundred images numbered consecutively. All attempts to identify the publisher have thus far been fruitless. The Indian portraits, however, are from W. S. Soule photographs.

The best printed series was distributed by the Little Chronicle Publishing Company (Chicago, 1904-06). Although 500 titles in sets of twenty-five cards were advertised, only two sets seem to be common. The original photographs were obtained from various sources, many from Griffith & Griffith. There are several unusual scenes such as "Finish of the American Derby, 1904—Highball Wins," (No. 302) negative by George R. Lawrence.

The following series suggest the variety of subjects that are to be found in monochrome half tone stereos:

Panama Canal 1906 25 cards
Continental Art Company
Three types of cards: first issue, glossy surface 1906; second issue gray bordered without publisher's imprint, 1907; third 1908-12 on plain white card, without publisher's imprint.

San Francisco Earthquake 1906 25 cards
World Wide View Company (Chicago)
Photographs copyrighted by Griffith & Griffith. After 1908 printed without credit to Griffith & Griffith on two types of cards.

San Francisco Earthquake 1906 25 cards
Metropolitan Series; negatives by Tom M. Phillips.

White House Wedding 1909 25 cards
Continental Series
Negatives by Clinedenst

New York City ca. 1908 25 cards
Unknown publisher

An Automobile Trip Around New York City 1918 25 cards
American Colortype (available also slightly colored)

Sears Roebuck Company 50 cards
First issued 1904, sold until ca. 1930.
A tour of their facilities.

T. Eaton Company, Toronto 50 cards Mail order retailer

A series similar to that issued by Sears Roebuck ca. 1906-10.

Kingston, Jamaica Earthquake 1907 25 cards

About 1910 several publishers issued small sets of views printed back to back on thick cards assembled in a two-ring looseleaf binder. The most common is a set sold to tourists at Niagara Falls. The format is reminiscent of the folders sold by Appleton in 1858-59.

Cartoons—monochrome and multicolored

Several sets of twenty-five cards of cartoons illustrating action in the World War and the life of a doughboy were sold quite extensively in 1917 and 1918. One poorly color printed set was produced by American Colortype. These issues are of slight interest as stereos except for their novelty as mementos of the war years.

Anaglyphs (Plastographs)

Anaglyphic stereo views are printed either in two contrasting colors or with the black and white images overprinted with contrasting colors. When viewed with an anaglyphoscope, an instrument with a pair of appropriate color filters, the images are seen stereoscopically. When viewed through a stereoscope, the illusion of three dimensions is heightened.

In the early 1920's there was considerable interest in anaglyphic photography, including its possible application to the cinema. During this period stereo half-tone images, one overlaid with green and the other with red, were produced by American Colortype. They were printed on very poor, off-white porous card but the stereoscopic effect is quite convincing.

Twentieth Century Stereo Collotypes

The popularity of half tone stereographs encouraged other photomechanical printing companies to produce stereos by collotype offset methods. Under magnification these images are semi-continuous, not broken into dots. The ink follows the surface of the paper or card. Very fine multicolored collotypes can be produced. I do not know of any colored stereo views made by this method after 1880.

Black and white collotype stereos were produced occasionally before 1880 and extensively after 1900. The best stereo views were printed in Germany but several series were manufactured by unidentified companies in the United States. Post cards were issued in this format.

The *glanceotype* (a registered trade name; *glanz, German*, meaning gloss or luster) was a printed image to which a high gloss was applied. Kresge & Wilson Syndicate (1904-10) distributed a large line comprised of scenes of the major cities of the United States. The views of each city were sold locally.

A very similar high gloss collotype series of California scenes, also printed in Germany, was published by M. Rieder (Los Angeles, California, 1904-06).

The greatest activity in half tone and collotype printing of stereo views occurred between 1902 and 1910. Despite the availability of at least a half dozen methods for printing stereographs, only the half tone competed with the mounted photo view. At no time did the ink printed stereograph displace the photographic view.

Serious collectors of stereographs have generally ignored half tone and collotype views simply because they are not photographs. In consequence of this neglect, very little is known about them.

It is true that many lithoprints are garishly colored and poorly printed. There are, however, some redeeming qualities. There are many scenes recorded in lithoprints that are not found in any other type of stereo views. Collectors and historians interested in city scenes, the United States Navy, early automobile and motor truck traffic, and children's toys—to name only a few subjects—will be surprised by the wealth of information in lithoprint formats.

More importantly, lithoprints, particularly three color, stereographs are among the earliest and finest products by the half tone method. Fine copies deserve preservation and greater appreciation.

CHAPTER SEVEN

CREATIVE PHOTOGRAPHY

Thus far we have considered stereographs of scenery, people and objects naturalistically—man and nature in real life. The photographer has recorded what he has selected for a picture. He may have used a romantic style or employed some device to capture an emotion but in his estimation the picture was faithful to nature. The camera was the recorder.

Grundy and Ogle consistent with artistic convention posed human figures in their views of pastoral scenes and ruined abbeys. The charm of their stereographs results from imaginative composition which implies peacefulness and contemplation.

A photograph of a still life arrangement, no matter how pleasing and intricate that arrangement may be, is still a picture of objects as they are.

There is an entirely different kind of imaginative photography which may properly be called creative. A combination of photographic techniques with the methods and traditions of the theater can create in the studio any scene desired. The photographer can, with stage set, accessories and models, arrange a tableau depicting a picnic, a harem scene or a ballroom crowded with dancers. With appropriate costumes and backdrops he can achieve an illusion of authenticity.

While many renowned photographers like H. P. Robinson, Roger Fenton and Lake Price experimented with "composition" photography, this approach was developed largely by lesser known and anonymous experimenters who were interested not in "art" but in "business."

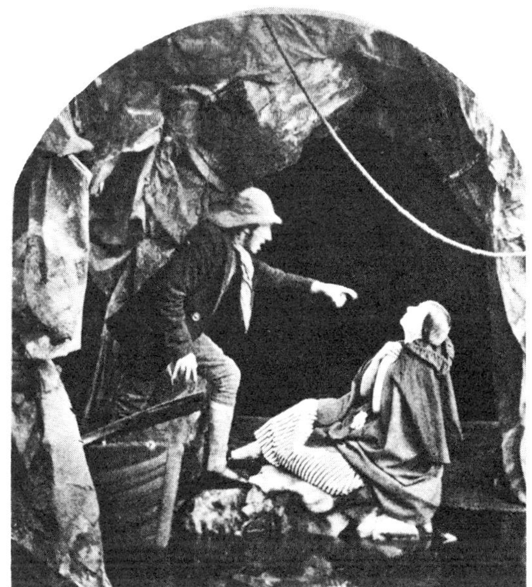

68. "The Colleen Bawn." Studio staged scene. Note the cave entrance. Unknown photographer. English, ca. 1857.

This is not an appropriate place to dwell upon conflicting opinions about the function of photography or what is art. Intellectuals in the nineteenth century were searching—sometimes foolishly—for "truth," truth in art, truth in science, truth in philosophy, truth in religion. The controversies among photographers as to what was art are but part of a much broader debate. Blind faith in absolutes, true or false, had not yet blended with relativism, pragmatism, individualism or modern humanism. Nor can we forget the nineteenth century intellectual snobbery against the artisan. Robinson's reference to those photographers who were "illiterate and ignorant tradesmen" is but one indication of the gulf between two traditions in photography, artistic and utilitarian.

Most "pure" artistic photographers could no more understand the innovative photographic manipulators than "pure" scientists could understand those who wanted to convert an idea into a practical application or make a profit from it.

The "secessionist" photographers of the 1890's who appealed for a return to nature were as much a product of their period as those they criticized were a mirror of their age.

With an open mind, then, we can try to look at composition stereographs in the same spirit and enthusiasm as those who produced them.

By 1858 a great diversity of "groups" and "compositions" were being produced by publishers catering to popular taste. James Elliott, Alfred Silvester, and "Phiz" (Hablot Knight) were excellent photographers and artists. Figures 54-63 illustrate fine examples of their work. The subjects of their stereos ranged from lovely brides to crude jokes, many in situations that required elaborate staging. Their competitors turned out huge quantities of comic and sentimental views, many being vulgar and poorly made. The editor of *Photographic News* called the compositions of the Truefit Brothers "the worst ever made."[1]

From the point of view of inventiveness, however, compositional photography had much more merit than contemporary critics recognized. Elliott's "Mary Queen of Scots—Compelled to sign Her Abdication" is a fine tableau with seven models in an impressive setting. His "Australian Recreations," washing clothes before a log cabin in the bush, although rather awkward, indicates the possibilities of simulating forest scenes in the studio.

Elliott and Silvester stand supreme in pioneering staged compositions for stereographs, 1856-1862. Elliott produced historical, fictional, sentimental, and comic

[1]Vol. *1*, p. 241, 1859.

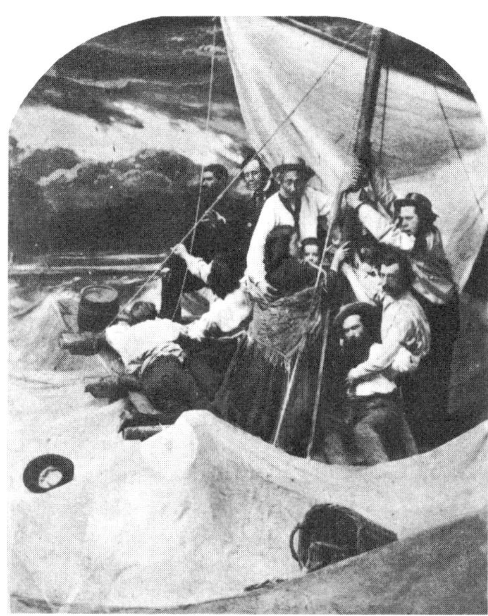

69. "Shipwrecked." Studio staged scene. Note painted storm background and waves in foreground. London Stereoscopic Company. ca. 1858.

scenes of great variety. He sought the advice of antiquarians to attain authenticity in two "English History Series," published by the London Stereoscopic Company.

In a serious vein Elliott produced "The Reception and Profession of a Sister of Mary" (Roman Catholic) with the permission and cooperation of the administrator of the Order. Elliott's "Sacking the Jew's House" (four scenes) may have been the first attempt to present a picture story in stereo. It is more probable, however, that the four scene "Little Red Riding Hood" preceded it.

Silvester's views are very similar in subject and technique. His series include "The Hero's Wife" (six scenes, 1859), "Look Before You Leap," Lodge 9581 (four scenes, 1858), a lampoon of Masonic initiation ceremonies, and "National Sports." This was a miscellaneous series, but mostly of horse racing, such as Epsom Downs, and Derby Day. His several "Artist's Studio" are satirical while his widow and child "In the Bitter Cold" is mawkishly sentimental.

Both Elliott and Silvester between 1858 and 1861 identified their views by a blind stamp imprint but many copies sold by the London Stereoscopic Company, especially after 1862 do not have the imprint. The stereos were usually very well hand tinted.

Comic views and jokes enjoyed great popularity. Silvester's "Provisions for the Monastery," depicts a monk attempting to smuggle into the monastery a young woman hidden in a bundle of faggots and a shocked brother crossing his arms in horror. "Fast Day" by Phiz portrays a priest dining on a sumptuous feast and a boy peering through a window. Both models are acting: The priest is hiding the roast duck under the table while the boy is grinning at the hypocrite. The importance of these stereos is their ability to imply action and reaction.

Many English and French photographers before 1860 undertook ambitious staging to produce stereos of ballroom scenes, with as many as fifty models arranged as dancing couples, orchestra and sitters. Some of the stereographs are montages made from several negatives but most of the ballroom scenes were made in spacious rooms with suitable camera distance. Figure 60.

The variety of composition stereos is incredible. J. Reynolds (1858) published a series illustrating Dickens' "The Old Curiosity Shop." The cluttered scene of "Little Nell" and her grandfather is overdone but striking. Punch and Gebhardt, Rotmann & Co. produced many splendid serious and comic views.

The London Stereoscopic published hundreds of compositions, generally well tinted, without a photographer identification. The series "Happy Homes of England," is especially beautiful in depicting upper middle class ideals.

Among the many popular themes not mentioned above are: courtship, marriage, unrequited love, bereavement, children sleeping or praying, musical duets, fortune telling and playing cards. Comic views of endless variety had wide appeal.

Strangely, these efforts were bitterly criticized by those photographers who remained purist. The notion that the camera records a scene truthfully, that is, just as the eye sees it, led to ridiculous controversy. Any photograph that involved an artifice was considered to be untruthful, dishonest. Even an instantaneous view that seemed to stop motion was suspect because it was unnatural. "The camera does not lie but liars photograph."

The so-called artist photographers sincerely believed that stereographic photography degenerated badly after 1860-62. What concerned them was the ever increasing intrusion of the photographer into his photographs. That intrusion is the mark of creativity.

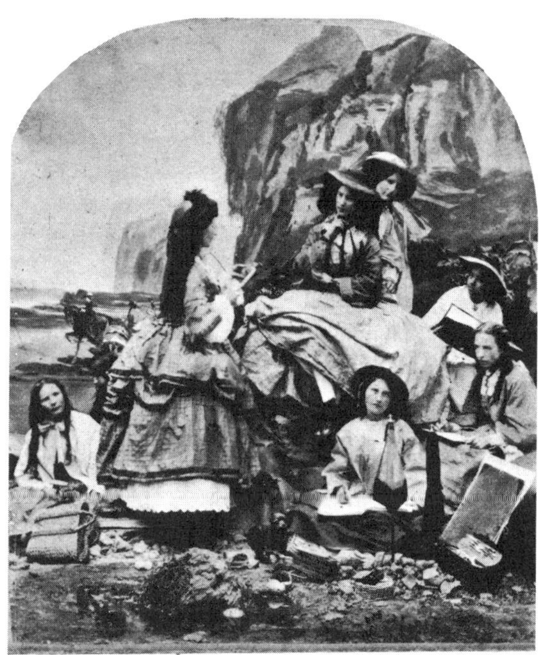

70. "Seaside Sketches—the Mermaid's Haunt." Studio staged scene. London Stereoscopic Company. 1858.

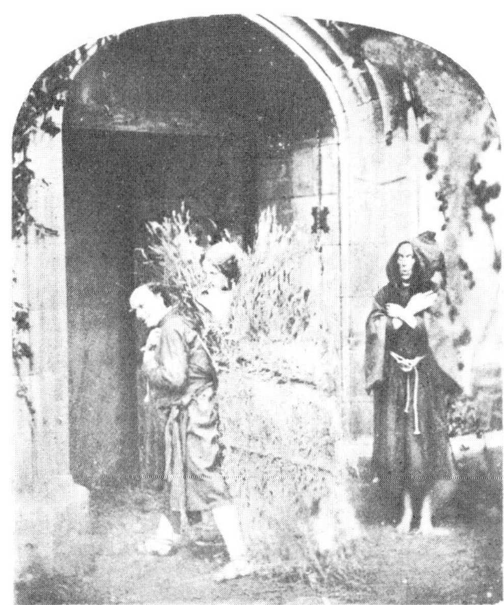

71. Alfred Silvester. "Provisions for the Monastery." 1858.

The possibilities of creative photography were not universally condemned. M. A. Root, more clearly than any other nineteenth century photographer recognized what was being accomplished and what greater achievements lie in the future.[2]

"In a vast atelier (sitting room) properly organized and fitted up with backgrounds, reflectors, and all requisite accessories, the intelligent and skilled photographer, aided by capable models, may therefore essay the most complicated and difficult pictures. . . ."

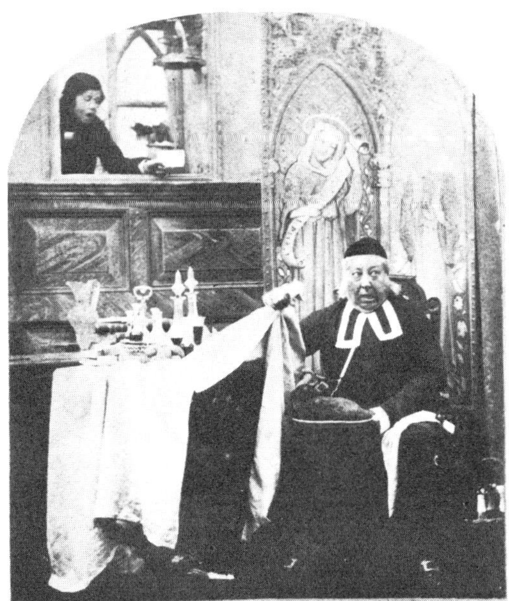

72. Hablot Knight ("Phiz") "The Fast Day." Note facial expressions. 1858.

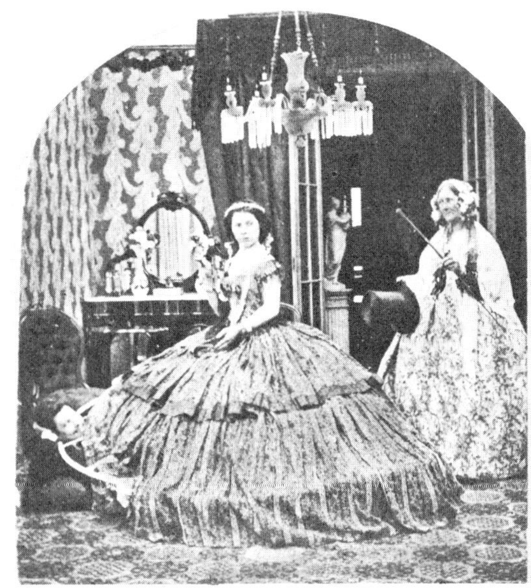

73. "Surprised." A convenient hiding place. London Stereoscopic Company. ca. 1860.

"For the stage men and women are carefully educated and disciplined . . . Why, then, may not education and discipline . . . fit men and women for models to represent such scenes and living groups as the photographer may wish to transfer to plate or paper? . . . No limit can be set to the possible development and progress whether of art or artists, and of the appliances required by them, whether inanimate or human. . . ."

"And the models required by the photographer for these large and complex representations, may serve besides to entertain and instruct the public, by composing and exhibiting "tableaux vivants." In these spectacles may

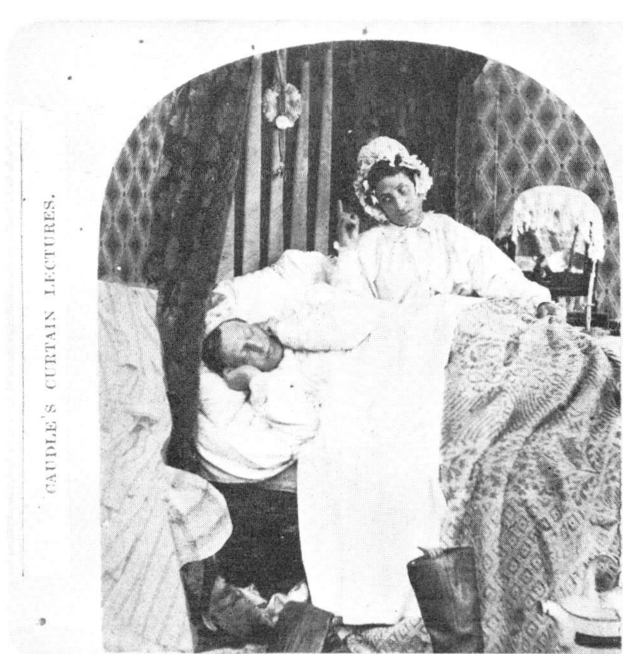

74. Humorous. "Caudle's Curtain Lectures" series. A quotation from the lecture is printed on the back. London Stereoscopic Company. ca. 1858.

[2] *The Camera and the Pencil*, pp. 445-449, 1864. See also Brewster, *The Stereoscope*, 1856, suggested the usefulness of compositions for instruction and amusement.

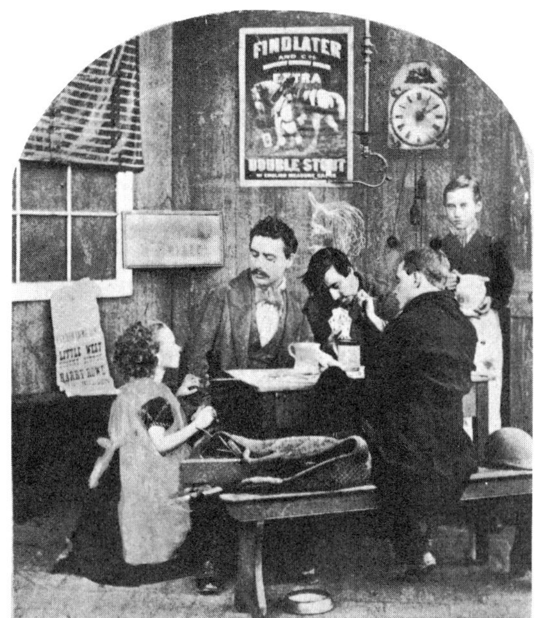

75. Social Commentary. Temperance. "Father Come Home." London Stereoscopic Company. ca. 1860.

be presented the sublimest and lovliest scenery of all lands, and the grandest and most beautiful monuments of human genius, skill, and labor, in both the ancient and the modern worlds, together with man himself . . . By the same flexible appliances, the most thrilling and critical scenes and actions that are commemorated in history or imagined in romance, together with the heroes or geniuses, the sages or saints or martyrs, who have borne a part therein, may be reproduced before the contemplation of the present generation with the vividness of living reality. What incalculable means and materials of instruction, of refinement, and of elevation, not less than recreation and amusement are here presented! And, after serving this primary and most important end, they may serve the photographer in producing pictures of whatever is most interesting and instructive, either in the vast and multifora world of reality, or the still vaster and more various world of imagination and inventive genius."

One need only recall some of the epic motion pictures to realize how well Root predicted the future of photography.

Returning briefly to the techniques of composition stereography, we can see how the studio evolved from the sitting room of a portrait photographer.

Several English and French stereographers attempted to stage scenes in a Turkish court and harem. The tableaus by Grundy, Fenton and Gaudin are remarkably similar. The actors in costume are posed in positions where they remain motionless until the photograph has been taken. The scenes are stiff, too posed. The faces are English and French, not Turkish.

The implication of emotion was often achieved quite convincingly. In such scenes as a mother tenderly looking down at the child nursing at her breast, we have the universal madonna.

Young lovers in embrace surprised by the intrusion of the girl's mother, elicit a universal response. We are "seeing" action and reaction. The producers of comics went further. An Irishman models the Irishman, black face models pose as Negroes. "Fitness for the part" is the basis for the selection of the model: young, old, fat, ugly, handsome, beautiful. These are but applications of theatrical techniques to composition photography.

Yet it must be recognized that nearly all of the compositions produced before 1865 have a stiffness that betrays some degree of artificiality. Probably only the illusions created by the motion picture could overcome this problem.

In the latter 1860's several notable series of compositions achieved charming realism with much simpler staging. Loescher & Petsch (Berlin, 1867-1873) produced their "Gems of German Life," a beautiful series of views mostly of young women and girls (occasionally with a grandfather or music teacher) engaged in a simple activity, such a reading, sewing or gathering flowers. The neatly dressed models, wearing starched aprons and petticoats, although obviously posed, show appropriate natural facial expressions. Loescher and Petsch used a stereo camera with lenses of different focal length, resulting in a slight size difference in the two images. Max Petsch abandoned photography in 1873 because of its supposed artistic limitations.

The Pauly Sisters (Berlin, 1869-74) produced a large series of fine views in the style of Loescher and Petsch. Their stereos were published by Sophus Williams.

F. L. Stuber (Bethlehem, Pennsylvania, 1871-72) published "Gems of American Life," obviously imitating Loescher and Petsch. The models used in these beautiful compositions are skillfully posed.

Notman published several unusual series, the majority utilizing his techniques for simulating snow and

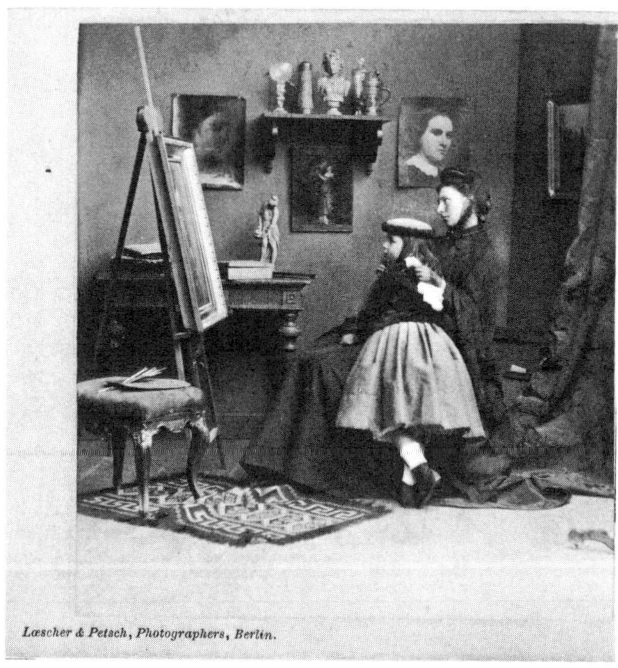

76. Loescher & Petsch. "Gems of German Life" series. Untitled scene. 1868.

snowflakes. Among the most striking are "Winter Sports," "The Skating Party," "The Trapper" and "Lumbering."

American stereographers were rather slow in working with the composition. Neither Langenheim nor Anthony bothered with it. On the other hand, Stacy and the New York Stereoscopic Company did.

The unknown photographers who produced the compositions for the Stacy and New York Stereoscopic Company frequently divided the stage into right and left "rooms" separated by a simple partition with a door. In one scene a housemaid with a broom in hand inquires at the door, to a bedroom, "Did you ring sir?" In another scene, "The Night Before Christmas," two children are asleep in bed while in the adjacent room Santa Claus is filling the stockings with gifts. The general effect is inferior to the English composition.

In 1867 Pollock Brothers produced a series of about thirty compositions of children, again imitative of the English photographers. Reviewers considered the views to have "natural charm."

About the same time, J. Gurney issued a series of clever comics, with minimum properties. One scene of a poker game depicts a player so surprised by the cards he has drawn that his hat has lifted three feet above his head.

M. M. Griswold in 1870 began to publish his "Life Compositions for the Stereoscope." Using only genuine properties, he was able to surpass all other attempts to photograph children in staged settings. Instead of papier mache rocks, cardboard fences and painted backdrops, he created realistic sets. A barn scene had straw, eggs, pails and lantern. The studio is completely concealed behind the set.

Griswold's first two compositions (1870) "The Hen's Nest" and "Blowing Bubbles," were followed by about fifty more. "The First Pair of Pants," "Mamma, Where was I when you were a little girl?", and "The Picture Book" were tremendously popular.

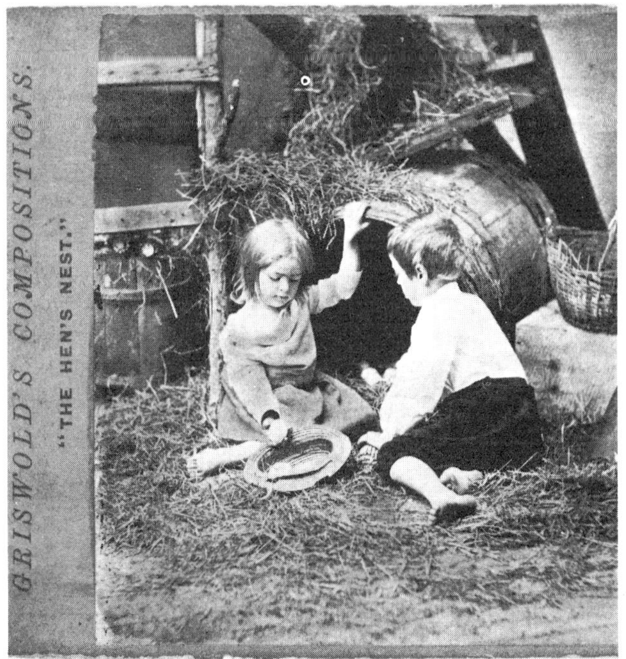

77. M. M. Griswold. "The Hen's Nest." 1870.

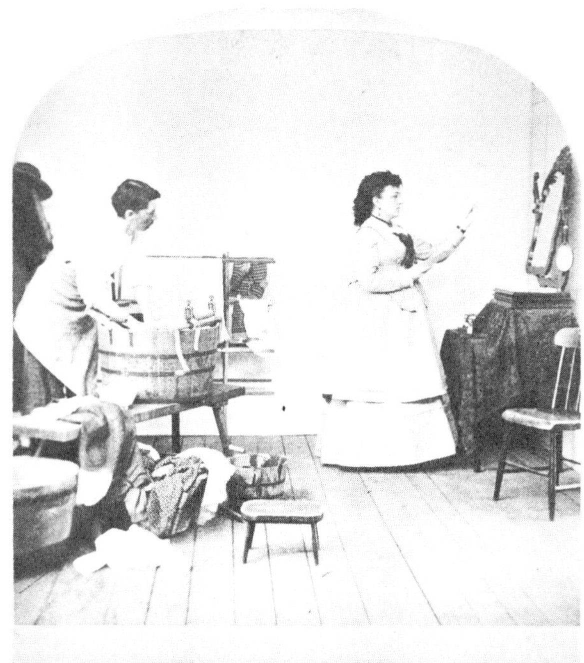

78. F.G. Weller. Satire. "Women's Rights, The Rehearsal." 1871.

In 1875, Benerman & Wilson offered to the professional trade a selection of twenty-seven of Griswold's most popular titles, with this comment: "These inimitable pictures are all natural compositions and touch the tender chords of human nature most wonderfully. They are attractive to everyone who has a heart, but *particularly instructive as studies for photographers* in grouping, posing and composition. They will help any man make better and easier pictures of children and should be studied."[3]

F. G. Weller in 1870 published a series of eight views illustrating the poem "The Night Before Christmas." Each scene was identified with a verse, as "The stockings were hung . . . " and "Then laying on his finger . . . " During the next three years Weller specialized in the production of sentimental and comic compositions. His views became the best known and most popular in America. Simple and touching is "Hope and Despair," two young women consoling each other, one a bride in white and the other a widow in black. "Just before the battle" is a school room with several frightened girls with their skirts gathered tightly perched on chairs and a mouse nearby. There are three similar scenes and three negatives of each, thus nine variants. Weller made several jibes at women's rights and the henpecked husband. Two of his early views are titled "The Rehearsal" and "Off to the Lecture Room" (Nos. 329, 330, 1871). Weller's most popular composition, "A Stitch in Time" with eight variants, depicts a little girl sewing a tear on her doll.

In the closing years of his career, Weller delved into purely imaginative compositions, attempting allegory and illustration of *Pilgrim's Progress* in stereo. During 1875 he produced such fanciful scenes as "The Fairy

[3] *Phila. Photogr.*, advertisement in consecutive monthly issues 1875. The series of twenty-seven titles was first mentioned in Mar. 1874, pp. 88-89.

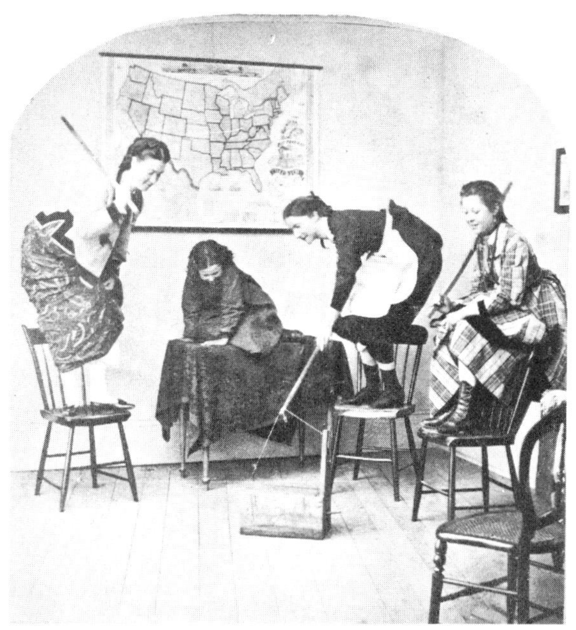

79. F.G. Weller. "Just Before the Battle." 1871.

Court," "Frostworkers painting windows," "The Water Nymph," "February," and "Spring." The figures and scenery are miniature objects made of wood and cardboard cut-outs. These curious stereos and the two series "The Rock of Ages" (three views, 1876) and *Pilgrim's Progress* (twelve views, 1877) were very popular.

Weller's negatives passed for a short period to G. H. Aldrich, then to the Littleton View Company and finally to Underwood & Underwood. Many of the stereos were in continuous production until 1897.

Several other American contemporary publishers issued compositions that were widely distributed, most

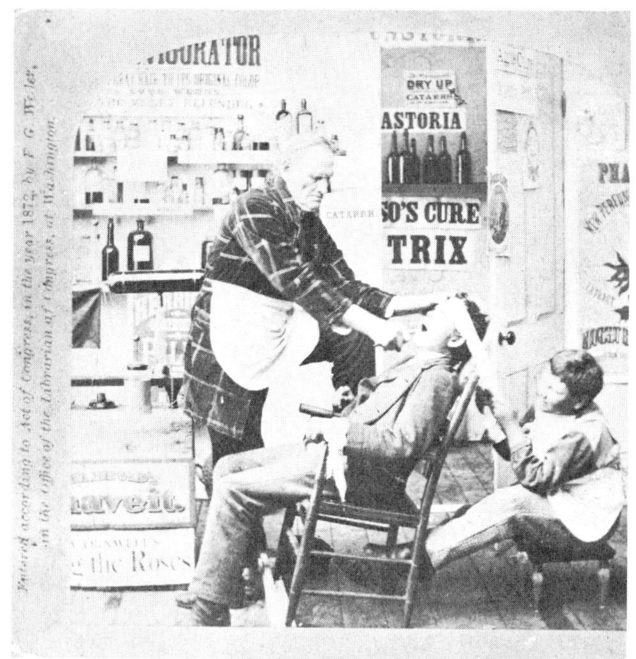

81. F.G. Weller. "An Effectual Remedy." 1872.

notably Melander & Brother (Chicago), L. E. Walker (Warsaw, N.Y.) and an unidentified photographer whose views were first sold by E. & H. T. Anthony under the title "Young Idea Series."

Melander & Brother photographed a series of forty-six compositions which were published (1874-5) by Lovejoy & Foster. The staging is well done but the posing is stiff. "The First Lesson in Knitting" and "The Spelling Match" are among the best of their early work. Far better is "Frontier Life After Supper" (No. 117, 1876), a family

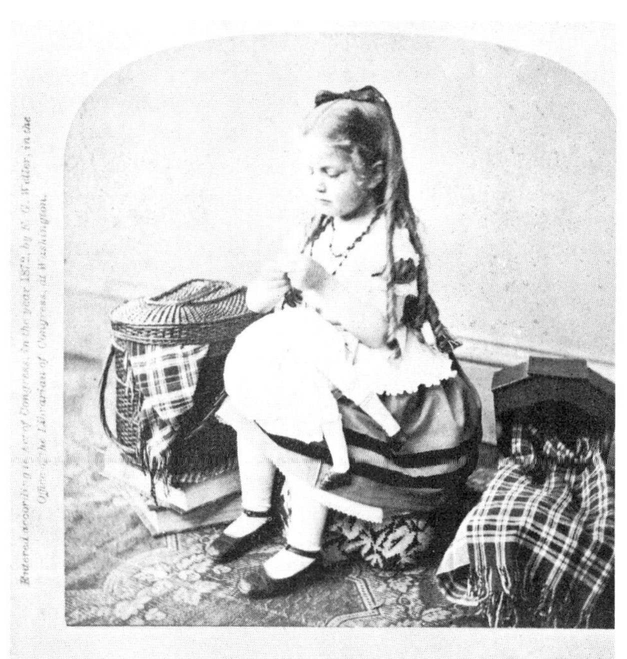

80. F. G. Weller. "A Stitch in Time." Eight negatives (1872, 1874 and 1876) of this view are known.

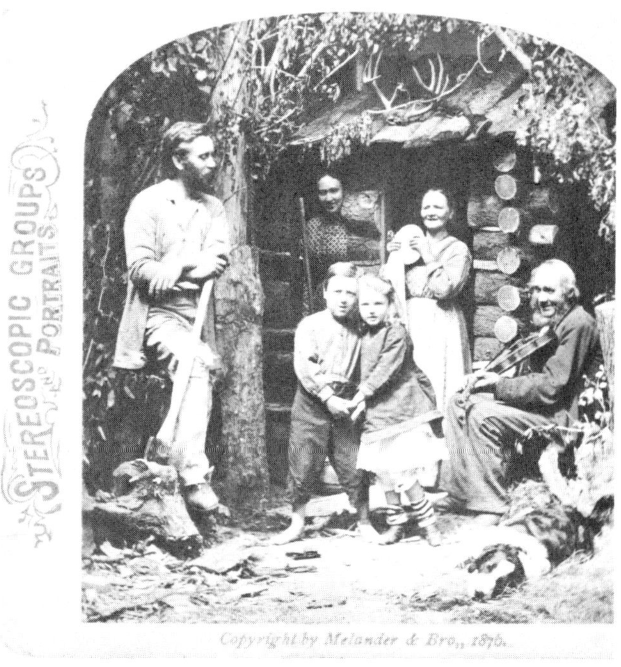

82. L.E. Melander. Studio group. "Frontier Life—After Supper." 1876.

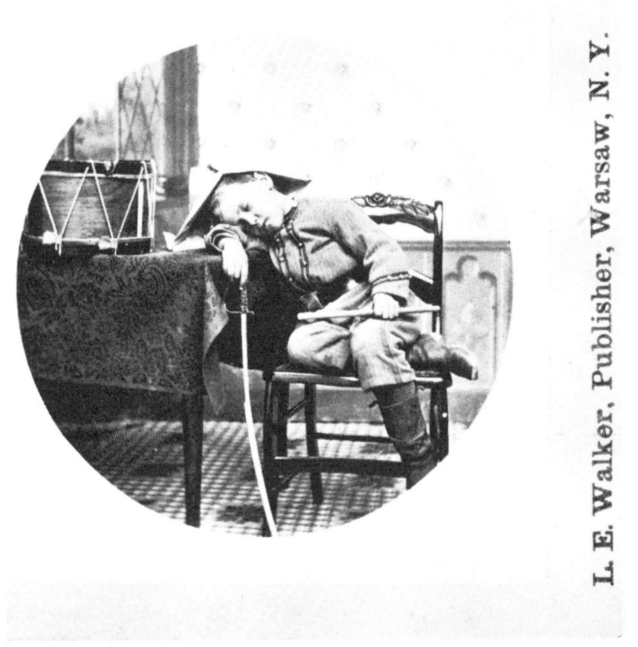

83. L. E. Walker. "Pleasing Studies for our Young Folks" series. "The Tired Soldier." 1873.

standing in front of a studio log cabin. Imitating Weller they illustrated, somewhat grotesquely, "The Ninety-Ninth Psalm" (Nos. 132, 133, 1877), reissued with new negatives in 1889.

L. E. Walker achieved more life-like poses in simple settings for his series, "Pleasing Studies for our Young Folks." There are about eighty titles of which the following are typical: "Shine Your Boots, Sir?", (No. 25) "We-we and Bob—the News Boys" (No. 26), "Fannie and William and the Album" (No. 48), and "The First Shave" (No. 58).

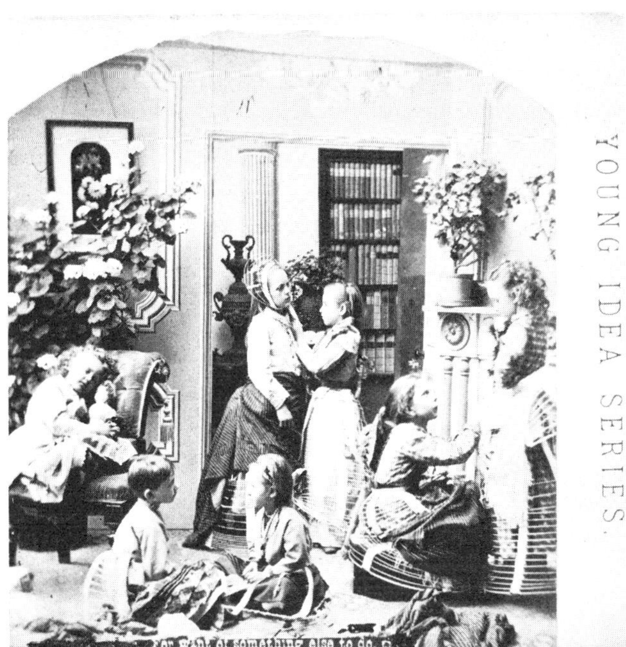

84. "Young Idea Series" "For want of something else to do." E. & H.T. Anthony issue. 1873.

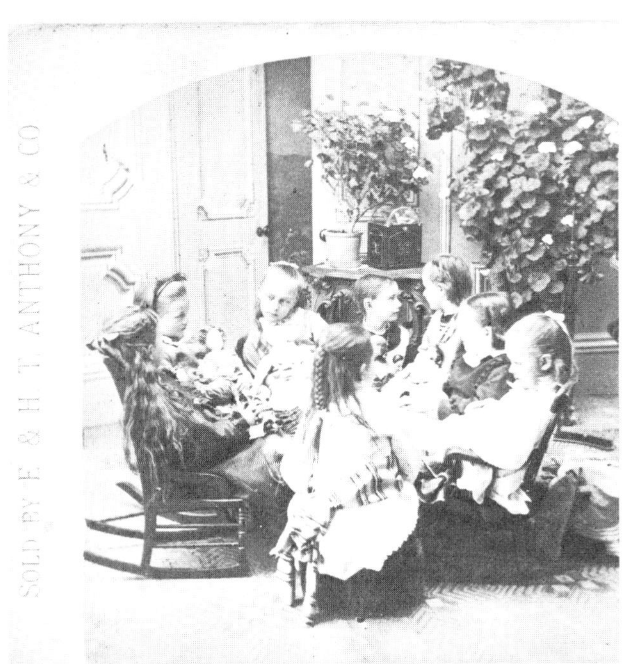

85. "Young Idea Series" "Waiting for the Committee on Prizes." E. & H.T. Anthony issue. 1873.

The Young Idea Series was distributed by Anthony between 1870 and 1874. After 1875 many cheap reprint and copy issues were available. The series is of considerable importance because a simple studio set with three walls was used to stage more than a hundred compositions showing children playing in as many different ways. In all, about a dozen boys and girls, between the ages of four and twelve, were used as models. Among the amusing scenes are: an orchestra of five children, four boys with two hobby horses, girls playing with dolls, mixed groups playing school—including such unusual classes as astronomy.

The ingenuity displayed in the arrangement of wall pictures, bric-a-brac, and furniture is remarkable. The panelling, fireplace and major pieces of furniture identify the studio in every view.

The stereographs are quite ordinary being simply cute. Yet the series is praiseworthy for the comfortable poses of the children who seem to be enjoying their roles immensely. The happy faces are genuine. Whoever the photographer was, he had an uncommon skill in working with groups of children.

S. Christmann (Berlin and Paris, 1868-1875) published many series of compositions oriented toward children. The scenes, although unsophisticated are clever. The views were nicely hand tinted. Several series illustrate adult occupations staged with children as the models. These include "Outdoor Work" (chimney sweep, gardener), "Housework Indoors," and "In the Workshop" (Basket maker). The views, which have titles in French, German and English, seem to have been sold only in Europe. They are seldom found in American collections.

Somewhat more common are the Christmann series "Dreams," such as "Dream of Hope" and "Past and Present," which were sentimental.

In addition to these series, Christmann published small

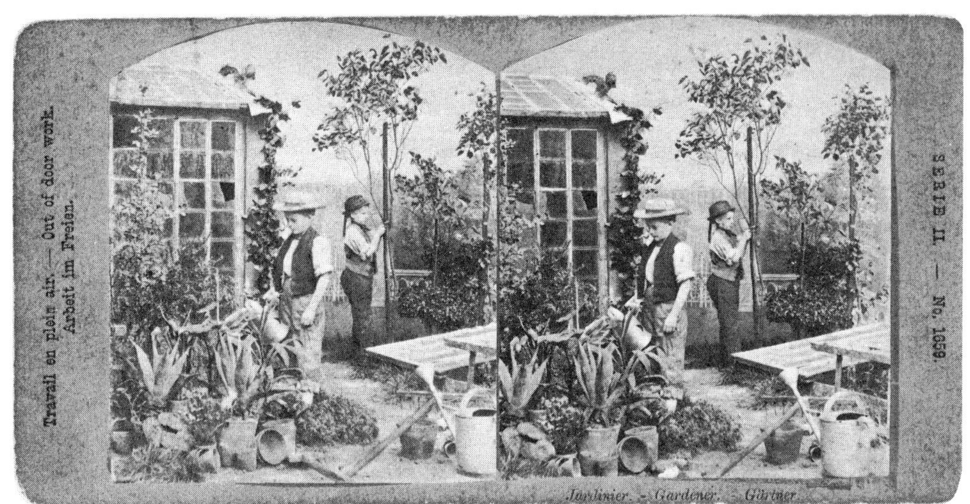

86. S.P. Christmann. Occupations series. "The Gardner." 1868. Note title in French, English and German.

sets illustrating fairy tales ("Cinderella", "Puss in Boots", "Hansel and Gretel").

Gaudin (London and Paris, 1862-70) produced a series of adult groups depicting many amusing and serious situations. The staging shows little variation, probably because of the few properties used by the photographer. Anthony distributed Gaudin composition in the United States for almost fifteen years.

Several other experimental techniques attracted the attention of stereographers. The earliest of these, "spirit photography," was discovered by Brewster.

When the exposure time for taking a photograph was ten or more seconds a transparent figure could be recorded in the negative if a person would quickly move into a predetermined place and withdraw in two or three seconds. The novelty of such ghost or spirit figures delighted many photographers. Scores of ghost stereos were published, some with "apologies to Sir David Brewster." Among the well-known photographers who produced them were Elliott, William England, Kilburn and Weller.

Another technique used rather infrequently in stereography is table-top photography, that is, staging of a scene with miniature models. Weller's use of them for his fanciful stereo compositions has been mentioned above.

The most famous "table top" scenes, are the "Diables," a French series "Journey in Hell" produced between 1868-1874 in tissue format. Satan's disciples are dolls and scaled figurines, many of which are dimunitive monsters. There are seventy-two numbers (not issued as a set) depicting the worldly sins and the punishments awaiting the sinner who is condemned to Hell. The mood is "tongue in cheek." Some of the punishments are quite enjoyable,

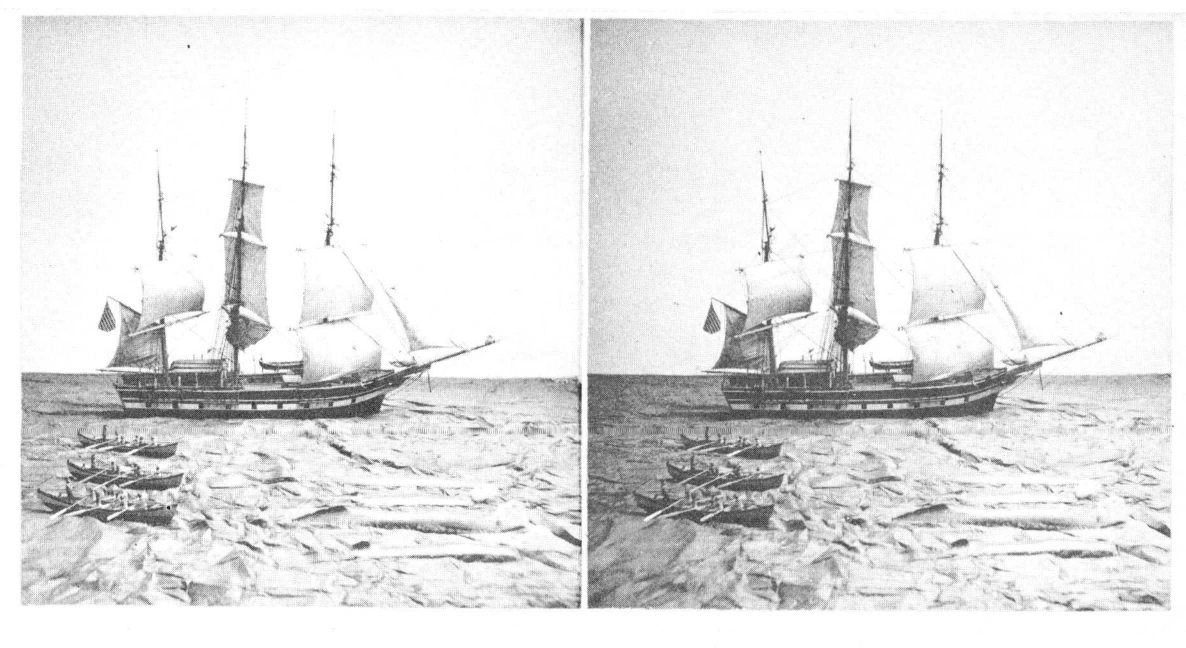

87. Table Top photography. "Chasing Whales" No. 2. in C.H. Shute's series, "Whaling Voyage." 1868.

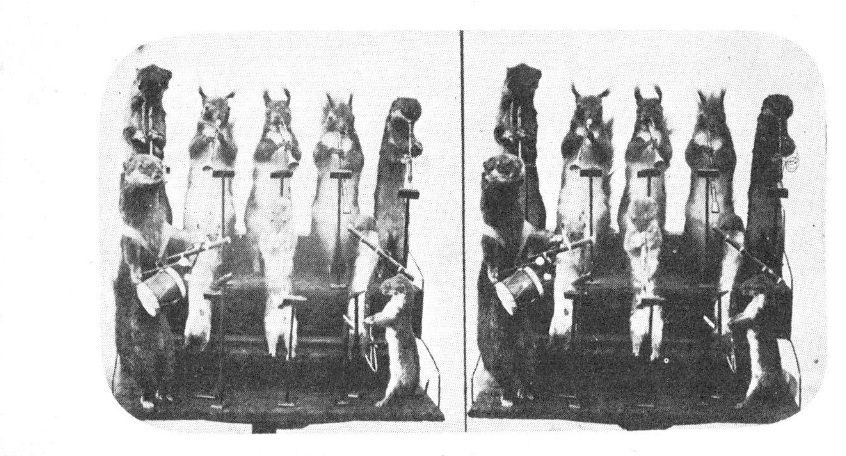

88. Humorous Group. Squirrel Orchestra. Unknown photographer. Gladwell issue 1855. The reverse of this view is shown in figure 6.

giving an ambiguously grim and comical effect. Many copy and pirated issues were published as standard card mounts between 1873 and 1880.

A similar miscellaneous series of comics were published in France, probably the work of the same photographer. One of the most clever is the "Dream of an Aeronaut," published also in England under the title, "Up in a Balloon." A slumbering scientist dreams himself, supported only by an umbrella, floating in the air far above the city below.

Both of these series were intentionally unrealistic, intentionally satirical.

Shute & Sons (Edgartown, Massachusetts, 1868-1870) published "A Whaling Voyage" in twelve scenes. The ocean is an oil cloth that has been roughened to simulate waves. So life-like are the whaling ship, fisherman, pursuit boats and whale, that the photographs might easily be mistaken for actual scenes at sea.

A few photographers used mounted animals to illustrate fables or arrange amusing compositions. One of the funniest, an orchestra of ten squirrels, was issued in 1855. E. A. S. Haines (Albany, N. Y., 1870-72) published a small series of amusing compositions including several of animal orchestras.

Illustration of such fables as Aesop's "The Lion and the Mouse," "The Wolf and the Lamb" and "The Town Mouse and The Country Mouse," of course, used mounted animals in staging.

Kilburn published a twelve card series (Nos. 1277-1288, 1874), "Illustrations of the Vision of Sir Launfal." These views are not compositions but are ice scenes accompanied by a verse of Lowell's poem. The fancied or symbolic implication, however, places this series with creative photography.

Interest in the composition stereograph declined noticeably in the latter 1870's. Although Kilburn continued to add varied titles to their trade list and several other photographers produced comics, not until the 1890's was there renewal of activity. Singley (Keystone View Company) and Rau began to issue sentimental and comic views, mostly unimaginative and dull at first. By 1898, however, the forgotten picture story returned to favor.

The basic idea in the late nineteenth century picture story is the conversion of a joke or "one-liner" into a comic situation.

A single example will demonstrate how the joke can be expanded and broken into a series of related scenes.

Rau's "Has the furnace man been here?" is a scene in which a mistress questions her housemaid. The maid is wearing a white blouse on the back of which are two large hand prints in soot. The viewer needs only a quick glance to answer the lady's question.

Compare now Underwood's "The New French Cook" (two versions ten and twelve cards, 1902, 1903). In the

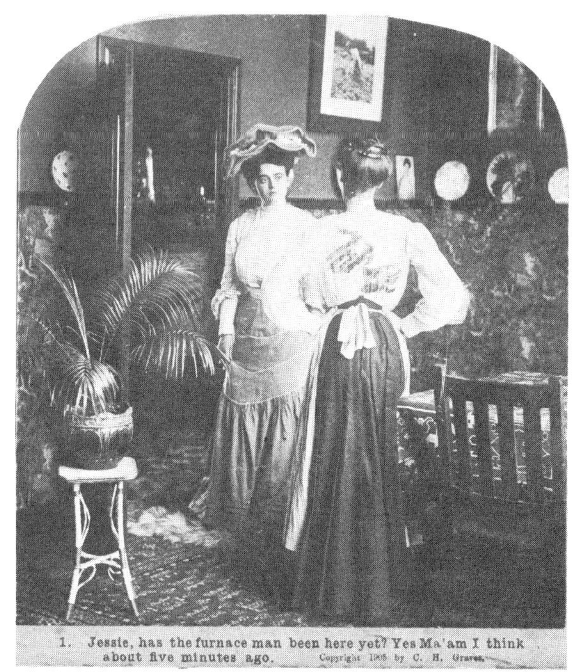

89. "Jennie, has the furnace man been here yet? Yes Ma'am I think about five minutes ago." C.H. Graves. 1905.

first scene, a pretty smiling maid is kneading bread dough in the kitchen. Her hands are covered with flour. The flirtaceous husband enters in the second scene. In quick succession the maid and husband kiss and embrace. Their startled faces show that the wife has called from the living room. The maid and husband separate but the tell-tale floured hand prints are on the back of his coat. The wife's discovery is followed by apology and reconciliation. The pretty maid is replaced by an older, fat, ugly one.

This set was so popular that eight competitors rushed to publish obviously imitated versions to market. Some versions substitute a Negro for the old fat maid (R. R. Whiting, 1902; Keystone, 1902; Rau, 1902; R. Y. Young, 1902, 03; C. H. Graves, 1903, etc.).

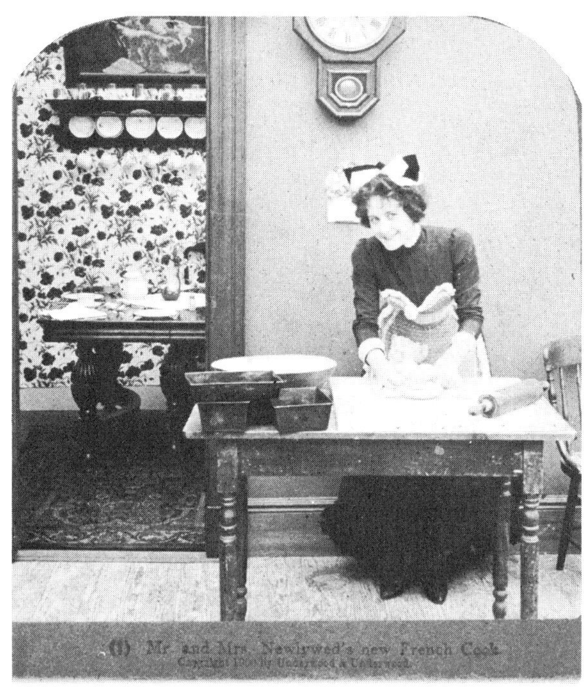

90.-99. (1) "Mr. and Mrs. Newlywed's New French Cook." A situation comedy in ten views. Underwood & Underwood. 1900.

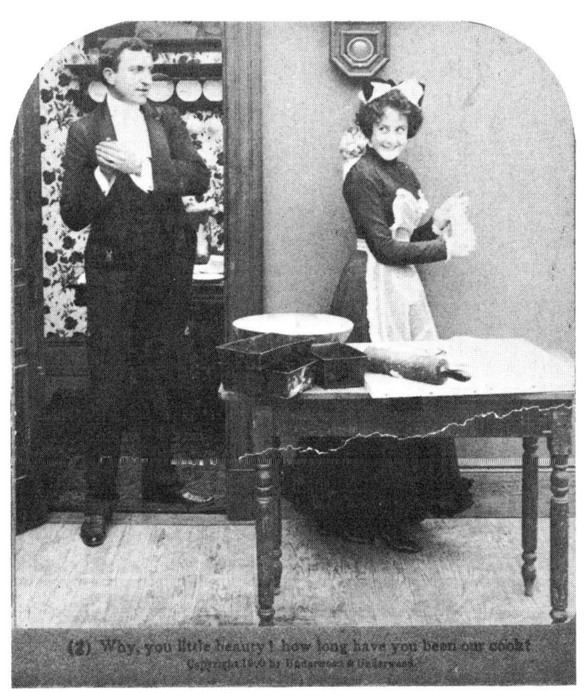

91. (2) Why, you little beauty! how long have you been our cook?

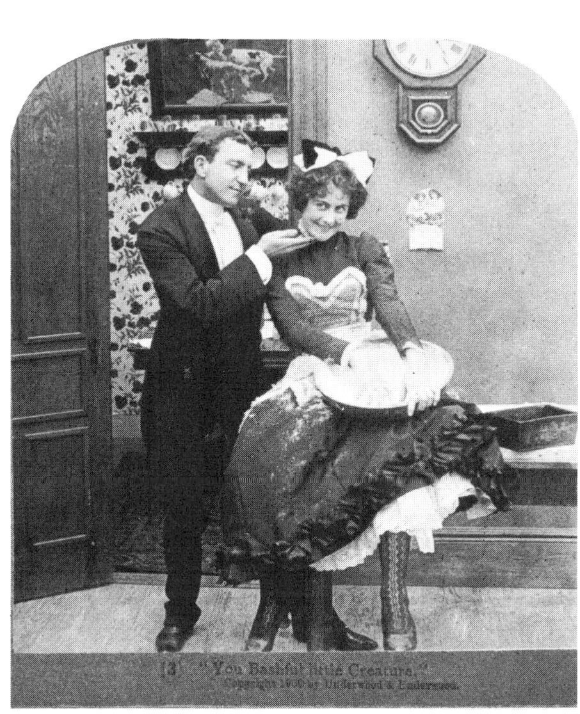

92. (3) You bashful little creature.

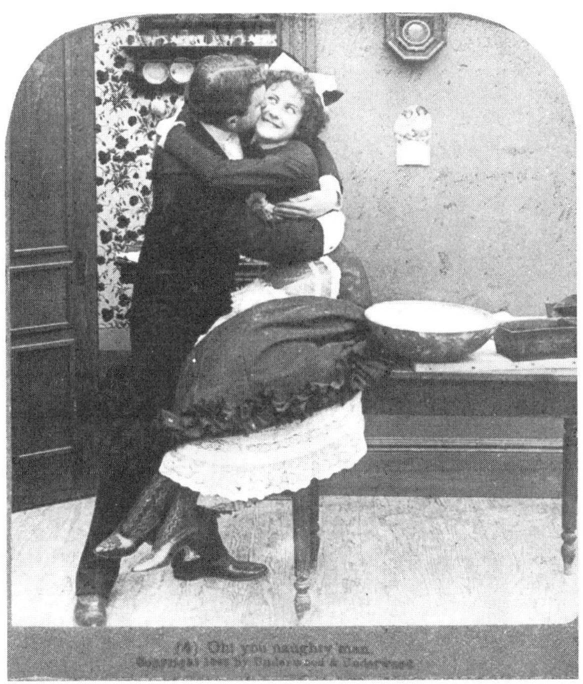

93. (4) O! you naughty man.

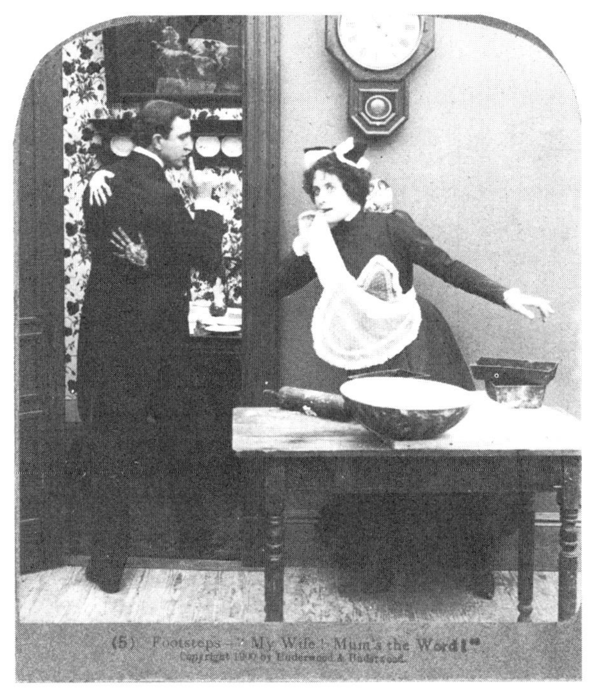

94. (5) Footsteps. My Wife! Mum's the word!

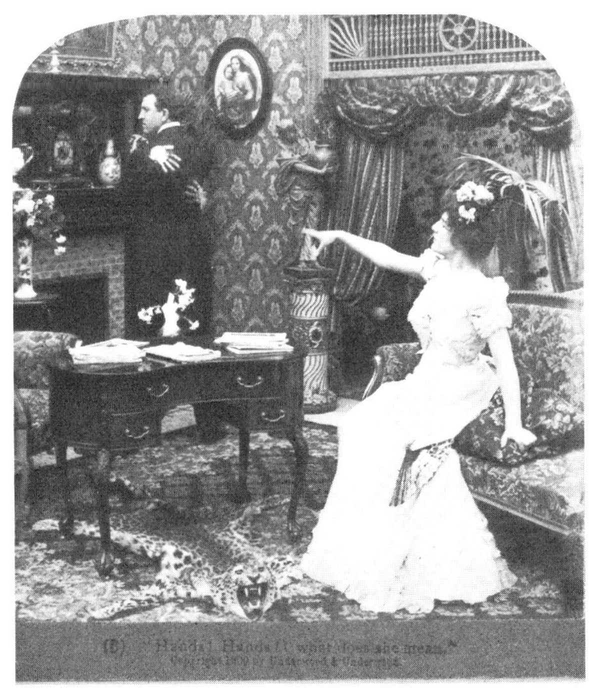

95. (6) "Hands! Hands! What does this mean?

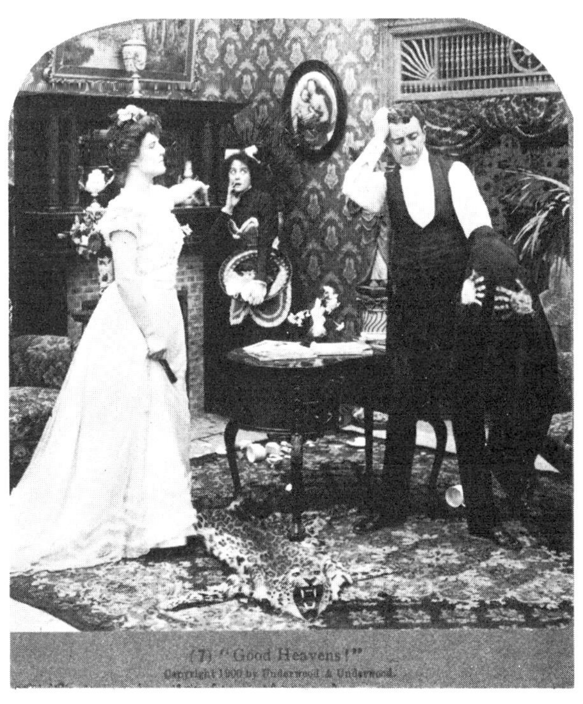

96. (7) Good Heavens!

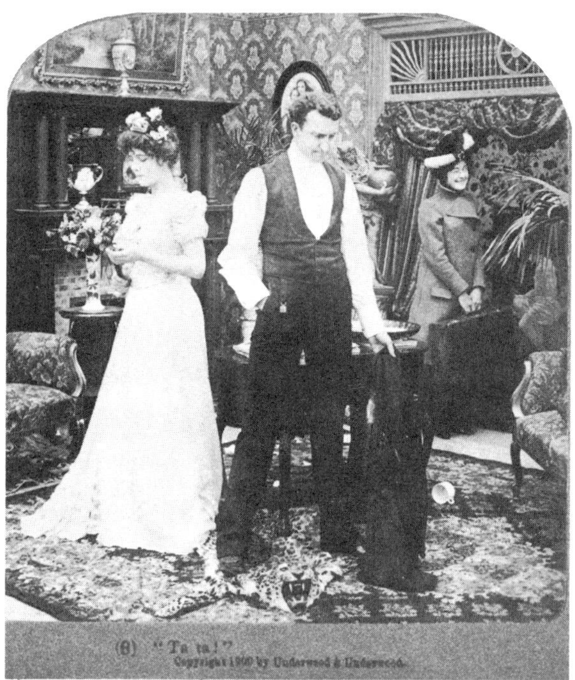

97. (8) "Ta-ta."

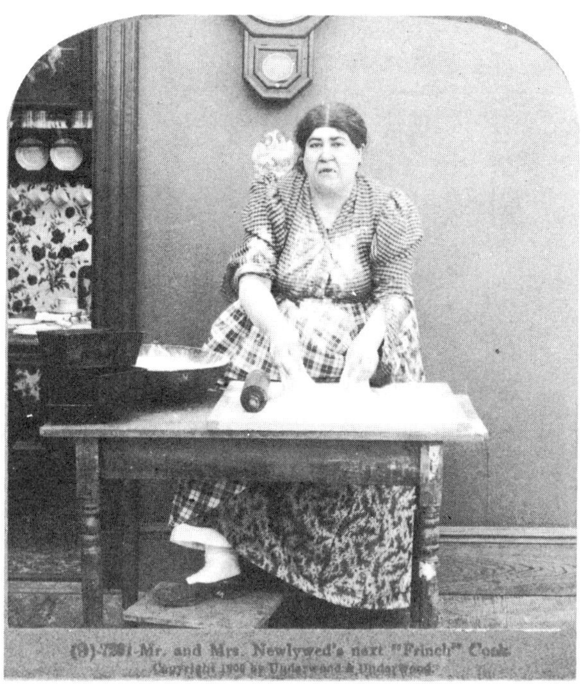

98. (9) Mr. and Mrs. Newlywed's next "Frinch" Cook.

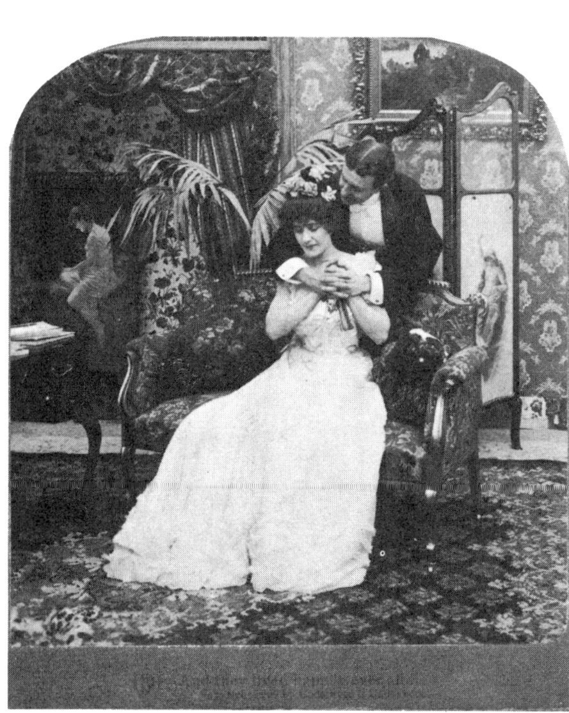

99. (10) And they lived happily ever after.

Many comic and sentimental sets were produced between 1896 and 1908. The following are among the best known:

"The Wedding," Kilburn, 1897, eighteen views.

At least a dozen photographers issued similar sets. C. H. Graves, 1897, ten views; Keystone 1900, ten, 1902, twelve; Underwood, 1902, twelve; H. C. White, 1902, ten; and C. L. Wasson, 1905, ten; are typical. This was the all-time favorite theme. How many maidens mooned over these romantic scenes?

"Married Life," Underwood, 1897, sixteen views, 1901, eighteen.

There were also many competitive series.

"The Shady Nook and Not a Man in Sight," R. E. Steele, 1908, ten cards.

This set is remarkable because the photography was entirely outdoors, "on location."

"The Dying Miner" (a "western") Sterro-Photo, 1906, six cards.

"Mr. and Mrs. Silas Green from Wayback, Ohio," H. C. White, 1903, eight cards.

"The Secretary" (another flirtation situation), Underwood, 1899, six cards.

"Reuben Visits His City Cousins," H. C. Graves, 1902, six cards.

There is an enormous variety of two to five card sets. Four examples will suggest the types of themes they illustrate.

"The Floorwalker" (by day and by night), Underwood, 1902.

"Greatness" (born great, achieve greatness, greatness thrust upon them.) Underwood, 1901.

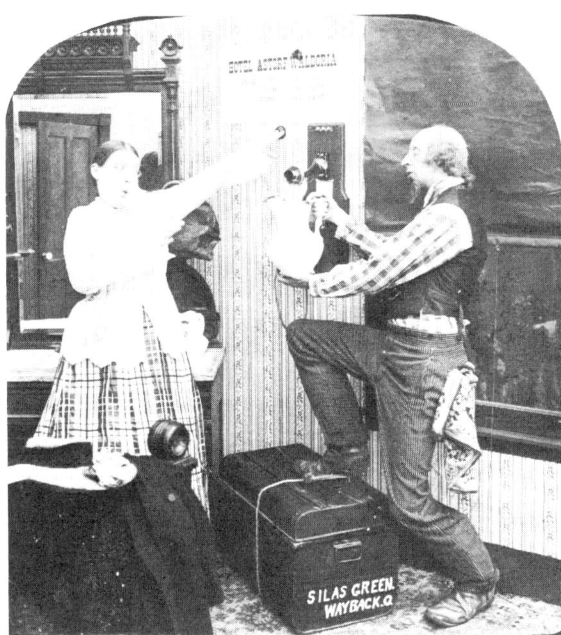

100. Comic. "Silas Green from Wayback, Ohio visits the City." One of a series of eight views. The couple are bewildered by the conveniences in the Astorf Waldoria Hotel. H.C. White Company. 1903.

"Three Ways to Spread the News" (slowest by telegraph, quicker telephone, quickest by gossip), H. C. White, 1903.

"The Five Senses," Underwood, 1905.

A technique for exaggerating comic effect was used by Herman Knudzen (Chicago, 1906) for a series of six-card lithoprint sets. The situations are staged with living models but the negatives are retouched to simulate explosions of fire crackers, spilled beer, spilled paint, etc. The viewer is not sure if he is looking at a cartoon or a photograph. Actually the scene is a combination of both. The situations are slap-stick comedies.

Comic sets enjoyed their greatest popularity between

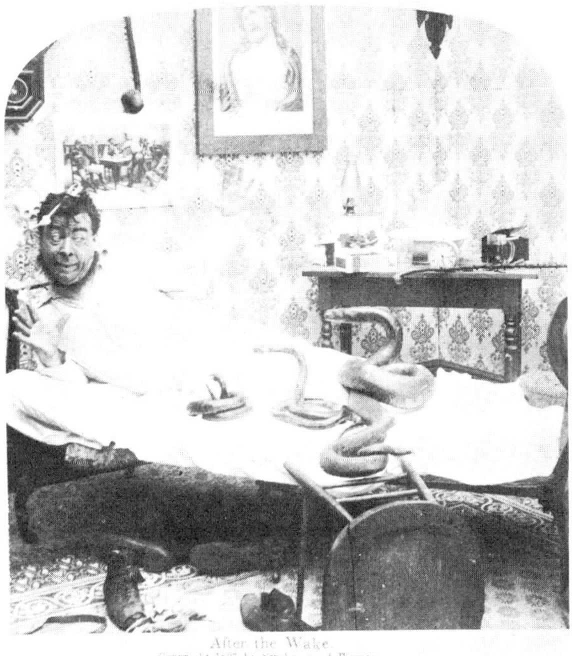

101. Comic. "After the Wake." Delirium tremens. A typical temperance view. Strohmyer & Wyman. 1897.

1898 and 1910, which coincides with the commercialization of the motion picture, Louis Lumiere (1895-98) and Georges Melies (1895-1900) produced hundreds of cinema shorts. Unquestionably the establishment of "nickelodeons" throughout the United States displaced humorous stereographs as entertainment.

The accumulated experience of compositional and creative photography in turn influenced the development of the cinema. There are too many parallels and too many shared techniques to deny strong interrelationships.

Composition stereographs represent one of the most intriguing and amusing areas for collection and investigation.

CHAPTER EIGHT

EASTERN UNITED STATES

GENERAL REMARKS

The topographic and scenic stereo views of the United States, so-called regional views, reflect the prevailing attitudes of the American people. First and foremost, they were proud of their home towns, proud of their country. And this pride, sometimes boastful, extended to bridges, factories, inventions and local landmarks, which, in essence, were symbols of progress. Second, and in some respects a feature almost uniquely American, they were drawn to the Frontier, those unsettled regions beckoning the courageous and ambitious.

Europe had no such frontiers. This great difference is shown in the freedom and mobility of the people depicted in stereo views. While it may be argued that much of this freedom was more imaginary than real, to the American of the nineteenth century it was an article of faith.

The frontier was essentially the West, roughly the land beyond the Mississippi River. The East was established; the West was being explored and settled. Although there were old cities like St. Louis and many early settlements in Texas and California, their ties and characteristics were transparently western.

Regional stereographs include five common categories.

(1) The land, regional scenery
(2) Large cities and towns
(3) Villages and their immediate vicinity
(4) Resorts and tourist attractions
(5) How people live and work

In attempting to generalize upon the regional views of the United States, we are confronted with the combined work of more than six thousand photographers. Roughly eighty percent of these are technically mediocre to poor, barely a fifth produced good to fine views. Artistically, even a smaller number are of high merit. Yet a very large proportion of the stereographs are historically significant, some of the poorest views being among the rarest.

Examination of the published trade lists of a random sampling of photographers and representative long runs of the views show a consistent pattern of subjects, so much so that a collector or historian can anticipate and predict what scenes of a given locale are available. The typical coverage of a town included panoramas, prominent buildings (town hall, churches, schools, Masonic temple), mercantile streets, mills and factories, railroad station, bridges, park or village green and cemeteries. The mansions of the rich are commonly photographed. Invariably, scenes of the surrounding countryside considered locally to be beautiful (promontories, rustic walks, ravines, streams) are well represented. In large cities coverage is less complete. Photographers generally neglected residential neighborhoods unless they were attractively terraced or planted with formal gardens. If a community had a prison, an asylum, a college or a religious colony—such as the Shakers—without question, it was stereographed.

The views of small villages are particularly charming. The village green, church, town hall and the center with a few mercantile shops are shown in winter and summer. Townspeople and horse-drawn vehicles indicate the tempo of rural life.

Local stereo views record fires, floods, snow storms, tornadoes and train wrecks. Commonly they depict celebrations, religious camp meetings, parades and conventions. In large cities the photographers usually were more selective in choosing their subjects, but in small towns virtually every event was recorded.

In addition to the usual types of local stereo views which were commercially produced for the trade, there were many custom-made to order. These range from views of a family farm or residence, with the family gathered on the porch or in the yard, to series of six to twenty cards. Such series record funerals, marriages and high school graduation exercises. More rarely, a son or daughter newly established in a distant location would engage a photographer to make a series of stereos to show the new home and community. The purpose of these custom-made views, in nearly all instances, was sentimental, a memento of an occasion or a means to show distant relatives where and how one lived. When accurately identified and documented, these sets are precious. Because they were issued in small numbers for purely private distribution, they are without exception rare.

John Soule produced scores of such sets for clients within a fifty-mile radius of Boston. These cards do not bear negative numbers but, so far as I am aware, always have the name of Soule printed on them.

One feature of city and town life was completely ignored by stereographers—the slums and run-down neighborhoods. Whether this was deliberate avoidance because of shame or embarrassment, we do not know. More likely it was dictated by the simple fact that there was no market for them. Social commentary in stereo views, except as satire, is very rare prior to 1905-1910 and uncommon thereafter.

The most popular regional stereo views between 1860 and 1880 were not the cities, excepting Washington, D. C., but the summer resorts and tourist attractions.

RESORTS AND SCENIC TOURIST ATTRACTIONS

Niagara Falls

No other single subject in the world has been more frequently stereographed than Niagara Falls. Daguerreotypists tried their skills here before 1850, and Langenheims' first glass and paper stereos were of this natural wonder (1854-1855). Figure 25.

Before 1860 six stereographers had established perma-

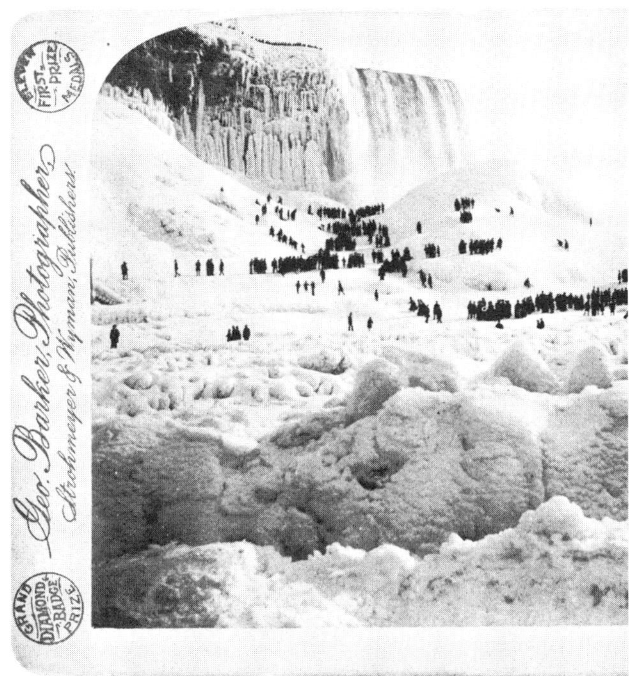

102. Niagara Falls. The great freeze of 1889. George Barker photo. The title on back is printed in six languages.

nent galleries at Niagara Falls to cater to the tourist trade: P. D. Babbitt, S. J. Mason, J. McPherson, J. J. Reilly, James Thompson and S. Davis (Canadian side). During the early 1860's George Barker, Charles Bierstadt and Thomas Barnett located here, and about 1870 George F. Curtis, O. B. Evans and L. F. Clegg opened studios. The volume and variety of their stereo views are incredible.

Yet these prolific photographers only half-tell the story. Anthony, Langenheim, Barnum, Heywood, Kilburn, Chase, Moulton and many more skilled operators issued great numbers of beautiful stereographs of the falls, hotels, the town, bridges, tight-rope crossings, etc.

Niagara Falls in winter was a favorite subject. The completely frozen falls provided spectacular scenery. There are stereos showing a dozen photographers with their cameras taking pictures of the ice formations (Bierstadt).

The bridges constructed over the gorge were engineering triumphs. Hundreds of views of each, from Roebling's suspension railroad bridge to the steel arch bridge, were published.

Likewise the many daredevil tightrope crossings of the gorge were well stereographed. The best covered were those by Blondin (1859-60) and Madam Spelterini (1872).

The White Mountains, New Hampshire

Next to Niagara Falls in popularity were views of the White Mountains. The mountains, divided by Crawford Notch into two ranges, the Presidential to the east and the Franconia to the west, are renowned for their beauty. Mt. Washington (6293 feet) is the tallest peak east of the Rocky Mountains and thirteen other summits exceed 5000 feet. Mt. Lafayette (5269 feet) is the tallest in the Franconia range.

Erection of the rude stone Tip Top House on Mt. Washington (completed 1853) and construction of the famous cog railway to the summit (1866-1869) increased tourism and provided almost unlimited opportunities for photographers. A score of large hotels and hundreds of small inns and tourist homes were scattered over the surrounding towns and foothills. There are many hundreds of views of these hotels, especially the larger, such as Fabyan House, Crawford House, Sinclair House, Profile House and "new" Summit House (1873).

Scenes of the cog railway (with prints mounted offperpendicular to exaggerate steepness), the engines, including "Old Peppersass," have delighted collectors for a century.

The cliff-hanging bridges of the Portland and Ogdensburg Railroad, especially the trains on Frankenstein Trestle, are among the most spectacular railroading views ever produced.

Before 1860 the Langenheims, F. B. Gage, Franklin White and the Bierstadt Brothers had produced fine stereos on glass and paper. Shortly thereafter John Moran issued a small series of beautiful scenic views.

Kilburn Brothers, of Littleton, became the most celebrated publishers of White Mountain views, beginning

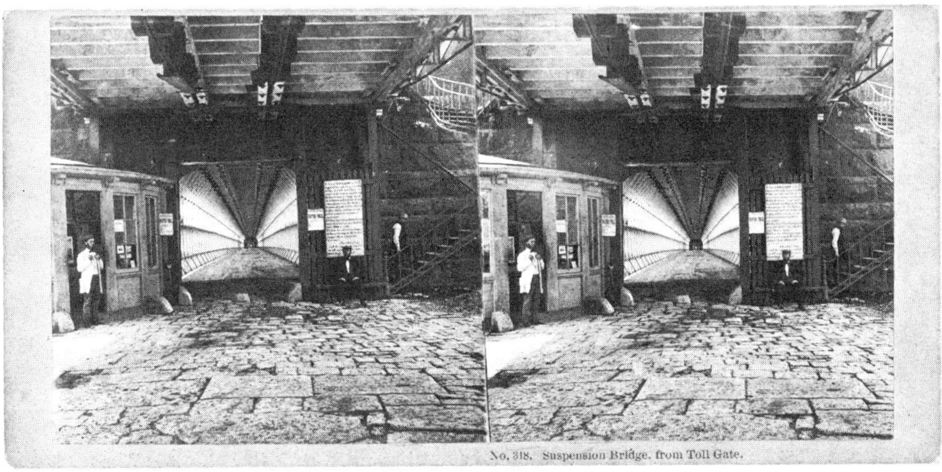

103. John P. Soule. Niagara Falls Suspension Bridge, Carriage level. The railroad level was overhead. 1862.

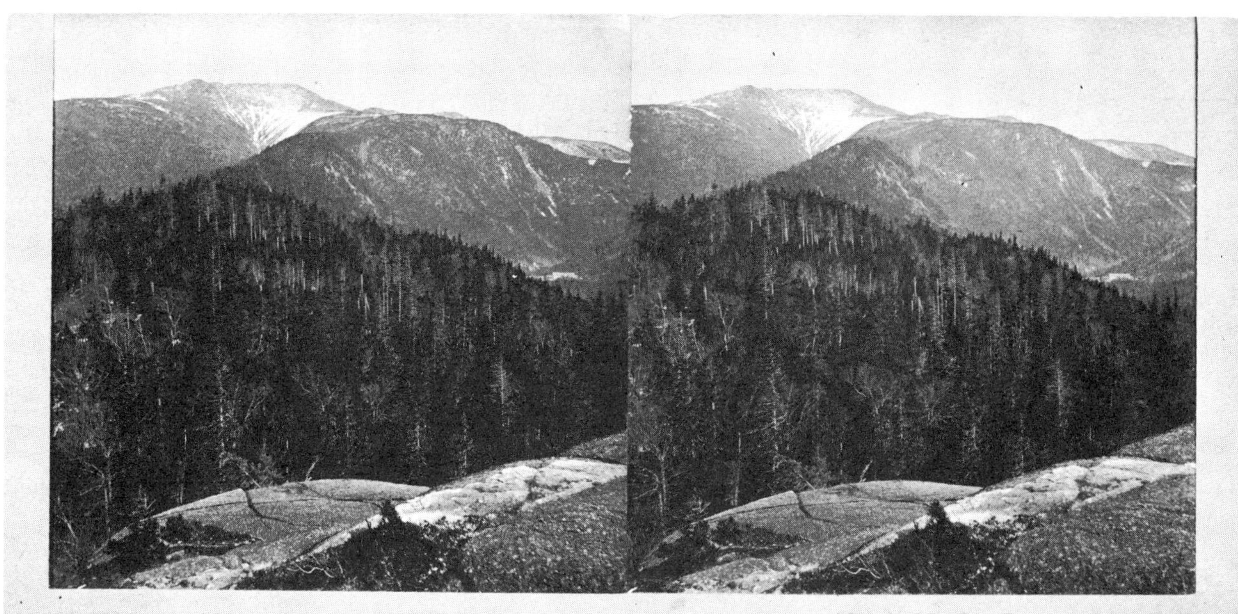

104. Kilburn Brothers, Negative no. 1. White Mountains, Mount Lafayette. 1865.

with a series of 175 titles in 1865. Ultimately the Kilburns issued more than 2000 views of northern New Hampshire.

F. G. Weller, (1867-73) a fellow-townsman, produced several hundred White Mountain views, but these do not compare with the fine work of the Kilburns.

Among the most beautiful White Mountain views are the smaller issues by John Soule, John Heywood, N. W. Pease, A. Marshall and O. R. Wilkinson.

Clough and Kimball published a remarkable series, "Summit of Mount Washington, Winter 1870-1871" (first issue 41 numbers, second issue 46), illustrating the meterological station and the crew making observations.

One of the most unusual photographic ventures was that of H. S. Fifield, who from 1867 to 1883, used the poised boulders in The Flume as the background for stereographing tourists. Although Fifield's stereo views are not rare, each title was issued in very small numbers. The boulder was carried away by an avalanche in 1883.

Other scenic resorts that were beautifully stereographed include

Lake Winnipesaukee (New Hampshire): photographed by Kilburn, Copeland
Mount Monadnock (New Hampshire): Scripture, Rice
Isle of Shoals (New Hampshire): Davis Brothers, Hobbs, Munger
Martha's Vineyard (Massachusetts): Bierstadt, Adams, Kilburn, Warren

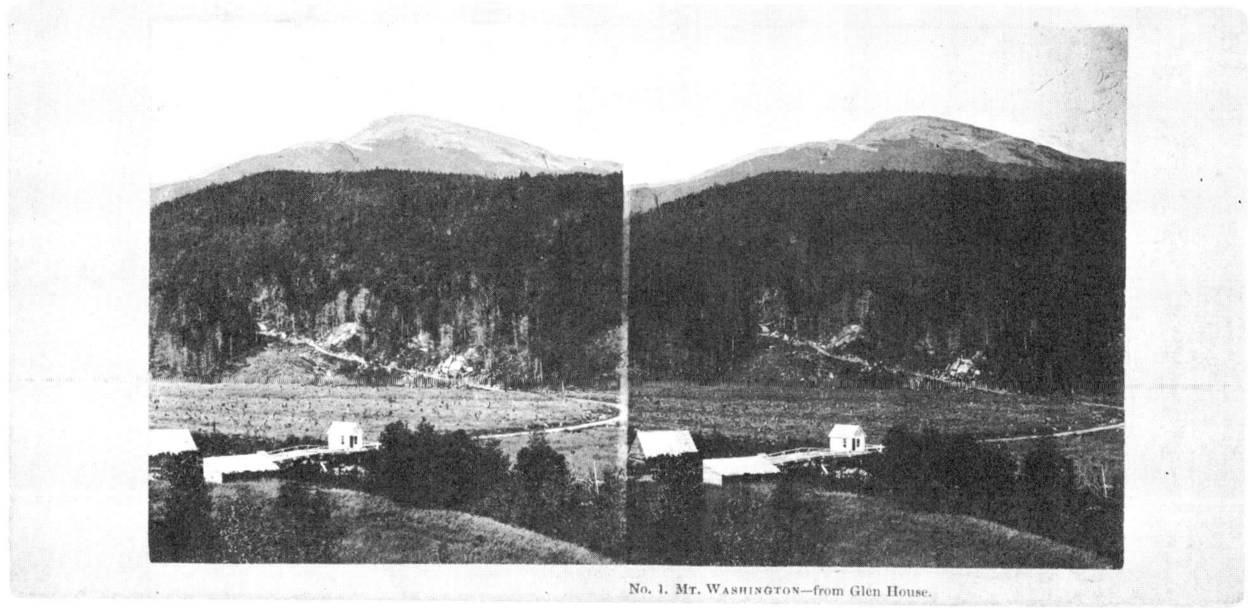

105. John P. Soule. Negative no. 1. "White Mountain Scenery: Mount Washington from the Glen House." 1861.

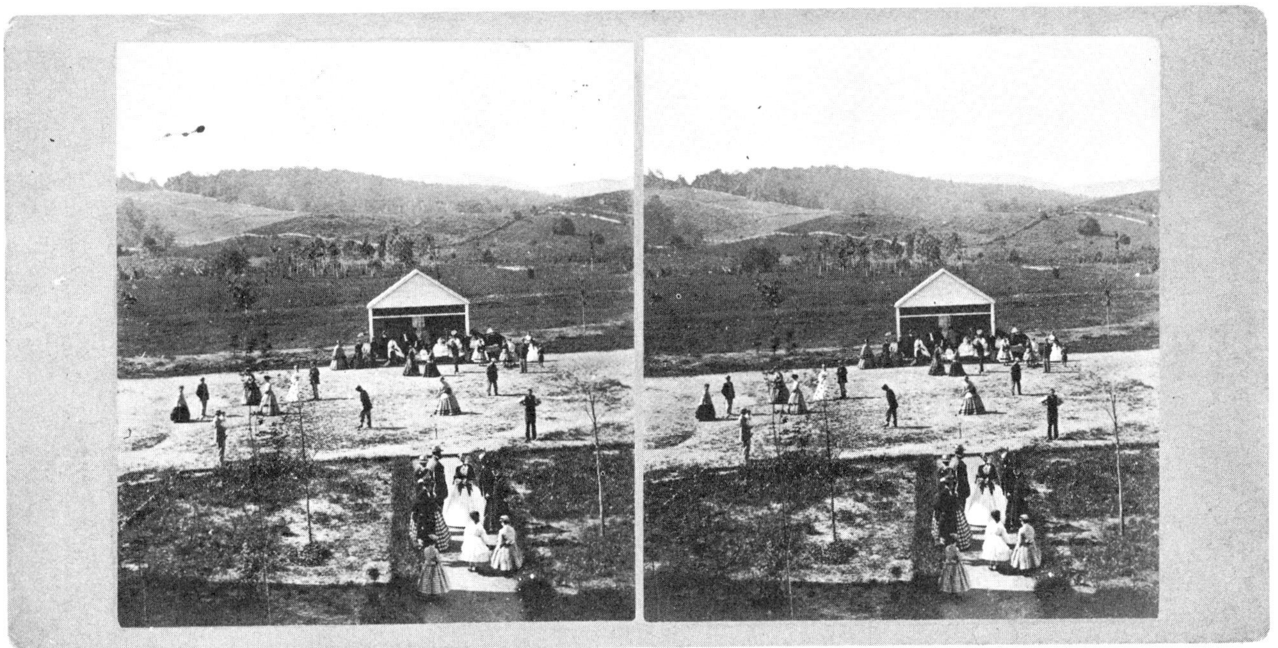

106. John Heywood. "Croquet Grounds at Mansfield House, Vermont. Green Mountain Scenery". 1863.

Catskill Mountains (New York): Langenheim, Anthony, London Stereoscopic Co., Loeffler
Thousand Islands (New York): McIntyre
Delaware Water Gap (Pennsylvania): Anthony, Moran, Graves Figure 31.
Mauch Chunk ("The Switzerland of America," Pennsylvania): Kleckner, Gates
Southern Appalachians: Morgan

THE GREAT CITIES: Washington, D. C., New York, Philadelphia, Boston, Chicago

A brief synopsis of the stereographic history of the principal cities in the East will suggest the similarities and differences in the range of subjects covered by photographers.

Washington, D. C., The Nation's Capital

Prior to 1875 Washington was the only American city with many impressive public buildings. The Capitol and the White House were so familiar there was scarcely a citizen who could not recognize a picture of them. Each federal department was housed in a commodious building of classic or contemporary architectural design, among the latter the controversial Smithsonian Institution. The District of Columbia had been laid out in graceful geometry, whereas such cities as New York, Boston and

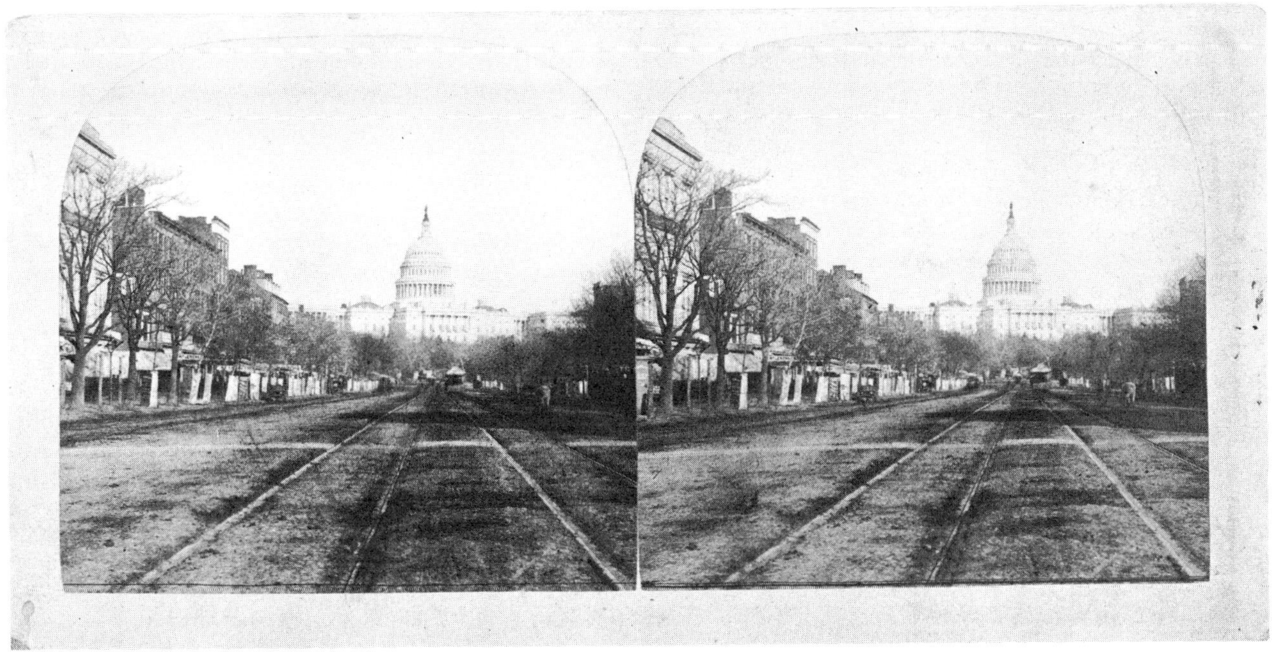

107. Washington, D.C. Pennsylvania Avenue and the United States Capitol. Bell and Brother photo, 1867.

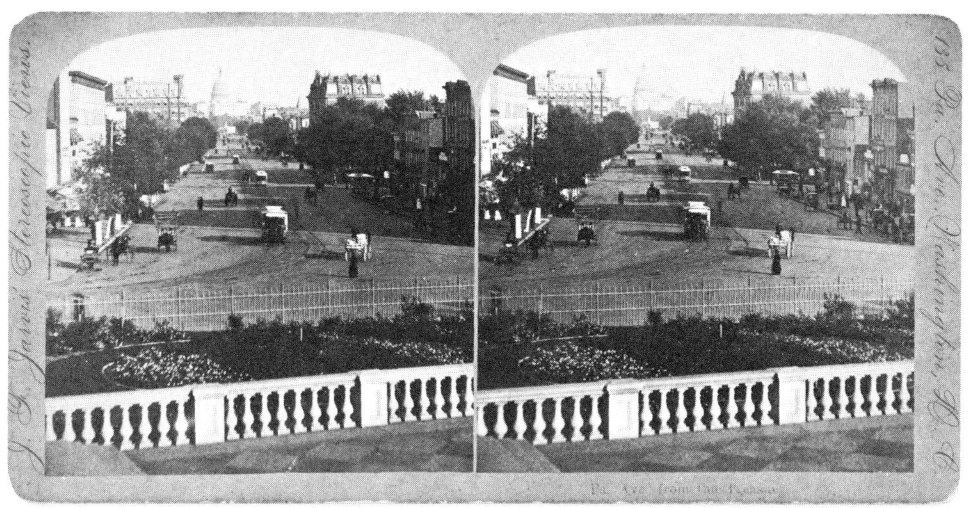

108. Washington, D.C. Pennsylvania Avenue looking toward the Capitol. J.F. Jarvis photo, 1873.

Philadelphia had simply sprawled over the countryside. Traffic circles with grass islands provided space for statues and fountains.

The earliest stereographs of Washington were issued by the Langenheims (1855-1858) and John McClees (1857-1859). These were followed in 1860 and 1861 by fine views by Anthony, Stacy and the New York Stereoscopic Company.

The finest views, however, were produced by F. A. Bell and Brother, C. M. Bell, (1865-1875) whose trade list ultimately exceeded a thousand titles. Their views of individual buildings are among the best architectural stereos made in the United States.

Of greater historical interest are the views issued by J. F. Jarvis (1870-1895), whose list included inaugural ceremonies, parades and street scenes of great variety. Among the most remarkable Jarvis views is his series of the rooms of the White House (issued 1873). The series includes approximately fifty views, but they were not regularly offered as a set. They were available beautifully (occasionally garishly) hand-tinted or untinted, singly or in "packages" of twelve or twenty selected views. Thus, twenty titles are to be found more frequently than the others in the series. Figure 50.

Jarvis was, for twenty years, the largest manufacturer of stereographs in Washington, indeed, for ten years one of the largest in the United States. He produced not only his own trade list and the stereo views of the government surveys in the 1870's but also views for many other photographers in Washington, including W. H. Jackson. Jarvis had established a photographic supply business in Omaha in the late 1860's and had dealt with the Jackson brothers there before moving to Washington.

Other noteworthy resident Washington photographers include:

C. S. & L. Cudlip 1871-1876
Alex Gardner 1863-1868
Walter Ogilvie 1868-1875
M. P. Rice 1871-1877
Albert Siebert 1875-1885
T. W. Smillie 1865-1873
W. M. Smith 1870-1876
G. D. Wakely 1865-(1869?)
H. E. Weaver 1868-1875

During the period 1865-1875 scores of excellent photographers visited Washington and issued stereo views. Most important were John Soule, D. Barnum, Kilburn Brothers, J. W. & J. S. Moulton and W. M. Chase, but there were many more.

No less important are the great number of fine views produced by Underwood, White and Keystone. These twentieth century stereographs show the growth of the city, the expansion of government, Presidents and their cabinets, conferences, Congress in session, the new buildings erected to house new activities, such as the Pan American and Red Cross Headquarters buildings, the Union railroad depot, and so on.

Three Washington operators served successively as "official" photographers for the Mount Vernon Preservation Association, Alex Gardner, N. G. Johnson and Luke G. Dillon. Their combined work represents remarkably complete coverage of George Washington's mansion and estate. Figure 26.

New York City

Like Washington, New York has been richly stereographed from 1855 to 1940. As the greatest American city, it has had an appeal peculiar to itself. The harbor, Battery, Broadway, Wall Street, the Hudson and East Rivers, Central Park and Greenwood Cemetery—these and many more features were known far and wide.

Anthony, of course, produced the finest and the largest variety of New York stereos. The trade list included cityscapes, harbor scenes, views of churches and public buildings, Fourth of July parades and regattas. With few exceptions the views show fine detail and excellent technique. His early street scenes of New York were unequaled by his contemporaries (Stacy, Fredericks, Gurney, Holt & Gray, Beers Brothers). Figures 27, 45.

The collector may be puzzled by the photographers' preoccupation with Central Park and Greenwood Cemetery—literally many hundreds of similar and repetitive views of them. This can be understood only in

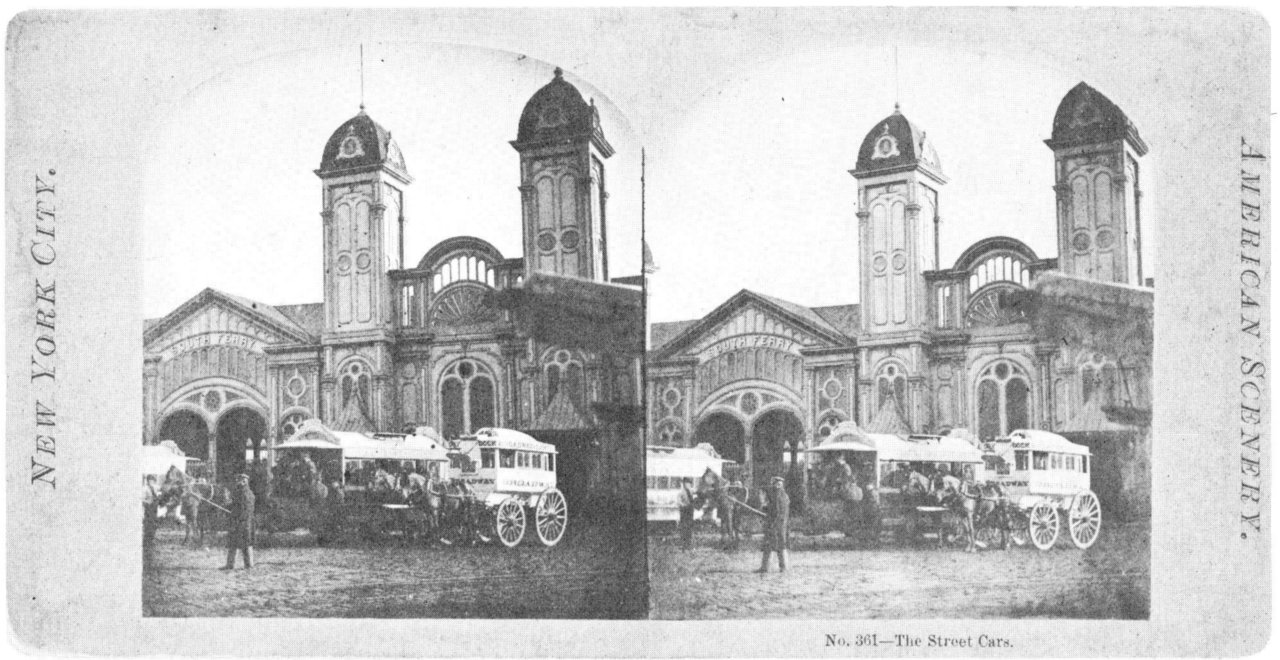

109. New York City. Street Cars at South Ferry. George Stacy, negative 1860, card issued 1869.

their contemporary context. The idea of setting aside a park for the permanent enjoyment by all the people was regarded by public-spirited citizens as a contribution to better living. New Yorkers were justly proud of Central Park. Indeed, many cities emulated New York by developing park systems; to name only a few (all repeatedly stereographed): Fairmount Park in Philadelphia, Druid Hill in Baltimore, Schenley and Highland Parks in Pittsburgh and park-systems in Boston and Chicago.

In a similar manner closure of churchyard burial plots by health authorities led to the creation of magnificent cemeteries, terraced, attractively planted with trees, shrubs and flower beds, lakes, walks, mausoleums and costly monuments by foremost sculptors. New York established Greenwood in 1840. Previously (1831), Boston had laid out Mount Auburn in nearby Cambridge. Thereafter every town and village in the United States established one or more cemeteries and, virtually without exception, photographed them.

One of the most interesting aspects of the stereo history of New York is the record of growth of commerce and with this, the constant improvement in transportation and communication. The great bridges connecting the boroughs were marvelous engineering triumphs. There is

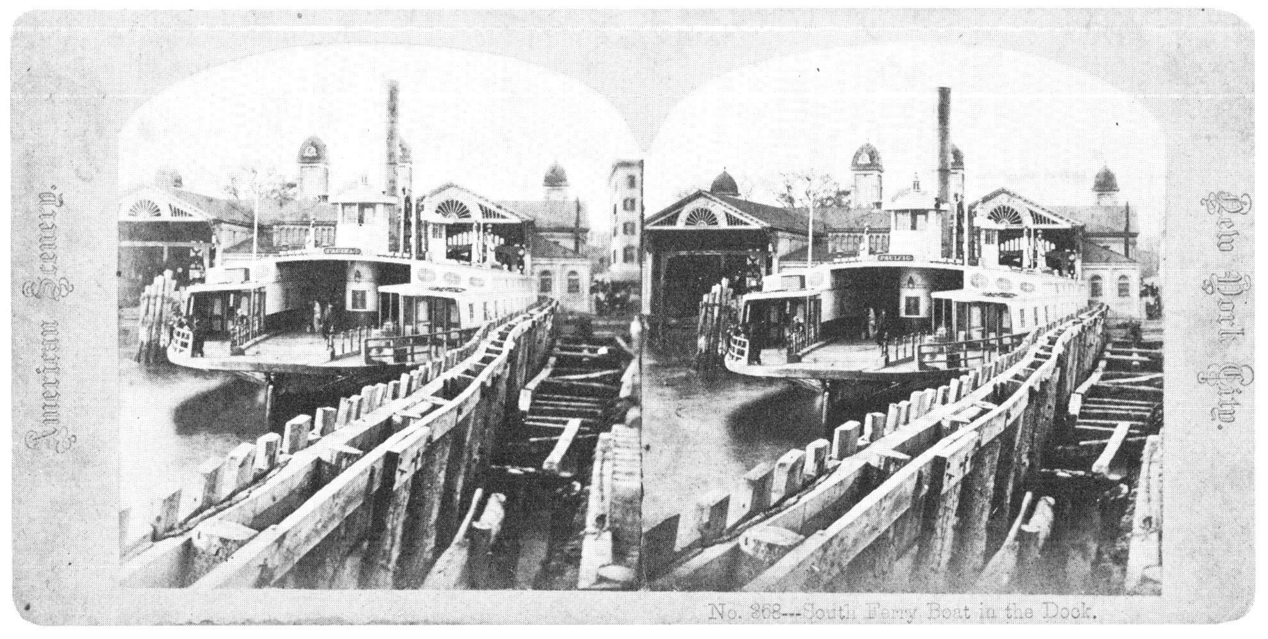

110. New York City. South Street Ferry, with boat in dock. George Stacy, negative 1860, card issued ca. 1868.

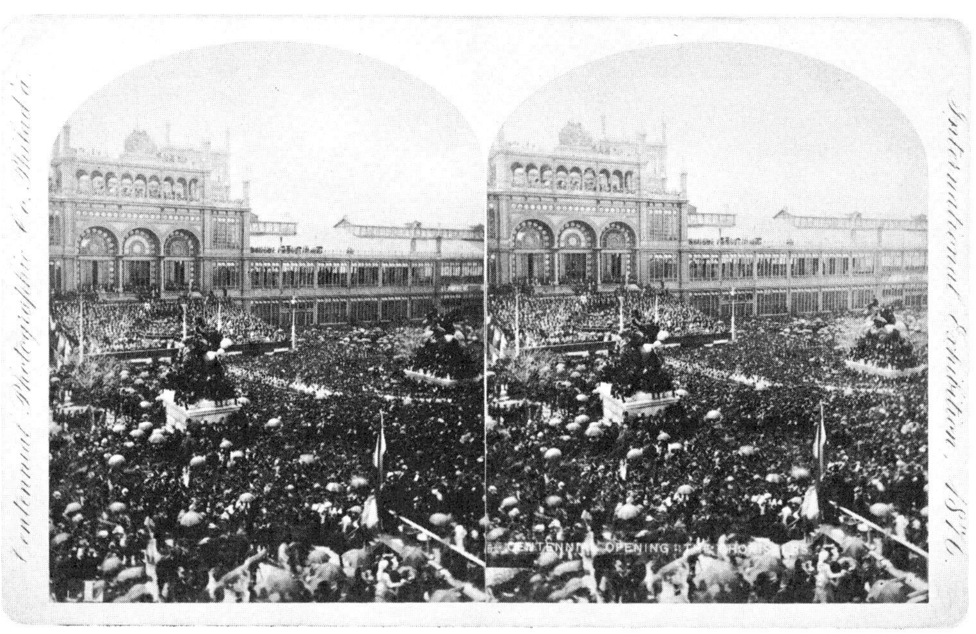

111. Philadelphia. Centennial Exhibition—"Opening Ceremonies—The Choristers." 1876.

excellent stereo coverage of the building of both the Brooklyn and East River bridges. Even the construction of the George Washington Bridge was photographed by Keystone.

The elevated subway and street railways of New York are well recorded, including rare views of subway tunneling.

The world-famous Manhattan skyline began to take form with the erection of skyscrapers.[1] The first skyscraper (1889-1892), the Tower Building, was only 129 feet tall. By 1900, 29 skyscrapers had been constructed. The Flatiron or Fuller Building (1902, 448 feet), Singer Building (1908, 612 feet), Woolworth Building (1912, 767 feet), Empire State Building (1931, 1250 feet) were world famous in their days.

The skyscraper was first developed in Chicago (Home Insurance Building, 1884, and the Masonic Temple, "the eighth wonder of the world," 1890). In 1900 Chicago had sixteen skyscrapers. Each of the notable buildings erected between 1890 and 1932 was beautifully stereographed upon completion.

About a score of aerial views of New York—spectacular novelties at the time—were issued by Keystone between 1922 and 1936.

New York as the "melting pot" of America has had many districts tenanted largely by immigrant nationality groups—Germans, Jews, Chinese, Italians, etc. Underwood produced nostalgic views of German and Jewish tenements in Brooklyn. Stereo Travel issued some interesting views of Chinatown.

[1] A tall building is not necessarily a "skyscraper." The term refers to the steel or "cage" construction by which the masonry walls do not support themselves. Instead, they merely enclose the building. The basic structural design—regarded as America's unique contribution to architecture—is shown in Keystone's V26106 (Underwood negative) "steel frame construction in erecting the Times Building, 23 stories, Times Square."

Earlier, Alfred S. Campbell (1890-1900) photographed groups of people and street scenes in these districts with remarkable human interest. The cards were cheaply produced, and many collectors disregard them in the mistaken belief they are poor copy prints. Campbell caught with his camera such street-figures as the candy man, ice cream vendor, organ grinder and monkey, fish monger and peddlers of many types.

Nor should we overlook the many stereo views of Coney Island and Luna Park.

Philadelphia

Philadelphia photographers were the pioneers in stereo in the early 1850's: Langenheim, McClees, Mascher, Germon and Hurn are only the best known. Between 1858 and 1865 John Moran, Frederick Gutekunst, M. P. Simons, R. Newell and Charles W. Hearn began producing local views. In the 1870's E. L. Wilson and James Cremer are outstanding. In the period 1860 to 1885 more than a hundred resident photographers issued local stereo views.

Yet the stereo coverage of Philadelphia is quite different from that of New York. More attention has been given to the Water Works, Independence Hall, historic churches and Girard College than to harbor and street scenes, although there are views of shipbuilding, the Navy Yard and street scenes. Langenheim produced (1856) a set of panoramas of the city taken from the tower of Independence Hall. Views of Wissahickon Creek and Fairmount Park outnumber by far those of the inner city. The best views of the city were produced by Moran (early 1860's), Newell (1860's) and Cremer (1870's).

The Centennial celebration in 1876 was preceded by several years of preparations, which included the erection of more than two hundred buildings on a portion of Fairmount Park and arranging for exhibits from every developed country in the world. Wilson and several associates secured exclusive rights to photograph the Cen-

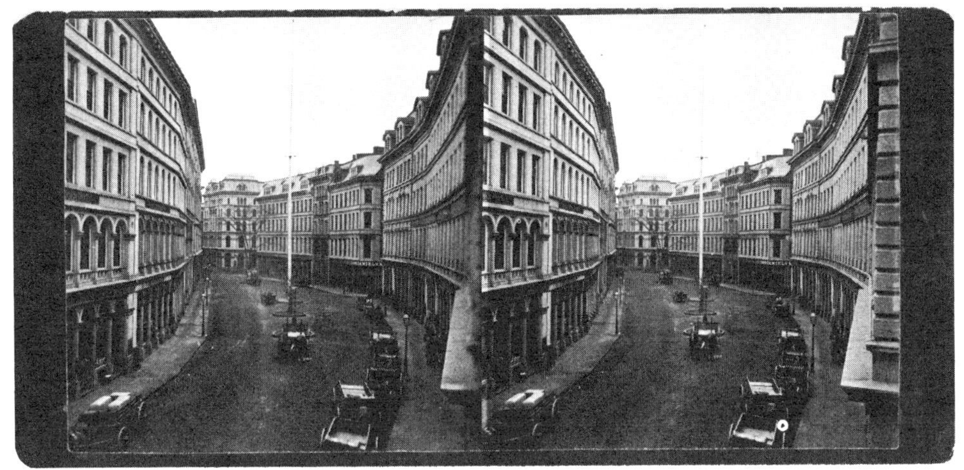

112. Boston, Franklin Street. John P. Soule photo, 1866.

tennial Exhibition. They issued stereo views from approximately 4000 distinct negatives. Despite the supposed Wilson monopoly, at least ten other photographers produced views of the exhibition grounds and some building interiors (especially Barker, Gates, Walker, and Beaman).

Preparations for the Centennial focused public attention on the deplorable deterioration of Independence Hall and surrounding historic buildings. Restoration was completed in time for the celebration.

In 1875 Cremer began issuing a large number of cabinet size scenic views of Independence Hall, the "old" Liberty Bell, the "new" Liberty Bell, buildings of Colonial and Revolutionary significance and downtown street scenes. The series was enlarged in 1876, including a remarkable sub-series on the animals in the new Zoological Garden.

Among the unusual Philadelphia views are those of the Sanitary Fair in 1863. Such fairs were held in a number of cities to raise money for soldier relief. Stereos were issued by Langenheim, Moran and Newell.

Overall, Philadelphia was not well covered by stereographers. Despite the large number of titles, the majority do not record the old city.

Boston

Boston, perhaps more tradition-minded than New York or Philadelphia, was keenly aware of its historic past. In 1859 D. Barnum published a series of stereographs of Colonial and Revolutionary landmarks in Boston, Charlestown, Quincy, Lexington, and Concord. Each card had a full description on the back.

Soule in the early and mid 1860's produced a magnificent series of views of Park Street, Tremont Street, Scolley Square, Cornhill, Faneuil Hall, churches of Boston and the harbor with its shipping.

Despite the more than seventy stereographers in Boston, only eight or ten are important. Besides Barnum and Soule, these are: John Heywood, Charles Pollock, C. Seaver, J. J. Hawes, C. E. & E. L. Allen, O. F. Baxter (Chelsea), Edward Knox (East Boston), E. R. Hills (Brookline) and Augustine Folsom (Roxbury).

Seaver (1866-1877) issued, among a very diversified trade list, fine views of the estates and formal gardens around Boston and Wellesley. Some were issued with the Seaver imprint, but the larger part of the negatives were published by C. Pollock without a Seaver credit.

Pollock also produced several very fine series of Boston and surrounding towns (1872-1876) without photographer's or publisher's imprint.

Heywood in 1859 copyrighted a small unknown number of views of Boston, issued on gray mounts. One of the most beautiful is of Fanueil Hall and its outdoor market.

In 1873 Boston suffered a disastrous fire that burned over a large area in the center city. Coincidently the fire halted at Soule's studio on Washington Street. There are at least two hundred stereos of the ruins, some showing fire engines, policemen and militia. The best series were issued by Soule, Pollock, Kilburn and Smith. Figures 238, 239.

Special events of interest well recorded by stereographers include the Peace Jubilees of 1869 and 1871, the

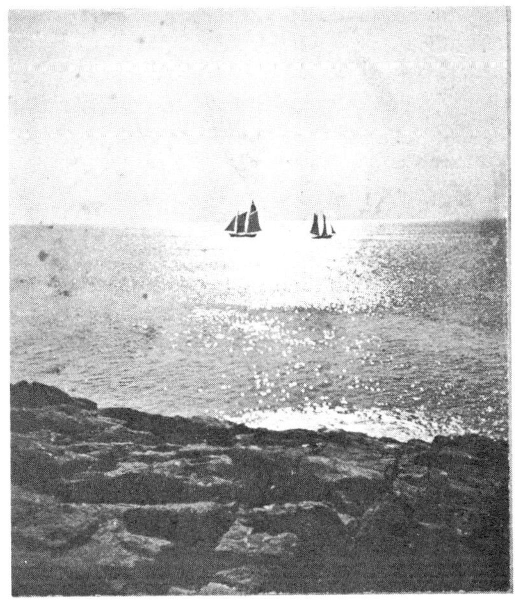

113. John P. Soule. Gloucester, Cape Ann, Massachusetts. "Marine Study by Moonlight." 1863.

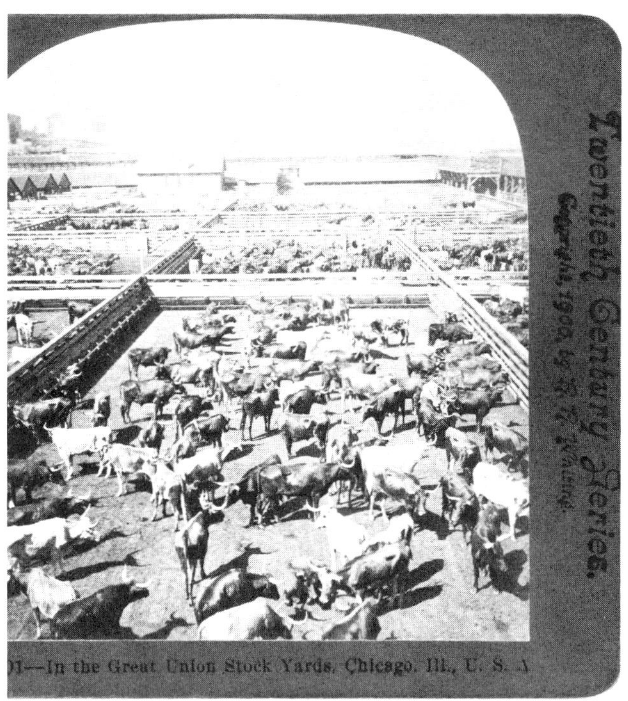

114. Chicago. The Great Union Stockyards. R.R.Whiting photo, 1900.

turned to photographing the West and then, in the later 1860's, to publishing the western views of other photographers. In 1870 he moved to Philadelphia, where he engaged in mechanical photoprinting and dealing in supplies for these processes.

On October 8-9, 1871, the great Chicago Fire wrought vast destruction. Lovejoy and Foster, recently established in the city, issued what is probably the best series of the burned-out district. A score of photographers hurried to record the devastation. Among the most interesting views are those by P. B. Greene and T. T. Sweeney. Figures 115, 277.

As an aside, dozens of photographers lost their studios, negative files and records. Many operators quit the business completely and others moved to new localities. Carbutt's old gallery was destroyed by the fire.

Rebuilding of the city was completed within a year. By municipal ordinance not a single building was of frame construction. Melander and Lovejoy & Foster stereographed the newly finished hotels and mercantile streets. By 1876 Melander had issued about one hundred and twenty titles.

The Union Stockyards and the meat packing establishments of Armour, Cudahy and Swift were photographed again and again from 1873 to 1925. Every stage of meat processing was well illustrated by stereo views.

The Columbian World's Fair in 1893 was covered by many photographers. B. W. Kilburn Company, designated "official photographer," issued about six hundred views of the exhibition.

The "Century of Progress" World's Fair held in Chicago in 1933 was illustrated by a fine 100-card Keystone set selected from approximately 200 available negatives.

Other Cities

Many other eastern cities have had fine stereographic coverage by more than one local photographer. Among those with excellent stereo views are: Worcester, Mass.; Buffalo, Rochester and Syracuse, N. Y.; Hartford, Conn.; Baltimore, Md.; and Cleveland and Cincinnati, Ohio.

Some cities like Pittsburgh have very spotty coverage. Kneeland produced several dozen spectacular views (1865-1869), and Purviance (1867-1870) included fine

many centennial celebrations of 1875 and 1876 and the hurricane damage of 1869. Figure 229.

The Boston Commons and Public Gardens have been richly stereographed from 1858 to 1900. The swan boats, Christian Endeavor conventions, other mass-meetings and peddlers of many kinds provide an interesting history of Boston's most famous park.

Chicago

Before 1870 Chicago had become the greatest railroad center in the United States. It was also center of the meat packing industry and vast agricultural commerce.

The classic views of Chicago were produced by John Carbutt in the mid 1860's. These splendid stereographs give an excellent view of the city and its principal buildings. Carbutt, one of America's greatest photographers,

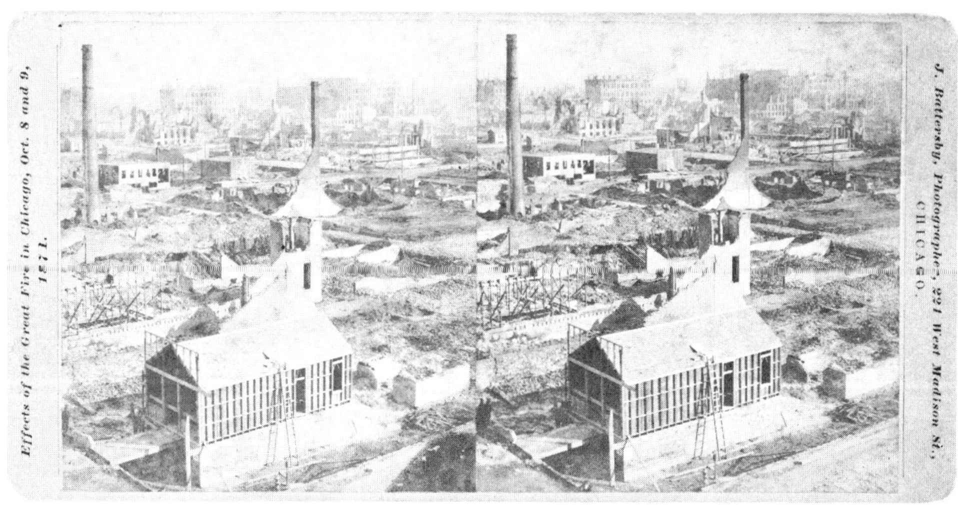

115. Chicago. The fire of October, 1871. J. Battersby photo.

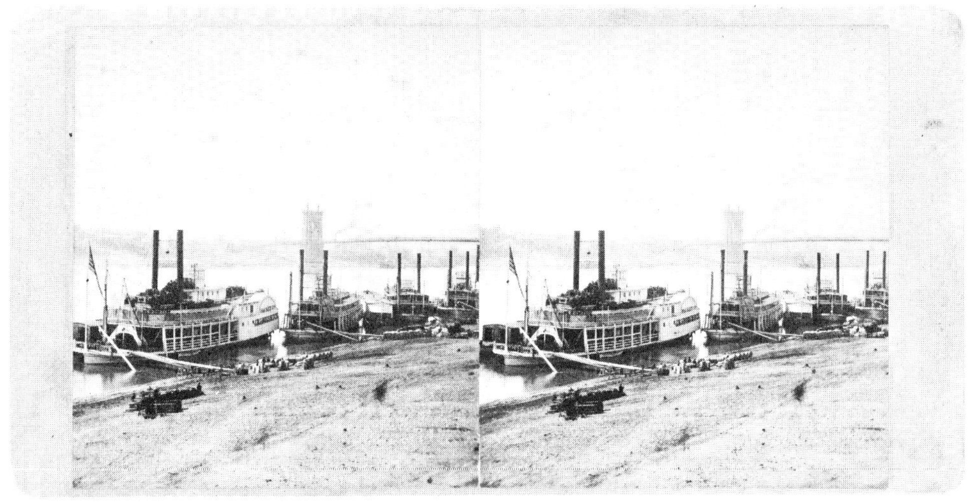

116. Cincinnati. The Ohio River, with the Suspension Bridge in the distance. Charles Waldack photo, 1870.

views of the bridges and several panoramas of Pittsburgh and the Union railroad depot in connection with his great series on the Pennsylvania Railroad. Stieren published (and probably photographed) downtown Pittsburgh in the mid and late 1870's. Albee and several other local photographers issued stereo views of the labor riots and destruction of the depot in 1877. The iron and steel industry centered in Pittsburgh was thoroughly stereographed by Underwood (1904-1908) and by Keystone (1923). Several small series depict flood damage in Allegheny City (Pittsburgh, north side) in 1873. Despite these scattered striking views, coverage does not compare with that of Baltimore or Philadelphia.

THE SMALLER TOWNS

It is utterly impractical to attempt an enumeration or synopsis of either the towns or their photographers. Approximately 3000 local photographers are listed in the appendix, but these represent barely forty percent of the known names.

Instead, the work of eight typical photographers will be summarized to show how each was influenced by the locality in which he operated and thus to suggest how to search for any desired subject of regional interest.

Hurd (Hurd & Sons, Hurd & Smith, Hurd & Ward, 1865-77, North Adams, Mass.)

North Adams is situated in western Massachusetts near the Hoosac Mountains, through which a railroad tunnel was dug between 1855 and 1873. The project was controversial, troubled by political connivery and delayed by complex litigation. Work was interrupted in the midst of the Civil War, when General Herman Haupt was forced to resign from the Army and abandon the tunnel construction he had planned and engineered.

Hurd was but one of a dozen photographers who recorded construction of the tunnel (1866-1874), but his series shows best the workmen, machinery and progress to completion.

J. Freeman, Nantucket, Mass. (ca. 1865-1885)

Nantucket, long famous as a whaling center was, by the 1870's a tourist attraction and place of summer residence. Freeman loved the town and its past. His panoramas and street scenes are exquisite. A view of the small early-Victorian Episcopal church shows children in their Sunday best standing on the steps. His fine whaling views, even though the industry had declined drastically, are exciting. The seaside scenes include fishermen and their huts surrounded by gear, lifesaving crews and equipment, sailing ships and stranded wrecks. The lighthouses, the old windmill and, of course, the bathers round out the wonderful unity and completeness of Freeman's stereographic output. Figure 300.

A. B. Hamor (successor to Lufkin & Hamor), Lawrence, Mass. (1867-1883)

In many respects Hamor was influenced in the same manner as Freeman. But Lawrence was a mill town, with huge factories and mill races. Hamor's stereo views depict all of the textile mills, interiors as well as exteriors, the stages in manufacture, the machines and the workers.

At the same time coverage of the city is extensive: the churches, schools, opera house (including beautiful interiors), covered bridges, parades, holiday celebrations and fires. His winter scenes are striking.

M. A. Kleckner, Bethlehem, also Allentown and Mauch Chunk, Pa. (1865-1876)

Bethlehem was settled by the Moravians in 1742, and the old town ("north side") retains even today much of the denomination's heritage. Kleckner, himself a Moravian, photographed an unusually broad scope of subjects and localities, but his Bethlehem views are among the best. He photographed the beautiful simple church, with several exceptional interiors (1866), the Sister House, the Burial Ground and charnal house and other historic structures. Yet his interest extended to domestic crafts such as cutting and drying "apple schnitz" and the Christmas tree "putz," a traditional "yard" around the base of the tree.

An enthusiastic fisherman, Kleckner produced many views, among them self-portraits, of trout fisherman.

Kleckner issued many views of Lehigh University, Lafayette College (Easton) and of the towns of Easton and Allentown. He photographed extensively the mills and foundries in Bethlehem, Allentown and Catasauqua and the zinc mines at Friedensville.

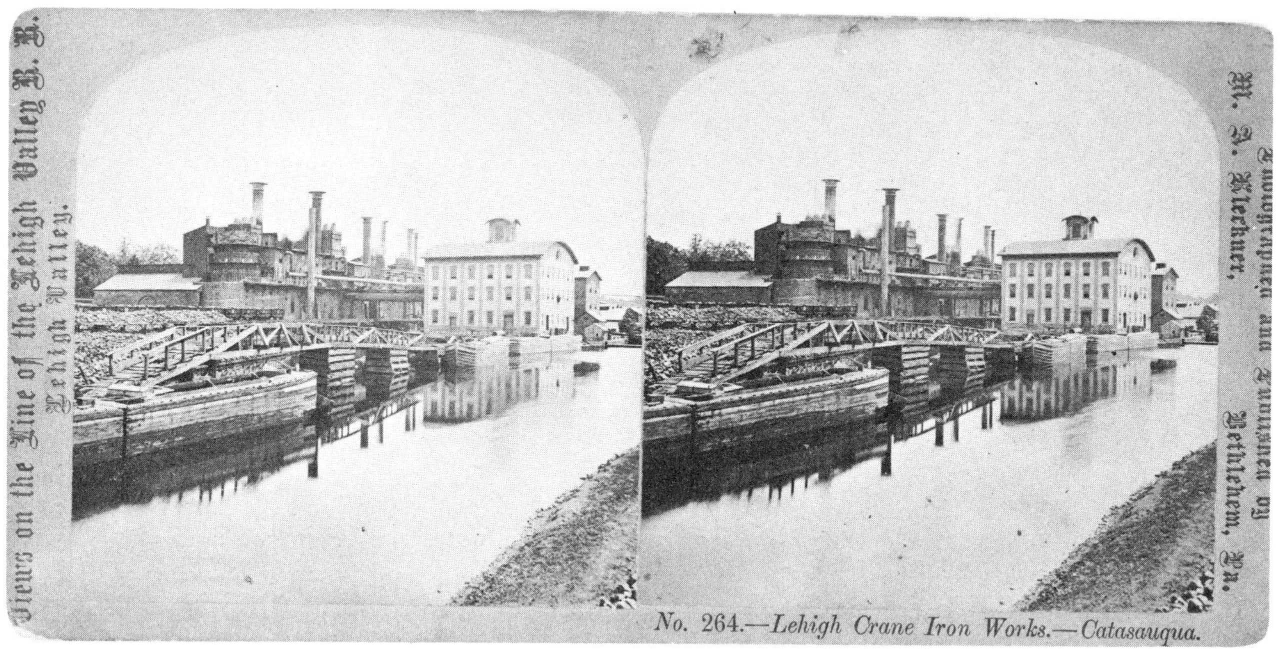

117. M.A. Kleckner. Catasauqua, Pennsylvania. Lehigh Crane Iron Works. Canal Boats in foreground. 1868.

In 1869 Kleckner opened a summer gallery at Mauch Chunk, where he sold thousands of stereo views from a trade list of about two hundred titles of the scenery of Mauch Chunk and vicinity, especially of the coal chutes and the navigation canal.

In 1877 Kleckner moved to Kansas, where he continued a career in portrait photography, producing some excellent frontier stereo views there (1878-1883).

John A. Mather, Titusville, Pa. (1862-1895)

Mather, renowned as the photographer of the Pennsylvania Oil Region, was attracted to it soon after the industry was born. He witnessed and recorded the growth of Titusville from a tiny village to a prosperous town with the fine mansions of wealthy oilmen.

Mather operated from a small floating gallery on Oil Creek to photograph the "oil farms" and then by wagon to follow the mad rush of speculation and boom towns from Petroleum Center, Pithole, Pleasantville, Tionesta, Tidioute and the rest. Among many thousand negatives there were at least six hundred stereos, a record of the first ten years of the industry, a coverage without equal in any nineteenth century technology.

William H. Tipton, Gettysburg, Pa. (1868-1900)

Tipton was apprenticed to C. J. & I. G. Tyson in 1863 at the age of twelve. A photograph by C. J. Tyson shows Tipton driving their photographic van, probably in the summer of 1863.

In 1868 Tipton and a fellow employee, Robert Myers, purchased the Tyson studio and the file of negatives including several hundred stereos dating from 1863 to 1867, one hundred of which were issued as a series in 1866 and 1867. Tipton continued to publish views from these negatives, without changing the numbers or titles, up to 1888.

Tipton became sole proprietor of the studio in 1870 and during the next twenty years produced two thousand stereo views, one-fourth of which were custom and copy work not included in his regular trade lists. Although his photographs were seldom technically excellent nor artistically well done, they are historically important.

Tipton was widely known as "the battlefield photographer," although he had some local competition (Levi Mumper and brothers). He stereographed every monument and memorial marker, in many cases recording the dedication ceremonies or the representatives of the State placing it.

His views of the town of Gettysburg were quite varied but were relatively few in number, mostly of Pennsylvania (Gettysburg) College and the Lutheran Seminary. The fine views of the churches, the jail and courthouse bearing his imprint were mostly from old Tyson negatives.

Tipton's custom views were produced for picnics, social clubs, camping parties and fishing outings, and a considerable number of tourists posed at Devil's Den.

In the 1880's Tipton issued under his own imprint copy (pirated) prints of English comics and sentimentals as well as a few from American sources for which copyrights had expired.

In later years Tipton advertised his business as founded in 1859 (the date the Tyson Brothers established a studio in Gettysburg). He claimed to have photographed the battlefield in 1863 (he would have been a twelve-year-old novice). There is no evidence that he made any commercial stereo negatives before 1868.

Rufus Morgan, New Berne and Morgantown, North Carolina (1866-1882)

Morgan's earliest views were of New Berne, a fine series including scenes of the harbor, ocean shipping, oyster boats and fishermen. In the early 1870's Morgan commenced extensive stereography of the scenery of "The Eastern Carolinas" and western North Carolina, producing more than four hundred views that compare favorably with the better White Mountain views.

He visited the principal cities of North and South

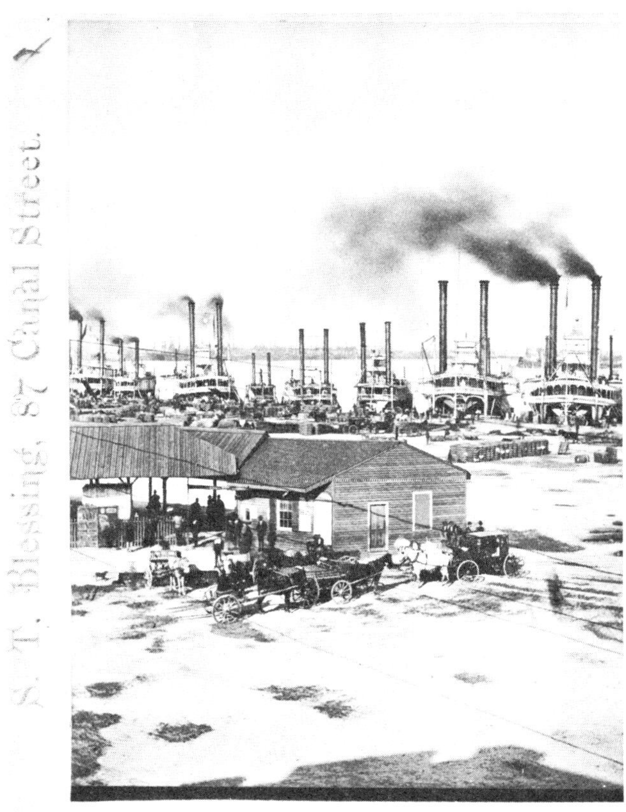

118. New Orleans. The levee, steamers and railroad station. S.T. Blessing photo, 1877.

Carolina, probably because of the relative few stereo photographers in the South after the Civil War. Small but representative series for each were issued. Especially notable are those of Asheville, Charlotte, Raleigh, Wilmington and Columbia.

Morgan was a sensitive observer who occasionally issued stereographs of simple, even homely subjects with little commercial potential. In the series, "Characteristic Sketches of Southern Life," there are views of fording a stream, negroes at leisure and primitive grist mills. He produced striking views of cypress swamps, rhododendrons in bloom as well as other plants indigenous to the southern Appalachian mountains.

In 1874 Morgan copyrighted a series of negatives of Yosemite that he had taken the previous summer. Twenty-five titles were issued on both standard and artistic mounts.

George F. Mugnier, New Orleans, Louisiana (1880-1888)

Of the three fine stereographers of New Orleans, Blessing, Lilienthal and Mugnier, Mugnier produced the most comprehensive coverage of the Deep South. His views of the cotton trade, from cultivation to shipping, are spectacular. The panoramic scenes of the New Orleans wharf, with stevedores among thousands of bales, loading picturesque steamers, are unequaled. In less complete fashion, Mugnier photographed sugar cane, sugar mills and rice cultivation. Although he was not particularly interested in natural scenery, he produced beautiful bayou landscapes and with them interesting views of alligators.

His New Orleans series includes fine views of St. Charles, Canal and Camp Streets, historical landmarks and public buildings.

These eight examples suggest how much the stereo photographer was influenced by the region in which he operated and the extent to which he was both observer and recorder of the events surrounding him.

THE VILLAGES OF AMERICA

There remains for consideration the vast reservoir of stereos of the small, even tiny, communities and the great number of photographers who produced these views.

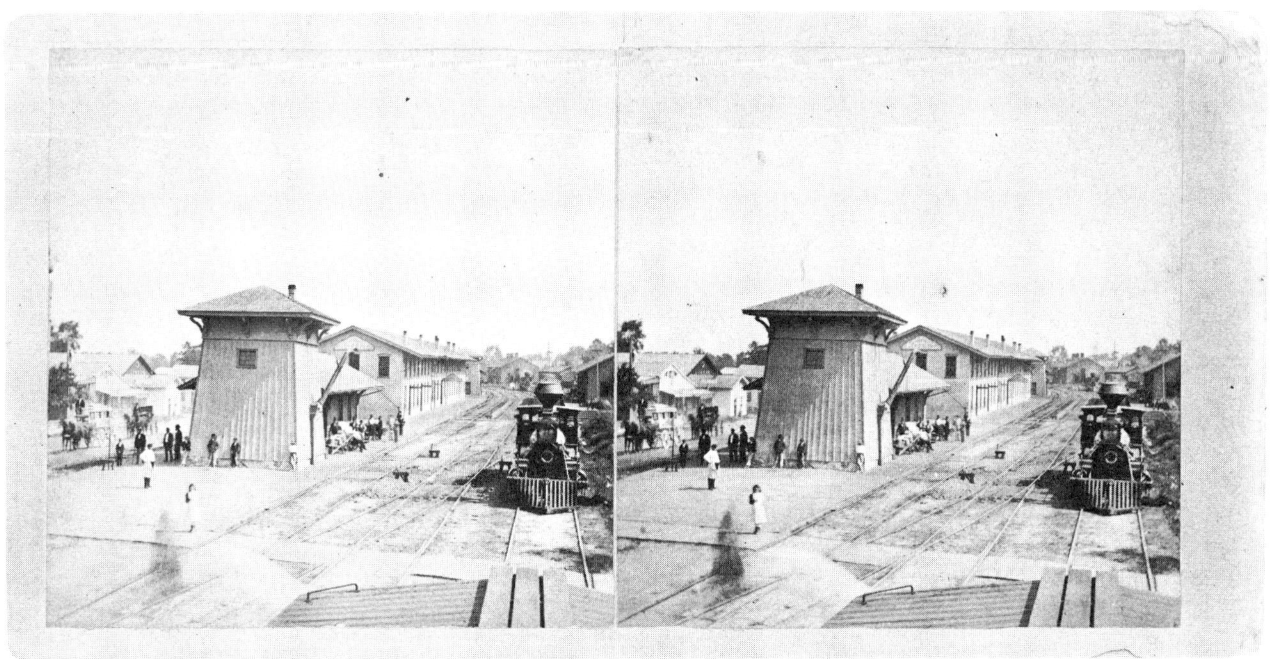

119. Avon, New York. "Railroad depot." T.D. Tooker photo, 1871.

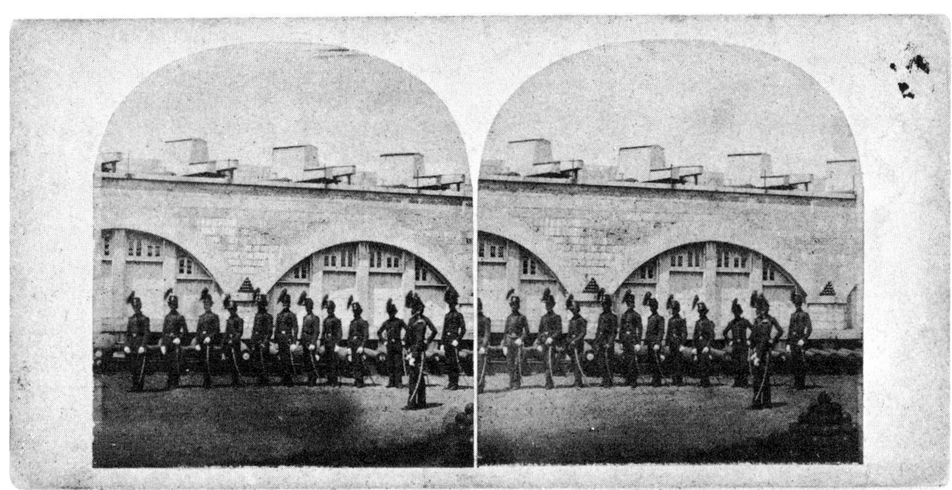

120. Fort Adams, Rhode Island. J. Appleby Williams photo, 1858.

Apparently, few communities were too small to attract if not support a photographer during the period 1860-1885. Of course, not all of these photographers issued stereo views, but almost half of them did. There is truly a remarkable stereographic record of rural and wilderness America. I have found stereo views produced between 1865 and 1875 by resident photographers of twenty-two Pennsylvania villages with fewer than six hundred inhabitants (1870 census). Five of these villages had two photographers operating simultaneously and eight had two photographers operating successively.

Itinerant Photographers

In addition to those photographers who established studios, there were hundreds of "traveling" or itinerant operators. They moved about in wagons, river boats, and portable galleries of great variety, visiting farms and remote outposts. While their stereo views seldom have much historical significance, the scenes of rural family life represent an aspect of rural America which contrasts markedly to village life.

Itinerant stereographers were active throughout the United States from 1865 to 1890. None produced a sufficient quantity of views to make the photographer well known.

The opportunities for assembling collections of regional views and searching for local photographers are virtually limitless.

CHAPTER NINE

WESTERN UNITED STATES AND CANADA

Stereographs of the West have fascinated collectors and historians for many years but no more than the public who eagerly purchased them when they were issued. These stereo views provided vicarious adventure: Indians, mining towns, homesteaders, cattle trade, railroads and magnificent contrasting scenery. The West had mountains, deserts, treeless plains and geological wonders such as the great waterfalls of Yosemite and Yellowstone and the canyons of the Colorado River, which inspired some of America's great scenic photographers to do their finest work.

BACKGROUND

The course of development of the American West was influenced by a series of events beginning in the late 1840's. The discovery of gold in California was a great stimulus, although population pressure had already been pushing settlements westward into the Great Plains. In the 1850's settlers became more numerous because of widespread hard times, exhaustion of fertility in eastern farmlands and increased immigration from Europe.

The adoption of "free soil" policies by the Federal Government attracted hordes of natives and immigrants, especially to Minnesota, Iowa, Kansas and Texas. The passage of the Homestead Act in 1862 opened the floodgate to settlement. Basically the act permitted the head of a family to acquire a homestead of not more than 160 acres by continuous residence for five years and the payment of twenty-six or thirty-four dollars, depending upon location of the land. By 1880 no lands suitable for agricultural homesteading, without irrigation, remained in the public domain.

The construction of railroads west of the Mississippi River created boom towns and markets for farm products and raw materials. A succession of gold and silver strikes in Nevada, Colorado, Dakota, Idaho and Montana enlivened the era from 1860 to 1880.

In 1862 Congress selected a northern route for the proposed transcontinental railroad and incorporated the Union Pacific Rail Road, granting to it rights of way, access to timber and financial guarantees. Similar privileges were granted the Central Pacific Railroad in California and to the Western Rail Road of Kansas.

The Homestead Act pertained to the surveyed lands of the public domain. In consequence of this limitation, the Federal Government engaged in four great surveys during the period 1867-1877, two under the jurisdiction of the War Department and two under the Department of the Interior. Although the objectives of these surveys differed somewhat, essentially they were organized to classify the lands of the public domain and determine their natural resources.

Meanwhile, in the latter 1860's in Texas, the cattle trade was evolving with its legendary round-ups and drives to Sedalia (Missouri) and Abilene and Dodge City (Kansas). The cattle drives tied into the railroads, creating huge stockyards, the greatest of all the Union Stockyards in Chicago.

Inevitably ranchers who raised cattle and drove them on the open range were in conflict with the homesteaders who fenced these lands and protected their waters. Hydraulic mining for gold involved the profligate waste of water and the ruination of great expanses of land. These interests, while interfering with each other, were collectively in conflict with the treaty rights of the Indians, who made vain attempts at retaliation against the encroaching white man.

Out of this mosaic there emerged villages, towns and great cities, vast agricultural pursuits and an amazing volume of commerce. Tourism, encouraged by the railroads and the new "national" parks became a profitable business.

All of these aspects of western development were thoroughly stereographed.

The photographers of the West fall into three groups:

(1) resident local photographers who, like their eastern colleagues, limited their views to their respective vicinities. Some of these men ranged over large areas, however.

(2) photographers employed by government agencies or private enterprises to document and publicize surveying and exploring expeditions.

(3) photographers who were employed by publishing companies, or who were themselves publishers, to obtain interesting negatives for trade lists.

Many photographers do not fit neatly into one or another of these groups. For instance, W. H. Jackson and Thomas Hine at different periods in their careers were involved in all three.

The local photographers will be considered first.

CALIFORNIA

Carleton E. Watkins was one of the most prolific stereographers in the United States and stands most important in California. He learned photography with the daguerreotypist R. H. Vance and opened his own gallery in 1858. Not later than 1860 Watkins began publishing stereo views of San Francisco and in 1861, of Yosemite. These early stereographs of Yosemite were issued on glass and ivory card mounts.[1] The views were praised lavishly by Oliver Wendell Holmes and received awards at the International Exhibition of 1862.

Charles L. Weed, while in the employ of R. H. Vance, took the first stereo negatives of Yosemite in 1858. Weed purchased the Vance gallery about 1861 but resold it several years later.

[1] Norton Russell, "Yosemite Photographs by Carleton E. Watkins, 1861," 14 pages, New Haven, Conn., 1976.

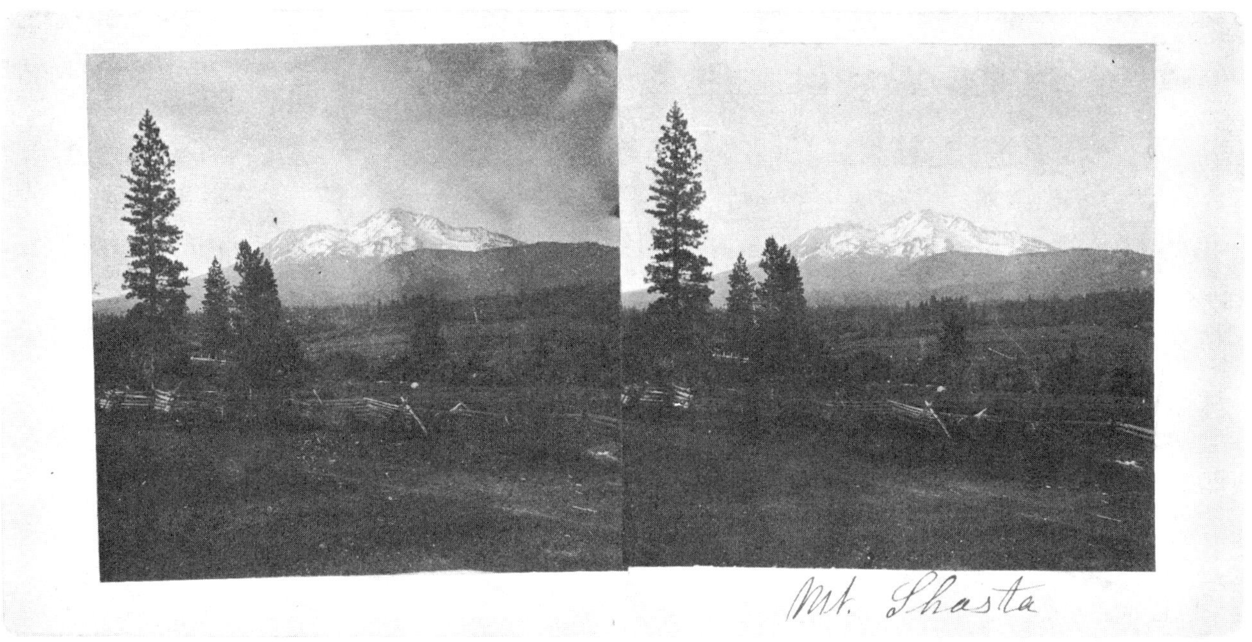

121. Mount Shasta, California. An early view, ca. 1857-1858, by an unknown stereographer, thin white card mounts.

Watkins' stereographs issued between 1860 and 1866 have manuscript titles in his handwriting. At first the workmanship, especially the mounting, is only fair to crude. Many of the images lack contrast. That this was the result of inexperience is shown by the beautiful prints he later produced from the same negatives.

In 1867 Watkins copyrighted 1400 stereo negatives, of which approximately 800 were taken between 1860 and December, 1865. Thereafter, an imprint appears on the right margin on the face of the card.

Watkins No. 1 is of Yosemite Falls with a tourist party on horseback in the foreground. No. 85 in the same series, "In Camp," shows a party of eight eating lunch. From a series of about a hundred negatives, Watkins selected seventy-two titles which were distributed as glass mounts. Over the years Watkins issued no fewer than 450—perhaps as many as 600—views of Yosemite and the mammoth trees.

Among his early issues are fine views of quicksilver mines (101-160) and San Francisco (162-175). Watkins' coverage of San Francisco from 1860 to 1880 is stunning. There are small series of many Fourth of July celebrations, such as 1862, 1865 and 1876. No. 755 shows the victory arch with huge portraits of Washington and Lincoln. The 1876 Centennial series includes the bombardment on July 3 and the yacht race on July 5. Among the many characteristic subjects are harbor scenes, prominent buildings, Chinatown and mercantile streets, interspersed with views of the nitroglycerine explosion in 1865 and the earthquake of 1868. Figure 259.

In 1869 Watkins purchased the A. A. Hart negatives of the Central Pacific Railroad and issued them under his own imprint. Meanwhile, he photographed extensively in the Sierra Nevada Mountains, Nevada and Arizona.

At this time (1871) Watkins suffered personal misfortune. While he was in the field, his gallery, including

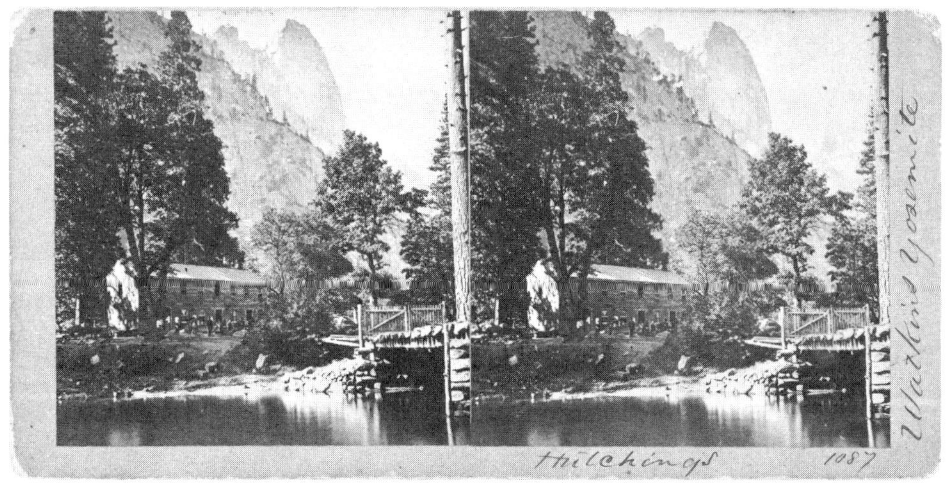

122. Carleton E. Watkins. "Yosemite, Hutching's Inn." Note Watkins' autographed title. 1863.

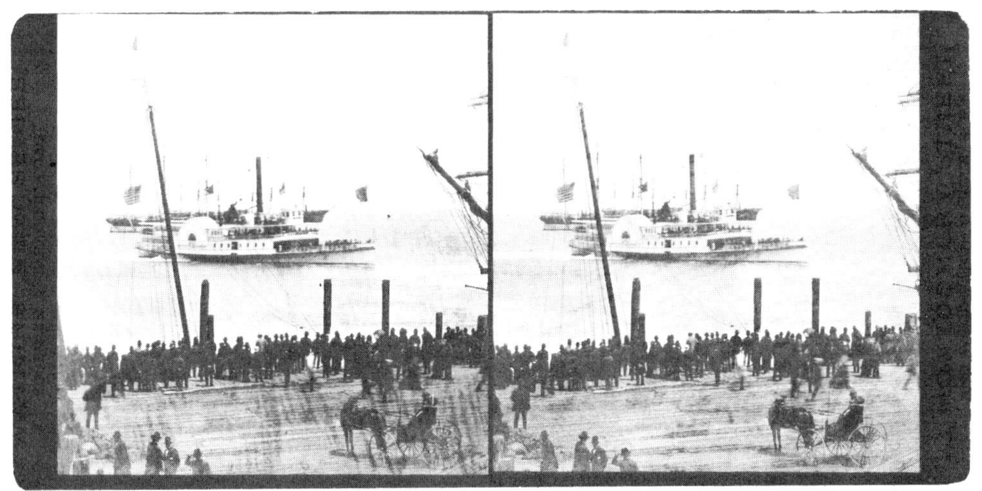

123. Carlton E. Watkins. "Centennial Celebration, San Francisco, 1876. The Yacht Race."

negatives and equipment was seized for non-payment of bills. Taber obtained the complete file of negatives, including those by Hart. Taber continued to publish stereos of many of these for six or seven years, without crediting either Watkins or Hart.

Watkins was forced to rebuild a trade list. His "New Series," commencing with a new "number one," ultimately exceeded 5300 titles. There were a few numbers assigned to negatives copied from old prints in the original series and some unassigned numbers reserved for late insertion of related titles. Approximately ninety percent of the numbers were actually used, indicating that Watkins issued well over 6500 different stereographs.

There are many wonderful runs in Watkins' New Series, to name only a few:

Chinatown (3761-3768)
Palace Hotel (3553-3570) with magnificent interiors
Virginia City (4170-4185)
Seattle (5219-5228)
Farallone Islands, with sea lions and birds (2021-2065)

There are scattered scenes of desert vegetation, specimen plants, mining, sailing ships, Indians and trains. No other western photographer recorded more fully the detailed character of his vicinity. Not even William H. Jackson of Denver produced comparable coverage of his Colorado.

Although Watkins deserves special recognition, he was by no means supreme in all areas of California stereography. Thomas Houseworth and Eadweard Muybridge were his peers.

Lawrence and Houseworth (succeeded by Thomas Houseworth) produced stereo views as early as 1862. These are ivory and cream mounts with manuscript titles. Some of these cards bear a blind imprint on the left margin on the face. These are followed by similar yellow or pink mounts with a small strip label with the title and with the blind stamp. Lawrence and Houseworth copyrighted their file of negatives in 1864 and in 1866 began to number them consecutively, from 1-1050. The negatives are not in chronologic order, although the date

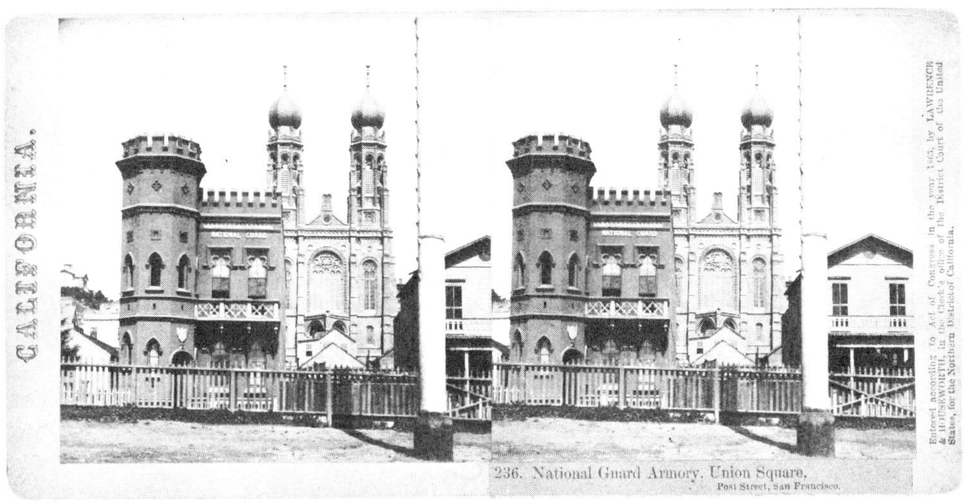

124. Lawrence and Houseworth. San Francisco. National Guard Armory, Jewish Synagogue in the background. 1865.

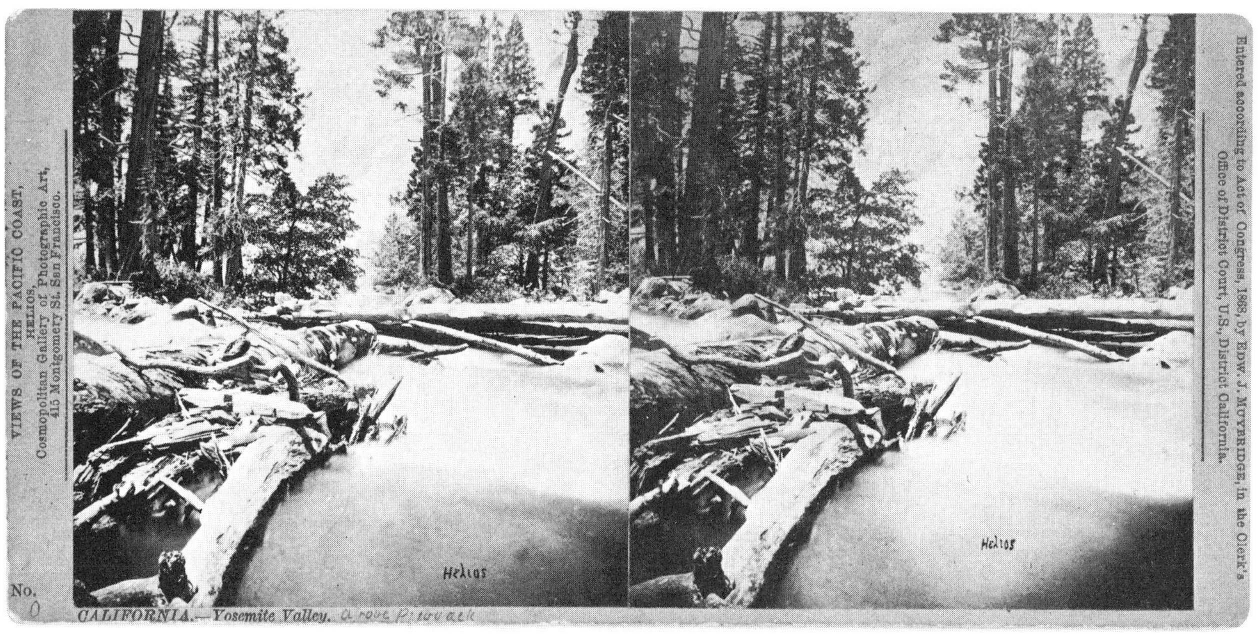

125. Eadweard J. Muybridge. Yosemite Valley. 1868. Note "Helios" scratched on the negative.

of each is accurately given in the copyright line. Figures 258, 281.

Thomas Houseworth succeeded Lawrence & Houseworth in 1867 and continued to issue the trade list without change. Between 1868 and 1873 he added approximately 800 numbers. Some new negatives replaced old numbers (for example, there are three No. 406, "Cliff House") without copyright application.

Houseworth's prints are beautifully made. The scenes are generally panoramic, with the more limited subjects carefully framed to emphasize detail. Among his most notable series are:

- Gold Hill, including the Gould and Curry Mill (many)
- Central Pacific Rail Road (many)
- Sutro Tunnel (1689-1710)
- Yosemite (1101-1121; 1581-1680)
- Hydraulic mining (790-805; 871-915; 968-1021)
- Big Trees (1741-1765)

Eadweard J. Muybridge, one of the most inventive and versatile photographers of all times, began issuing stereographs in 1867 and obtained copyrights for approximately 500 titles in 1868. This series included more than a hundred views of Yosemite and an interesting run of San Francisco, such as No. 256, "Grading Telegraph Hill." Like Watkins and Houseworth, Muybridge photographed San Francisco, railroads, Yosemite, the mam-

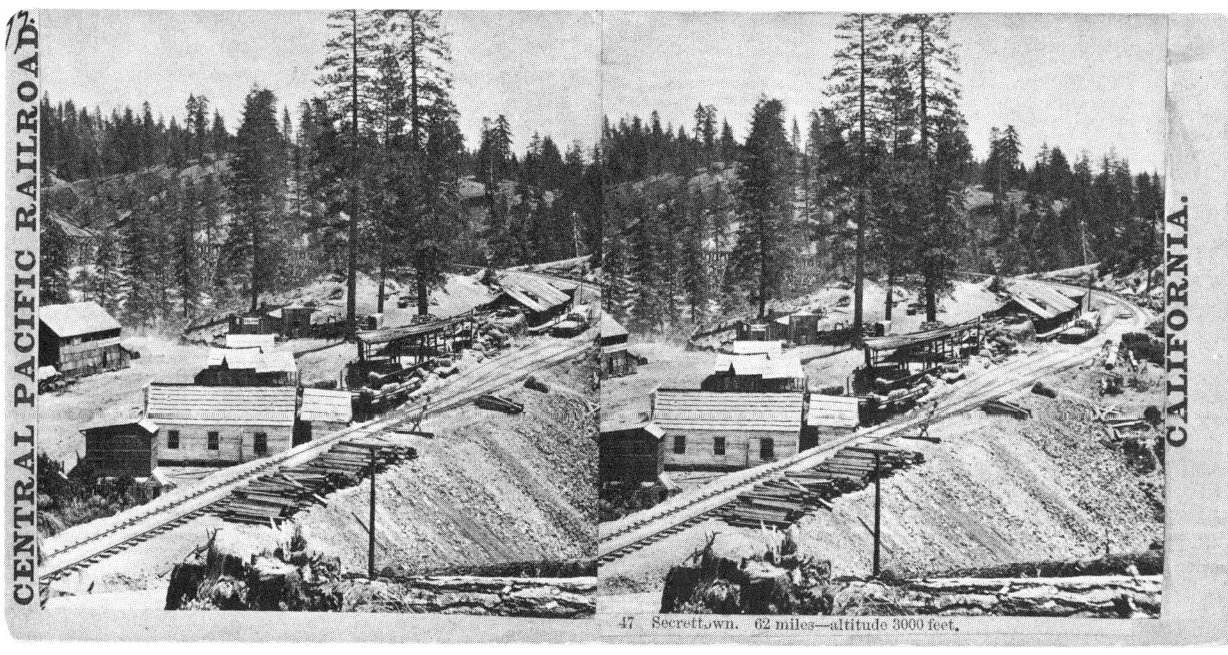

126. Alfred A. Hart. Central Pacific Railroad Series. Secrettown, California. 1866.

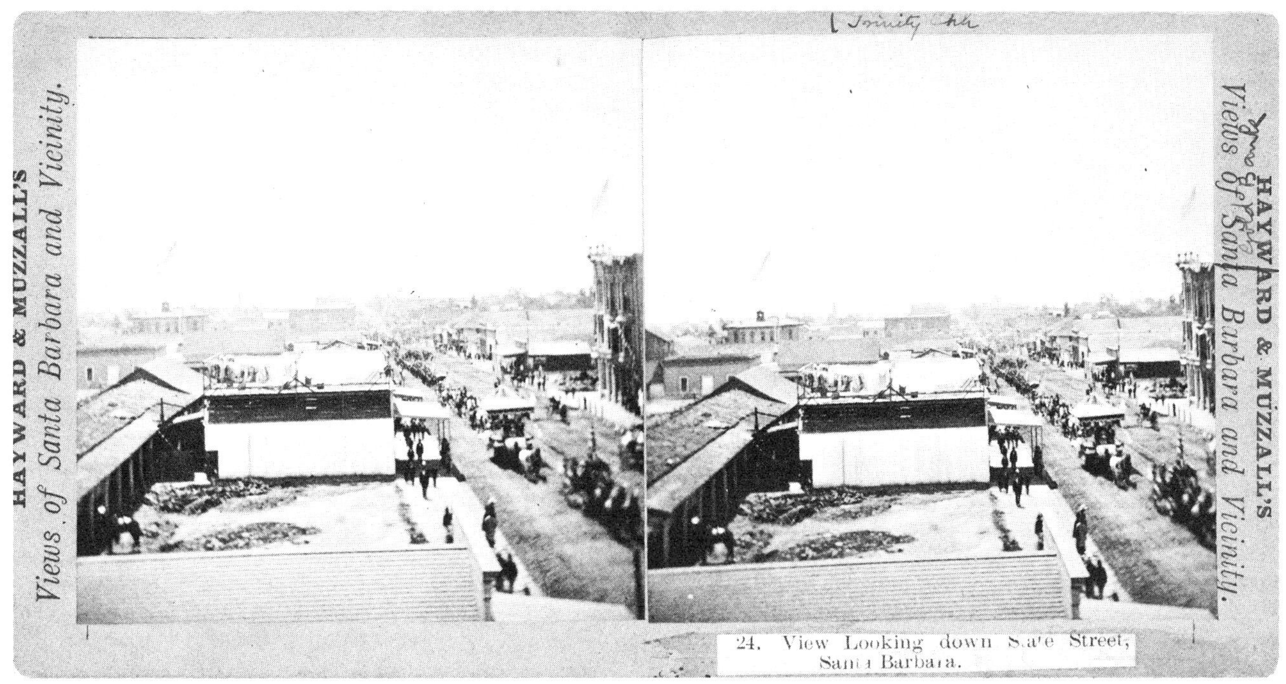

127. California, Santa Barbara. "Parade on State Street." Hayward and Muzzall photo, 1876.

moth trees and events such as the San Francisco earthquake of 1868.

Custom work includes some of Muybridges' most unusual stereo views. He produced a set of thirty-six views of the Alfred A. Cohen estate, "Fernside," in Alameda County. This set illustrated the mansion, billiard house, stables, landscaped grounds and fine interiors. Mr. and Mrs. Cohen are shown seated informally in several rooms. Muybridge produced other custom sets, such as the fine series on the Leland Stanford mansion and family.

The War Department in 1872 engaged Muybridge to photograph the "Modoc War." He issued a set of fifty stereo views selected from about a hundred negatives.

Muybridge's scenic views are exquisite, joining the best of Hart, Watkins, Reilly, Houseworth and Bierstadt. Most of the stereos by Muybridge were manufactured and distributed by Bradley and Rulofson, a company of excellent photographers.

Alfred A. Hart (Sacramento) began issuing stereo views about 1863. The earliest series is titled "The World as Seen in California—illustrated for the stereoscope and album," followed by "Scenes in the Sierra Nevada Mountains." Both series bear the imprint of 135 J. Street. Later series were issued from 65 J. Street. Figure 15.

In 1865 Hart became the official photographer for the Central Pacific Railroad. He published approximately 400 views in this series, for which three different imprints were used. Each includes the line "photographed and published for the Central Pacific Railroad." Hart retained ownership of the negatives with rights to sell prints made from them. The engineering works, such as the curved Secrettown trestle, and railroading views taken between 1865 and 1867 are among the best ever published.

J. J. Reilly (Stockton), whose name is intimately associated with Yosemite Park, began his photographic career at Niagara Falls and moved to California about 1870. He produced more stereo views of Yosemite than any other single photographer. Between 1873 and 1883 Reilly operated several studios in Yosemite and in neighboring towns through which tourists passed. His stereographs were sold wholesale and in job lots throughout the United States.

He also published spectacular railroading views, some of which were staged with the obliging cooperation of company officials. These interesting views show trains on trestles or two or three trains with engines in full steam

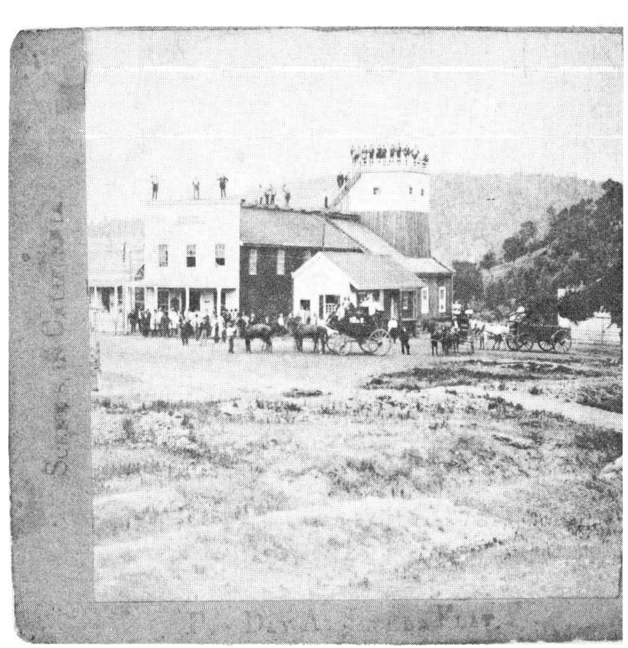

128. California. "Pay Day at Sucker Flat." Mains and Shippy photo, 1868.

traveling in opposite directions. Figure 286.

There were at least two hundred resident California stereographers operating between 1865 and 1885. Many of these are known only by a few surviving stereo views. Nevertheless, remarkable scenes were recorded by them.

Hayward, E. J., Hayward & Muzzall, Santa Barbara, 1870's
: a fine series of more than 200 views, including many of the missions of Santa Barbara, San Fernando, San Gabriel and San Miguel; also of Indians and Chinese.

Parker & Parker, San Diego, 1870's
: a series of more than 300 views, with many of the "Old Town."

Godfrey, W. N. Los Angeles, 1860's and early 1870's

Payne, H. T., Los Angeles, 1870's and 1880's
: about 250 numbers, including many of the missions.

Mains & Shippy, Sucker Flats, early 1870's
: interesting views of the robbery of the Blue Point Mining Company, July, 1871; "Pay day," and of hydraulic mining.

Price, Andrew, Geyser Springs, 1870's and 1880's

Johnson, A. P., San Francisco, 1860's

Dowe, L., Petaluma, 1870's into 1880's

Varela, A. C., Los Angeles, 1870's

Spooner, J. Pitcher, Stockton, 1870's

Scripture, J. C., Big Trees, 1870's into 1880's
: Scripture deserves some attention because he was primarily a publisher, deriving negatives from many sources. His trade list of more than 4000 numbers includes many fine California and Nevada views not available elsewhere. For example, No. 3443, "Devil's Gate, Devil's Gate Toll Road, Nevada," shows traffic waiting to pay the toll.

Photographers from other states who toured California to take negatives for their trade will be reviewed later.

UTAH

Utah was fortunate in having two master stereographers, Charles L. Carter, who began in Salt Lake City in 1859, and Charles R. Savage, who in 1861 joined Marsena Cannon, a daguerreotypist in Salt Lake City since 1851. The combined work of Carter and Savage is a truly remarkable stereographic record of Utah and surrounding states from 1860 to 1885.

Carter's extensive coverage of Salt Lake City illustrates the construction of the Mormon Temple and Tabernacle, the progressive growth of the city and its commerce. He published many fine views of Indians and of mining settlements.

Savage, in 1863, took into partnership the artist-photographer George M. Ottinger, who remained with him until 1870. The Savage trade list is more diverse than that of Carter. An overland trip in 1866 rewarded him with a fine collection of negatives.[2] Savage's views of the driving of the Golden Spike linking the Union Pacific and Central Pacific into a transcontinental railroad at Promontory Point brought him immediate fame. His views of snowbound trains are spectacular.

There were a score of lesser Utah photographers who produced stereographs of their vicinities between 1867 and 1885. T. B. Cardon (Logan), James Fennemore (St. George), Jens C. Gasberg (Brigham City), O. P. Huish (Payson), Johnson & Sainsbury (Salt Lake City) and Edward Martin (Salt Lake City) are the more important.

After Hyrum Sainsbury withdrew in 1893, C. E. Johnson began large-scale manufacture of "Johnson's Stereo Views of Everything," until about 1910.

In addition to the stereographs issued by known photographers, there are many very excellent views by unidentified itinerants or local photographers. Operators with portable tent galleries combed the network of Mormon settlements in the 1870's and early 1880's.

COLORADO

Stereographs of Colorado by resident photographers

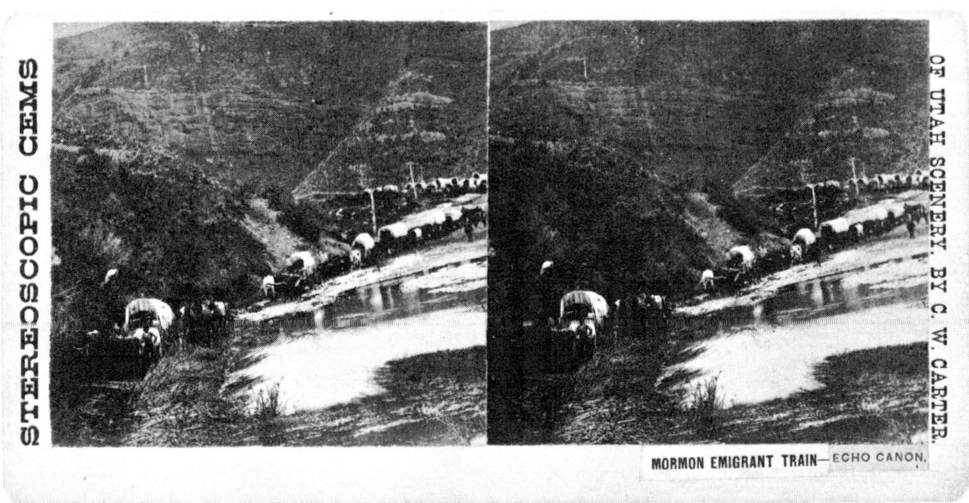

129. Utah. "Mormon Emigrant Train". C.W. Carter photo, 1872.

[2] *Phila. Photogr.* Vol. *4*, pp. 287, 313, 1867.

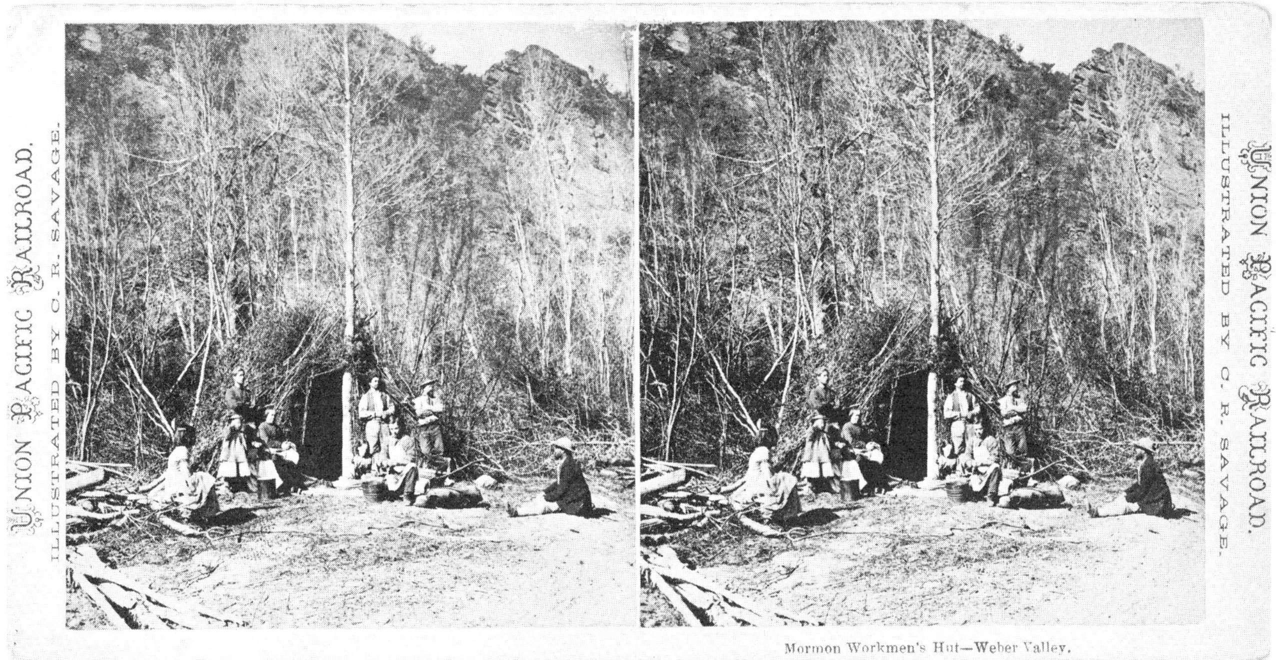

130. Utah. "Mormon Workmen's Hut, Weber Valley". C.R. Savage photo, 1870.

are much fewer in number and less diverse than those of California. The main categories are Rocky Mountain scenery, Denver, the mining towns and scenery along the Denver & Rio Grande Rail Road. The Park region and the Garden of the Gods were well-developed tourist attractions and as such were frequently stereographed. More than sixty Colorado photographers are known to have published views of their localities.

The most important of these was W. G. Chamberlain (Denver, 1861-1880), whose trade list included approximately 750 numbers. He issued many excellent panoramas of Denver. Among his more spectacular scenic subjects are Gray's Peak, Pike's Peak, Mountain of the Holy Cross (No. 601) and views along the Denver & Rio Grande Rail Road. He also produced fine views of mining towns and Indians. Figure 250.

J. Collier (Central City, 1871-1878; Denver, 1878-1890), whose trade list ran to fewer than 300 numbers, is next in importance to Chamberlain. Among his best views are the interiors of the Caribou Mine, mule trains and ranching.

B. H. Gurnsey (Colorado Springs, 1872-1880) published about 250 titles, including Leadville, silver mining and cattle raising.

J. Thurlow (Manitou, 1874-1880) is primarily noted for his views of Colorado Springs, but his list includes many interesting Indian subjects.

C. W. Talbot (Canon City, 1874-1877) produced 200 titles, including some unusual views of dinosaur skeletons in the rock formations in which they were discovered.

B. E. Hawkins (Denver, 1872-1877) produced some excellent stereos of Ute Indians.

Perry & Bohm (Denver, 1872-1875) produced mostly scenic views, but there are fine stereos of Denver and Central City.

Charles Weitfle (Central City, 1878-1885) issued about 300 interesting views, including a remarkable series on Utah towns.

Between 1877 and 1885 there were many first-rate photographers located in the boom towns who delightfully recorded the activities there. The better-known include Luke & Wheeler (Leadville), Barnhouse & Wheeler (Lake City), Frank Kuykendall (Silver Cliff), E.

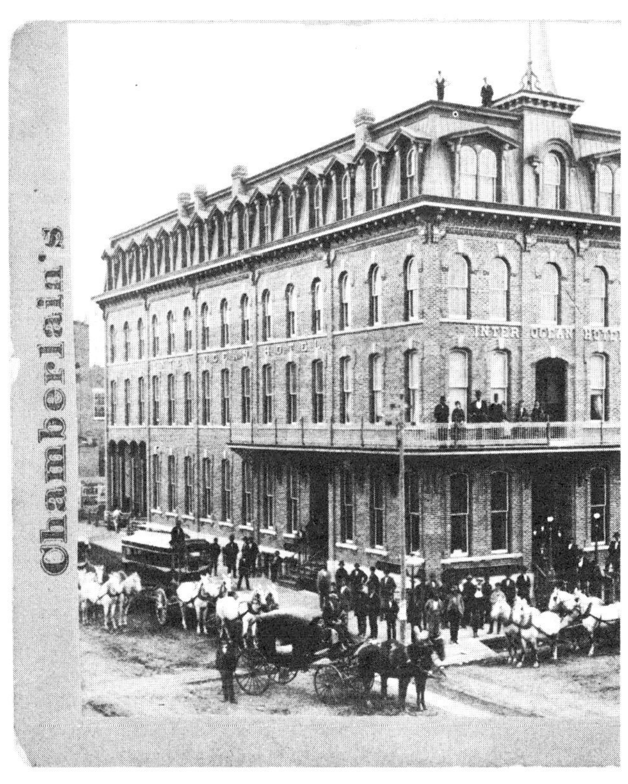

131. Colorado, Denver. Inter Ocean Hotel. W.G. Chamberlain photo, 1878.

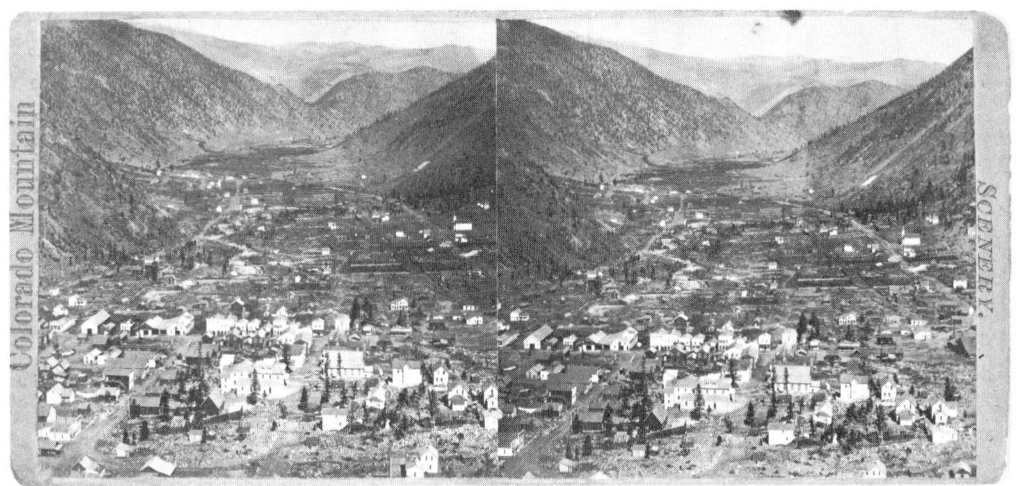

132. Colorado. Georgetown. W. G. Chamberlain photo, 1873.

A. Wilder (Rico and Durango), D. B. Chase (Trinidad) and Charles E. Emery (Silver Cliff).

Emery photographed Silver Cliff by moonlight on the night of January 12, 1884. This stereo view was a genuine triumph, not a printed fake from composite negatives.

William H. Jackson settled in Denver in 1880, where he became known as America's foremost scenic photographer, a reputation he himself did much to encourage. He ranged from Denver and Leadville to Mexico and the northwest coast to build a huge file of stereo and other negatives. He became primarily a publisher and continued the manufacture of stereographs into the early 1890's.

NEBRASKA

Omaha was the eastern starting point for the Union Pacific Rail Road, and construction of the road bed was begun in 1863. The city, laid out in 1854, was not incorporated until 1867. As a bustling outfitting place for the gold rushes and prairie freighting and with heavy river traffic, Omaha supported several daguerreotypists in the 1850's. Two local photographers produced a few stereos in the mid 1860's, E. L. Eaton and J. H. Hamilton, who also operated galleries in Sioux City and Council Bluffs, Iowa.

Jackson went to work for Hamilton in 1867 and, with his brother, purchased the studio the following year. In 1869

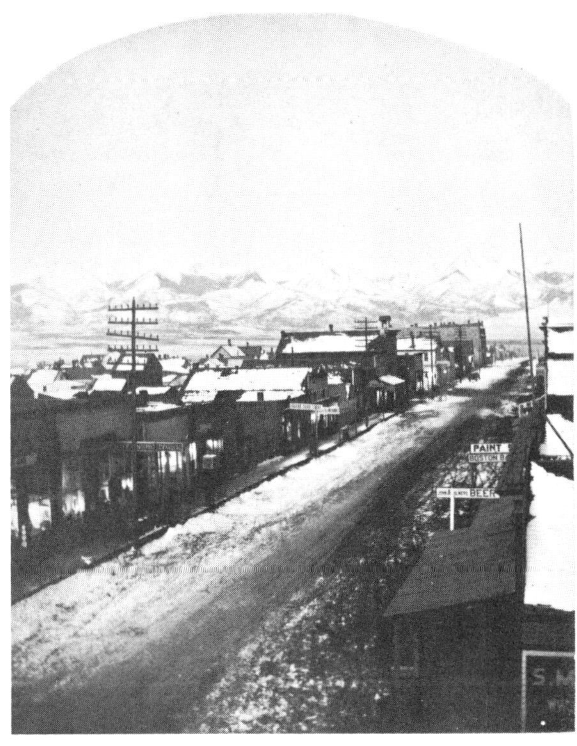

133. Charles E. Emery. Silver Cliff, Colorado photographed by moonlight, night of January 12, 1884.

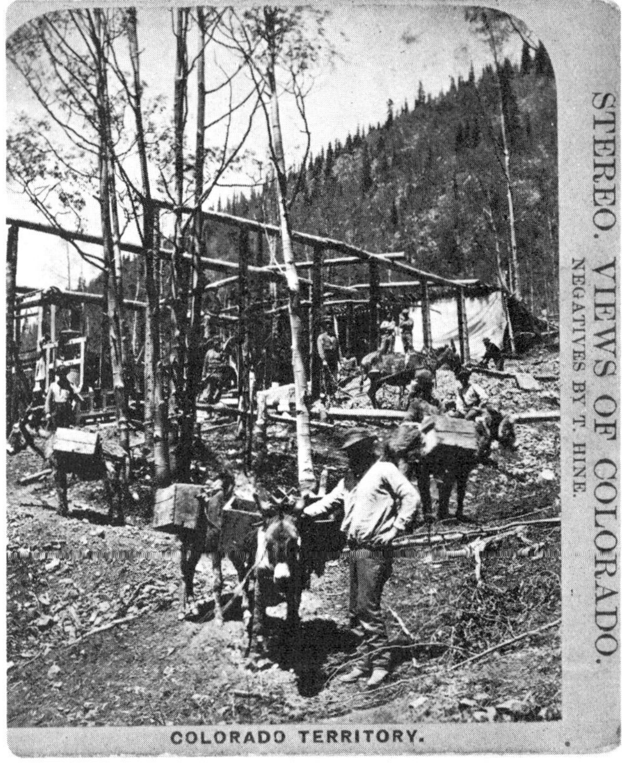

134. Colorado. "Silver mining camp." Thomas Hin photo, 1873. Copelin and Son publishers.

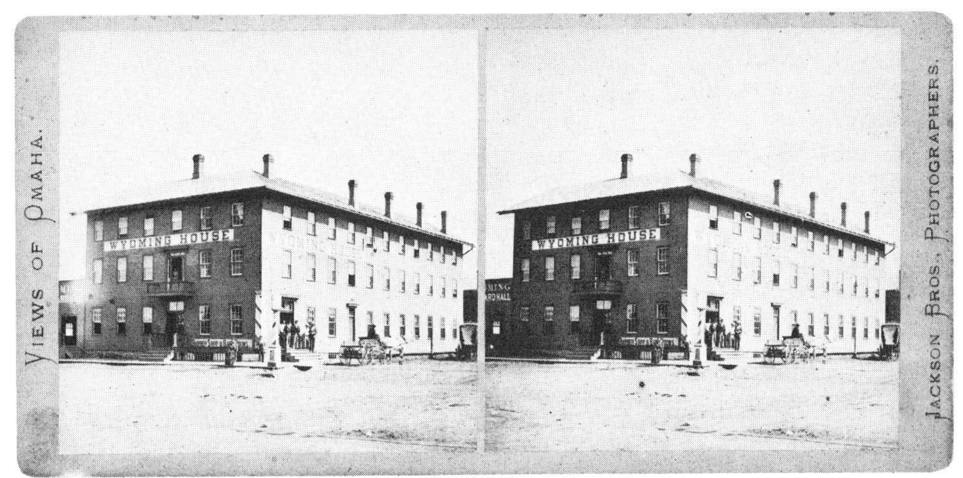

135. Jackson Brothers. Omaha, Nebraska. A view from their first issue on gray cards with small white strip label on back. 1868.

Jackson purchased that of Eaton, also. During the summer of 1868 William and Edward Jackson followed the route of the Union Pacific Rail Road to take a large series of stereo negatives of the railroad, Indians and plains countryside. So popular were the stereos issued by Jackson Brothers that Anthony purchased (1869) 10,000 prints for mounting on standard cards. William Jackson joined the Hayden Geological Survey in 1870 and sold his gallery in Omaha, October 1872.

One of the most prolific and unappreciated western photographers was W. R. Cross (Niobrara and Norfolk, 1870's and 1880's). He covered much of Nebraska and Dakota Territory, recording in a trade list of more than 2000 views everything of interest from Indians, sod houses, windmills to fossil mammal skeletons. He published a set of twenty views of Sitting Bull's camp at Fort Randall, where the Indians were held as prisoners of war. The quality of the images by Cross is generally mediocre, but this does not lessen their historical significance.

M. A. Kleckner moved from Bethlehem, Pennsylvania, to Atchison, Kansas, in 1878 and for five or six years issued a beautiful series, "Life and Scenes in Kansas"—"prairie life, dugouts, log cabins, sod schoolhouse, sheepherding, prairie flowers, and everything on the frontier." The publisher's imprint is Conklin & Kleckner.

The stereographs of Cross and Kleckner were conscious efforts to depict frontier life, how settlers adjusted to and utilized an unfamiliar and often inhospitable environment.

There are scores of photographers who were located at military outposts and short-lived communities. Their stereo views are very rare but deserving a diligent search. William Soule, for instance, published fine views of Fort Sill (1868-69).

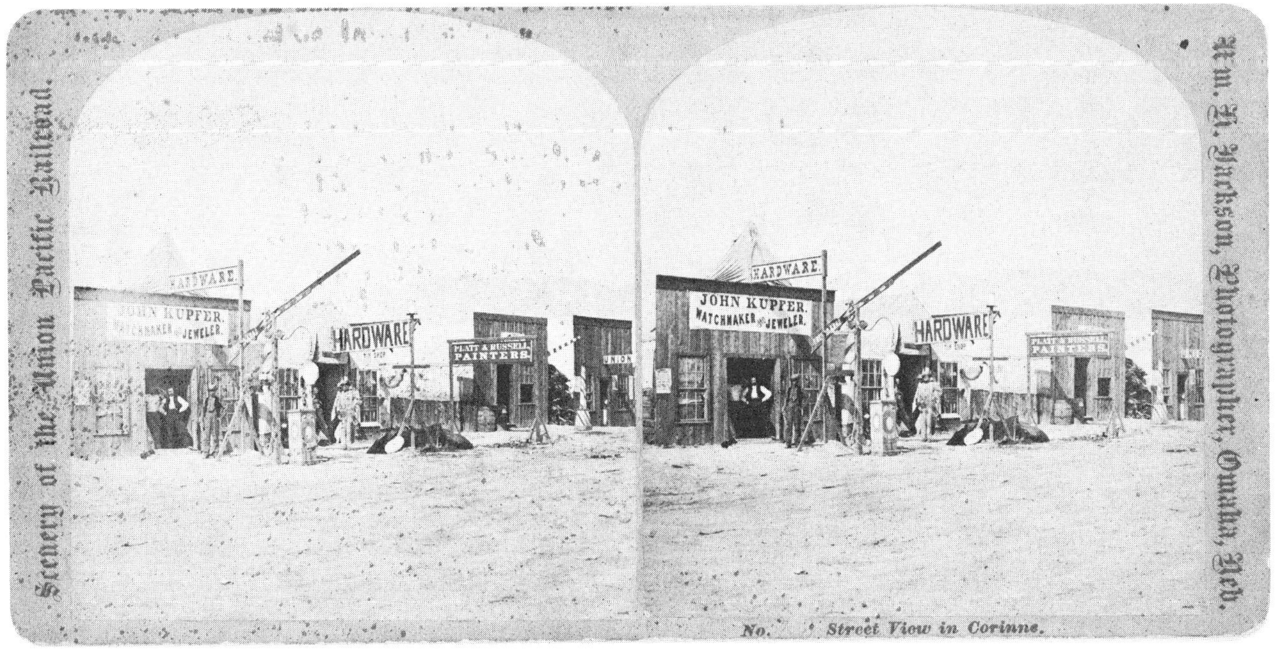

136. William H. Jackson. Union Pacific Railroad Series. Corinne, Utah. (first station on the Central Pacific division), boom town. 1869.

EXPLORATION OF THE WEST

As wondrous as these scenes may have appeared to the nineteenth century Easterner, the spectacular wonders of the West lay between the Rocky and the Sierra Mountains. Although only a part of the vast public domain, the wildness between the 98th and 120th meridians was the special concern of four Federal geographical and geological surveys, alluded to earlier. The immediate objective of these surveys was to explore and map the areas assigned to them. The combined work, however, led to the establishment of government agencies and Federal policies that controlled the future course of western development. Each survey employed photographers for at least a part of its existence.

There were earlier Federal exploring expeditions which had more limited objectives. After 1858 nearly all of these were accompanied by photographers. The first successful stereographic venture was that by Albert Bierstadt, the celebrated artist who in 1859 accompanied the Col. F. W. Lander Expedition. Only recently, through the persistent research of H. F. Bendix,[3] has the existence of surviving copies been verified.

The series includes about eighty numbers, many depicting Indians, published in 1860 by Bierstadt Brothers (New Bedford, 1860-1866). The series was issued in three formats until the partnership (Charles and Edward) was dissolved in 1866 and the studio sold to S. F. Adams, an employee. Adams continued to produce stereos from some of the negatives until the early 1870's.

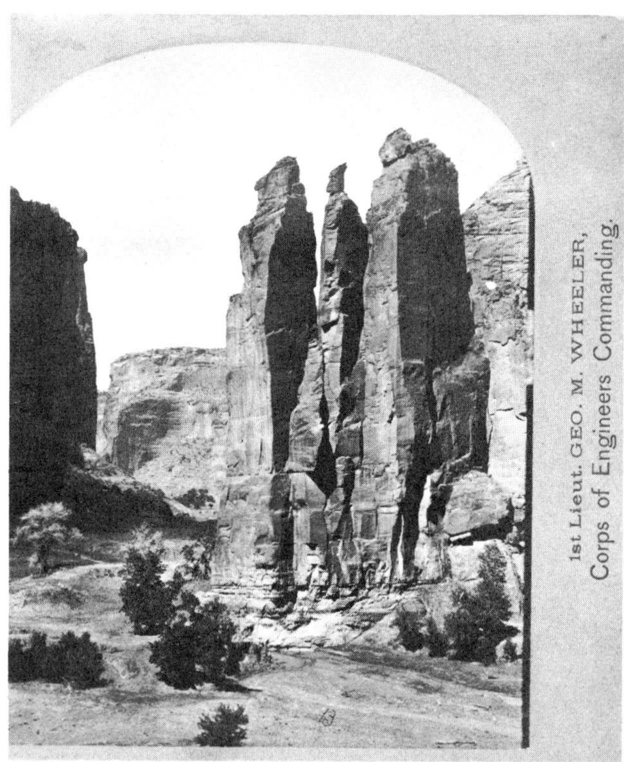

138. Wheeler Survey. "Canyon de Chelly," Arizona. T.H. O'Sullivan photo, 1873.

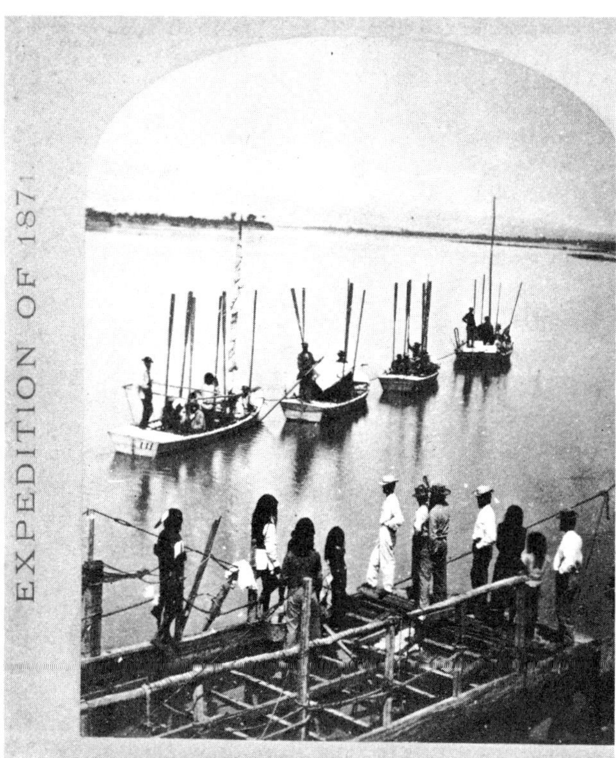

137. Lt. Wheeler Survey West of the Hundredth Meridian. "The Start from Camp, Arizona, September 15, 1871". T. H. O'Sullivan photo, 1873.

Much better known is the series of about forty views taken by Illingworth and Bill, who accompanied the Capt. J. L. Fisk Expedition to Montana in 1866. The party was organized to find a safe overland route from Minnesota to the gold fields of western Montana. William H. Illingworth (St. Paul, 1864-1885) and his assistant, George Bill, left the expedition at Fort Union. Upon his return to St. Paul, Illingworth published his remarkable series of views of forts, Indians and wagon trains. The first issue, on ivory mounts, has only manuscript titles, with Illingworth's unique misspellings. The second issue on gray or gray-brown cards has a printed imprint, but these titles also are in manuscript.

Late in 1866 John Carbutt published a selected series of twenty-seven of Illingworth's views on his standard yellow mounts (Nos. 234-260) with printed titles. Whereas the images produced by Illingworth lack contrast, those by Carbutt are excellent. Carbutt seems to have purchased the negatives (or copies of them), because he took great care to mask or crop from the prints any clue to Illingworth's identity and deliberately claimed them as his own. Figure 9.

There is at least one other authorized issue of the Fisk Expedition series, that by B. H. Gurnsey (Sioux City, Iowa, ca. 1863-1873). Illingworth was associated with Gurnsey in 1863-1865 and in partnership with him briefly, 1869-1870. There are two formats, one with Carbutt numbers printed on the cards, the other with unnumbered manuscript titles. Both formats bear the inaccurate imprint "Photographed and Published by B. H. Gurnsey." This example of multiple issues with false claims demonstrates some of the pitfalls in research.

[3] Bendix, H. F., *Photographica* 6 (8): 4, 5; 6 (9) 7, 10; 6 (10) 7; 7 (1), 41; 1974-75.

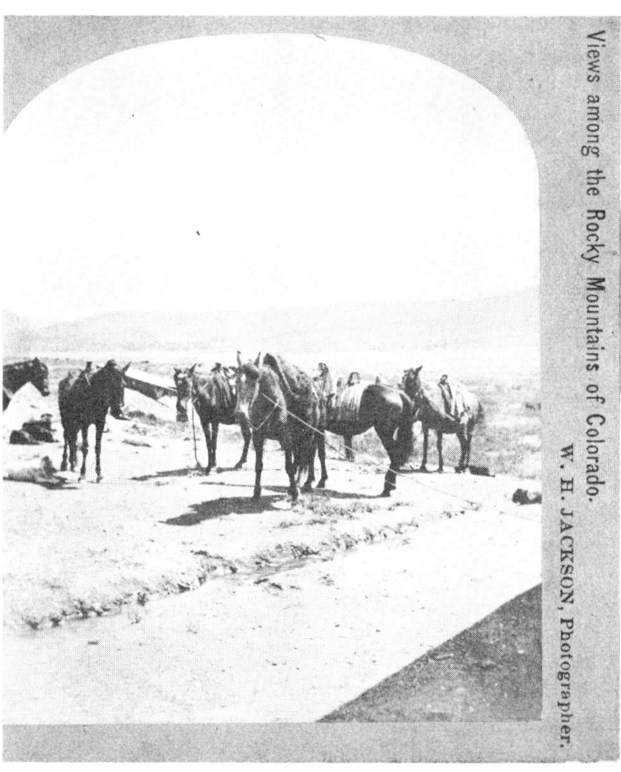

139. Hayden Survey of the Territories. "Our Horses in Camp." W.H. Jackson photo, 1871.

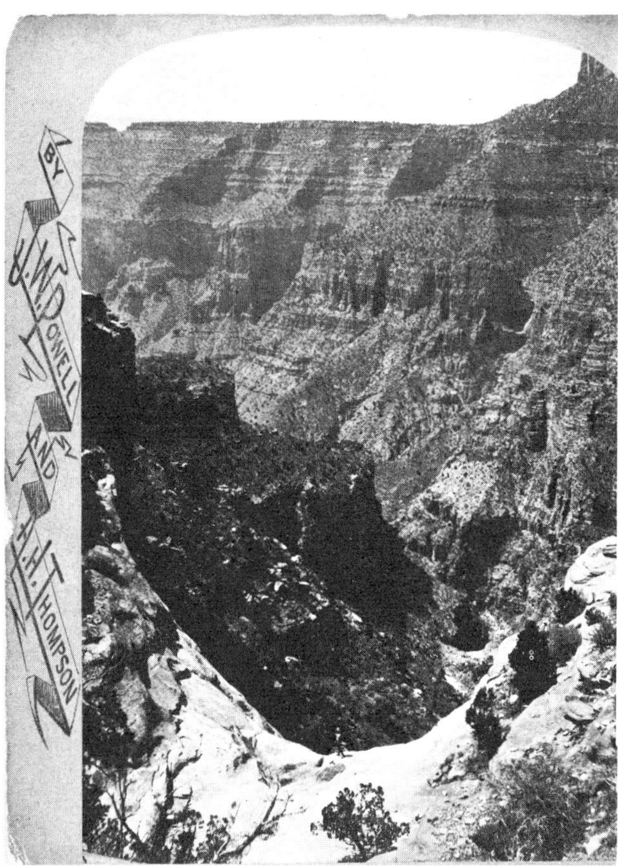

140. Powell Survey of the Colorado River. "Grand Canyon of the Colorado River, Arizona." J.K. Hillers photo, 1872.

The stereographic work of the major government surveys can be summarized briefly, even though the number of negatives ran into the thousands.

The Survey of the Fortieth Parallel, under the geologist Clarence King, employed the well-known Civil War photographer, T. H. O'Sullivan. Most of the photographs were intended for official records and illustrations of reports. Only a relative few stereographs were distributed. It is probable that they were not regularly sold commercially.

When the field work of the King Survey had been completed, O'Sullivan joined the Lt. Wheeler Survey already in progress. He photographed from 1871 to 1875 except for the summer of 1872. William Bell took O'Sullivan's place on the Wheeler Survey in 1872. Approximately 700 stereographs were produced by the Survey. Most of the existing cards bear a War Department imprint. These were distributed generously among members of Congress, officers in the War Department and their friends. A selection of more than a hundred titles was sold commercially through the publishing houses of Jarvis and Anthony between 1872 and 1876.

The Hayden Survey of the Rocky Mountain Region engaged William H. Jackson as chief photographer from 1870 to 1878. There were several assistants, of whom T. J. Hine (Chicago) was the most able. Jackson's finest stereo scenic work was done during his eight years with Hayden. His spectacular mountain scenery, geological features of Yellowstone and outstanding views of Indians fall within this period. A sense of artistry, appeal and detail characterize this work. Jackson, who held full rights to his negatives, was able to commercialize his views. Cards bearing his Washington imprint were manufactured by Jarvis. Several hundred of the more than 2200 Jackson negatives were published by Anthony with a Hayden Survey imprint. Hayden presented sets of stereographs to Congressmen and friends to publicize the importance of his Survey. Figure 283.

Major Powell's Survey of the Colorado River experienced considerable trouble with the photographers until Jack Hillers, a boatman, aptly learned the art. The first expedition in 1869 did not include a photographer. Indeed, photographic equipment and supplies would not have survived the first third of that incredible passage of the Colorado River. The second expedition, 1871-1872, was organized with the intention of securing an adequate photographic record.[4] E. O. Beaman, who had been recommended by Anthony, disliked the arduous work involved in climbing canyons and withdrew after taking about 350 negatives. His place was taken by James Fennemore, an operator for Savage in Salt Lake City. Fennemore, too, found the physical labor unbearable but, before quitting the expedition, taught Jack Hillers the rudiments of wet plate photography.[5]

[4] Darrah, W. C., *Utah Hist. Quart. 16-17:* 491-497, 1949. Fowler, Don D. (ed): "Photographed all the Best Scenery," Jack Hiller's Diary of the Powell Expeditions, 1871-1875, Univ. Utah Press, 1972.

[5] Walter Clement Powell, a nephew served as an assistant to Beaman and Fennemore but he showed little aptitude for photography. At least three of Clem's negatives were used to print stereographs.

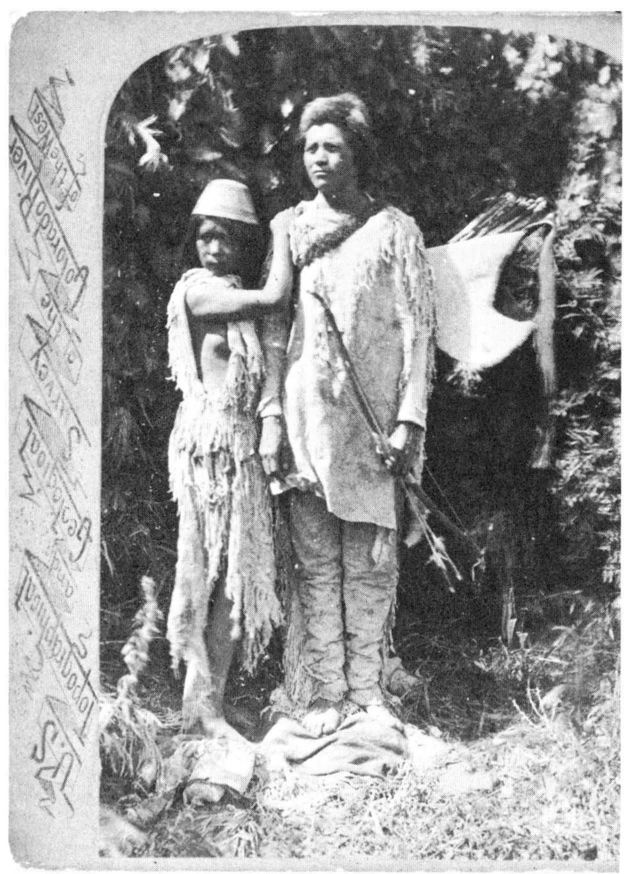

141. Powell Survey. "Nuaguntit Indians, Southwestern Nevada." J.K. Hillers photo, 1874.

Jack Hillers quickly became a master of scenic photography, equaling the best. He remained with the U. S. Geological Survey as a photographer until his retirement in 1900 and for almost twenty years more (until 1919) served on a *per diem* basis whenever his experienced skill was desired. Hillers' stereo work, however, was entirely with the Powell Survey.

Under Powell's direction Hillers achieved with his photographs a sense of natural process—a continuity that no single view can imply. For instance, Powell desired successive negatives of a small side canyon from its head to mouth to visualize the origin and development of a canyon. I know of no other nineteenth century photographer who applied this approach to imply continuity in natural phenomena. Muybridge's study of locomotion in the horse and human was a much greater achievement, of course, because he developed *experimental* photographic techniques to *analyze* motion.

Powell was quick to recognize the commercial potential of stereographs for academic instruction as well as recreation. Jarvis manufactured great numbers of the card mounts, which were sold with the labels of many dealers scattered throughout the United States.

Stereographs from at least 1400 negatives taken by the Powell Survey photographers are known. Approximately 650 were regularly issued for commercial sales and complimentary distribution. These depict the most interesting scenery, geologic formations and Indian anthropology. Approximately 600 additional titles were mounted for internal use and limited distribution. About 150 other titles were apparently distributed among members of the expedition and their families or used for study by the personnel of the Surveys.

It should be noted again that the rights to use the photographic negatives made on these and other government surveys were granted to the photographers, in some cases in lieu of salary. When, however, the King, Hayden, Wheeler and Powell Surveys were abolished and the U. S. Geological Survey established in 1879, all negatives were supposed to be deposited in the Departments that had sponsored the surveys.

This pictorial record of the public domain is of inestimable historical importance. To suggest only one implication—the damming and silting of the Colorado River since 1925 has forever hidden many of the features of the canyons photographed in 1871 and 1872.

There were approximately twenty other western expeditions organized by the War and Interior Departments for more limited objectives. Usually a photographer accompanied the party, sometimes an amateur or semi-professional.

Illingworth accompanied Gen. Custer's reconnaisance to the Black Hills in 1874 and issued a celebrated set of fifty-five stereo views of this controversial expedition.

The geological expedition of W. P. Jenney and Henry Newton, authorized in 1875 by the Interior Department to determine the extent of valuable mineral deposits in the Black Hills, was really a follow-up of Custer's superficial appraisal of the gold field. The physician accompanying the party, Dr. V. T. M. McGillycuddy (St. Louis), also served as the photographer. A series of approximately sixty stereo views were published by R. Benecke (St. Louis). The subjects include Indians, forts, personnel at work and typical scenery.

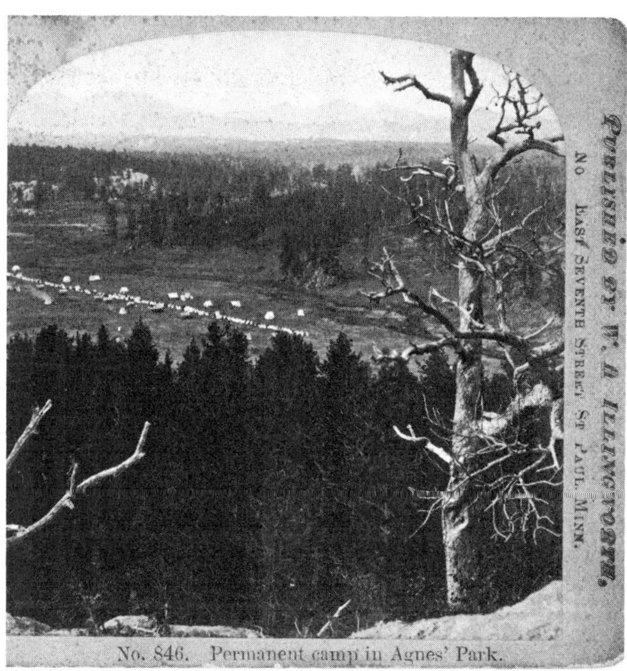

142. Custer Expedition to the Black Hills, 1874. "Permanent Camp in Agnes Park." W. H. Illingworth photo.

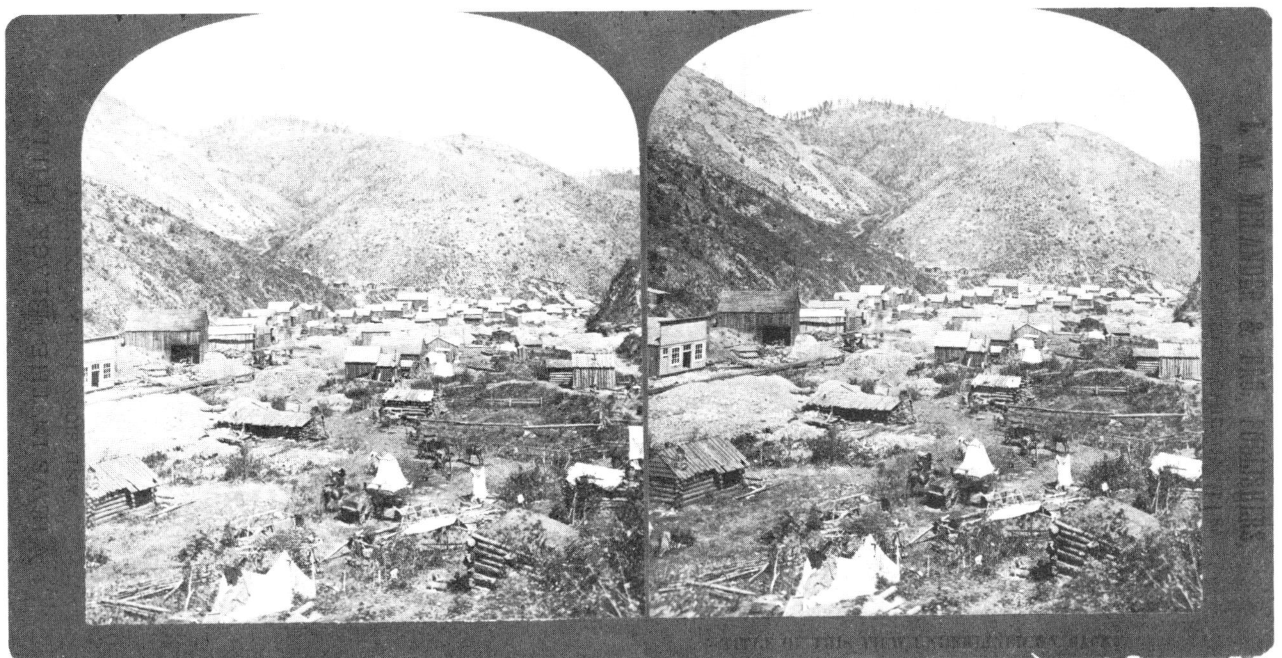

143. Dakota Territory. Gold Mining boom town. "South Bend, Deadwood Gulch." Rodacker and Blanchard photo, 1879. L.E. Melander and Brother publishers.

Following the massacre of Custer and his men at Little Big Horn in June, 1876, Gen. George Crook was sent in pursuit of the Sioux who were responsible. S. J. Morrow accompanied this military expedition and issued a series of thirty-two remarkable views, including wounded troops.

S. J. Morrow (Yankton, D. T., 1870-1890), who was one of the most important photographers of the Indians, was with the Gen. D. S. Stanley Yellowstone expedition of 1873. Morrow also stereographed the Custer massacre site in 1877, recording for posterity the gruesome littered field.

DAKOTA TERRITORY

When the Black Hills gold district was opened to settlement in 1877, thousands of fortune-seekers swarmed into the region, taking up claims in every gulch in which stream action might have freed gold from the parent rock.

A marvelously comprehensive record of this madness is to be found in the series of seventy-nine views by Rodacker & Blanchard (Deadwood) taken in 1878 and published by Melander and Brother (Chicago) in 1879. This spectacular issue, "Views in the Black Hills Mining Company and in the Sioux Indian Country," includes fine panoramas of Deadwood, Gayville, Hills City, Montana City, Custer City, Central City, Galena City and Lead City; Gayville in ruins after a fire, settlers, stockades, Indian camps, Camp Robinson, placer mining and even the Union Beer Garden at Deadwood.

Other photographers who published fine but smaller series include: Albert Pollock (Deadwood), Ben Oppenheimer (a mute, Deadwood), A. A. Rounds (Sioux Falls), P. G. Anderson (Redfield) and W. W. Delong (Yankton). Figure 240.

Agricultural settlements and towns may seem more commonplace, but several have been well photographed.

The town of Groton was photographed by two local operators, F. Q. Miller (1883, fifteen numbers) and C. H. Carli (1885, twelve numbers). These sets give a remarkably complete picture of the town, its hotels, granaries, civic band and famous artesian well. Surely, diligent search would find that many other small communities were equally well photographed.

In 1889 North Dakota and South Dakota were sepa-

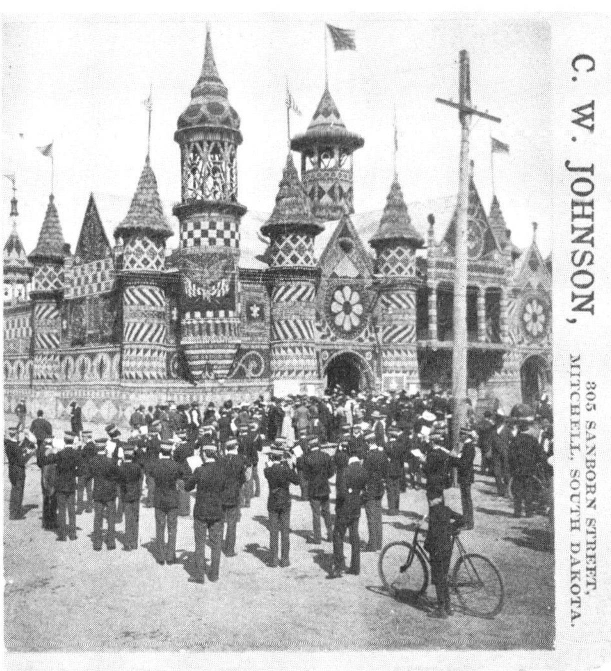

144. South Dakota, Mitchell. "Corn Palace." Wooden building decorated entirely with ears of corn cut lengthwise. C.W. Johnson photo, 1903.

rated and granted statehood. Several stereographers produced local views of interest. Only one, however, C. W. Johnson (Mitchell, S. D.) will be cited here. In 1903 he issued a small series of the Corn Palace, an imposing building completely covered with multi-colored ears of corn, cut length-wise and nailed to the siding. Other views show the interior and exhibits.

Somewhat later, ca. 1906-1912, N. H. Forsythe of Butte, Montana, published an excellent series of about a hundred views of "the richest hill in the world," including the town, smelters, mills and underground copper mining operations. Placer gold mining here was worked out by 1867. Silver mining, which followed in the mid-1870's, was by 1895 supplanted by copper, with zinc and lead important by-products of ore treatment. Forsythe also stereographed the cattle trade and Indians.

RAILROAD CONSTRUCTION

We have already noted that local photographers like Hart, Watkins, Houseworth, Muybridge, Jackson and Savage took full advantage of the exciting and picturesque railroad projects in their areas. The public eagerly followed the progression of the various rail lines, and the railroad companies found the stereograph to be an excellent promotional instrument.

Hart had begun photographing the Central Pacific in 1864. John Carbutt published a series of one hundred spectacular views, "Union Pacific Rail Road Excursion to the 100th Meridian, October 1866." This jaunt had been organized by the Union Pacific promoters to entice capital from eastern bankers and investors. The following year Carbutt made an independent trip to obtain additional negatives of the plains, Indians and railroad construction.

In 1867 Alex Gardner photographed the line of the Eastern Division of the Union Pacific Railway across Kansas and published a fine series of 160 views.

The Union Pacific Rail Road employed two "official" photographers, A. J. Russell (1868-1870) and J. B. Silvis (ca. 1873-1876). Russell's more than 500 fine negatives comprise an important record of the construction and scenery along the transcontinental railroad. There are excellent views of tracklaying, Chinese laborers, work-trains, snow sheds and boom towns. The views were published under a Russell imprint from 1868-1872, on mounts of various colors. The early issues bear on the back a large imprint: "Pacific R. R. Views Across the Continent West from Omaha." Later issues have a printed list of titles on the backs of the cards, in fourteen sub-series, beginning with Omaha and ending with Sacramento, California. The imprint closes with "A. J. Russell & Co., New York." Figure 17.

In 1873 S. J. Sedgwick became the publisher of these views on mounts and imprints identical with those of Russell but with Russell's name deleted. About 1875 the negatives passed to O.C. Smith, who continued to produce views until 1878.

During the mid-1870's Russell's negatives, or copies of them, were used to print stereos mounted on plain yellow cards with white backs. The manuscript titles and numbers are those of Russell. The name of the publisher is unknown. An indication of the enduring interest in Russell's views is the fact that they were in print continuously for a decade.

While some of the novelty and excitement of railroading had worn off after completion of the transcontinental line, the progressive extension of side-lines and branches continued at a great pace until 1900.

F. Jay Haynes began photography in Moorhead, Minnesota, in 1877 and moved to Fargo, Dakota Territory, in 1879. In the latter year he became the official photographer for the Northern Pacific Railroad. Haynes boasted that in 1879 alone he had sold 60,000 views. The Northern Pacific held the concessions in Yellowstone National Park. Thus, Haynes became the official photographer of the Park. His trade list exceeded 4800 numbers, almost eighty percent of which were scenes in Yellowstone National Park. Figure 251.

Other railroads and the scenery adjacent to their lines, such as the Denver & Rio Grande, the Atcheson, Topeka and Santa Fe, were repeatedly and beautifully stereographed.

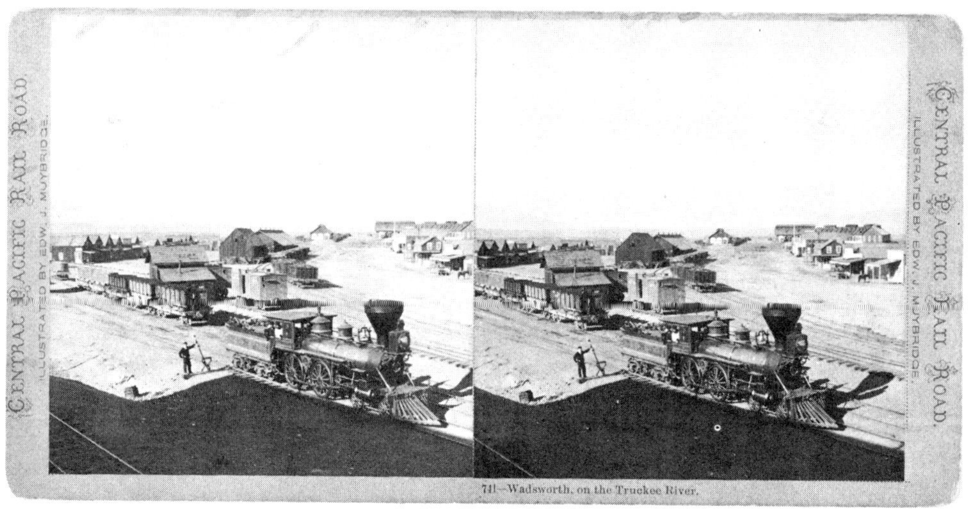

145. Central Pacific Railroad. "Wadsworth on the Truckee River." California. Eadweard J. Muybridge photo, 1869.

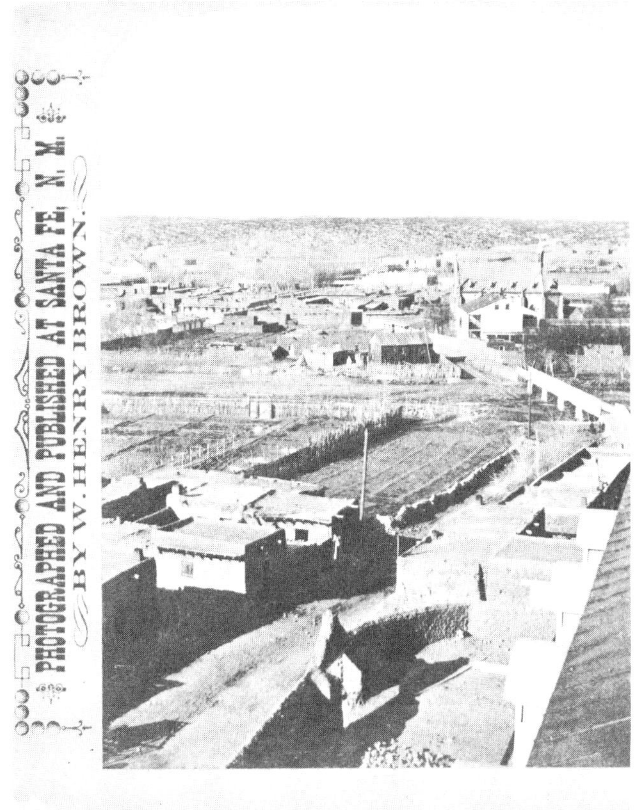

146. New Mexico. Santa Fe. W. Henry Brown photo, 1877.

OTHER WESTERN STATES

The chief centers of stereoscopic photography were, of course, in California, Colorado, Utah and Nebraska. The great "events"—railroads, Indians, exploration, gold and silver—were taking place there.

More routinely, perhaps, the photographers in countless communities in other western states followed their trade and accumulated negatives from which many interesting stereo views were published.

TEXAS

For uncertain reasons relatively few stereographs of Texas are known. Doerr and Jacobson (succeeded by H. A. Doerr, San Antonio) produced views from the latter 1860's to the late 1870's. Barr & Wright (succeeded by C. J. Wright, Houston) were active in the 1870's. Also located in Houston was the firm of J. B. Blessing and Brother.

During the 1870's interesting local views were issued by: F. A. Bailey (Huntsville), E. Finch (Waxahatchee and Alvarado), P. Rose (Galveston) and Louis dePlanque (Corpus Christi).

E. Parker (El Paso) produced excellent views of the town in the 1870's.

In the 1880's there were many local photographers who produced a few views of their localities. Two examples will suggest the possibilities: M. Cumming (Corsicana) and J. H. & J. Selkirk (Matagorda).

NEW MEXICO

New Mexico is surprisingly well represented in stereo. The several government surveys photographed extensively, as did many Colorado photographers. Among the latter were Jackson, F. A. Nims, Gurnsey and Gillingham, all of whom followed the route of the Atcheson, Topeka and Santa Fe Rail Road. Their combined lists of Arizona views exceeds 600 titles.

The most prolific local photographers were Bennett & Brown (W. Henry Brown, successor, Santa Fe, early 1880's), who published more than 550 titles, most of which were in four series: "Among the Ancient and Interesting Scenery of New Mexico," "Santa Fe and Vicinity," "A Trip from Trinidad, Colorado through New Mexico to Paso del Norto, Mexico," and "Atcheson, Topeka, and Santa Fe Rail Road Scenery."

Representative series were published by H. T. Hiester (Santa Fe, 1870's), "Views of the Great South West," by A. S. Addis (Silver City, early 1880's), "New Mexico Scenery," and by M. Schuster (Las Vegas, 1880's.).

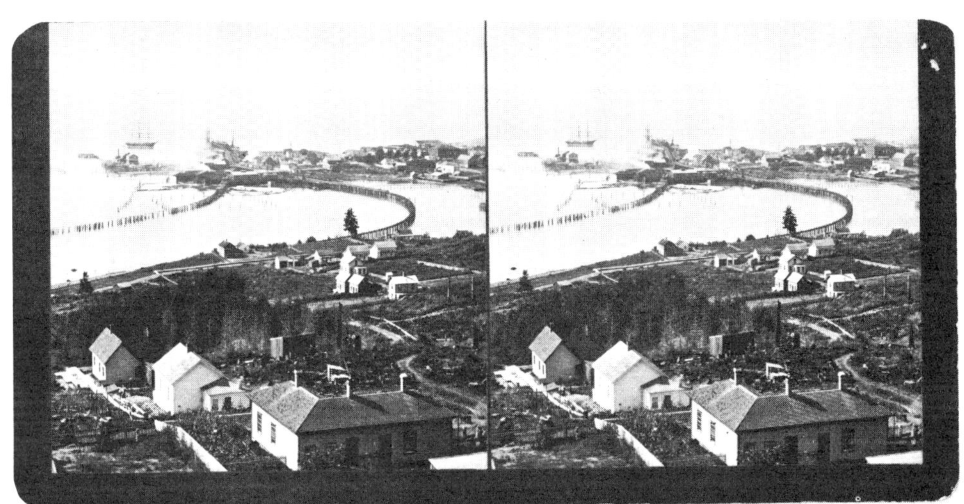

147. Washington. "Seattle and Puget Sound." C.E. Watkins photo, 1873.

ARIZONA

The government survey photographers were the most important contributors to the stereographic history of Arizona. Following them in importance were Watkins and Savage, who also operated in the 1870's. There were some excellent local photographers as well, the best known of whom were G. H. Rothrock (Phoenix and Prescott), H. Buehman (Tucson), D. F. Mitchell (Prescott) and Wittick & Russell (Albuquerque, N. Mex., early 1880's).

THE NORTHWEST COAST: OREGON AND WASHINGTON

The earliest known stereo views of Oregon were issued in the late 1850's on thin white bristol card by an unidentified photographer who also took views of Mt. Shasta in California and around the little settlement, Ashland. The images are of rich velvet-black texture, suggesting the workmanship of a skilled daguerreotypist. Figure 121.

During the period 1868-1880 a number of California photographers ventured up the coast, recording seaports, salmon fishing, lumbering, Indians and characteristic scenery. C. E. Watkins and M. M. Hazeltine did notable work in the region. Haynes' views of Portland and Seattle (1882) have already been mentioned.

Important series by local photographers include those of Frank G. Abell (Portland), Buchtel (Portland), J. G. Crawford (Harrisburg and Albany), I. G. Davidson (Portland), M. M. Hazeltine (Baker City), A. B. Paxton (Albany), Ball & Sons (Seattle), S. W. Beers (Walla Walla), J. D. Maxwell (Dayton and Walla Walla), Peterson and Brother (Seattle) and A. B. Woodard (Olympia).

EASTERN PUBLISHERS OF WESTERN STEREO VIEWS

Catering to the popular demand for stereographs of the West, the large publishing houses sent photographers into the field to build files of negatives for the trade. Anthonys sent their chief photographer, T. C. Roche, across the country in 1870 with special instructions to obtain a set of negatives of Yosemite and the mammoth trees. In addition, Anthony purchased 10,000 prints from Jackson. The Roche views were published on both standard and cabinet mounts, 1871-1874.

J. P. Soule of Boston went to California in 1870 and returned with a series of more than 250 titles. There is some uncertainty as to how many of the series were from negatives by Soule and how many were purchased. Careful examination of the stereo prints suggests that these were negatives by two, perhaps three, photographers. Soule's imprint indicates ambiguously that he was "publisher," not necessarily photographer and publisher. Figures 148, 224, 243.

Edward Kilburn, not to be outdone, covered much the same ground, and in 1871 Kilburn Brothers issued an excellent series, 917-986, of about seventy titles, most of Yosemite but a few of San Francisco and Sacramento.

In 1873 Charles Bierstadt (Niagara Falls) issued a beautiful series of approximately a hundred views of Yosemite and Sierra Nevada Mountain scenery, comparable with the best of Muybridge and Watkins.

Many other publishers issued smaller series of views between 1873 and 1880. The series distributed by J. S. & J. W. Moulton (Salem, Mass.) is probably most frequently encountered.

The Continent Stereoscopic Company (New York, ca. 1875-1885) published a large trade list of more than 2000 numbers, about a third of which were Western scenes. It is a very curious series, a majority of prints being from copy negatives—probably purchased—but many from original negatives taken for the company. Readily recognizable are scenes by Watkins, O'Sullivan, Brown, Haynes and Jackson. Most of the titles were available both on standard and white mounts of cheap quality.

About 1880-1885 T. W. Ingersoll (St. Paul) issued a

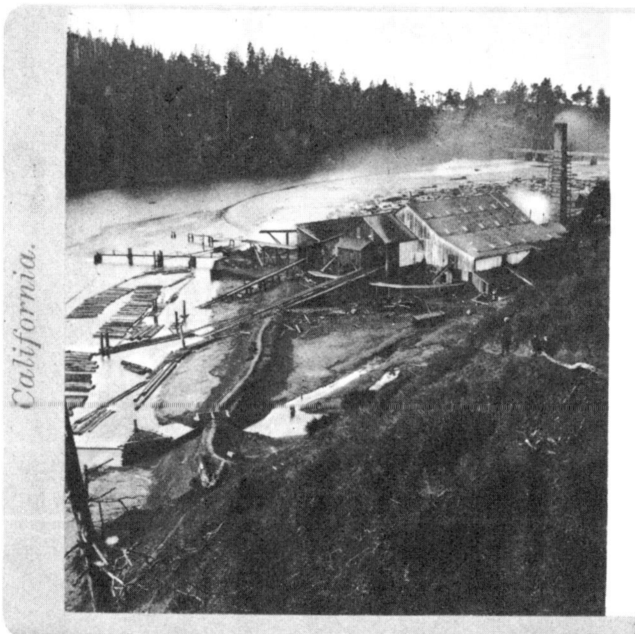

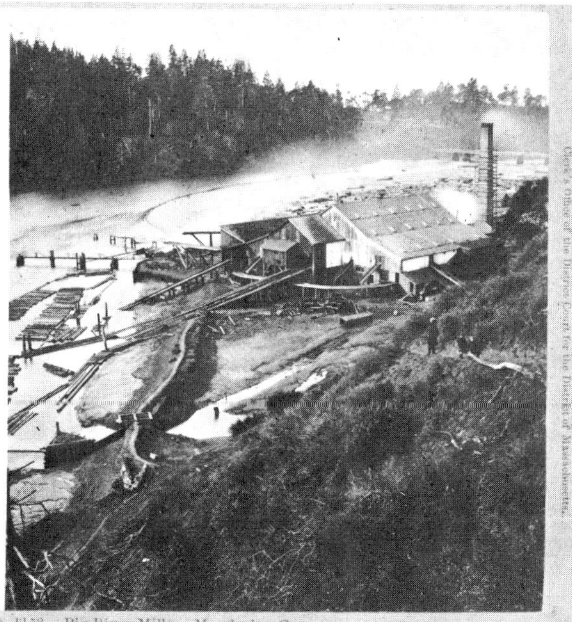

148. John P. Soule. California series. "Big River Saw Mills, Mendocino County, California." 1870.

series of 300 numbers of Yellowstone Park and hundreds of other views of the West. Yellowstone attracted many able eastern photographers. Lovejoy & Foster (Chicago, 1875, one hundred titles), Wm. M. Myers (Iona, Michigan, 1875, forty-eight titles), W. I. Marshall (Fitchburg, Massachusetts, 1876, 120 titles) and C. D. Kirkland (Cheyenne, Wyoming 1883, about one hundred views).

During the resurgence of popularity of stereo views between 1900 and 1920, the great publishers, Underwood, Keystone and White issued literally thousands of views of the West, with emphasis on the National Parks. Their trade lists, however, were not confined to scenic subjects. Every event of modest local significance was stereographed: "Pickfair," the home of the motion picture stars Mary Pickford and Douglas Fairbanks, the "parades of the roses" at Pasadena, naval bases and petroleum fields. Of course, major events, such as the San Francisco Earthquake, 1906, and the Pan Pacific Exposition in 1915 were very well photographed. Figure 230.

ALASKA

As far as is known, Alaska had no resident stereographers before the Klondike Gold Rush of 1898. Very few photographs of the territory had been published. Most famous of the early views was the series issued by Muybridge in 1868. His views show well the Russian influence, especially in Sitka.

The Continent Stereoscopic Company produced a small series of original views of Sitka and its vicinity about 1878.

There are several little-known rare series which are important for their detail of specific subjects. For example, H. H. Brodeck (Walla Walla, Washington) produced at least fifty numbers for the Northwest Trading Company in the mid-1880's. I. G. Davidson (Portland) also issued an interesting series in the early 1880's. T. W. Ingersoll published several hundred views of Alaska between 1885 and 1905.

The gold rush lured many photographers to the region to "scoop" the market with exciting stereo views. Unquestionably the best were produced by Keystone. B. L. Singley copyrighted more than 300 titles, capturing the hardships and the faces of the gold seekers in his pictures. Kilburn issued more than 250 titles in three series, 1898-1902.

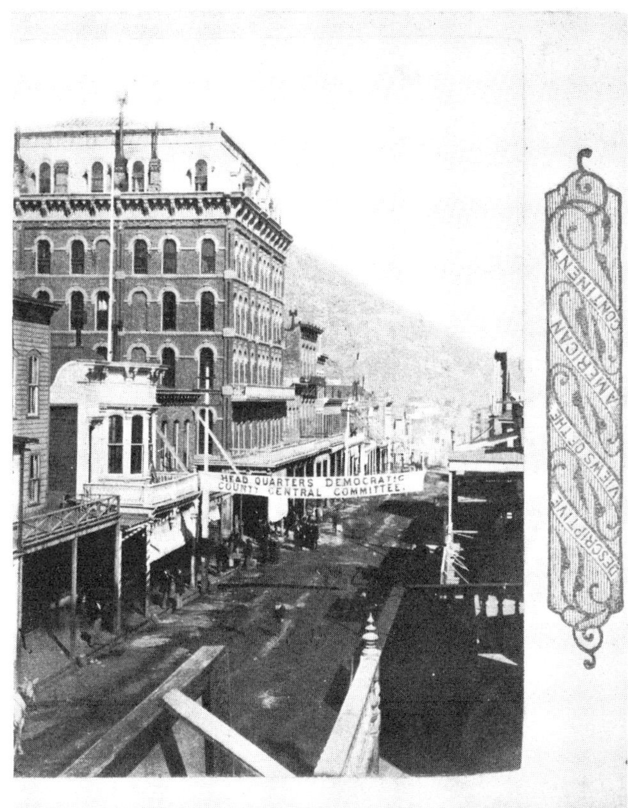

149. Nevada. "Virginia City, C. Street. Continent Stereoscopic Company." 1878.

Keystone View Company in 1923 published a hundred card set of President Harding's visit to Alaska. Half of the titles were of characteristic scenery. A somewhat similar set, but with substitutions for most of the Harding cards, was issued in 1928.

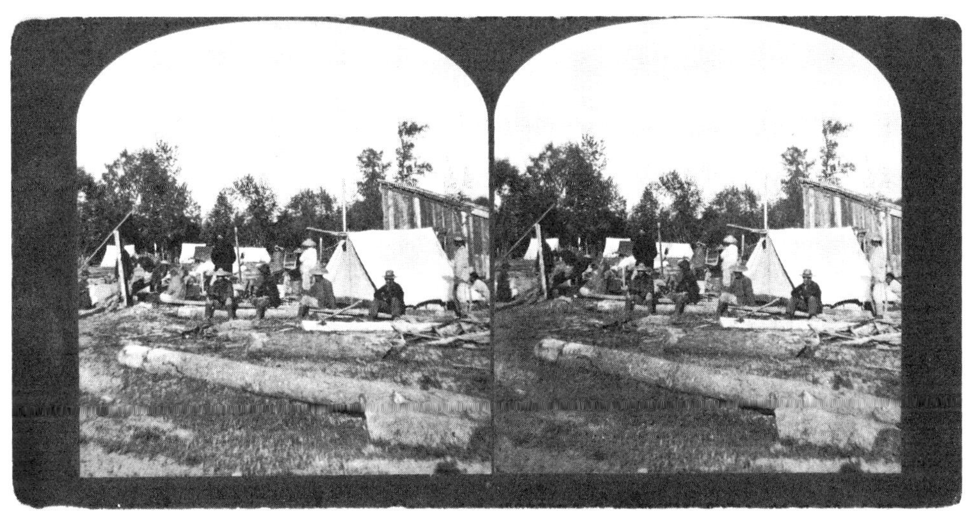

150. "Chinese Encampment in California." Continent Stereoscopic Company. 1876.

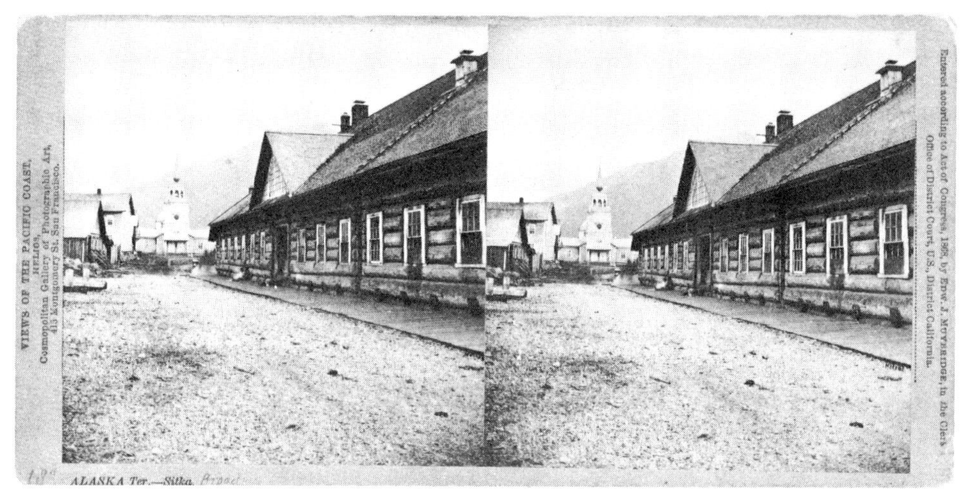

151. Alaska, Sitka. Eadweard J. Muybridge photo, 1868.

CANADA

The stereographs of Canada demonstrate several remarkable relationships. The earlier views produced in the eastern provinces are more comparable in subject and style to the views by English rather than by United States photographers. Emphasis is on panoramic scenery, fine architectural studies and studio poses. Nevertheless, opportunism is evident. William Notman (Montreal, 1856-1885) began his commercial stereo work with views of the construction of the St. Lawrence bridge. L. P. Vallee (Quebec, 1865-1880), J. G. Parks (Ottawa, 1865-1880), Alex Henderson (Montreal, 1860-1875) and H. L. Hime (Toronto, 1858-1860) produced beautiful views of their respective cities.

Notman, like Anthony, was primarily a publisher of stereographs. He purchased many negatives, including some from Anthony, dispatched staff photographers to various locations and made many himself. In addition to the scenic and documentary views with which we are here concerned, Notman produced ingenious studio groups with painted backgrounds and trick effects.

The famous photographic venture of William England for the London Stereoscopic Company resulted in a fine series of 150 Canadian views published in 1859 and 1860.

By the 1870's Canadian photographers were doing the same kinds of stereo work as their colleagues in the United States. The present and the timely took precedence over the artistic. Harbor scenes, fires, market places and novelties held more appeal.

In St. John, New Brunswick, J. S. Climo, James McClure and James Notman were actively producing fine local views. Both McClure and Climo issued large series of the great fire of 1877.

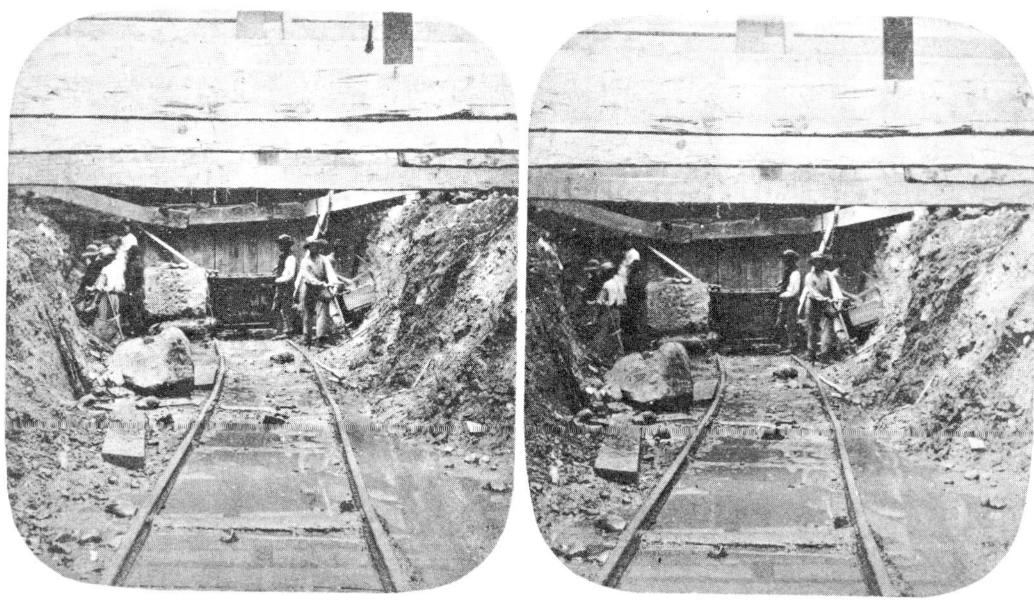

152. Canada, William Notman. "Construction of Victoria Bridge. Coffer dam twenty feet below surface of the River." Montreal. 1857.

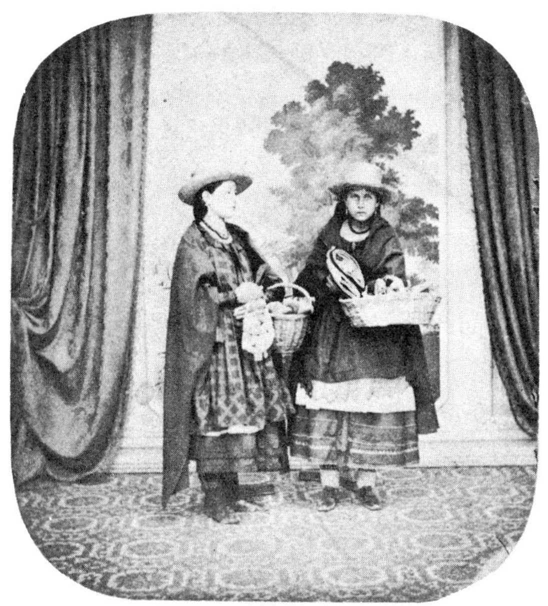

153. William Notman. "Indian Squaws." Studio pose. 1857.

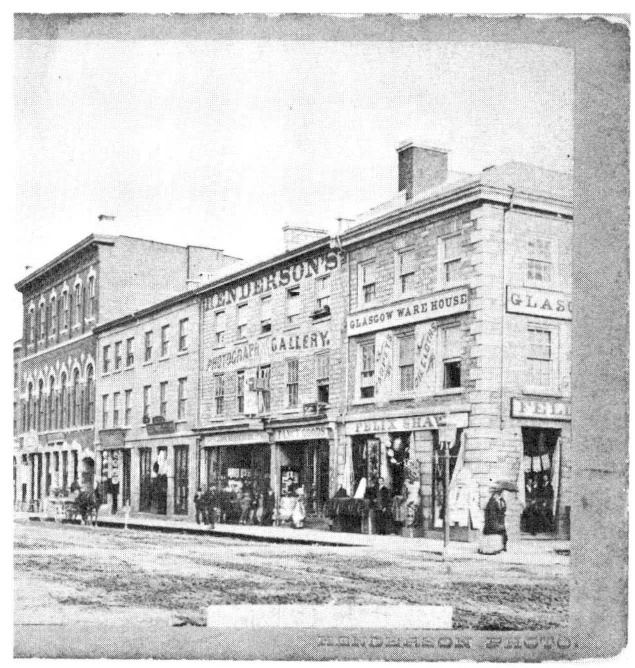

154. Ontario, Kingston. Gallery of H. Henderson. Henderson photo, ca. 1870.

Nova Scotia had several stereographers, of whom L. G. Swaim (ca. 1863-1873) is the most important. Also notable in this period were E. W. Lyon (St. Johns, Newfoundland and Truro, N. S.) and Ross Brothers (Charlottetown, Prince Edward Island).

James Esson (Preston, Ontario, latter 1870's and 1880's) published a large line of varied views including scenics, Indians, groups and sentimentals.

There is a third aspect of Canadian stereographs which parallels those of the United States, development of the West between 1870 and 1890. The Canadian Pacific Railway was completed in 1885 and settlement of the western provinces followed quickly.

The Alfred Selwyn Geological and Pacific Railroad Survey, under government auspices in 1871, was accompanied by two photographers, B. J. Baltzly and John Hammond, the latter in the employ of William Notman. A series of nearly one hundred views of this survey were published by Notman in 1872.

Stereo views of British Columbia are seldom seen although excellent views were produced by R. Maynard (Vancouver, late 1860's and 1870's), G. R. Fardon (Victoria, 1860's) and F. G. Claudet (New Westminster, 1860's).

Perhaps as many as thirty local photographers scattered in the western provinces issued stereo views of their communities. Those of Duffin and Caswell (Winnipeg, about 1880) are typical.

Kilburn Brothers published a small series of about thirty titles of Montreal and Quebec in 1867.

In the early 1900's the H. C. White and Underwood Companies issued magnificent views of British Columbia and the Canadian Rocky Mountains, with fine panoramas of glaciers. Underwood produced a set of one hundred cards as a tour of the country. This set includes detailed stereographs of characteristic Canadian industries and skilled craftsmen.

CHAPTER TEN
GREAT BRITAIN

Great Britain has been more completely and beautifully stereographed than any other country in the world. Furthermore, to a remarkable degree, this photographic record preserves the poetic and sentimental characteristics of the Victorian Age. On the one hand the emphasis is beauty, yet on the other it is tradition.

The earliest views were of subjects chosen for their natural beauty. Scenes depicting romantic rustic villages and ruins of antiquity, overgrown with vegetation, held a special appeal.

The British people are constantly reminded of their historic past. Nearly every community is built upon or is situated near an ancient abbey, castle or fortification. Preserved among the ruins are doorways and windows of surpassing beauty. The great cathedrals—altered, enlarged and rebuilt time and again over five to ten centuries—retain features of Norman, Early English and Perpendicular architecture. The labels accompanying early stereographs of these cathedrals and abbeys commonly accurately identify the style of each feature illustrated. Fine details of tracery, wood carving and stained glass windows were faithfully recorded.

Another aspect of British tradition, the literary landmarks, was everywhere at hand. The scenes of the plays of William Shakespeare and the novels of Sir Walter Scott were favorite subjects of the photographer, but scarcely more so than the scenes of the poems of Robert Burns or Robert Southey.

M'Glashon (Edinburgh) published (1857-1863) a series of about four hundred numbers titled "Realities of the Waverly Novels, Burns' Poems, Scottish Songs, etc." The legends accompanying the views provide full descriptions, usually with an appropriate quotation. R. Boning (London), ca. 1862, entitled a fine series of rustic scenes of the Isle of Wight, "She Stoops to Conquer." This allusion to Goldsmith's play was based on the simple rustic countryside, fancying the cottages to be reminiscent of Goldsmith's imagery.

This literary interest extended to the dwellings of Shakespeare, Scott, Burns, John Knox, Charles Dickens, Charles Darwin and many lesser-known personalities. The London Stereoscopic Company published (1872) shortly after Dickens' death a fine series of views of Gad's Hill, which were still being sold to tourists in 1888. The graves and headstones of the writers and those written about were not overlooked by photographers.

The Lake District (counties of Cumberland, Westmoreland and Lancashire), renowned for its natural beauty, was associated with scores of English writers, among them Wordsworth, Ruskin, Keats, Shelley, and Tennyson. This region was photographed both for its natural appeal and for its literary connotation.

Simple panoramic views of busy seaports, towns and popular resorts were issued by many photographers. Views of prominent buildings, especially cathedrals and churches, were published in great variety. Street scenes are rather infrequent, and these seldom show people going about their business. Even the great buildings in the center of London are pictured without human figures. In fact, relatively few British stereographs published before 1890 include people in a manner that portrays or even suggests the vitality of a community. Instead, human figures are posed among the ruins of an abbey to increase the illusion of solitude and contemplation or lend scale to the scene.

There are, however, some notable exceptions. G. W. Wilson's instantaneous views (1857-1862) show groups of people on the streets of Aberdeen and Edinburgh and at the piers. William Grundy depicts the unity of man and the land. Hesketh (Pembrokeshire) has some interesting views of foundrymen and slate workers standing with their tools.

British photographers seldom recorded disasters, although there are two series of scenes of flood damage at Leeds (1864). Still, there is nothing comparable to the tornado, fire and wreck views so avidly purchased in America.

The contrast between the settled British and the restless American temperaments is strikingly demonstrated in their respective topographic and scenic views.

BRITISH STEREOGRAPHERS

More than eight hundred photographers in Great Britain are known to have produced stereo views commercially. The actual total number is certainly much greater. It is easy to single out ten or twelve of the most outstanding scenic photographers because contemporaries lavishly praised their work. But to select fifty or sixty to suggest a cross-section of the types of views, techniques and geographic regions is extremely difficult. No fewer than three hundred photographers have left a wonderful pictorial heritage, artistically and technically of great merit.

At the outset, we must clarify the role of the early publishers, especially London Stereoscopic Company and the firm of Negretti and Zambra, both publishers and distributors of the views of many photographers—generally unnamed.

Between 1854 and 1860 the London Stereoscopic Company sold several thousand different views of the British Isles. Many were printed from negatives taken by staff photographers, but greater numbers were from negatives by independent photographers. From 1856 to 1859 cards by the London Stereoscopic Company bear on the back a strip label with a border of repeated designs, printed usually in red (occasionally in blue). Beginning in 1857 the company used a blind stamp to identify the cards they sold as well as those of their own manufacture. There are four basic designs with several variants of each. A blind stamp was used consistently until 1864, excepting the extensive series of Exhibition views (1862) and several small issues which had a credit line, "London Stereoscopic Company," printed on the face of the card. Earlier issues on thin cards, 1858 and earlier, have the strip label. The thicker gray mounts of 1858-1862 may have either, occasionally both, strip label or blind stamp. The blind stamp does not necessarily indicate that the London Stereoscopic Company itself is the publisher—often it merely records London Stereoscopic as seller.

Among the early issues are fine views of government buildings in London, ruins of famous castles and abbeys and scenes in many cities and town. For instance, there is a beautiful tinted series of all of the seaports of the Isle of Man. The trade list included views of every part of England, Wales, Scotland and much of Ireland.

William England was the chief photographer of the London Stereoscopic Company from 1858 to 1863. After that date he operated independently. England was a skillful artist in virtually all areas of photography, but especially landscape, architecture, interiors and sculpture. His most notable stereo work is embodied in four great series: America (1859), Paris (1860 and 1861), International Exhibition (1862) and the Alpine Club issues with their continuations without the Club sponsorship (1863-1868). There are other fine series including Ireland (1858), statuary (1872-1873) and many small runs of London and English scenery.

Negretti & Zambra published a smaller variety of British views than did the London Company. There is scarcely any duplication of titles. In many respects, however, their series of London is more impressive. The cards do not have an imprint but may be recognized by the gray rectangular label pasted on the back. Negretti & Zambra also published a fine series of Irish scenery.

There were several other publishers who produced stereographs from their own negatives and from those of other photographers. Two of these will be mentioned here, J. Elliott and C. E. Elliott, who have sometimes been confused or erroneously considered as one concern.

J. Elliott is best known as a photographer and publisher of genre group views, but he issued many fine London views from his own negatives (1860-62). More important, he published the famous stereo views by William M. Grundy (Sutton Coldfield near Birmingham, d. 1859). Grundy, a patent leather manufacturer, began in 1854 to take stereographs of rural England and created an almost unique style. More than a thousand negatives were taken over the span of five years. The prints were distributed in several distinct issues. The earliest are on thin card with manuscript titles in Grundy's hand, with or without his signature. These were followed by an issue with a small white strip label on the back (Example: "In Sutton Coldfield Park, W. M. Grundy"). Shortly before and after Grundy's death, J. Elliott published about four hundred of Grundy's titles, mostly "Rural England" but including geographic localities such as "on the Lledr, North Wales," all of them available tinted or untinted. These rural artistic scenes were not intended to illustrate specific locales, rather, they typify peaceful nature. Figure 33.

The J. Elliott issues bear an imprint naming both Grundy and Elliott. Grundy usually scratched a number on the negative, often preceding it with the letter "G". The London Stereoscopic Company distributed these Elliott issues wholesale during the early 1860's.

J. Elliott also published a most beautiful series of twelve interior views of Westminster Abbey by Victor A. Prout (1860). See also Figure 41.

C. E. Elliott (London) published more than a thousand numbers between 1858 and 1872, exclusive of an unknown number of small issues produced for other photog-

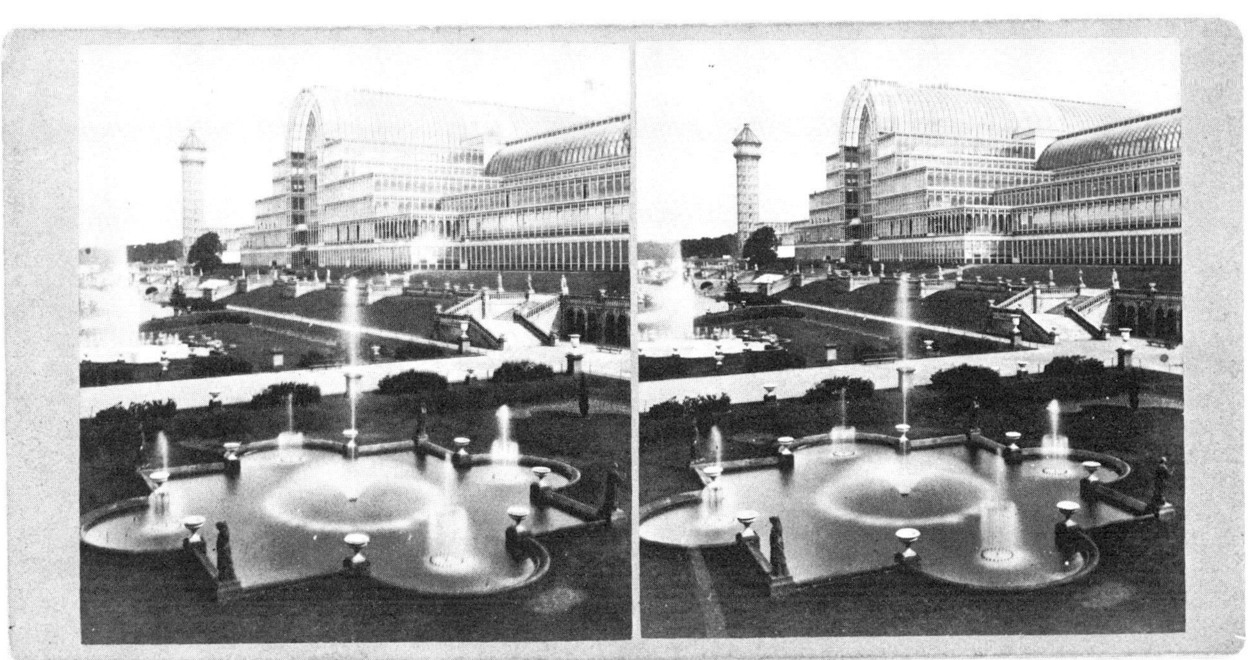

155. The Crystal Palace, rebuilt at Sydenham. William England photo, ca. 1860. London Stereoscopic Company publisher.

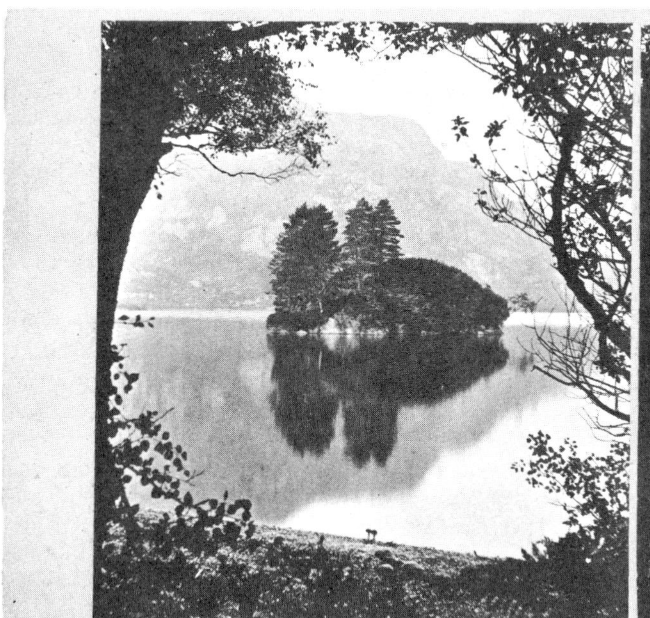
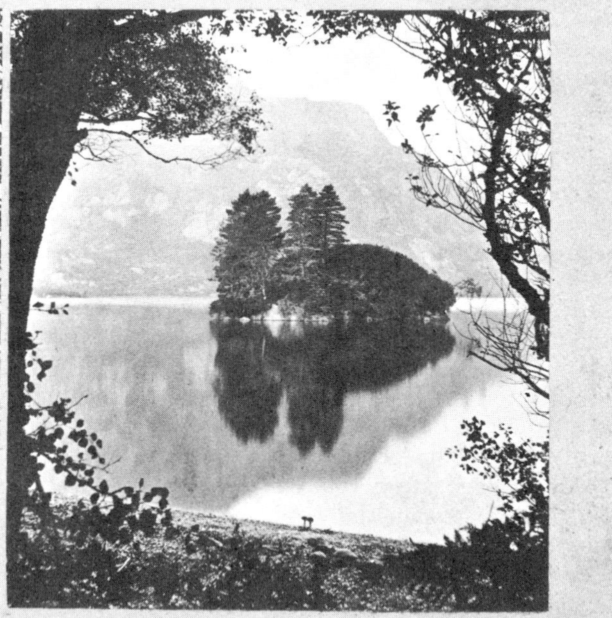

156. George W. Wilson. "Loch Katrine, Otter Island." 1858. Note framing and composition.

raphers. He seldom credited the photographer, a practice for which he was criticized by the editor of *Photographic News* (6:22, Jan. 10, 1861). In this instance the editor believed—correctly—that the negatives were by V. Blanchard. Among the unusual views published by C. E. Elliott is a fine series of the exhibits in the British Museum photographed by Blanchard.

. . . . . .

The two giants among British stereographers were George Washington Wilson, who had no peer in scenic photography, and Francis Bedford, a master of architectural photography.

George Washington Wilson (Aberdeen)

Wilson produced more than 2000 numbered titles between 1858 and 1872, but there were many more negatives used in his printings. For some numbers there were as many as eight or ten distinct negatives, some taken years apart, of the same or similar scene. Particularly among the earlier numbers, the substituted negatives were identified as 121A, 121B, 121D, etc.

While not confining his field work to Scotland, Wilson certainly loved his homeland. His outdoor views are picturesque and panoramic. The viewer is not conscious of boundaries—the scene is almost limitless. His beautiful interiors are also extensive. Although interest is emphati-

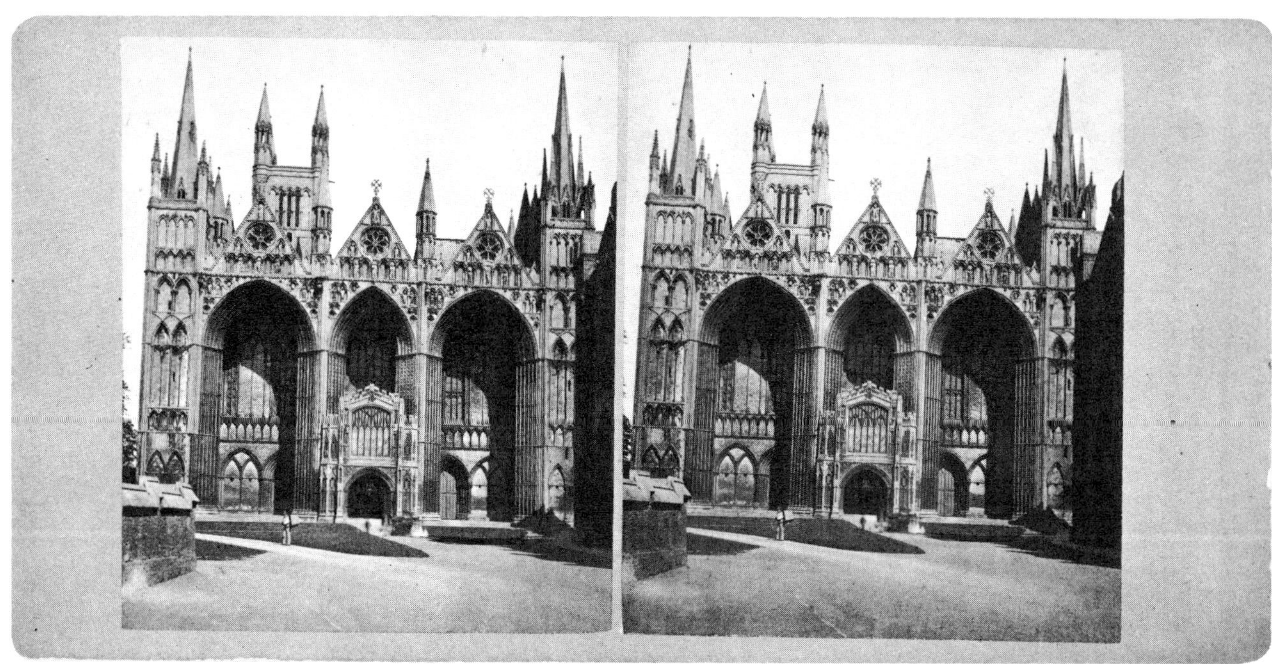

157. George W. Wilson. "Peterborough Cathedral, West Front." 1860.

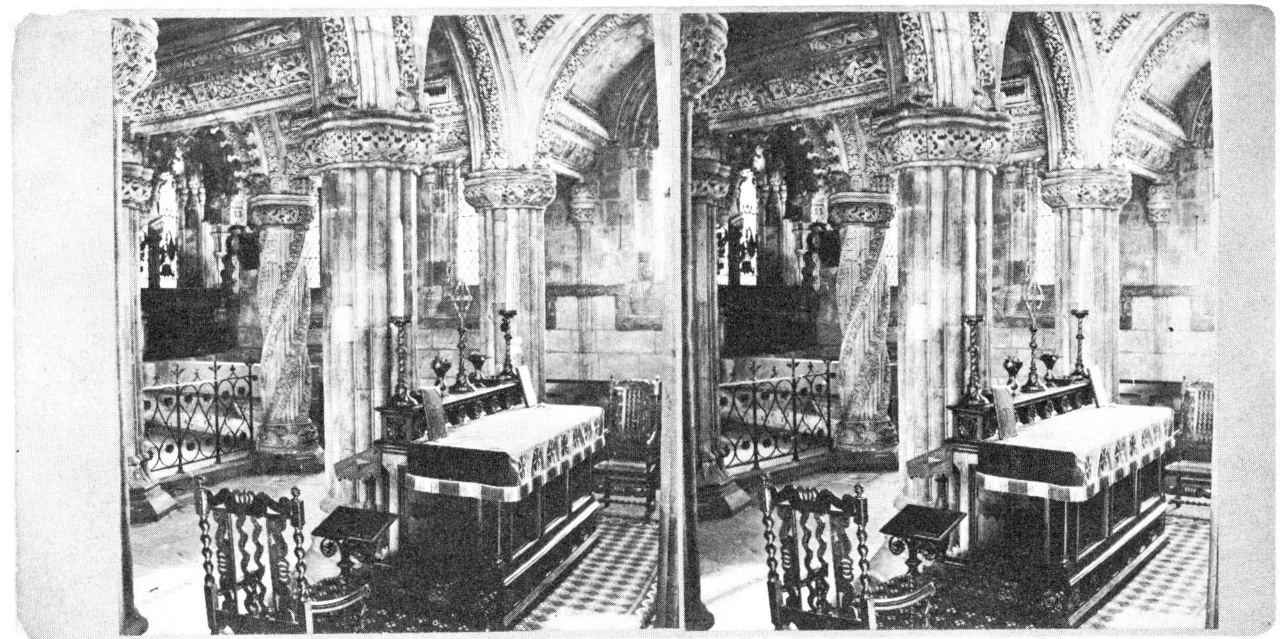

158. George W. Wilson. "Interior of Roslin Chapel." 1859.

cally directed to a center, the lateral detail, sometimes simple line, sometimes intricate, never detracts from the central object. Many photographers attempted to imitate Wilson's artistry, some quite successfully.

Wilson was among the first to achieve "instantaneous" photography. In 1857 he issued stereographs of the crowded pier at Greenwich, "Waiting for the boat," and ships of the Royal Navy firing broadsides. These famous views were at approximately one-fifth of a second exposure.

Francis Bedford

Between 1857 and 1863 Bedford produced more than two hundred stereographs, including both interiors and landscapes, mostly of Warwickshire. These magnificent views, which were published by Catherall & Pritchard (Chester), received awards "for great excellence" at the 1862 Exhibition. During the next seven years, Bedford covered England and Wales, building a huge file of negatives from which more than 3000 numbers were issued.

In 1862 Bedford began to arrange the views into approximately twenty-five series illustrating a county, town or district and bearing a uniform title and distinctive yellow mount. The following typical series suggest the breadth of his interests:

Bristol Illustrated
Chester Illustrated
Clifton Illustrated
Devonshire Illustrated
Exeter Illustrated
Gloucester Illustrated
Herefordshire Illustrated
Ludlow Illustrated
Monmouthshire Illustrated
North Wales Illustrated

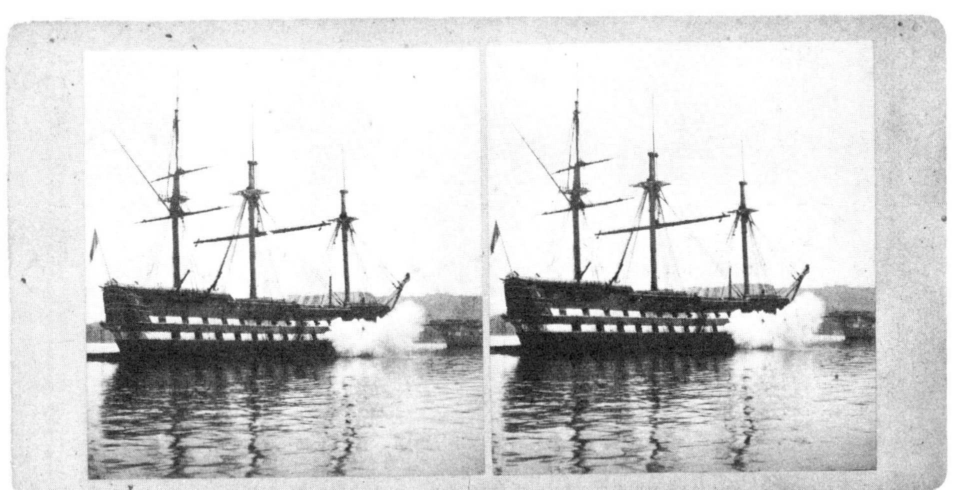

159. George W. Wilson. "H.M.S. Cambridge—Great Gun Practice." "Instantaneous," 1857.

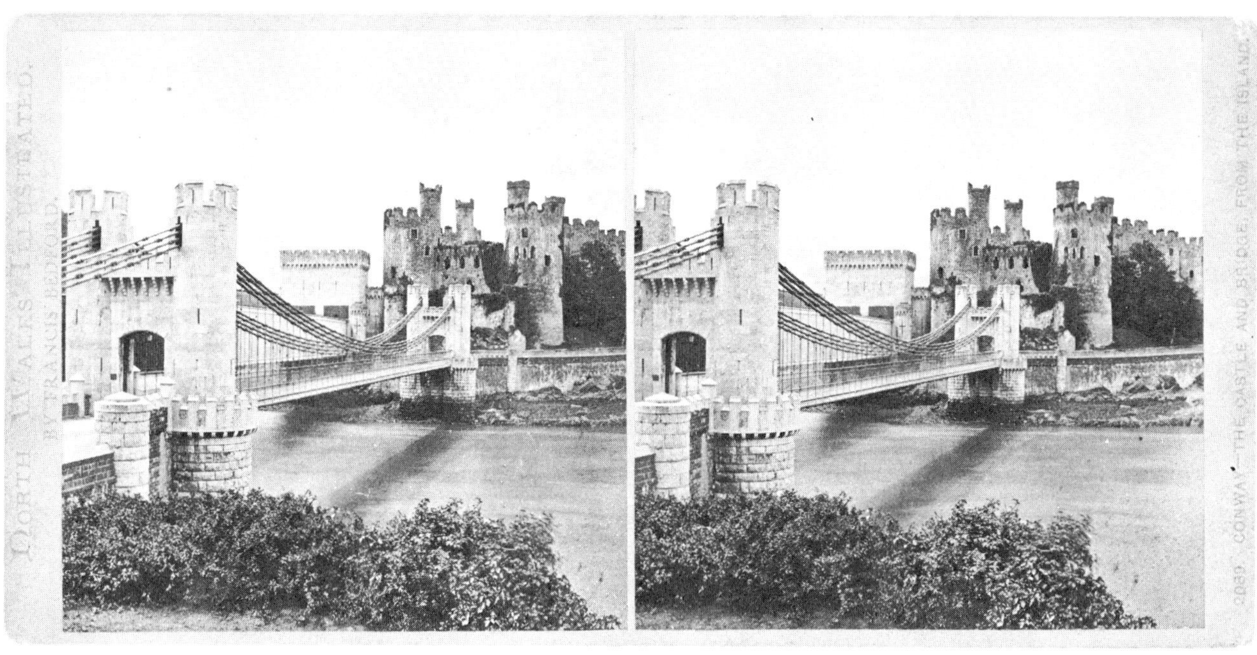

160. Francis Bedford. "Conway Castle." 1864.

South Wales Illustrated
Warwickshire Illustrated, etc.

One small sub-series was entitled "Welsh Costume,"

The majority of Bedford's stereographs include buildings, relatively few being purely natural scenery. The images are sharp, massive, yet with remarkable detail and center of interest. His cathedral interiors are among the finest ever produced.

William Russell Sedgfield

"English Scenery," a beautiful series photographed between 1855 and 1866, includes more than a thousand numbers. They were published by A. W. Bennett and sold exquisitely tinted and untinted. Sedgfield's views of cathedrals and abbeys are very different from those by Wilson. The effect is miniature, the surroundings framed. The interiors are more delicate and distant, the effect is total, not sharp, detail. Figure 42.

About 1870 prints from Sedgfield's negatives were offered for sale without a photographer's or publisher's imprint.

H. Petschler (Manchester, 1858-1865)

Petschler photographed extensively in England, Wales and Ireland, producing more than 1100 titles. He was succeeded in 1866 by the Manchester Photograph Com-

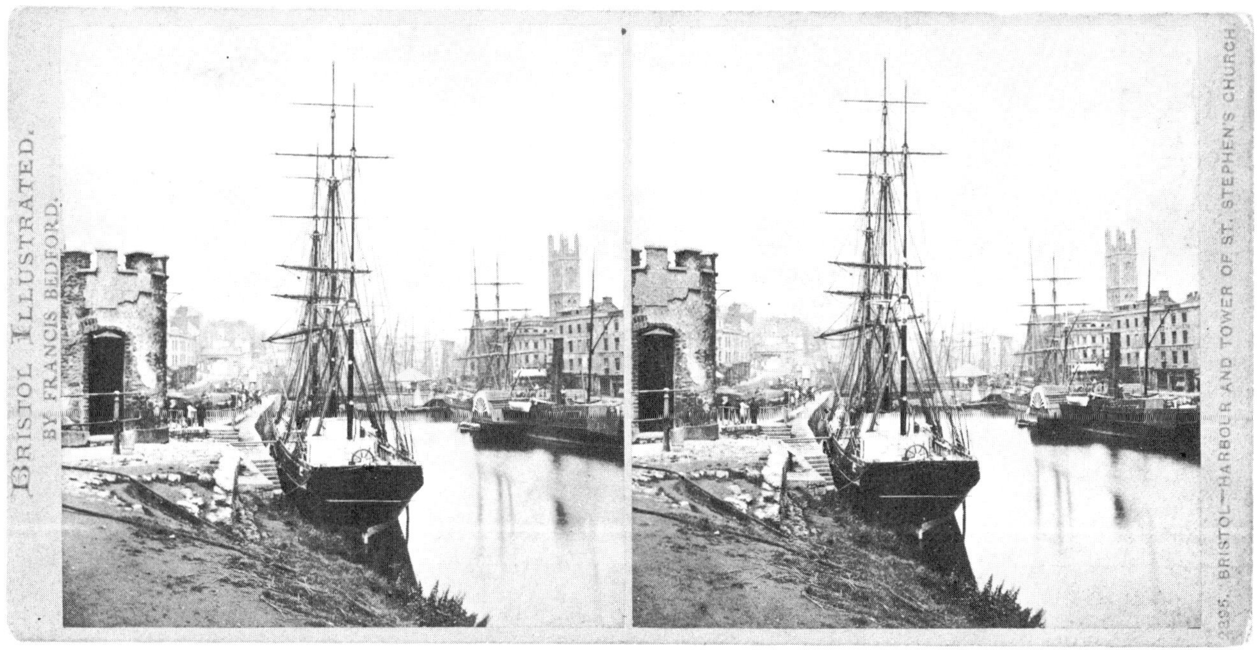

161. Francis Bedford. "Bristol Harbor." 1863.

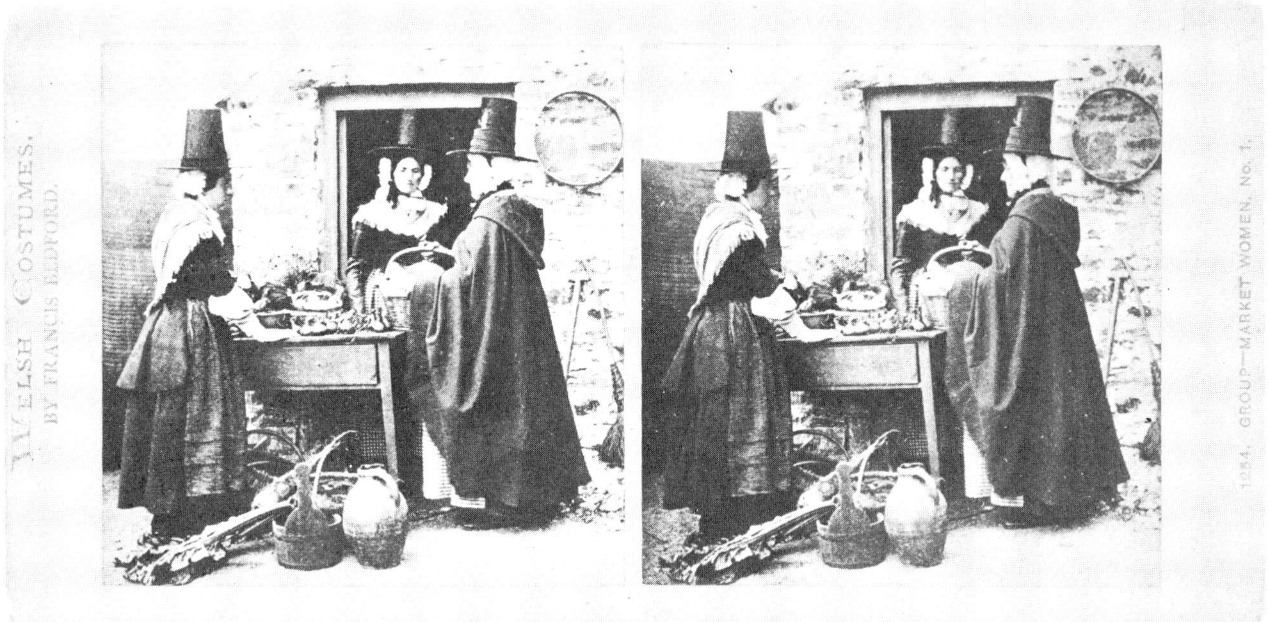

162. Francis Bedford. "Welsh Market Women." ca. 1864.

pany, which continued to publish his stereo views until 1875. The scenic views are picturesque and beautifully printed. Petschler deserves much greater recognition.

Ogle and Edge (Preston, Lancashire)

These two fine photographers, Thomas Ogle and Thomas Edge, in 1857 began issuing landscape and topographic views, in many respects similar to the work of Grundy and Fenton. The negatives are usually identified by the initials OE or, more rarely, TE. The trade list, which exceeded 500 numbers, was largely English and Welsh scenery, including beautiful views of castle and abbey ruins.

Among remarkable rustic scenes are

No. 58, "Old Mill on the river Stock Ambleside"
No. 88, "On the River Brock, near Preston"
No. 149, "The Crow Trees, Newby Bridge, Windermere"
No. 247, "Kirkstall Abbey, from the south," shows beautiful reflection in a placid stream.

They are usually found tinted but were also sold untinted. The series was distributed between 1857 and 1866. Figure 35.

Valentine Blanchard (London), ca. 1860-1872

Blanchard ranks close to Bedford in the production of fine architectural and scenic stereo views. The cards were published by C. E. Elliott, who did not credit Blanchard

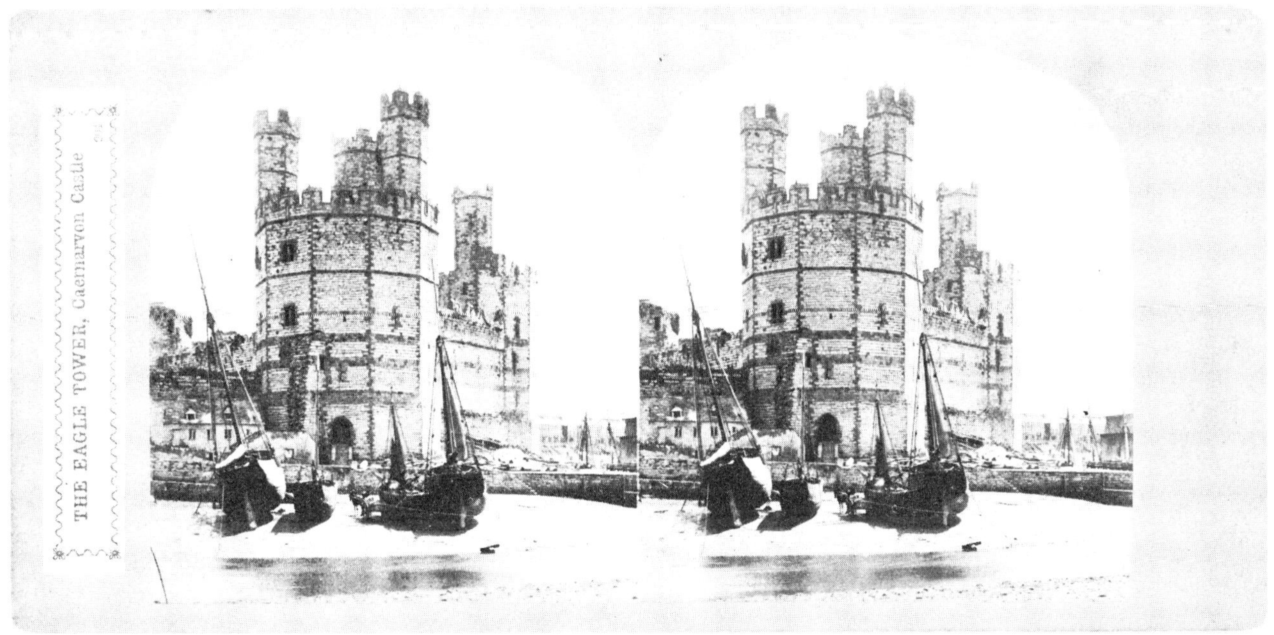

163. William Sedgfield. "Caernarvon Castle." Wales. 1862.

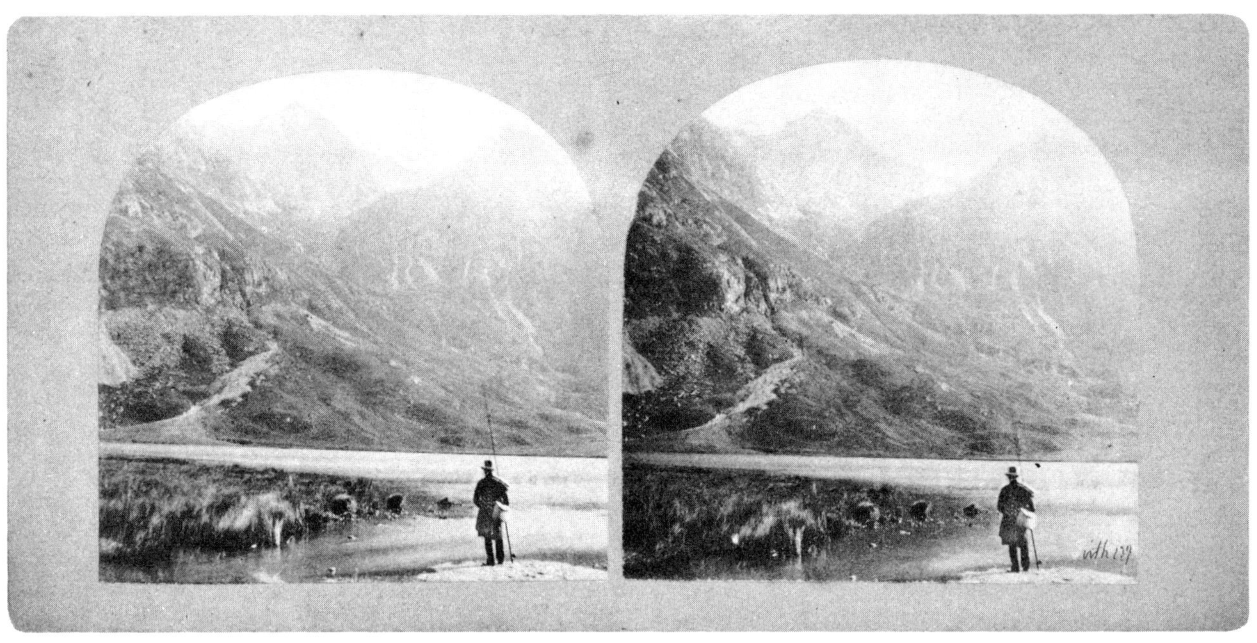

164. Francis Frith. "Glencoe, The Lock, Scotland." Negative ca. 1856.

in the earlier issues (1861). Beginning in 1863, however, Blanchard's name is usually given. The town scenes, especially those of London (Nos. 140-240), Ramsgate and Margate, taken by instantaneous photography, are interesting. No. 146, "Evening the Port of London," and No. 274, "An Angry Sea," are striking.

Francis Frith. ca. 1854-1863

Francis Frith produced several hundred scenic views of England and Wales. The earliest issues are on thin lavender cards with titles written in Frith's hand. These precede his Egyptian and Near East views.

About 1860, when Frith commenced to publish independently, the English views were reissued on light gray card mounts. The prints are generally light, lack contrast and technically do not compare with his Egyptian work. As was his custom, Frith signed his negatives. In their time, these English countryside scenes were greatly admired, but today they seem to have been less imaginative than the views by Wilson, Ogle and Edge or Bedford.

Roger Fenton

Although Fenton is best known for his Crimean war photography and for his still life stereos, he produced many exquisite scenic views of England and Wales. Figure 38.

Local Photographers

Between 1856 and 1872 nearly every town in the British Isles had at least one resident stereographer. The following photographers issued local or regional views of excellent artistic and technical qualities.

Allen, R.	Nottingham
Ambrose, J. W.	Beaumaris
Bainbridge, J. T.	Bradford
Baldry, W.	Grasmere
Bampton, Eugene	Chatsworth
Barber & Marks	Bristol
Barker, W. B.	Leamington
Beck, J.	Leamington
Beckett,	Scarborough
Bell, W.	Peterboro
Bennett, A. W.	London
Boole, A. & J.	London
Booth, H. C.	Bradford
Bowness	Ambleside
Britton	London
Browne & Wheeler	Cowes
Buckman, C. H.	Dover
Burns, Archibald	Edinburgh
Burton, J. Davis	London
Campbell, G.	Edinburgh
Carlyle	Grasmere
Child, W.	Leeds
Clark, John	Matlock
Clark, W.	Bristol
Clarke, J. S.	Peterborough
Collen, H.	St. Albans
Collister & Kieg	Douglas
Cooke, H. T.	Warwick
Cramb, J.	Glasgow
Crowe, A.	Stirling
Daniels, W.	Tingrith, Woburn
Day, Robert	Bournemouth
Deighton, G.	Worcester
Delamotte, P. H.	Oxford
Diamond, H. W.	Kent
Dixon, H.	London
Downey, W. & D.	New Castle-on-Tyne
Drayson	Canterbury
Drury, H.	Canterbury
Dutton, J. J.	Bath
Earl, F. C.	Worcester
Ewing	Kinross
Fergus	Largs
Ferguson, W.	Keswick
Findlow, A.	Warwick

Fisher, W. T.	Yarmouth
Foster, P.	Surry
Garnett, J.	Windermere
Glaisby, W. P.	York
Godfray	Jersey
Gordon, A.	Aberdeen
Gray & Hall	Brighton
Groves & Little	Cardiff
Gulliver	Swansea
Gutch	Scotland
Haylor, W.	Pimlico
Heath, G.	Leamington
Hesketh, W. T.	Pembroke
Hills & Saunders	Oxford
Howe, T. L.	Cardiff
Hudson, F.	Ventnor
Hughes, Jabez	Ryde
Hutton, T. B.	Guernsey
Jamblin, John	Penmaenmawr
Jones, Frederick	London
Latham, John	Matlock
Lennie	Edinburgh
Manson, A.	Bridge of Allen
Marion, A.	London
May, W.	Devonport
Mayland, William	Cambridge
Mayle	Liverpool
Minshell & Hughes	Chester
Mowbray	Oxford
Napper	London
Ogier, E.	Jersey
Palmer, W.	Lynton
Paton, A.	Edinburgh
Pettitt, A.	Keswick
Poulton, S. & Son	London
Prince, W. L.	London
Robinson & Thompson	Liverpool
Seeley, A. & E.	Richmond Hill
Smith, Theophilus	Sheffield
Spreat, William	Exeter
Stearn	Cambridge
Stuart, F. G. O.	Norwood
Stuart, J.	Inverness
Symonds, J.	Ryde
Taylor, W. F.	Windsor
Taylor, J.	London
Twyman & Son	Ramsgate
Valentine, James	Dundee
Wallis, G.	Whitby
Warwick, J. A.	Derby
Waters, G.	Windermere
Way & Sons	Torquay
Wheeler & Day	Oxford
Widger, W.	Torquay
Willis, George	Scarborough
Wilson, Alexander	Leamington
Wingrabe, J.	Coventry
Winter & Sons	Beverly
Wiseman	Southampton
Woodward, William	Nottingham

Brief comments on a few of these may suggest what treasures can be found among the issues of such photographers.

Beck issued several hundred charming views of Leamington between 1858 and 1863, perhaps achieving a nearly complete photographic survey of the town.

Burton produced a magnificent series of twenty-four views of the Tower of London, illustrating the structure, individual rooms, crown jewels, the costumed guard and ceremonies.

Cramb was one of the earliest stereographers in Glasgow, issuing fine card views as early as 1853.

Delamotte, whose stereo work was largely confined to the 1850's, produced a very wide range of subjects. His beautiful views of Oxford placed him among the best local photographers.

Poulton produced some interesting stereographs of personalities as well as of scenes around London. His most unusual production was a large series (about 600 numbers) of the conservatories and specimen plants at Chatsworth. Photographically the series is of variable quality, there being many mediocre and even careless photographs. Even so, the series is probably the most complete pictorial record of living plants ever taken in a greenhouse collection.

William Woodward, who, like Delamotte, was an experimenter in the 1850's, produced magnificent scenic views and for a time was in the employ of the London Stereoscopic Company. Figures 34, 39.

Many additional English photographers will be cited in other sections of this book.

It has been widely believed that the popularity of stereographs in England had so declined by 1870 that production of them had almost ceased. This is completely untrue. A great change in the stereo trade had taken place. Although interest in novelties had diminished, tourist and export markets kept business at a profitably high rate.

The classic views by Wilson, Bedford, William England, Blanchard, Good, York and Sedgfield were exported in huge quantities to the United States, where a steady demand continued until the late 1870's. Wilson, England, Good and York actually added hundreds of titles to their trade lists after 1870.

Moreover, new photographers and publishers entered the field, although most of them catered to a cheaper trade. Fortescue Mann, for example, commenced operations about 1872 and remained active until 1900.

After 1896, following the renewed enthusiasm for stereographs in America and the invasion of European markets by American publishers, a number of English photographers produced stereo views in relatively large quantities. A few of the better series are listed here.

H. D. Girdwood's international enterprise (1908-1916), cited on page 52, was the most successful British stereo publisher in the twentieth century.

A. Seaman & Son (Chesterfield), ca. 1892-1905, advertised 1500 titles, "all natural subjects, no made up effects."

A. Saynor (Liverpool), ca. 1895-1908, for a time agent for Griffith and Griffith (1897-1900), was also a publisher of stereo views.

Erdman & Schanz (London)

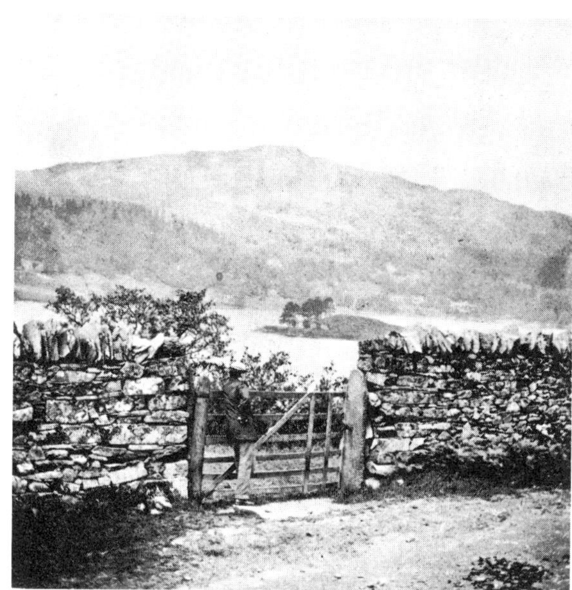

165. "The Wishing Gate." Grasmere. Baldry photo, ca. 1863. Autographed on back.

Frank Nicholls (Shanklin)
Bunney (Liverpool and Llandudno)
Alfred Newton (Leicester)

IRELAND

The London Stereoscopic Company in 1858 sent William England to photograph extensively in Ireland, although most of his negatives were from counties Killarney and Cork. About the same time Negretti and Zambra (1858) published a series of views, including a number of scenes of Dublin and Belfast. Beginning in 1859 H. Petschler (Manchester) issued a beautiful series, both tinted and untinted, ultimately including nearly 250 Irish titles (on yellow mounts, 1860-1870; also on green mounts, 1864-1870). W. D. Hemphill distributed a small series of beautiful Irish scenery ca. 1861-1864.

Stereographs published by Irish photographers, particularly before 1870, are quite rare. James Magill (Belfast) produced excellent scenes of the city between 1862 and 1872. E. G. Mare (Dublin), photographer-publisher-dealer, produced a series of views of that city about 1870-1872. The negatives may have been taken by James H. Burke, who issued a few Dublin scenes under his own imprint, 1863-1870. William Mansfield (Dublin) issued a series, "The Lakes of Killarney," in the later 1860's. He is presumed to have taken the photographs. Somewhat earlier, Yeates & Son (Dublin) published a "Series of views at and near the Giant's Causeway, county Antrim." The photographer has not been identified but is assumed to have been Yeates, Senior. A. Lesage and W. Lawrence, both of Dublin, published views about 1870.

The largest and best-known popular series was "Hudson's Irish Scenery," an extensive run of more than 900 titles. They were in continuous production from 1862 (earlier?) to 1872, at which time the stereo views were being sold without publisher's imprint.

Beginning in 1872 the reprinted Hudson views were issued as the "Eblana Series—Gems of Irish Scenery," appearing first on yellow or green mounts and in 1874 on inferior orange-brown mounts. William Rodman & Company (Belfast) was the publisher and distributor, at least for the period 1872-1875. The series was enlarged by the addition of a few original titles and some replacement negatives. Many of the titles were produced from copy negatives made from old prints. The quality declined progressively, yet the series was in production until 1890, probably later.

It is rather surprising that the several thousand different stereographs of Ireland taken between 1856 and 1875 seldom show the Irish people. Of course, one can find an occasional view of a cottager or a cart with a driver and a passenger, but the record is essentially scenic and architectural.

Not until Underwood sent a staff-photographer to Ireland just before 1900 did we have stereographs of cottagers, peat cutters, linen workers, children at play, cobblestone village streets or the hard, simple life. Only then did the photographer record a faithful picture story in stereo.

Foreign Photographers

Few non-British photographers before 1880 issued stereographs of the British Isles on a commercial basis. Probably, the large number of able natives discouraged outsiders.

J. Queval (ca. 1868-72), who had studios in London and Paris, issued a series of approximately 150 numbers with titles and imprint in both French and English. The prints are excellent but the subjects are commonplace.

E. Linde & Co. (Berlin) maintained a London branch (ca. 1865-1875) and also issued a small series of views of London and vicinity, with titles in English and German.

B. W. Kilburn in 1877 issued a series of views on both standard and cabinet mounts. The subjects include ruins of castles, abbeys and city views of England, Scotland and Ireland. The photography is good but, again, the subjects are of the usual tourist sites.

Throughout the 1880's and 1890's, Kilburn added several hundred views of England and Ireland to his trade list. The most important of these concern Queen Victoria, but there are also some excellent harbor scenes of Liverpool and views of busy London.

Jarvis (Washington, D. C.) in the early 1880's produced approximately 150 titles from negatives he had taken on a trip to England.

With the advent of the boxed sets of a hundred views, issued by several American publishers, a large number of negatives were taken by a score of photographers. There is great similarity in these sets, primarily because, as tours, they cover the same ground and the same scenes. The two most interesting are the sets issued by Underwood & Underwood and H. C. White. Both include exceptional graphic scenes of London and Southampton.

The British photographers were pioneers and practitioners in every category of stereography. They toured many countries in the 1850's and 1860's and contributed substantially to artistic aspects of stereographs. Many additional first-rate British photographers will be discussed under appropriate headings throughout this book. Similarly, British involvement in Colonial enterprises, the Boer War and World War I will be considered under those headings.

CHAPTER ELEVEN

CONTINENTAL EUROPE

Stereographs of Continental Europe are not as well known as those of England and North America. Even though French photographers were pioneers in stereo and stereographs were popular fully a year earlier than in England, the work of individual photographers is only sketchily known.

Most of the European stereographs distributed in the United States prior to 1890 were imported. Relatively few were purchased as mementos by American tourists. As a result the familiar views were produced by a few large publishers, and the works of local photographers are scarce.

There are some peculiarities in the scope of stereography in Europe which must be noted. Europe between 1840 and 1880, indeed, throughout the nineteenth century, was torn by political unrest. Ethnic cultures sought political independence. The struggle for civil rights permeated all aspects of national life. France, Switzerland, Italy, Germany and Austria experienced not only internal difficulties but also hostilities with their neighboring countries. Not until 1870 and 1871 were Italy and then Germany unified as nations. Religious strife, including restriction of the Papacy, further complicated the times.

In many countries it was necessary to obtain from the police a permit to own or use a camera. Thus photographic documentation of these underlying currents is virtually absent. Stereo views with even a hint of political implications are extremely rare. While there are many beautiful series showing imperial residences, cathedrals, historical landmarks, market places and peasants, these are invariably serene and picturesque. Of course, there are views of armies, parades, international exhibitions and occasional natural disasters, but these, in themselves, are innocuous.

Portraits, compositions, the humorous and the burlesque were common in France and Germany but virtually absent in all other European countries, excepting Italy. Nevertheless, the artistic quality of many of the stereographs between 1850 and '80 ranks among the best.

FRANCE

Louis Napoleon declared himself Emperor Napoleon III in 1852. The political ineptness and difficulties that ensued were hidden behind an external magnificence symbolized by the Imperial palaces and the rebuilding of Paris.

In 1853 George Haussmann was appointed to transform Paris from a decaying city into a glorious capital (1855-69). Twenty thousand houses were demolished and twice that number of new structures were erected. Broad boulevards, designed for military security as well as convenience, traversed and encircled the city. Haussmann planned the Bois de Boulogne, one of the most famous public parks in the world. "Paris Nouveau" became the pride of France, despite the staggering cost.

In 1855 the International Exhibition, patterned after the London Exhibition of 1851, was held on the Champs Elysees. The exhibits were housed in the Palais d'Industrie, already under construction, and the Rotunda, which stood in the public gardens. To accommodate the displays of machinery, a sprawling one-story building nearly three-quarters of a mile long was erected on the bank of River Seine. In 1867 another International Exhibition was held in Paris. This most ambitious project established the pattern for all subsequent exhibitions. There were buildings by foreign governments, structures to house special exhibits, concessions for food service and for the sale of souvenirs. Figures 23, 24, 235.

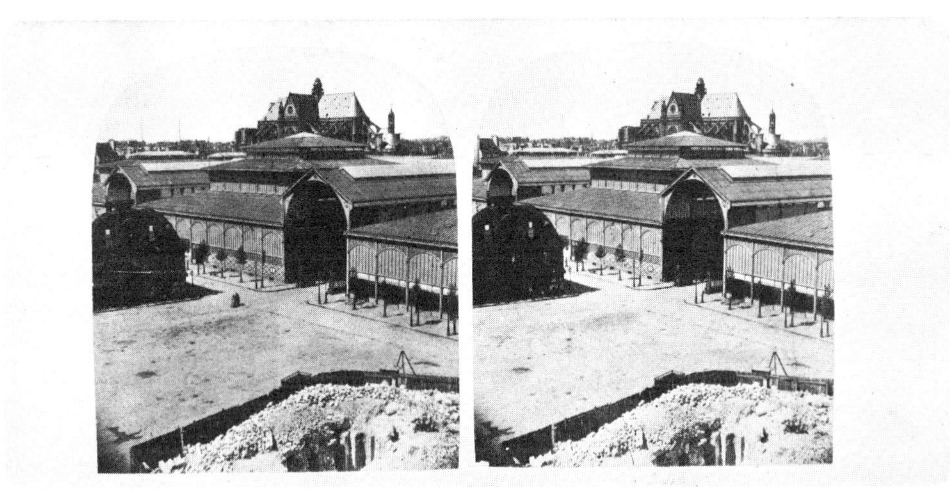

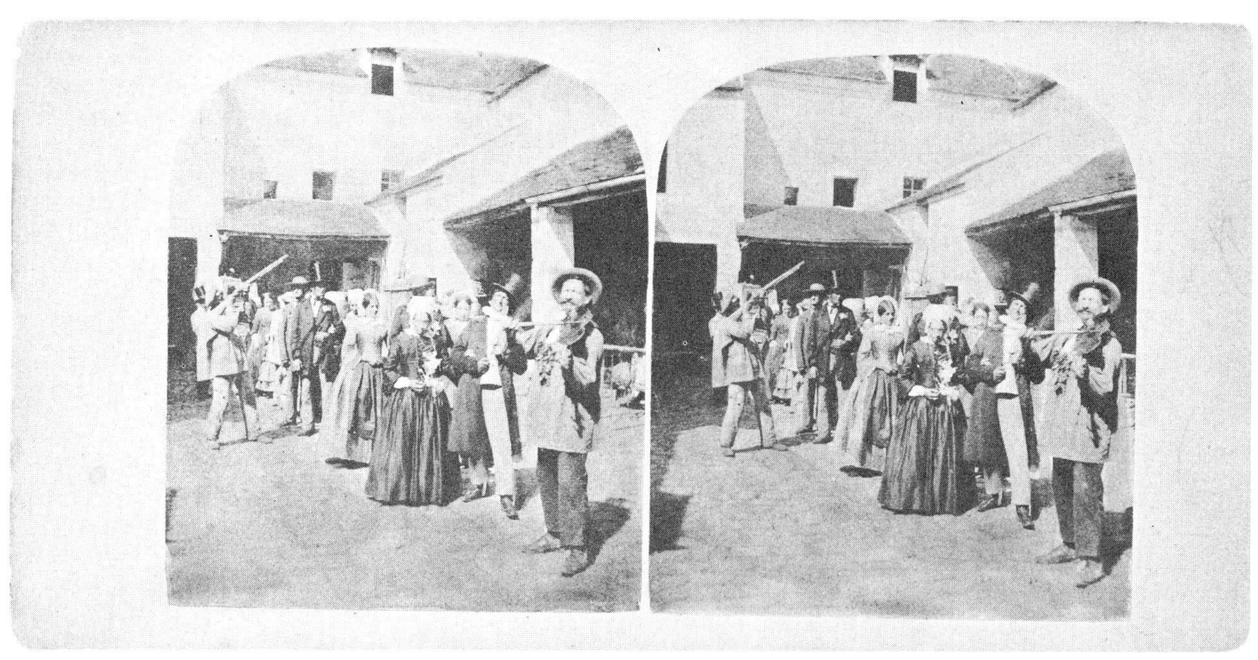

167. France. "Peasant Wedding." Unknown photographer, ca. 1856.

France was ineffectually involved in the Crimean War (1855), Austro-Italian War (1859) and in Mexico (1866-67). The war with Germany (1870-71) was quite different. France declared war on Germany, but things went badly from the start. Napoleon III was captured with his troops at Sedan. Paris was besieged for four months, and the victorious German army entered the city on March 1, 1871.

The tragedy of civil war followed. On March 28 the Commune seized Paris, and the French Royalist armies began the second seige of Paris. The embattled communards set fire to the city on May 23, creating a period of terror. Peace was restored gradually, and on June 29, 1871, 120,000 government troops marched in review along the Longchamp Race Track.

Yet with incredible speed the historic buildings were restored to their former magnificence. By 1875 few scars of the civil war remained.

Peasant life remained almost untouched by these political events. There are many charming views of the work and simple pleasures of the peasantry, especially by Malizard. Figures 166-168, 272.

The stereographs of France record a considerable part of this story. The great decade of Haussmann's transformation of Paris was thoroughly photographed. Many beautiful series of views bear the title "Paris Nouveau."

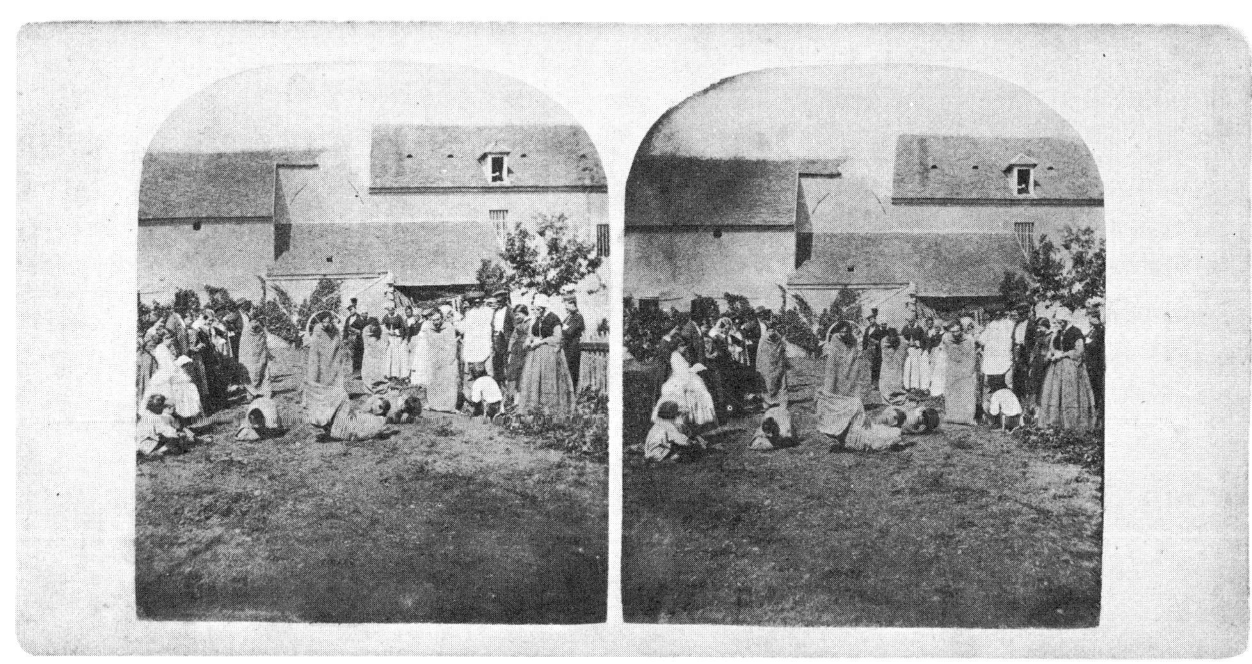

168. France. "Sack Race." Unknown photographer, ca. 1856.

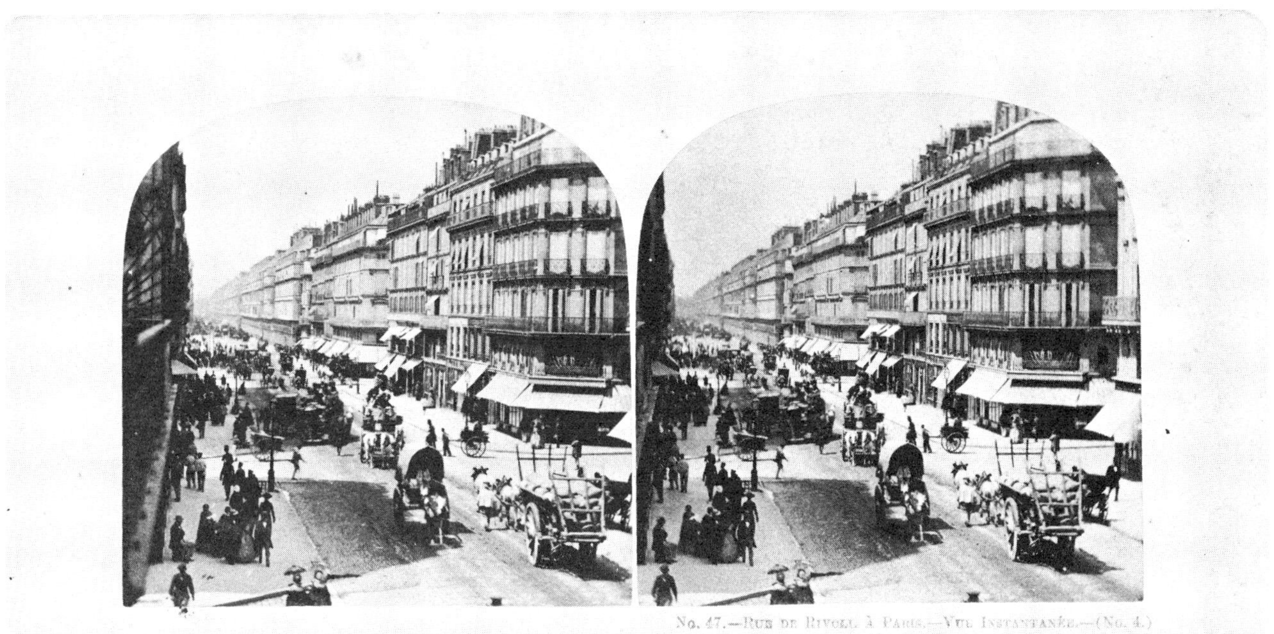

169. France, Paris. "Rue de Rivole." William England photo, 1860.

The boulevards lined with fine structures six or eight stories high were impressive. The finest views of Paris Nouveau, however, were not made by a Frenchman but by William England (1861, 1862).

The 1855 International Exhibition was stereographed by at least five, probably more, photographers. The contemporary prints are calotypes mounted on thin blue, green, gray or brown card stock. None that I have examined bear the name or initials of the photographer.

There are many views of French military forts, troops on parade and in camp and in humorous poses at leisure. The best known, but rare, views are those of Camp de Chalon issued by Le Gray in 1857 and '58 on buff or off-white cards. Cards of the first issue bear a small blue-bordered white label. Later issues have only manuscript titles on the backs. Figure 254.

To tourists, Paris was its great churches, the Louvre, the Seine and its bridges, the Arc de Triomphe and Place de l'Opera. These landmarks were photographed hundreds of times, as were Place de la Concorde and Place de la Bastille. Many views show architectural detail, stained glass windows and statuary. Versailles was likewise repeatedly photographed.

Views of the Franco-Prussian War are generally of towns damaged by bombardment and bridges blown up to impede troop movements. I have seen no French views comparable to the American Civil War battlefield scenes by Gardner or Brady.

The destruction of Paris under the Commune was well photographed. Panoramic and detailed views of burned-out buildings attest to the ferocity of the struggle. Many of the scenes showing street barricades, especially those manned by fighters, were staged and as such must be considered to be fakes. The series by M. Appert is suspect.

Notable French Stereographers

Richebourg between 1852 and '60 published a wide variety of views of Paris, much of France, Rome, Pompeii, Athens, Russia, Spain and Algeria. His views are generally identified by the letter "R" in many variants, blind-stamped and printed. Richebourg also used hand-stamped imprints. Many of his early calotypes have faded. Figure 201.

Theodorine d'Harcourt in 1858 published a beautiful series of views of Paris. Descriptive notes in French and English are printed on the backs.

Mayer and Pierson (1858) produced fine stereo portraits of Emperor Napoleon and Empress Eugenie. An extensive series illustrating the Imperial residences is attributed to Mayer and Pierson, although their imprint does not appear on the mount. The series may be identified by the royal crest embossed at the upper center of the card face.

Olivier (1858-62) published on waxed cards an excellent series illustrating historical monuments of France. The titles are given in French and English

Much better known than these early photographers are the great publishers, Ferrier, Soulier and Braun.

Claude M. Ferrier (later, Ferrier Pere & Fils & Soulier)[1] produced the world's finest glass stereographs, although all known titles were available on card mounts. Fine ivory card mounts were issued between 1857 and '62. The trade list ultimately exceeded 40,000 titles. The Ferrier production includes a wide selection of scenes from Europe, the Near East and North Africa.

In 1867 the stereographic department of the Ferrier company passed to Leon & Levy, who continued to manufacture glass views of the highest quality and a huge variety of card stereographs. Leon & Levy printed the glass views for many foreign photographers, including those of F. York and Frank Good.

Leon & Levy held the official monopoly for photo-

[1] Alexander Ferrier and Charles Soulier.

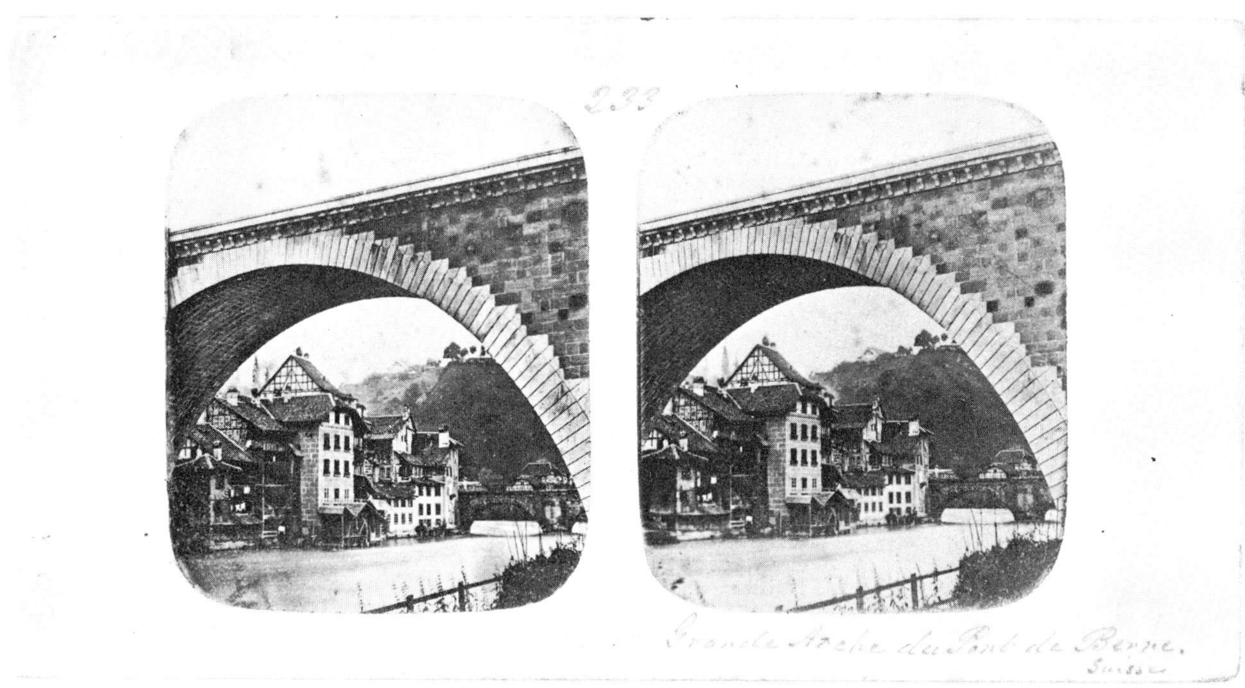

170. C.M. Ferrier. "Grand arch of the bridge at Berne, Switzerland." 1859.

graphing the International Exhibition of 1867. Many remarkable series identified by the letters "LL" were issued by them between 1867 and '80.

A. Braun of Dornach (Upper Rhine, French until 1871; thereafter, German) began publishing stereo views in 1856. Braun achieved fame for his magnificent alpine scenic views. By 1866 his trade list exceeded 6000 titles and by 1871, 8500. The earlier images do not show the striking composition, shadows or panoramic impact that delighted viewers for a quarter of a century. About two-thirds of the trade list are of alpine scenery, the remainder includes fine views of Belgium, Holland and the Rhine Valley. In 1868 Braun published a splendid series, "Costumes of Switzerland" (sixty numbers). About 1871 Anthony published under its own imprint a selected series of Braun's Swiss views from prints purchased from him.

Little-known but deserving of recognition was Jouvin (ca. 1860-68), who published a large number of views grouped into small series, such as "Voyage en Normandie," "Voyage en Bretagne," "Midi du France," "Voyage en Italie," etc. The early issues are on lavender, blue or green mounts with boxed titles on the face. Only the early issues bear a Jouvin imprint. These beautiful views resemble the English artistic genre. Figure 40.

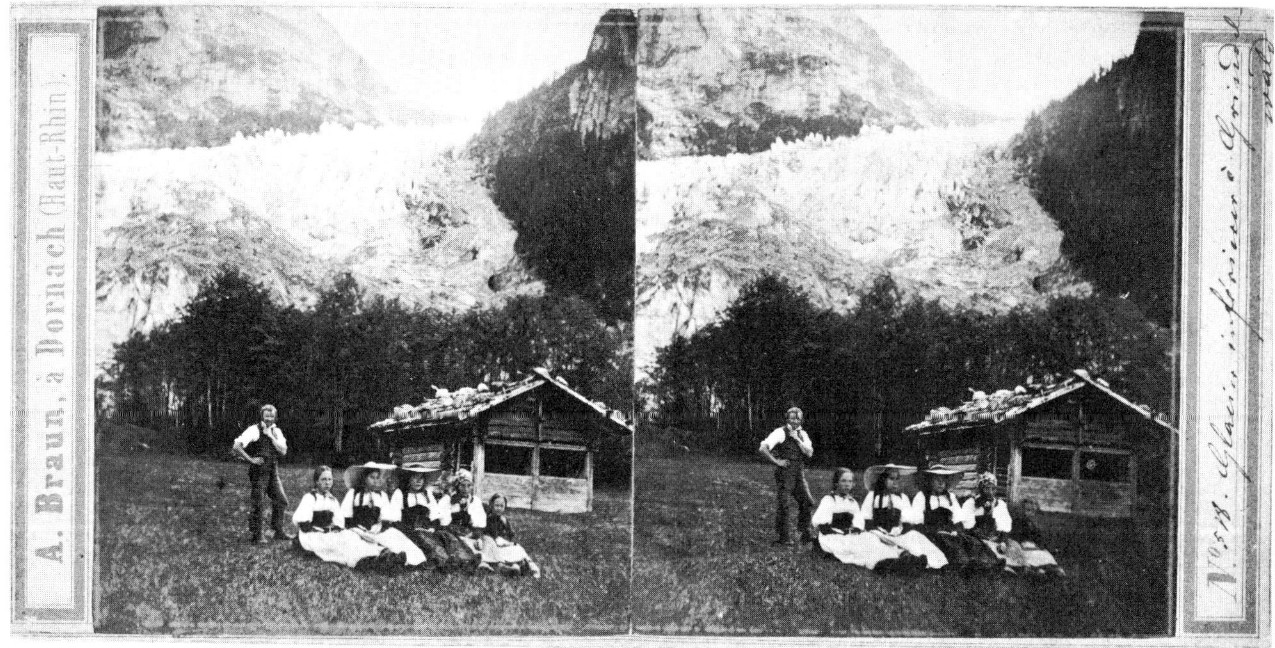

171. A. Braun. "Base of the Grindelwald Glacier, Switzerland." A fine typical example of Braun's composition. 1858.

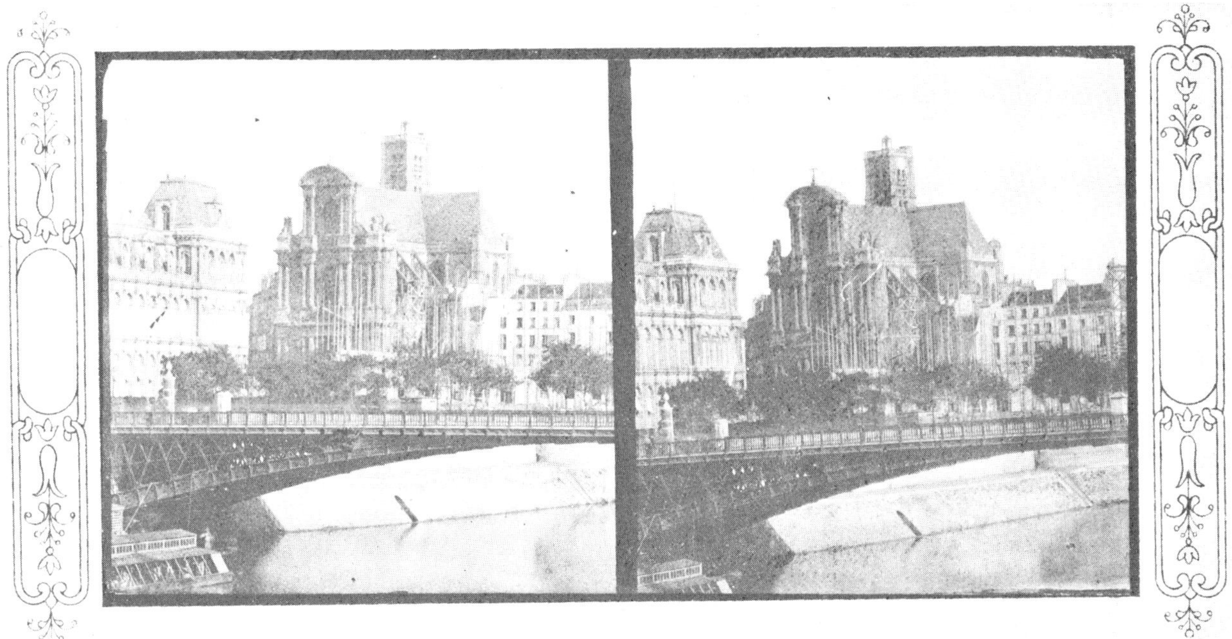

172. France, Paris. "Church of St. Gervais." Descriptive notes in French and English on back. Olivier Brothers photo, 1860.

Baldus (1856-68), official photographer for the Louvre, issued many fine views of the galleries in the museum and of individual pieces of statuary.

Bisson Freres (1860's), under the title "Collection Bisson," issued many fine views of France and Switzerland. Their later negatives of scenes in Syria, Damascus and Egypt were published by Leon & Levy.

Lallemond, in collaboration with Hart (Paris, London & Strasbourg, 1862-66), produced a remarkable series, "Galerie Universelle des Peuples," intended to illustrate the native costumes and peoples of the world. More than 600 titles are known, but the project never extended beyond Europe and North Africa. The cards were available tinted and untinted. Although the quality of tinting is variable, the best are exquisite. Figures 47, 48.

During the period 1865-80 there were several hundred active stereographers in France. Some of these, like E. Frioux of Lourdes, catered entirely to local interests; but many others developed successful large-scale publishing businesses.

Most notable of these was J. Andrieu. Early issues bear his name, but later on the initials "JA" appear on the

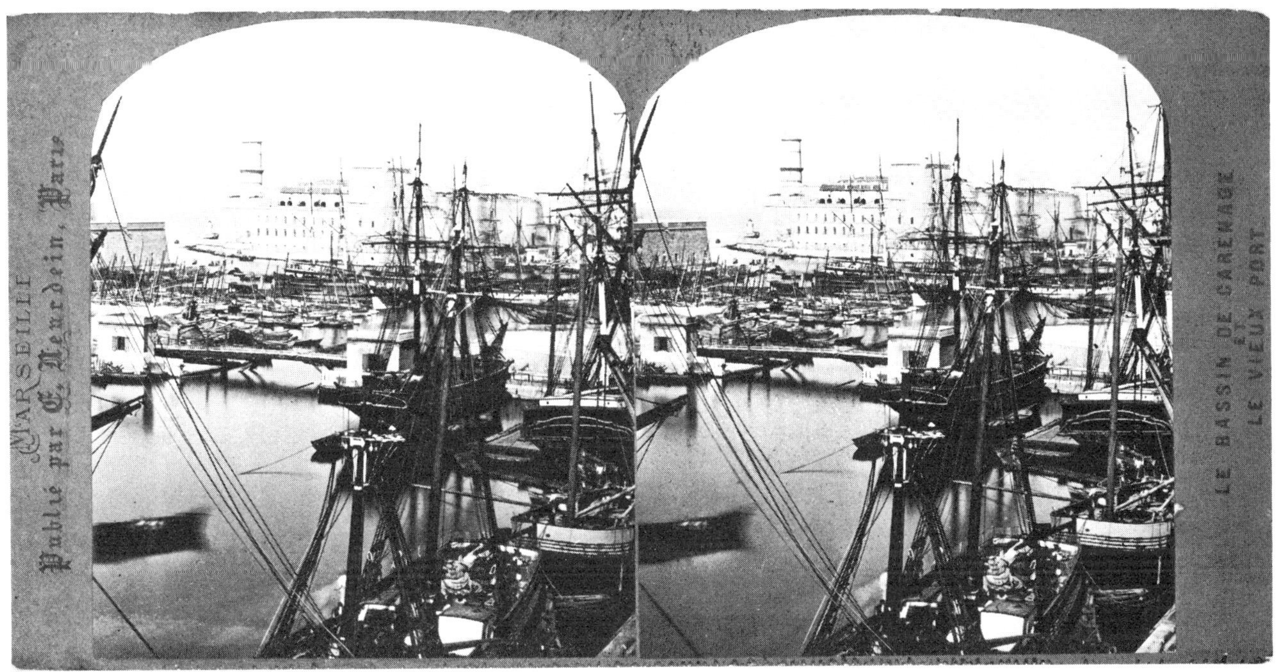

173. France, Marseilles. The Harbor. C. Neurdein photo, ca. 1865.

cards. Andrieu ultimately accumulated a trade list of more than 9000 titles, covering much of Europe, Egypt, Algeria and the Near East. Among his more important issues are the series on the destruction of Paris during the Commune.

E. Lamy also ranks as a master photographer with fine series on France, Belgium, Holland, the Rhine and Italy.

Notable Parisian photographers who produced excellent stereo views include:

Numa Blanc
Champaign
D. Charnay
Edward Delepert
Delton
A. Disderi
Drier
Duroni & Maurer
F. Fescourt
Leon Foucault
F. Franck
Gaston & Mathieu
Charles Gerard
Gouin
Henry Guerard
A. & M. Hanriot
A. Hautecoeur
Herve & Debitte
J. Kuhn
Ch. Lallemond
A. J. Liebert
A. Marion
Charles Marville
Adolphe Moreau
A. Quinet
Thibault
Jules Valecki
Vimard
Walevy
E. Ziegler

The following list includes notable local photographers who produced unusually striking stereo views of their vicinities between 1860 and '80.

Bohm	Mulhouse
Chartier	Nice
de Charley	Renaison
G. Dardel	Mulhouse
L. N. DeCroix	Boulogne-sur-Mer
Davanne & Aleo	Mentone
E. Degand	Nice
DeMay	Aix les Bains
Dumas	Nismes
Falkenstein	Strasbourg
Fescourt	Paris, Nismes
E. Fietta	Strasbourg
E. Frioux	Lourdes
Froissart	Lyon
Furne, Jr.	Cherbourg
Gallot	Cherbourg
J. Garnier	Avignon
Grenier Bros.	Bischweiler
Hamelaine	Rouen
C. Jacquard	Sedan
A. Michaud	Oisant
L. Moilessier	Montpelier
Muzet & Joquet	Lyon, Grenoble
E. Neurdein	Paris, Marseilles
Oberthur & Fils	Rennes
F. Peter	Strasbourg
V. Platel	Toulon
Tairraz & Savioz	Chamonix
Visconti	Nice
Mme. V. Weill	Strasbourg

Hamelaine's fine series "Midi de la France" was available exquisitely tinted.

Excellent seaport scenes are to be found in Platel's "Les Bordes de la Mediterrane."

There are two practices in French stereography, that inevitably puzzle the collector or historian. The identical view may be found as both a fine sharp image mounted on an enameled card of the best quality and a mediocre or poor image on several cheap grades of card, ranging from thick to thin, flimsy porous stock. Inexperience might confuse these thin mounts with thin cards manufactured in the 1850's.

The trade in stereographs in Paris was plagued by the

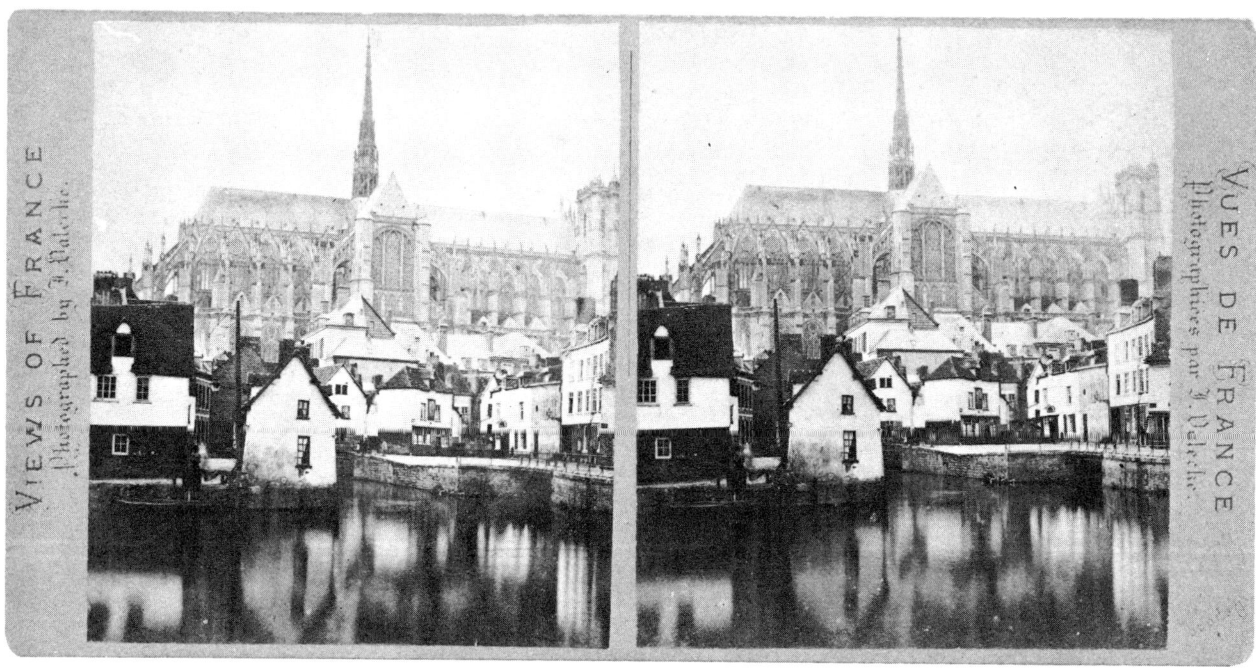

174. France, Amiens. The Cathedral. J. Valecki photo, ca. 1865.

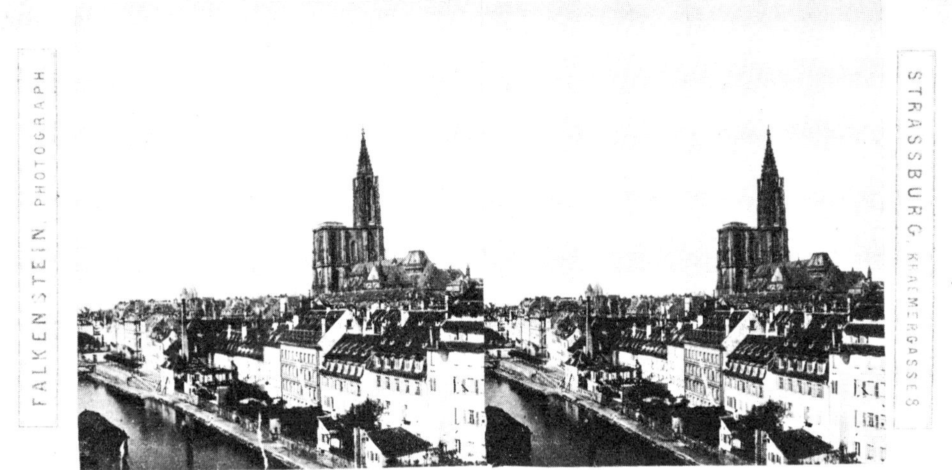

175. France (Germany) Strassburg. Falkenstein photo, negative ca. 1868, card issued 1872.

most brazen piracy. A fine view introduced by a reputable publisher was almost certain to be copied within two or three days by unscrupulous competitors. Thousands of such pirated views were sold to unsuspecting tourists at reduced prices. To combat this situation, some publishers printed the same series on two or three grades of card stock, which then could be sold wholesale at different prices.[2]

The only useful criteria for interpreting views which have no publisher's imprint are the relative quality of the image and card stock. Generally, if an imprint appears on the mount it is an original issue, but the reverse is not necessarily true.

The second problem confronting collectors arises with those views that have neither photographer's nor publisher's imprint. In the early and mid 1850's few photographers identified their own stereo work. This omission continued throughout the 1860's in much of Europe. The French in particular seemed inclined to omit their names. Many who did identify their views used only initials, sometimes so minutely printed or hidden that they escape notice. About 125 sets of initials have been recognized in French stereographs; barely one-third have been identified with certainty. Even among the "known" initials there is cause for confusion. At least three early photographers used "LL" as did Leon & Levy.

"JA" for J. Andrieu has been noted previously. Eight additional examples will be cited:

A H	A. Hautecoeur
C G	Charles Gerard
C.M.	Charles Marville
F.F.	F. Fescourt
J.L.	J. Laurent
L.F.	Leon Foucault
M.A.	M. Appert
N.B.	Numa Blanc

Some combinations of initials apply to more than one photographer:

A M	A. Marion, Adolphe Moreau
E.L.	Ernest Lacan, Ernst Ladry

Ultimately, French historians of photography will unravel the confusion of these important early stereographs.

Large-scale manufacture of stereo views in France continued into the mid 1880's. The decline in interest experienced in England did not affect the Continent. In fact, in 1872 the editor of *Photographic News* noted, "Every class and description of picture is to be purchased . . . of stereos in any multitude."[3]

There was noticeable decline in trade during the latter 1880's and '90's; but the International Exposition in Paris in 1900 excited considerable stereo activity, including the last commercial issue of glass views of standard size.

By this time, however, the enterprising American publishers, especially Underwood & Underwood and H. C. White, had firmly entrenched themselves as the leading distributors of stereo views. The Underwood "France" set, 100 cards, first issue 1900, is an outstanding example of travelogue photography. Monaco and its gambling casino at Monte Carlo were beautifully stereographed by Keystone View Company (1900-02). There are thirty numbers, including interiors of the gaming rooms.

Attention is directed to the role of France in World War I. France was the Western Front, the area in which American soldiers were primarily involved. Scattered among the hundreds of World War views are many of French towns and French people. See also, World War I, page 195.

ITALY

A large proportion of the stereographers operating in Rome, Florence and, to a lesser degree, other Italian cities were foreigners—French, German, English and

[2] Both Anthony and Wilson in the United States imported two grades of French views for their *wholesale* trade but retailed only first quality in their own emporia.

[3] *Photo. News* 16: 364, 1872.

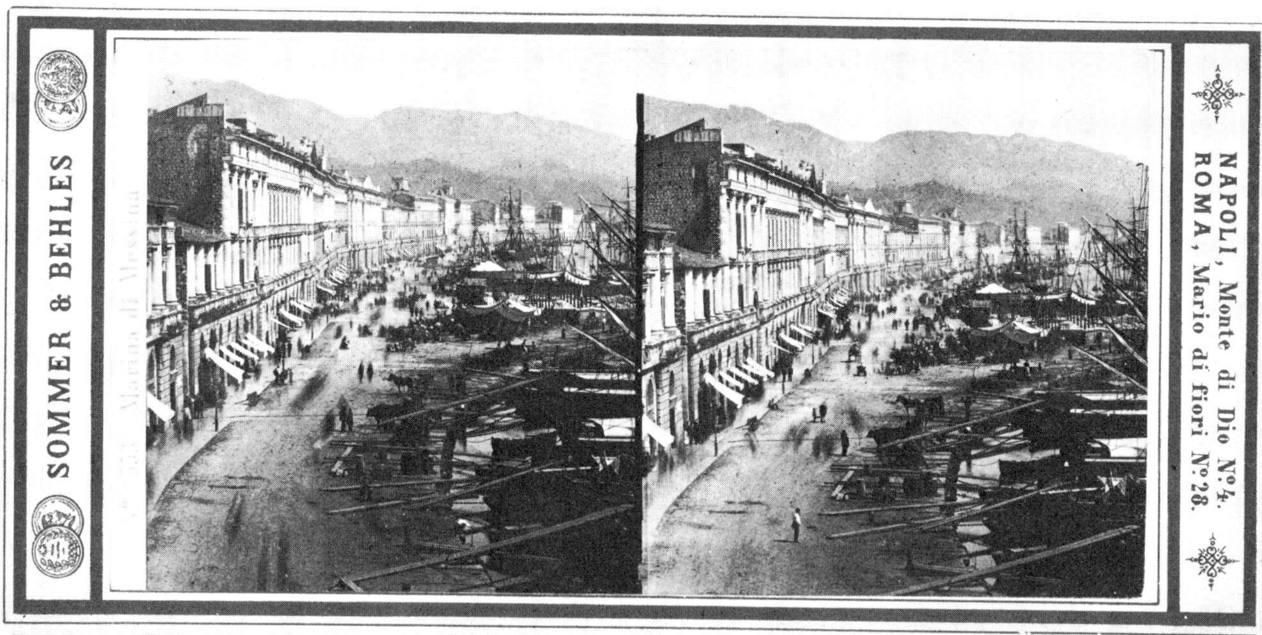

176. Italy, Messina. "The Marina." Sommer and Behles photo, ca. 1866.

American. In addition to these resident operators, hundreds of photographers visited Italy throughout the 1850's and '60's to take views of classic ruins of Rome and Pompeii and the famous buildings, especially in Florence and Venice. Elliott published about sixty views of Pompeii taken by C. E. Goodman in 1857-58. Most of the early views, as in France, have no photographer identification. There are, however, fine views by Charles Goodman, Richebourg, Ledot Jr., Melhuish and many others. The London Stereoscopic Company published a beautiful series simply titled "Italy" about 1857. S. Thompson in 1858 issued a fine series of Venice.

The following Italian photographers, selected from about 125 known to have issued stereographs, produced excellent views of their vicinities:

Alessandri Brothers Rome 1860's and '70's
Alinari Brothers Florence 1860's to '90's
Amodio & Sprungli (Amodio Brothers, Michele Amodio) Naples 1850's to '70's
G. Bacmeister Lake Maggiore 1860's
O. Baratti Milan 1860's
Bardi Florence 1860's and '70's
P. Barelli Milan 1860's
Alphonse Bernoud Naples and Florence 1850's to '70's
very fine early views, including scenes of Livorno
E. Bressanini Verona latter 1860's to '80's
more than 4600 numbers, including fine views of Milan, Pisa and Turin
C. Coen & E. Figlio Venice and Trieste 1860's to '70's
Giorgio Conrad Naples 1850's and '60's
Cuccione Rome 1860's and '70's
including views of Milan and Naples
Degoix Genoa 1860's and '70's
Duroni Milan 1860's (succeeded by Icilio Calzolari who continued to print from Duroni negatives)
Emilia Bologna latter 1860's and '70's
F. Fassina Milan 1860's
Ferrando Rome 1860's
Patrini Galeazzo Crema 1860's
Genazzini Bellagio 1860's and '70's
A. Godard Genoa 1850's and '60's
Hodcend Genoa 1860's
Paolo Lumbari Siena 1860's and '70's
Luswergh Rome 1850's and '60's
M. Mang Rome 1860's and '70's
Molins (Altobelli & Molins) Rome 1860's
Monaldino & Calisti Rome 1860's
C. Naya Venice 1860's and '70's
very fine images, especially noted for architectural detail and artful composition
Nessi Como 1860's
Alfredo Noack Genoa 1860's and '70's
approximately 3000 numbers
G. A. Ottico Rome 1860's
P. Passina Milan 1860's
A. Perini Venice 1850's into '60's
Carlo Ponti Venice latter 1860's to '90's
an excellent photographer, also publisher and dealer. Many issues bear titles in French, others polyglot in four languages (Italian, French, English, German). More than 4000 numbers many published from Naya negatives in the latter 1870's and '80's. Ponti's workmanship similar to that of Naya.
Giovanni Brampton Philpot Florence 1850's and '60's
Powers Brothers (L. Powers, successor) late 1850's to late '60's
These sons of the celebrated American sculptor Hiram Powers, who resided in Florence, published beautiful stereos of their father's sculpture and that of some of his pupils as well as scenic views of the city.

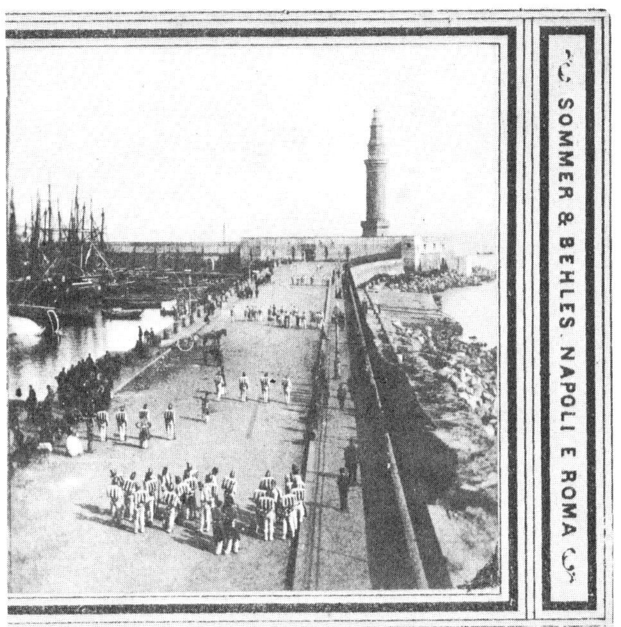

177. Italy, Naples. Harbor scene. Sommer and Behles photo, ca. 1866.

R. Rive Naples 1860's and '70's

Georgio Sommer; Sommer & Behles Naples and Rome 1860's into '70's
probably the most important Italian stereographers

Sorgato Bologna 1860's

Joseph Spithover Rome 1850's to mid '70's
one of the best early stereographers

Stabil Milan 1860's

Suscipi (Suscipj) Rome 1850's to '70's

Toncker Rome 1860's

O. Ufer Rome 1860's

Van Lint Pisa 1860's and '70's

Enrico Verzaschi Rome 1860's and '70's
more than 1100 numbers

In addition to these photographers, there were many others located in the smaller cities and towns throughout Italy, including Sicily.

Occasionally, besides being recorders of their times and mores, the photographers revealed their own "personalities." Noack's gallery in Genoa was located behind the statue of Columbus. A huge sign identified the establishment. Hodcend, a local competitor, took several fine views of the Columbus statue but carefully blocked out Noack's name on the negatives before making prints!

Sommer & Behles

A rich source of information is preserved in the stereographs published by this firm. During the early 1860's Sommer operated a gallery in Naples and Behles had an establishment in Rome. About 1867 they joined in partnership, each continuing at his own location. An ornate boxed mount was adopted and a joint trade list was released. Consequently, the same image on a similar card mount may have the imprint of G. Sommer, Sommer & Behles or Behles. Those with only the Behles name are rather infrequent; Sommers continued trade in stereos after the partnership terminated in 1874. The trade list included about 2000 numbers, most of them from negatives by Sommer. The striking images are among the best stereos ever produced. Unlike most of their Italian contemporaries, Sommer and Behles photographed peasants, street urchins and tradesmen.

Scattered among the great diversity of stereographs of Italy are views of the Austrian-Italian War, especially of departing and returning troops, Vesuvius, picturesque harbor scenes. Predominently, however, the views are of Roman antiquities, churches and palaces and street scenes. The architectural and sculpture treasures of the Italian Renaissance were beautifully stereographed again and again, often in exquisite detail.

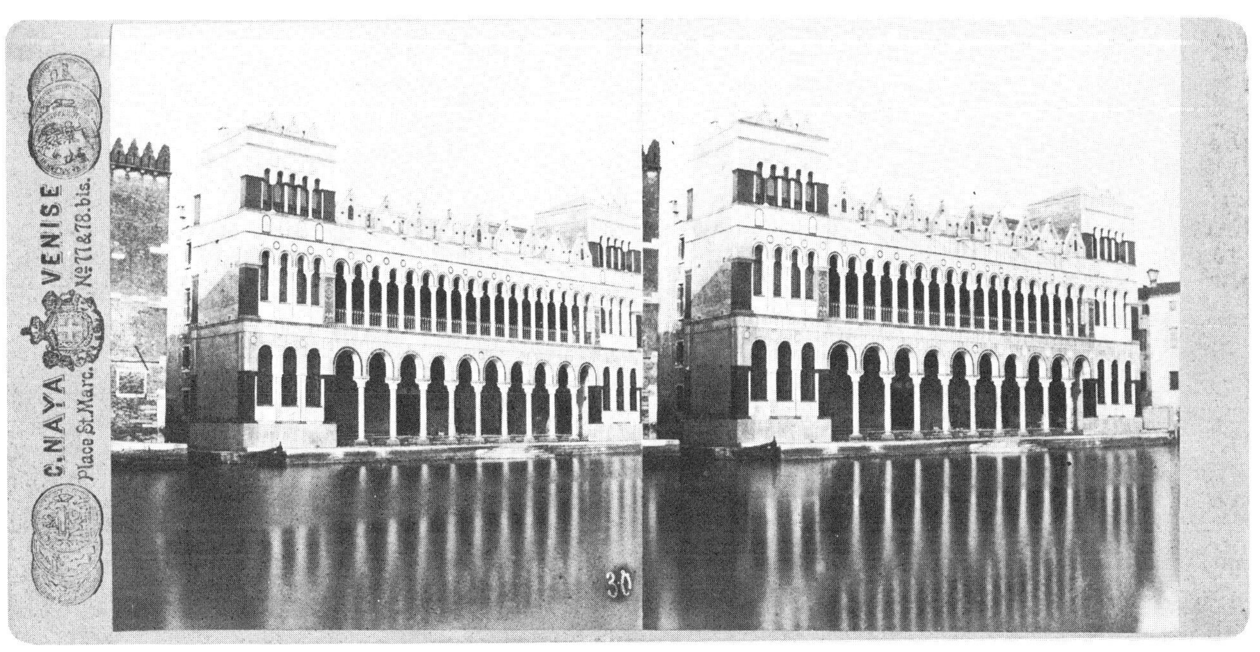

178. Italy, Venice. "The Grand Canal." C. Naya photo, ca. 1865.

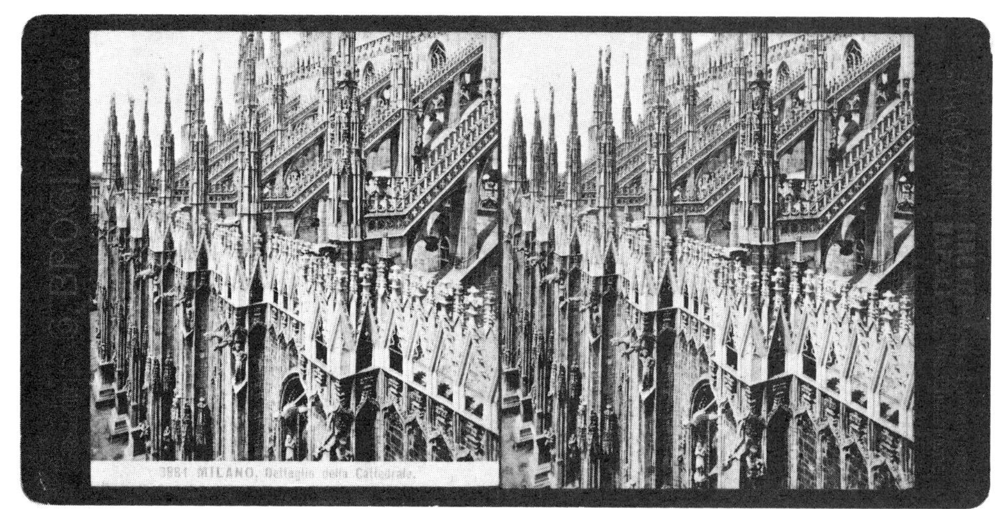

179. Italy, Milan. The Cathedral, architectural detail. G. Brogi photo, 1863.

Foreign publishers who issued excellent series include Sophus Williams (E. Linde), Berlin (1870's and '80's), who produced an exceptional series, "Florence and Its Edifices." S. P. Christmann, Berlin in the 1870's, produced an extensive series titled simply "Italie-Italien." Other noteworthy series were published during the 1870's by A. Gabler (Interlaken), E. Lamy (Paris) and, of course, by J. Andrieu.

Attention is called to an American issue, "Roman Antiquities," of sixty titles published (1868-72) by A. F. Styles (Burlington, Vermont). The source of the negatives is not known.

The most important set of boxed views was the 100-card selection "Sicily," published by the Stereo-Travel Company (1913).

The Vatican and the activities of the Roman Catholic Church were richly stereographed. D'Alessandri published a small series (1863) of portraits of Pope Pius IX (1846-78) wearing the vestments of his various offices. There are countless views of St. Peter's Cathedral, the Basilica and throngs gathered in the Square. J. Andrieu published fine views of the Vatican gardens. There are many beautiful interiors of the Vatican, including the Library, art treasures, chapels and throne room.

Stereo views of Pope Leo XIII (1878-1903) are very scarce, but his successor, Pius X (1903-14), was frequently photographed. J. B. Hewitt took several views of Pius X (H. C. White, No. 10356) and of the body of Leo XIII lying in state (No. 10357). Underwood and Underwood issued a set of twelve cards in 1903 (negatives by Bert Underwood) portraying the Pope, his principal ministers and the Swiss Guard. In 1908 the set was expanded to twenty-six titles and renamed "A Pilgrimage to See Pope Pius X," using negatives gathered between 1897 and 1907.

SWITZERLAND AND THE ALPS

The most majestic scenery in Europe is to be found in the Alps, a series of mountain ranges and valleys extending from France to Austria and embracing northern Italy and much of Switzerland. Nineteenth century photographers referred to the regions as French or Savoy, Swiss, Tirolean and Italian or Penine. A huge variety of stereographs, published by hundreds of photographers, cover every notable village and feature. Alpine scenery was a favorite subject for photographer and viewer alike. Glaciers, mountain-climbing, picturesque agricultural villages were thoroughly covered.

Without question, the series by William England published under the patronage of "The Alpine Club" stand foremost. The first set of 130 numbers, published in 1863, was lavishly praised. England returned to Switzerland and Tirol in 1865 and '67 and photographed extensively, ultimately producing more than 550 numbers.

A. Braun issued nearly four thousand views of the French and Swiss Alps. His views of glaciers and mountain-climbing are exceptional. The Bisson Brothers also produced beautiful alpine views in the early 1860's.

Several French photographers limited their scenic stereo views to the Alps. Most notable among these were Tairraz of Chamonix and Savioz, his partner and successor.

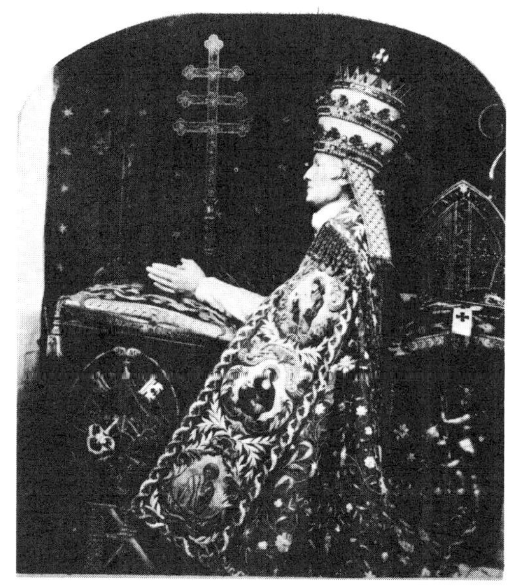

180. Pope Pius IX, with the vestments of his office. D'Alessandri photo, 1863.

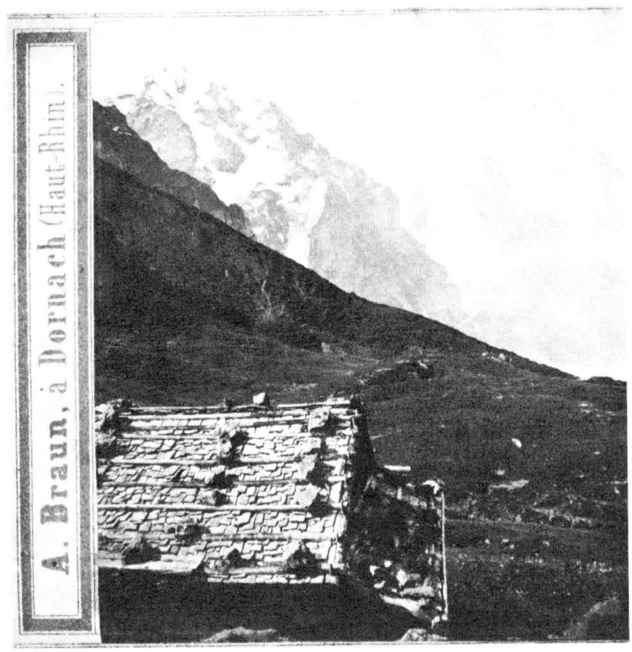

181. Switzerland, La Mouche. A. Braun photo, ca. 1862.

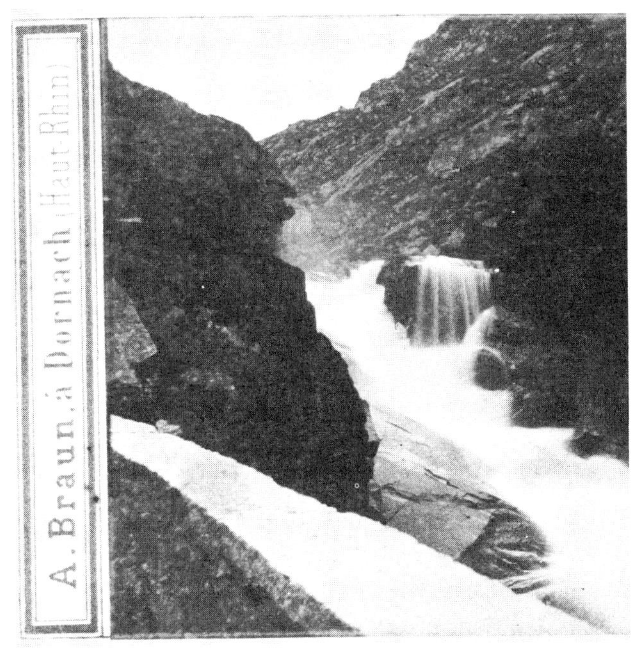

182. Swiss Alps. "Chute de la Reuss a Pont du Diable." St. Gotthard. A. Braun photo, 1860.

There are about sixty known Swiss stereographers who operated between 1855 and '80. Each restricted his work to his own neighborhood. The more important are therefore listed by geographic location:

Basel	Hoeflinger
Berne	M. Vollenweider & Sons
Einsiedln	P. Rossier
Geneva	Leon Bloch, F. Charnaux (later Charnaux & Sons), A. Garcin, J. Jullien, Felix Morel, Reyman & Pricam, F. Richard
Interlaken	B. Leuthold
Lucerne	Jules Bonnet, Fisher & Mathis
Neuchatel	Bruder Bros.
Ragaz	J. Fetzer
Zurichsee	R. Mannedorf

There are many very fine views of Swiss cities and villages taken by French and English photographers in the latter 1850's and early '60's. Wehrli (Zurich) produced a series of views in the early 1900's.

Several series illustrating Swiss peasant costumes and occupations, by Braun and Lallemond & Hart, have been mentioned previously (p. 115).

The travel sets produced by American publishers after 1900 are generally excellent. The Underwood 100-card set gives special attention to Swiss crafts, showing men and women performing their skills.

GERMANY

Stereographs of Germany and central Europe are poorly represented in American collections. Despite the large German-American population, there was very little

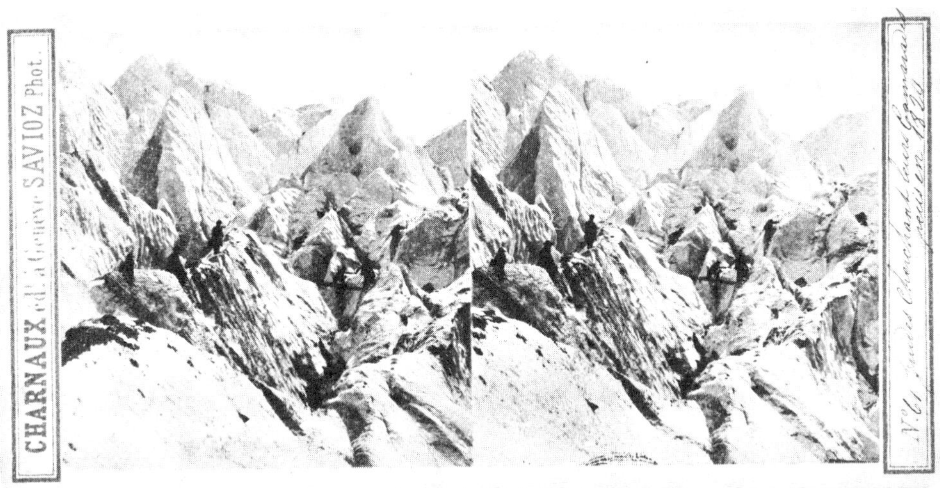

183. Switzerland. "Guides searching for lost comrades." Savioz photo, ca. 1865, Charnaux publisher.

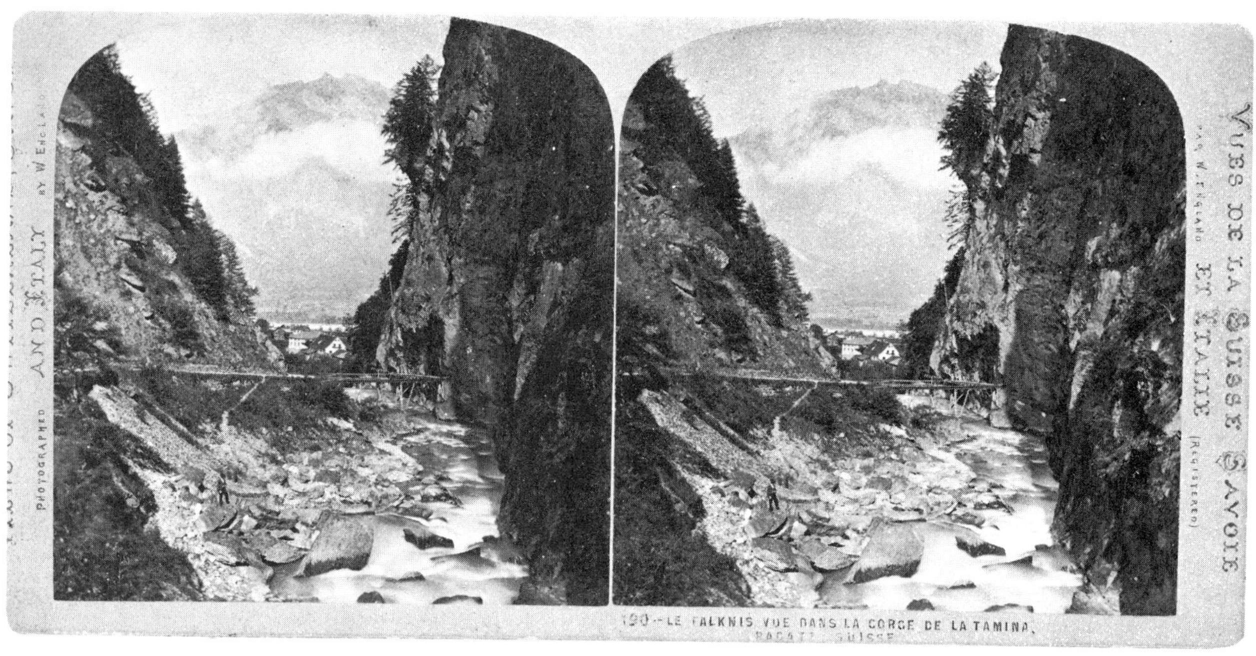

184. Switzerland. La Tamina Gorge. William England photo, 1865.

American tourism in Germany and Austria. Even so, German photographers published an enormous volume and variety of stereo views. The larger publishers maintained branches in Paris and London but, so far as I am aware, none had a branch in the United States.

The greatest German publisher was Sophus Williams of Berlin, who was succeeded by E. Linde. The company issued views from approximately 1862 to '95, with the most active period 1865-80. The trade list, which included all categories from documentary to comics, was much larger than that of Anthony but smaller than that of the London Stereoscopic Company. Individual photographers are seldom credited, although several series are acknowledged as the works of J. F. Stiehm and E. Linde.

Berlin

Excellent views of Berlin are numerous. The subjects range from street scenes and public buildings to the zoological gardens. Moses (also Moses & Senftner) produced notable interior views of the National Gallery of Art. The series includes many unusual stereographs of paintings.

Other Berlin photographers of importance include: E. Biegner, Burchard Brothers, S. P. Christmann, F. A. D. Gallrein, L. Haase, C. Eckenrath and Clemenz Kauffmann.

Germany has many cities with medieval streets, guild houses and famous Gothic cathedrals. Several of these cities were beautifully stereographed in the period 1855-75.

Cologne, especially its cathedral and street scenes, was photographed by W. Afsenheimer, Th. Creifelds, F. C. Eisen, L. Haase, A. Schmitz and T. Schoenschidt.

Nurnberg, with its castle and elaborate Gothic churches, was one of the favorites of German photographers. Buildings associated with Hans Sachs and Albrecht Durer were frequently photographed. The charm

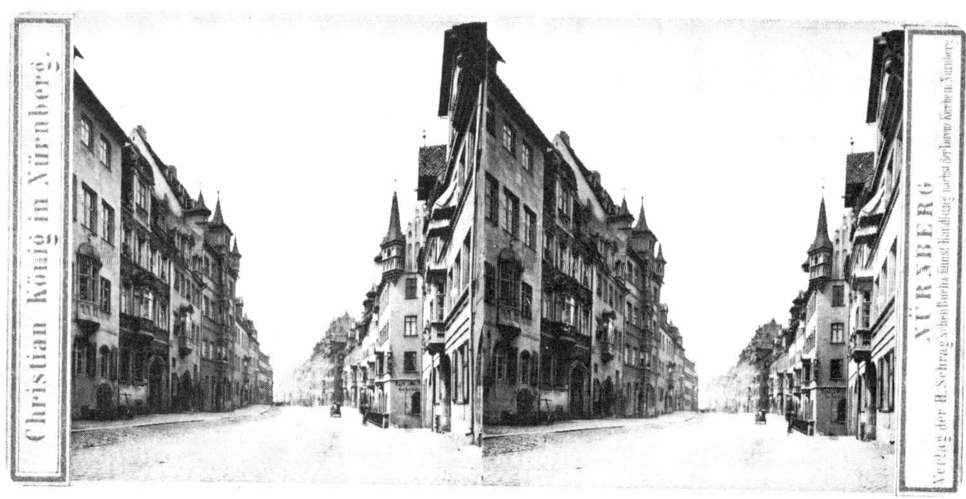

185. Germany, Nuremburg. Christian Koenig photo, ca. 1865.

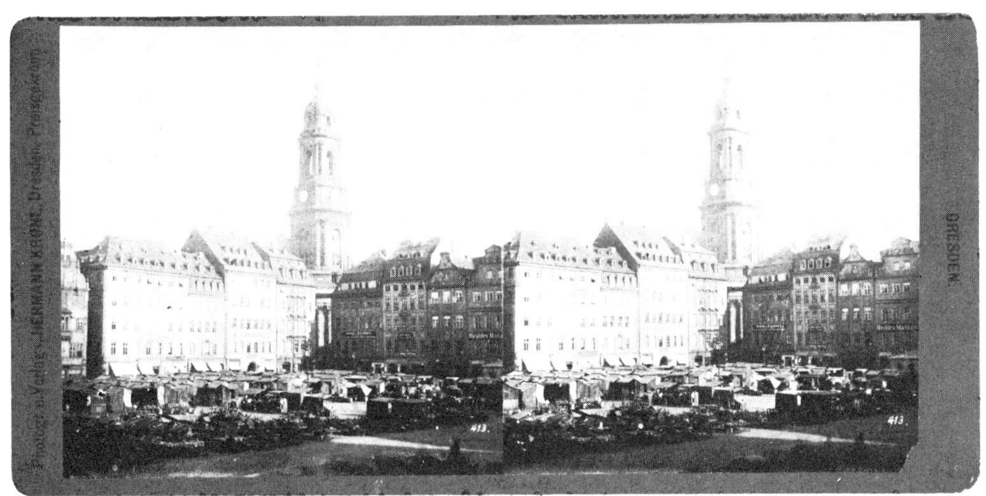

186. Germany, Dresden. Market place. Hermann Krone photo, 1868.

of the ancient city is recorded in the views by Koenig, Leidig, F. Schmidt and C. Smidt. Interesting, but less artistic views were issued by Popp and Schultze.

Heidelberg's great castle and courtyards were stereographed by many photographers from virtually every point of view. The University buildings and the ancient churches were also well illustrated by stereo. G. M. Eckert, L. Meder and F. Richard are the most important resident photographers.

Munich had many excellent photographers, notably J. Aumiller, O. Bir, C. Bottger, B. Kostler, E. Reulbach, Hanfstangl and W. Widmayer. There are fine views of the old town and of the principal public buildings.

Germany, like England and the United States, could boast of a competent photographer in almost every village. Many of them produced stereo views of only local interest. The following list suggests the names and locations of first-rate stereographers. All operated between 1860 and '80.

Berctesgaden	Ney
Bingen-am-Rhein	J. B. Hilsdorf
Breslau	L. Haase
Constanz	Wolf
Creuznach	Jacobi
Dresden	F. & O. Brockmann, H. Hanfstangl, Hoffmann, H. Krone, O. Schmidt
Flensburg	F. Brandt
Frankfurt-am-Main	C. Abel, G. Keller
Guntersblum	W. Glock
Hamburg	Boock, Kruss, V. R. Noodt
Hannover	L. Herzog, E. Lulves, G. Reese, F. Reinecke
Kempton	Zabuesnig
Kissingen	F. Harren
Leipzig	Thiele
Lubeck	J. Noring
Maenedorf	T. Richard
Mainz	C. Hertel
Meran	P. Moosbrugger
Partenkirchen	B. Johannes
Potsdam	H. Selle
Regensberg	F. Schmidt
Salzungen	R. Hoefel
Stuttgart	L. F. Brandsep, L. Schaller
Thuringen	E. Schuler
Wiesbaden	L. Bender, C. Borntraeger
Worms	C. Holzamer

An unidentified photographer ca. 1858 issued several remarkable views of Thorwaldsen's statue of Gutenberg, erected in the town square of Mainz. The images, mounted on thin brown cards, are brilliant. Holzamer's views of Worms include many associated with Martin Luther.

The well-known spas of central Europe were extensively stereographed by photographers who established galleries catering to the patrons. Typical examples are Bad Kissingen (C. W. Cronenburg), Bad Elster (E.

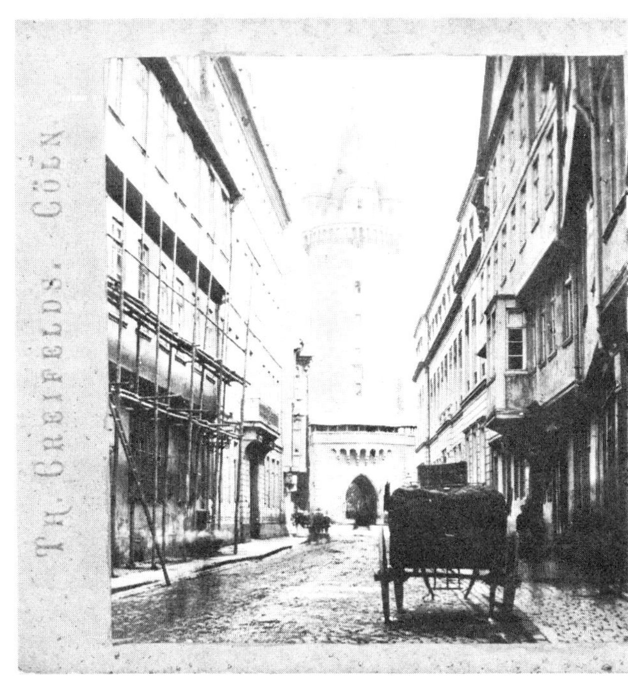

187. Germany, Frankfurt. "Eschenheimer Tower." Th. Creifelds photo, ca. 1868.

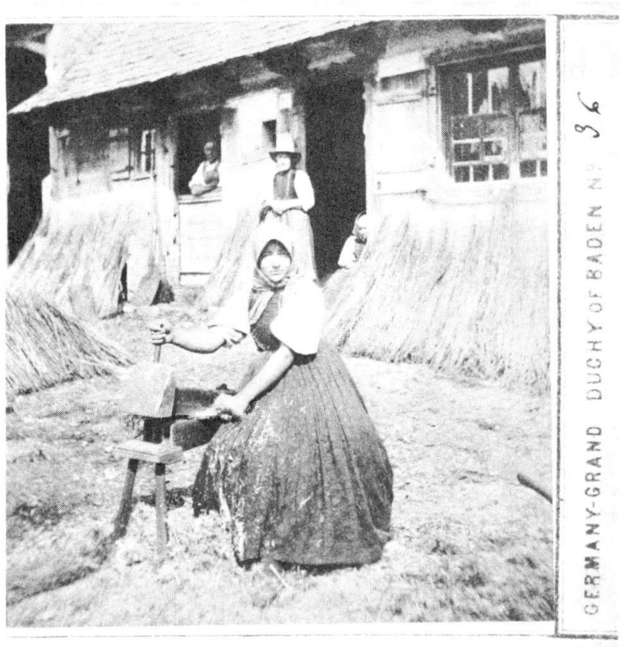

188. Germany, Baden. Breaking flax to free the fibers. Lallemond and Hart photo, 1865.

Tietze) and Marienbad (A. Guntner). Although most of the views depict buildings and landscaped grounds, many show patrons gathered in the plush lobbies and drawing rooms.

Views of Germany by foreign photographers

Some of the best views of the Rhine Valley were produced by the Frenchmen A. Braun, E. Lamy, Ferrier and two others known only by the initials C. G. (Charles Gerard?) and Ferrier issued many magnificent glass views of the Cologne and other German cathedrals.

Kilburn Brothers between 1873 and '96 published approximately 300 views of Germany. Those manufactured between 1883 and '92 are technically inferior, often lacking contrast. Nevertheless, there are some unusual scenes among them, for example, the bustling harbor of Hamburg.

The boxed sets published by Underwood, White, Stereo Travel Company and Keystone are excellent. They contrast the historic pastoral Germany with the industrialization achieved in barely fifty years.

Stereographs of World War I are reviewed on page 195.

OTHER EUROPEAN COUNTRIES

Only a cursory survey of nineteenth century stereographs of other European countries will be attempted. Two factors dictate this procedure: views of these countries are relatively scarce; and the majority of familiar views were produced by French, German and English photographers, not by resident operators. Collectors in these countries should be able to recover and collate significant data about native photographers who have been long forgotten.

BELGIUM and HOLLAND

About a score of Belgian photographers are known to have produced stereo views in the 1860's and '70's. Unfortunately, one-third of them failed to identify their fine work.

Antwerp	F. Tessard, began in the 1850's
Brussels	Bernheim, Brand Brothers, A. F. Deloeul, Dechamps, Eurgard, E. Fierlants, H. Plaut
Ghent	Ch. d'Hoy
Liege	Damy

Unidentified photographers in Bruges, Malines and Mons produced local stereo views during the period 1865-75.

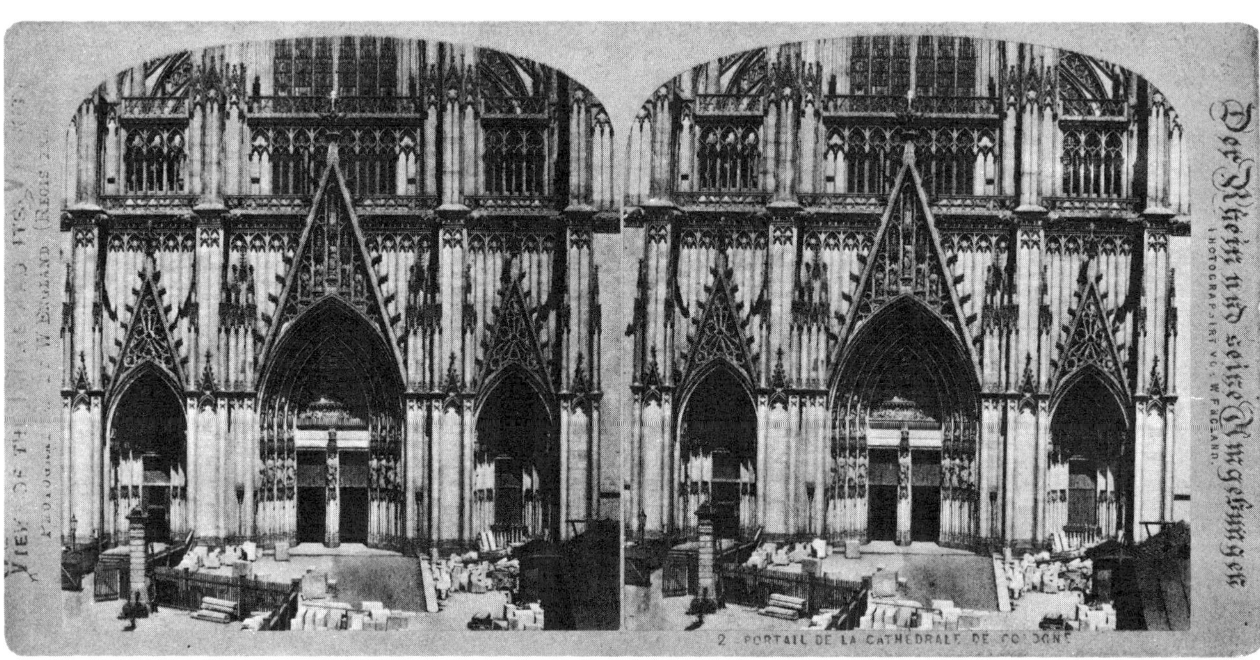

189. Germany, Cologne. The Cathedral. William England, photo, 1866.

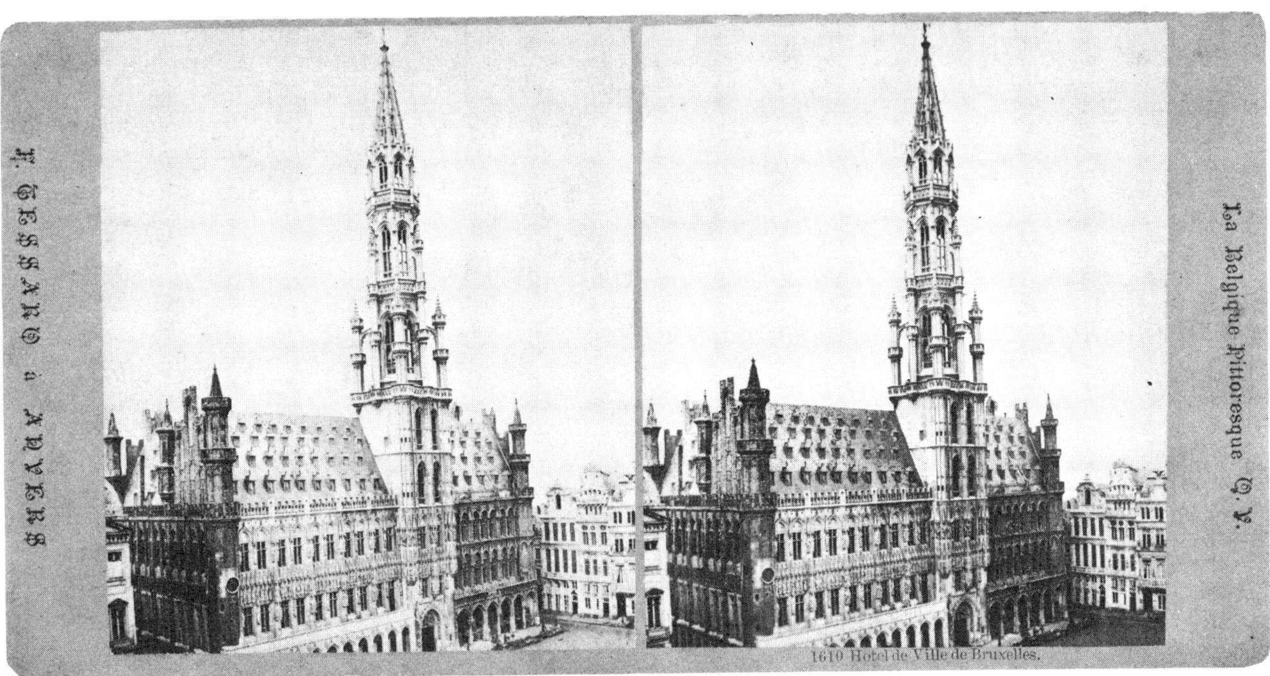

190. Belgium, Brussels. Hotel de Ville. F. Tessaro photo, 1866.

The majority of town views illustrate cathedrals and castles with fine interiors of both, medieval streets and excellent views of canal and river traffic.

A series of approximately twenty views of the Waterloo battlefield was issued by an unknown photographer about 1862. The cards bear manuscript titles in French or English, which suggests that they were intended for visitors to the site of Napoleon Bonaparte's defeat (1815).

The finest views of Belgium were published by the Frenchmen Ferrier, J. Queval, J. Valecki, Leon & Levy, those known by the initials B. K. and B. T.

Holland seems to have been sporadically covered by stereographs. Only four local photographers are known to me, but there were probably many. A. Jager operated in Amsterdam, M. M. Couvee in The Hague and J. Schaarwacter in Nijmengin. The fourth, J. Queval, maintained a gallery in Amsterdam, although his main studio was in Paris. Dutch views are characteristically of windmills, canals and canal traffic. There are some fine views of market places, including flower and cheese markets.

As in the case of Belgium, the best views of Holland were published by foreign photographers, French and German: Braun, Lamy, Leon & Levy and Sophus Williams.

SPAIN and PORTUGAL

The most important stereo views of these two countries were published by J. Laurent, who operated in Madrid and Paris. Laurent issued a beautiful series on the museums and costumes of Spain and Portugal (ca. 1868-72). There are exquisite views of Moorish architecture, especially of the Alhambra at Granada.

The Englishman Joseph Forrester (Lisbon) published a small number of excellent views in the late 1850's. In Spain another Englishman, Charles Clifford, produced fine stereo negatives. Probably the series published in 1859-60 by the London Stereoscopic Company were from Clifford Negatives. The more popular titles were available until 1870 and are, therefore, to be found on many different types of card mounts.

Luis Masson (Seville, late 1850's to '70) published an extensive series of Spanish scenery, including the Pyrenees Mountains. The quality is mediocre, but in many cases they represent the only known contemporary stereographs of the localities illustrated. Masson usually identified his cards with a hand-stamped imprint, but many copies were sold without an imprint.

B. Caro (Malaga, 1857-62) produced fine images on thin white cards. E. Julia (Madrid, 1860's) also published good views of his neighborhood.

Relvas (Lisbon) 1860's and 70's published a series of views of his neighborhood.

Marrao, operating in Cintra, Portugal, in the latter 1870's published a modest series of his vicinity.

Somewhat later, Alberto Martin (Barcelona, 1880's and '90's) issued an extensive series covering much of Spain.

The largest selection of scenes of Spain and Portugal was issued by J. Andrieu (Paris) between 1868 and 1877.

H. C. White Company published (1908) an outstanding boxed travel set of Spain. The series includes a dozen views of the wine industry at Jerez.

GIBRALTAR

J. H. Mann, who operated here in the 1860's and 70's, published many beautiful views of "The Rock," harbor and settlements.

NORWAY, SWEDEN and DENMARK

K. Knudsen (Bergen, Norway) published more than 750 views in the 1860's and '70's. The images are excellent. The scenes are mostly of Bergen and vicinity, with many different views of the same landmarks taken at different times. Waldemar Selmer, also of Bergen, between 1885 and 1900 produced large numbers of

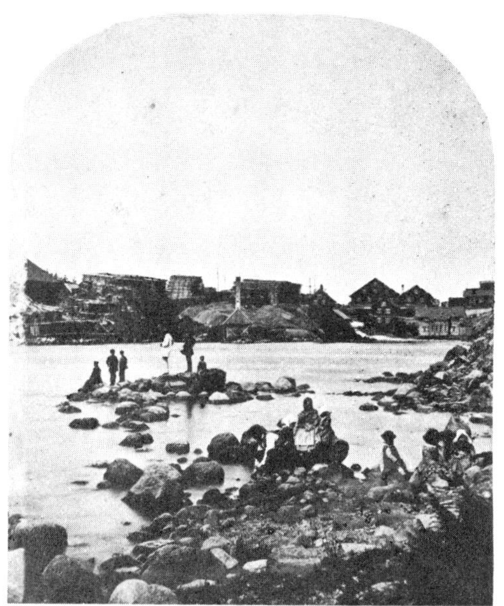

191. Sweden, Gothenburg. Harbor scene. Boeckman photo, ca. 1862.

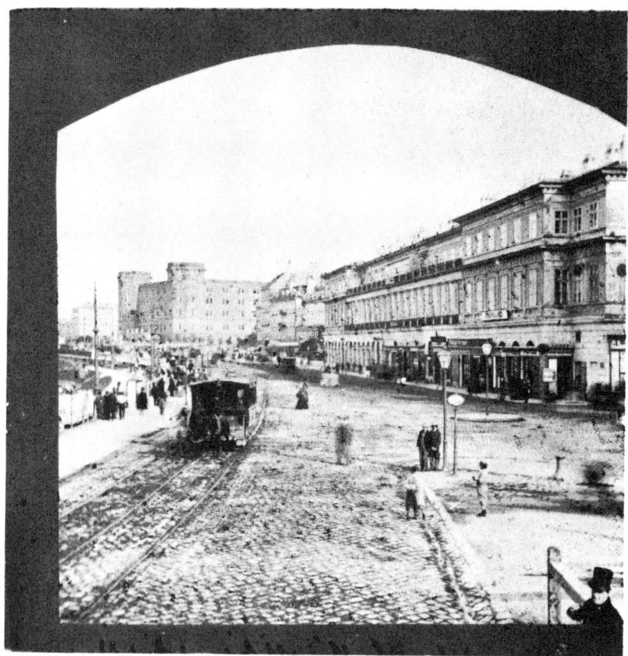

192. Austria, Vienna. "Franz-Joseph Quay." A. F. Czihak photo, 1868. Title on back printed in German, French and English.

mediocre views, many of which were sold to Norwegian families who had emigrated to the United States.

Sweden had several notable photographers in the 1860's. Best known for excellent stereographs are: Joh. Jaeger, Stockholm; Boeckmann, Gotheberg; and Vogel & Dienstbach, Gotheberg. Generally the views are of towns and harbors.

Denmark was very well covered by stereographers, but the overall quality of the views was mediocre. The best stereos were published by Vilhelm Tryder, Copenhagen, who was noted for his fine views of Thorwaldsen's statuary. Other photographers operating in Copenhagen were Vilhelm Tillge, J. C. Farrer and the firm of Muller, Budtz & Co. All were active between 1860 and '80.

P. Fangel, Middlefart, was primarily a publisher, using mostly negatives by other photographers. The most prolific publisher, however, was Peter Elfelt, who, between the latter 1880's and early 1900's issued more than 4000 Danish views, a strange mix of unusual and commonplace subjects.

AUSTRIA

The Austrian Empire in the second half of the nineteenth century included Austria, Hungary and those

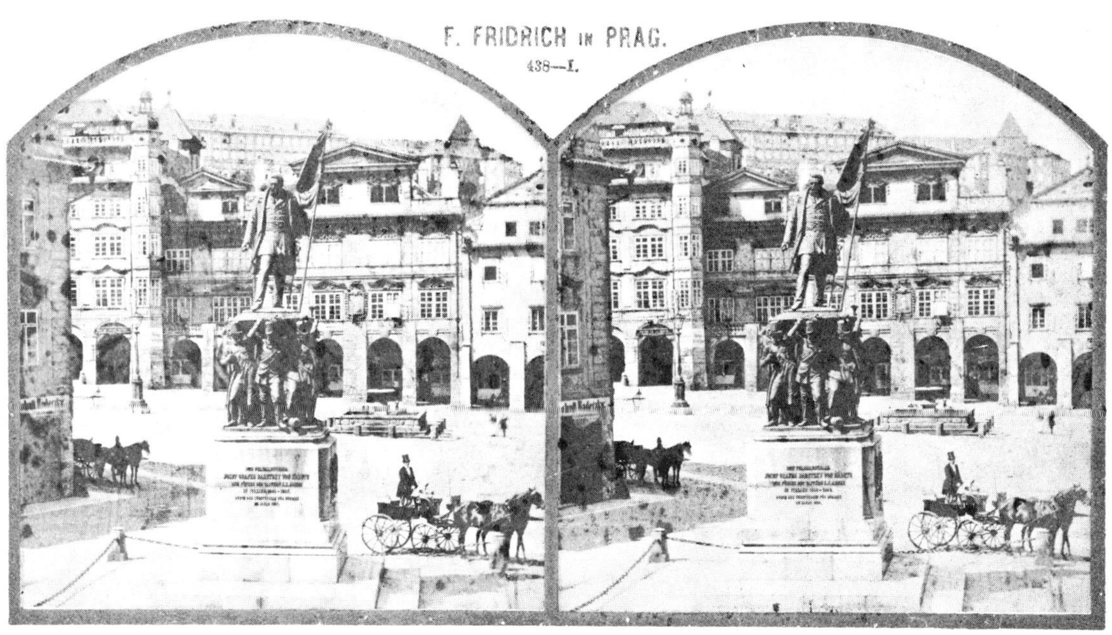

193. Austria (Czechoslovakia), Prague. "Radetsky Monument." F. Fridrich photo, 1859.

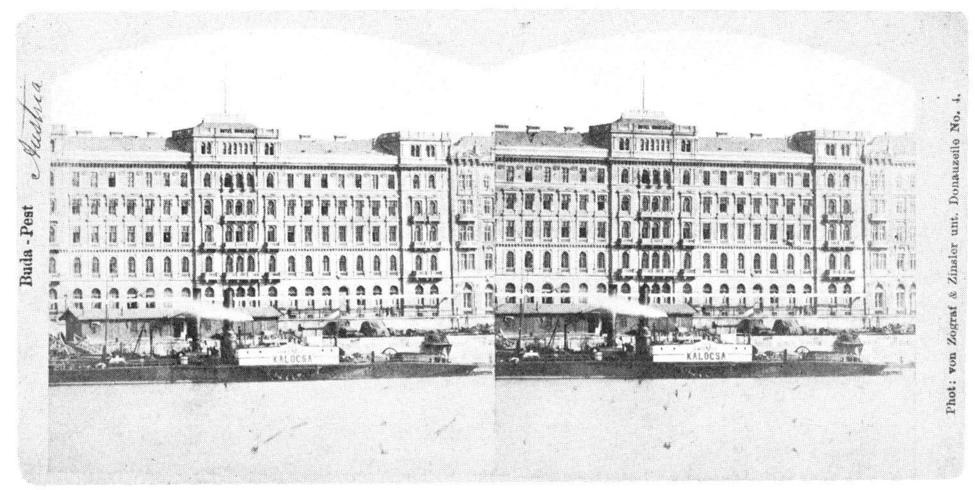

194. Hungary, Budapest. "Grand Hotel." Zograf and Zinsler photo, ca. 1870.

areas presently known as Czechoslovakia and portions of Yugoslavia and Poland.

Vienna and Budapest were the principal seats of government and social life. As such, they were the most frequently photographed.

There is no hint in the stereographic record of the political unrest and suppression which were most intense in the Austrian Empire. Ethnic groups are almost never identified in the scarce views of peasants.

Nevertheless, there were many first-rate stereographers operating in the 1850's and '60's.

Victor Angerer and Ludwig Angerer (Vienna) published fine images in a variety of card mounts. They also published the views of other photographers, such as W. Frankenstein, under both their own and the photographer's imprints.

In the 1860's Vienna had many able photographers. The better stereographs were those by J. Lowy, Eduard Oberhausen, C. J. Rospini and D. Schoefft. For some years Rospini used a full-card imprint showing his shop. Figure 16.

F. Fridrich (Prague) between 1855 and '68 published beautiful images, notable for brilliance and composition. Many of his views of Prague and Dresden are gems. Two other Prague photographers issued notable stereographs, Lachman (1860's) and M. Klempfner (1870's).

During the 1870's several Vienna photographers published broader coverage of Austria than scenic and architectural. Fritz Luckhardt, most famous for his beautiful female portraits, "Luckhardt's Heads," issued fine scenic views which seem to be quite rare. Oscar Kramer published an extensive scenic series. Wilhelm Burger, A. F. Czihak, Miethke & Wawra, Louis Schrank and C. Sonnenthal are also noteworthy.

Innsbruck, a popular resort, had several excellent stereographers. Fr. Unterberger produced fine thin card mounts, 1859-65. C. A. Czichna issued beautiful scenic views of the Tirolean Alps. About the same time M. Endres and Anton Gratl published many views of the town and countryside.

Salzburg was beautifully stereographed by Ludwig Hardtmuth, Karl Boos and Baldi & Wurthle, who also published a large scenic series of Berctesgaden.

W. Jerie issued an extensive series depicting Carlsbad.

Benque & Sebastienutti were operating in Trieste.

The best-known Hungarian stereo photographers were the partners VonZongraf & Zinsler who were active in the 1860's and '70's.

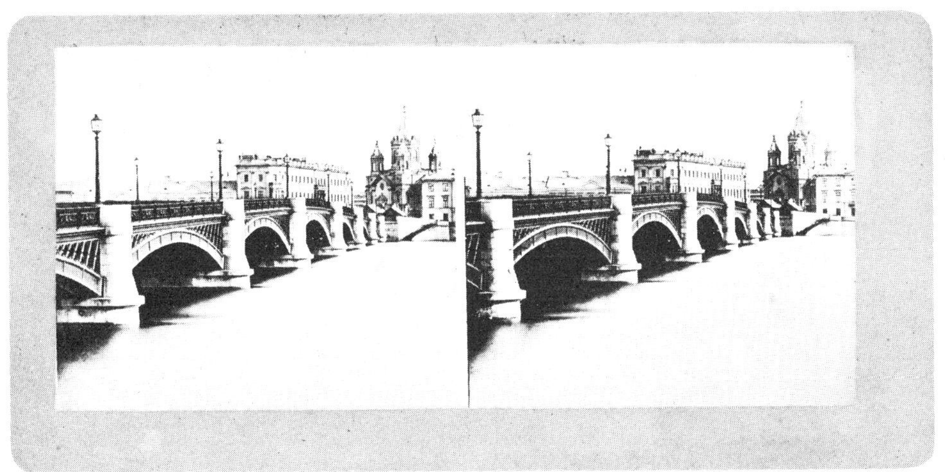

195. Russia, St. Petersburg. English series, unidentified photographer, ca. 1857.

In 1873 the International Exhibition was held in Vienna. It was a spectacular undertaking, with the nave of the main building more than a half-mile in length and crossed by sixteen transepts. The structure was surmounted by a colossal cast iron dome. The splendidly landscaped grounds were not equaled by any other exposition, before or since. Exclusive rights were not granted to a single photographer or publishing company. Instead, the Vienna Photographic Association was awarded the privilege. More than 450 fine stereographs illustrating every feature of the occasion were issued. In addition to the "official" series, views were also issued by Sophus Williams and Leon & Levy.

In 1923 Keystone published a beautiful set of fifty views of Czechoslovakia. Complete sets are seldom seen because the sales of this issue were very disappointing.

In Bulgaria D. A. Karastoyanov produced views of Sophia in the 1870's.

RUSSIA

The earliest known stereographs of Moscow and St. Petersburg were published in England and France in the early 1850's. The typical scenes are of the Kremlin (some entitled "The Citadel"), cathedrals, palaces and the Hermitage. Many of these early views are calotypes mounted on thin off-white, gray, green, blue, buff or brown cards. Very few bear any clue to the photographer. Fenton and Richebourg, however, are known to have issued some of them.

Langenheim Brothers published a small series of approximately twenty views of Russia (1857-59). It is believed that some of the negatives were taken by Frederick Langenheim himself, but others seem to be of English origin.

About 1860 Elliott published a series of at least forty numbers of Moscow and St. Petersburg. A very fine French series (about fifty numbers, ca. 1858) bears the simple title "Russie" on the left margin of the face and a printed label "Voyage en Russie" on the back.

During the 1860's and early '70's E. Linde published for L. Gothe (Frankfurt-am-Main) a series of about 200 views, "Ansichten von St. Petersburg," on buff cards with green backs. Another fine series without a photographer's imprint (ca.1873) has cards with red face and lavender backs.

In 1875 D. R. Clark (Indianapolis, Ind.) published a series of ten views of Vladivostok, Siberia.

Stereographs by Russian photographers are seldom seen in America. Enough is known, however, to indicate that careful search would recover data on a fair number of local operators.

In the latter 1860's A. Alassine issued a series of views of Moscow and vicinity.

An unnumbered series of about 200 titles was published between 1868 and '75 by A. Felish of St. Petersburg. The cards bear titles in Russian and German.

A few views of Warsaw by J. K. Walowsky (late 1860's) are known.

About 1874 Kloch & Dutkiewicz of Warsaw (prior to 1918, Poland was part of Russia) published a good series of the city and its surroundings.

A local photographer produced a small series of the ancient city of Kiev. Titles are hand-stamped in Russian and German.

Not until the period following the coronation of Nicholas II (1894-1918) do we have stereo views of the Russian people. Kilburn in 1897 issued nearly 200 views from negatives taken between 1894 and '96. There are twenty-five scenes of Coronation Week, including gruesome views of the 3000 people trampled to death when a crowd gathered to receive free food stampeded (Nos. 12012, 12013).

Bert Underwood personally photographed the Royal Family, official occasions and striking views of the principal cities. These were incorporated in the Underwood 100-card "Russia" set.

Stereographs of the Russo-Japanese War will be described on page 187.

GREECE

Although Greece had few native stereographers between 1850 and '75, the classic ruins of Athens, Epidaurus, and other famous sites were handsomely recorded by foreign photographers.

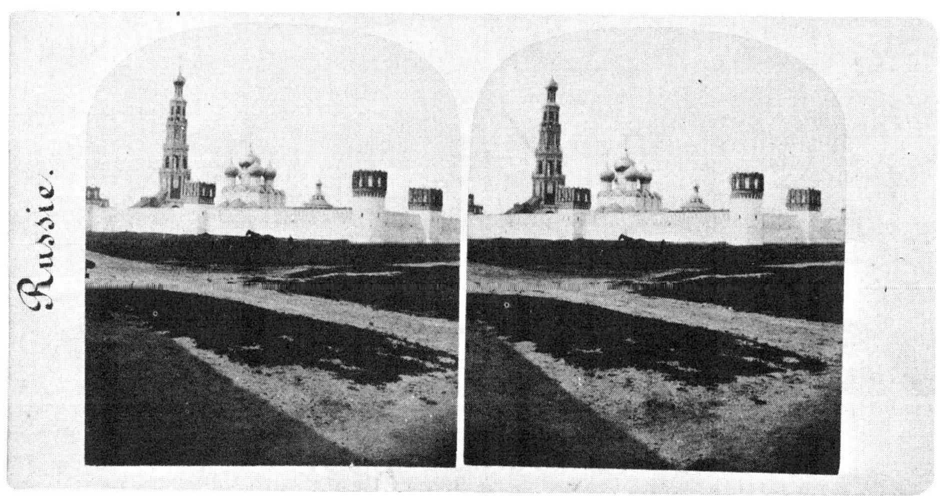

196. Russia, Moscow. French series "Voyage en Russie" (no. 59). Unidentified photographer, ca. 1856.

D. Constantin (Athens, 1850's into '70's) is the best known of the native photographers. His many fine stereos were sold to tourists.

P. Moraites (Athens, mid 1850's into 80's) also produced views which are less frequently seen than those by Constantin.

Gerard (Paris) in the 1860's published about 200 views on yellow mounts. Somewhat later, ca. 1872, Leon & Levy issued an unusual series, "Grece & Turquie." Unfortunately, the prints are light and flat, inferior to the usual high standards of this firm.

As with most pre-1856 views, many excellent views of the Acropolis and its buildings bear no clue to the photographer.

During the period 1896-1910 the major American publishers produced very fine sets of Greece, with coverage more truly representative of the country and its people than is recorded by the sum of all earlier views. The Underwood set (72 cards, 1901; 100 cards, 1908) is the best, with that by H. C. White (100 cards, 1905) a close second. The set by Stereo-Travel Company, while technically inferior, includes many scenes not available elsewhere.

Both Underwood and Jarvis photographed rebel Macedonian bands and government troops in the mountain recesses of northern Greece, 1896-97. Figure 66.

On the whole, Western Europe was more thoroughly stereographed than Central and Eastern Europe. In the latter there is a much narrower range of subjects. Purely scenic and cautiously documentary views predominate.

CHAPTER TWELVE

THE NEAR EAST, AFRICA, ASIA, AUSTRALIA, LATIN AMERICA AND ATLANTIC ISLANDS

The nineteenth century witnessed continued expansion of Western European influence throughout the world. Central and South America had long been under European domination. There were colonial possessions on every continent, even on small islands in the most remote oceans. Africa, the so-called "dark continent," was carved up and claimed for colonies during the later 1800's.

The races of man and their cultures aroused great interest in Europe and North America. Who are these peoples? Where do they live? How do they live? Long before 1800 explorers and missionaries had acquainted Europeans with the religions and customs practiced in many parts of the world.

As the interchange of raw materials and products played an ever greater part in world commerce, information about them was sought in many ways. The emigration of millions of Europeans to North America, Australia, New Zealand and South Africa contributed to the changing face of the earth.

Sometimes unexpected consequences attended political events. Napoleon Bonaparte's Egyptian campaign was a military failure, but it provided the foundations for the study of Egyptology. Struggle between the Eastern Orthodox and Roman Catholic hierarchies over the Holy Places in Palestine had far-reaching repercussions in the Islamic and Christian countries, most importantly in the Near East.

Thus, many influences were to present opportunities for photographers to establish galleries in virtually all of the seaports and larger settlements throughout the world. Daguerreotypists toured the Near East in the 1840's and their successors with the glass wet plate visited Central America, Africa and Asia, making known ancient cultures and picturesque landscapes.

The overwhelming majority of these early photographers were Europeans. Except in Turkey and Egypt, very few natives acquired the technical skills in photography before 1870. After that date proficient individuals took up the art in slowly increasing numbers.

THE NEAR EAST: PALESTINE, SYRIA AND TURKEY

Palestine, the traditional homeland of the Jews, included the Holy Places of Christendom and many sites revered by the Moslems. It was a poorly defined area within the Turkish Ottoman Empire. Since 1740 Roman Catholics and other Christians had been guaranteed access to the Holy Places, then under French protection. From 1790 onwards, the Eastern Orthodox Church progressively encroached upon the Roman Catholics and openly attempted to gain control of the Holy Places. Napoleon III precipitated the Crimean War by exploiting this religious quarrel.

The regime of Abdul Mejid (1839-61) was marked by social reforms and a rapid westernization of Turkey. French and English photographers were welcome in Constantinople and in most cases were able to obtain permission to take pictures in Syria and Palestine.

Simultaneously, the development of Biblical scholarship and the Protestant Sunday school movement created a demand for photographs of the Holy Land.

Francis Frith, although not the earliest stereographer to visit the Near East, was the most celebrated. After a highly successful venture in Egypt in 1856, Frith went from Jerusalem to Damascus and Baalbec, taking several hundred fine negatives (1857-58). Negretti & Zambra issued a beautiful series of one hundred views.

In the mid 1860's Frank Good published his excellent

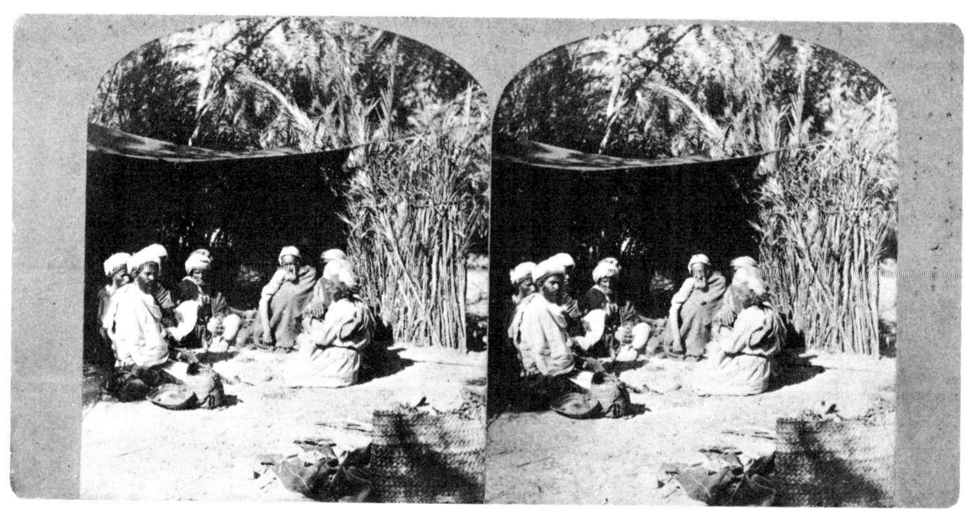

197. Sinai. "Bedouin Encampment." British War Office Topographical Survey, 1869.

"Eastern Series" of about 250 titles. Whereas Frith placed his camera at a distance to emphasize perspective and skillfully used shadows to show architectural detail, Good isolated the subject from its nearby surroundings. By limiting composition, the detail is precise.

An excellent series, obviously imitating that by Frank Good, was published by P. Bergheim (Jerusalem, 1863-73). The views are somewhat inferior, but there are many fine titles.

About 1868 Felix Bonfils began publishing a large series, ultimately exceeding 700 numbers, ranging in quality from very fine to mediocre. Nevertheless, the coverage was so thorough that there are many scenes not recorded by any other stereographer.

The earlier stereo views, which were much more limited in subject matter, are primarily of historical and sentimental interest. Maxime Du Camp issued calotypes on thin off-white card stock in 1852 or '53. Salzmann (Jerusalem, 1855-58) published beautiful tinted views of Jerusalem, showing the town almost wholly within its ancient walls before the period of modern building had begun. C. F. Spittler (Jerusalem, mid 1860's) issued a small series of fine views.

The British War Department (1868-69) undertook a topographical survey of Sinai and published a series of more than 150 stereographs, including many of Bedouins, desert and geological formations.

Although many photographers published excellent series of views of the Holy Land, mostly in the 1870's and early '80's, none of them approached the artistic skill of Frith and Good.

Charles Bierstadt (1872) toured the Holy Land and the coast of North Africa and obtained a set of 250 original negatives, the most popular of which were in continuous production until 1895.

Kilburn Brothers published (1875) a series of about eighty views of Jerusalem and twenty-five of Syria. Two other Americans issued stereographs from original negatives. William E. James (1866) issued about 150 titles, primarily intended for Sunday school instruction and lyceum programs. E. L. Wilson published his "Eastern Series" of more than 650 titles on fine artistic mounts (1883). These are quite scarce today because of a diminished interest in stereos at that time. The Wilson views are important because they depict modernization of many parts of the Near East in barely twenty years.

Leon & Levy and Braun issued noteworthy series of Palestine.

At least seventy-five photographers are known to have published stereo views of the Holy Land prior to 1900. The majority, however, photographed the same familiar landmarks over and over again.

The most vivid stereographs of the Holy Land are not the classics but, rather, the inspired work of Bert Underwood (1896). Underwood's stereos of Jerusalem show Moslems, Jews and Christians, natives and pilgrims. Palestine is not merely the site of Holy Places; it is a land inhabited by nomads, shepherds and villagers. Maidens are drawing water, merchants are weighing grain, as they had been doing for more than two thousand years. The Underwood 100-card set (first issue, 1897) was so popular that various subsets, such as "Jerusalem" and "Life of Jesus," also were made available. Figure 65.

H. C. White, Stereo Travel and Griffith & Griffith published very good series and sets of Palestine. The Keystone sets are reissues of the original Underwood set.

We should not overlook the multicolored lithoprints manufactured in the United States between 1902 and 1916. A 200-card "Holy Land" (also called "Palestine") series sold by Sears Roebuck & Company is notable because of its true-to-life coloring and the breadth of coverage.

TURKEY

Nearly all nineteenth century views of Turkey refer to Constantinople (now Istanbul) and vicinity. Situated at the southern extreme of the Bosporus and erected on seven hills, Constantinople was for 2500 years the crossroad of cultures, Byzantine, Greek, Roman and, after 1453, Turkish. The city has many ancient Christian churches, most of them converted as mosques. The renowned Byzantine basilica St. Sophia is one of the most beautiful buildings in the world. Interspersed throughout the city, Roman engineering works, such as aqueducts, still remain.

The stereographs, many taken during the 1850's, show all of these features as well as fine harbor scenes, the Golden Horn and the Golden Gate.

Two capable photographers who operated in Constantinople issued stereos: P. Sebah (1860's and '70's) and Abdullah Freres (1860's to 90's). A few excellent views were published by B. Kargopoula (Constantinople, ca. 1870).

The foreign photographers, however, are better known. Sophus Williams (E. Linde) produced a fine series (1870's).

Underwood published a forty-eight card set, "Constantinople," which Keystone republished, with minor changes, as "Turkey" (fifty cards, 1923; seventy-two, 1927).

EGYPT

Francis Frith's stereographs of Egypt, published by Negretti & Zambra (1857-59) as both card and glass mounts, were probably the most lavishly praised and famous series in the history of stereography. The unity, technical quality and artistic excellence have made them truly classics. Frith scratched his name with a number on each negative, a practice he had begun about 1855. After 1861, when Frith established his own photographic publishing company, the Egyptian and Near East series were published under his imprints. These Frith views were in continuous publication until 1880, available in many formats including miserable pirated copy issues. Figure 22.

F. Good had many fine views of ancient Egyptian monuments in his "Eastern Series."

Earlier than Frith and Good, Maxime Du Camp issued scenes of Egypt and Nubia along with those of Palestine and Syria. Robinson & Beato and Frank Haes published stereos of Cairo in 1858. Those of Haes were available tinted and untinted. C. E. Goodman (ca. 1858) also produced fine views of Egypt.

Construction of the Suez Canal began in 1860, with a large part of the work being done by forced labor until

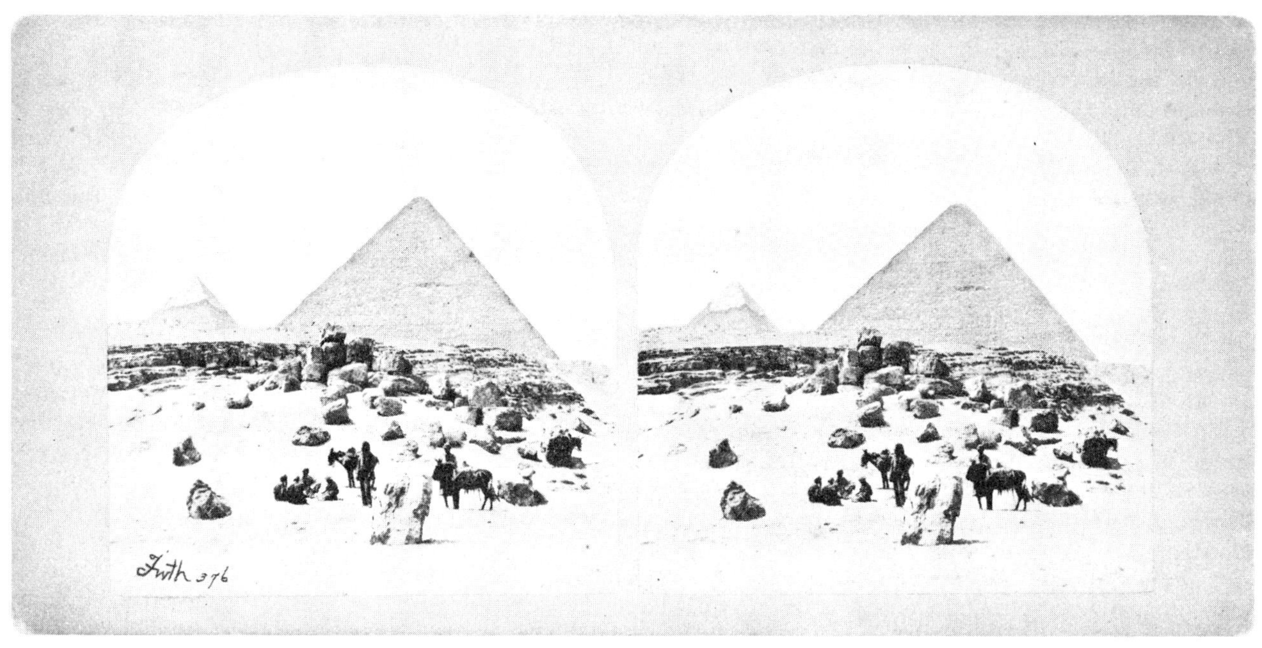

198. Francis Frith. "Views in Egypt and Nubia," "The two largest pyramids at Geezech." 1858.

1864. There are several stereo views showing scores of men carrying baskets of excavated sand up the sides of the great ditch. The celebration of the opening of the canal in November 1869 was stereographed by J. Andrieu at both Port Said and Suez, including the procession of vessels that made the first passage. Andrieu's small series of tinted tissue mounts is spectacular. Figure 13.

The Suez Canal increased general interest in Egypt. C. Gerard in the latter 1860's produced a series of about 150 views, "Egypte en Stereoscope." Other excellent series were published by Ferrier & Soulier, Braun, Leon & Levy, Bisson and W. Hammerschmidt.

Kilburn Brothers (1875) issued about ninety scenes of Egypt and Nubia. Subsequently (1890's) they added another hundred titles.

Several Egyptian photographers published extensive series of stereo views, largely for the tourist trade. The most important were G. Lekegian (Cairo, 1870's to mid 1890's) and J. Heyman & Co. (Cairo, 1890's to 1915). Heyman's images are high gloss prints. Both made views of natives engaged in daily work.

There are many Egyptian stereographs of unusual interest. The explorer Sir Samuel Baker and Lady Baker, seated on dromedaries, were photographed near Ezion Geber, Sudan in 1863. Anthony included this view in their Near East Series. Charles Piazzi Smyth's illustrations of astronomical experiments begun in 1856 in Tenerife, Canary Islands, were followed by others in Egypt (1865) including views of the interiors of the Great Pyramid.

Bert and Elmer Underwood toured Egypt in 1896 to secure a large series of stereoscopic negatives. They believed that they were the first to photograph Upper Egypt. The Underwood boxed set (1900) is the best stereo representation of the region ever published.

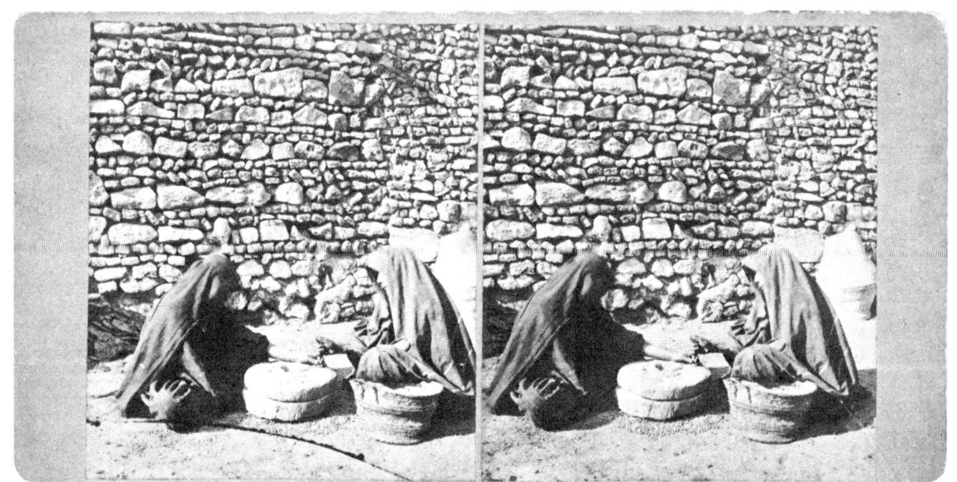

199. Egypt, Cairo. "Two Women Grinding Corn." Frank M. Good photo, 1865.

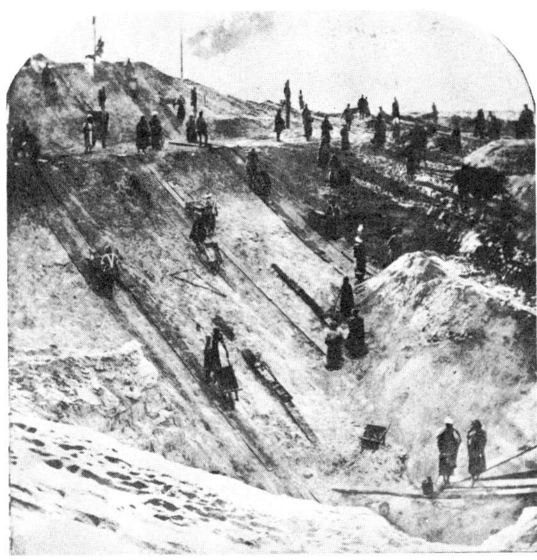

200. Egypt. "Digging the Suez Canal." H. Ropes and Co. issue, 1865. Source of negatives unknown.

THE BARBARY COAST: TUNIS, ALGIERS, TRIPOLI AND MOROCCO

Ferrier & Soulier published magnificent glass views of the Moorish settlements on the Mediterranean coast of North Africa. The scenes are mostly architectural, many with exquisite detail. All of the titles were available also as card mounts.

There are many early calotypes of Tunis and Algiers, tinted and untinted, by unidentified photographers. Very rare stereos by Richebourg were published about 1856.

J. Garriques, who had a studio in Tunis, issued stereo views in the 1860's and probably made negatives for several European publishers.

Bierstadt (1873) issued a few stereos for his American trade.

SOUTH AFRICA

Prior to 1900 the region included two British Colonies, Cape Colony and Natal, and two independent republics, Orange Free State and Transvaal, settled by Dutch and Huguenots. The British occupied Transvaal from 1877 to '84. After the Boer War (1899-1902) the region was reorganized as the Union of South Africa. These settlements were largely agricultural until the discovery of diamonds about 1870 and gold in 1875. Gold was not extensively mined, however, until 1884. The native peoples, Bantu, Hottentot, and Bushmen, were thinly scattered throughout the area.

Stereographs of South Africa before 1900 are quite rare, but those that are preserved record the transformation of the region.

Early in the 1860's two photographers had established galleries in Cape Town, E. Burmester and Arthur Green. Burmester issued an excellent series of town scenes.

G. Burger (Berlin, about 1872) published a varied series of nearly 400 titles of the Cape of Good Hope with titles in German and French. Another large series of views of considerable scientific interest illustrating the Orange Free State, Bechuanaland and Griqueland, was published by Dr. Stoltze (Berlin). The negatives were made by the natural history expedition organized and directed by Dr. Gustav Fritsch, 1863-66. There are fine anthropological views, especially the portraits of some of the native peoples. Figure 218.

Much rarer than the stereos of the Fritsch expedition are those taken by James Chapman during his exploration of the Upper Zambesi River (1860-64). Chapman in 1851, when only twenty years old, had begun his expeditions into the Zambesi region, and the Chapman "Pictures of African Travel" series on thin white card mounts recaptures some of these adventures.

About 1900-10 George B. Neilson (Boksburg North) issued a large number of local views, including extensive coverage of gold mining that showed underground operations in detail.

Scattered among the trade lists of Underwood, Keystone, Kilburn and White, there are many excellent views of gold and diamond mining. The set on "South Africa" published by Stereo-Travel Company (1908) conveys the best impression of the busy towns of South Africa.

So far as stereographs are concerned, however, it was the Boer War that brought many photographers to South Africa. The war views will be discussed later. Hundreds of scenes showing Pretoria, Johannesburg and Cape Town and many other towns were issued. There were also many views of the landscape, natives and agricultural pursuits.

CENTRAL AFRICA

There are very few stereo views of Central Africa before 1900. After that date the great American publishers sent photographers to Rhodesia and the Congo. Keystone employed a photographer to make a journey from Cape Town to Cairo, anticipating the preparation of several

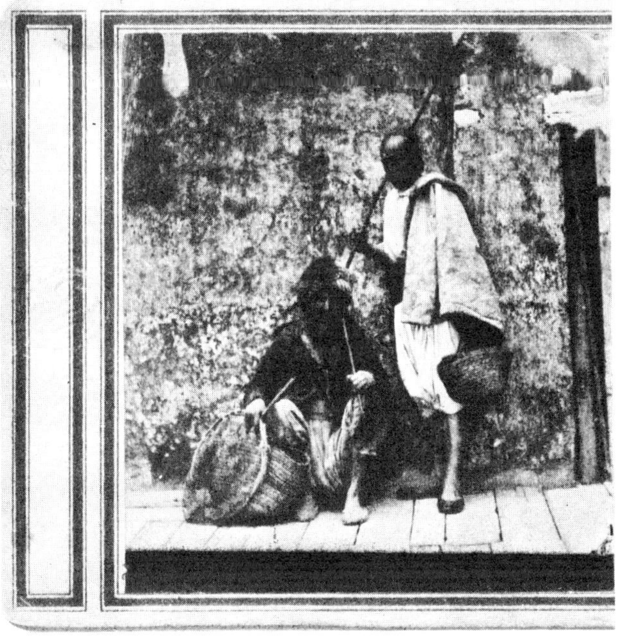

201. Algiers. "Ill-tempered Fisherman." Richebourg photo, ca. 1858. Note blind stamp monogram at middle of box on left margin.

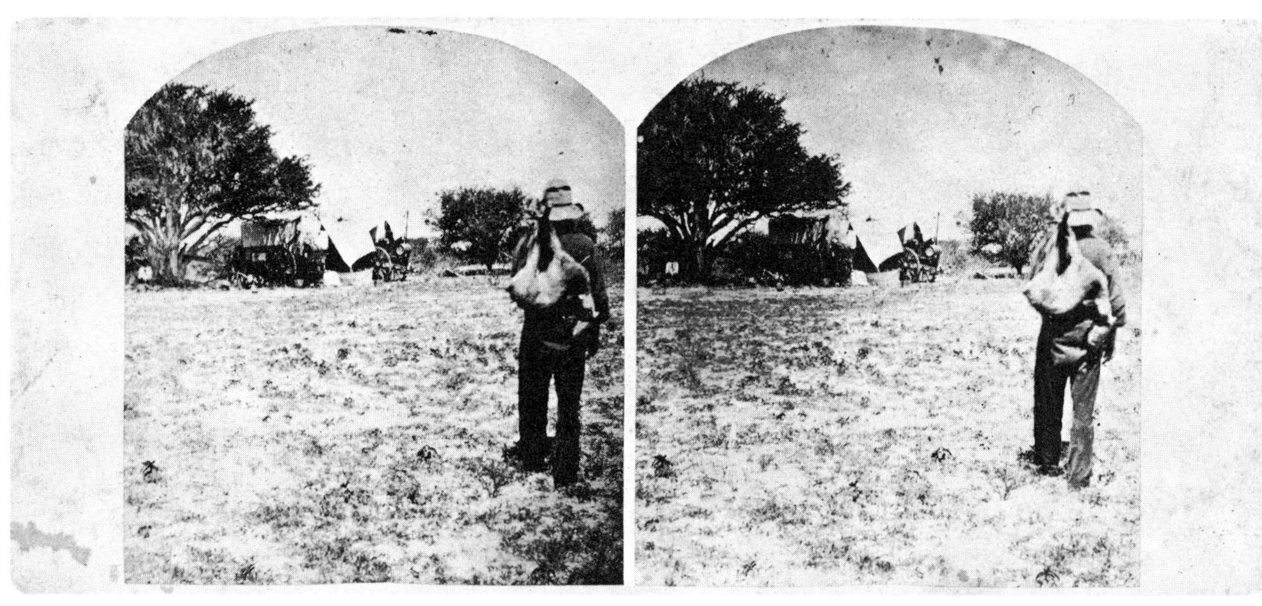

202. Africa, Zambesi. Chapman Expedition, 1860-1864. "Encampment at Elephant Valley. John Laing carrying a steenbok. Motlopie tree at left." J. Chapman, publisher. 1864.

travel sets. Spectacular views of the ivory trade, grass-hut villages and tribesmen were obtained.

Construction of the Victoria Falls Bridge over the Zambesi River was stereographed by an unknown photographer, possibly one of the engineers supervising the project in 1904. The railway bridge was complete in 1905. Keystone published a view of the bridge (No. 11063) about 1910.

There are two fine African travel sets, each with one hundred views, Underwood (1909) and Keystone (1923, revised 1927).

INDIA

To appreciate the magnificent range of stereo views of India, it is helpful to recall the the diversity of peoples and religions, the caste system and the marked distinction between British India and the Native States governed by Indian princes and chiefs. The more powerful princes lived in luxury, raised armies and ruled with almost complete independence of England.

The East Indian Company, founded in 1600, began commercial settlements in 1612. Over a period of almost 250 years the Company increased political control over the Indian continent. Frequent wars with native states occurred between 1800 and '50, as did mutinees by native troops. Although the Company's inability to administer the country politically had long been apparent, it was the mutiny of native troops in the Bengal army in 1857 that led to the abolition of the East India Company. In 1858 Queen Victoria proclaimed sovereignty over India, recognizing "the Native Princes of India."

At the height of the Great Mutiny, Negretti & Zambra issued a splendid series of stereographs, "Our India Empire . . . illustrating the social customs and religious ceremonies of the natives . . . by permission of the Honourable East India Company." The earliest issue is on gray cards and the second on enameled ivory cards.

There are many early stereo views of India, including fine calotypes, 1854-58, mostly by unidentified photographers. Some were produced by amateurs. Views by Samuel Bourne (ca. 1865-80; many published under the imprint Bourne & Shepherd) are well known.

During the 1860's and early '70's many photographers visited India to secure stereo negatives. The most extensive series was published by F. York ("York's Views in India," 1867-68, about 450 titles). Anthony's "Views in India" are from York's negatives.

G. F. Gates (Watkins, New York, 1868-70) issued a fine series from original negatives.

Burma, though part of continental India, was, nevertheless, often considered separate from India be-

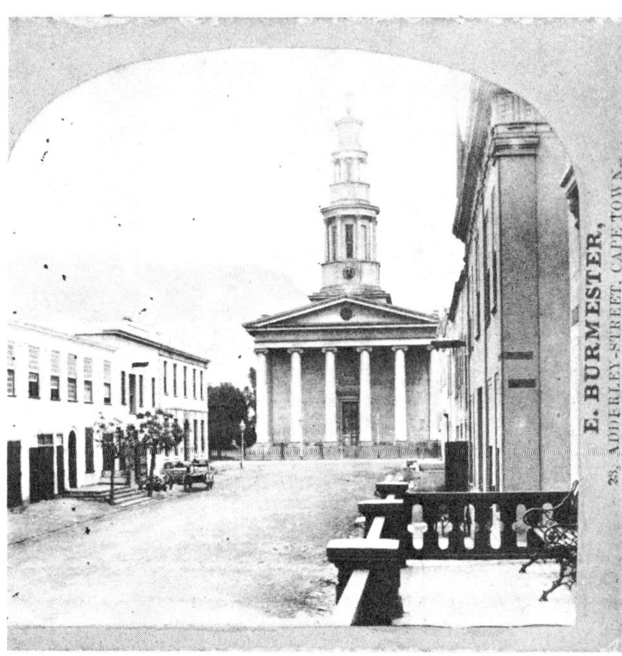

203. South Africa, Capetown. E. Burmester photo, ca. 1867.

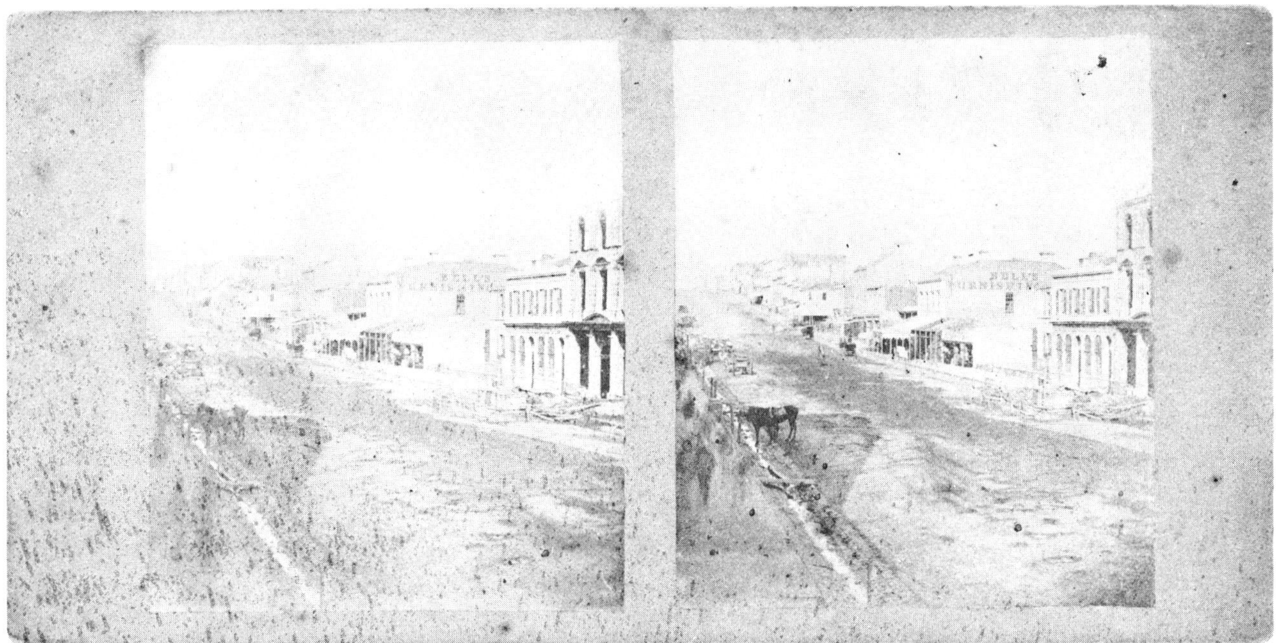

204. Australia, Melbourne. "Collins Street, East." McGlashon photo, ca. 1860.

cause of its many Oriental (Chinese) characteristics including its mongoloid native population.

Burma was frequently photographed between 1856 and '85. One of the most unusual series was published by the Women's Baptist Missionary Society (Boston, Massachusetts, 1872-76) from excellent negatives taken by Reverend A. Bunker. There are about seventy-five titles, including many of missions, Christian schools and native villages.

As we have noted before, stereographers after 1900 were more concerned with people than with places. The Underwood India set (100 views, negatives by Ricalton) is a masterpiece of photographic narration. Among the titles of unusual interest are several of the Great Durbar at Delhi in 1903. This colorful formal reception of the opulent native princes by the governor general typifies the zenith of the British Empire.

CEYLON

Although there are numerous views of Ceylon from about 1857 to '80, no extensive series seems to have been published until 1909 (Underwood, thirty cards). Keystone reissued the set without important changes in 1923. A much more representative coverage is to be found in the fine 100-card set issued by Stereo Travel Company (1910, 1913). Apparently there was little change in the outward appearance of the country from 1870 to 1910. A small series of twenty-one titles published by D. C. Clark in 1874 is especially informative in this respect.

AUSTRALIA

The vast expanses of Australia were thinly populated and much of its interior unknown before 1890. Even so, there are many early stereo views of Australia issued between 1856 and '75. Unfortunately, the majority of those examined have no photographer's or publisher's identification.

Perhaps the best known but a very rare series is that by McGlashon (early 1860's), probably the Scotsman Alexander McGlashon of Edinburgh. There are several sub-series, such as "Melbourne" and "Sydney." J. H. Newman (Sidney) published some local views about 1870. Moira and Haigh published a series of about 150 views in 1863.

Fine ivory mounts of the 1860's depict prominent buildings of Sydney, the Mohawi River and the harbor. Another series includes a fine view of "Carrier's Camp," and still another series has one of "Lal Lal Falls."

An early series on thin white cards, earlier than 1865, shows Queensland scenery, Brisbane and Moreton Bay. A titled series, "Bush Scenes in Queensland," was issued in the early 1870's.

Somewhat later, about 1878-80, an unidentified series issued on both standard and artistic mounts includes fine views of Dandenong National Forest.

Even after 1880 the majority of Australian views bear no photographer's imprint. There are excellent logging scenes, probably photographed in Victoria. There are good views of the Sandhurst gold field (ca. 1890).

Henry B. Merlin (American Australian Photographic Company) took several thousand negatives of the frontier on a trip from Sydney to the gold fields of New South Wales. How many stereo negatives were made is not known.

Some Australian photographers did identify their stereo views. Kerry & Jones (Kerry & Co., successors, Sydney) issued a large series, "Peeps in Sunny New South Wales" (1890's). They also published beautiful views of Jersey Cave. Ludovico W. Hart (South Yarra, Victoria, 1885-1905) also issued large varied series, "Australian Stereoscopic View," and "Hart's Centennial Views."

Kilburn included a number of views of Australia, among them the Charters Tower Gold Mine in Queensland in the earlier 1880's.

The rapid development of Australia, especially in en-

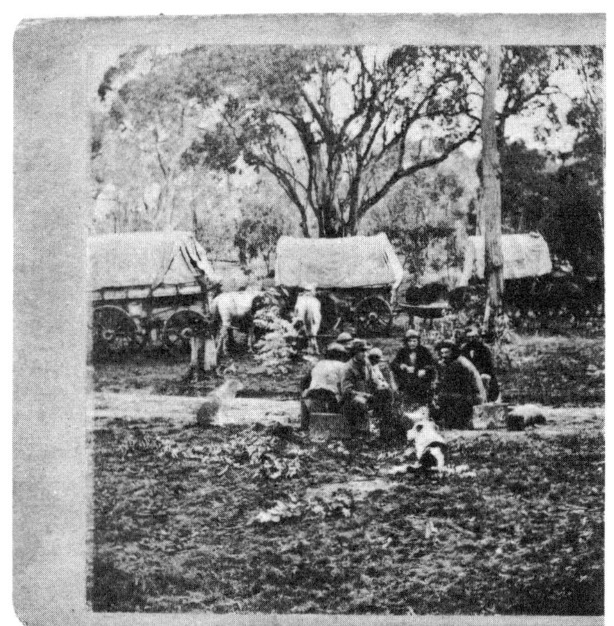

205. Australia. "Carrier's Camp." "Australian Scenery" series, unidentified photographer, ca. 1870.

gineering and industry, is shown beautifully by the Underwood set (eighty-four titles, 1906). The negatives passed to Keystone, which continued to publish them after 1923. Subsequently Keystone added several hundred Australian scenes to their trade list. Most of these are scattered in the World Tour, educational and natural history sets (1923-35).

TASMANIA

Most stereo views of Tasmania (united with the Commonwealth of Australia in 1901) are of Hobart and of the surrounding countryside, taken between 1865 and '90.

The earliest known to me were published by G. Cherry (ca. 1868), but there were undoubtedly other operators who preceded him.

At least two series were produced during the 1870's by local photographers. One of these, on green mounts, is very well done.

An astronomical station to photograph the transit of Venus was set up at Hobart in 1874. John Moran (Philadelphia), the chief photographer with the party, published about thirty views of the station and the Hobart vicinity.

NEW ZEALAND

Stereographs taken before 1880 are seldom credited to a photographer. Thomas E. Price (Masterton), best known for his portraits of natives, issued fine local scenic views.

Tait Brothers (Greymouth and Hokitika) produced views of these towns.

In the early 1900's J. Thompson (Auckland) distributed views of Auckland, including many of Albert Park.

Underwood included sixteen scenes of New Zealand in its "Australia" set.

CHINA

Stereographers began visiting China about 1860. There had been two periods of localized war ("Opium Wars") between China and England and France which resulted in treaties granting to foreign governments privileges of residence and trade in designated ports. Foreigners, including missionaries, were permited to travel into the interior. F. Beato was active in the Far East ca. 1855-1862.

Negretti & Zambra were the first to place on sale a splendid series "Views in China" on cream card mounts (about 200 titles), available tinted and untinted. The series includes many portraits of people posed in surroundings which illustrate in wonderful detail how they lived. Some of the scenes are of historical importance, such as "Pey Kwei, The Governor of Canton, Manderin of the Red Button, or the first class, with Mr. Commissioner Parkes, and attendants on Pey Kwei" (No. 38). The accuracy of the legends add much to the importance of these negatives by F. Beato. Figures 46 and 207.

In 1862 Anthony published a small series of fine "Views in China and Japan" (twenty-seven of China, seven of Japan) from negatives by M. Miller. Among the unusual titles are cases of leprosy (No. 18) and elephantiasis (No. 17) at the Missionary Hospital, Canton.

By the later 1860's photographers were able to range beyond Canton, Shanghai, Peking and Tientsin to record more of the occupational and religious aspects of China. Several French series are notable. BK (1868-72) published "Chine & Japon," including more than 250 numbers. The prints are mostly light and lack contrast. Another series, better printed, is simply titles "Vues de Chine." No. 19, "Chaise a Porteurs de Pekin," is typical of the care with which the photographer selected groups of people at characteristic occupations.

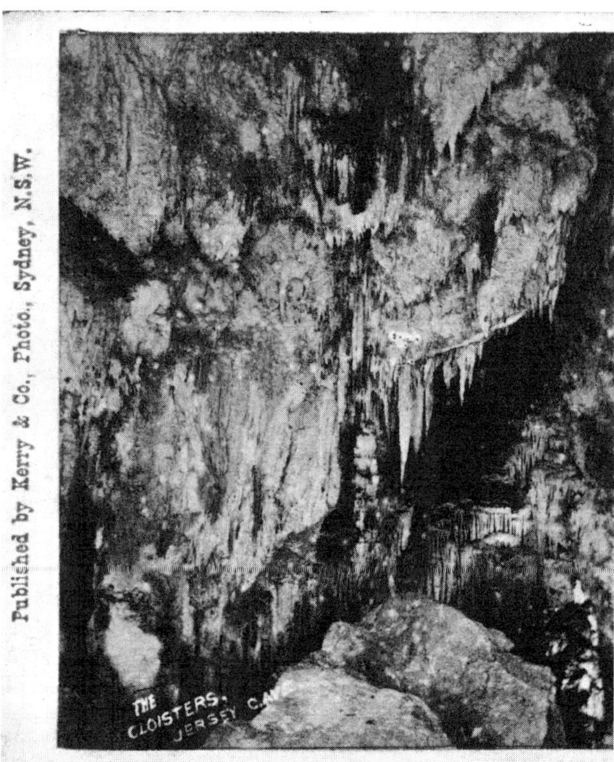

206. Australia, New South Wales. "Cloisters, Jersey Cave." Kerry and Jones photo, ca. 1890.

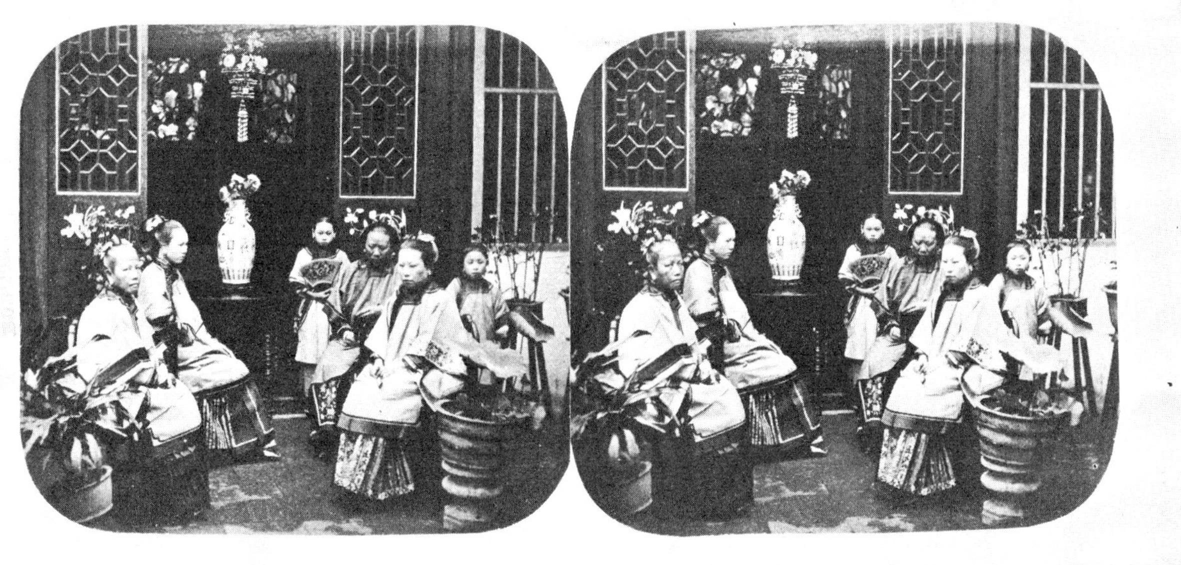

207. "Group of Chinese Ladies of Rank, evening Costumes." Canton. F. Beato photo, 1860. Note dealer's imprint (Joseph L. Bates, Boston).

W. Burger (Berlin) in 1868 issued approximately a hundred views of China in his sub-series "China and Japan" in the grand "Tour of the World." The titles are usually in German and French but are known also in German and English. The excellent prints are mounted on cards with red face and lavender back.

Thomas Houseworth published in 1869 an excellent series, "Views in China and Japan." These stereos differ from all others taken in China during the 1860's by their panoramic approach to the landscape.

Hong Kong, ceded to Great Britain in 1842, has been stereographed frequently from the late 1850's into the 1900's. Most of the early scenic views, of unknown origin, are unimaginative, the majority being of the harbor, government buildings and St. John's Place. Floyd, who had a gallery in Hong Kong, ca. 1865 to 1875, published views of the vicinity.

The aggressive ambitions of Russia and European trading nations increasingly threatened traditional Chinese life. Brief war with Japan (1895) resulted in not only the defeat of China but also a bitter reaction by Russia against Japan. Various groups in China, conservative and extremist alike, sought to oust all foreigners. This movement exploded in 1899, commencing with attacks on Christians, and culminated with the Boxer Rebellion in 1900. In June combined foreign troops seized Taku to gain access to Peking and Tientsin. Thousands, mostly Christians, were murdered. Without declaration of war the allied forces captured Peking and negotiated agreements for the future protection of foreigners.

James Ricalton hurried from the Philippine Islands, where he had been photographing for the Underwoods. He arrived at Taku in time to take excellent views of the action. His scenes showing refugees, prisoners, soldiers and horrible executions are among the most graphic war views published up to that time. Underwood assembled a twenty-six card set, "Boxer Rebellion," and incorporated them in the splendid "China" set (100 titles). Kilburn, among others, published excellent documentary views of the rebellion and of China more generally, 1900-04.

Underwood included eighteen views of Manchuria in the China set but sold them also as a separate set.

JAPAN

Japan entered into trading agreements with the United States in 1854, 1857 and 1859, opening Nagasaki and Yokohama to American ships and giving rights of resi-

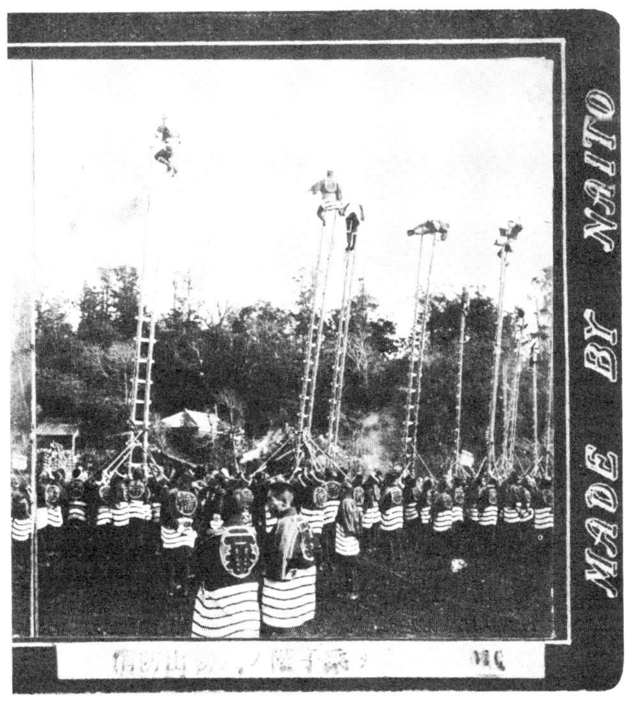

208. Japan, Tokyo. Exhibition by firemen. Naito photo, ca. 1900.

dence in several cities. Japan sent its first envoys to a foreign country to Washington in 1860. This was an exciting event, richly photographed in New York and Washington by Anthony, Fredericks, Stacy, Gurney, Brady and others.

At the same time that concessions were granted to the United States, similar privileges were extended to British, French, Dutch, German and Russian traders.

Japan very rapidly expanded participation in Asian affairs. Korea, although independent, came under Japanese domination in 1885. In Manchuria, Russian and Japanese interests were antagonistic. Japan supported the Western countries against China in the Boxer Rebellion, gaining favor with the European powers but thereby increasing its difficulties in Asia.

Russia's uncompromising position with respect to mutual interests in Manchuria and Korea led to a declaration of war against Japan in February, 1904. The annihilation of the Russian fleet and the capture of Port Arthur were but two of the brilliant Japanese victories. The stereographic record of the Russo-Japanese War portrays battle action, materiel and strategy more strikingly than any other war stereos—including World War I. The most notable views are by Underwood and H. C. White.

It will be remembered that Negretti & Zambra, Anthony, Burger, Houseworth and "BK" published series of China and Japan. Thus, the general comments as to issues and dates and quality of mounts need not be repeated.

There are several early issues which have no publisher's or photographer's imprint.

Excellent views of Nagasaki, Tokyo and Yokohama were issued between 1860 and 1867. The earliest series recognized is mounted on thin white card. The sharp images have manuscript titles in English. Another series, with English titles, is on canary-yellow card mounts (ca. 1865). A somewhat similar series on darker yellow mounts has the titles in Japanese characters. Still another series (ca. 1867) has fine prints on brownish yellow mounts. The landscape style and workmanship indicate that these are four unrelated issues.

Two nice series were published in England during the early 1860's: London Stereoscopic Company and Melhuish.

American photographers were more active in Japan in the 1870's. Anthony published its second series in 1871, and P. W. Weil (New York) produced about a hundred titles, 1873-74.

About 1873 there appeared on the American market a series of views of Japan on rather thick cards with yellow enameled face and soft white back bearing brief manuscript titles and a number ("760, Jeddo"; "765, View of Nagasaki"). This was possibly a copy issue, but I have not recognized stereographs from which they could have been copied.

A seldom seen, but very fine, series of about twenty-five titles was published by H. H. Bennett (Kilbourn City, Wisconsin) under the title, "A Summer in Japan." The negatives were taken by William H. Metcalf.

A few Japanese photographers produced stereographs during the 1860's and '70's. The Japanese Photographic Association (Yokohama) in the early 1870's issued fine scenes of the harbor, city and natives. The images are on yellow mounts typical of the period. R. Shimooka (Yokohama 1868-72) also published stereos of the city.

H. Uyeno (Nagasaki, 1870's) produced stereos of natives, including unusual tinted views of wrestlers and actors.

In the early 1900's Naito (Tokyo) issued a large variety of views illustrating Japanese life. The images are mounted on very thick card stock, with square cut corners. The card face is black and the back white, gray or black. The images are found tinted and untinted. The titles are in Japanese characters, sometimes printed on a strip label pasted to the bottom of the card face.

Owariya was either the successor or predecessor of Naito. He issued similar views on black cards with white backs. All of the examples I have seen are untinted. Some of the subjects are from the same negatives as Naito's views. The Naito-Owariya series includes many scenes not found among the stereos by foreign photographers, as, for example, "The Street of Pleasure," a street scene in a brothel district of Tokyo.

Despite the excellent views of Japan which were widely distributed before 1875, a much truer conception of the Japanese people is to be found in Underwood's beautiful 100-card set, one of their very best productions. Underwood's forty-eight card "Korea" set is also noteworthy.

Fine series of stereos of Japan, which supplement each other remarkably, were published by Keystone (1900-04, 1923-29), H. C. White (1900-10), Griffith & Griffith (1896-1902) and Stereo-Travel (1906-10).

ISLANDS OF THE PACIFIC

The Philippine Islands

The Philippines remained virtually unphotographed until the outbreak of the Spanish-American War. At that time a score of American photographers, mostly in the employ of stereo publishers, took thousands of negatives, about 2500 of which were ultimately used commerically. Most important were those by James Ricalton, who took, over the period of a year, "nearly 1900 negatives of war, life and industrial scenes" for Underwood.[1]

Although the majority of stereos were war-related, the natural landscape, natives, agriculture and industries were very broadly covered. Many Filipino personalities, such as Aquinaldo, were photographed. See also, SPANISH AMERICAN WAR, page 190.

A fine set entitled "Our Pacific Possessions," published by H. C. White (1905), is essentially a tour of the Philippines, Hawaiian Islands and Samoa, with scant attention to the war. Underwood issued a "Philippine Island" set of 100 cards (1901, revised 1909) which includes views of the Hawaiian Islands. Keystone, although copyrighting many good negatives between 1899 and 1903, did not issue a Philippine set until 1923 (fifty titles).

The Hawaiian Islands

American influence in the Hawaiian Islands extends to the 1830's largely through the activities of Christian missionaries. Hawaii sought annexation to the United States in 1893 but was not accepted by Congress until 1898. Two years later Hawaii became a Territory of the United States.

[1] Ricalton, James, *China Through the Stereoscope*, p. 12, 1901.

The splendid stereographic record of the Hawaiian Islands during and after the Spanish-American War has been mentioned above.

Much more important are the earlier views published by several resident photographers. J. W. King (Honolulu, 1860's) published a number of scenes but was apparently more interested in Americans living there than in natives and the natural landscape. M. Dickson (Honolulu, 1870's) produced many fine views of Honolulu and native villages. A. A. Montano (Honolulu, 1870's-80's) published more than 450 varied stereos in his series "Photographs Illustrating the Hawaiian Islands," which was issued on both standard and artistic mounts.

THE SOUTH SEA ISLANDS

Java, Sumatra and the Dutch Indies

Early views are very scarce, although a few scenes of Java were distributed by the London Stereoscopic Company before 1862. Burger published a series of views of the East Indies, 1870-1872. The best series is certainly Keystone's "South Sea Islands" set of 100 views (1923). More restricted in scope, but excellent, is the Underwood "Java" set (thirty-six views, 1903).

The Moluccas (Spice Islands)

Several views of native villages were sold by the London Stereoscopic Company about 1862. Copied views, probably made in the United States, were distributed about 1878.

Tahiti

A small number of scenes were issued by French and English publishers. Some of the earliest have been attributed to Gustav Viaud (ca. 1860).

LATIN AMERICA

South America, Central America and Mexico share a common Indian and Spanish heritage.

SOUTH AMERICA

Stereographs of South America reveal many relationships with the history of the continent. The over-all impression is a land that is thinly populated, largely by mixed blood Indian-European people, rugged Andean mountains, deserts and tropical rain forests. Yet its great cities, with deeply rooted Spanish influence, Rio de Janeiro, Buenos Aires, Lima, La Paz and others, were founded a century before any city in North America.

Although many photographers established galleries in the larger cities of South America before 1865, relatively few of their stereographs reached the United States before 1900. Equally strange, even the works of many North American photographers who operated there are seldom seen. This is not easily explained because there was considerable commerce with Chile, Brazil and Argentina. Yankee whalers and sailing ships made the long journey around the Horn. In this connection, two fine views by Underwood are of special interest: "Rounding the Horn" (No. 11200), showing a square-rigger in full sail, and "In the Straits of Magellan, looking Southeast to Snow-Covered Mt. Sarmiento" (No. 11201).

ARGENTINA

The most frequently encountered series, illustrating the city and harbor of Buenos Aires, is found on both yellow and buff mounts. The cards which have manuscript titles in Spanish, are probably of local origin (ca. 1875-80). In the early 1900's E. Widmayer issued a large series of "Views of Buenos Aires" as glossy prints not mounted on card.

BRAZIL

Brazil had been the possession of Portugal for three hundred years by the early 1800's. Hence, language and custom were largely influenced by this relationship. Rio

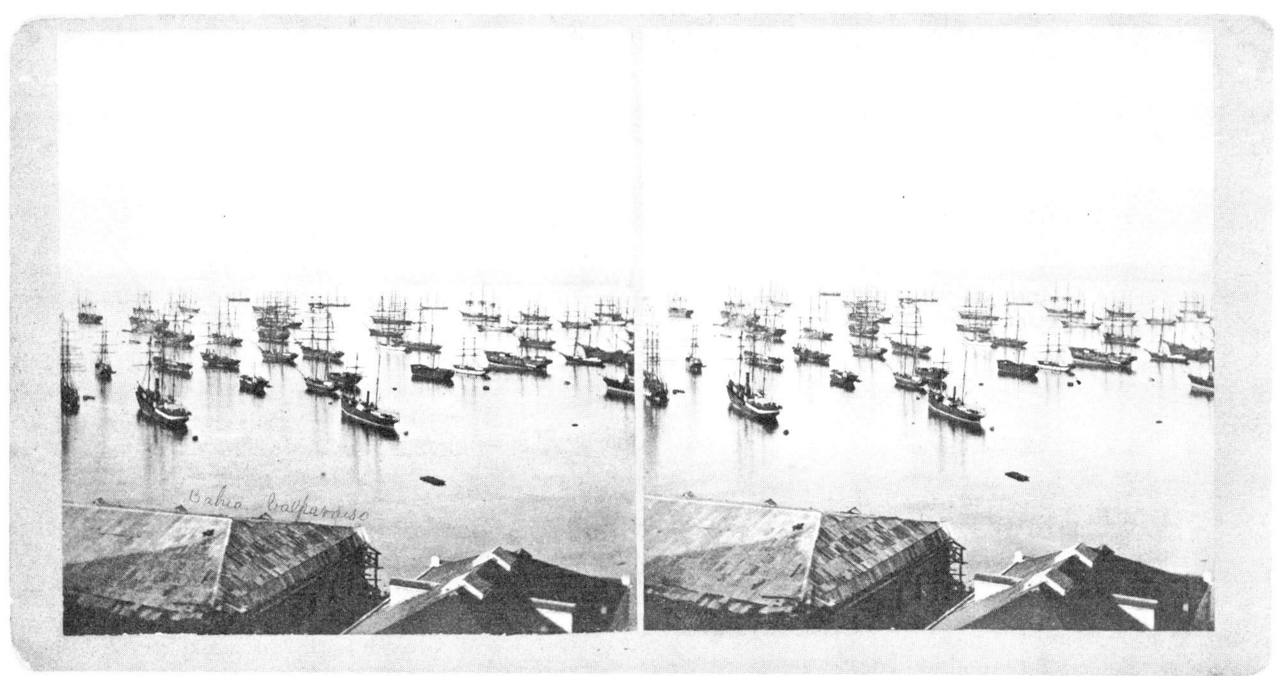

209. Chile, Valparaiso. Harbor scene. Bischoff and Spencer photo, 1873.

de Janeiro was the most cultured center in South America, mostly because of the influence of Dom Jogo VI, who lived there from 1808-22. His son, Dom Pedro, proclaimed Brazil's independence from Portugal in 1822 and remained in power until 1889. Dom Pedro, who was greatly admired in the United States, was treated with pomp when he visited the Centennial Exhibition in Philadelphia. Several stereographs show him at the opening ceremonies.

There are at least three fine series of stereos of Rio de Janeiro issued between 1855 and '65. The images depict palm-lined streets, the National Library, street scenes and the Botanical Gardens. The two earlier issues are on thin, soft, white card. The titles are in Portuguese and are undoubtedly of local origin. A few of the views which have reddish-brown images have the imprint of R. H. Klumb. A few views of later date (ca. 1875) are on yellow mounts. R. H. Fuhrman (ca. 1863-1875), G. Leuzinger (1860's) and Henschel and Benque (1880's) produced views of Rio de Janeiro and vicinity.

CHILE

The earliest stereos of Chile and Juan Fernandez Island were taken by Wm. G. Helsey (Liverpool) in 1860.

Bischoff & Spencer operated galleries in Valparaiso and Santiago. They published many excellent stereos, especially of the harbor with many ships in view (1870's into '80's). Valparaiso suffered bombardment by the Spanish in 1866, extensive destruction during civil war in 1891 and severe earthquakes 1873 and 1908. These circumstances place considerable historical value on the Bischoff & Spencer views. Their trade list includes many scenes on the Juan Fernandez Islands.

Spectacular views of the transcontinental railroad from Valparaiso to Buenos Aires, opened to traffic in 1911, were published by Keystone. Most of this series illustrate the engineering feats in the rugged Andean sections.

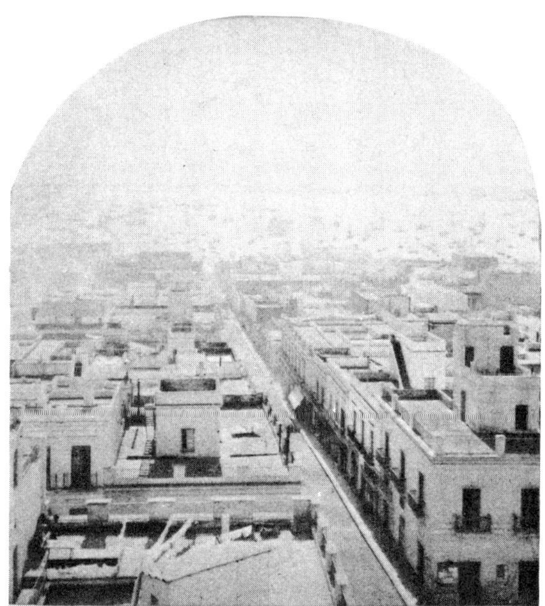

210. Uruguay, Montevideo. "Panorama." Chute and Brooks photo, ca. 1868.

COLOMBIA

Anthony published a series of fifteen scenes in "New Granada," the name by which Colombia was called in 1861 (Granadine Confederation 1858-61, New Granada 1861, Colombian Republic 1861-). I have not seen any other nineteenth century views of Colombia. After 1900 excellent stereos were published by Underwood and Keystone.

ECUADOR

Anthony produced a fine series of seventy views in 1863. Most of the views are of Quito but these are mountain scenery, including several volcanoes. Underwood published a forty-two card set in 1908.

PERU

Several excellent photographers operated galleries in Lima prior to 1875. V. L. Richardson (about 1859-64) and "E B" (in a caduceus logo, about 1860) published cityscapes. A few views by H. P. DeWitt and Amandus Moller are known. E. Courrett (1870's and '80's) issued at least 225 numbers illustrating Lima and vicinity. The titles and negative number appear on the left image.

A. D. Moulton and B. F. Pease published series in the 1860's.

Spectacular views of the pre-Inca massive stone works and other ruins at Cuzco are to be found in the Underwood "Peru" set (1908).

The excellent coverage of Peru suggests that the other countries of South America were photographed much more extensively than the meager existing collections record. By way of contrast, very few views of Uruguay and Venezuela are known to me.

URUGUAY

Chute & Brooke, who operated in Montevideo, issued a modest set of the city in the 1870's.

VENEZUELA

John L. Gihon (Philadelphia) published a small series of views in the early 1870's.

General South American Issues

The great North American publishers of the twentieth century treated the whole of South America as a single entity rather than a number of separate, individual countries. Underwood issued a 100-card set selected from hundreds of negatives. Apparently fewer than five hundred South American titles were commercially produced by Underwood.

The subjects documented by the photographer are fascinating: astronomical observatories, primitive bridges, nitrate mining, Indians, rubber and quinine cultivation, all of which supplement the usual scenes of town and country and give a beautiful cross-section of South American life.

Keystone continued publication of the Underwood views along with the best of a huge file of negatives taken by A. S. Iddings in 1912.[2] Prints from about 700 of Iddings' negatives were published, nearly all of these widely scattered through world tour and educational sets.

[2] Erwin, P. F., "Andrew S. Iddings, Explorer," 1967, pp. 303-330.

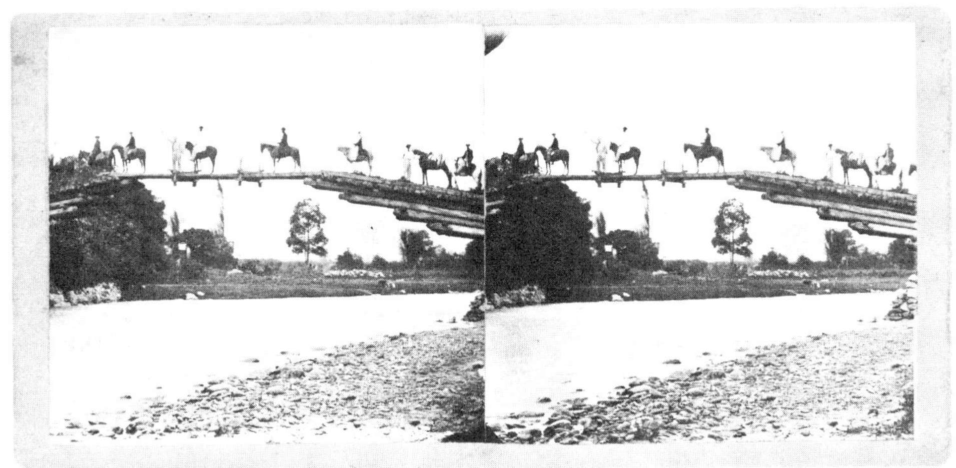

211. Venezuela. "Bridge over the Bocono River." Unidentified photographer, ca. 1870.

CENTRAL AMERICA

Only two areas of Central America have been extensively stereographed, Panama and Mexico.

PANAMA

Soon after the California gold rush, the narrow Isthmus of Darien was recognized as the possible location for a canal connecting the Atlantic and Pacific oceans. A railroad was constructed in 1850-55 by American interests but a ship canal that would eliminate the long difficult route around Cape Horn was essential. In 1870-71 the United States government authorized an expedition to explore and survey a possible route for a ship canal. Commodore T. O. Selfridge, the commander, was accompanied by two photographers, T. H. O'Sullivan in 1870 and John Moran in 1871. An official series of seventy-six views was published on artistic mounts distributed by Anthony. Jarvis published a "Tropical Series" comprised of Selfridge Expedition views, also on artistic mounts. There are about a hundred titles in the Jarvis series.

In addition to these, there is a considerable series on standard buff mounts published by Moran in 1872, without the photographer's imprint. All copies I have seen have manuscript titles in Moran's handwriting. None seems to be identical to the views published by Jarvis and Anthony.

There are, accordingly, no fewer than 200 stereo views of the Isthmus in the early 1870's—natives, villages and scenery, probably the most complete extant coverage of any Central American area.

After several abortive attempts by French companies to construct a canal across Panama, the United States resumed the project in 1904. The military advantages of a ship canal were evident during the Spanish-American War. Actual construction took seven years, and the canal was opened in August, 1914.

Hundreds of outstanding stereo views cover every detail of the building of the Panama Canal. Underwood issued a thirty-six card set of work in progress in 1909. A forty-five card set was published in 1912. Both Keystone and Stereo-Travel produced fine 100-card sets in 1912. Several printed half tone twenty-five card sets (1906-10) are worthy of mention.

COSTA RICA

Photographers operating in San Jose (1860's and early '70's) are known to have produced stereos of local scenes: F. Albar, L. Fortino and Edwardo Joej. These views are very scarce. M. C. Keith and A. S. Taylor issued small series in the 1870's.

Somewhat later, H. N. Rudd (San Jose, branch studio at Alajuela) issued about 1880 a series of approximately fifty views of these two towns and coffee trading.

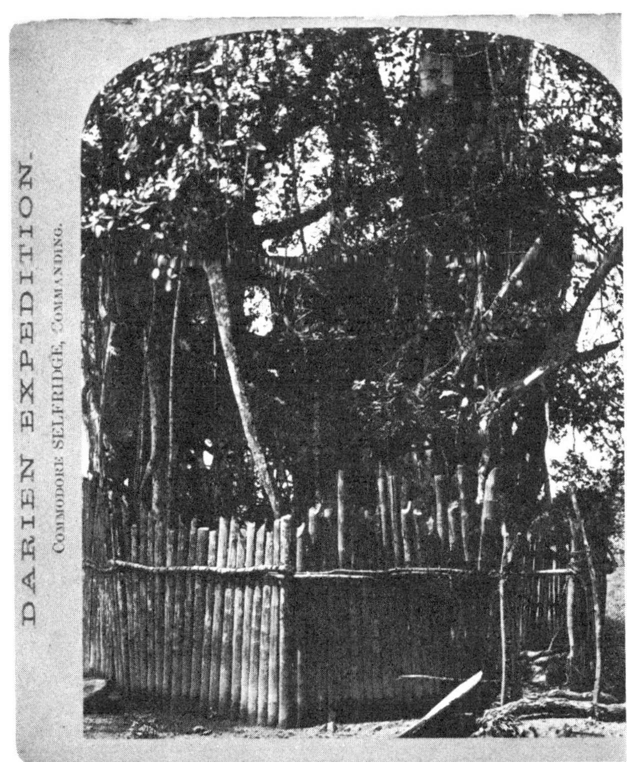

212. Panama. Selfridge Darien Expedition, 1870-1871. "Ruins of Old Spanish Fort and Martyr Tree." T. H. O'Sullivan photo, E.&H.T. Anthony publisher.

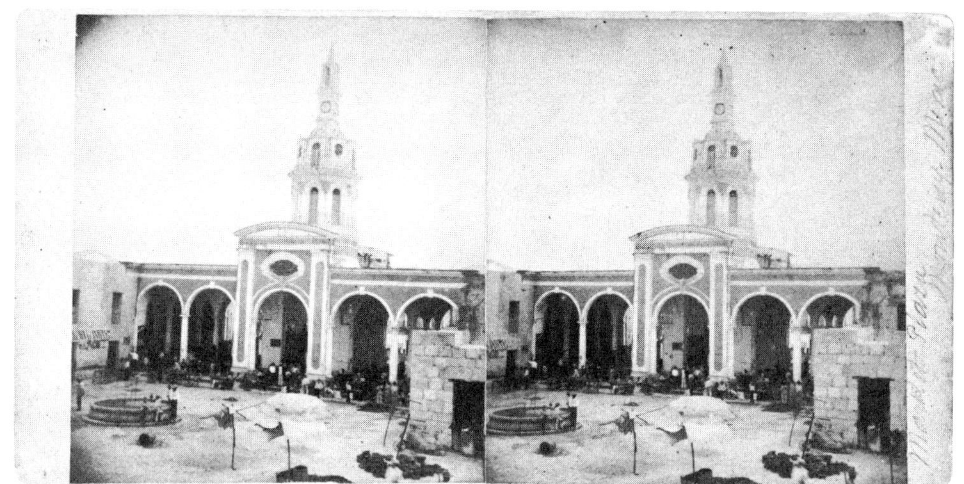

213. Mexico, Monterey. "The Plaza." Lagrange and Hermano photo, ca. 1868.

E. Herbruge (Antigua, 1860's into 1870's) published views of this city.

GUATEMALA

G. A. Hawley (successor to W. C. Buchanan, Guatemala, 1860's) published fine views of the city. A few views by Enrique Seeligman (San Miguel, 1860's) are also known.

MEXICO

Between 1860 and 1880 scores of photographers, the majority Europeans of French and German origin, settled in the principal towns, especially the seaports, of Mexico. How many of these published stereographs is uncertain, but many did.

The following produced views of their vicinities:

Barroeba	San Luis Potosi
Carlos Clausnitzer	San Luis Potosi
V. Contreras	Guanjuato
Alberto Fahrenberg	Monterey
A. Lagrange & Hermano	Monterey
Juleo Michaud	Mexico City
G. L. Zuber	Mazatlan

These views are very rarely seen in the United States. Apparently their sale was limited to their own localities. Far better known are the many Mexican series published by United States photographers.

The most ambitious series (157 titles) was published by Kilburn Brothers (1873). The negatives, which were made by Edward Kilburn, include people at work, Mayan monuments and village scenes. The implicit activity and coordinated sequence anticipate the later tour technique developed by Bert Underwood.

Melander (Chicago, 1875) published a series of about a hundred views "by a special artist."

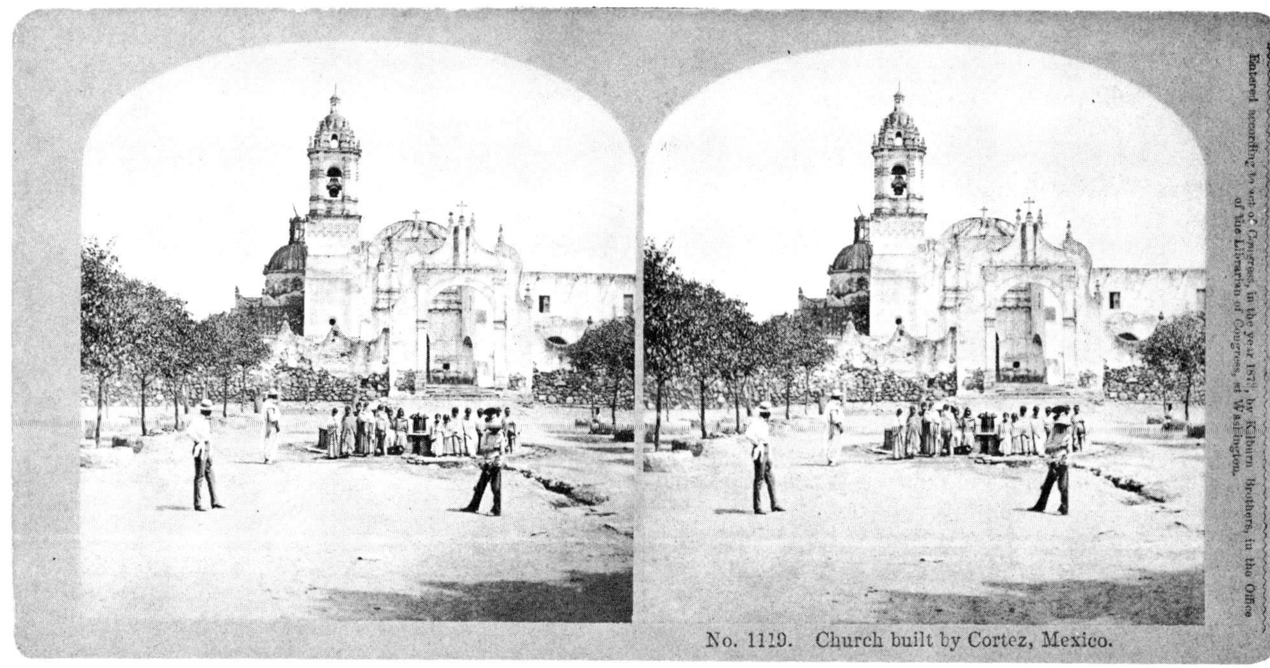

214. Mexico. "Church built by Cortez." Kilburn Brothers photo, 1873.

In the mid 1870's Joseph H. Downing (Healdsburg, California) published at least fifty stereos of Lower California.

Several Colorado photographers traveled in northern Mexico to take stereo negatives. Wm. H. Jackson (mid 1880's) issued about a hundred titles. Nims and D. B. Chase produced smaller series.

Somewhat later, E. L. Clement (Chicago, 1890's) published a series of 100 views "On the Line of the Mexican Central Railroad." Barker (Eureka Springs, Arkansas, 1880's) issued views of Juarez. Chihuahua was stereographed by F. Parker and H. A. Doerr, both of El Paso, Texas (late 1870's and early '80's).

Of the boxed travel sets published in the twentieth century, those by Underwood (100 cards, 1909) and Stereo-Travel (100 cards, 1910) are best.

THE WEST INDIES (ANTILLES)

The islands of the Caribbean Sea are grouped into the Greater and Lesser Antilles.

Cuba

The earliest known stereographs of Cuba are excellent intense black images mounted on thin off-white card 1855 or earlier. The manuscript titles are in Spanish. A somewhat later series on thin white card have the titles in German. M. E. A. Mestre (Havana, ca. 1860) published views of Cuba but apparently did not use an imprint to identify his work.

In the mid 1860's C. F. Fredericks, who had studios in New York and Havana, sold views of Cuba on yellow mounts. Probably the negatives were made by one of his employees in Hàvana. There is neither a publisher's nor a photographer's imprint on the cards.

Anthony (1862) published a series of nearly 200 views of Cuba including a wide range of subjects but notably thirty excellent views of the sugar industry.

Vere F. Campbell (Washington, D. C., 1871) published a small series of Cuban views.

The sinking of the *U. S. S. Maine* by a mine in the harbor of Havana (February, 1898) precipitated the Spanish-American War. American troops invaded Cuba and quickly defeated the Spanish garrisons. The Spanish fleet was destroyed in the Battle of Santiago Bay. American administration of the island continued until 1902. Cuba was probably the first nation to have its birth photographed. Underwood published the historic scene, "The Cuban Republic's Birth, Noon, May 20, 1902, Havana." The negative passed to Keystone, which continued to publish it under No. V 14493.

The Spanish-American War created a tremendous demand for stereo views in the United States, a demand that accelerated mass production of stereographs.

Underwood issued a 100-card set, including Puerto Rico in 1901 (revised 1909). Stereo-Travel produced a set of 100 cards in 1912. These represent but a small fraction of the many hundreds of views issued by Underwood, H. C. White, Keystone and Griffith & Griffith. Although most of the scenes pertain to the war, many portray Cuba and its people.

Puerto Rico

All of the views of Puerto Rico known to me were taken after the American occupation in October, 1898. Puerto Rico became a Territory of the United States in 1917. As indicated above, the stereos are usually seen in the "Cuba" and "World Tour" sets published by Underwood, Keystone and H. C. White.

Haiti

J. Wheeler (1860-65) produced a few stereos of Haiti. W. Watson (Port au Prince, 1875-85) published a greater variety including views of coffee cultivation and personalities, among them, General Hirau.

Jamaica

At least two photographers who operated galleries in Kingston issued stereo views of their vicinity, A. Duperly & Sons (1860's) and George W. Davis (ca. 1870). P. Sarthou (Lucea, latter 1860's into '70's) also published local views.

H. C. White published a very fine 100-card set of Jamaica in 1909. Another, entirely different 100-card set was issued by Stereo-Travel in 1913. Smaller sets were issued by Underwood (twenty-four, 1909) and Keystone (thirty-six, 1923).

The Kingston earthquake (1907) was extensively stereographed. The best set is a lithoprint series of twenty-five views.

The Lesser Antilles

Despite the fact that stereographs of only a few of the islands are known, photographers were probably active in all of them.

A very fine diverse series, "Six Months Tour of the Tropics," was published by Holt and Gray, 1860-1861, includes views of many islands.

There are about a dozen scenes of St. Christopher, St. Croix and St. Thomas in Pollack's "America Illustrated—Tropical Series" (1874). The stereos are too few and too scattered to give more than a superficial impression of these islands.

In the mid 1860's J. W. Clement published a few views of St. Thomas. Another series with tinted images by an unidentified photographer was issued about 1868.

J. W. H. Campion, in the 1870's issued views of Barbados.

Martinique

Stereographs of the eruption of Mont Pelee are among the most famous ever produced. On May 8, 1902, after threatening for several months, the volcano erupted with tremendous violence, emitting a cloud of super-heated gases which snuffed out the lives of 30,000 people and devastated the town of St. Pierre. Many photographers rushed to the scene of the disaster and recorded awesome pictures of the volcano and the destruction. The stereos by Keystone are the best. Underwood issued twenty-five views, a selection of eighteen were sold as a boxed set (1903). Figure 299.

La Soufriere, on nearby St. Vincent, which also erupted in May, 1902, was stereographed by H. C. White, Underwood and Keystone.

OTHER ATLANTIC ISLANDS

Bermuda

Four very fine series of views of Bermuda were published between 1866 and '85. The earliest series, with

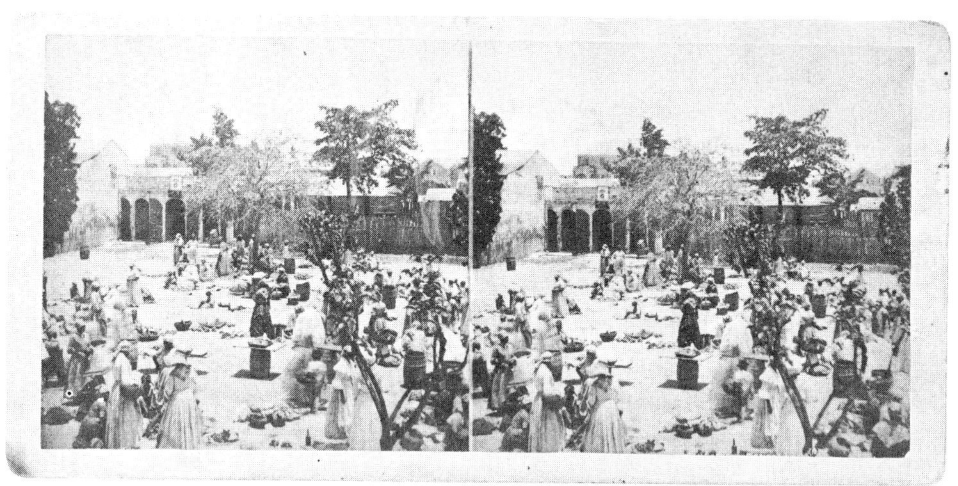

215. St. Croix, West Indies. "Fredericksted, Market Day." "Six Months Tour in the Tropics" series. Holt and Gray photo, 1860-1861.

more than 100 titles, was issued by Balch. A larger variety were published by J. B. Heyl (Hamilton, 1870's). A very similar series was produced by H. L. Chase (Hamilton, later 1870's and '80's). In some respects the series by Kilburn Brothers (ninety-five titles, 1875) is more pleasing because the veiws represent a tour of the island, rather than a miscellany of interesting scenes.

A few views by T. Frith (Hamilton) are known.

The Azores

The large Portuguese ethnic population in New Bedford and other fishing towns in Massachusetts had emigrated from the Azores, Madeira and the Canary Islands, rather than directly from Portugal. The desire to retain sentimental ties with relatives and the former homeland resulted in a truly remarkable stereographic heritage.

In the early 1860's R. A. Miller (Boston) issued fine, probably the best, views of the Azores and Madeira.

M. Goulart (Horta) began publishing local stereos in the 1870's, most of them destined for sale in the United States. About 1885 Goulart settled in New Bedford, where he continued issuing stereo views until the late 1890's. His trade list ultimately exceeded 600 numbers, with titles in English and Portuguese. Goulart had views of each of the nine islands of the Azores. He also visited Madeira to take views of the island and its chief town, Funchal. Regrettably, the technical quality of most of Goulart's views is rather poor. Nevertheless, the scenes record vital detail.

Views of Funchal by S. Wit (ca. 1870) are occasionally found.

. . . . . .

The regional stereographs so sketchily summarized in the last four chapters can only suggest the wide scope and variety of views that are available. In no sense is this summary complete or comprehensive. We can assume that in every country of Europe and in every part of the world touched by Western Culture, photography was practiced between 1845 and 1860. Almost as certainly, some photographers in each area produced stereographs. Most of these views probably remained in the countries of their origins.

Reasonably complete surveys of stereographs country-by-country can be accomplished only by resident investigators.

A SUBJECT GUIDE TO STEREOGRAPHS

GENERAL COMMENT

The encyclopedic subject guide which follows is arranged in alphabetical sequence. Eighty subjects, of unequal magnitudes, have been selected to accomplish three objectives:

1. to provide a cross section of the kinds of stereographs that comprise a tremendous resource of pictorial documentation;
2. to indicate the extent to which this stereographic heritage can be useful to historians, scholars and librarians, as well as to satisfy collectors;
3. to suggest what kinds of views are available and by citing photographers, series and specific titles to convey a "feeling" for associating time, place and probability.

Most experienced collectors develop a "sixth sense," an intuitive skill—a kind of serendipity by which one hint triggers another, often unrelated, in the search for specimens and information.

Some readers might object to the historical and social comments that accompany each topic. I have tried to relate the stereographs to the periods in which they were produced and to imply the circumstances that inspired photographers to publish them.

ADVERTISING

Stereo views have been used in various advertising and promotional activities. In the most direct form, a stereograph illustrated the product being offered for sale. Such items as glassware, silverware, furniture, carriages, and machinery were often advertised by stereo views. The most unusual examples are to be found in a series (1868) of about fifteen machine tools manufactured by the Brown & Sharpe Company of Providence, Rhode Island. A complete technical description of the machine is printed on the back of each view.

Real estate was occasionally sold in this manner. Dr. H. E. Bennett of Boston distributed a view of his Rockport property in 1872 (J. Wing photo). About 1880, J. Austen of Fergus Falls, Minnesota distributed a view of a water power dam which he was offering for sale.

Several companies issued sets of views illustrating their manufacturing facilities and products. Most of these were intended for the instruction of salesmen but some were distributed more generally. Such products as corsets, shirt collars and umbrellas were stereographed. H. C. White Company issued a fine set of its own stereograph and stereoscope factory.

The best known series, however, is the fifty card tour of the Sears Roebuck Company. A similar, much rarer, series was issued by T. Eaton & Sons of Toronto, also a mail order house.

There are many views of stores, photographic galleries and other business establishments. Some of these portray the proprietor and clerks. There are fine interior as well as exterior views. Grand openings and anniversary sales provided occasions for most of these stereos.

During the period 1875-1885, views in several cheap and reprint lines were used extensively in advertising. A merchant (typically a dry goods, notions, or drug store) merely printed his address or message on the backs of cards which were sold to customers at two to five cents each.

Briefly, between 1878 and 1885, several advertising companies sold space on the backs of stereo views. Thus a card might have as many as eight or ten brief notices by a group of local merchants.

The use of lithoprints as free premiums, especially by cereal manufacturers (1904-12) is described on page 54.

AGRICULTURE

The stereographic record of agriculture is so extensive that only a brief synopsis will be given here. Touring photographers invariably made negatives of the characteristic crop plants and farming methods of every culture and geographical region.

There are fine series, all issued after 1900, illustrating cotton, sugar, wheat and rice, not only as crop plants but also as commodities in world trade. Maize or Indian corn was not covered by a series of views, but hundreds of stereos show every aspect of its cultivation from primitive Indian methods to Iowa hybrid varieties in the early 1930's.

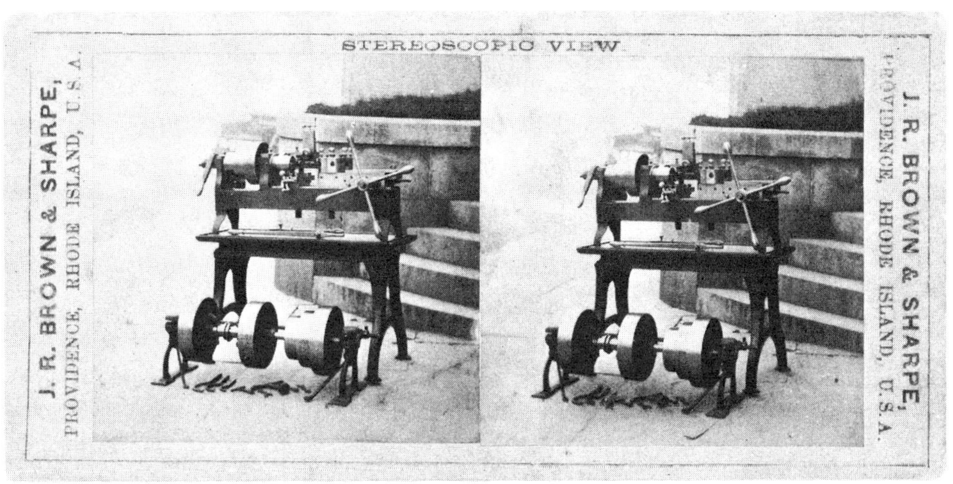

216. Advertising. Brown and Sharpe Company. "Screw Machine for Manufacturing of Fire-Arms and Sewing Machines." Technical description and specifications on the back. 1868. Photographer unknown.

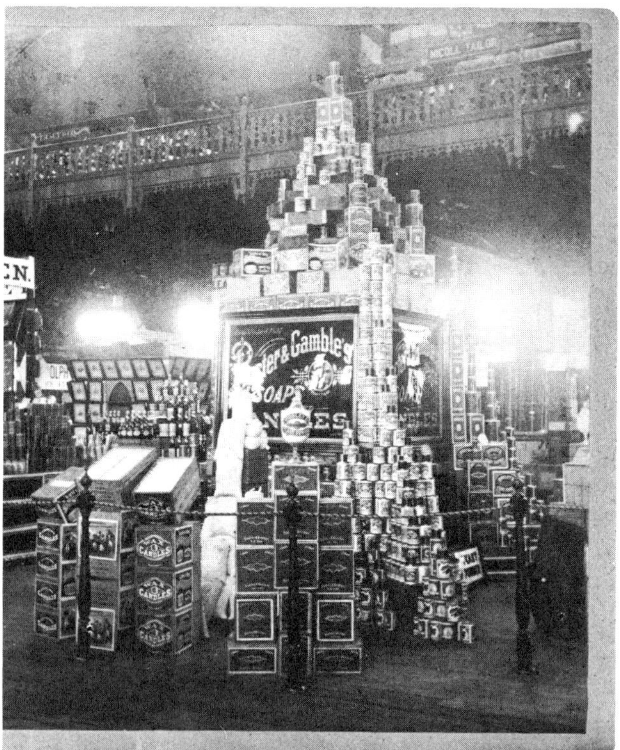

217. Advertising. "Procter and Gamble Soap and Candle Display, Mechanics Institute Fair, San Francisco, August-September, 1878." Unknown photographer. View distributed by W.A. Hepburn, Manufacturers' agent.

All vegetable crops from lettuce and cabbage to melons and peanuts (ground nuts) have been stereographed.

Types of cultivation such as dry farming, irrigation, rice paddy, and milpa (Central America) are well illustrated. The complete range of farming tools from digging stick to twenty-horse reapers and motorized tractors may also be found in stereos.

Views of fruit culture and semi-wild trees such as coconut palm, in temperate and tropical climates are plentiful. Grape vineyards and hop culture have been photographed in many countries. Keystone published several views of spraying equipment in fruit orchards (ca. 1925).

Animal husbandry is an integral part of farming throughout the world, in terms of milk, meat and work. Stereographs of horses, mules, oxen, water buffalo, sheep, goats, camels, hogs, are to be found in the travel sets.

There are many collateral aspects of agriculture that should not be overlooked. Several of the Land Grant Colleges and Experiment Stations (Kansas, Iowa, Illinois, Nebraska, Cornell) have been the subjects of small series of views. There are scenes of experimental farms, herds and flocks of animals as well as of service buildings. Many agricultural fairs, mostly county fairs, have been stereographed from about 1865 to 1885. The agricultural buildings and exhibits in the American world fairs, especially the centennial and Columbian Exhibitions, are of great historical interest. The progressive mechanization of agriculture can be readily visualized, by comparing the displays of farming equipment.

AMATEUR STEREOGRAPHS

There were two periods during which amateur stereography was popular. The most exciting period extended from 1850 to 1870 when hundreds of persons from all walks of life experimented with the medium. Both in England and in the United States amateur exchange clubs were organized (see page 27). Hundreds of amateurs, however, did not join societies. We cannot always be sure that a person was an amateur or a semi-professional, that is, one who sold views for profit.

During the second period, roughly 1905 to 1925, two stereo formats were widely used by amateurs, the standard card mount and the small Richard type (glass or paper) positive prints. The majority of these views record family outings, vacations, and travels to foreign countries. The large majority of surviving stereo views were manufactured by professional photofinishers. For example, Julius Wendt (also Wendt Brothers) of Albany, New York processed the film, made the prints and mounted the cards for scores of amateurs.

Generally, the historical interest of these later amateur views is slight, but there are exceptions. There are series of expositions, carnivals, fires and personalities. An amateur produced a fine informal series of Harry S. Truman with his cabinet and friends and provided a set for each member of the party.

ANTHROPOLOGY

No special comment on this category is necessary. Traveling stereographers were primarily interested in peoples. The photographer was usually well aware of small or minority groups and made appropriate arrangements to photograph them. Thus we find excellent views of the Ainu of Japan (Keystone - White W33912), the Pygmies of Africa, Indians of Terra del Fuego and many others. Mere knowledge of the historic location of a given people is sufficient to begin a search for views of them.

The archeology and pre-history of peoples are well stereographed within the time limitations of photography. The monoliths of the Easter Islands, Mayan pyramids, Stonehenge, remains of Swiss lake dwellings are examples of the types of subjects available.

The cultural aspects of national and regional populations were basically the features that captivated the imagination of photographers, marriage ceremonies, family groups, occupations of women, hair dressing and hunting are but a few of the practices that have been stereographed.

Perhaps the single most significant stereo pictorial record concerning cultural anthropology is the phenomenon of social change brought about through contact and communication.

ARCHITECTURE

A large proportion of the stereo views produced between 1854 and 1880 were essentially architectural. Specifically or incidentally cathedrals, palaces, public buildings and monuments were depicted in great detail. The full range of religious, royal and administrative buildings is available in stereo. Every notable structure in the world in existence between 1850 and 1930 has been stereographed. This sweeping generalization is literally true. For examples, one need only cite the Taj Mahal, Eiffel Tower, Great Wall of China, St. Sophia, and the Alhambra.

The rich coverage of domestic architecture from medieval Europe to Yokohama in 1860, including the rapidly changing styles in the United States from 1850 to 1930 is almost incredible.

There are hundreds of views of the mansions of the rich but just as many of more modest residences. A majority of these nineteenth century American structures have been destroyed.

Construction methods, from simple carpentering to the modern skyscraper, are thoroughly documented. One can also find many views illustrating the use of native building materials as well as of brick, cement and concrete.

ARCTIC AND ANTARCTIC

Many attempts to find a northwest passage to the Pacific Ocean were made before the development of photography. Public interest was heightened by the loss of the John Franklin expedition in the 1840's and by the British and American search efforts to determine what had happened to Franklin and his men. Dr. E. K. Kane's expedition (1853-55) encouraged several American parties to venture into the Arctic.

In July 1860, Dr. I. I. Hayes, who had accompanied the Kane expedition, sailed from Boston with "a photographer sent by the American Photographic Society." A remarkable series of about eighty stereo views, copyrighted by Hayes, was published by T. C. Roche.[1]

Exploring parties were sent to Greenland between 1858 and 1885 by Sweden, Norway, Great Britain and the United States. Few stereographs were made by them. Even the remarkable international cooperative circumpolar stations (1882-83) involving ten nations seem to have been neglected by stereographers.

Meanwhile, in the 1870's William Bradford published about sixty views of Greenland and Laborador (negatives taken 1869). In 1875, H. N. Robinson (Reading, Massachusetts) issued a series of forty-six views, "Laborador Life and Scenery" from his own negatives.

The period of "modern" polar explorations, 1890-1930, fared much better photographically because it was no longer necessary to work with the wet plate techniques.

Robert E. Peary 1886-1909, North Pole, 1909
  Underwood issued about twenty views of the Peary expedition at Cape Sabine in 1899 (4681-4700).

A. W. Greely (American, 1881-84)
  Kilburn issued several, including a model group at California mid-winter Exposition (9622). These views were not taken in the field.

Fridtjof Nansen (Norwegian, 1893-96)
  Views by Underwood (1897)

Roald Amundsen (Norwegian, Arctic 1903-06; 1918-22, Antarctic, with Gerlach 1895-96; South Pole 1912).
  Keystone, including a view of "Amundsen inspecting an ice field (13327, 1912).

Adrien de Gerlach (Belgian) 1895-99
  There are excellent views of Gerlach and the *Belgica* by Keystone.

Robert F. Scott (British, with Schackelton 1901-04, Antarctic, reached continental land 1901. Separate expeditions, Scott 1911-12, Schackelton 1908, 1921) A few views were issued by Underwood.

It is probable that stereographs of other expeditions and their leaders have been published. There are views of Eskimo natives and Greenland settlements, by Underwood and Keystone. Included in Underwood's views of Peary at Cape Sabine, Ellesmere Land, are several of Eskimo families. An excellent view of an ice-bound steamship in Baffin Bay was published by Keystone (4224).

ASTRONOMY

There are three categories of stereo views of astronomical interest: (1) our solar system and the constellations in our galaxy, (2) astronomical research expeditions, and (3) astronomical observatories and instruments.

J. W. Draper (1840) and J. A. Whipple (1849) made daguerreotypes of the moon. The first stereograph of the moon was produced by Warren De La Rue at the Cranford Observatory in 1858.

In 1860 J. A. Whipple produced telescopic images of the moon on February 5 and on April 6, thereby obtaining sufficient change in position to achieve the effect of rotundity. Whipple's stereograph was not exploited commercially but L. M. Rutherford, who had experimented with astronomical photography since 1857, published a magnificent stereograph in 1862. He used Whipple's method but shortened the time interval, taking negatives on December 17, 1861 and on January 16, 1862. Permission to publish this view was granted freely. There are thus a dozen issues, including Beer Brothers, Bierstadt Brothers and Anthony. In 1864 Rutherford published several additional stereos of the moon. Draper made stereoscopic negatives of the phases of the moon which were published under several imprints, most notably by Charles Bierstadt.

The solar eclipse of August 7, 1869 was stereographed by the Philadelphia Photographic Eclipse Expedition under the direction of Professors Henry Morton and J. H. Coffin, USN.

An international cooperative project to photograph the Transit of Venus in 1874 aroused considerable popular interest. Small series of views were published from stations set up in Tasmania (John Moran, photos) and Siberia (D. R. Clark photos).

Keystone View Company published approximately thirty views of the sun, planets, comets and meteors. Eight titles are relatively common, having been included in the "600" Educational Set. Most spectacular are the stereos of Mars (16766) and Saturn and its rings (16767).

Among the views of observatories there are many unusual

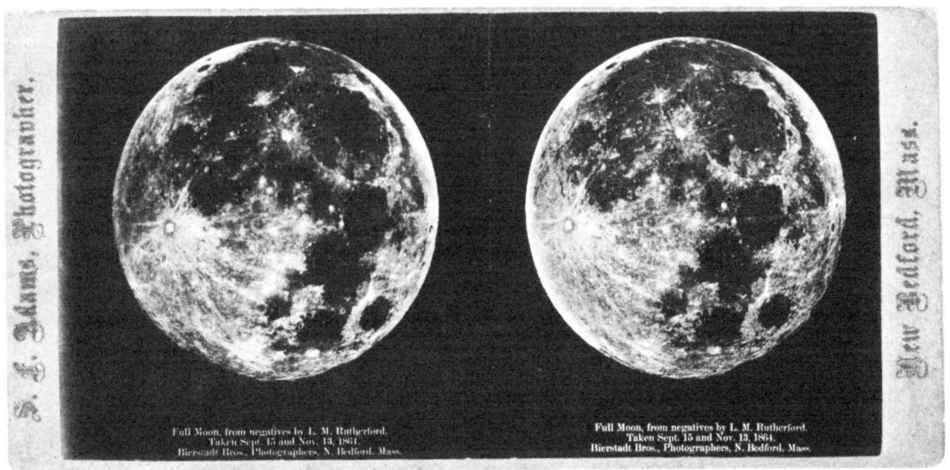

218. Full Moon. Negatives by L.M. Rutherford, 1864. Stereograph by Bierstadt Brothers. Card issued by S.F. Adams, successor to Bierstadt Brothers.

[1] Russack, Richard, "Dr. Isaac Hayes: Explorer, Photographer, Bigot," *Northlight* 2 (2) :5-7, 11; 1975.

subjects, such as the observatory at San Domingo Convent, Lima, Peru (Underwood 9226, 1906) and the magnificent bronze instruments in the Imperial Observatory, Peking, China (Underwood, 1901).

AUTOMOBILES

Beginning about 1896 stereo cityscapes show automobiles parked or moving in traffic. Until 1900, the number of views with motor vehicles is very small. Thereafter, with each passing year they become more common. By 1906, the automobile became an influential part of urban life. With few exceptions, however, the automobiles in the stereo views are incidental.

The prize gem of stereo automobiliana is an eighty card set, simply titled "Motor," published by Stereo-Travel in 1909. Half of the series records the first races at the Indianapolis Motor Speedway, August 19-21, and the other half, the races at the Lowell (Massachusetts) Speed Carnival at The Automobile Course, September 5-7. The views are primarily of automobiles and their drivers in actual racing. Each scene is identified with the make of car, the drivers, and the racing times of the winners.

These views represent a superb cross-section of cars—Marmon, Apperson, Moon, Benz, Simplex, and many more—and famous drivers, Oldfield, Borque, Christie, Aiken, Robertson, and many more. There are fine close-ups of individual automobiles, starting line-ups, and finishes. All cards in the series are very rare. Only one incomplete boxed set is known to me.

Various stages in the manufacturing of automobiles have been stereographed. The most extensive series (about forty titles) shows the Chandler Motor Company plant in Cleveland, Ohio, published by the Corte-Scope Company in 1916. Keystone issued views of assembling operations in the Ford and General Motors plants in Detroit. Keystone also published excellent views of tire manufacturing in Akron, Ohio.

The motorizing of buses, trucks, fire-fighting equipment and ambulances developed rapidly after 1905. Simultaneously the development of paved roads, highways, the gas station (Keystone 29359) and the inevitable garish road sign boards are also faithfully recorded in stereo. The motorcycle policeman and the highway patrol (Keystone 29221) are there too.

The application of motor vehicles to warfare occurred in World War I. The monstrous contraptions that served in frantic mobilization, lorry caravans moving to the front and mechanized equipment, culminating in the tank are strikingly recorded in stereo views.

AVIATION: AIRPLANES, BALLOONS AND DIRIGIBLES

The history of heavier-than-air flying machines is fairly well documented by stereographs.

Ascensions of balloons inflated with hot air were popular attractions at fairs and celebrations. There are stereos of scores of such ascensions in France, England and the United States from about 1860 to 1890.

Attempts to develop lighter-than-air ships that could be self-propelled and steered were not successful until 1898, when Alberto Santos-Dumont (Brazilian living in France) and Ferdinand Zeppelin (German) both constructed dirigibles. Dumont used a flexible gas bag whereas Zeppelin designed a rigid frame within which were gas compartments (bags.). There are at least a dozen stereos of Dumont and his dirigibles, including his famous "No. 4" and "No. 6."

Some of the forgotten pioneers and their airships are recorded in stereographs, among them:

"Baldwin's Air Ship," St. Louis 1904, Keystone 15168

"Francois Airship," St. Louis 1904, White 8002

"Astronaut Tomlinson sailing away for Washington," St. Louis, 1904

An unusual craft in flight at the Jamestown Exposition, 1907, is shown in Underwood 9842.

The best-known views of Zeppelin dirigibles are those used by Germany in World War I, the famous "Graf Zeppelin" and the ill-fated "Hindenburg." A crashed military Zeppelin (Keystone 18632) reveals the rigid framework. The bombing damage inflicted on England during Zeppelin raids was recorded by Underwood. There are beautiful stereos of the "Graf Zeppelin" especially one showing the craft high above the pyramids of Egypt (Keystone 17398).

There are several views of the "Hindenburg" which exploded

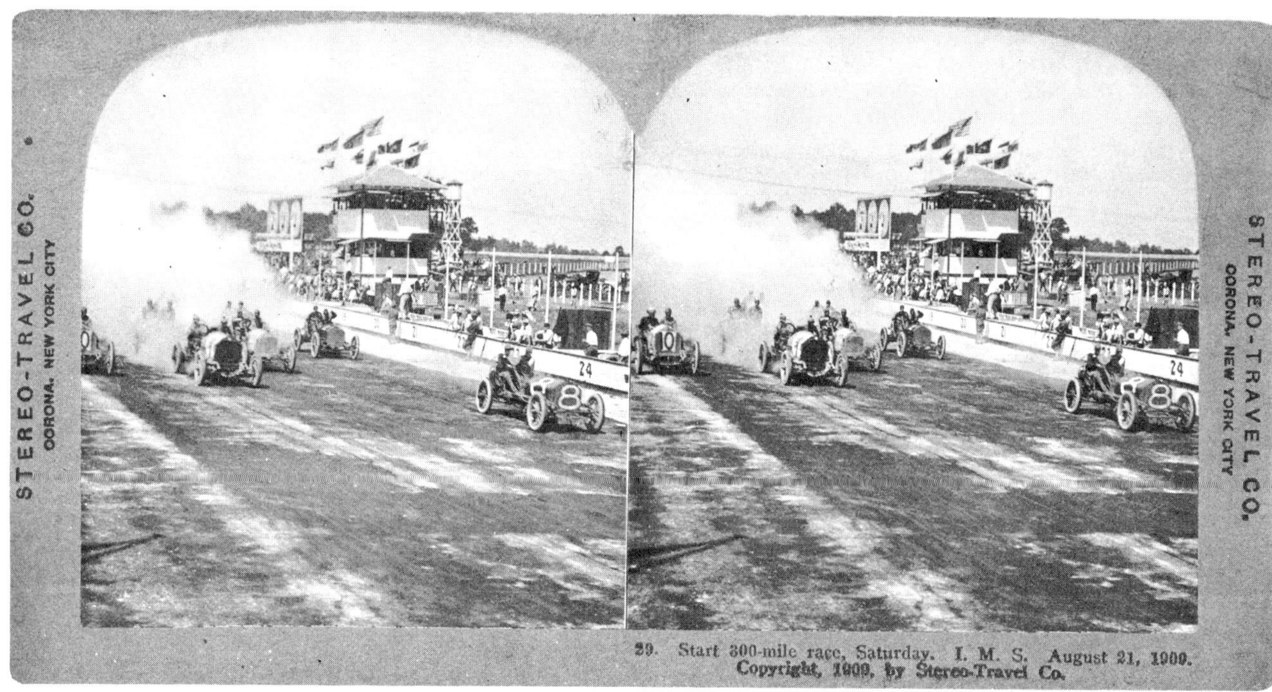

219. Automobiles. Race at the Indianapolis Motor Speedway, August 21, 1909. The first year of this famous track and races. Stereo-Travel Company.

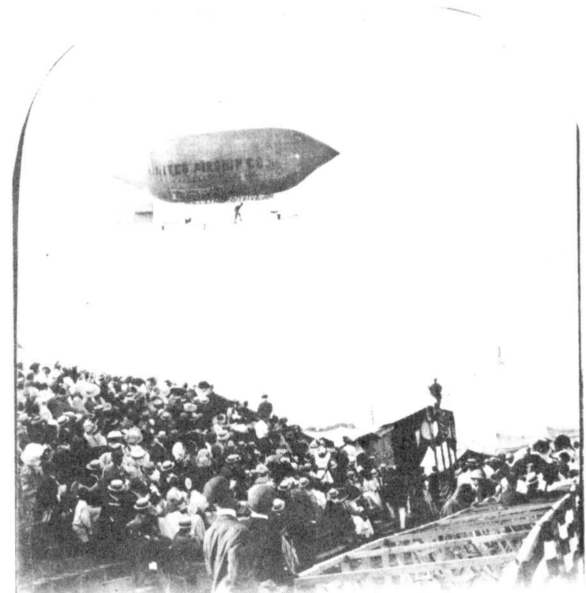

220. Aviation Meet. United Airship Company's dirigible balloon. Asbury Park, New Jersey, 1906. Keystone View Company, Underwood negative.

and burned at Lakehurst, New Jersey, only a year after being placed in trans-Atlantic passenger service.

Several American dirigibles were stereographed. The "R38," built in England in 1919 and purchased by the United States in 1920, crashed in 1921. The "Shenandoah" (1923) was destroyed in a storm in 1925 and The "Los Angeles" (ZR3) built in Germany (Keystone 17397-17401). Two American-built dirigibles, the "Macon" and the "Akron" (ZR4, Keystone 32740) were both lost at sea, the "Macon" in the Pacific, February 1935, and the "Akron," in the Atlantic, April, 1933. Although these accidents discouraged further development of dirigibles, it was the mechanical superiority of airplanes that made lighter-than-air craft obsolete. The high speed, fixed wing, maneuverable airplane in peace and war completely outclassed the balloon and the dirigible.

There are excellent views of early airplane flights by the Wright Brothers and Curtis. Among the best are:

"Wright Brothers" biplane flying at 45 miles per hour, Gouvernor Island, N.Y., 1909" White 22002

"Wright Brothers at Dayton, Ohio" Keystone 16644

"Wright Brothers in Flight, Ft. Myers, Va." Keystone 26102

"Curtiss and his biplane, Long Island, 1909" Underwood 11228

Air shows and races held between 1910 and 1920 were occasionally stereographed. There are small series of the show at Asbury Park, New Jersey, August 1912 (Keystone) and of the Sharon Speedway, May 30, 1917. A fine view of Ruth Shaw and her plane is among the titles in this amateur series.

The development of commercial aviation is recorded in many excellent Keystone views:

"Charles Lindberg and the 'Spirit of St. Louis' " 32062

"Lt. Smith and the crew of the "Chicago' at Bolling Field after encircling the Globe" 26407-26409

"Inaugurating transcontinental Air-Travel Service, leaving Columbus, Ford Tri-Motor Plane, July, 1929" 32372

"Air mail plane, Cleveland, 1927" 29446

The military aircraft used extensively in World War I were completely stereographed. The various types of planes, Allied and German, and many pilots are identified in the views by Underwood, Keystone and Trautman. Equipment adapted for aircraft include machine guns, armor and photographic apparatus. These are views of the 37 mm "Quickfire" gun (e.g., Underwood 12310) and of aerial cameras (Keystone 14326).

There are remarkable views of helicopters ("autogyros")—Keystone 32689; aquaplanes (including the Navy Curtis Seaplane)—Keystone 19119, 19144, 27318; gliders—Keystone V26755; and parachutes—Realistic Travels.

A few views of plane assembling plants are available, notably at Wichita, Kansas (Keystone 32318) and Handley-Page Works, London (Realistic Travels).

After 1912 there are increasing numbers of aerial views of cities, especially in the United States. Keystone published many fine stereos of New York, Washington, Boston, Philadelphia, Cleveland, Chicago, San Francisco and approximately twenty other cities (1923-1935).

BOER OR SOUTH AFRICAN WAR

The South African War between the Boers of Dutch descent and the British began in 1899 with the invasion of Natal by the Boers. A see-saw struggle continued until 1902 when peace was ratified at Pretoria.

The war was extensively stereographed by American—not by British—photographers. Underwood obtained several hundred negatives from which 50, 100 (1904) and 150 (1905) card sets were issued. These were sold in considerable numbers until 1910. Keystone published approximately 150 titles and H. C. White about 80 titles. Smaller issues were produced by Kilburn, and William H. Rau (sold by Universal View Co., and by Griffith & Griffith).

The stereographs include views of clumsy vehicles, transportation problems, observation balloons and improvised artillery. There are scenes with notable personalities and of many towns throughout the area.

See also SOUTH AFRICA, page 133.

BOTANY

Stereographs showing plants are of two main types, (1) vege-

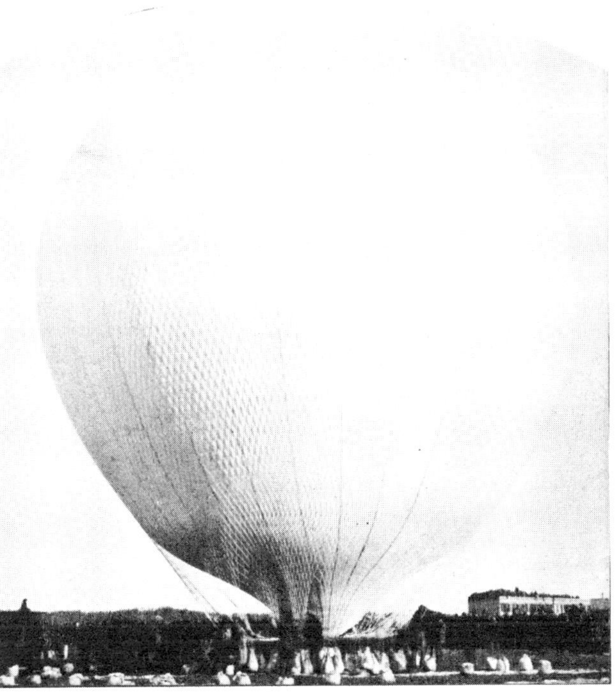

221. Balloon Ascension. Minneapolis, Minnesota. H.R. Farr photo, 1882.

tation, the total plant cover of a locality which is thus a characteristic aspect of the environment, and (2) specimen plants, that is, one or several individuals of a kind or species. Specimen plants may be wild or cultivated.

Vegetation is typically described as forest, grassland, swamp or desert but there are many variations of each, such as an alpine meadow or a mangrove swamp. Virtually every outdoor view records incidentally some aspect of the local vegetation.

There are literally thousands of views of the mammoth trees of California. The redwoods, some with ages greater than 3,000 years, have held us in awe. The giant douglas fir of the American northwest, the kauri of Australia, the tree ferns of Tasmania, New Zealand and the Hawaiian Islands have likewise been stereographed many times. In contrast, the pampas, veldt, savannas and prairies, each with their unique plant associations have been less frequently photographed.

Specimen plants, generally, have not been systematically stereographed. Most photographers operating in the American west did produce views of cactus, yucca, agave and mesquite, chiefly because of their bizarre habits. Throughout the world, handsome trees have been photographed for their unusual forms, banyon tree, breadfruit, coconut, palm, banana and cedar of Lebanon, are but a few of these.

Poulton's remarkable series illustrating the plants in the Conservatories of Chatsworth (1860-66) has previously been mentioned (page 109). There are at least 600 subjects, each card bearing an accurate botanical identification and the date of introduction of the species into England. Figure 52.

A fine series of tinted "Blumen und Bluthen," photographed by Stiehm, was published by Sophus Williams ca. 1870.

Keystone published a hundred card set, "American Wild Flowers," beautifully tinted and with full descriptive notes. An additional seventy-five titles were available untinted. The plants were photographed close-up in their natural habitats. The views are superior to illustrations in flower guidebooks. The tinted Wild Flower set was first issued in 1922 but as early as 1908 Keystone offered a hundred card selection for school instruction. The titles were entirely different from those in the later tinted set.

Many unusual and admired plants were stereographed between 1860 and 1890. Frank Good produced charming studies of mosses and ferns. Kilburn Brothers issued scores of views of mosses, lichens and ferns in the White Mountains. Native water lilies, cat-of-nine tails, pitcher plants and orchids vied with the night-blooming cereus, Victoria water lily for popular appeal.

Botanical gardens and their conservatory collections were extensively photographed. Kew Gardens (London), Shaw Gardens (St. Louis), Phipp's Conservatory (Pittsburgh) are but three examples. F. York issued at least 150 views of Kew Gardens, ca. 1870. There are attractive views of the Papal Gardens and formal gardens at Versailles, Hong Kong, and Monte Carlo.

Seaver (C. Pollock, publisher) stereographed the formal gardens of the estates in Wellesley and other suburbs of Boston (1873-75). Mugnier issued fine views of the gardens of the Louisiana Jockey Club, New Orleans (ca. 1882). The variety is almost limitless.

Horticultural Hall at the Centennial Exhibition in 1876 was a veritable cross-section of the plants of the world. With some justification its managers boasted that the displays were the most varied and extensive ever assembled in the United States. There are about 200 "official" stereographs of the Hall and plant exhibits.

Useful plants—sources of dyes, medicines, fibers, waxes, latex and lumber—exploited as growing naturally or under semi-wild conditions have been extensively stereographed. Most travel sets include several views of this type. A few examples will suggest the range: maple sugar, manila hemp, bamboo, quinine (chinchona), wild rice. To search for views of a desired plant, it is necessary to know only the country or region in which the plant is native.

The professional botanist will find remarkable documentation of the dispersal of weed species throughout the world. For instance, the American cactus *(Opuntia)* was established in Palestine and Sicily before 1880.

The enormous increase in world population and the destruction of wilderness is recorded in stereos between 1860 and 1930. A comparison of stereo views of a given non-urban locality at twenty-year intervals can be a shocking experience.

BRIDGES

Of all engineering work none shows more imagination in combining utility and beauty than bridge building. Wherever man has found it necessary to move people and vehicles over a river or chasm, he has spanned it with a bridge.

There are hundreds of stereo views of stone arches and viaducts in Italy, France, Spain and England, especially where Roman armies carried their skills. Indigenous architecture in many parts of Renaissance Europe added many picturesque bridges to the landscape.

In the nineteenth century technological developments ushered in an era of great bridge building. The availability of wrought iron and, after 1865-70, structural steel provided new building materials. Before the end of the century, portland cement, concrete and reinforced concrete also became important materials.

Pile drivers operated by steam engines, caissons and coffer dams constructed on the bed of a river, made it possible to work far below water level. In quick succession, massive bridges capable of supporting railroad trains, withstanding great floods, many more than a thousand feet in length, were built over the largest rivers.

The first ambitious bridge building project covered by stereographs was the Victoria Tubular Bridge (1854-59) over the St. Lawrence River at Montreal. Notman between 1856 and 1859 issued a classic series recording the methods and progress of construction, including excavation and building piers. Figure 152.

Earlier notable completed bridges, such as the Conway Tubular Bridge (Wales) were stereographed in the 1850's.

Each new great bridge incorporated innovative features adding to the accumulative experience that would benefit later engineers.

Wooden arch bridges, some of considerable size, were constructed in the United States before 1800. "Long Bridge" at Georgetown-District of Columbia and the Susquehanna River Bridge at Harrisburg, and the Scotia Bridge of Schenectady were truly remarkable structures that were stereographed frequently.

The wooden trestle bridge at Genessee, New York was stereographed by fifty photographers beginning with Langenheim in 1854. It was destroyed by fire in 1875 (recorded in stereo) and replaced with an iron bridge.

The steel suspension bridge over the Niagara River, designed by J. A. Roebling was the forerunner of the famous Brooklyn Bridge also constructed by Roebling. Langenheim, Barnum, Reilly, Anthony and many others issued views of the Niagara Bridge. There are many stereos recording the construction of Brooklyn Bridge. The completed bridge was a tourist attraction well into the 1900's. Stereo views of other early suspension bridges include St. Johns, New Brunswick (by Climo), Binghampton, New York (Beckwith), and Pittsburgh (Purviance).

The Mississippi River Bridge at St. Louis (1869-74), designed by J. B. Eads was the first major steel arch bridge. Benecke published a fine series of views of the construction of the bridge and the dedicatory exercises upon its completion. Many steel arch bridges are recorded in stereo, among them: Niagara Falls; Berne, Switzerland;

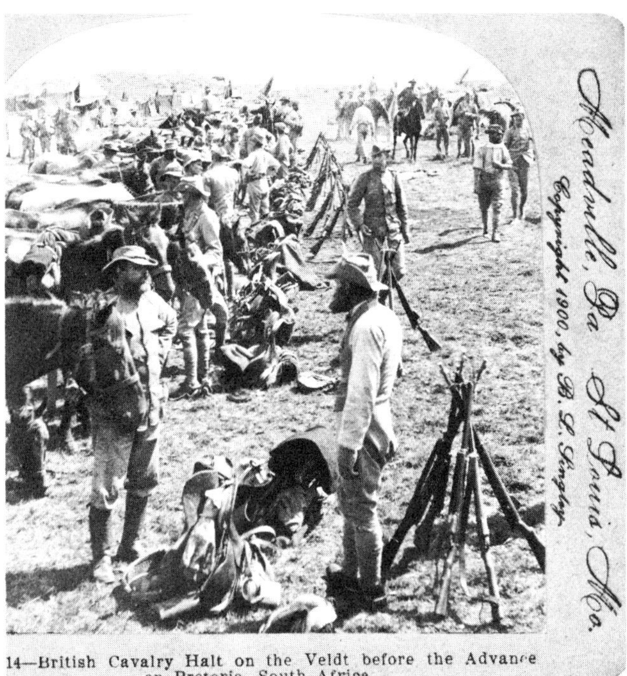

222. Boer War. British Cavalry before Pretoria. Keystone View Company, 1900.

and Lee's Ferry over the Colorado River, Arizona.

Views of unusual types of steel bridges include:

Frankenstein Trestle, New Hampshire (Kilburn)

Loop Bridge, Georgetown, Colorado 1881-82 pier and tower design (many)

St. Paul, Minnesota, steel truss

Examples of wrought iron truss bridges include spans at Hannibal, Missouri; Augusta, Maine; Omaha, Nebraska and Kinzua, Pennsylvania. J. West published excellent views of the construction of Kinzua Bridge in the early 1880's.

The classic Bollman iron truss bridge at Harpers Ferry was often stereographed (Langenheim, Anthony, Chase, Kilburn).

Of the thousands of covered bridges built in the United States, relatively few remain today. The surviving structures are small picturesque bridges that do not display the ingenuity or skill involved in constructing the much larger bridges that once crossed the Delaware and Susquehanna Rivers. Hundreds of covered bridges were stereographed, generally by local photographers.

Purviance, photographer for the Pennsylvania Central Railroad, produced stereos of all the bridges on the line and of other notable bridges in the cities served by the railroad. His fine view of the Sharpsburg Bridge over the Allegheny River near Pittsburgh (1868) shows the magnitude of a large covered bridge. Other striking examples include the Manchester, New Hampshire and the Wilkes Barre, Pennsylvania bridges.

Stone Bridges. London Bridge was stereographed virtually every year after 1854 until 1930. The changes in the pattern of traffic are self-evident. Fine examples of stone bridges include:

Starucca Viaduct, Pennsylvania, (Bierstadt, Anthony)

Toledo, Spain; Old Roman Bridge, Palestine; Dinan Viaduct, France; Soo Chow, China.

Primitive bridges of great diversity—practically each example is of unique construction—are to be found in the travel sets. The famous rope bridge at Carrick, Ireland has been stereographed scores of times. Beautifully tinted views of this curious bridge were sold by the London Stereoscopic Company and Negreth & Zambra in the 1850's.

The Underwood "India" set (1908) includes a view of a rope bridge and another of a cribbed bridge in Cashmere.

A stereo of a huge narrow log arch over the Bocono River in Venezuela shows twelve mounted riders standing on the bridge (ca. 1865). Figure 211.

The stereo coverage of bridge construction in the twentieth century is much more limited. Even so, there are remarkable views of the building of the George Washington Bridge (Keystone). Views of all great modern bridges built before 1935 are available.

Those collectors interested in the history of bridge building should be aware of the importance of bridge testing ("performance testing"). The only method of testing a railroad bridge was to run a loaded train over it. There are incredible views of heavily over-loaded trains, far exceeding the specified "maximum" weight limit of the structure. Fine examples may be found in L. E. Walker's views of the new iron bridge at Portage, New York (1875). Figure 232.

Bridges wrecked by ice jams and floods are occasionally encountered but views of bridge failures are rare. Several stereos of the St. Paul, Minnesota bridge cut by a cyclone in 1904 were published by Ingersoll.

CATTLE TRADE, COWBOYS

The cattle trade in the United States divides into two phases, the early romantic cattle drive period from 1867 to 1875 and the railroad period from 1875 to 1935. After 1935 motor trucking displaced much of the railroad commerce.

During the 1870's photographers gave scant attention to the cattle trade. There are stereos of stock yards in Kansas, unloading cattle from railroad cars and scattered ranch scenes with cowboys, round-ups drives and chuck wagons. Stereos of mounted cowboys with lariat and with rifles are fairly common.

The most comprehensive coverage is to be found in an excellent set "Cowboys" published by Keystone in 1934 (two versions, 72 and 100 views). The scenes were selected from a negative file gathered over a forty-year period. There are cattle ranges in Texas and Montana, cowboys, roping and branding, round-ups and shipping cattle to the Chicago stock yards. About fifteen titles depict cowboy rodeo events such as broncho busting, and trick riding at the World's Fair in Chicago, 1933.

Champion personalities identified in the views include Chester Byers, Hardy Murphy, Homer Hocum and Mrs. Tad Lucas with three of her women trick riders (no. 32907).

Keystone, Underwood, White and Kilburn published many views of cattle and cowboys in the 1890's, most of the scenes being from Texas, Oklahoma, Kansas and Montana. N. A. Forsythe (Butte, Montana 1905-10) published a remarkable series of cattle raising in Montana.

There are many views of cattle raising and trading in the travel sets. Keystone (1923) photographed the trade in Argentina, with good scenes of the pampas and gauchos.

The method of loading live cattle on ships by their horns is shown in several views of Cuba (Strohmeyer & Wyman, 1899) and Costa Rica (Keystone, 1910).

Cattle exhibited at fairs and expositions were frequently stereographed. "Samson, Largest Steer in the World," was exhibited by the Kansas Agricultural College at the Louisiana Purchase Exposition, St. Louis, 1904 (Kilburn 16232). Underwood issued a dozen views of prize cattle at this exposition.

CAVES

Cave photography involves a source of artificial illumination, a problem which had to be solved before negatives could be taken within a cave.

In 1866, Charles Waldack (Cincinnati, Ohio), with magnesium light made about eighty stereo negatives of Mammoth Cave. A selection of forty-two card views was published by Anthony. The cloud of magnesium oxide resulting from each

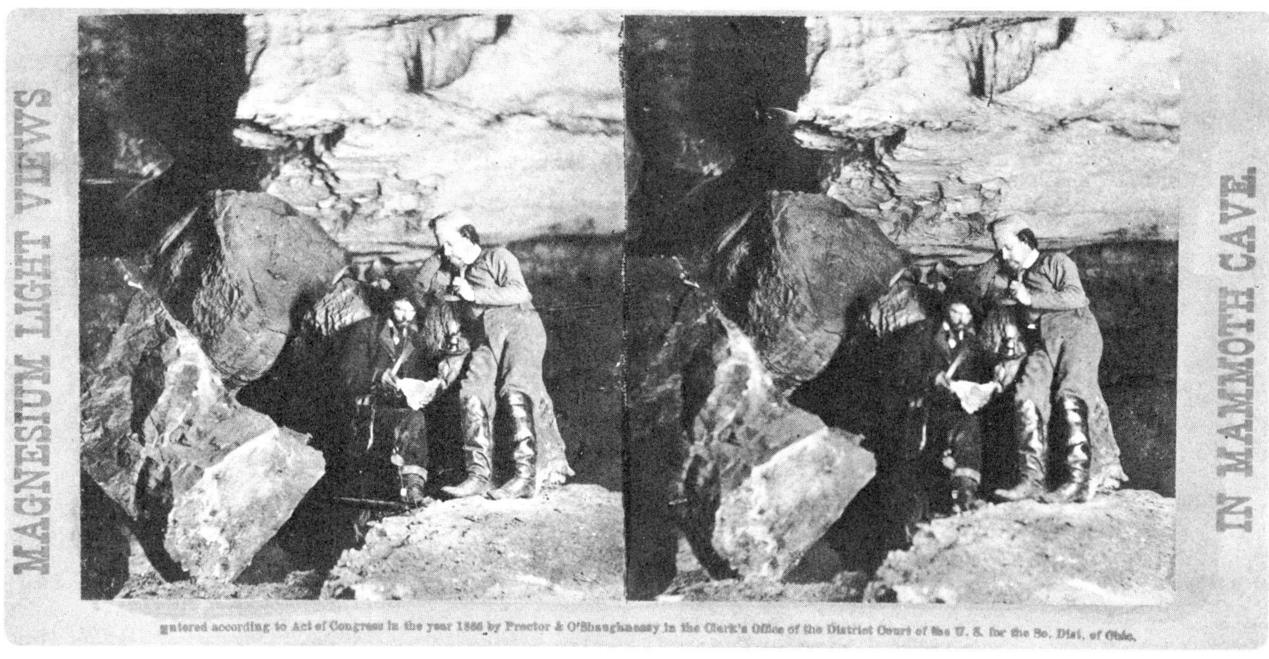

223. Mammoth Cave. Photographed by magnesium light by Charles Waldack, 1866.

flash had to dissipate before another picture could be taken. The Waldack views were highly praised and remain today the finest cave set ever issued. Waldack published (1866) under his own imprint an unknown number of Mammoth Cave views, some of which were not included in the Anthony series.

Twenty years later, Ben Hains (New Albany, Indiana) issued a larger series of views of Mammoth Cave taken by magnesium light.

Luray Caverns, Page County, Virginia, was stereographed by electric light by C. H. James (Philadelphia). James published an excellent series of thirty-seven scenes (1882-83, 1889).

A. Veeder (Albany, New York, 1877) published a series of twenty views of Howe's Cave photographed by calcium light.

The stupendous Carlsbad Caverns, New Mexico, possibly the largest in the world, were stereographed by Keystone (1932). Luray and Carlsbad Caverns are noted for the spectacular stalagmite and stalagtite formations formed from limestone, marble and travertine.

Fine views of cave formations in the Jenolan and Yarrangobilly caves of New South Wales, Australia were published by Kerry & Jones (ca. 1885). Underwood issued several views of Bellamar Cave in Cuba. Figure 206.

Other types of caves that were extensively stereographed include:

Manitou Caverns, Colorado (Jackson, Thurlow, Hook)
Pluto Cave, Portage County, Ohio (H. D. Udall, 44 nos. 1878)
Caves in the Grindewald Glacier, Switzerland were favorite subjects for photographers (Braun 1160, 1810 and Gabler 1106).

Among caves associated with folklore and history, there are:

"Cave prison of Socrates," Athens (H. C. White 4134)
"Ear of Dionysus," Syracuse, Sicily (Underwood 8588)
Fingal's Cave, many, especially by G. W. Wilson.

CIRCUS AND CARNIVAL

Stereographs of circuses and carnivals are quite rare. There

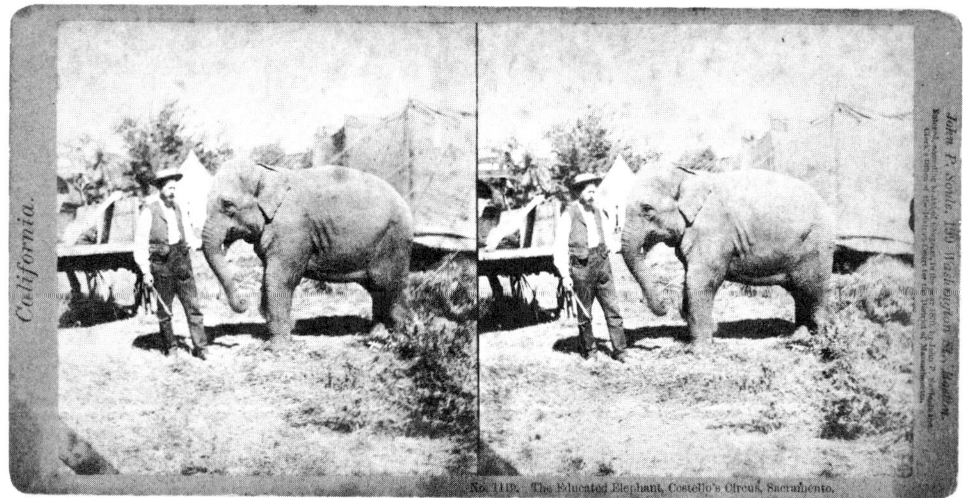

224. Circus. "The Educated Elephant, Costello's Circus, Sacramento, California." John P. Soule photo, 1870.

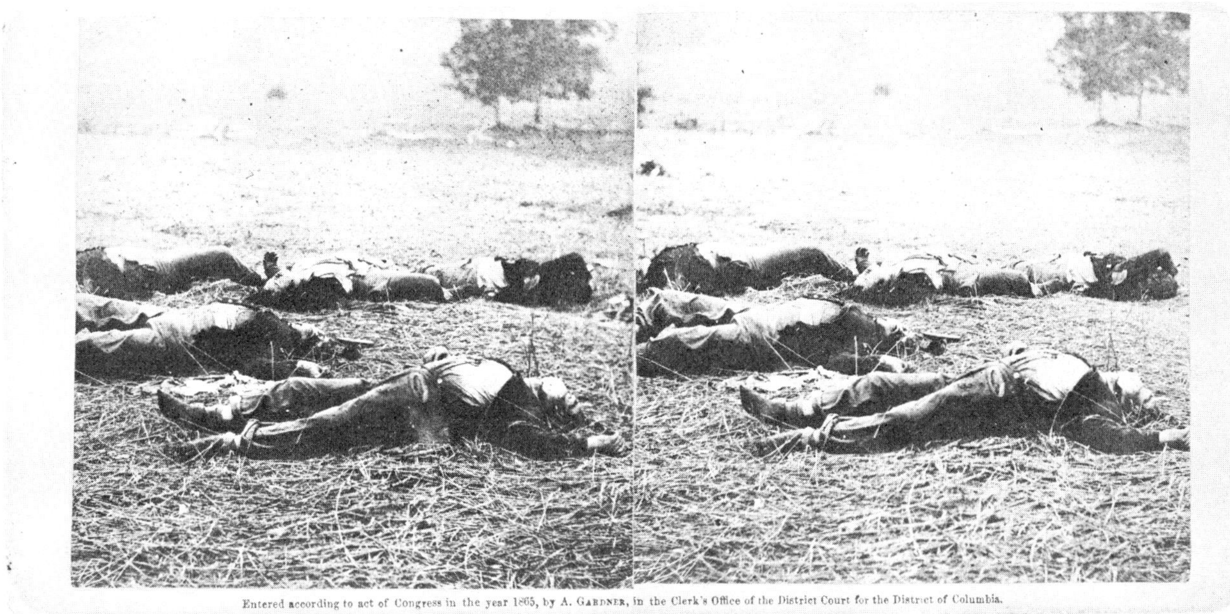

225. Civil War. Battle of Gettysburg. "Federal Soldiers as they Fell." July, 1863. James F. Gibson negative, Alex Gardner publisher, 1862.

are occasional views of circus parades and street carnivals. Somewhat more frequent are views of trained animals such as horses, dogs, bears and monkeys. These are usually photographed with their trainers. There are also stereos of clowns and acrobats, often traveling in small troupes rather than with a circus.

A parade of the Barnum and Baily circus at Foxcroft, Maine was stereographed by S. J. Chase. Circus elephants were photographed by Soule, Gates, W. H. Chase and many others.

There are local views of carnivals in many communities in New York and New England. A majority of these show small carousels or merry-go-rounds. Travelling and permanently erected ferris wheels have been frequently stereographed.

Views of the midways and amusement areas of the Columbian and Louisiana Purchase Expositions preserve many details of sideshows and the crowds attracted to them.

CIVIL WAR

The Civil War retains a romantic hold on American traditions. Civil War buffs have organized societies to study the war or to reenact the battles and skirmishes. It is not surprising that collectors seek all types of stereographs relating to the Civil War.

Mathew Brady's role in documenting the war photographically is well known. Failing to obtain an official appointment to execute the work, Brady proceeded at his own expense. He employed a corps of photographers who worked in small teams. The best known assistants were Alex Gardner, T. H. O'Sullivan, James F. Gibson, George N. Barnard, William Bell, J. Stanley Morrow, Thomas Hine and Louis Landy.

Anthony in 1862 published the first large series of "Brady" views both in stereo and carte de visite formats. Ultimately Anthony published about 2,000 Civil War views, about 900 of which were by the Brady corps (2275-2522; 3030-3630).

Early in the war (1861-62) Anthony issued several hundred "War Views," photographed by T. C. Roche, mostly camp scenes and soldiers on guard duties on the vicinity of Washington (scattered numbers between 810-1510).

Brady found himself in severe financial straits in 1863. He could not pay his men who were already unhappy over Brady's unwillingness to credit their work. Just prior to the Battle of Gettysburg (July 1-3), Gardner, O'Sullivan and Gibson separated from Brady. They, not Brady, photographed the battlefield littered with dead. F. Gutekunst (Philadelphia) arrived on the field on July 5 and Brady not until July 15.[2]

Gardner, who acted as principal for the trio, carefully credited each negative to the photographer. The views were pub-

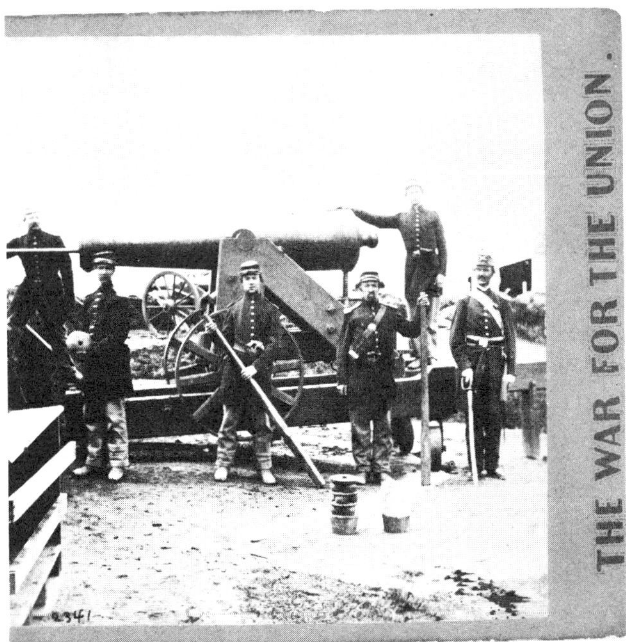

226. Civil War. "General Ingalls, 4th New York Artillery, loading a cannon." Brady Company negative, E. & H.T. Anthony publisher, 1862.

[2] See Frassanito, W. A. "Gettysburg: A Journey in Time," 1975, a remarkable chronicle ingeniously using photographs in exhaustive and rewarding research.

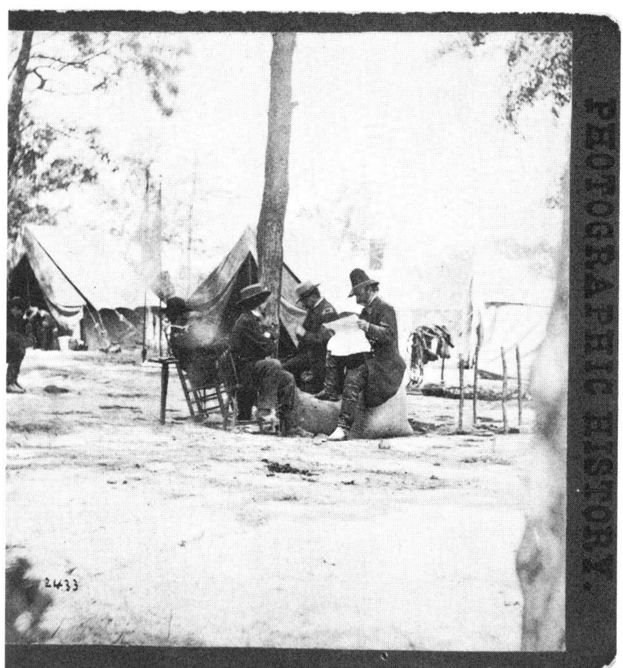

227. Civil War. Personalities. "Maj. Gen. Burnside and Mathew Brady at Headquarters of the Army of the Potomac." Richmond, 1865. Brady Company negative, E. & H.T. Anthony publisher, 1865.

lished by Philp and Solomon but were distributed also by Anthony.

Sam A. Cooley, photographer for The Tenth Army Corps, remained in South Carolina after the war and operated galleries at Beaufort, Hilton Head, Folly Island and in Jacksonville, Florida. He published under his own imprint at least a hundred war views, none, however, of battle scenes.

In April 1865, Soule travelled from Richmond to Charleston to stereograph the war damage and the sites of action. His series of about seventy-five titles is excellent. Many photographers recorded the ruins of Fort Sumter, outstanding among them were views by Quinby and S. T. Souder.

Other photographers visited battle scenes to obtain views for their trade. One of the more extensive series is W. F. Larrabee's thirty-five views of Fortress Monroe.

Stereographs of the Confederate armies are exceedingly rare. I have been able to examine only a few. The most informative do not have a photographer's imprint. There is a view at Corinth, Mississippi, probably 1862, showing troops sitting in small groups, resting. Another shows soldiers guarding supplies at a railroad siding at Chattanooga, probably 1863. The mere existence of these views indicates that much can be rediscovered with patient searching.

After 1868, popular demand for war stereographs virtually ceased. Anthony continued to issue a few cards in the "Brady" War of the Rebellion series until 1873.

In 1879-80, General Ordway obtained the Anthony file of Civil War negatives intending to reissue the views. Unfortunately, the cards produced under several imprints between 1881 and 1890 are indiscriminately credited to Brady. The successive imprints are: John C. Taylor (Hartford, Connecticut), and Taylor & Huntington. The promoters believed that the twenty-fifth anniversaries and reunions would create a brisk market for the old views. They were to be disappointed.

Quite different was the situation at Gettysburg, Richmond and Vicksburg. Tourists in increasing numbers eagerly purchased views of these battlefield sites.

Tyson Brothers and Samuel Weaver and his son Peter had published stereo views of the Gettysburg battlefield in 1863, including some scenes of the dedication ceremonies of the National Cemetery. After the war, C. J. Tyson issued a set of approximately a hundred views of the battlefield and town, including some taken in 1863. The negatives passed to W. H. Tipton who continued to publish them for many years along with a large series of his own negatives made between 1869 and 1889.

Their fellow-townsman, Levi Mumper also produced an extensive series of battlefield views (1866-1889). Peter S. & Hanson E. Weaver (1866-67) published a series of approximately 135 views of the Gettysburg battlefield, including some negatives taken several years earlier.

Although less extensively covered, other battlefields were well stereographed. Anderson's views of Richmond (1867-1875) were widely circulated.

Arlington National Cemetery, established in June 1864, attracted many stereographers. The best early series was published by Bell & Brother (Washington, 1866-1872). Chase (Baltimore) also issued fine views (ca. 1870-73).

Many types of views issued after 1870 are considered to be war-related and as such are classed as "Civil War." The chief categories include:

(1) views of battlefield monuments and markers
(2) veterans' organizations, reunions and parades, especially the Grand Army of the Republic
(3) dioramas, paintings and other memorabilia copied by stereo.

In this category there are many examples, notably the cycloramas of battles by Philipiteau stereographed by Kilburn, Bennett and others.

CONVENTIONS

There are two main types of conventions that have been frequently stereographed: those organized and scheduled and assemblies that are more or less spontaneous.

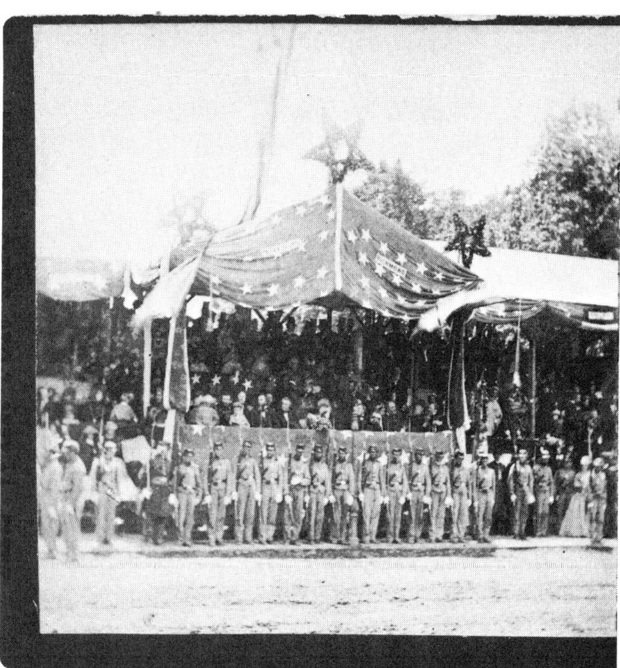

228. Civil War. "Grand Review of the Great Veteran Armies, Washington, May 23, 24, 1865. President Johnson, the Cabinet officers, Generals Grant and Sherman in the Reviewing Stand." E & H.T. Anthony publisher.

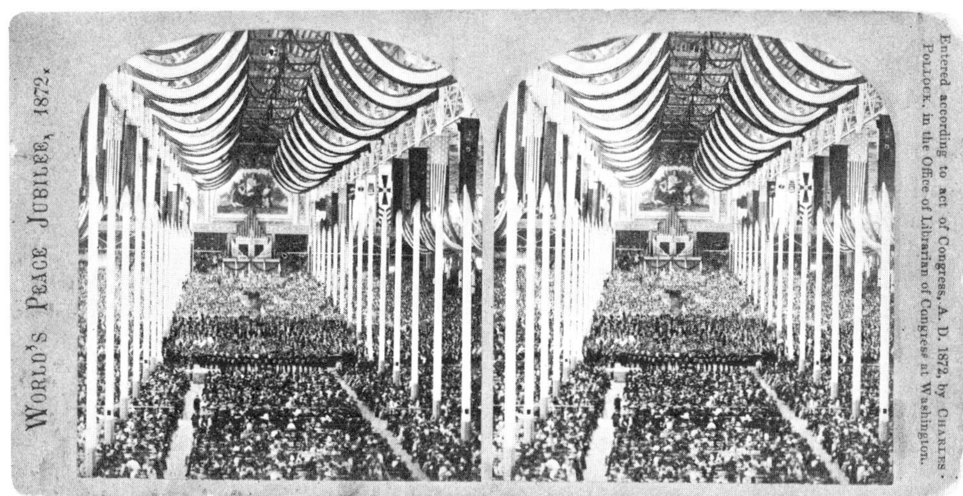

229. Conventions. World Peace Jubilee, Boston, 1872. Massed choir of 20,000 voices and 2000 musicians. Charles Pollock photo.

Political conventions, Peace Jubilees, national annual conventions such as by the Christian Endeavor Society are attended by delegations and by crowds of visitors. Several Republican and Democratic political conventions have been photographed. Keystone (14264) recorded the 1908 Republican Convention in Chicago.

The remarkable World Peace Jubilees held in Boston in 1869 and 1872 were extensively stereographed (Towle, Seaver, Soule, Allen, and others). Gilmore's Band, the Chorus of a Thousand voices, and the throngs were recorded.

The spontaneous mass meetings and gatherings are quite diverse. Anthony (no. 909) stereographed "The Great Union Meeting" in New York on April 20, 1861, following the surrender of Fort Sumter. Quite different was "Coxey's Army" of unemployed who in 1894 marched to Washington. Kilburn and Jarvis published several views of the marchers approaching Washington and the stragglers idling on the Mall.

COPY PHOTOGRAPHY, Stereographs of paintings, etc.

Copy photography refers to the copying of paintings, drawings, photographs, documents, pages of books and broadsides. It has become the most extensive and highly diversified aspect of modern commercial photography.

In stereography copying was principally of two types: copied stereo views and original views of copied subjects. The legitimate and pirated copying of stereographs to obtain new negatives was extensively practiced. "Copy issues" are those printed from negatives made by copying stereo views. Generally these were poorly made and sold cheaply.

There were some remarkable applications of copying in the production of stereographs. A few typical examples are:

1. Stereographs of paintings and engravings. Famous paintings hanging in museums and in private collections. Paintings deliberately made to be stereographed. There are great numbers of such views. Those by Weller and Melander are typical.
2. Stereographs of printed pages, such as of the Bible. In the 1860's and 70's a score of American photographers issued views of the Bible opened to a favorite passage (such as the Twenty-third Psalm). Sometimes a magnifying glass was placed over a verse to emphasize the selection.
3. Stereographs of architects' sketches, such as of houses, mausoleums, etc.
4. Stereographs of pictures (usually lithographs or engravings) of factories intended for advertising.
5. Stereographs of famous documents, such as the Declaration of Independence.
6. Stereographs of cartoons drawn for stereo.

An unidentified New England photographer issued a small series of hand tinted copied Currier & Ives prints (ca. 1868).

Several photographers copied the cyclorama and other paintings of Civil War Battles and issued small series of views (Kilburn, Bennet, Rau), all in the 1880's.

Bennett also published a series of fifteen painted scenes of the Crucifixion.

Note: Because the object stereographed is printed or engraved on a flat surface, the stereoscopic effect suffers accordingly.

COSTUME

Virtually all stereographs that include people automatically record the costume characteristic of the time, place and social position of the wearers. The well-known travel sets include thousands of excellent views showing costume of every description.

The category described here, however, emphasizes the special series prepared to illustrate costume.

The ambitious—but never completed—"Galerie Universelle des Peuples" by Lallemond & Hart (late 1850's to mid 60's) has been mentioned on page 115. Figures 47, 48.

In 1921 Keystone issued a beautiful hand colored hundred card set, "Costume." The set was also available untinted. Keystone first offered a seventy-two card selection illustrating native costumes of the world in 1906. Most of the views were incorporated in their "600 Educational Set."

There are many stereographs showing the uniforms, robes and dresses worn by kings and queens, for coronation and other state ceremonies.

DAREDEVILS

Adventurous persons who earn a livelihood or notoriety through foolhardy stunts have occasionally been stereographed.

In the United States, until forbidden by law, crossing Niagara Falls was a perennial challenge. Emile Blondin's tightrope crossings in 1859 and 1860 were stereographed by a dozen photographers, including Langenheim and William England. Blondin walked the tightrope with a man on his back, tied in a sack, and pushing a loaded wheelbarrow. Each attempt was recorded in stereo views.

The ten or so daredevils who crossed the Niagara gorge by tightropes were stereographed by local photographers. Best

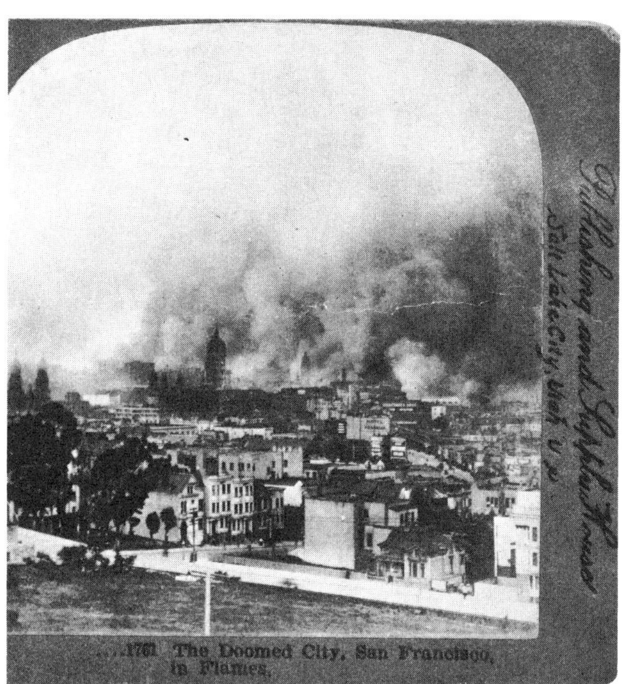

230. San Francisco Earthquake. "The Doomed City in Flames." Pan-American Publishing Company, 1906.

covered were Signora Spelterini, Bellini, Calverley, Peer, Dixon and McDonel.

Keystone (14207) recorded Ivy Baldwin crossing Boulder Canyon, "The highest and longest tightrope walk on record—580 feet high and 555 feet long.

DISASTERS

Public, almost morbid, curiosity about disasters has always provided the stereographer with a market for views documenting death and destruction. Perhaps our awe of unforeseen natural forces contributes to the fascination.

Natural disasters include hurricanes, tornadoes, cyclones, floods, ice jams, earthquakes, tidal waves and volcanic eruptions. After 1900, the ease of travel made it possible to hasten to the scenes of destruction. Consequently, the Messina earthquake (1908, 77,800 killed), the Jamaica earthquake (1907), and the San Francisco earthquake (1906) were extensively stereographed.

Several volcanoes in eruption are recorded in stereos. The Mont Pelee disaster (1902) was the only modern eruption causing extensive loss of life.

There are many series of American views recording flood damage. The greatest loss of life occurred at Johnstown, Pennsylvania (1889) (stereographed by nearly twenty photographers). The Mill Creek flood (Massachusetts), Pittsburgh and Allegheny Flood were also photographed by several photographers. The Oil Creek disaster—flood and fire—which caused great damage to Titusville and Oil City, Pennsylvania (1892) was the subject of stereos by at least six photographers. Figures 231, 232.

"The Great Storm" (hurricane) along the New England Coastline (1869) toppled trees and church steeples which were stereographed in many towns.

Technologic disasters are caused by failure of structures made by man or by accidents which result in loss of control of energy.

Structural collapse of bridges and buildings do not ordinarily cause great loss of life. Failure of water storage dams were the immediate cause of both the Johnstown and Mill Creek floods.

Fires and explosions frequently result in costly disasters.

Trainwrecks and shipwrecks are frequently considered disasters when there is loss of life. There are hundreds of views of accidents caused by collision, derailment or grounding of ships in a storm.

See also: FIRES, VOLCANOES

EDUCATIONAL STEREOGRAPHS

The category described here is limited to views specifically prepared for use in formal education (primary, secondary and collegiate). Views which are educational in a broader sense are excluded.

A case can be made for considering Frith's Eastern Views to have been the first educational series because the publishers, Negretti and Zambra recognized the potential use for them in the classroom. The series, however, was really issued for the educated and cultured gentleman and lady.

Probably the most important project, but probably not the first, to apply stereographs to formal instruction was the Hurst & Son Natural History Series of birds and mammals "for use in schools." (1870).

The views illustrated mounted specimens, usually of several related species. Each card was provided with a scientifically accurate description and taxonomic notation. The Hurst series was published about the same time that natural history instruction was introduced in public high schools and

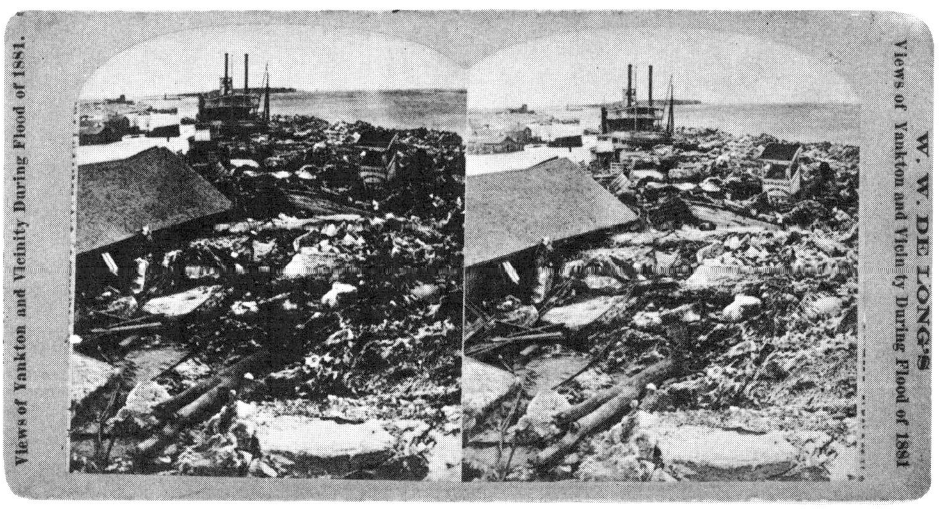

231. Floods. Yankton, Dakota Territory, 1881. W.W. Delong photo.

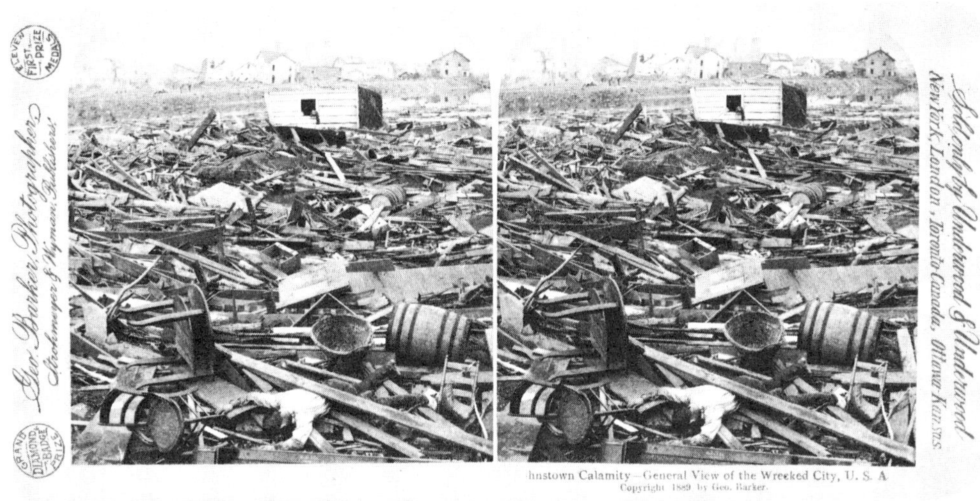

232. Floods. The Johnstown Flood, 1889. General view of the city. Note posed "victim" in the foreground. George Barker photo.

the use of so-called visual aid materials was encouraged.

Also in the early 1870's, several attempts were made to apply stereo views to instruction in history and geography. The idea was, basically, to compile a "reader" of selected published writings and accompany the book with a Beckers type stereoscope and a series of views illustrating the assigned readings. The stereoscopes were constructed to hold 100 or 200 views.

W. S. Clark (1871) published *Elements of Geography and History . . . Illustrated by Stereoscopic Views* and a year later A. Hart, Jr. (1872) published *The World in the Stereoscope . . . written and compiled to accompany sets of stereoscopic illustrations for the use of schools.*[3]

Hart sold one hundred cheap copied views with a Beckers stereoscope. Clarke included 103 cheap copied views with a Beckers stereoscope that held 200 cards. The teacher or school board could purchase additional views from Hart. Neither Clark nor Hart credited the sources of the stereographs which were probably pirated.

The great demand for educational views did not develop until the late 1890's when a revolution in school curricula was taking place. The introduction of courses in economic geography, the assimilation of large numbers of children of foreign born parents and universal education created need for novel methods and at the same time provided a ready market.

B. L. Singley (Keystone View Company) was the first to sense the vast potential in educational stereographs. See page 49.

The H. C. White Company (ca. 1906-1908) published "Geography Visualized by the Stereoscope," a series of four-card sets in ring binders, prepared by L. L. White, PH. D. About twenty sets, American and foreign, are known in this format. The views were also issued on standard card mounts.

ELECTRICAL ENGINEERING

This category included stereographs that record the application of electricity to practical uses. Electrical engineering including the invention of telegraphy by S. F. Morse (who was a pioneer daguerreotypist) falls wholly within the age of photography. Actually there were few practical uses for electricity before 1870.

Friction machines capable of producing an electric current were familiar laboratory instruments in the 1840's and 50's. Parlor models were used to amuse guests who, holding hands, received a mild shock. Several comic stereoviews depict them in action.

The electric generator ("dynamo") which converted mechanical energy to electrical energy was developed commercially after 1870. The Centennial Exhibition featured displays of the telephone, dynamos, electric arc-lighting and electroplating.

In 1882 the Edison Pearl Street Station in New York City, the first power generation-transmission distribution system, was put in operation. Between 1891 and 95, the hydroelectric plant at Niagara Falls transmitted power to Buffalo sixteen miles distant. In rapid succession electric traction companies installed street car trolleys. By 1900 there were 600 municipal power plants operating in the United States. There is a remarkably rich stereoscopic documentation of this rapid development. There are views of Pearl Street Station, many of the Niagara hydroelectric plant and hundreds of cityscapes showing trolley cars, telephone wires and streetlights—a peaceful revolution in less than twenty years.

In 1900, Germany exhibited its "Great Engine and Dynamo, 2,500 Horsepower" at the Paris Exposition (White, 10325). That same year "The Great Power House, Niagara Falls" had a capacity of 50,000 horsepower (White, 320).

The military use of electric lighting, the telephone and telegraph in the trenches in World War I were incidentally stereographed.

There are spectacular views of electrical illumination at night. The successive international exhibitions, particularly those at Chicago (1893), Paris (1900), Buffalo (1901) and St. Louis (1904) illustrate the phenomenal advances. Views of Broadway and Manhattan at night and Luna Park, Coney Island (1900-1912) thrilled many who were unable to visit New York City.

The collector with patience will find scenes of power dams, electrification of railroads, elevators and electric automobiles, to name but a few other common applications. More unusual stereographs of electrical interest include the "Electric Bath at the Battle Creek Sanitarium (Michigan, C. S. Baldwin, ca. 1876) and the dazzling ice palaces, such as at St. Paul (1886), illuminated from within. Keystone stereographed the Edison Celebration at Pittsburgh, October 1929, including a magnificent panorama of the city at night (32412).

ENGINEERING

Stereographs document the progress of engineering ingenuity and skill in ways that books cannot describe. In the early 1800's engineering was largely concerned with canal and road

[3] Clark, W. S., copyright James H. Clark, Clark, Lake & Co., Rockford, Illinois. Hart, A., Jr., Hart & Anderson, New York, second edition, with slight changes, also 1872.

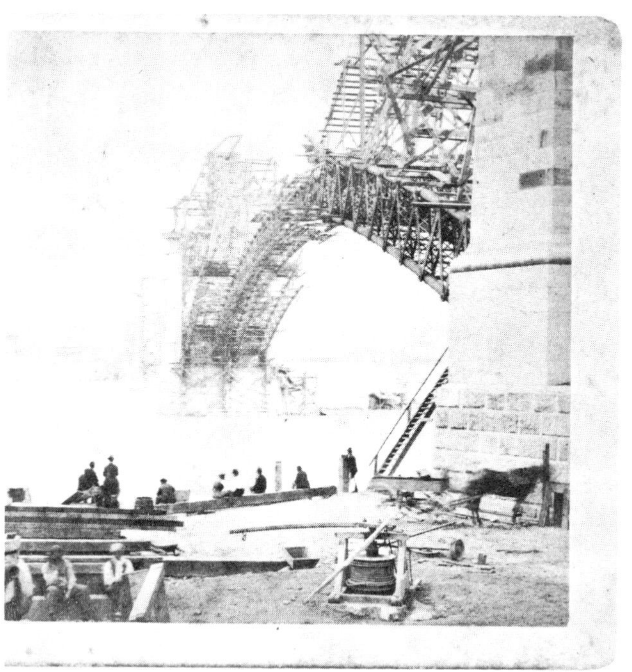

233. Bridge Engineering. St. Louis Bridge over the Mississippi River. Designed and supervised by James B. Eads. Arch erection. R. Benecke photo, 1871.

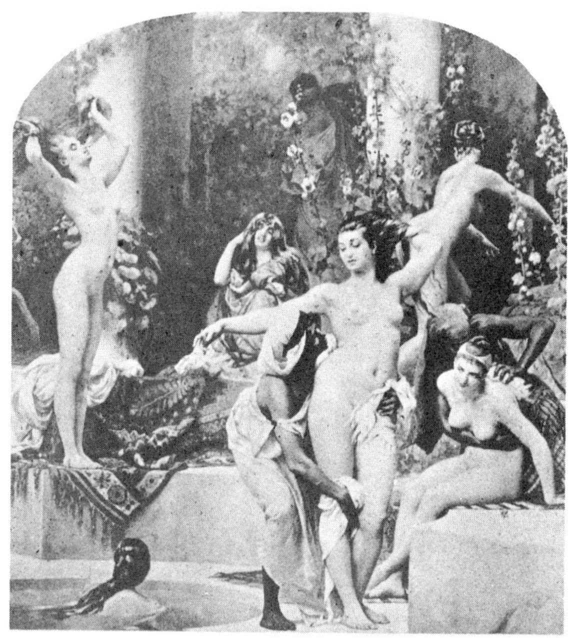

235. Erotica. "A Summer Bath, Pompeii." Copy of a painting by Boulanger. "Art Series," unknown American publisher, ca. 1900.

building, mills and mining. The growth of railroading by 1850 had necessitated improvements in bridge building and the digging of tunnels. The invention of telegraphy and simple electrical generators quickly led to practical applications in many fields.

Engineering gradually specialized into civil, mechanical, mining, electrical, and chemical. By 1876, the year of the Centennial Exposition, these professions were already defined. Yet the great engineering undertakings, which required ever greater specializations, involved all of the engineering skills.

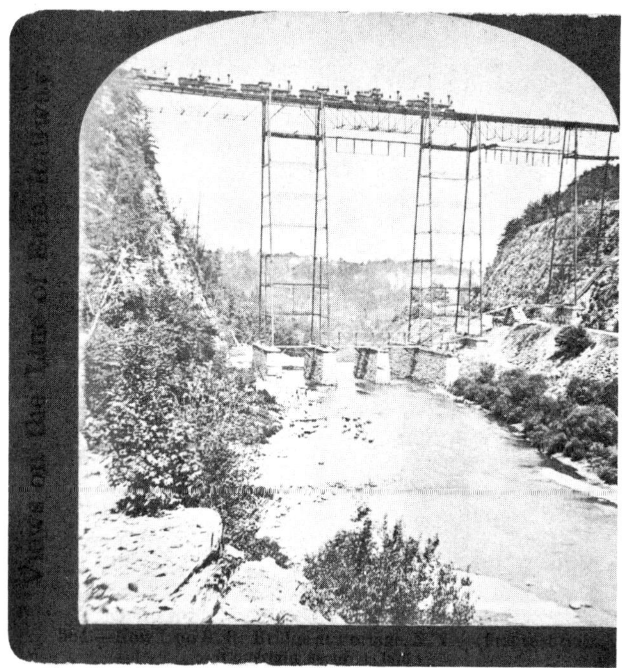

234. Bridge Engineering. Performance testing a steel bridge. Genesee, New York. First test train. L.E. Walker photo, 1875.

After 1865 the availability of shaped steel products, rails, I-beams, wire, boiler plate, etc. greatly accelerated improvements in railroads, bridges and factory construction.

The growth of cities demanded ambitious water works. Philadelphia (1822) and the Croton Reservoir (1842) were great accomplishments. The following heroic projects illustrate the social importance of engineering. Each was well stereographed during construction.

The *Great Eastern* steamship, 1853-1859
Victoria Bridge over the St. Lawrence River, Montreal 1854-59
Laying of the Atlantic Cable 1865-66
Hoosac Tunnel, 1855-76
Massachusetts, first use of nitroglycerine and pneumatic drills in the United States
Mt. Cenis Tunnel, Italy 1857-71 pneumatic rock drill
Mississippi River Bridge, St. Louis, Missouri 1869-74
The Corliss Engine 1875-76 operated at the Centennial Exhibition
Brooklyn Suspension Bridge 1869-83
Firth of Forth Cantilever Bridge, Scotland 1883-90 considered by many to be the greatest of all bridges
The Panama Canal 1904-14
"The greatest liberty that man has ever taken with nature" (James Bryce)

Most of the stereographs of these projects depict men at work and the tools available to them.

Engineers, by the way, were among the first professionals to utilize photography as part of their work.

EROTICA-PORNOGRAPHICA

Stereographs intended to be erotic or pornographic were produced almost as soon as views were commercialized. The subjects range from nudes in conventional artistic poses to what is today called hard-core pornography. Pornographic views were seldom, if ever, distributed by reputable publishers.

In 1859, the editor of *Photographic News*[4] complained, "Stereographs of 'fast' young men looking from their hiding place in the cliffs at girls preparing to bathe in the sea, or 'ladies' in full dress leaning over a balcony, their development exaggerated by a well-known stereoscopic trick . . . have neither novelty or superior skill to atone for their intense vulgarity."

The same journal (1870) reports the arrest of a man who was selling a series of "Thirty badly colored vulgar slides . . ." "to school boys, soldiers and sailors." Such views were sold on the streets, not in shops. Vigilant ladies reported offenders to the police.

I have never seen a pornographic stereograph manufactured in the United States prior to 1905. About that time they do appear on cheap gray or black card mounts, nearly always without a publisher's imprint. C. E. Johnson issued vulgar views under his standard imprint, but the subjects cannot be considered "hard core." The Climax View Company (perhaps there is innuendo in the name) sold a variety of suggestive and pornographic stereos in the early 1920's. Most of the scenes show women in various stages of undress, bathing, or in teasing poses.

Another series, which includes a twelve-card set of a black woman undressing in an inviting manner, is more ludicrous than erotic.

Some years the Williams Book Store in Boston owned a ten-card set showing a naked young couple engaged in intercourse. The views were manufactured in France about 1918-20.

There is a large variety of mildly erotic stereographs. Many of these were produced by well-known American publishers, who, however, omitted an imprint even though the negative number is printed with the title. The majority of these views are copy-photography, that is they are copied from paintings. This device avoided the implication that the photographer used living models.

Probably the most frequently encountered stereos are in the "Art Series" ca. 1895-1910 which can be identified by a pink or white label:

"Art Series—This is a series of pictures reproduced from the finest works of American and foreign Art. For the admirers of fine Art works, and particularly for those who have not the opportunity to see the original painting." There follow a number, title and artist name. For example, 106 "A Summer bath Pompeii,"—by Boulanger. Figure 235.

There are about sixty titles in the series which was distributed for about fifteen years.

Many merely suggestive views were probably issued to ridicule hypocrisy rather than to titillate.

EXHIBITIONS AND EXPOSITIONS

Popular and commercial stereography received its initial impetus at the International Exhibition in 1851. The incredible Crystal Palace was disassembled and reconstructed at Sydenham in 1853. Several thousands of views of the Crystal Palace and its exhibits were taken between 1851 and 1870.

Thereafter, until 1935, every international and important exhibition was recorded in stereo, in every instance by more than one photographer or publisher.

1855 Paris (page 111)	1889 Paris
1862 London (page 103)	1893 Chicago
1867 Paris (page 114)	1900 Paris
1873 Vienna (page 128)	1901 Buffalo
1876 Philadelphia (page 84)	1904 St. Louis
1878 Paris	1915 San Francisco
1886 London	1926 Philadelphia
	1933 Chicago

Managers of several of the exhibitions granted exclusive rights to photographers, others designated "official" photographers without exclusive privileges.

The Centennial Photographic Company, organized by E. L. Wilson and William Notman and their business associates obtained the official concession at the Centennial Exhibition. They erected a studio building and published views from more than 4,000 negatives but only about 3,200 numbers. This extensive series records the construction, the various buildings exhibits, individual objects, and events (opening ceremonies, Pennsylvania Day, Women's Day, etc.), the narrow gauge railroad, and throngs of people.

The Columbian Exhibition was officially stereographed by B. W. Kilburn (approximately 1,100 views) but a score of other photographers collectively produced several thousand views. Film with faster exposure time permitted extensive candid photographing of people on the promenade's midway and at the amusement concessions.

The Paris Exposition of 1900 was noted for its splendid ornate buildings and the exhibits of large machines. The stereographic record is more limited than that of Philadelphia (1876) and Chicago (1893). There are many series, however, the best of which was issued by Underwood.

The Pan-American Exposition was marred by the assassination of President McKinley. Many stereographs of the exposition and of McKinley interest were produced. Those by Kilburn and Keystone are especially noteworthy.

The Louisiana Purchase Exposition in 1904 was remarkable for its emphasis on agriculture, stock-raising, mechanical exhibits and aeronautics, all of which were fully stereographed. There are many excellent series including multicolored lithoprints. Hundreds of amateur views of the exposition have been preserved.

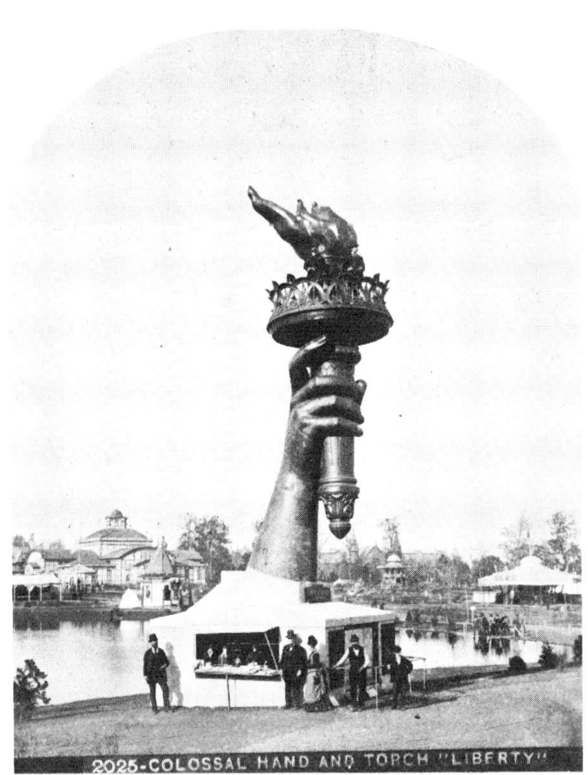

236. Centennial Exhibition. Hand and Torch of Liberty, 1876. Bartholdi's Statue of Liberty. Centennial Photographic Company.

[4] *Photo News* 1:254, Feb. 4, 1859; 14:551 1870

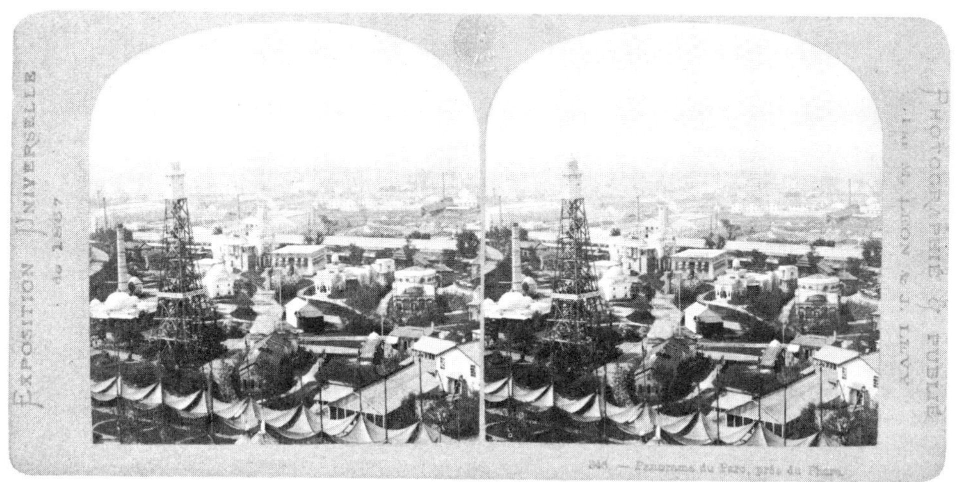

237. International Exhibition, Paris, 1867. "Panorama of the Park." Leon & Levy publisher.

Keystone View Company issued a series of views of the Pan-Pacific (1915) Sesquicentennial (1923) and World's Fair, Chicago (1933).

Hundreds of regional and local exhibitions have been stereographed. There are four common categories:

historical celebrations
state fairs
agricultural fairs, including "corn palaces"
mechanical fairs

Historical fairs include exhibition such as the Sanitary Fairs (1863 and 1864) organized to raise funds for the care and relief of soldiers of the Civil War. The Philadelphia Fair was stereographed by five local photographers. Small series of views record various national expositions such as the Trans-Mississippi (Omaha 1898), Jamestown (1907), Alaska-Yukon (Seattle, 1909). The Cotton Centennial Exhibition (New Orleans, 1884) was well stereographed.

Industrial and Mechanic Institute Fairs, although not as frequent as agricultural fairs, were organized as annual events in many American cities, 1868-1885. There is a wealth of information in the views of exhibits. The devices and products depicted indicate the changing nature of eating habits, sanitation and public health and the origins of many manufacturing companies. To cite one example, the Mechanics Institute Fair at San Francisco in 1878 include a Procter and Gamble Company exhibit of its products—soap and candles. Figure 217.

EXPEDITIONS

The various exploring and mapping government surveys in the United States and Panama have been described in previous chapters. Several other expeditions such as in Africa and Polar regions have also been considered. The more important are listed here in chronological sequence.

1859 F. W. Lander, Wyoming
1860 I. I. Hayes, Labrador
1860-64 J. Chapman, Zambesi Africa
1861-65 S. Baker, Egypt and Sudan
1863-66 G. Fritsch, South Africa
1866 J. L. Fisk, Dakota Territory and Montana
1867 C. King, Hundredth Meridian

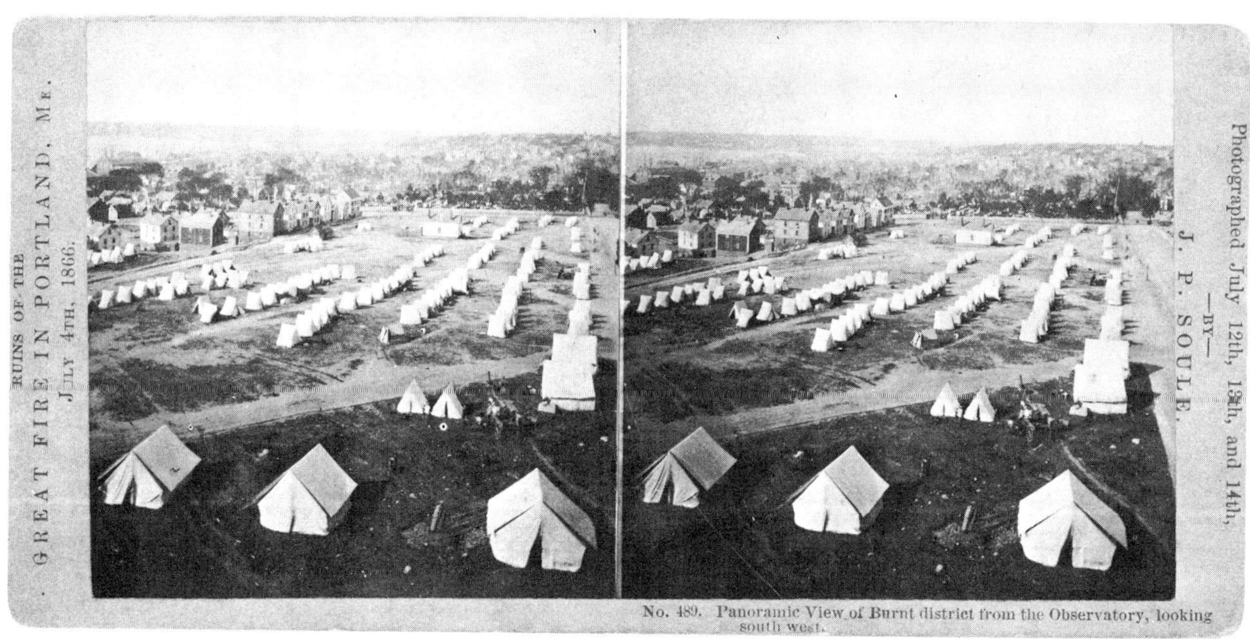

238. Portland Fire, July, 1866. John P. Soule photo.

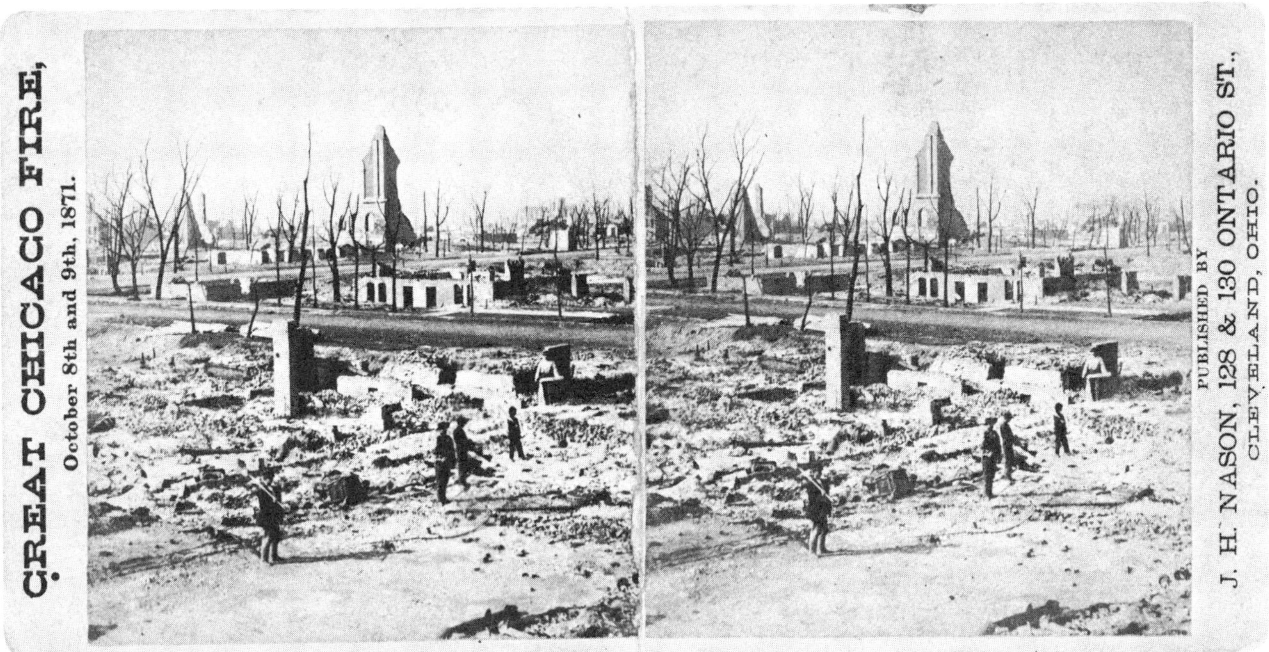

239. Chicago Fire, October, 1871. "Cass and Indiana Streets." J.H. Nason photo.

1868-69 War Department, Great Britain, Palestine and Sinai
1870-78 F. V. Hayden, Rocky Mountains
1871 A. Selwyn, Western Canada
1871-72 T. O. Selfridge, Isthmus of Darien
1871-75 G. Wheeler, Fortieth Parallel
1871-78 J. W. Powell, Colorado Riverion
1873 D. S. Stanley, Yellowstone National Park
1874 Transit of Venus, Siberia, Tasmania
1874 G. Custer, Black Hills
1875 W. P. Jenny-H. Newton, Dakota Territory
1877 Princeton University, Colorado
1893-96 F. Nansen, Arctic
1899 R. Peary, Arctic
1903-06, 18-22 R. Amundsen, Antarctic

At least forty additional minor expeditions under government or public institution support have been stereographed but only a few views of each are known.

Expeditions organized for personal enjoyment, hunting game, or simply photographing have been excluded from this list.

FIRES AND FIRE FIGHTING

Fires that destroyed entire towns or devastated large areas of cities were a scourge of the nineteenth century. Any community consisting mostly of frame buildings was vulnerable.

The first such fire to be stereographed occurred in Portland, Maine in July, 1866. Six photographers are known to have issued views of the damage. The best series was published by John Soule. Fine views were also made by S. Towle and S. W. Sawyer. Figure 238.

In October 1871, the Chicago Fire, the most destructive in American history, leveled much of the city. Thirty photographers, hurried from New York, St. Paul and St. Louis to stereograph the ruined city. Among the better series are those by Lovejoy & Foster, P. B. Greene, J. H. Nason, G. N. Barnard, Sweeney and Copelin & Melander. Figure 239.

About seventy-five Chicago photographers lost their studios and files of negatives in the conflagration.[5]

At precisely the same time a forest fire in Peshtigo, Wisconsin killed nearly 1,200 people. No stereo views of this disaster are known, the greatest loss of life by fire in the United States.

The following year Boston (November 1872) suffered a disastrous fire centering in the downtown area. The series by Soule, whose gallery stood one door from the limit of fire on Washington Street, is the best photographically. The "Boston Fire" set by Pollock is more extensive, however. Kilburn and E. F. Smith also produced excellent series. Details of heat damage to granite walls, fire-fighting equipment and police guards are recorded in these views. Figure 240.

The Chicago and Boston fires inspired several photographers to issue "before and after" views, one side of the card having a print of the building before the fire and the other side, showing the ruins.

The fire that destroyed nearly half of the St. John, New Brunswick (June, 1877) was stereographed by James McClure and J. S. Climo.

The Baltimore fire (February, 1904), fortunately without loss of life, was photographed by Underwood, Rau and White. A few stereo views by local photographers are also known.

The San Francisco earthquake (April, 1906) was followed by a tremendous fire which burned for several days. There are hundreds of stereo views recording the care of refugees in addition to the earthquake and fire damage. Fine series were published by Underwood, Keystone, White and Kilburn. Two excellent lithoprint series are also available, a multicolored set by W. B. Smith and a black and white half-tone set.

Hundreds of lesser fires that destroyed blocks of cities, mills and factories, schoolhouses and churches have been stereographed. Typical examples include:

Haverhill, Massachusetts, A. W. Anderson (1870, 1882)
Concord, New Hampshire, W. G. C. Kimball (1887)
Atlanta Exposition, Hagenbeck Building, Kilburn (1895)
Toronto, Canada, Underwood (1904)

Unusual fires include several burning oil tanks and derricks in

[5] *Phila. Photogr.* 8:365, 1871; with appeals for funds for the relief of them in subsequent issues.

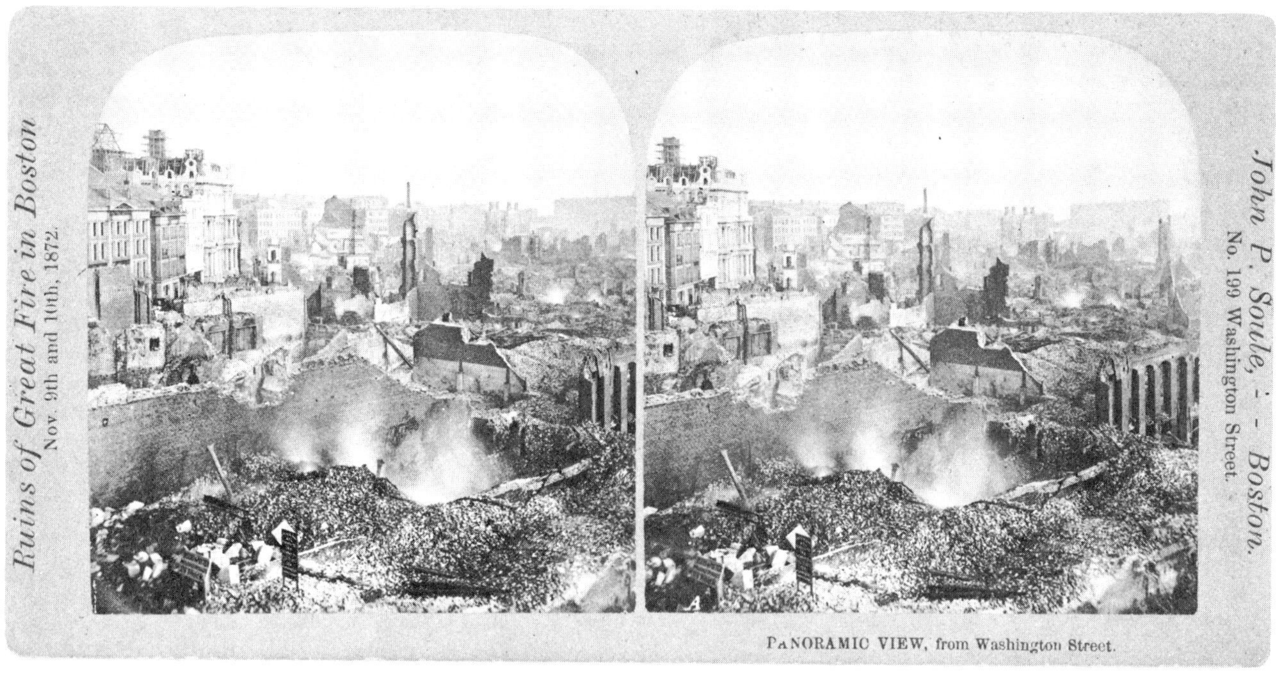

240. Boston Fire, November, 1872. John P. Soule photo.

the petroleum regions of Pennsylvania, New York and Oklahoma.

Stereo views of fire engines, fire companies (often in parade formation) and firemen in action are fairly common. A few examples will suggest the range of subjects:

- The South Gardner (Massachusetts) Fire Company uniformed members, hand pumper and hose (T. Lewis, 1873)
- The steam fire engine of A. L. & G. W. Brown & Co. (lumber), Whitefield, New Hampshire (F. G. Weller no. 435; 1872)
- Fire engines in action, Boston Fire, 1872 (Moulton no. 369)
- Light hose carriage for a private estate, Syracuse, New York (Ranger & Frazee ca. 1873).

FISHING

Commercial and sport fishing will be here considered separately.

Commercial Fishing

Almost every harbor scene stereographed before 1900 includes fishing boats. Fishermen drying and repairing nets were occasionally recorded in Europe. In the United States, the abundance of fish along the New England coast led to a considerable degree of specialization, that is, fishermen concentrated upon one or two species having high market value.

Gloucester, Provincetown and Nantucket fishermen specialized in cod and mackerel. There are many stereos of Cape Ann and Gloucester but none more picturesque than those by E. G. Rollins (1870's). The great sun-drying yards in Gloucester photographed by Keystone in 1920 are identical to those recorded in 1870. Nickerson (Provincetown, Cape Cod) and Freeman (Nantucket) also published views of cod drying. Their scenes of fishing villages, boats and gear are noteworthy.

The bustling Boston Fish Pier, long a center of fish trading, has been stereographed by Keystone. The striking contrast

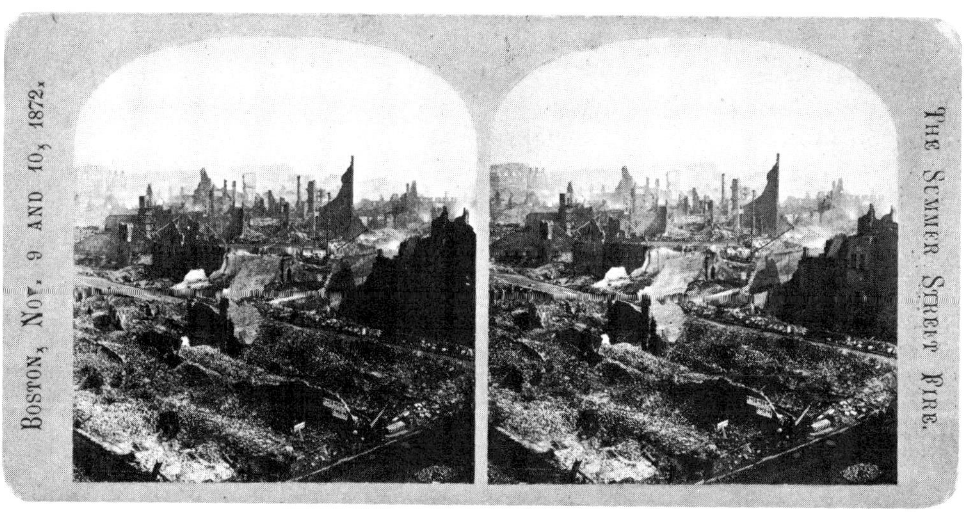

241. Boston Fire. "Panorama looking east towards Sailor's Home." Charles Pollock photo, 1872.

between American and European methods is shown in Keystone 22520, unloading halibut in Boston and Underwood's view "Receiving fish . . . in a warehouse, Aalesund, Norway" (ca. 1908).

Salmon fishing along the Pacific coast from California to Alaska is recorded in hundreds of views, ranging from harpooning and fish weirs by Indians to canning factories in the latter 1920's.

The travel sets include typical fishing scenes in Japan, Norway, Spain, Portugal and Italy.

The various types of specialized "fishing," squid, lobsters, oysters, marine turtles, and sponges have been stereographed wherever they were practiced commercially.

Sport Fishing

The earliest pastoral scenes found among stereo views depict gentlemen, in the tradition of Isaac Walton, quietly fishing in a brook. Grundy produced several charming views of such fishermen. Bedford (1410, ca. 1862) issued a view of a trout angler in Devonshire. In the same spirit Anthony (1860-61) issued several nostalgic fishing scenes. Figure 37.

Trout fishing was a popular sport in the United States, so much so that an unending variety of stereo views was published from 1860 to 1910. Kilburn issued scores of views of fishermen and their catches. Kleckner, himself a devotee, published self-portraits standing in midstream. McIntire (Thousand Islands, New York) and Ingersoll also issued many views of fishermen.

Long pole fishing from the seashore of Cape Ann is depicted in the views by Proctor Brothers (Salem, 1871-2). There are several hundred lithoprint fishing views, about a third of them comical.

The development of fish hatcheries to replenish the supplies in over-fished streams are nicely shown in Kilburn 669 (1879), the New Hampshire State Hatchery and Webster & Albee 209 (1892), the New York State Hatchery. Releasing ("planting") trout in Wayne County, Pennsylvania is shown in Keystone 29215 (ca. 1925).

See also: MARKETS; WHALING

FOOD PROCESSING

No attempt will be made here to list the many native methods for preparing foods for storage or shipment. The natural rapid spoilage and decomposition of foodstuffs led man to devise means to dry, smoke or otherwise preserve them. Sun-drying, smoking meats over a fire, and grinding flour and meal are as old as civilization and virtually similar throughout the world.

After 1850, improvements in mechanical and chemical technology, and advancements in public health, correlated largely with urbanization, hastened the development of a dependable year-round food supply, and world trade in grain, fruits and meat.

The unique American meat packing industry, was rationalized in Chicago in the 1870's where the great Union Stockyards received and processed cattle and hogs from the midwest and Western States. The names of the principal packing companies, Swift, Armour and Cudahy, are a century later still household names. Kilburn (1885-95), Underwood (1890-1910) and Keystone (1894-1930) are but a few of the publishers who stereographed every phase of the beef and pork industry.

The shift from the farmyard, milk cow and home butter-churning to a vast dairy industry is shown in many views of Vermont, New York State and Wisconsin, especially by Kilburn and Underwood.

There are excellent views of cheese manufacture by the Shakers of New Hampshire and the large-scale commercial production in New York and Wisconsin.

In contrast, the minor importance of milk in cities of Europe prior to 1920 is suggested by the stereos of dog carts of milk vendors in Belgium and France.

The shift from the grist mill powered by a water wheel to the huge flour mills like those at Minneapolis is shown in stereos from 1870 to 1900.

The related developments in refrigeration, railroad rolling stock, and packaging for shipping are well documented in stereographs. Canning factories were frequently photographed.

See also: MARKETS

FOREST INDUSTRIES

Eastern North America at the time of colonization by Europeans was covered by extensive forests. Much of this forest was removed to clear land for farming. There was a need for lumber to build housing but the huge surplus cuttings were profitably exported. Many parts of the Middle Atlantic and Northeastern states have been lumbered over three or four times since 1740.

Logging, lumbering and sawmill operations in Maine, New Hampshire and Pennsylvania between 1860 and 1890 have been extensively stereographed. Similar scenes in Michigan, Wisconsin and Minnesota were also photographed.

The lumbering of giant redwoods and Douglas fir in California, Oregon and Washington involved flumes to carry logs from mountain sides to sawmills, great log rafts, and teams of mules or

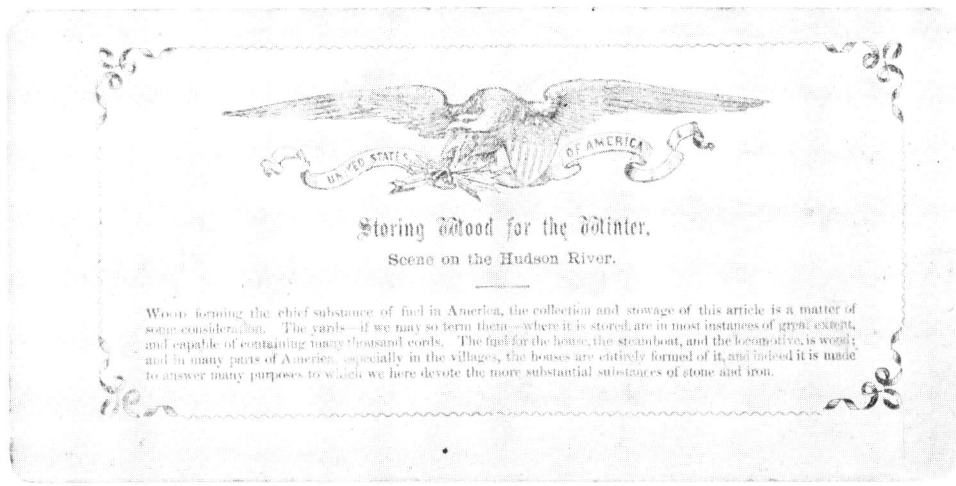

242. Forest Industries. "Storing Wood for the Winter-Scene on the Hudson River." Descriptive notes explain the importance of wood in American domestic life. William England photo, 1859.

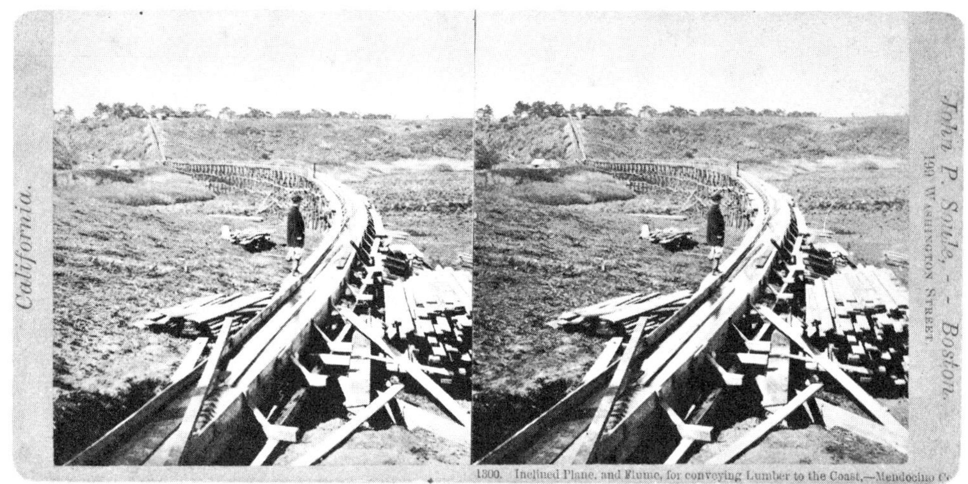

243. Forest Industries. Flume for transporting lumber, Mendocino County, California. John P. Soule photo, 1870.

oxen. In no other part of the world in the late nineteenth century was lumbering on such a scale.

A few examples which indicate the diversity of views follow:

logging camps —Michigan J. A. Jenney, 1870's
Wisconsin T. Ordemann, 1870's
Florida 1870's
New Hampshire Keystone, 1905

cutting timber —Washington (fir) Kilburn, 1890's
California (redwood) 1860's-90's

log driving —Maine S. S. Vose, 1870's
Minnesota Upton, 1863

hauling lumber —muleteams, California Underwood 1898
oxen, California Keystone 1897
oxen, Arkansas Keystone, 1899

flumes —Oregon Keystone, 1900

sawmills —Clarion Pennsylvania F. M. Lewis, 1880
Oregon H.C. White, 1905
California J. Soule, 1870
Michigan M. Hiler, 1870's

shipping lumber by sailing ships —Washington, Keystone 1918

pulpwood —Ontario, Canada Keystone 1925

teakwood —Burma, Keystone, 1904

Keystone issued a fine educational set, "Lumbering" comprised of twenty-four views (1912, revised 1921).

No stereo views of forest fires are known to me, despite the fact that every year great fires ravaged forests in the United States and Canada. Keystone published a view of burned over timberland near Duluth, Minnesota (29231, ca. 1926).

Other forest industries well documented with stereographs include:

naval stores, turpentine, rosin and pitch (Georgia, North Carolina, South Carolina, France)
charcoal burning (many localities)
tapping rubber (Brazil, Malaya)
cork (Spain and Portugal)
maple sugaring (New England, New York, Pennsylvania)

FRANCO-PRUSSIAN WAR, See WARS.

FRATERNAL

Although many fraternal organizations in the United States have been stereographed, only the Masonic orders were extensively covered. Masonic English and American photographers even incorporated Masonic symbols in their imprints.

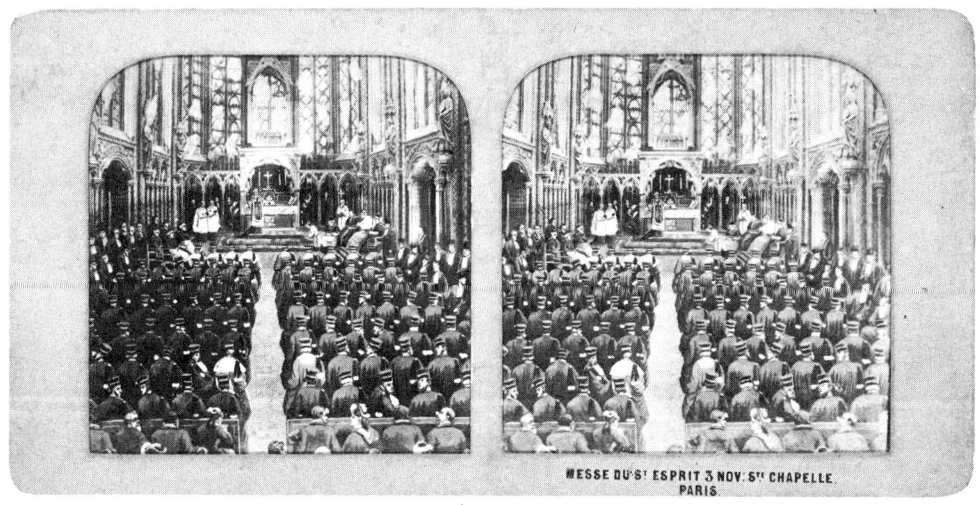

244. Franco-Prussian War. Military Mass, Ste. Chapelle, Paris. Tinted tissue mount. J. Andrieu photo, 1870.

The dedication of a Masonic Temple was usually the occasion for a dress parade, banquet and celebration. The most comprehensive series depicting a Temple dedication was published by Anthony (New York City) in 1875. Cremer and Gutekunst stereographed the dedication of the new Masonic Temple in Philadelphia in 1873. Fine interior views of many temples are numerous, among the best are those in Boston, New York, Philadelphia, Chicago, San Francisco, and a beautiful series of that in Melrose, Massachusetts (R. J. Chute).

The hundredth anniversary celebration of the Mount Vernon Lodge (New Hampshire), July 15, 1873 was handsomely stereographed by B. Carr.

Some photographers issued still life arrangements of Masonic symbols and accessories. Views by Kilburn and Singley (Keystone) are typical.

The Centennial Exhibition (1876) scheduled many fraternal celebrations, such as "Odd Fellows Day," "Red Men of America Day," and "Knights of Columbus Day." The participating organizations paraded from Independence Square to the Exhibition grounds. Stereographs of a score of these ceremonies were issued.

The Odd Fellows Fair, Georgetown, Massachusetts, 1874, was photographed (about ten views) by A. W. Anderson.

In addition to scenes of the meeting houses and members, there are widely scattered views of fraternal homes maintained for widows, orphans, and aged members (e.g., the Masonic Home, Utica, New York, 1906).

While not strictly fraternal, youth organizations such as Boy Scouts, Girl Scouts and Camp Fire Girls, have occasionally been stereographed. About fifty views depicting scouting have been recognized among the Keystone issues and several of Camp Fire Girls, mostly of the period 1917-1925.

GEOLOGY

Physiography, the study of the features of the earth's surface is the basic descriptive aspect of geology. All that we appreciate as scenery is the unity of land form and vegetation cover, if any.

Stereo views of glaciers, deltas, volcanoes and deserts are not static features, they imply dynamic action. The trained eye can interpret the structure recorded in a photograph although not as accurately as in nature.

The rocks and minerals which compose the crust of the earth may be seen in two types of stereographs, views of mining and quarrying and in views of individual specimens. The latter are more rare because hand specimens do not lend themselves to stereography and because there was little market for them. Academic instruction in mineralogy requires actual handling of specimens, not photographs. Nevertheless there are fine views of calcite and quartz crystals, meteorites and ore minerals.

Paleontology is better represented. One early venture illustrated the shell fossils excavated in London (1860). Figure 245. There are many stereos of fossil vertebrate skeletons in the rock matrix where discovered, in museum collections, and reconstructed for exhibit. There are also views of various fossil plants, especially fossil tree trunks.

Geological processes such as erosion, cave formation, volcanic eruptions and their products, peri-glacial phenomena and displacement by earthquakes can be illustrated by many excellent views.

Applied geology, including mining and quarrying and tunnelling, has been extensively stereographed. Views of open pit and strip mining often record unweathered rock strata. The recovery of salt by mining and by evaporation of sea water is shown in many views. The nitrate beds of deserts of Chile are of related interest. The mining of peat, coal and recovery of petroleum have been thoroughly illustrated between 1860 and 1930.

Keystone assembled an educational set of 200 views illustrating geology for schools and colleges (1921-1933). The same set may be found titled "Physical Geography," "Physiography" or "Physiography & Geology," depending upon the purchaser.

The work of government geological surveys (King, Hayden, Powell, Wheeler) has been described in Chapter Nine.

See also: DISASTERS-EARTHQUAKES; EXPEDITIONS; MINING AND QUARRYING; VOLCANOES.

HORSES, HORSE DRAWN VEHICLES

Horses are of two general types, work and pleasure. Stereographs illustrating the breeds and uses of horses are of great diversity.

Work horses have been used singly or in teams to pull plows and other farming implements, wagons, carriages, hearses, and coaches; and, in time of war, artillery and materiel.

Small family farms commonly had a multipurpose horse, using the animal for farming and transportation, such as for marketing and attending church.

The importance of horses in the development of the American West cannot be exaggerated. Distances were so great and the country so rugged that speed and safety were critical. The cowboy and his horse are legendary.

There are many excellent stereos of six- to twenty-horse teams pulling wheat reapers, stage coaches and heavy lorries.

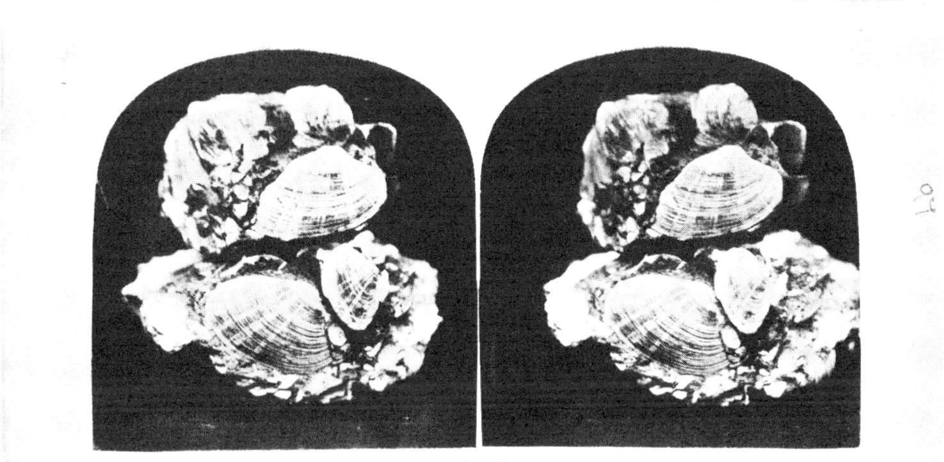

245. Geology. "Fossil Seashells, *Cyrenia dulwichiensis*, excavated at Dulwich" London. J. Warner photo, 1860.

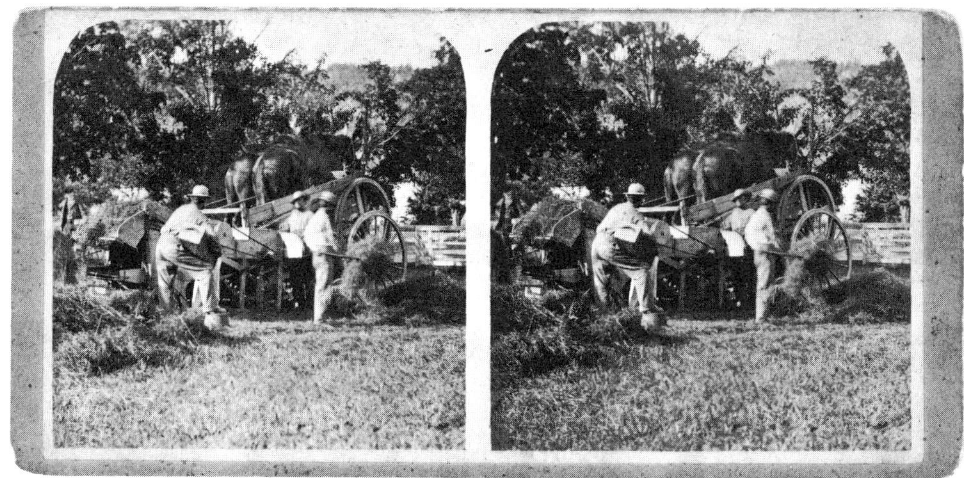

246. "Horse Mill." "Scenes from the Farm and Busy Life" series. Oxford, New Hampshire. A.F. Clough photo, 1870.

Examples include the great coaches carrying tourists to Yellowstone National Park.

Horse drawn street cars, (before 1900) fire engines, and mercantile wagons were part of every busy cityscape before 1915.

Pleasure horses are of three types, riding, including hunting, horses; carriage horses, including those used for royal coaches; and race horses.

In some armies the horses of cavalry officers and parade horses were handsome thoroughbred animals.

Schreiber & Son (Philadelphia, 1870-74), noted for animal photography, published a series of views, "The Principal Race Horses of the Country." Scattered among the many issues of Kilburn, there are views of many thoroughbred horses, for example, 5332-5336, "Mr. Bonnar's Race Horses"(1890).

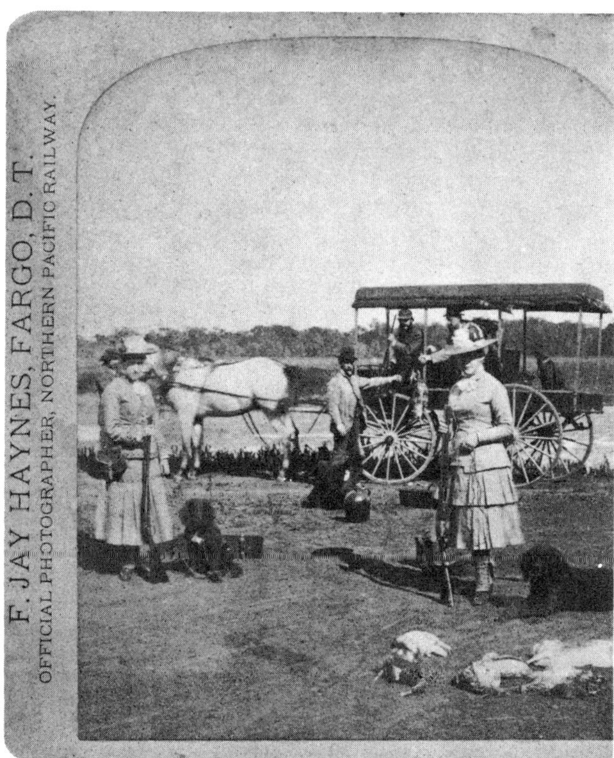

247. "Hunters' Return." Dakota Territory. F. Jay Haynes photo, 1878.

Attention is directed to the stereos of horses exhibited at the International Expositions, particularly of those at the Louisiana Purchase Exposition (1904).

In England, Frank Good (1863-66) published scenes of Derby Day and Epsom Downs.

The mule (hybrid between the horse and ass) was extensively used in American farming in the nineteenth century. It was the animal typically used by the black farmer after the Civil War.

HUNTING

Pleasure hunting in Europe has traditionally been the sport of kings and noblemen. In the United States the pastime has been available to anyone who desired to participate. The abundance of game and the expanses of wilderness contributed to such open freedom.

All travel sets illustrating lands inhabited by peoples with primitive cultures include views of natives hunting animal food—the aboriginal Australian, the American Indian, the Eskimo. We are concerned here, however, with sport hunting.

Big Game Hunting

The majority of stereographs depicting big game hunting were published between 1880 and 1910, although there were many earlier views, particularly in the United States. The wanton waste of animal life is a sorrowful episode in history. "A Night's Bag" (Keystone 17010) shows a pair of dead elephants at a water hole in East Africa. Keystone also issued a small series of views (17012-17015) of an American hunter in Rhodesia, assisted by twenty-three native guides, beaters and porters. In one scene, twelve slaughtered hippapotami lie upon the ground.

"Hunting the Royal Bengal Tiger" is a set of twelve excellent views published by Underwood (1904). Underwood also issued a boxed set of forty-two views of big game hunting in East Africa (1906).

The animals considered as big game in the United States include deer, elk, moose, mountain sheep, bear and buffalo. The buffalo, formerly extensively hunted for hides and meat, especially during the period of railroad construction, was nearly exterminated by 1900.

There are excellent stereo views of moose, elk, deer and bear hunting. B. L. Singley (Keystone, 1890's), an avid hunter, photographed himself and friends in scores of scenes of deer and moose hunts. George Barker, another hunting enthusiast, produced remarkable views of hunting camps (bear and deer) in the 1880's.

Hunting excursions from eastern states to Minnesota, Dakota

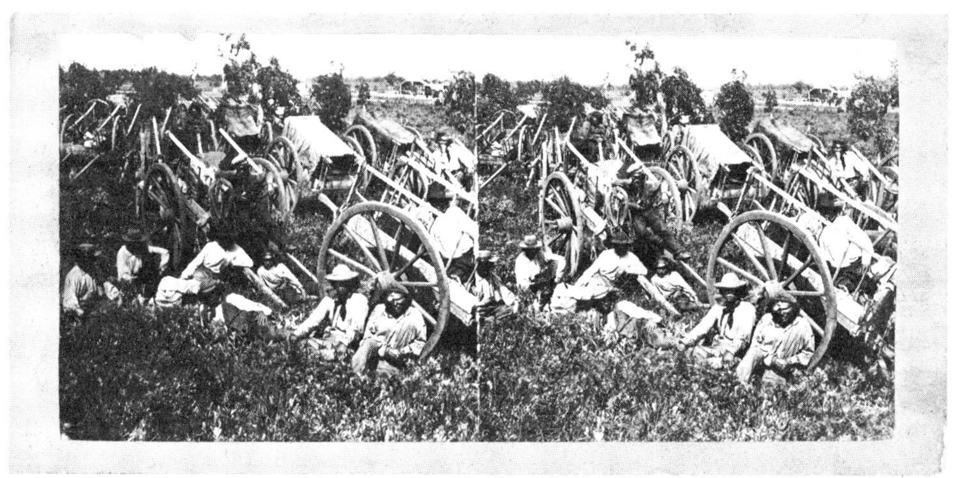

248. Indians. "Pembina Half-Breed Indians on a 600 mile trading tour to St. Paul." B.F. Upton photo, 1862.

Territory and Montana, were common during the late 1870's and 80's. The Worcester (Massachusetts) Excursion Car Company organized annual hunting tours. E. O. White, who accompanied the excursion of 1882, published a series of forty-two views, including scenes of the incredible array of skins, carcases and trophies shot by the men and their wives.

Kilburn Brothers, both of whom enjoyed hunting and fishing, issued many views of deer and small game hunting.

Small Game Hunting

Small game include water fowl and other migratory birds as well as rabbits, squirrels and opossum. Stereographs are numerous. The most extensive series, about 350 numbers, was issued over a period of twenty years by Ingersoll. A great variety of views are widely scattered among the work of many local photographers.

There are several hundred multicolored lithoprints depicting hunting scenes, including many from Ingersoll's regular trade list. A considerable number are humorous.

There are fine views of English fox hunts. Underwood (1905) published a notable scene in Wiltshire showing huntsmen and their dogs pursuing an otter pack.

There are similarities between the hunting scenes recorded in stereographs before 1890 and the genre of hunting paintings by American artists of the nineteenth century. Whether this merely reflects a common interest or records some deeper relationship is worthy of study.

INDIANS

The Indians of the Western Hemisphere, especially those of North America, have fascinated photographers and collectors. Thinly scattered small tribes, grouped in a score of linguistic stocks, populated the continent prior to the arrival of white men. Gradually pushed from their hunting grounds and subsequently placed in reservations, the Indians lost much of their culture. The last unspoiled tribes, the Utes and Paiutes of the Colorado Plateau region were stereographed by O'Sullivan and Hillers between 1873 and 1875.

A number of photographers issued fine stereographs of Indians. The most notable of 1860-1892 include:

G. Barker, New York, Iroquois, Onandaga
H. H. Bennett, Wisconsin, Winnebago
Bennett & Brown, New Mexico, Navajo, Pueblo, Kiowa
C. Bierstadt, New York, Iroquois, Tuscarora
J. Carbutt, Pawnee and others
C. W. Carter, Utah, Shoshone
B. F. Childs, Michigan, Chippewa
W. R. Cross, Nebraska, Sioux and others
F. J. Haynes, Dakota, many tribes
J. K. Hillers, Arizona, New Mexico, Ute, Piute, many others
T. Houseworth, California, Washoe and others
W. H. Illingworth, Minnesota, Dakota and others
W. H. Jackson, Colorado, Wyoming, many tribes

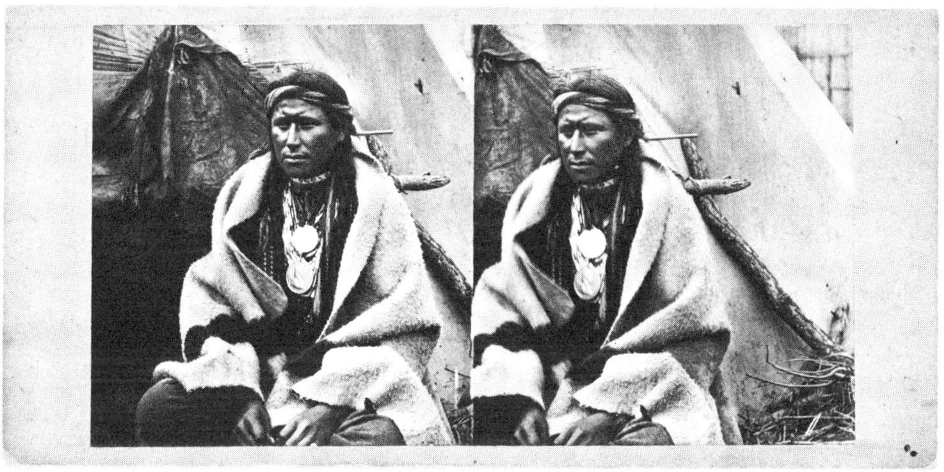

249. Sioux Indian. Joel E. Whitney photo, 1862.

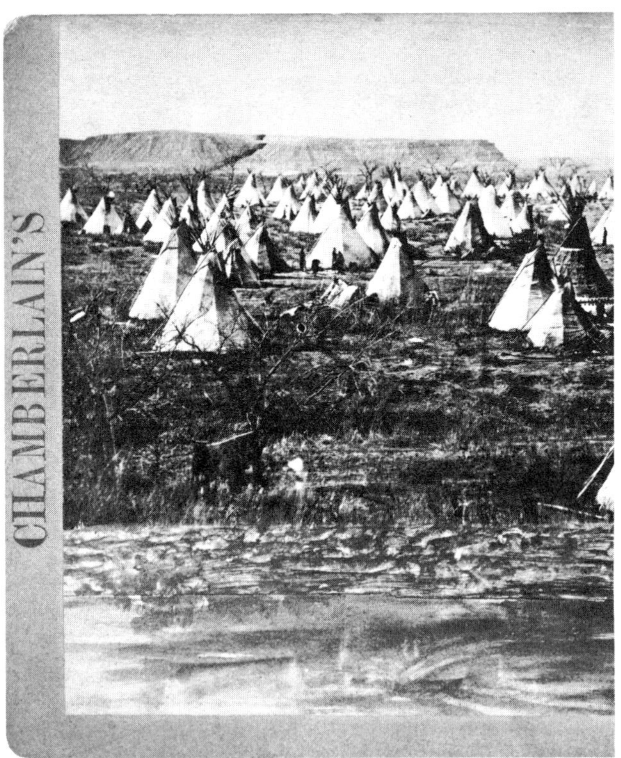

250. "Indian Encampment in Middle Park, Colorado." W.G. Chamberlain photo, 1877.

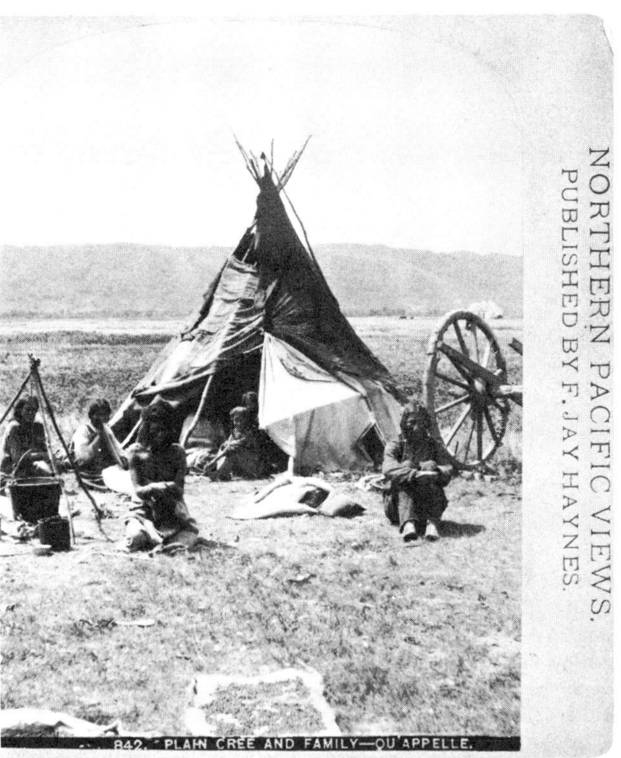

251. Cree Indian Family. Dakota Territory. F. Jay Haynes photo, ca. 1878.

Kilburn Brothers, Mexico; Maine, Penobscot
J. S. Mitchell, Florida, Seminole
S. J. Morrow, Dakota Territory, many tribes
T. O'Sullivan, Arizona and New Mexico, Navaho, Zuni, and others
G. L. Rose, Arizona, New Mexico, Pueblo
A. J. Russell, Utah, Shoshone
C. R. Savage, Utah, Shoshone, many others
B. F. Upton, Minnesota, Chippewa, Winnebago, Sioux
C. E. Watkins, California, many tribes
J. E. Whitney, Minnesota, Sioux, Winnebago
J. R. Woodburn, Nova Scotia

In the twentieth century, Keystone, Underwood and White published many views of Indians on reservations. These stereos are important because the elder people especially among such tribes as the Blackfeet (Glacier National Park) and Pueblos retained traditional skills, dress and pure features of their people.

Most stereos of the Eskimo were photographed after 1898, by Underwood and Keystone although in the 1860's Muybridge visited Alaska and Hayes obtained views in Labrador.

No catalogue of types of views is necessary because every aspect of Indian life from hunting and cooking, crafts to burial customs has been recorded. Stereos of mothers with papooses (Bierstadt, Curtis, Barker) were sold in great quantity.

Studio portraits of hundreds of Indian personalities, most of them carefully identified, are available.

The Indians of Mexico, Panama and South America are depicted in the well-known travel sets.

INDUSTRIAL ARCHEOLOGY

This relatively new field of historical research attempts to recover information about technological processes, mills, tools, locations and related data. Strangely, thus far, the vast resources recorded in stereographs have been neglected in the research. Technology between 1850 and 1920 has been stereographed in incredible detail.

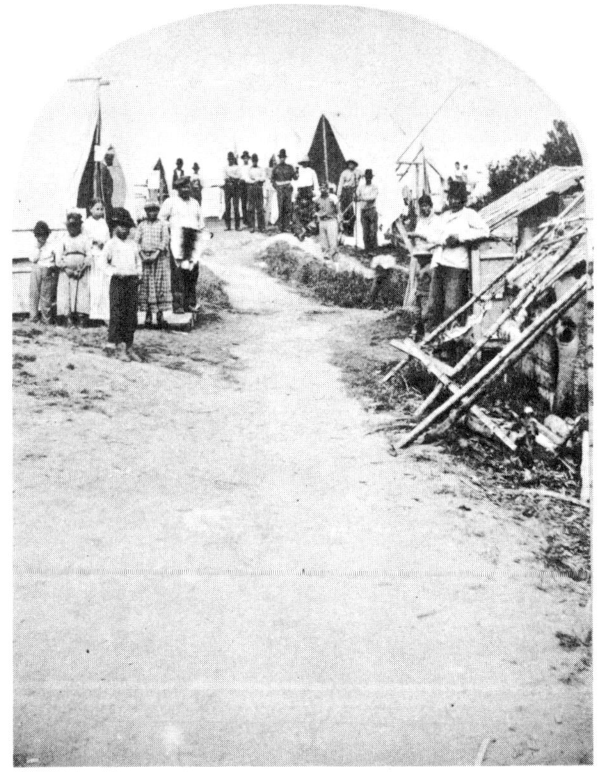

252. Penobscot Indians. Encampment at Bar Harbor, Mt. Desert, Maine. B.W. Kilburn photo, 1879.

The skilled tradesmen in every culture have been photographed at their work. Since most of these were photographed again and again over a period of fifty years, the persistence or change of methods is discernible.

Major occupations and types of labor also have been thoroughly photographed. Farming, mining, railroading, factory workers are especially well recorded.

The factory buildings, characteristic of every "mill town," the "company towns," and mill races are handsomely illustrated.

Those industries which exhaust a resource and move elsewhere, leaving "ghost towns," have also left a stereographic record. The petroleum industry in western Pennsylvania, lumber towns, nitroglycerine factories located near great construction projects, hydraulic mining and many other semi-temporary works are but a few of very many examples.

See also: AGRICULTURE; CIVIL ENGINEERING; ELECTRICAL ENGINEERING; ENGINEERING; MINING and QUARRYING.

LIBRARIES AND MUSEUMS

The extent of stereographic illustration of the interiors of libraries and museums is seldom realized. While collector interest in these views is slight, the details of organization, patronage and techniques have considerable academic interest.

The great libraries of the world have been stereographed beautifully. The buildings, halls of statuary, the shelves of books and maps and the reading rooms are shown from many points of view. The Vatican Library, the Library of Congress, National Library of France, and those of many universities (Oxford, Cambridge, Harvard) were stereographed repeatedly before 1875.

Interior views of private libraries in Boston, Providence, New York and in many small towns are available. For example, the Putnam Library (Richmond, Indiana) was stereographed by Nute Brothers (four views, ca. 1882).

Views of public libraries, generally exterior scenes, are found in nearly all local series. A view of the old Boston Public Library opposite the Commons (built 1855-57) in the "Boston Illustrated' series by C. Pollock (1872-4). Another typical view is Robinson's "Circulating Library, Lowell, Massachusetts" (1872).

Among the unusual subjects may be cited "Sailors' Free Reading Room" (Edgartown, Massachusetts (C. H. Shute, 1870) and "Apprentice's Library" (Boston, Pollock, 1873).

Public museums are of two general types, art and natural history. Both types have been extensively stereographed.

The galleries and exhibits of the Louvre, Vatican and the museums in Florence, Naples, Berlin are depicted in hundreds of stereo views. The statuary and mural paintings in the United States Capitol have been repeatedly photographed.

Natural history museums involve more complicated procedures than art museums in that preparation and preservation of specimens precedes displaying exhibits. Furthermore, most of the scientific collections, which are held in systematic storage, are seldom exhibited.

The British Museum has been extensively stereographed. The two largest series are by C. E. Elliott and F. York (ca. 1870). The Smithsonian Institution and the Academy of Natural Science (Philadelphia) have also been stereographed (1865-1880).

Views of college and university museum exhibits are quite common, among the best Oxford, Yale, Harvard, Dartmouth, Amherst and McGill—but there are many others. The majority of such views depict displays of minerals, fossils, insects and mounted birds.

The taxidermic and diorama methods recorded in these views are of interest to historians of science. Attempts to exhibit plants and animals in so-called habitat groups were rather crude in 1865-75. More natural and realistic techniques developed slowly. The "Group of American Elk by Prof. Dyche" (Kansas University Museum, Berry, Kelly & Chadwick, no. 1475, ca. 1908) is a fine example of its period. R. Y. Young's "Tiger Cat and Deer" 1902, is another excellent group.

The ingenious Zoographicon, invented by F. Gruber, displayed at Woodward's Garden, San Francisco, had eight dioramic panels illustrating the characteristic animals of the world (Asia, Africa, etc). The exhibit included models of mammals and birds moved by mechanical devices. Lange and Newth published a series of eight stereos of the Zoographicon.

Several famous private museums were stereographed. One of the most unusual was that assembled by Mrs. M. A. Maxwell (Denver) illustrating the fauna, rocks and minerals of Colorado. Chamberlain published several fine views most of which were sold to visitors at the museum. There are eight views of Mrs. Maxwell's attractive displays at the Centennial Exhibition.

Cremer in 1876 issued two fine views of the exhibits in the "National Museum in Independence Hall."

Historical museums which often are merely historic houses will not be described in this book. Those interested in a particular house can readily locate a view among the issues by local photographers.

LITERARY

Popular literary personalities were widely known in their own times. The educated masses were familiar with their lives and works through newspapers and periodicals. Popular interest and national pride provided ample reasons for stereographing the homes and haunts of deceased and living poets and novelists.

The landmarks mentioned in the works of Sir Walter Scott and Robert Burns were beautifully stereographed. The cottages of Burns, Shakespeare and Ann Hathaway were favorite subjects.

American stereographers followed suit. The homes of Longfellow, Whittier, Cooper, Hawthorne, Irving and many others were repeatedly photographed.

There are many excellent stereo portraits of literary figures living between 1860 and 1930. The series by Anthony, Gurney, Sarony and Holmes include European as well as American authors. Underwood and Keystone (1910-1930) issued views of many personalities.

Collateral subjects of literary interest extend to monuments, graves, and statues of ancient and modern authors.

The common use of verses of poetry as appropriate legends for a stereo view and the many attempts to illustrate literary works by stereographs may also be considered in this category.

MACHINERY

Brief reference to the wide range of stereo views of machines, machine tools and machine shops will be made here.

Vehicles which utilize steam engines or gasoline engines have been noted under aircraft, automobiles and shipping.

The interior views of factories and machine shops illustrate a great variety of machines such as saws, planers, lathes, grinders and rollers. The various forms of each basic type of machine used in different industries (lumber, steel, glass) have been fully stereographed.

The machinery involved in minting coins, grinding optical and telescopic lenses, manufacturing jewelry are but a few of the many specialized devices that are very well recorded.

The huge machine shops associated with railroads (such as Altoona, Pennsylvania with views by Purviance, Gutekunst and Bonine) were photographed with men at work.

Domestic machines such as those used for sweeping, washing, sewing, peeling apples, churning butter, have been incidentally stereographed. For examples one must search through interior views of homes, especially of kitchens, to find them.

Attention is called to views of many ingenious devices and scaled models, often built as an avocational activity. "The 8th Wonder Engle Clock" built by J. Reid (Philadelphia, 1874-78) was stereographed a dozen times.

See also: ENGINEERING; MILLS and FACTORIES.

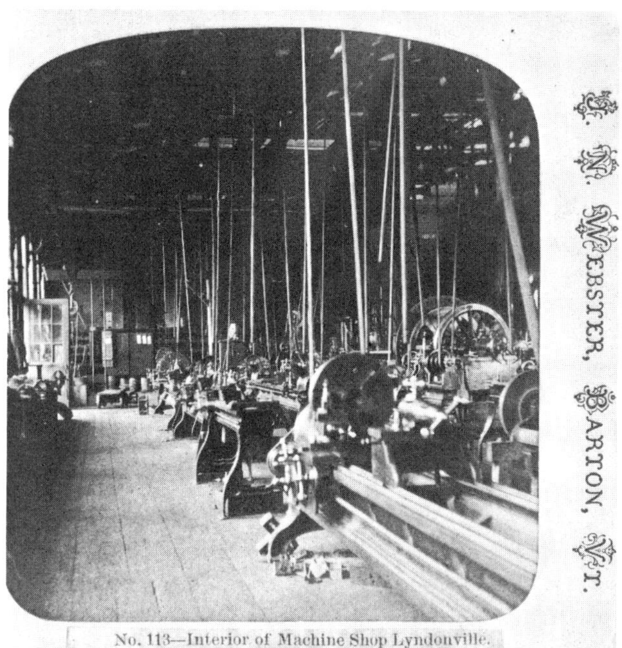

253. Machinery. Railroad Machine Shop, Lyndonville, Vermont. J.N. Webster photo, 1868.

MARKETS

Modern food distribution and shopping centers are taken for granted. In many parts of the world it is still necessary to purchase food daily because of lack of refrigeration and storage facilities. Markets of great diversity are traditional activities that have continued with little change for two thousand years.

Bartering in Greece (Argos), (H. C. White 4188, 1898), the fruit market in Tunis (White 3006, 1901), and the Swahili native market at Nyanza, Lake Victoria (Keystone 17011, ca. 1910) show how enduring such customs persist. The Old World markets where buyers and sellers come together have their origin in the Middle Ages. The one-product vendor and one-product market are recorded in many scenes in Europe and Latin America. A few examples will indicate their diversity.

cabbage market, Germany, C. H. Graves, 1901
vegetable market, Moscow, Russia, White, 1902
dish market, Mayence, Germany, Griffith, 1903
flower market, Brussels, Belgium, White, 1908
old clothes market, Moscow, Russia, White, 1901
sombrero market, Puerto Rico, Underwood, 1900

Panoramic views of various busy outdoor markets include:

Quebec, Champlain market, Vallee, 1867
Strassburg, Germany, White, 1901
Nuremberg, Germany, Keystone, 1904
Guyaquil, Ecuador (canoe stalls) 1910
Cape Town, South Africa (auction market), White, 1901

In the United States farmers' markets and municipal markets were usually in commodious buildings. From 1840 to 1930 they were found in nearly every American city. Some cities still maintain them. The renowned Faneuil Hall market with a hundred wagons lining the streets was stereographed by Heywood in 1858 and a score of other photographers thereafter.

The Keystone view of the "Farmers Market, Washington, D.C." 29495, ca. 1928, is a vivid example. Other city markets with distinctive features include the Fulton Fish Market (New York, A. S. Campbell, 1895) and the Kansas City Market (Missouri, Kilburn, 5473, 1890).

Stereographs of push carts and other street vendors are not common. They are occasionally depicted in New York scenes (Campbell, 1894-1902; Stereo-Travel, 1909-11).

MEDICAL

The application of stereography to medical instruction began about 1900 with the publication of the "Edinburgh Stereoscopic Atlas of Anatomy" which was followed by a set on obstetrics and then other subjects. Each stereoscopic image was mounted on a card measuring 7 inches by 9 inches, with a detailed printed text. The sets were available until the late 1950's.

A similar "Stereoscopic Atlas of Neuro-Anatomy" prepared by Doctors H. S. Rubenstein and C. L. David, was published by Grune & Stratton Company in 1947. Unlike the Edinburgh atlases, however, this set has half-tone stereo views.

There were other experiments with medical stereographs. The most remarkable was a 160 card set of multicolored lithoprints illustrating "Diseases of the Skin" prepared and published (1910) by S. I. Rainforth, M.D. of New York. The coloration of pathologic conditions are highly accurate. The diagnoses and treatments printed on the backs are, however, obsolete. The views include all common skin diseases from allergic conditions and fungal infections to carcinomas and syphilitic lesions.

Nineteenth century views of hospital interiors are fairly numerous. Among them are scenes in municipal, Catholic, and private hospitals.

Military medicine and associated equipment such as ambulances, litters, tent hospitals and wounded is recorded in hundreds of views of the Spanish-American, Russo-Japanese and World (I) Wars.

MILITARY

Peacetime activities of standing armies and navies range from garrisons, camps and manned forts to guard duty and ceremonial parades in dress uniforms.

The army forts located in the western territories of the United States commonly had a resident photographer. William Soule, for example, published fine views of Fort Sill and of the families stationed there.

United States Army maneuvers in peacetime were stereographed by H. C. White (6501-6510, 1905) at Manassas, Virginia. This small series illustrates the tremendous advances in

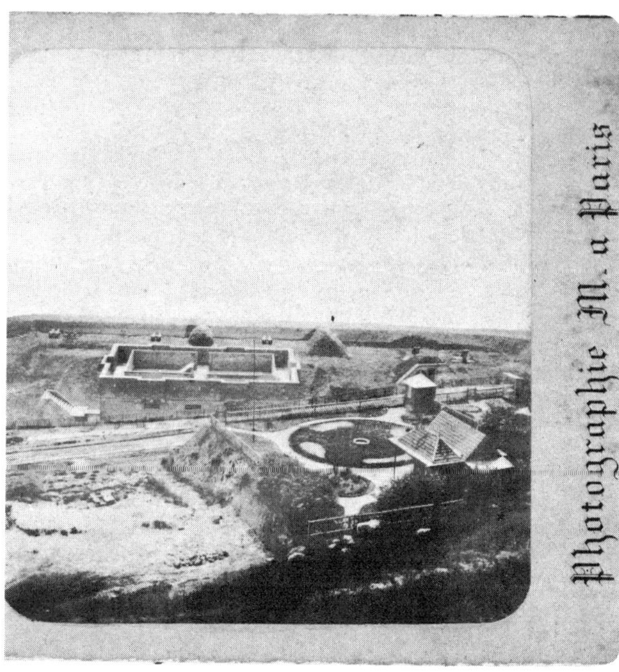

254. Military. Fort Ste. Adresse, Loire, France. Moreau photo, 1867.

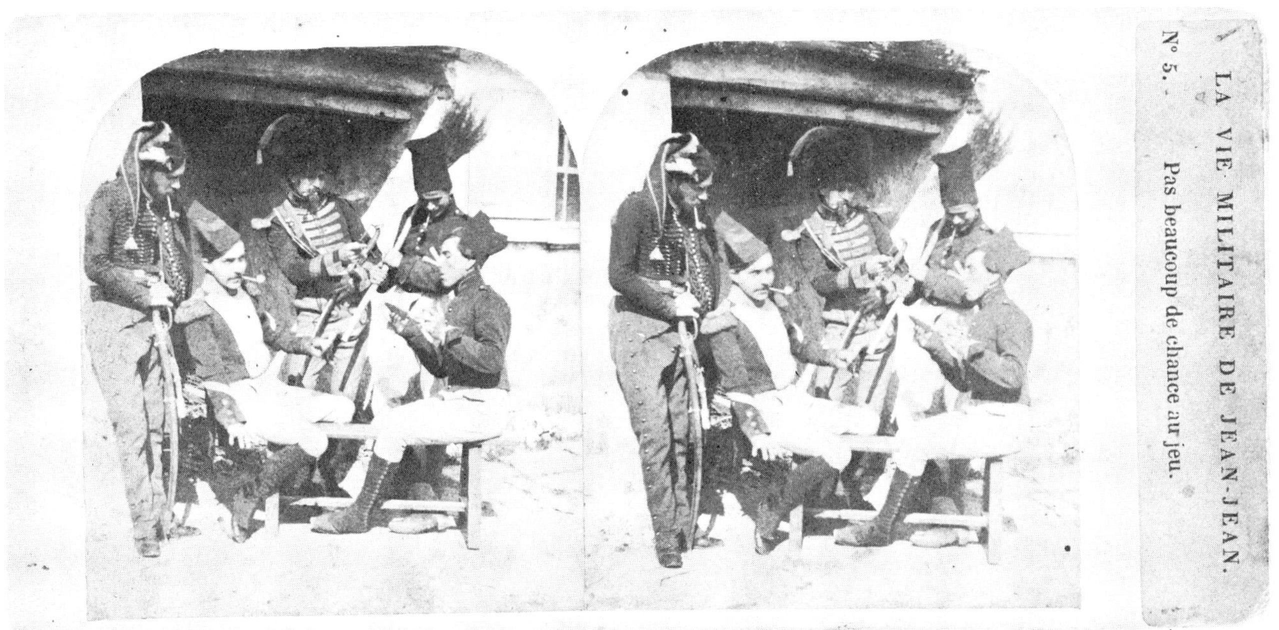

255. "La Vie Militaire de Jean-Jean." "Not much luck at play." Unknown photographer ca. 1857.

training and preparedness over conditions existing in 1898.

The life of the common soldier and sailor from 1854 to 1925 has been the subject of hundreds of serious and humorous views. Reference to Camp de Chalons has been made earlier. A semi-humorous series "La Vie Militaire de Jean-Jean" is a delightful picture story of boredom and occupations of a French soldier (1857-59).

MILLS AND FACTORIES

Pre-1890

The factory system which developed in America integrated all of the operations from receipt of raw material to shipping of finished products into one or several inter-connecting buildings. The famous "Waltham System," which grew out of the Boston Manufacturing Company and its complete cotton factory (established 1813) involved not only manufacturing industry but "paternalistic" control of the employees through rigid supervised boarding houses, education and recreation. The textile mills founded between 1820 and 1870 in Massachusetts, New Hampshire, and Maine employed young farm women recruited from all parts of New England. Revulsion against the sordid conditions prevalent in English and French factories made it desirable—so the mill owners and parents believed—to maintain a more humane and moral environment for female employees.

Many industrialists constructed rows of houses adjacent to the mills to provide for the families of married employees.

It is difficult for us to believe how much towns prided them-

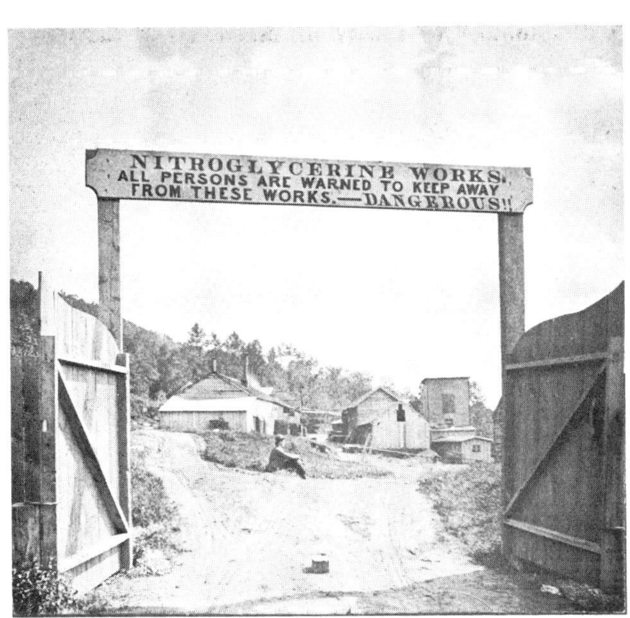

256. Mills and Factories. Nitroglycerine Works, Hoosac Tunnel Construction, Massachusetts. H.D. Ward photo, 1868.

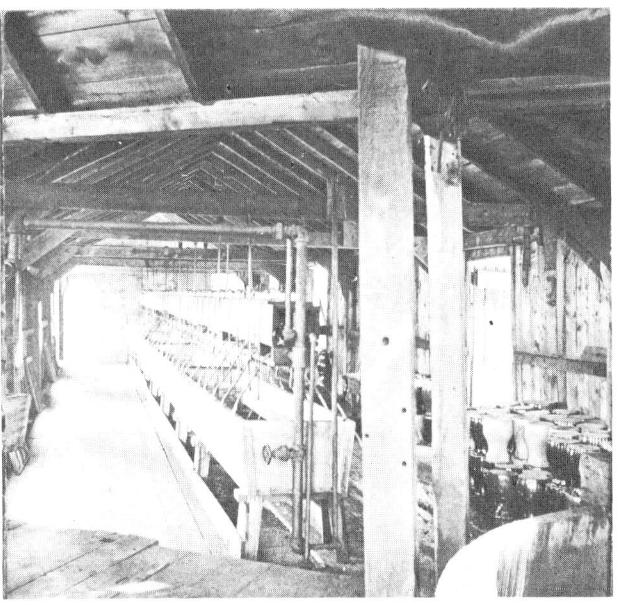

257. Nitroglycerine Works, interior of converting room. Hoosac Tunnel, Massachusetts. H.D. Ward photo, 1868.

selves over their factories and company houses. These were not poverty areas but prosperous attributes of the community. As such they were enthusiastically stereographed.

The majority of textile mills in Lowell, Lawrence, Manchester and Saco were illustrated in great detail. The factories, machinery, employees and the sense of community are vividly recorded in hundreds of views.

Many manufacturing companies were illustrated by series of views. Generally these were intended to be informative and were not issued as advertising material.

The Waltham Watch Company was stereographed by T. Lewis (43 cards, 1873).

The Sanders, Frary & Clute Cutlery Works, Hartford (12 card set, Prescott & White, 1873).

Willimantic Linen Company Thread Works (about 10 views, Prescott & White, 1872).

Excelsior Straw Works, Medfield, Massachusetts (27 views, O. M. Perrigo, 1874).

P. H. McGraw & Son, corset manufacturers, McGrawville, N.Y. (10 views, 1882).

There are views of hundreds of iron works, furniture factories, shoe factories, nitroglycerine plants, carriage shops recording with great fidelity how products were manufactured.

Historic mills like "Old Slater" at Pawtucket, Rhode Island were repeatedly photographed.

Post 1890

The educational sets of stereo views assembled by Keystone and Underwood emphasized economic geography, including world trade and industries. Such industries as iron and steel, silk, wool, cotton were illustrated to show the source of raw materials, transport, processing and manufacturing operations and finished products. Primitive methods were contrasted with the most advanced as practiced in the most modern plants.

These sets are significant historical documents inasmuch as they are complete pictorial records, many of which are of obsolete processes and factories since abandoned.

The assembly plant system developed in the automobile industry is recorded in a number of Keystone views.

The paradox of labor conditions in the United States in the early 1900's is illustrated by the zenith of the paternalistic employer. H. C. White published "A Visit to the White Oak Cotton Mills at Greensboro, North Carolina, the Largest Denim Mill in the World," as a loose-leaf stereo-pack, 25 views (1909). The Proximity Manufacturing Company operated two mills at Greensboro, the White Oak and the Proximity. The photographer and editor were remarkably successful in recording the spirit of the enterprise. The mills were run by electricity generated by the company's own power plant. The machinery and operations were clearly depicted and described in accompanying notes. The company built a substantial grade school for each mill, maintained a kindergarten, employed seventeen teachers including music, cooking, sewing and manual training. There were after-school activities for younger children, crafts for the older and a boys' club with a gymnasium for the boys. Each of the mills had uniformed baseball teams and brass bands.

Many mills and factories have been stereographed but none so completely or vividly as the White Oak Mill at Greensboro, North Carolina.

See also: OCCUPATIONS

MINING & QUARRYING

The mad rush for gold in California inspired the scaling of simple devices such as pans and screens to colossal sizes, and the diversion of water from mountain streams through sluices and flumes to wash native gold from sand and gravel. The greedy ingenuity created a wasteland. The act was repeated in the Dakotas, Idaho and Alaska. Hydraulic mining of gold gravels, one of the most spectacular technologies of the nineteenth century, was accomplished without the use of fuel-driven power machinery.

Traditional methods of open-pit mining did not require elaborate equipment or much capital. When the demand for iron and copper ore increased to the extent that power machines, deep mines, and railroads were indispensable, great industrial complexes replaced the neighborhood furnace or smelter. Processing plants were constructed close to the ore mines or to the source of fuel, whichever economic factors dictated.

The famous metal mining districts in Michigan (copper), Minnesota (iron), Missouri (lead), Colorado (silver, lead, gold), Arizona (silver and copper), Idaho (silver, lead), Nevada (silver) were extensively stereographed. Individual mines and their operations are recorded in detail.

Views of more restricted deposits in Pennsylvania (zinc, iron) and New Jersey (zinc), Alabama (iron) and small ore banks in many states are also available.

Deep mine interiors were stereographed by O'Sullivan and Jackson in the 1870's.

Coal mining methods, including deep mining were well developed in Europe before 1800. When anthracite coal was discovered in eastern Pennsylvania, Welsh miners were recruited

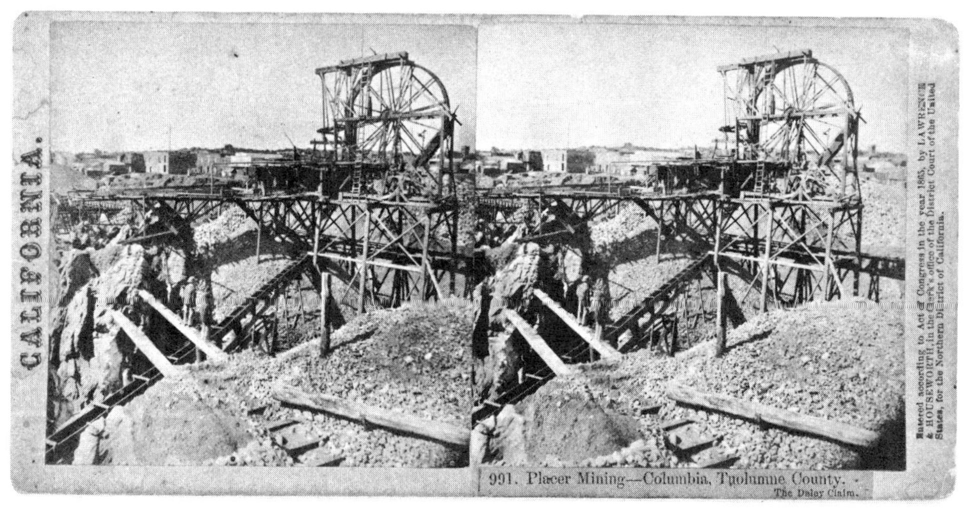

258. Placer Mining, Tuolumne County, California. Lawrence and Houseworth photo, 1865.

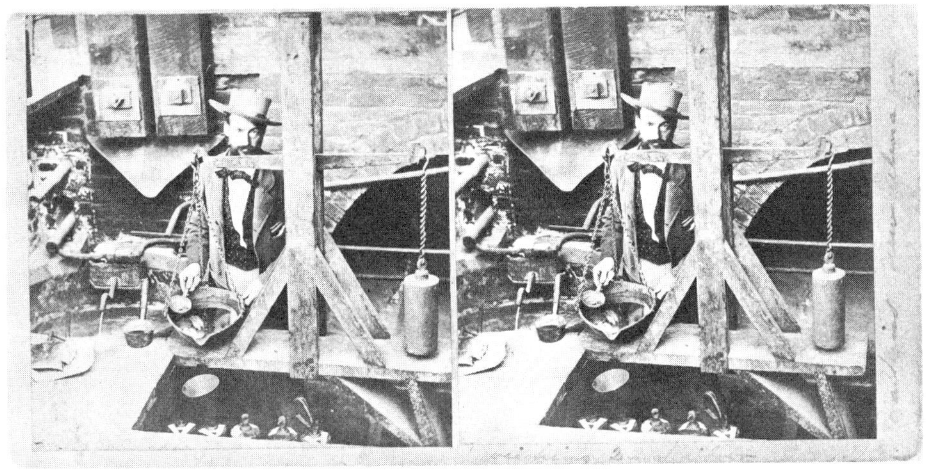

259. Mining. "Weighing Mercury, New Almaden," California. Carleton E. Watkins photo, 1861.

to bring their experience to America.

There is splendid stereo coverage of the anthracite basins of Pennsylvania by dozens of photographers, especially Langenheim, A. M. Allen, Josiah Brown, Schurch, and Johnson. Because no open flames can be permitted, no interior mine views could be taken prior to the invention of the incandescent electric light. Nevertheless, the method of mining and the associated coal breakers is clearly recorded. Keystone published several series of interior views between 1906 and 1925, some of which illustrate electrification of some mines.

Mining bituminous coal is basically similar to anthracite mining except that before 1920 stripping was more frequent. Various strip mining operations were stereographed by Keystone.

There are extensive series illustrating diamond mining in South Africa.

The travel sets usually include a selection of views illustrating important or unusual mining industries (such as nitrate and guano in Chile).

Quarrying differs from mining in that rock is removed from the open face of a hill or cliff or from the surface in an ever enlarging open pit. Granite, marble, limestone, sandstone, slate and asbestos are the principal quarried rocks. Except for machine hoists, machine drills and explosives, the methods employed have changed little from those of antiquity. Obelisks and great stone blocks were quarried in Egypt. Many ancient monuments and adorned temples (Acropolis, Athens) attest to the incredible human labor involved in quarrying and erecting massive blocks of stone.

Hesketh in the 1860's published excellent views of slate quarries in Wales. The granite quarries of Massachusetts, Rhode Island and Maine were frequently stereographed, especially those on Cape Ann (Lanesville and Rockport).

The Vermont and Tennessee marble quarries have also been well recorded.

In mining, as in all other aspects of technology, the introduction of power machinery, the utilization of energy, transformed the industry to vast proportions requiring railroads, lake or river shipping and international commerce in the span of barely fifty years. The steps and stages in this transformation have been handsomely documented in thousands of stereo views.

MONUMENTS

The term monument is here used in a narrow sense, referring to statues, columns and markers erected to memorialize persons or events. Imposing buildings are excluded.

Monuments in most countries are preserved by government regulation. Many are placed in public squares, near public buildings or in parks. Many are erected at the location of an event. Monuments are often works by renowned artists and

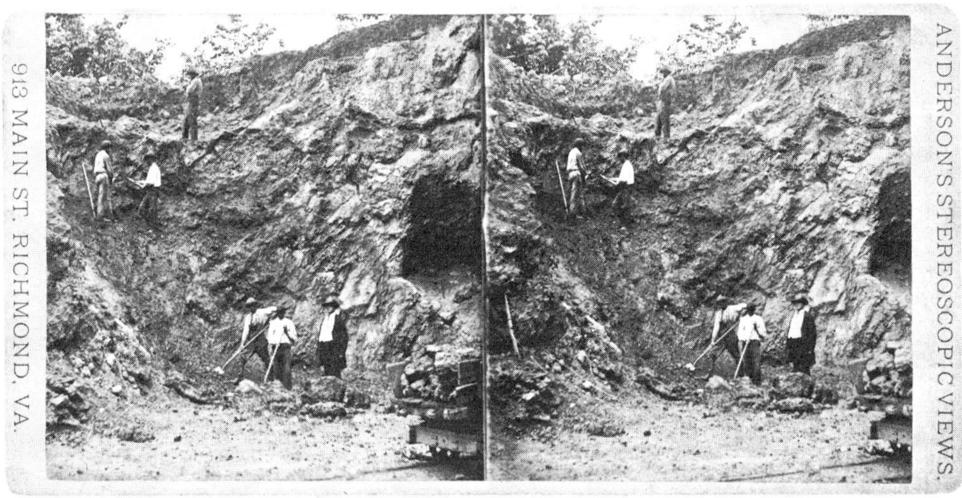

260. "Iron Ore Pit, West Virginia." A typical 19th century ore bank. Anderson photo, ca. 1870.

often reveal much about the culture of the period they commemorate.

Simple obelisks like Bunker Hill Monument and the Washington Monument on the Mall in Washington, D.C. are known to every American. Ancient Egyptian obelisks (Cleopatra's Needles) were moved from Alexandria to London (1877) and New York 1879). The column commemorating Napoleon at Place Vendome, Paris is also well known.

One of the most beautiful monuments is the Albert Memorial (London, 1872-76) which was stereographed by F. York (50 views) and by many other English photographers.

Every city in the world has its statues and markers to men and women, royalty, artists, soldiers, benefactors and folk heroes. Among the great monuments are statues of:

Christopher Columbus with America kneeling at his feet, Genoa, Italy

Dante, by Michaelangelo, Florence, Italy

Gutenberg, by Thorwaldsen, Mainz, Germany

Andrew Jackson, equestrian statue by Mills, Washington

Famous allegorical monuments have also been frequently stereographed.

"The Minute Man," at Concord, Massachusetts, by David French

"The American Volunteer" exhibited at the Centennial, later erected on the Antietam Battlefield

"Statue of Liberty," New York Harbor, by Bartholdi. There are fine views of the arm and torch exhibited at the Centennial. Figure 236.

Monuments marking events are extremely varied. "The National Monument to the Forefathers" erected at Plymouth, Massachusetts is an example of an imposing monument. The simple bronze marker on a pedestal commemorating Lincoln's Address in the Gettysburg National Cemetery is annually visited by more than a million people.

Triumphal arches in Rome, Paris, Berlin and the monument studded cities like Rome, Florence, Venice and Washington have been stereographed hundreds of times.

MUSICAL INSTRUMENTS

History of the instruments that man has used to produce music is one of the neglected fields of musicology. Stereographs record virtually every native instrument, often being played by groups of performers. A band of alang-alang players in Java is recorded in Underwood 9084 (1907). The Japanese harp-like koto which is played horizontally may be seen in Keystone (White) W33908.

The familiar stringed instruments such as harp, violin family, guitar are depicted in hundreds of stereographs. Keystone (13424, 1903) recorded the Norwegian hardanger violin with six strings beneath the standard four.

The whole range of harpsicords, virginals, spinets and pianos are richly photographed. Views of Victorian parlors and furnished historic homes usually show several musical instruments.

Without attempting to catalogue other types of instruments, the following are available in many views: drums, tomtoms, bagpipes, zithers, zimbalims, and horns of every variety.

Stereographs of church and concert organs are often accompanied by descriptive notes concerning construction, cost and history. The Murray organ (Congregational Church, Gloucester, Massachusetts) imported from England in 1778 was stereographed by Cook & Friend in 1872. The colossal organ in the Boston Colosseum (Peace Jubilee, 1872) required eight pumps powered by a gas engine. There are scores of views by a dozen photographers. The famous organ in the Mormon Tabernacle in Salt Lake City was beautifully photographed by Savage and Carter.

Stereographs of groups of musicians, trios, quintets and large orchestras are not common but there are many fine views. F. M. Good (125, 1863) issued a scene of a quintet performing at the Royal Sandrock Hotel, Isle of Wight. Celebrated bands, such as those of Gilmore and Sousa were frequently stereographed. Hall Brothers published an excellent view of Gilmore's Band at Grand Hotel, Saratoga. There are scores of stereos of home town marching bands, 1860-1885.

For those interested in choirs, attention is called to fine views of church choirs, oratorio societies and combined choruses at religious conventions. A typical example, The Salem (Massachusetts) Oratorio Society, was stereographed by Whipple & Smith in 1868.

Finally, among the stereographs of displays at the international exhibitions there are a considerable number of ancient and modern musical instruments. The London Exhibition of 1862 had a fine display by Distin & Company (London Stereo, 339). There are several views of the remarkable exhibit of Egyptian instruments at the Centennial of 1876.

NATIONAL PARKS

National parks reserved by Acts of Congress after 1900 were stereographed under the names by which they are now known. The scenic areas, of course, were well photographed in the 1870's and in subsequent years. Such views must be sought

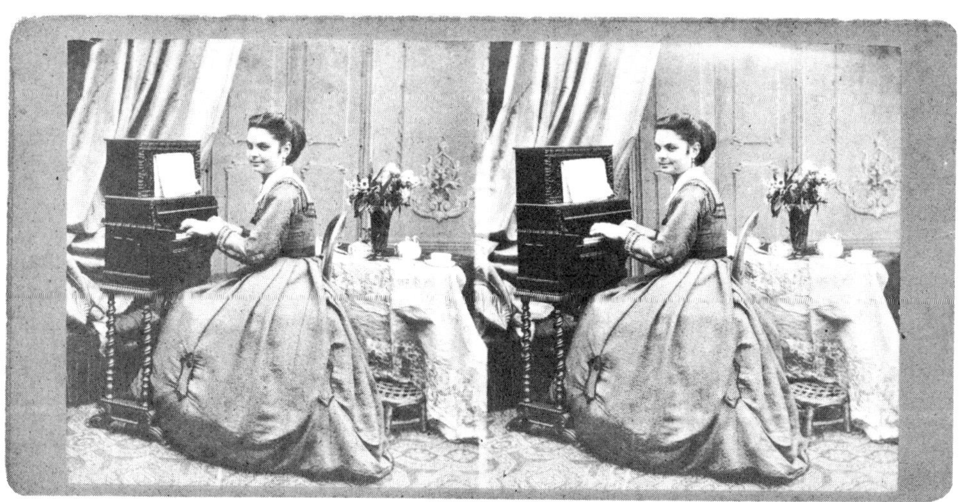

261. Musical Instruments. Unusual spinet parlor organ. French. Unknown photographer, ca. 1865.

among those produced by government surveys and local photographers.

Yosemite was a California state park for many years before it was returned to the Federal Government in 1890. The extensive stereo documentation of Yosemite Valley has been described on pages 84, 86, 98.

Yellowstone, the first National Park, was set aside in 1872 to preserve for posterity a wilderness area with animal life and geological features unequaled in North America, perhaps in the entire world. Jackson's stereographs, which helped to promote creation of the park, are justly famous.

Mount Rainier was reserved in 1899; Crater Lake, 1902; Mesa Verde, 1906; and Glacier Park (Montana) in 1910. Many stereo views of these parks were published by Underwood, Keystone and White. Additional parks were established including Rocky Mountain, 1915; Hawaii (volcanic), 1916; Grand Canyon, 1919; Acadia (Maine) 1919; and Zion (Utah) 1919.

There are many small boxed sets of views of various parks. Underwood issued a series of Yosemite (twenty-four cards, 1912) and Grand Canyon (eighteen views, 1912). Keystone issued a fifty view set of Yosemite (1914), another of Mt. Rainier (thirty views, 1914).

Keystone issued nearly a thousand titles between 1921 and 1936. "Our National Parks", a splendid set of 100 views, was published in 1926.

Hot Springs, Arkansas, reserved (1832) for use of all the people, has been extensively photographed, mostly 1872-1885.

NAVAL

Stereographs illustrating the navies of the world from 1850 to 1930 are of great variety. During periods of war, views of battleships and auxiliary vessels are common but in peacetime the scenes are usually of national celebrations and training cruises.

Wilson's famous instantaneous views of gunfire from British warships of the Channel fleet (1857) are classics. The cannon were fired for the convenience of the photographer. Figure 159.

Various Civil War vessels, Union and Confederate, including the ironclads *Monitor* and *Merrimac* were stereographed. There are scenes of transports and prison ships.

The Spanish-American War involved navies more than armies. There are hundreds of views of the Atlantic Squadron at Santiago Bay and of the Pacific Squadron at Manila Bay. Keystone sold more copies of their views of the wreckage of the *U.S.S. Maine* than any other titles they published. The American views include every class of vessel: battleships, cruisers, torpedo boats, mine layers, mine sweepers, colliers and troop transports. The ruined ships of the Spanish fleets were repeatedly stereographed. No battle action stereos were taken.

The most complete coverage of naval warfare was accomplished during the Russo-Japanese War during the Siege of Port Arthur. Close views of actual bombardment and sinking ships were published by White and Underwood. The destruction of the Russian fleet is shown in spectacular scenes.

President Theodore Roosevelt sent "The Great White Fleet" around the world in 1907-08 to call attention to the naval strength of the United States. There are several views of the fleet, including a scene in the harbor of Sydney, Australia (Keystone, 15948). Between 1906 and 1910 several excellent lithoprint series depicting the life of a sailor were widely distributed. The scenes were photographed on board various ships of the Great White Fleet.

Naval activities in World War I were not stereographed systematically. The super dreadnaughts were generally photographed in harbor. There are many views of troop transports and naval escort ships. Submarines, including wrecked German ships are shown in about twenty scattered views.

Navy yards in the United States have been extensively stereographed, especially at Boston, Brooklyn and Philadelphia. There are many scenes of chain yards, anchor yards and shot parks. Sailing ships used by many nations for training sailors have provided many opportunities for unusual stereographs. Spectacular scenes with sailors perched or lined up on the rigging were issued between 1875 and 1910 (Littleton, 1898).

The United States Naval Academy was photographed many times. The most extensive coverage, at least seventy-five views, was published by W. M. Chase between 1870 and 1885.

There are many attractive views of naval reviews. The review celebrating the coronation of George V, 1911, was beautifully photographed by Underwood.

Collateral subjects are varied and numerous. The rotting hulks of the *Constitution* and *Constellation* were stereographed in 1876. The public outcry at the neglect of these historic ships led to the restoration of the *Constitution*. There are fine views of naval shipbuilding, drydocks and launchings.

Keystone (28372) records "The Final Session of the Naval Conference, St. James Palace, London, April 22, 1930."

NEGRO-BLACK CULTURE

The native black peoples of Africa have not been stereographed systematically. The best series is that made by the Fritsch expedition to South Africa, 1863-66. This series includes identified portraits of men and women of various tribes. Between 1905 and 1925 Underwood and Keystone published many scenes of Central African villages and tribesmen, usually engaged in characteristic occupations. There are staged as well as actual hunting scenes. The best views were taken in Congo, Uganda, Kenya, and Nigeria. There are many excellent views of children and aged people.

Scenes showing black slavery in the United States are very rare (I have never seen one) although there are many views of slave quarters on plantations, and slave markets, without human figures in them, photographed during and after the Civil War.

Between 1865 and 1880 a wide range of stereographs record the negro at work: in the cotton field, on the tobacco plantation, on the levee toting cotton and molasses, in the ginning mills and presses. The scenes recorded by southern photographers are best because they show the boss system and the methods of field and mill work (Upton, Barnard, Morgan, Wilson, and Palmer).

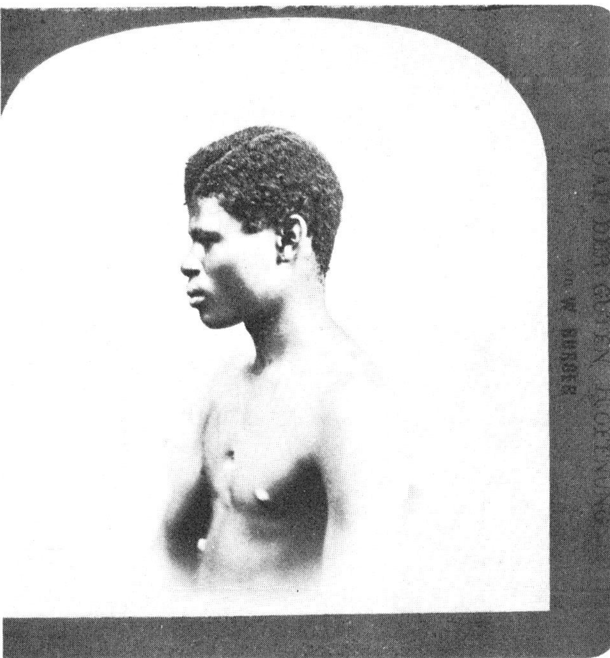

262. Negro. Native Kaffer, Cape of Good Hope, South Africa. W. Burger, photo ca. 1870.

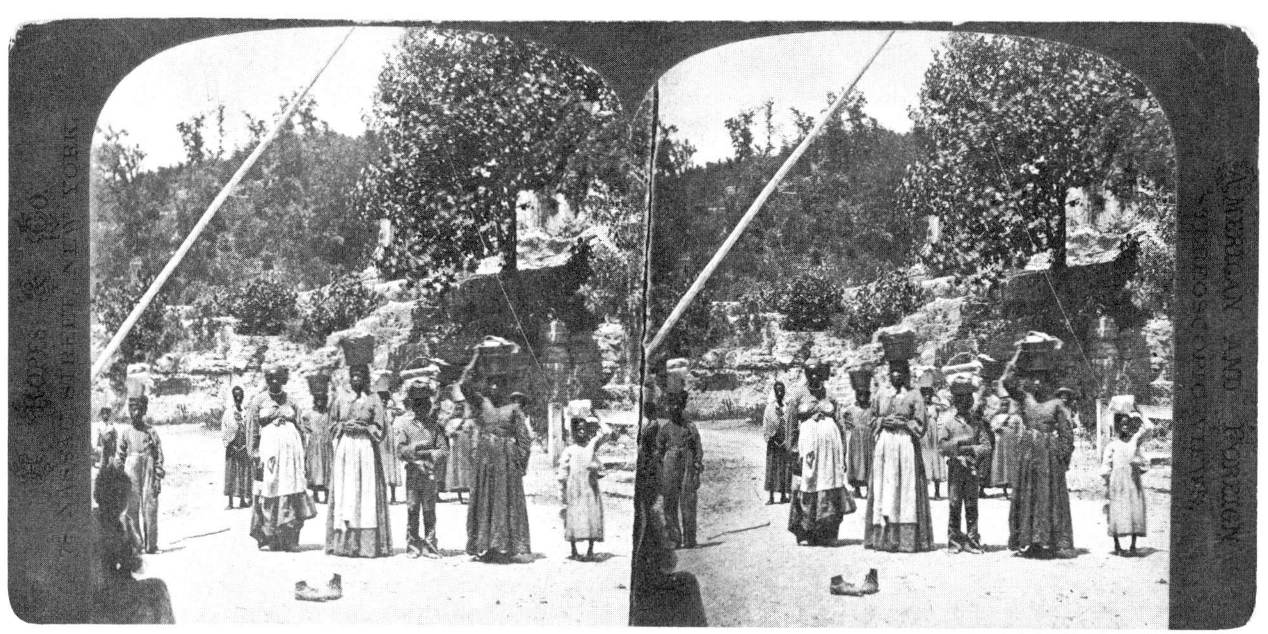

263. Negro, Kentucky. J. Mullen photo, 1866.

Views of negro cabin life and amusements in North Carolina, South Carolina, Georgia and Louisiana are more frequently encountered than in other states.

Following the Emancipation Act of 1863 there was a rash of views depicting a negro in a cart drawn by a mule. The accompanying title was frequently humorous or derisive. Ignoring the titles, we can see in such views revealing detail of faces. Rufus Morgan caught with his camera a charming picture of two men in their carts abreast, earnestly talking to each other. The title is simply "Gossiping on the Way."

Kilburn published many unusual views of black interest, although some of his titles would today be considered to be in poor taste. "Our Blackberries," twelve beautiful children, 7635, 1892; "Five Generations," a family including members aged from one to 120 years, pupils at a Negro School (6584) and convicts in striped uniforms (10813), suggest how Kilburn was interested in people.

There are views of many other aspects of negro life, such as: black regiments in the Civil, Spanish-American and World Wars; blacks employed as civilians by the Union Army; college students, singing groups and after 1890 many types of employment in hotels, railroad Pullman cars and musicians. The Fisk

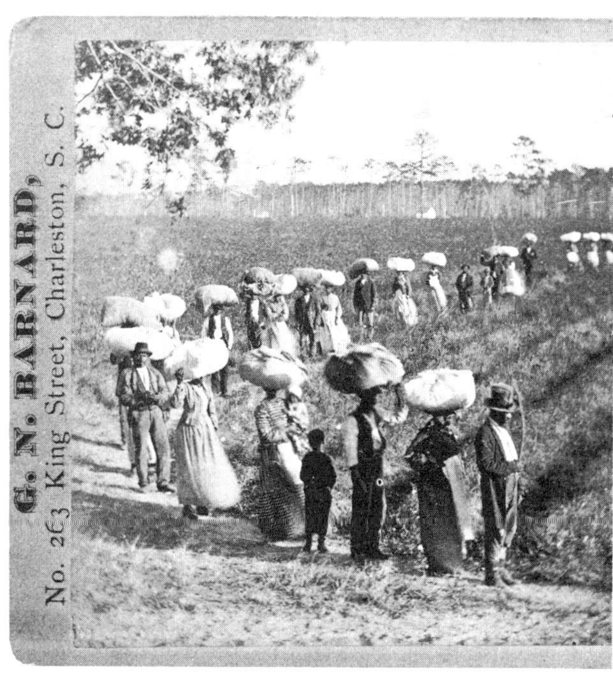

264. Negro. "Laborers Returning from Picking cotton at Sunset on Alex Knox' Plantation, Mt. Pleasant, near Charleston, S. C., November, 1874." G.N. Barnard photo.

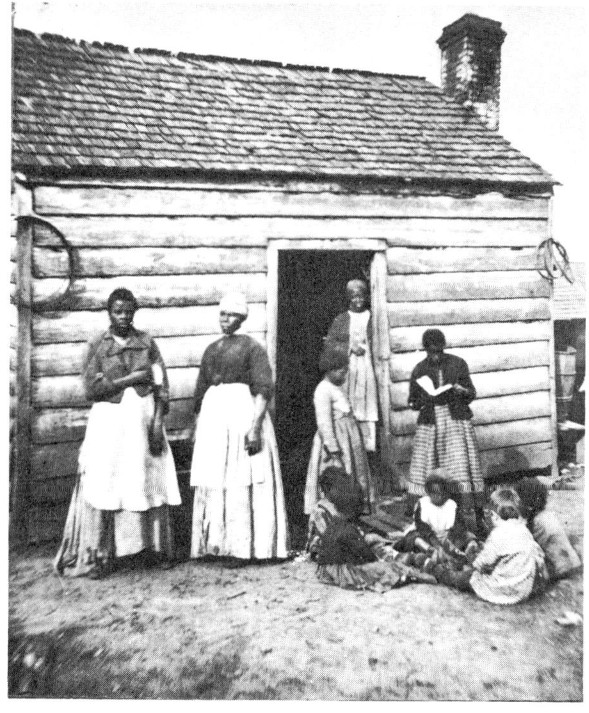

265. Negro. "Aunt Betsy's Cabin." Aiken, South Carolina, J.A. Palmer photo, 1876.

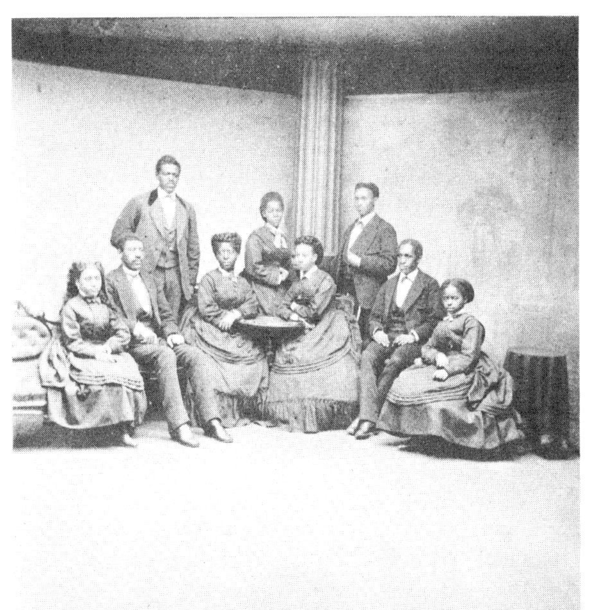

266. Negro. "Fisk University Jubilee Singers." Negative by J.W. Black (Boston), published by the American Missionary Society, 1872.

College Singers on tour were stereographed in Boston by J. W. Black (1873).

The Atlanta Exposition (1894) featured the Negro Building in which were displayed a wide range of products, art works and historical objects associated with the negro in America.

A few negro personalities have been stereographed, most notably Booker T. Washington.

The black populations of the West Indies were, of course, fully documented in the travel sets.

Humorous and comic views with black models are of two types: sympathetic appealing to universal humor and ridiculous, which often were derisive or offensive. One must recognize, however, that in these crude jokes the black man fared no worse than the Irishman or the white "country rube." Among the sympathetic humorous views are cakewalks at street fairs, children eating watermelon, musicians at the New Orleans Mardi Gras. Whatever poking fun occurs in these views, is gentle, without traces of scorn.

As yet there has been no concerted effort to compile the stereographic history of Black American Culture. There are certainly several thousand titles.

NOVELTIES

Occasionally one encounters among the countless stereographs images that defy classification. Some were experimental or innovative. Others were photographed whimsically or are so unusual as to be practically unique.

Four examples will be described to indicate a few of the possibilities.

John Towler distributed a few copies of his "Strobonic Stereograph" which was reproduced in *The Silver Sunbeam* (1864, page 319).

A fine portrait stereo, "Old Abe," the American eagle mascot of the Eighth Wisconsin Infantry, 1861-64, was published by the Centennial Photograph Company (1876). Old Abe, exhibited at the Centennial, was the subject of a published biography, probably the only bird to have been so recognized.

The Lincoln Monument designed by Clark Mills—but never built—was "stereographed" in a fake sense. A composite photograph shows the architect's conception of the monument in the foreground and the Capitol in the background (c Clark Mills, 1869).

I. N. Rood, while a member of the Amateur Photographic Exchange Club, produced "a stereo photomicrograph of a piece of granite smaller than the head of a pin" (1861). Copies of this view, however, were not exchanged with fellow members.

OCCUPATIONS, including child labor

Stereographs of men and women at work are among the earliest, commercially produced views. In many pastoral scenes the distant human figures are incidental, haying, mowing, draying, or fishing. City scenes often include vendors and hawkers or market places. Harbor scenes include sailors, fishermen and stevadores. There were relatively few attempts to depict an occupation although there are French views of stone masons at work and British views of slate quarry men in the 1850's. Beggars (begging is an occupation in some cultures) shipbuilders and basketmakers were also stereographed.

In the latter 1860's, several English, German and French photographers published views of children acting out adult occupations. The best of these is an extensive series by S. P. Christmann (1868-72) showing the gardener, carpenter, boat builder, brick mason, chimney sweep and many more. The staging is elaborate and realistic. The titles are given in English, German and French. Figure 86.

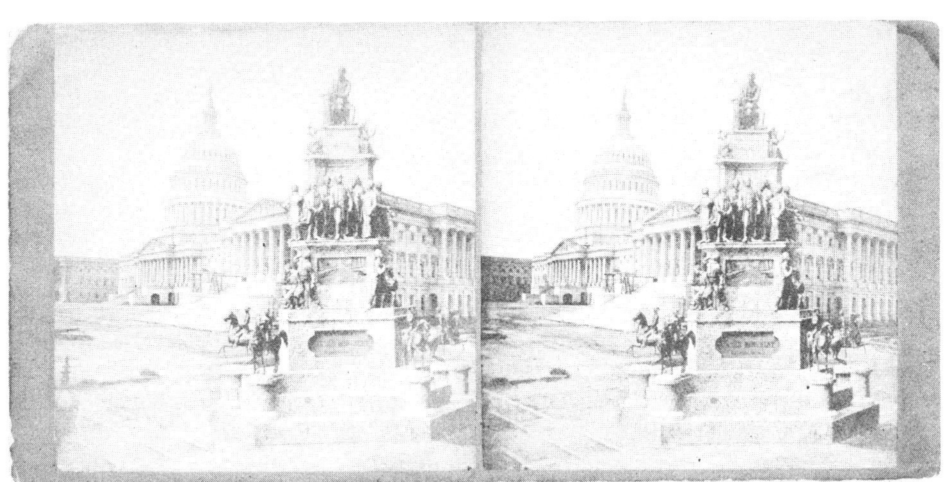

267. Novelty. A composite stereograph of a proposed Lincoln Memorial which was never constructed. Designed by Clark Mills. Unknown photographer, copyrighted by Clark Mills, 1868.

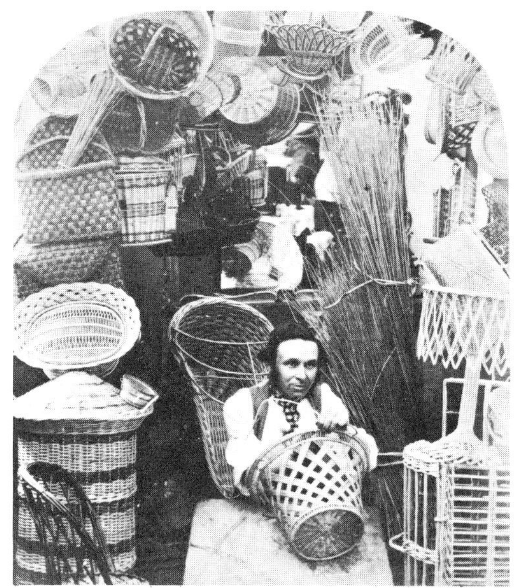

268. Occupations. "The Basket Maker." Unknown photographer, English, ca. 1856.

Approximately half of the hundreds of views of American mills and factories taken between 1865 and 1880 include mill hands and other employees. Commonly the labor force is lined up in front of the factory or shop. Many series that illustrate a particular mill include scenes of the various manufacturing operations and workers performing them.

The Underwood photographers deliberately recorded the artisans and laborers of each country. A woman is not a figure. She is spinning, milking goats, working in the field or engaged in some domestic task. Whether she is Persian, Zuni Indian, or an American textile worker, she is doing something.

The technology sets and series assembled by Underwood follow this theme. Mining, weaving, shoe making, meat packing and farming are human activities. The man and his tools or machines are depicted as he used them.

The rich documentation of laborers in such industries as the wool, silk, cotton, porcelain, bronze and lace making are shown in contrasting cultures, primitive, traditional, automatic machined, and so on. A scene of a blacksmith, forge and helper photographed by W. H. Rau in 1896 is very different from Underwood's view of a smith, bellows and helpers in the Congo (9959 ca. 1906).

The importance of water carriers in dry regions, such as in Egypt, Palestine, Mesopotamia, and Peru is seldom considered in the western world.

Working conditions and the use of child and women labor have generally been stereographed incidentally. There are views of children nine to twelve years old, in American cotton mills, breaker boys under fourteen at anthracite coal mines and widely scattered views of helpers, newsboys and shoeshiners. One of the most revealing scenes records children making shoes at "The Western House of Refuge," Rochester, New York, ca. 1875 (Woodward 133).

The employment of women in coal mines (Belgium), as stevadores loading iron ore on steamships (Cartagena, Spain, Underwood 11174, 1900), are but two examples of heavy labor performed by women.

See also: MILLS & FACTORIES, MINING

PARADES AND PROCESSIONS

In many countries holidays and celebrations are occasions for street parades or processions, often organized into divisions of participating units. Military parades, especially following victory, are traditional. The Anthony series (twenty titles) the Grand Review of the Armies in Washington, May 23-24, 1865 is probably the most complete parade coverage. Similarly there were many views of the German armies marching in Berlin (1871) and victory parades in numerous American cities in 1898. Figure 228.

Coronations, presidential inaugurations, state funerals represent other occasions which are marked by parades.

In Catholic countries, holy days and Saint Days may be celebrated with processions bearing religious statues or relics. Dozens of views of such processions, mostly in Italy, Switzerland, Austria and Spain are available. Many non-Christian Asian religions also encourage processions. Stereographs of typical celebrations are to be found in the travel sets.

In the United States parades have had wide public appeal. In 1860 Anthony and Stacy stereographed parades welcoming the Prince of Wales and the Japanese Embassy, and the annual Fourth of July event. In 1858 a grand parade marked the laying of the first short-lived Atlantic Cable.

There are views of many local parades that are typical Americana:

- political electioneering, 1860-1875 (stereos of the traditional torchlight parades unfortunately were not attempted)
- Fourth of July parades, many! Figures 45, 127.
- firemen's parades

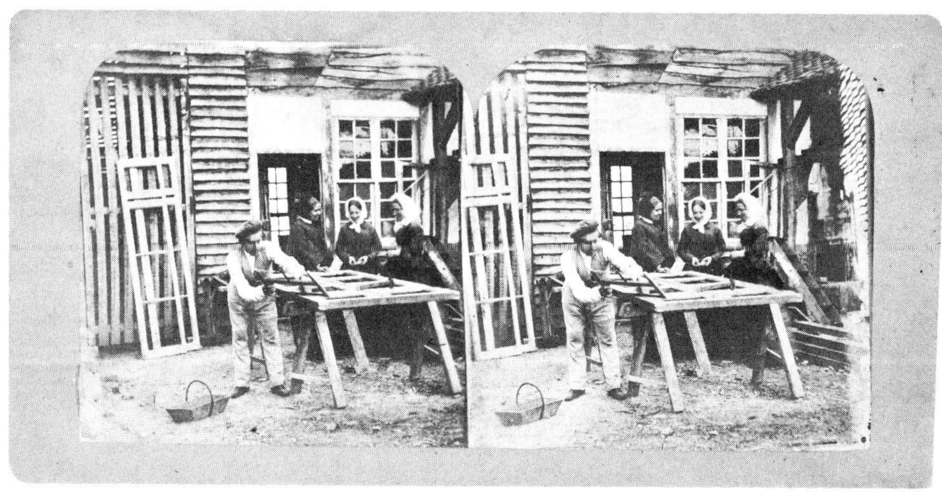

269. Occupations. "The Carpenter." Unknown photographer, French ca. 1862.

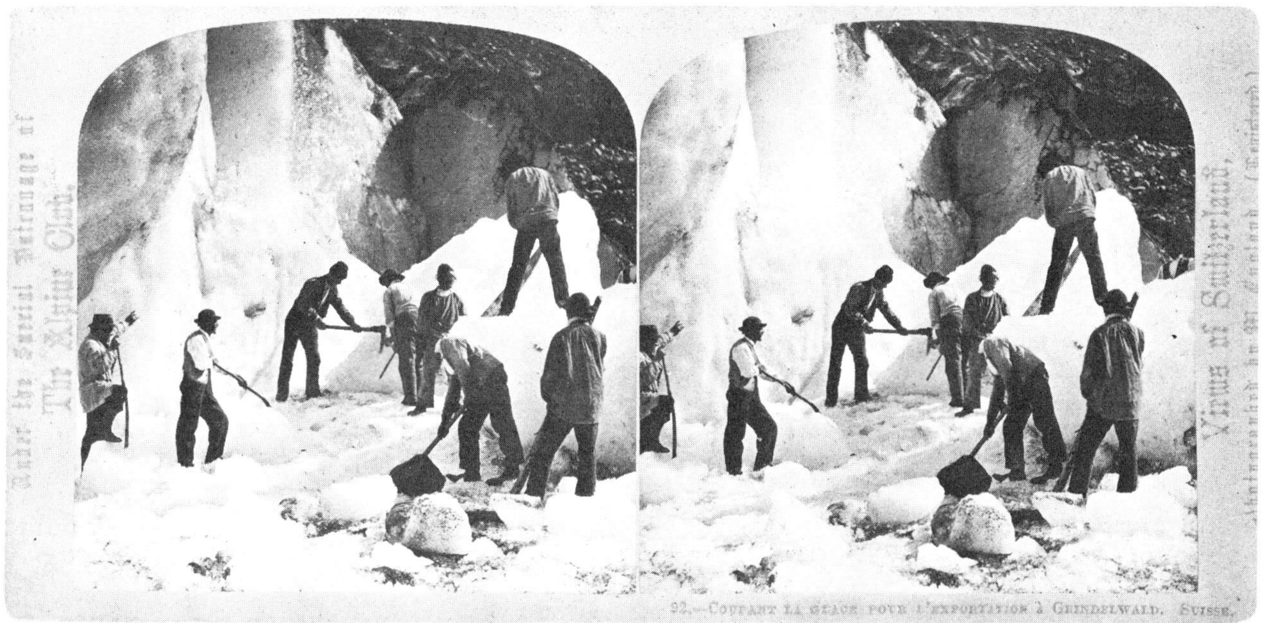

270. Occupations. "Cutting Ice for Export, Grindelwald Glacier," Switzerland. "Alpine Club Series." William England photo, 1863.

Masonic parades
amusement parades, such as baby parades, Tournament of the Roses, Mardi Gras, Mummers (Philadelphia)
dedications of buildings, bridges, monuments, etc.
conventions, such as the annual reunions of the Grand Army of the Republic.

PERSONALITIES

Stereographs of identified personalities as a category are relatively common, occurring as approximately in one of 150 views (or 0.67%). Yet, very few stereos of famous persons are common. Instead, except for a few presidents of the United States and Allied generals of World War I, views of specific persons are rare.

I have personally examined at least fifty different views of each of the following categories:

actors
artists
athletes
aviators
champions
daredevils
educators
engineers
explorers
Indians (American)
industrialists
inventors
literary
musicians
military
nobility
oddities
photographers
physicians
presidents
religious
scientists

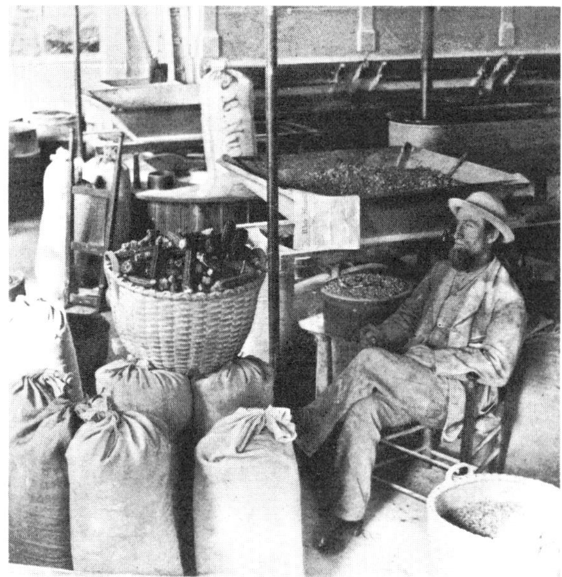

271. Occupations. "The Miller at Home." Kilburn Brothers photo, 1867.

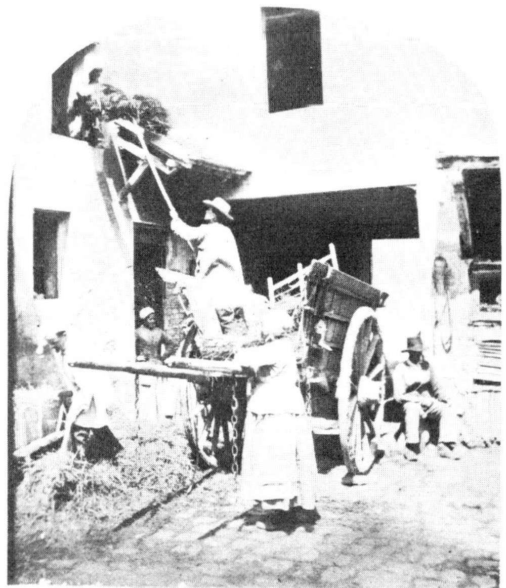

272. Occupations. "Putting Wheat in the Barn." Unidentified photographer, French, ca. 1858.

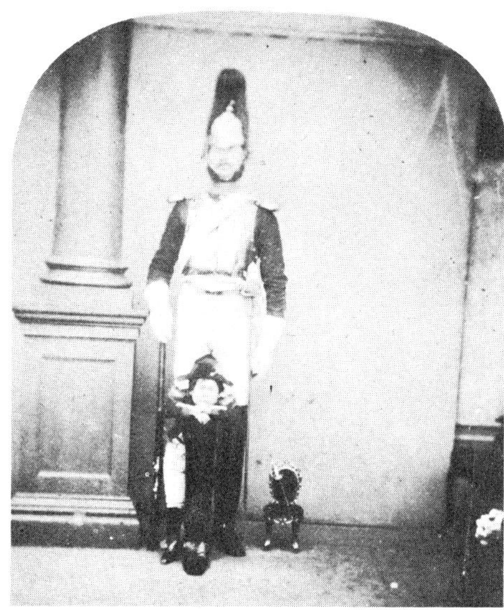

273. Personalities. Tom Thumb leaning behind a guard's boot. Unknown English photographer. Card issued ca. 1857.

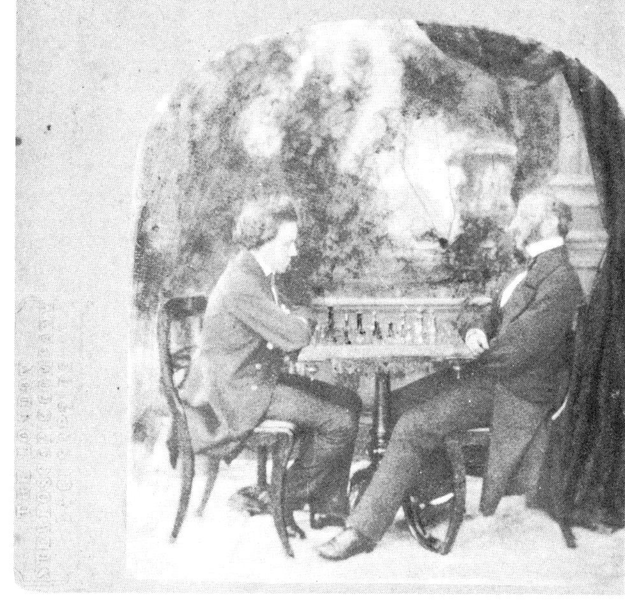

274. Personalities. Paul Morphy, the great chess champion, with M. Lowenthal, London. London Stereoscopic Company, 1859.

socialites	statesmen
sportsmen	women

Categories with fewer examples include labor leaders, newsmen and negroes.

Some collectors include with "Presidentials" scenes showing wives, children, cabinet members, and houses in which presidents lived.

"Oddities" include giants, dwarfs and "freaks."

In 1898 Underwood published a series of individual portraits of the members of the United States Congress, a truly remarkable venture.

In the 1860's, coincident with the fad for collecting carte de visite portraits of prominent personalities, several publishers issued large series of stereo portraits. Many of these were actually paired images made from carte de visite negatives. Anthony published the largest "Celebrities" series. Gurney also issued a large variety. In the 1870's W. H. Holmes, Sarony, and L. E. Walker published fine portraits, mostly theatrical, literary, and religious personalities.

A few examples may suggest the wealth of information available in stereographs.

"Stanley and Major Bartellot in the Tent, Upper Congo," Bert Underwood, 1904

"Dr. Anita Newcomb McGee, with American Red Cross Nurses in Field Hospital in Japan" H. C. White, 1905

"Paul Morphy, the American Chess Champion and M. Lowenthal whom he defeated during his European Visit" London Stereo Co., 1858

"Sir Erasmus Wilson, at his Establishment in Malvern" unidentified photographer, ca. 1882.

Doctor Wilson (1809-84) celebrated surgeon and dermatologist, was largely instrumental in the introduction of Turkish baths in England, and publicizing daily bathing. He defrayed the costs of moving "Cleopatra's Needle" from Alexandria to London.

It is far more important to find and preserve portraiture of forgotten men and women than to locate additional copies of views of well-known personalities.

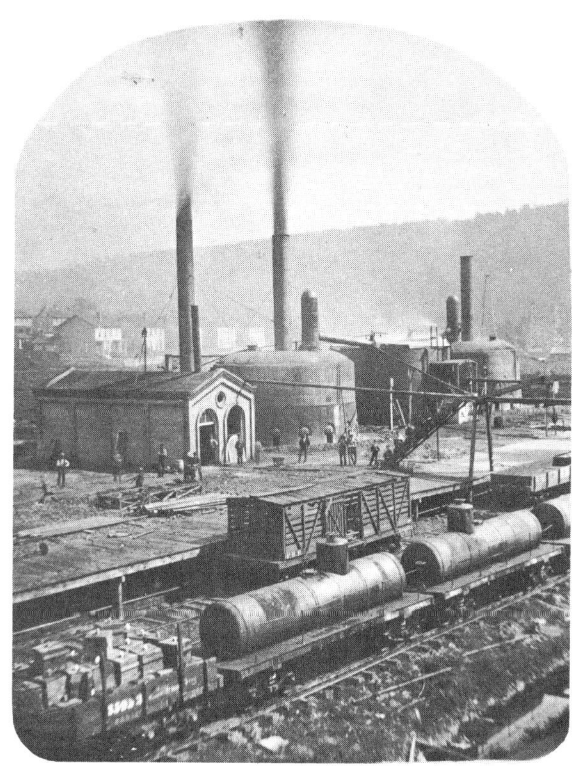

275. Petroleum. Refining oil. This view, taken in 1878, shows the remarkable progress in the petroleum industry in less than twenty years. Oil City, Pennsylvania. Frank Robbins photo.

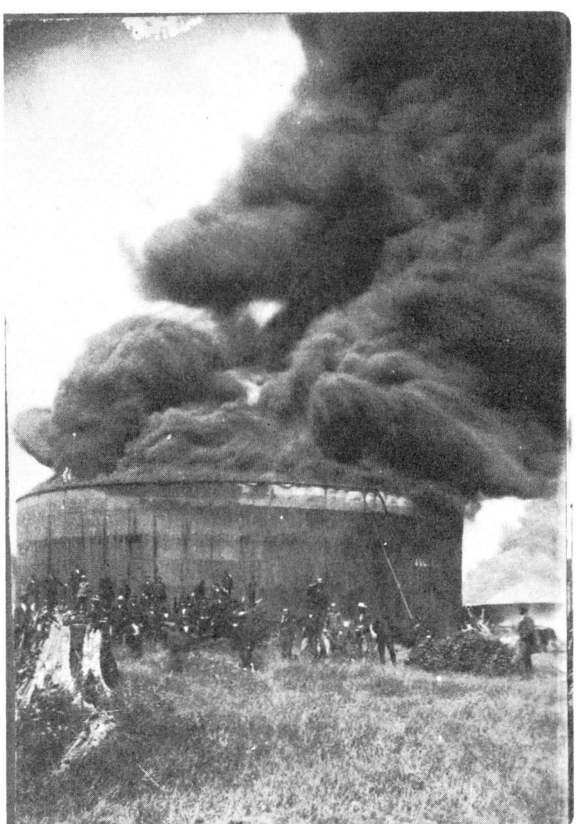

276. Petroleum. Burning oil tanks, struck by lightning, Olean, New York. Detlor and Waddell photo, 1879.

PETROLEUM

The petroleum industry had its meteoric rise in northwestern Pennsylvania between 1859 and 1870. By the mid 1870's all of the basic methods for recovering, refining and transporting oil had been developed.

J. A. Mather (Titusville) became the unofficial photographer of the industry. Between 1860 and 1900 he made thousands of photographs, including about 600 stereo views of every boom town along Oil Creek and eastward as the rush for oil moved to Warren and Bradford.

Scores of local and touring photographers produced fine stereo views of the oil region (Deming, Wilt Brothers, Robbins, West, Detlor & Waddell are the most notable.

Petroleum was drilled also in Canada in the late 1850's. A few stereos of these strikes are preserved. In the early 1860's oil was discovered in Ohio and West Virginia.

Titusville remained the center of the oil industry until 1895 even though the production of oil in the immediate area had diminished drastically.

The "Spindletop" Field near Beaumont, Texas was developed in 1901. By that time California had become an important oil producing state. Stereo coverage was not extensive because the public had become accustomed to the various visible aspects of petroleum refining and transportation.

The technological innovations, however, did interest photographers. "Shooting wells with nitroglycerine is recorded in several Keystone views (20054, 20354). Early off-shore drilling near Summerland, California, is shown in views by White and Keystone (1906). The master power-distributor "grass-hopper" linkages operating several wells from a single engine is recorded in Keystone 23264.

No other industry has been so fully documented by stereographs.

PETS

Stereographs of pets, especially dogs and cats, have provided vicarious pleasure for generations. There are many views of children and adults with their pet animals, including lambs,

277. Pets. "Waiting for Dinner." Strohmeyer and Wyman photo, 1897.

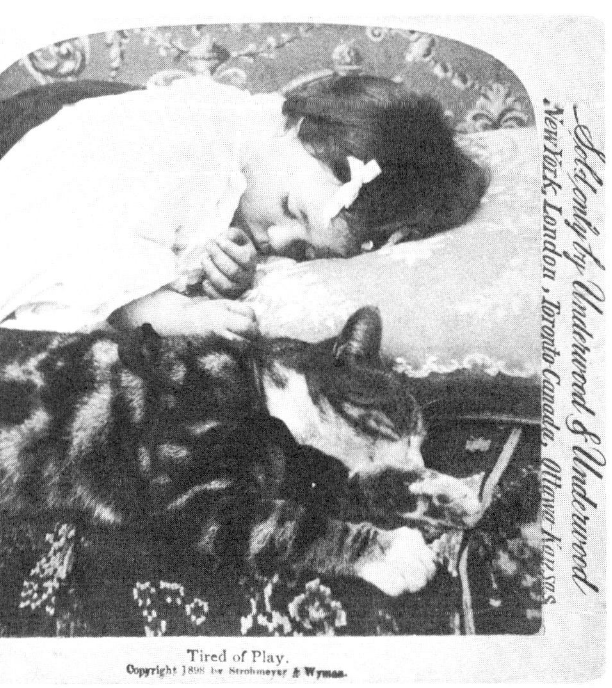

278. Pets. "Tired of Play." Strohmeyer and Wyman photo, 1898.

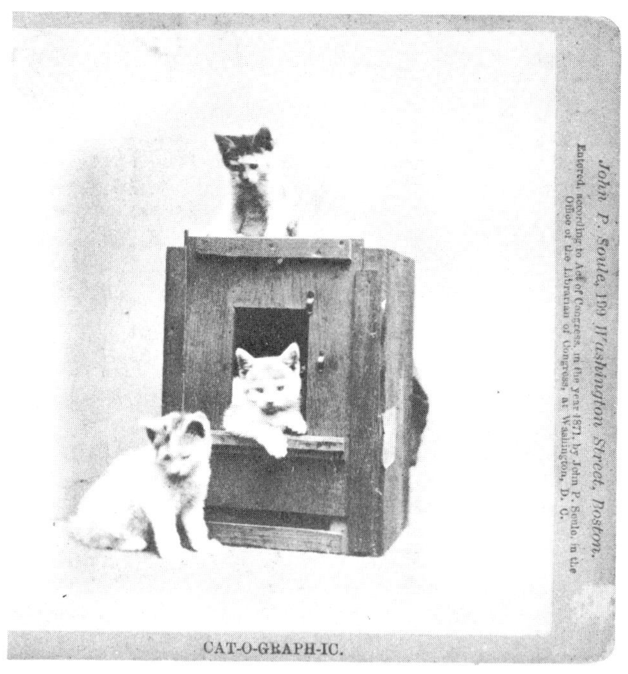

279. Pets. "Cat-o-graph-ic" John P. Soule, "Kittens" series, 1871.

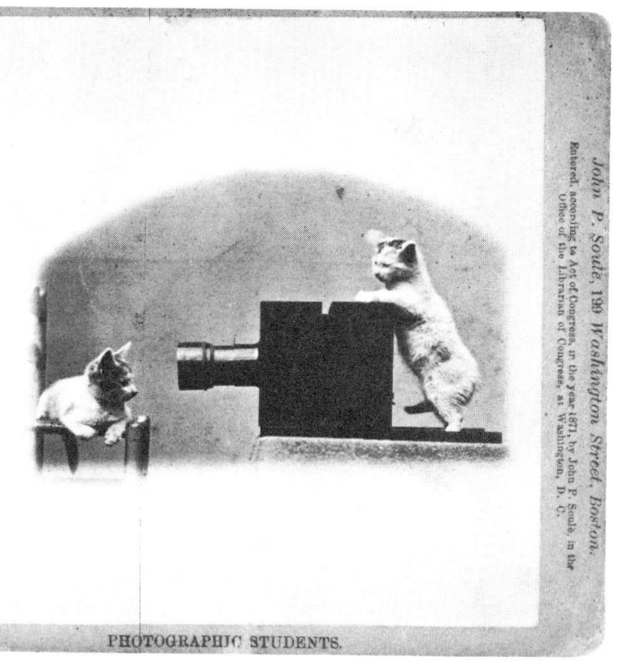

280. Pets. "Photographic Students." John P. Soule, "Kittens" series, 1871.

goats, ponies, rabbits, raccoon, and others. Only dogs and cats, however, will be considered here.

In the 1860's, Coonley & Wolfersberger (Philadelphia) issued views of prize-winning dogs. Schreiber (1868-73) published similar views of champion dogs. Kilburn probably published the greatest number of stereos of dogs and cats, at least several hundred titles widely scattered through the trade list. Littleton issued a view of "Prof. Gentry's Trained Performing Dogs" (no. 1478, 1889).

Hunters and their dogs were favorite subjects for photographers before 1900. Keystone published many such stereos.

Work dogs, although not strictly pets, were frequently stereographed as if they were. Carts drawn by dogs were common in Western Europe. The Saint Bernards of Switzerland were stereographed many times. Also, there are many scenes showing dog teams pulling sleds in the Yukon and more generally in Alaska.

A. S. Campbell (1898) issued a view of "A Life-saver's Dog on Beach, Long Island."

There are fewer stereographs of cats but the diversity is remarkable. Soule (1869-72) produced an imaginative series of playful "Kittens." The fifty titles include many delightful

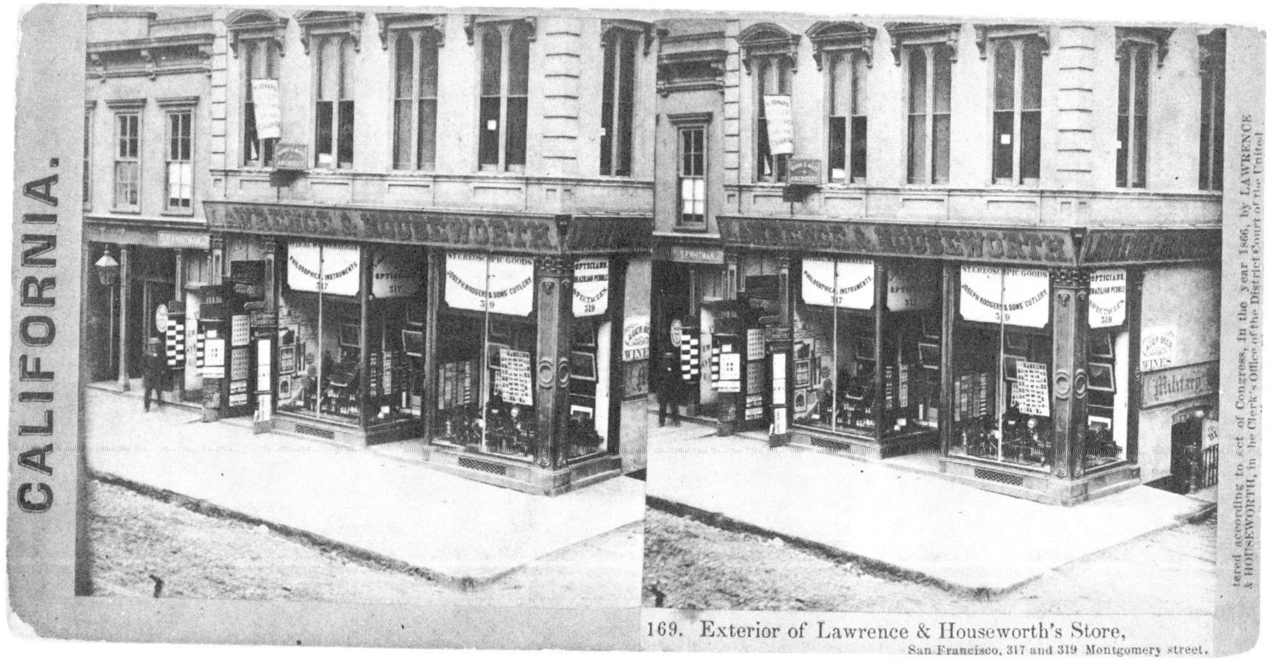

281. Photographica. The shop of Lawrence and Houseworth, San Francisco, 1866. Panels of stereographs are displayed along the left side of the store entrance.

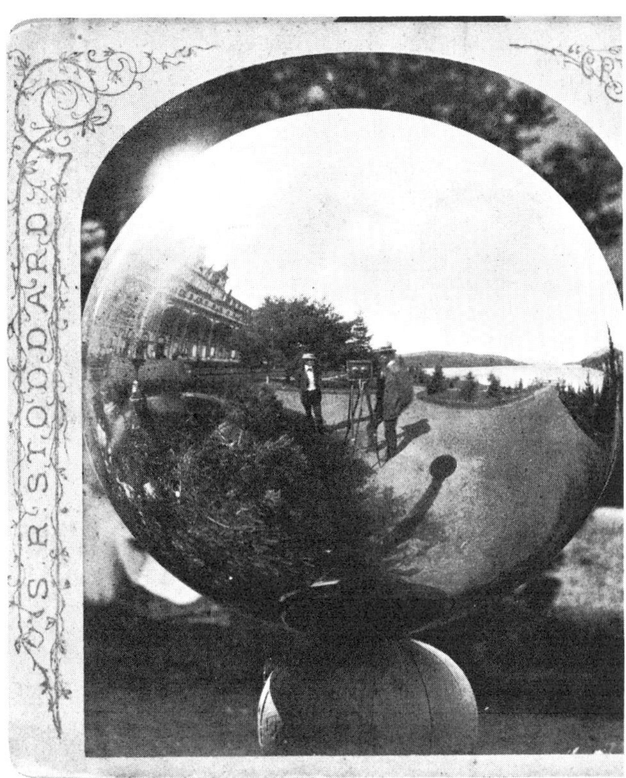

282. Photographica. S.R. Stoddard, reflected self portrait with a stereo camera. Glen Falls, New York. 1875.

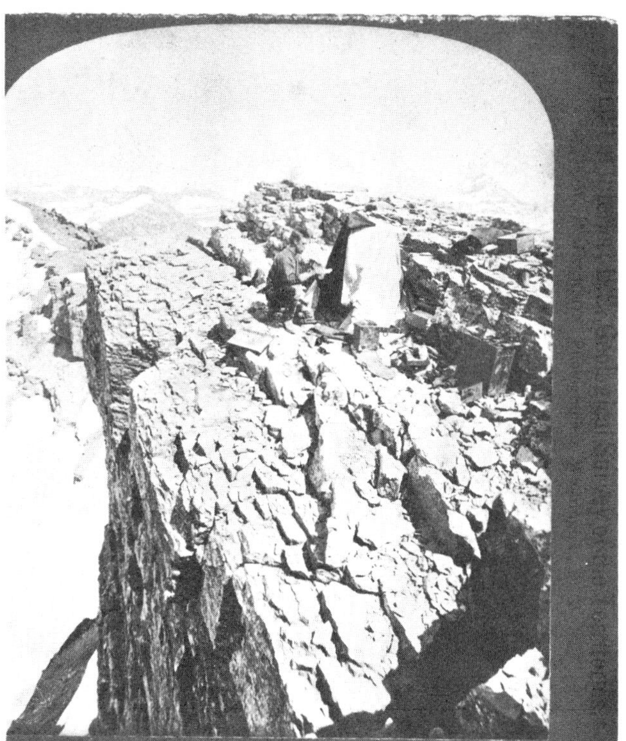

283. Photographica. William H. Jackson, "Photographing in High Places," Grand Tetons. Hayden Survey of the Territories, 1872.

groups, such as, "Cat-o-graph-ic"—three inquisitive kittens exploring a camera.

PHOTOGRAPHICA

Photography has recorded its own history to a degree only recently recognized. Images showing any aspect of photographers at work have become one of the most active fields of stereo collecting. The number of such views runs into many hundreds. Eight categories are distinguished:

1. Photographers with their cameras and other equipment
2. Studios, interiors and exteriors including portable and floating galleries, railroad cars, etc.
3. Manufacturing facilities, including factories producing stereoscopes and stereographs
4. Views of stereoscopes and people using them
5. Photographic exhibitions and conventions of photographers
6. Portraits of photographers, especially self-portraits
7. Stereographs autographed by the photographer
8. Stereographs of still-life arrangements that have photographs in them. (See also SKELETON LEAVES)

The list can be extended to include views with imprints or labels with vignettes of studios, cameras or symbolic heliographic figures. Figures 1, 2, 3, 20, 154.

PORTRAITS

Portraiture in stereographs is fairly limited. The stereo portrait offers little advantage over the carte de visite or the larger cabinet photograph so popular from the 1860's to the 1890's.

Even so, there are several notable series of portraits. The most famous views are the "Luckhardt Heads" (1868-72). Fritz Luckhardt, an accomplished artist as well as a photographer, left the employ of Oscar Kramer in 1867 and opened a portrait studio. He published about 200 portraits of beautiful young women.

Two English series are comparable, one by J. Elliott and the other by the London Stereoscopic Company. The models are portrayed full bust or half-length, however. These portraits were widely criticized because many of the models selected for their beauty were of menial position. Snobbish critics argued that only women of high rank or accomplishment should be so photographed. See also Figure 53.

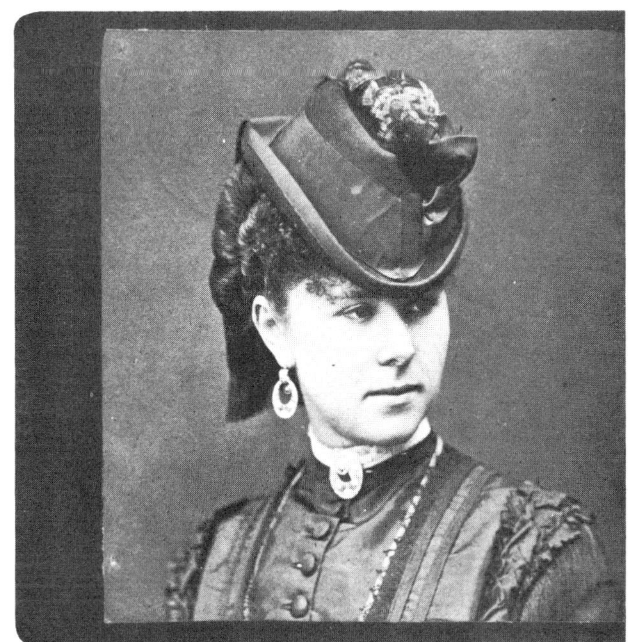

284. Portraits. An example of Fritz Luckhardt's "Heads," ca. 1870.

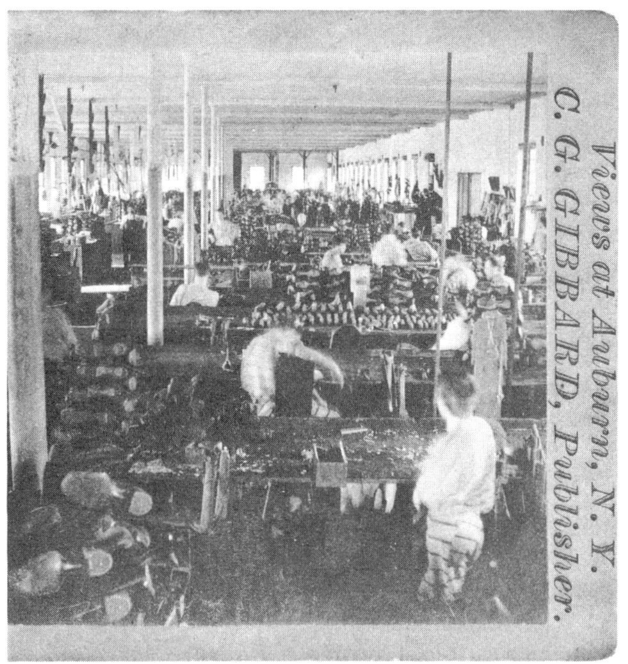

285. Prisons. "Auburn Prison Shoe Shop" Auburn, New York. C.G. Gibbard photo, 1873.

Series of prominent personalities generally include head or bust portraits. Fine series were published by Anthony, Gurney, Holmes, Sarony and others. The Mascher type stereodaguerreotype was primarily adapted to portraiture.

Attention is called to the Underwood stereo portraits of the members of the United States Congress (1900).

See also: PERSONALITIES

PRISONS AND PUNISHMENTS

Stereographs of American prisons reflect the widespread concern for reform of penal systems. In the United States these reforms involved prison design, occupation of prisoners and other treatment of prisoners.

In the Auburn (New York) State Prison in the 1870's the prisoners were confined to individual cells at night but in daytime they worked together in prison shops. The cells were arranged in tiers in "blocks."

The Auburn system, which became generally accepted for larger prisons in the United States, was in opposition to the older "Pennsylvania System" which was based upon solitary confinement without employment. The prison was structured to have central corridors with cells lined on both sides.

The Elmira (New York) Reformatory (1877) for young male first-offenders guilty of lesser felonies, classified prisoners and provided both academic instruction and physical training.

There are excellent series of views illustrating these institutions and many other prisons in the 1870's and 1880's.

The Auburn Prison complex was stereographed by J. D. Eagles (Glenora, New York, about fifty titles), C. G. Gibbard (Auburn, forty views) and L. E. Walker (Warsaw, New York, twenty-four views). There are many scenes of men at work in the shops.

A small series of views of the Elmira Reformatory was published by C. Tomlinson, a local photographer.

Sing Sing Prison, famous for its harsh discipline, was constructed by prisoners from Auburn. Anthony published about thirty scenes in Sing Sing, including the mess hall, chapel, hospital and workshops. Prisoners at work in the marble quarries are shown in 4298. There is an external view of the Female Prison (4313). Havens (Sing Sing, 1873) issued a series of twenty-five views and Pach (1875) published about twenty views. At least one of the Pach stereos depicts women prisoners. Littleton View Company also issued a stereo of a group of women prisoners (no. 1325, 1877).

Many state prisons were stereographed. The most informative include:

New Hampshire (Concord) a fine series by H. A. Kimball (ca. 1880, about fifty numbers). The carpentry shops, especially the bed shop (no. 31) indicates how extensively prisoner labor was used.

Vermont (Windsor). The best series, though comprised of only eight views, ca. 1878, is remarkable. One scene shows about a hundred prisoners lined up in lock step in the yard, ready to march into the building.

Connecticut (Hartford), a fine series (twenty titles) by Prescott & White, ca. 1870.

Fortress-like jails and prisons with massive stone walls and towers were built in many cities between 1800 and 1860. Trade lists of local stereographers usually include a few views of the county prisons. Fine examples are stereos by W. L. Gill (Lancaster, Pennsylvania, ca. 1868), C. Kneeland (Pittsburgh, 1867), and many of "The Tombs" in New York City.

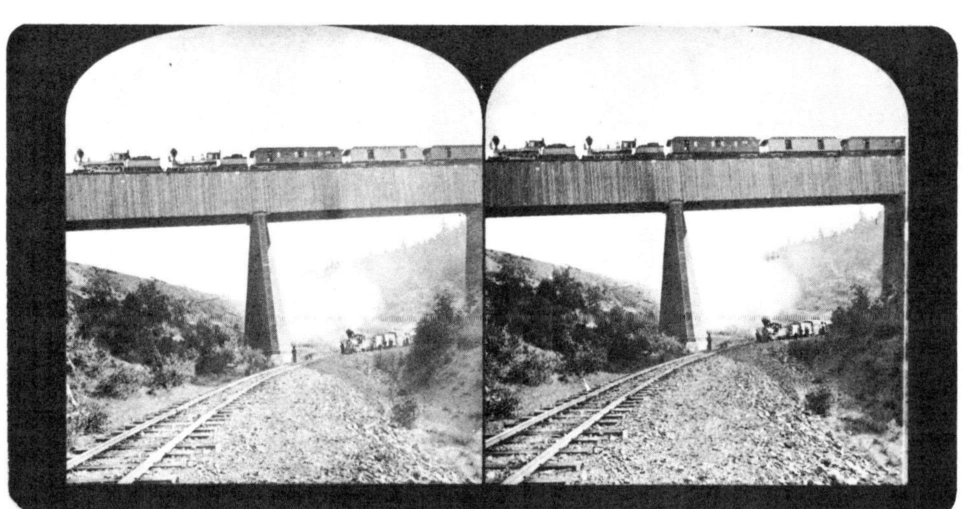

286. Railroads. Central Pacific Railroad train on bridge, narrow-gauge train approaching. Staged for J.J. Reilly, photo 1876.

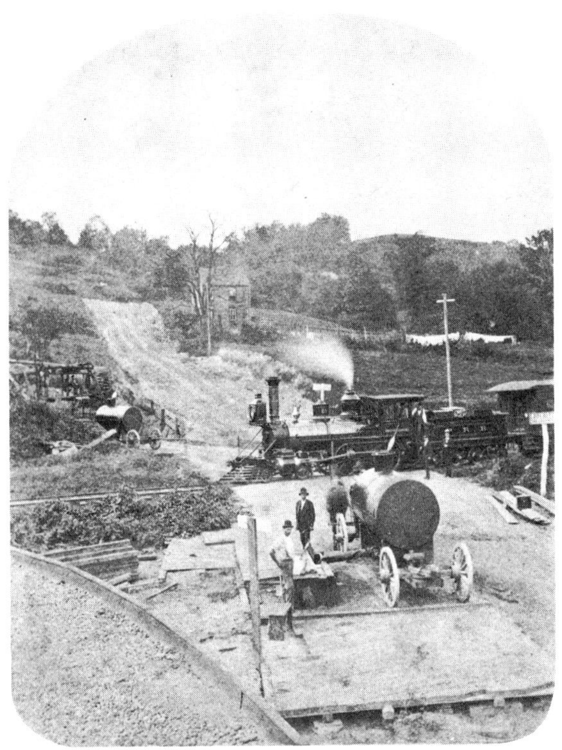

287. Railroad-Pipeline war, 1874. The West Penn Railroad refused to permit the pipeline to cross under its tracks. It was therefore necessary to transfer the oil to tank wagons, pull the wagons over the tracks (on the public highway) and then pour the oil into the pipeline again. Fairview, Pennsylvania. Frank Robbins photo.

In contrast to the treatment of prisoners afforded by the institutions described above, the older traditional Old World dungeons, cages, and stocks are well-recorded in the travel sets. In some sets there are gruesome scenes of executions, torture and cruel punishments. In 1900 Ricalton ("China," Underwood) stereographed a convicted murderer being slowly strangled in a bamboo cage.

There are scattered American views (notably by Kilburn) of prison chain gangs and prisoners garbed in striped uniforms and caps.

RAILROADS

Railroads and railroading have been favorite subjects for stereographers. Scenes of locomotives in full steam and trains on bridges have always had great appeal. The following categories of views are widely collected:

locomotives	repair shops
trains	signals and safety devices
rolling stock	railroad construction
train wrecks	bridges and tunnels
narrow gauge roads	freight handling
rail lines, including stations	special railroads (in mines, inclines, etc.)

The majority of American railroad companies in the nineteenth century employed or designated "official" photographers. Generally the company or the photographer published a series of stereo views which were sold from display racks in the waiting rooms of every station or at newsstands located nearby. The series usually included scenic views along the route, towns and bridges. If one can visualize a traveler making his first long railroad journey, the popularity of such views is readily understood.

Anthony was the first publisher to issue series of views along the lines of established eastern railroads (Pennsylvania Central, Erie, New Haven & Hartford, Delaware & Lackawanna, and others) (1862-66).

Purviance became the official photographer for the Pennsylvania Central Railroad in 1867. Later he produced fine series of the Lehigh Valley Railroad and Central Railroad of New Jersey.

Many very small lines, such as the Catawissa, were surprisingly well stereographed.

The transcontinental railroad, the Central Pacific and Union Pacific lines, joined in 1869 at Promontory Point, Utah, was of course the most exciting and fascinating. We have already considered the many photographers who have left a wonderful historical record (Hart, Watkins, Jackson, Savage, Muybridge, Carter and Carbutt). Figures 15, 126, 145, 286.

There was scarcely a railroad line in operation in the United States before 1890 that was not well stereographed. Among those especially well covered, not mentioned above, are the Baltimore & Ohio; Atcheson, Topeka & Santa Fe; and Northern Pacific.

Similar series were published in England and France, but never on the scale prevalent in America.

Scenes of unusual railroads enjoyed enormous popularity. Kilburn's stereos of the cog railway on Mount Washington were perennial favorites.

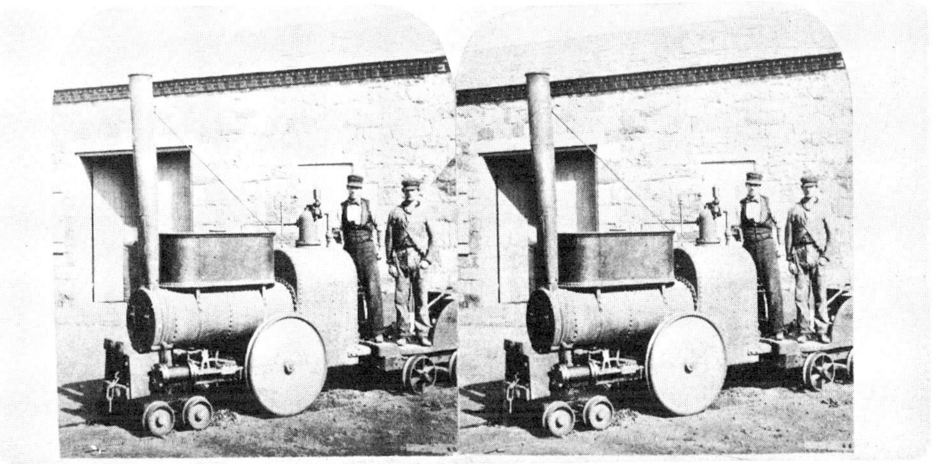

288. Railroads. Locomotive "Samson Junior," Philadelphia Gas Works, 1861. Unknown photographer.

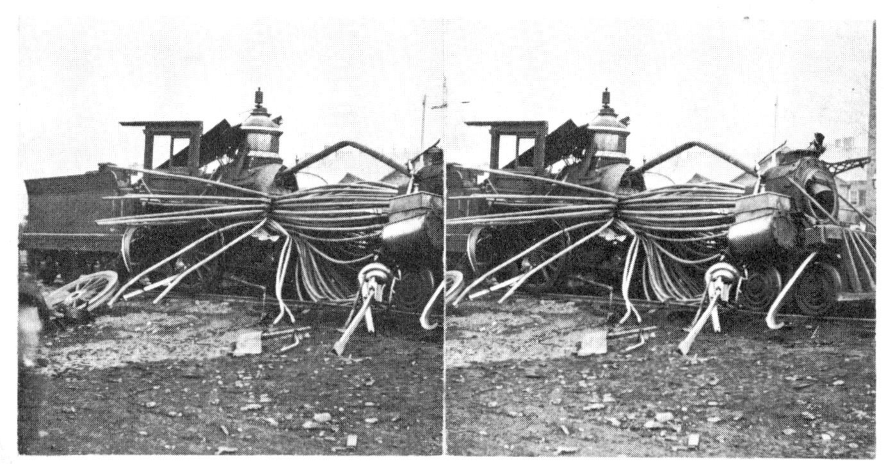

289. Railroads. An exploded locomotive, Watertown, New York. C.S. Hart photo, 1868.

There are stereographs of scores of train wrecks. The Ashtabula (Ohio) disaster was recorded in a series of twelve views. Exploded locomotives, completely disintegrated trains, head-on collisions and collapsed bridges have been photographed. Figure 289.

Locomotive manufacture is illustrated in fine views of the Baldwin Works in Philadelphia. Repair shops, especially those of the Pennsylvania Central at Altoona, are spectacular (Bonine, Gutekunst).

No railroad buff should overlook the Keystone hundred card set issued in conjunction with the Railroad Centennial in 1922. Many early original locomotives and working replicas were illustrated, along with the most modern giants.

RELIGIONS

The major religions of the world have been richly stereographed as integral parts of the cultures illustrated in the travel sets. There are thousands of much earlier views but most of these are isolated and scattered scenes, rather than series of related views. Characteristically, the religious views in the travel sets record the churches, mosques and temples, worshippers, and symbolism, including shrines and statues.

The Roman Catholic Church is most extensively stereographed. Hundreds of photographers published views of the Saint Peter's Cathedral, the Vatican and the Papacy. Many of these views were sold to pilgrims but greater quantities were sold to tourists of all faiths. Underwood's *Visit to Pope Pius X* has already been described, page 120. Keystone issued a set of twenty-four scenes illustrating the Roman Catholic Mass.

The great cathedrals of Europe have been stereographed again and again. There are fine interior views of most of them. Stereographs of congregations attending mass are relatively rare. J. Andrieu issued a scene of a military mass in Paris (1870). Figure 244.

There are thousands of views of Protestant churches, especially interiors. The structures range from simple New England meeting houses to imposing buildings with ornate sanctuaries. In many scenes, the minister is posed in the pulpit.

As for individual denominations, no catalogue is feasible. Every parish was proud of its new sanctuary, just as every town boasted of its various churches. Three denominations were unusually well stereographed: the Mormons or Latter Day Saints, the Shakers and the Moravians.

Carter and Savage, both Mormons operating galleries in Salt Lake City, left an incredible record of the Mormon Temple and Tabernacle, Mormon settlements, personalities and church activities. J. B. King (1906) published a series of thirty-six views illustrating Mormon history, including buildings in New York,

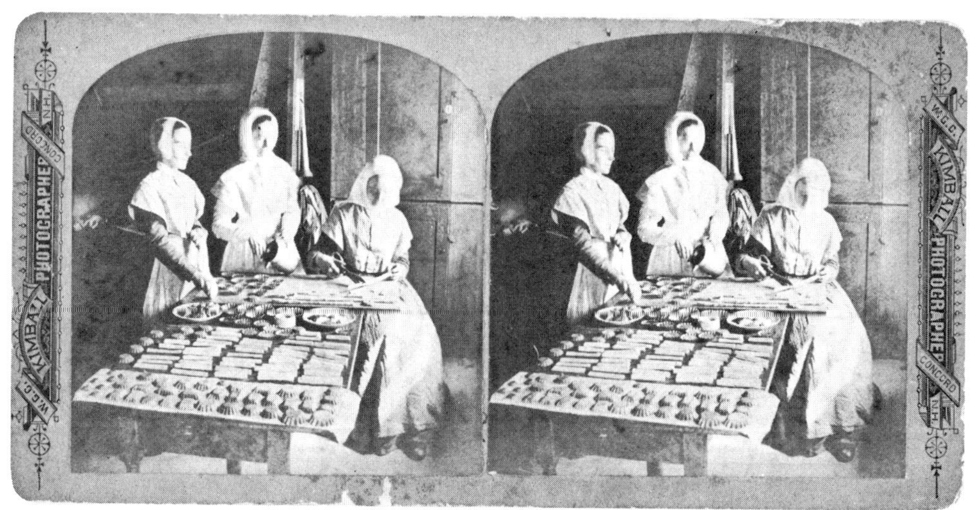

290. Religious. Shakers. Canterbury Village, New Hampshire. "Maple Candy Makers." W.G.C. Kimball photo, 1872.

Ohio, Illinois and Missouri in which the Mormons resided before settling in Utah.

Views of Shaker communities are much scarcer but fine series depicting the colonies at Mount Lebanon and Oneida (New York), Canterbury (New Hampshire), Harvard (Massachusetts) and a small series of Sharon (Maine) are known. The most extensive coverage is that of Canterbury by W. G. C. Kimball (1869-72).

The coverage of the Moravians is due entirely to the interest of M. A. Kleckner (Bethlehem, Pennsylvania, 1865-76). He issued fine views of the beautiful simple church, the sister and brother houses, school, charnal house, and cemetery. He recorded also the trombone choir in the steeple and typical Pennsylvania German crafts.

There are excellent diversified views illustrating the Jews and Judaism. The religious aspects are best seen in the stereos of Palestine. Bert Underwood photographed the role of the rabbi in village life, many scenes in Jerusalem including Jews at the Wailing Wall, and many of scrolls, symbols and customs.

Synagogues built in American cities before 1880 are recorded in many views, notably in those by Anthony, Watkins and Muybridge.

The Moslem religion has been equally well stereographed. Views of Mecca, exquisite interiors of mosques, crowds praying and customs are found in the travel sets of Islamic countries.

Other categories of religious interest include:

1. Missions and missionaries, mostly Christian, in foreign countries.
2. Camp meetings, denominational summer colonies.
3. Christian Endeavor and other conventions. For example: Cook & Friend stereographed the Universalist centennial Convention of Gloucester, Massachusetts in September, 1870.
4. The Passion Play, Oberammergau. White and Underwood issued various views, some identifying the actors cast as Jesus and Mary.
5. Personalities such as clergymen and evangelists.
6. Allegorical views and series, such as the three-card set "Rock of Ages" (Weller, 1873).
7. "Life of Christ" series.

   In the late 1860's a series of twelve tissues illustrating the life of Jesus was published in France. The scenes were paintings copied as stereo. The views were in turn copied many times. In addition, similar sets, including two lithoprint series were prepared and produced by several publishers. Great quantities of these views were sold in the United States until 1915.

RUSSO-JAPANESE WAR

Stereographs of the Russo-Japanese War are, in many respects, the most action-packed and successful war views ever published. Although many World War I stereos record carnage and civilian refugees which indicate greater dimensions of war, scenes of the siege of Port Arthur convey feelings of involvement and immediacy.

The siege culminated in "History's greatest bombardment" (—up to that time). Underwood's views of the two hundred gun bombardment (e.g., no. 7585) are spectacular. Such views as carrying shells to siege guns, sailors placing naval guns in position and troops in battle position are more than just informative.

Underwood published about 300 titles, a hundred card selection being offered as a boxed set. H. C. White published an excellent eighty card series. The U. S. Stereograph Company (also of North Bennington, Vermont) produced a series of fifty views. Keystone issued about a hundred titles but only about thirty are seen frequently. There are also a few views by Kilburn.

The naval views in the harbor record gunnery at close range, exploding shells, direct hits upon Russian battleships and sinking ships.

There are among the White and Underwood views many excellent informal views of Japanese officers and men.

The Peace Conference held at Portsmouth, New Hampshire, 1905, was stereographed by H. C. White (8448).

The rapidly evolving technology in many branches of warfare from artillery to the medical care of wounded, from safe drinking water to field generals studying maps, is recorded in remarkable detail.

SCHOOLS AND COLLEGES

Categorically it is safe to say that every college and university in the United States and Canada between 1850 and 1900 has been stereographed. Harvard, Yale, Princeton, Pennsylvania, Cornell and Wellesley were photographed many times. Colleges that have merged, changed their names or disbanded are fully recorded. There is no comparable coverage of educational institutions in Europe, especially on the continent, although Oxford and Cambridge and the schools of Eaton and Harrow were frequently stereographed.

In the United States, local photographers almost without exception took views of the public school buildings, academies, and colleges. There are many scenes with students and graduating classes posed on steps or in the school yard.

It should be noted that the establishment and extension of public education in the United States between 1840 and 1875 was a national movement of great importance.

Interior views showing students and classrooms are much less common. T. Lewis published a series of views of Wellesley College (1874) among which are scenes in art and science classrooms. No college was more frequently and thoroughly stereographed than Girard College (Philadelphia 1854-1898).

A few exceptional series of more than ten views each include:

Amherst, J. L. Lovell, 1868-70
Dartmouth, D. A. Clifford, 1870-72; H. O. Bly, 1873
Grinnell, Everett & Co., ca. 1873

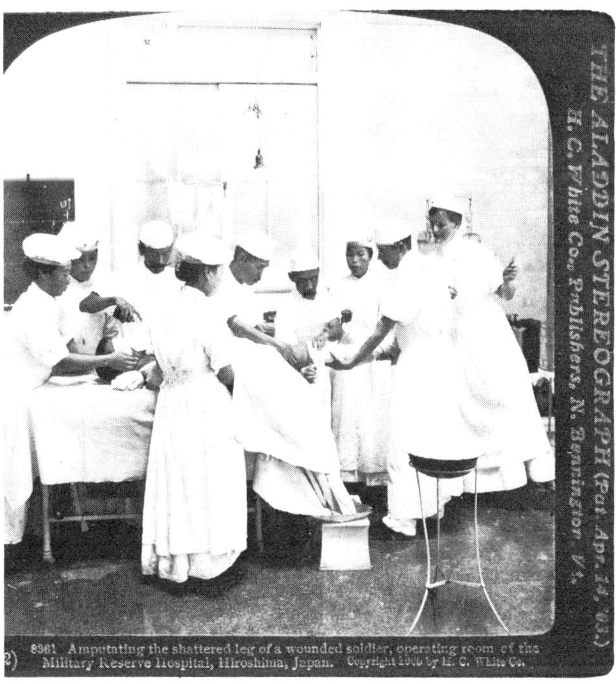

291. Russo-Japanese War. Surgical team amputating a leg, Military Reserve Hospital, Hiroshima. Contrast the state of medical care to that in the American Civil War. H.C. White Company, 1906.

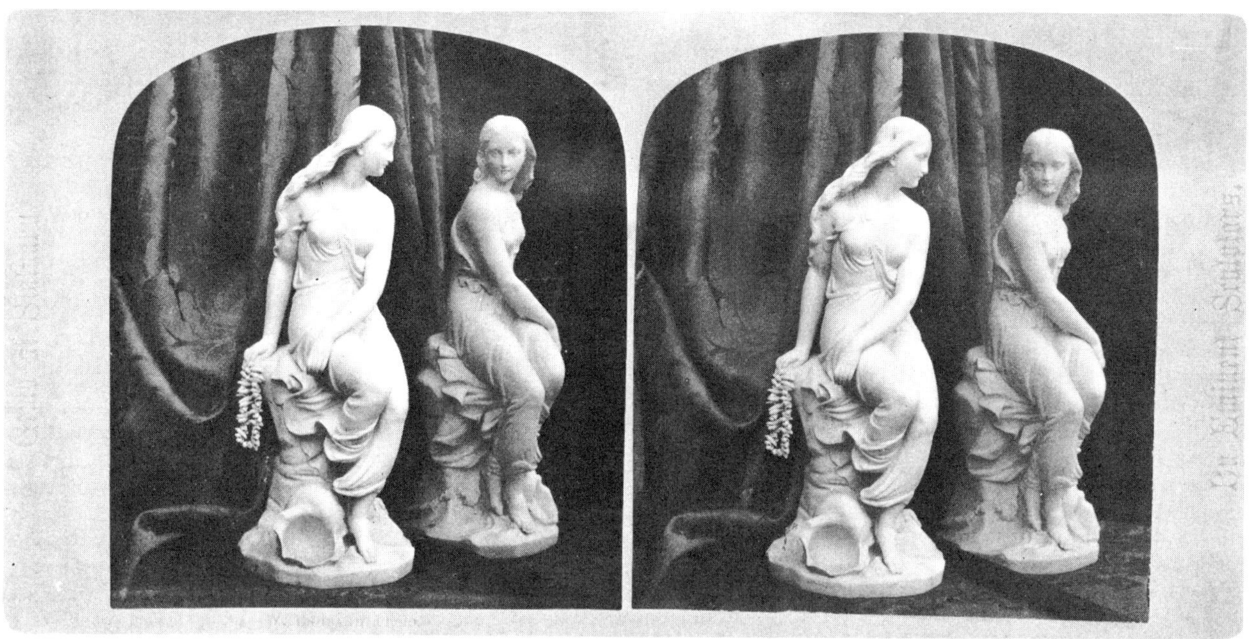

292. Sculpture. William England photo, "Miranda." Note the mirrored image technique. Negative 1858, card 1863.

Harvard, R. E. Lord, 1874
Lehigh, M. A. Kleckner, 1870's; H. T. Clouder, 1880's
Marietta, J. D. Cadwallader, 1868
Mount Holyoke, Knowlton Brothers, 1873
Notre Dame, unknown photographer, fine artistic mounts, ca. 1878
Oberlin, Platt & Co., 1868-72; L. W. Upton, 1874
Wellesley College, T. Lewis, 1874; Seaver, 1878

Pach issued a fine series of twelve views of the Eastman Business College at Poughkeepsie, New York (1877).

Travel sets published after 1900 usually include views of national universities and native schools. Underwood (8559, 1897) is an excellent scene of a boys' class at Palermo, Sicily Underwood issued views of Roberts University in Constantinople (1903) and White issued scenes of University of Bombay (1901).

Views of American missionary schools in China, Burma, India, Egypt and the Hawaiian Islands are evidence of the importance church bodies attached to the mission movement.

There was some effort to record innovations in education, especially in the land grant colleges. Keystone, for instance, issued a view of "The Hydraulic Laboratory of the Cornell University School of Engineering" (32574, ca. 1932).

Underwood, for use in sales promotions, distributed several clever views of high school pupils in geography classes using stereoscopes and stereographs.

Other types of schools have been stereographed. There are scenes of schools for American Indians, negroes and orphanages. There are fine views of denominational schools, Roman Catholic, Quaker, Shaker, and many others. Rural one-room schools are to be found in hundreds of views.

SCULPTURE

The Victorian passionate admiration of sculpture in all its forms has been mentioned in connection with the earliest stereographs. Photographers catering to this taste, published huge numbers of views, especially before 1880.

The classical statues preserved in the great museums, such as the Louve and the Vatican, were individually stereographed many times. Art treasures became familiar to thousands of persons who could not travel beyond their home towns.

Sculpture posed many technical problems for the photographers. Light and shadow are paramount. Fenton placed a mirror behind the object in such manner that the stereo image recorded full roundness. William England was particularly successful with this method. Fig. 292. The London Stereoscopic Company published many of the views by Fenton, England and Goodman.

Critics (1859-65) considered Fenton to be foremost in stereographing contemporary sculpture and Goodman to be supreme in taking views of classical works in museums.

Michelangelo's *La Pieta* in the Basilica of St. John at the Vatican has been stereographed by a hundred photographers but never more movingly than by Alinari (ca. 1868-70). More accessible are the fine views published by Underwood (1897) and White (1901).

While Americans generally did not share the Victorian appreciation for classic sculpture, the rising middle class and newly rich families decorated their homes and filled museums with original works and reproductions of classics. Beginning about 1890 art history was taught in a few American colleges.

Folk art, however, enjoyed an enormous appeal in the 1860's. Thereafter taste for fine arts increased rapidly, especially after the Centennial Exhibition.

Every international exhibition had its hall of sculpture, the precedent established at the Crystal Palace was continued at the London Exhibition in 1862. The Centennial at Philadelphia boasted a Fine Arts Building that received so many exhibits that two annexes had to be hastily erected to display them. Treasures on loan from the Louve, Vatican and British Museum opened the eyes of thousands of people who literally had never before seen a classic work of art. The Centennial exhibits, with the art objects grouped by countries, were handsomely stereographed in approximately 600 views.

The most popular exhibited sculptures and stereos were *The Birth of Love*, *Beggar Boy*, *Blind Man's Buff*, *Pharaoh's Daughter*, and *Out in the Rain*. These statues were simple, unsophisticated, yet beautiful.

Nationwide, the greatest popularity fell however upon the small statues by John Rogers, a self-taught sculptor. Plaster casts of "Rogers' Groups" adorned American homes from the 1860's well into the 1890's. Somehow Rogers had appealed to the sentimental feeling of beauty in the commonplace. A few titles will indicate the mood: *The Village Schoolmaster*, *Courtship in Sleepy Hollow*, *The Slave Auction*, *The Council of War* (Lincoln and Grant), *The Town Pump*, *Sharpshooters*, and *The Checker Players*.

There are at least ten original issues of stereographs beginning with J. B. Aiken (1863), John Soule (1866), Bierstadt (1868), Gurney (1868) and many copy issues published in the latter 1870's.

Other popular American series illustrated "Palmer's Marbles" in the 1860's.

Several sculptors used simultaneous multiple images of a person to assist in achieving a life-like bust or statue. There are a few stereographs which identify this method of "photo-sculpture."

The examples cited above are stone or clay sculpture. The range of stereographs is far more extensive. Many works in bronze, wood carving and other media were photographed in fine detail.

F. Brandt (1868) issued a set of twenty views of the Altar Shrine in Schlesweg Cathedral, carved by Hans Bruggemann (ca. 1520). Bronze sculpture, such as the door of the United States Capitol by Randolph Brothers and the great horse at the entrance of St. Mark's Cathedral in Venice have been beautifully stereographed.

Perhaps the most unusual temporary sculpture was Caroline Brooks' *Dreaming Iolanthe*, carved in butter. Mrs. Brooks of Helena, Arkansas, displayed the carving preserved by cracked ice in the Women's Pavilion at the Centennial of 1876. Several stereographs of this work were published.

As noted earlier (page 17), it is possible to locate stereographs of the works of every great sculptor from Ancient Greece to 1900, among them Phidias, Praxiteles, Michelangelo, Canova, Danecker, Thorwaldsen, Powers, French, Baily, Greenough and hundreds more.

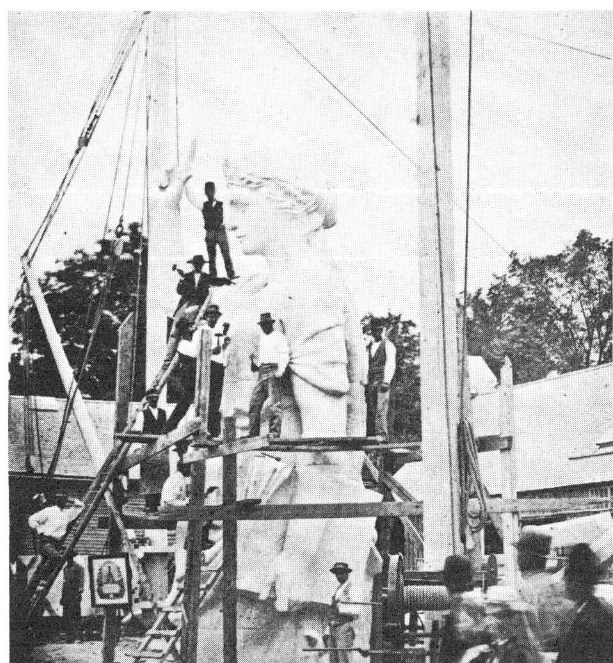

293. Sculpture. The sculptor Joseph Archie and his carvers working on the "Statue of Faith" for the Plymouth Monument. Hallowell Granite Company, Hallowell, Maine. Morse and McIntosh photo, 1877.

SHIPS AND SHIPPING

Ships are among the most popular subjects for topical collectors. The transformation from wooden sailing ships to great steamships is handsomely recorded. All kinds of steamboats plied the lakes and rivers of western Europe and North America: pleasure craft for summer tourists, freighters on the Great Lakes, and the highly ornamented steamers that worked up and down the Mississippi River and its tributaries in the Missouri and Ohio River basins. Figures 116, 118.

The great wooden men of war of the Royal British Channel Fleet were stereographed by Wilson in 1857 and several times thereafter. Figure 159.

The famous four mast schooners that made the long journey around the Horn in the trade from New York and Boston to San Francisco and the ports of China are best seen in the many views of the harbors of Valparaiso, Chile and San Francisco. Figure 209.

The maiden voyage of the Great Eastern was stereographed at Southampton and at New York (1860). Howlett (London Stereoscopic Company) issued a series illustrating its construction. There are hundreds of views of famous ships, to name a few, the *Lusitania* and its sister-ship the *Mauretania*, the *Leviathan* (the *Vaterland* seized by the United States during World War I) and the ships of the Cunard, White Star and German-American Lines. Figures 30, 297.

The several coastal shipping lines operating between New York, Boston, Portland and Halifax were nicely stereographed.

Harbor views of every continent are numerous. Among them one can find dramatic scenes of stevadores, tugs, lighters and commercial activities.

Collateral subjects related to shipping are of considerable variety: lighthouses, breakwaters, docks, piers and other engineering works.

Replicas of historic ships such as those of Columbus, Henrik Hudson, and the *Mayflower* have been stereographed during the celebrations for which they were built.

A few ship disasters have been recorded in stereo views. The best known is the small series of the *General Slocum* which burned in the East River, New York, with the loss of more than a thousand persons (1904), issued by H. C. White. There are many scenes of shipwrecks, mostly along the coast of New England.

Finally, sets of views taken during world cruises were popular between 1900 and 1935. In most cases the sets were produced for the participants only but some were offered for general sale. A typical example is "Our Cruise Around the World, S. S. Cleveland," produced by Underwood. Most of the sets include scenes of recreational activities of the members of the cruise. See also: NAVAL; YACHTING

SKELETON (PHANTOM) LEAVES

One of the curious fads of the mid-Victorian era was the preparation and display of skeletonized leaves. The soft tissues of leaves, flowers and seed pods were removed by any one of several fermentation or chemical maceration methods, leaving a delicate tracery of vascular tissue. The plant parts were then dried and arranged in artistic still-lifes.

Enthusiasm for stereo views of these arrangements was incredible. The first issue (1858) of William England's "Beautiful in Death" was simply titled "Skeletonized leaves." Huge quantities of the view were sold by the London Stereoscopic Company until 1870. Pirated copy issues were widely distributed in the United States in the latter 1860's and 70's.

Mrs. I. L. Rogers (Springfield, Massachusetts, 1870's) copyrighted about thirty skeleton leaf arrangements, most of which were stereographed by Soule. Subsequently B. W. Kilburn obtained rights to them and continued issuing stereos until 1895. Mrs. Rogers' earlier arrangements were symbolic, such as

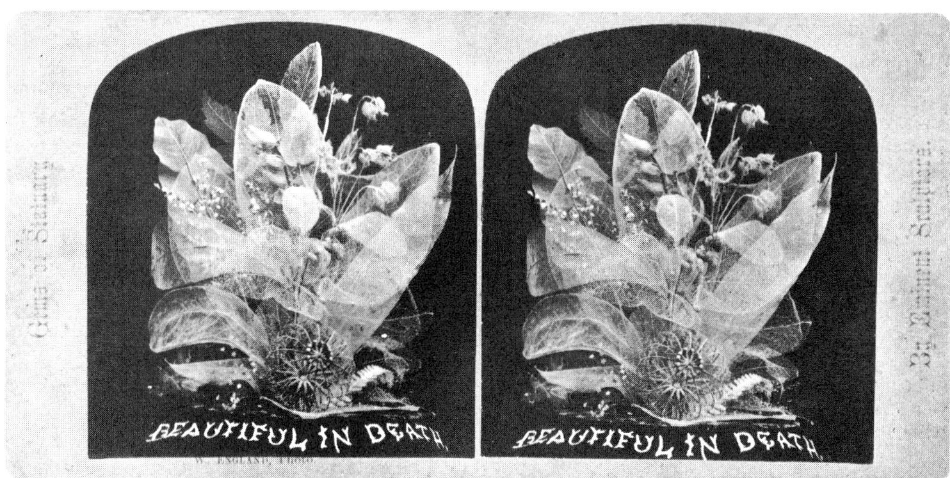

294. Skeleton Leaves. "Beautiful in Death." William England negative, ca. 1858.

Christian and Maltese crosses, Masonic, etc. (all 1872-73). More typically each arrangement was built around a cabinet photograph of a prominent personality (Lincoln, 1874; Charles Sumner, 1874; "Charles Ross, the Stolen Child," 1877).

Kilburn added at least thirty views of skeleton leaf arrangements to his trade list. Nearly all are wreathed portraits, such as of James Garfield, Robert E. Lee, Queen Victoria, and Pope Leo XIII.

The appeal of skeleton arrangements may be judged by the excellent photographers who produced stereos of them: Soule, Anthony and Charles Bierstadt. Scores of funeral skeleton leaf arrangements, especially wreaths, with a portrait of the deceased, are widely scattered in the trade lists of American photographers 1867-1878.

Close inspection of interior views of Victorian parlors and sitting rooms will occasionally reveal a skeleton leaf arrangement under a glass dome on a table or mantlepiece.

SPANISH-AMERICAN WAR

The sinking of the Battleship *Maine* in Havana harbor on February 15, 1898 was followed by protests that resulted in a declaration of war by Spain on April 24. A call for volunteers brought more than a hundred thousand men to training camps at Tampa, Chickamauga and New Orleans.

The war which lasted barely four months was fought in and about Cuba and the Philippine Islands. Men and materiel had to be transported by coordinated navy and army operations. The decisive turning points of the war were the naval battles at Santiago Bay and Manila Bay. In these engagements the Spanish fleets were completely destroyed.

The brief but bitter land action in Cuba, including the feats of Colonel Teddy Roosevelt's "Rough Riders" (First Voluntary Infantry) were given wide publicity.

There are more stereographs of the Spanish-American than that of any other war. Underwood published more than 2,000 views, including the issues with Strohmeyer & Wyman and Littleton View imprints. Next in importance are the thousand titles published by Kilburn. Smaller series, but in each case with more than 200 titles, were issued by William H. Rau (Universal View Company), H. C. White, C. H. Graves (Universal Photo Art Company), C. L. Wasson (International View Company), Webster & Albee, and Whiting View Company.

There are at least a score of other publishers who issued a few views related to Spanish-American War.

Although no single photographer or publisher attempted to assemble a complete or systematic record of the war, the combined coverage is marvelously complete, excepting scenes of battle actions. The views of mobilization and training camps, identify the majority of regiments with their officers and flags. There are many views of men practicing military tactics and many showing recruits at play.

The naval views are spectacular, scarcely a battleship or auxiliary vessel was neglected by stereographers. Even improvised guns and armor were recorded. Close-up views of guns and their crews and deck scenes are numerous. Troop ships leaving American ports and disembarking units in Cuba and the Philippines are also illustrated.

Historically important are the stereos of sick and wounded, the field hospitals and medical care in general. Typhoid, malaria, and yellow fever inflicted much more suffering and casualties than fighting.

Public celebrations such as victory marches, Admiral Dewey receiving a ceremonial sword from President McKinley, and burial of the victims of the *Maine* were extensively stereographed.

Finally, there are several hundred views portraying personalities associated with the war, military, political, newspaper correspondents, and others.

SPORTS

Stereographic coverage of sports is very erratic. Generally there are relatively few views of a particular sport, excepting hunting and fishing. Team sports are poorly represented.

Golf has been illustrated by two excellent series, each including more than a hundred card views. The Bay State Publishing Company (Boston 1906-10), issued a remarkable series of "amateur" champions, including Walter J. Travis, Harry Vardon, Alex Campbell and about 200 others. A boxed set of a hundred selected titles was distributed. The Stereo-Travel Company published a similar boxed set (100 titles, 1910) which illustrated different golf strokes and body positions being demonstrated by prominent golfers. Cards of the Stereo Travel series are occasionally found without a publisher's imprint but with the regular series number and title ("Teeing Off," 53).

The following were stereographed often enough to provide at least a sketchy history of the sport:

billiards
boxing
bull fighting
croquet
foot racing
horse racing
mountain climbing
polo
rowing
rugby and soccer
skiing
swimming and diving
yachting

After 1910 a few views of college and professional baseball and football teams were published. Automobile racing also became popular after 1908.

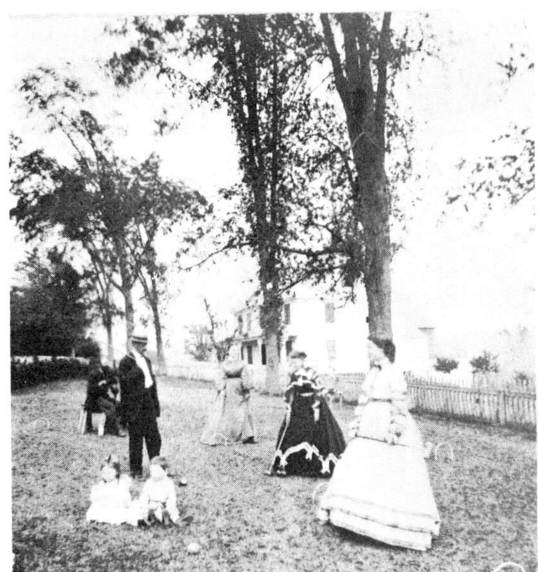

295. Sports. "Croquet Party, Mount Monadnock," New Hampshire. Unidentified photographer, ca. 1867.

College rowing matches have attracted many stereographers. Poulton issued views of the Henley Regatta in 1859. The Harvard-Yale and Harvard-Amherst races were photographed many times.

Croquet was a favorite adult pastime at the summer resorts of the 1860's and 1870's. Scores of excellent views are available. Realistic Travels (ca. 1910) published unusual views of skiing at St. Moritz.

The list could be expanded to include competitive games like chess (of which there are many stereographs) and games played by children (baseball, etc.) but I have excluded them.

See also: AUTOMOBILES, FISHING, HORSES, HUNTING, YACHTING

TECHNOLOGY

What we call modern society, is the condition of man in a world transformed by technology. Not all nations have been equally affected, nor have all citizens in a country shared equally its benefits or disadvantages.

The progressive industrialization and mechanization that have so materially changed the world in a little more than a century are uniquely recorded by stereographs. The following major categories of views are summarized in greater detail elsewhere in this book:

See Also:

AUTOMOBILES	MILLS AND FACTORIES
AVIATION	MINING
BRIDGES	OCCUPATIONS
CIVIL ENGINEERING	RAILROADS
ELECTRICAL ENGINEERING	SHIPS AND SHIPPING
ENGINEERING	TRANSPORTATION

TEXTILES

Food, clothing and shelter constitute the basic needs of mankind. From prehistoric times to the present, plant and animal fibers have been woven into fabrics which were used not only for making clothing but also for many other products.

The important plant fibers have been cotton, cultivated since ancient times in India, Egypt and Central America and flax grown in Europe since Neolithic times. Coarse fibers such as jute (India) and sisal (Mexico) have many domestic uses. Manila hemp has also found extensive use for rope, twine and nets.

Animal fibers include wool, alpaca and vicuna from mammals and silk from an insect, the silkworm moth.

In the nineteenth century the traditional primitive methods of weaving persisted in many parts of the world at the same time complex factories increased tooling and power for mass production. The travel sets invariably depicted native weavers and their looms. Local photographers, particularly in the United States, documented every new large factory and mechanical innovation.

Primitive looms of great variety have been stereographed, including the horizontal looms used by the Ainu of Japan and in some African tribes.

There are many stereo views of the methods used to prepare fibers for market, such as ginning cotton to remove seed and

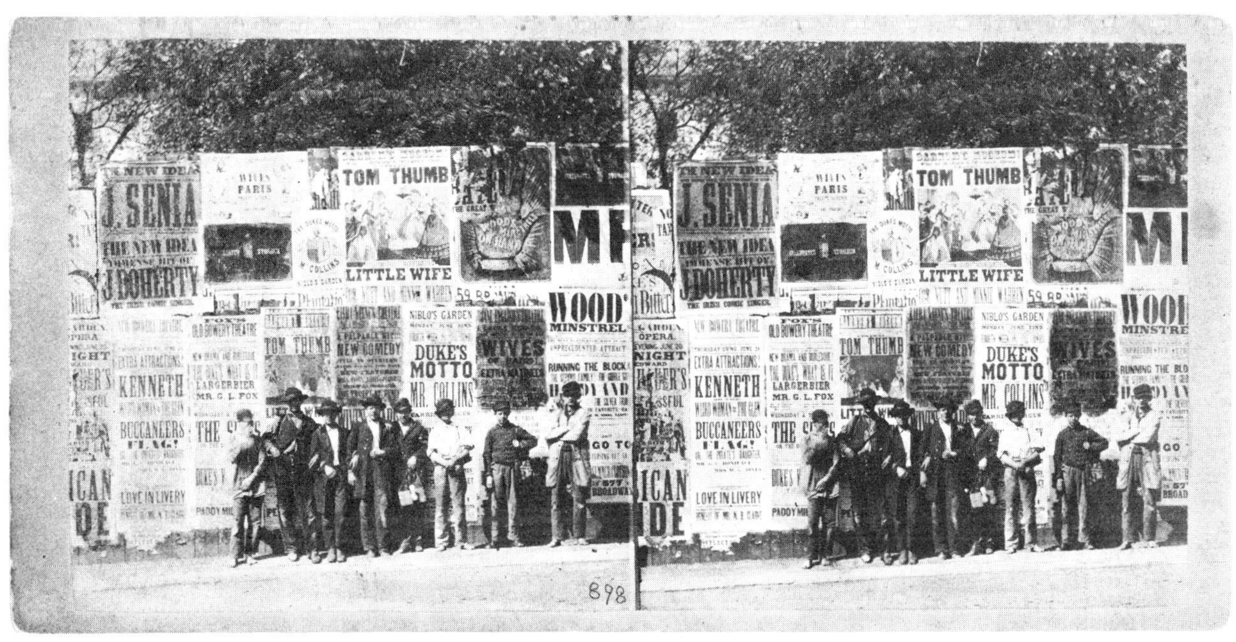

296. Theatrical. Billboards with playbills. New York City. The boys are shoeshiners. E. & H.T. Anthony, photo, 1860.

retting flax. Fine scenes of retting in Belgium, Holland and Ireland are available.

Manufacturing, other than by hand tools, is well illustrated by stereos. The Gobelin Tapestry Works (Paris), machine embroidering, carpet looms, machine lacemaking and other types of textile manufacture have been stereographed many times.

Primitive methods are very well recorded. Among the picturesque, spinning with the distaff, colonial spinning wheels, weaving pina cloth (Philippines), weaving rugs of Vicuna wool (Bolivia) and rug weaving by American Indians.

Those interested in examples of textiles rather than methods of fabrication will find an incredible array of titles. The ultimate purpose for which the textile is intended is not always self-evident. A woven garment may become the plain dress of a farmer's wife or the brocaded and jeweled robe of a queen. In the field of industrial uses the variety ranges from burlap of jute for cotton bales, awnings, tents, nets and sails. Artistic uses include altar cloths, silk hangings, and the vestments of emperors and popes. There are many surprises in store for those who examine stereographs carefully.

See: MILLS & FACTORIES

THEATRICAL

Theatrical stereographs are of four general types:

personalities, including actors, actresses, concert artists, playwrights and composers

performances, scenes from plays, operas and ballets

theaters, interiors and exteriors

theater advertisements, posters, billboards, etc.

Anthony's series of "Prominent Portraits" (1862) includes nearly seventy-five of actors, dancers and singers. Nearly all of the celebrities performing on the American stage in the 1860's were represented. Among them are likenesses of Lester Wallach, John Gilbert, Edwin Booth, Adelina Patti and Stella Bonheur.

Other stereo series including many portraits of performers were published by Gurney (1860's) and Sarony (latter 1870's). A fine series of German actresses photographed by Stolze & Company was published by Linde-Sophus Williams (1868-75). Similarly a French series, "Celebrites Theatricales," without a publisher's imprint was distributed (1867-73). London Stereoscopic Company also issued a series (1872).

There are many stereographs of plays *(Hamlet, MacBeth)* operettas *(Pinafore)* and grand opera *(Faust, L'Africane)* some of which were posed by the acting companies currently performing in the city. The majority of these views, published between 1865 and 1875, were beautifully hand tinted.

A fine series of "*The Black Crook*," the first American musical comedy (1866), was issued in 1867 or 1868. Copy issues were widely distributed in the 1870's.

A tinted series "Actualities Theatricales" of scenes from plays and operas was published by Marion (Paris, 1866-1872).

Stereographs of theaters include both interior and exterior views of famous buildings such as the Grand Opera in Paris, La Scala in Milan and Ford's Theater in Washington where President Lincoln was assassinated.

Cityscapes occasionally show theater marquees and billboards advertising stage attractions. Such views may be found throughout the period of commercial stereography, i.e., 1854-1935.

Collateral to theatrical subjects are a great variety of performers and their acts: punch and judy shows, magicians, Bali dancers, Japanese kabuki.

TOYS

The toys of childhood have remained remarkably unchanged until the twentieth century. Dolls, toy animals, balls, rattles and drums are found in all cultures and all periods of history.

The advent of mass production of such objects as wooden animals for Noah's Arks, glass marbles, china dolls and cast iron pull toys supplanted improvisation and traditional craftsmanship.

Stereographs of children at play—sentimental and amusing—are of two sorts, those with toys and those depicting games and improvised activity. There are thousands of views of both kinds.

Dolls are among the more common and at the same time most diverse. F. H. Foss (Dover, New Hampshire, 1873) issued "There was an old lady who lived in a shoe," a clever arrangement of eleven dolls in a large wooden shoe. W. L. Hall (Trumensburg, New York ca. 1872) published a view of a six-room furnished doll house which would delight any little girl today. Stereos of "doll parties" are especially interesting because they can be used to date dolls with considerable accuracy.

Among the unusual views ("Standard Series" ca. 1895) is "The Doll's Favorite"—fifteen dolls grouped around a child's toy model of a Singer sewing machine.

One of the best sources of illustrations of toys are stereographs of Christmas trees surrounded by presents: Kilburn issued a score of beautiful scenes, especially nos. 11633-11635 (1897).

The German toy makers display "The Children's Paradise" at the Paris Exposition of 1900 is a gem.

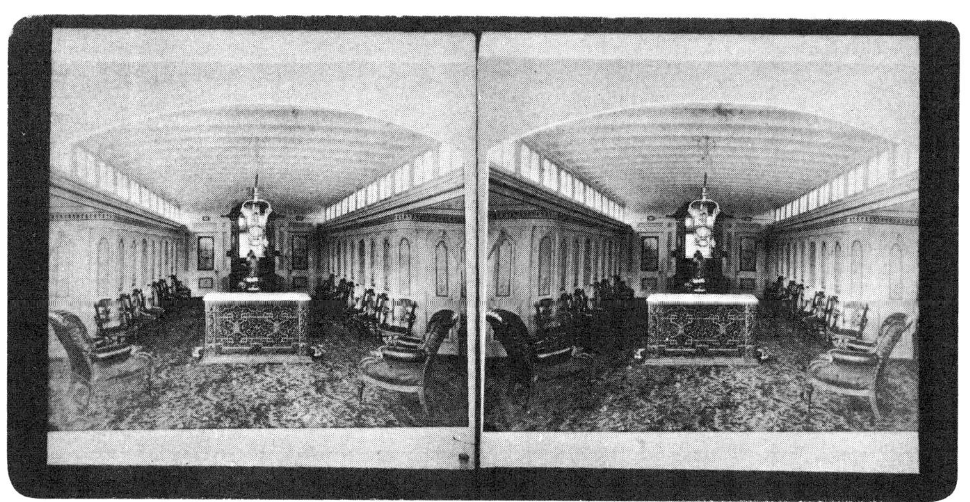

297. Steamship. "Ladies Cabin of the *Wide West*." Portland, Oregon. I.G. Davidson photo, ca. 1876.

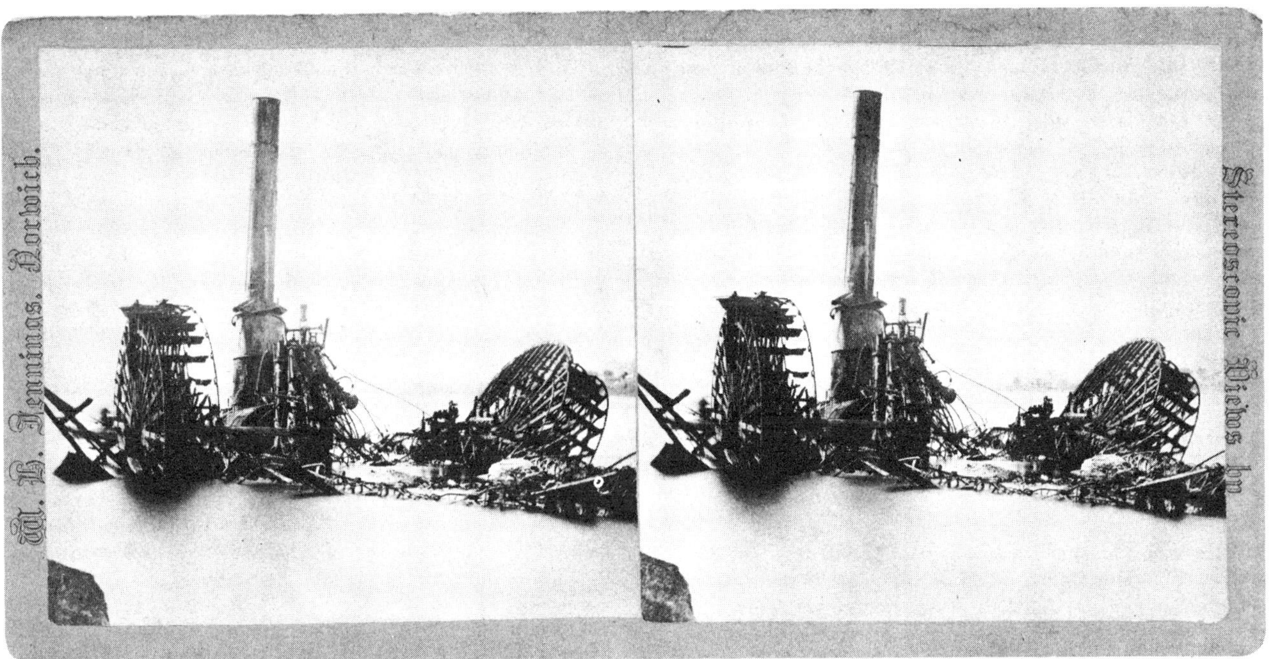

298. Steamship. "Wreck of the *New London*" River Thames, Connecticut. November, 1871. (See also figure 11). W. H. Jennings photo.

Twentieth century stereo views should not be neglected. Two examples will indicate the possibilities.

Keystone 11917 (ca. 1910) depicts a family of seven persons, including a boy playing with an Erector set, while the grandmother is using a Holmes-type stereoscope. Keystone 34406 shows a child playing with a Lionel electric train (ca. 1934). This view (P. 9, in the "Pastime" series) replaced two earlier ones, the first of which (1902) illustrated a train with a mechanical key-wound locomotive.

TRANSPORTATION

The story of transportation, the methods for moving man and his materials over land and water, is one of marvelous ingenuity. Coincident with the Industrial Revolution, changes in the speed and efficiency of transportation and communication unified nations, changed ways of life, increased international trade, and spread information throughout the world. Transportation played a key role in the political, economic, and social revolution begun in the 1840's.

In those parts of the world in which the horse was not domesticated, other animals like the camel, reindeer and elephant were used in various ways as beasts of burden. Ships rowed by men or moved by sails in the wind developed in many ancient cultures, were still prevalent in the early part of the twentieth century.

The steam engine, burning wood or coal and later by oil or gasoline, transformed both land and water transportation, railroad locomotives, automobiles and aircraft; river boats and colossal ocean ships.

The activity and mobility of modern man are so dependent upon and involved with transportation, it is self-evident that a large proportion—approximately half—of all stereographs record directly or indirectly some aspect of transportation.

Most major categories have been considered under more specific headings.

See also: AUTOMOBILES; AVIATION; HORSES; RAILROADS; SHIPS & SHIPPING

VOLCANOES

Active volcanoes are among the most awesome physical features of the earth. The eruption of Mount Vesuvius in 63 A.D. buried the city of Pompeii under nearly twenty feet of dry ash and dust, and nearby Herculean under sixty-five feet of material that turned to mud under heavy rains. The site of Pompeii was discovered in 1600 but excavations of this ancient Roman city did not begin until 1763.

Stereographs of Pompeii and the artifacts recovered from the site were extremely popular in the 1850's and 60's. Vesuvius in eruption was stereographed by Cuccione (1868) and White (1908). Many publishers produced fine scenes of lava fumaroles and other features. Views of Mount Etna in eruption in 1865

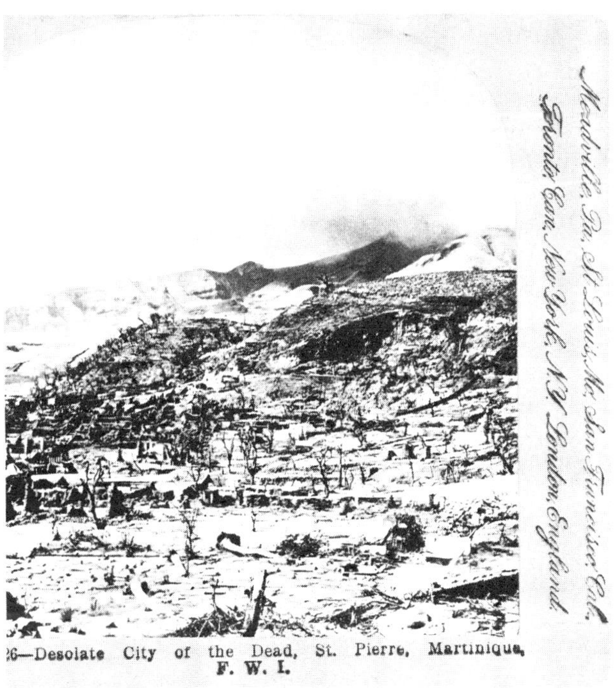

299. Volcanoes. Eruption of Mont Pelee, Martinique. 1903. Keystone View Company.

were issued by an unidentified French photographer. Vogel (Berlin, 1871) issued views of the semiquiescent crater.

Realistic Travels (London, 1908) published excellent views of boiling lava in Mount Pazzuoli, Italy.

The most spectacular coverage of a destructive eruption was the catastrophe on Martinique in 1902. Mont Pelee erupted with devastating force sending a cloud of super-heated gases that leveled the city of St. Pierre and killed 30,000 people. The best series (18 views) was issued by Underwood. Keystone published good views of La Soufriere, on nearby St. Vincent, which had erupted one day earlier than Mont Pelee.

Other notable eruptions recorded by stereo include: Asama-yama, Japan (Underwood, 1904), Mt. Lassen (Keystone), and an unidentified volcano in Java (Keystone no. 16400). This latter view shows fine details of the cinder cone and dense cloud of dust.

Nearly all of the great inactive volcanic peaks of the world have been stereographed. Travel sets invariably include views of those in the area illustrated.

WARS

Stereographs of the many wars and military incidents between 1855 and 1920 are among the important documentary photographs. These have always fascinated collectors. Generally, these stereos sold well during the war period and for a brief time after hostilities ceased. Only World War I was an exception, the views being in demand until 1929.

Photographers seldom were able to take negatives during battles. Thus, most scenes before 1900 show the battlefield after the fighting has ceased. Even so, there are many scenes of dead and wounded amply recording the horrors of war.

Attention has already been directed to the questions about stereographs of the Crimean War (page 20). It is known that more than twenty photographers recorded incidents of the war. Assuredly some stereos were produced.

Views of the Austrian-Italian wars were issued by many Italian and French photographers. Scenes of dead on the battlefield, prisoners, departing troops and returning victorious armies are known (1859).

The American Civil War, however, was the first struggle to have been covered more or less systematically. Even here, however, the coverage is unbalanced. There are very few views from the Confederate viewpoint and the entire western theaters of operations is sketchy.

Stereographs of the Franco-Prussian War have been mentioned previously. The German viewpoint was recorded by E. Linde. French views, by a score of photographers are more common.

The Turkish-Greek or Macedonian War was stereographed by several Americans. The best views are by Bert Underwood, although Keystone and Kilburn obtained good negatives.

The Spanish-American War was exceptionally well recorded. Every aspect of the war was illustrated.

The Boer War was also extensively illustrated by stereo views. American photographers were responsible for the splendid range of views.

The spectacular action-filled stereographs of the Russo-Japanese War were produced by American publishers, most notably Underwood (negatives by Ricalton) and H. C. White.

World War I was well stereographed but with some limitations. The Western Allies mobilized hastily in response to Germany's invasion of Belgium. Underwood and several British photographers recorded mobilization, Belgium in 1914, fighting in Flanders and various actions well into 1916. By the time that the United States entered the war and American troops arrived in France, Underwood had drastically restricted stereographic publication. Not until the war had ended did Keystone obtain permission to send its photographer (Iddings) to France to record the war scenes. Under this circumstance, the Iddings views are remarkable. The advancements in military technology from food handling to medical care, from submarines to aircraft are recorded in fine detail. The series of views by Troutman supplement rather than duplicate the Underwood and Keystone issues.

There are few commercially produced stereographs of World War II (1939-45). Keystone issued a number of views of American generals and political figures which had a limited sale to collectors.

Many minor hostilities were stereographed. Best covered was the Boxer Rebellion or Tsien Tsien Incident (Underwood, White, Keystone, Kilburn).

There are two lithoprint series of the Mexican Border Incidents (1912-16).

See also: BOER WAR; CIVIL WAR; RUSSO-JAPANESE WAR; SPANISH-AMERICAN WAR; WORLD WAR I.

WHALING

There are very few stereographs of whaling, probably because the industry which had centered for many years in Nantucket and New Bedford, Massachusetts, had severely declined by 1860.

The finest views, now very rare, are the twelve scenes issued

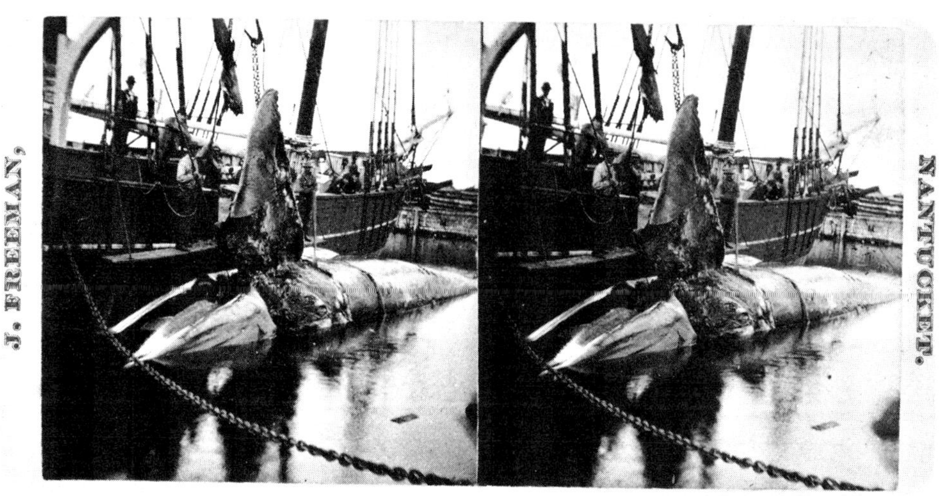

300. Whaling. "Skinning a fin-back whale." Nantucket, Massachusetts. J. Freeman photo, ca. 1870.

by Bierstadt Brothers in 1861, and the twenty additional views published by them during the next four years. The scenes include whaling ships tied to the pier, anchored in the harbor, dock scenes and gear.

Shute & Son (Edgartown, Massachusetts) in 1868 published a famous series (twelve titles), "A Whaling Voyage." The scenes are staged with miniature models on an oilcloth ocean. The mother ship, pursuit boats, whales, fishermen and harpooners are so convincingly accurate that individual views have been mistaken for actual whaling scenes. Although a complete set is composed of twelve cards, the Shutes staged several scenes more than once. Two or more variations are known for six titles. This series is one of the classic examples of table-top photography. Figure 87.

Freeman (Nantucket) published about thirty exceptional views of whaling interest, including skinning, cutting blubber, boiling oil, ships arriving with whale catches and fishermen (1867-1876).

In the twentieth century the industry mechanized with steamships and harpoon guns. Underwood (4700) photographed a gunner on an Arctic whaler in Baffin Bay. Underwood also published a view of whalers cruising in Dexterity Harbor (reissued by Keystone V27198). Keystone issued a view of a floating whaling station near Spitzbergen (15768).

One of the best stereographs of whale skinning shows a beached whale on Long Island (Underwood 11232, ca. 1900).

WORLD WAR I

Almost every collector is familiar with the scenes of World War I (1914-18) by Keystone View Company, published in great quantities from 1919 to 1929 and in diminished numbers until 1935. Less familiar are the nearly 2,000 views by Underwood & Underwood although it is well-known that the Keystone sets incorporated many Underwood titles.

Underwood photographers were active in Belgium and Flanders in 1914. They followed also the opening of the Dardanelles and Balkan campaigns in 1915. Inasmuch as the United States was not yet at war, the American photographers were able to do limited traveling in Russia and Germany. Mobilization in England, the first Zeppelin air raids and the naive inexperience of the first British troops sent to France are strikingly recorded.

In 1916 Underwood issued two small sets of war views (24 and 48 views). The following year expanded sets of 36 and 72 views were published. Underwood had severely curtailed manufacture of stereographs by this time, although many scenes of American "preparedness" and mobilization were photographed.

Keystone View Company did not obtain permission from the War Department to send a photographer to France until after the Armistice had been signed. Andrew S. Iddings, a former staff photographer, was persuaded to leave his law practice, to undertake a stereographic tour of the battlefields. He obtained nearly 1,100 negatives, an incredibly realistic coverage, considering the handicaps.

The first Keystone sets (1919) were not unusual (24, 48 and 72 cards, each larger selection including the smaller). The first 100 card set was published in 1921. In 1923 the familiar 100-200-300 sets were assembled to illustrate the history of the war. The negatives were approximately two-thirds by Keystone and one-third by Underwood. An important guidebook, "The World War Through the Stereoscope" was prepared by Major Joseph M. Hanson (1st edition, 1923; 4th, 1927). Although Keystone had obtained the entire file of Underwood negatives, only a small percentage of the war scenes were actually used. The reason was deceptively simple. The Keystone sets were devised to appeal to American war veterans and their families. The sets emphasized localities in which Americans participated. The larger part of Underwood's file were photographed before the first contingents of American Expeditionary Force landed in France.

Keystone accumulated an extensive holding of World War negatives, many of which were never published commercially. Sets of 400 and 500 views housed in velvet lined boxes were assembled to order. I have seen one "500" set. It is difficult to determine how many distinct stereo views bear a Keystone imprint. Of 900 known to me, thirty percent are from Underwood negatives.

The Keystone sets include several views of the Great White Fleet, mostly copyrighted in 1908. Some collectors have been puzzled by this anachronism. In 1914, when the war began, this *was* the American fleet. Superdreadnaughts were still on the drawing board.

A third publisher, W. E. Troutman (Reading, Pennsylvania) produced sets of World War I views. The more common is a 100 card set but there was also a 300 card set. Generally, the photography is inferior to that of Underwood or Keystone. The chief interest in the Troutman views is the considerable number of scenes, especially of aviation not available elsewhere.

There are several series of English stereographs illustrating the war. The most extensive is a fine series of more than a hundred titles by Realistic Travels (London, 1914-16). Few of the various series bear a photographer's imprint. Possibly some were published by amateurs. Typical scenes include parades, mobilization, refugees, bomb damage in England and subjects peripheral to the war.

Only a few German views are known to me, mostly helmeted troops, cavalry and horse-drawn artillery, issued 1914-15. The scenes appear to be parade grounds and camps rather than locations in France.

In addition to views on standard card mounts, there are many lithoprint issues both black and white half-tones and multicolored and stereo cartoons—all of American origin. These are of minor importance except as historical documents of propaganda and attitudes toward war.

At least two series of small glass views of the war were issued for use with Richards type stereoscopes which never gained wide acceptance in the United States.

YACHTING

Brief reference to stereographs of yachting is included here to suggest the depth of coverage of almost any activity that has enjoyed popularity or had some prominence. Pleasure yachting as a sport was especially popular in England and America.

Many regattas in New York Harbor were stereographed by Anthony (1859-1865) and in the harbors of New England by scores of photographers (1860-1880). Among the most charming scenes are those of Bar Harbor (Bradley, 1877-78).

All of the "American Cup" ("International Yacht Races") held between 1885 and 1903 were stereographed, notably

1885 *Puritan* and *Genesta*, Kilburn
1899 *Columbia* and *Shamrock*, Keystone
1901 *Columbia* and *Shamrock II*, Underwood
1903 *Reliance* and *Shamrock I*, R. Y. Young
and *Shamrock III*, Underwood

Underwood published a fine view of Sir Thomas Lipton standing on the *Erin*, watching *Shamrock II* at Sandy Hook, New Jersey (1901).

There are views of many other cup races, as for example, the Goelet Race, Newport, Rhode Island (1895, Kilburn) and of individual racing contenders such as the *Valkyrie* (ca. 1905) and the *Defender* (A. S. Campbell no. 271, 1896).

ZOOLOGY

Animal photography, especially in the wild, was very difficult prior to the invention of high speed emulsions. Once this technical problem had been solved, many photographers attempted to record songbirds, mammals, and reptiles in their natural habitats.

Another factor that delayed progress in animal photography

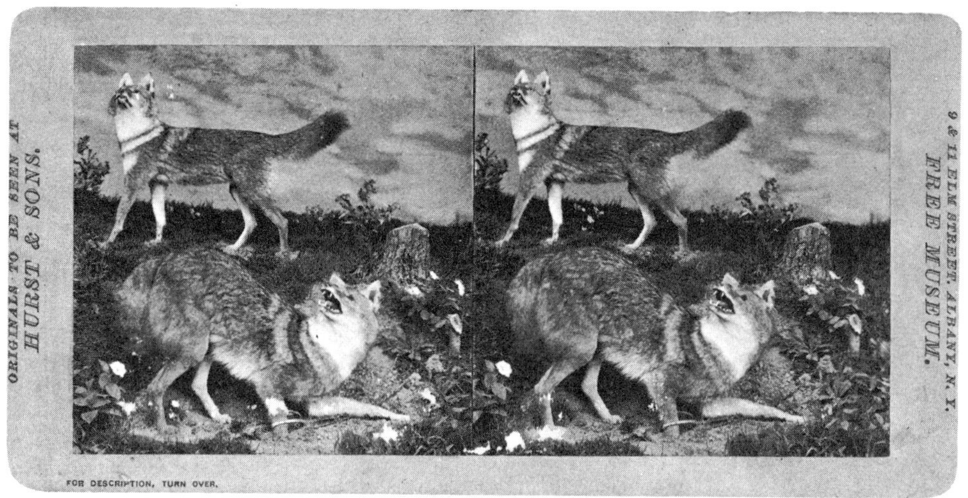

301. Zoology. Hurst's Natural History Series. "The Prairie Wolf." Haines photo, 1870.

was the limited interest in natural history as such prior to 1870. Although botany, conchology and entomology were popular avocations in England and the United States, amateurs were interested in collecting specimens rather than studying nature.

The great natural history museums reflect the change from buildings to display curiosities to institutions for research and education. This was strictly a development of the nineteenth and twentieth centuries. The extinction of many species of birds and mammals and the modification of the wilderness areas of the earth had, by 1900, stimulated world wide concern for conservation. This concern, in turn, resulted in the introduction of various types of nature study in primary and secondary schools and in youth movements.

The first significant attempt to stereograph animals was made by Frank Haes in 1864.* Using an exposure time of one-third of a second, he was able to obtain negatives of twenty-two animals in the London Zoological Garden. In 1865, Haes obtained views of forty animals, some duplicating the earlier series. These views attracted much attention at the Paris Exposition in 1867, especially those of the orangoutan, tiger and cheetah which won honors. In addition to familiar animals, Haes issued fine stereos of the python, boa constrictor, condor vultures and the American bullfrog. The series was originally published by McLean & Haes. Pirated copy issues were distributed in the United States during the 1870's.

In the early 1870's F. York published a fine series of animals in the London Zoo. More expressive than either of these is a splendid series of fifty animals in the Philadelphia Zoological Garden taken by Schreiber & Sons and issued on cabinet mounts by James Cremer in 1875.

There are many other stereos of animals in zoos and menageries (New York, Paris, Berlin, etc.), mostly published in the 1870's.

Exhibits of taxidermic mounted birds and mammals are of greater historical interest because they illustrate the techniques and theories of museum display. No series is more justly famous than the "Stereoscopic Studies of Natural History," "for schools and popular entertainment" by James A. Hurst (1870). The series includes approximately 200 subjects, half of mammals and half of birds. Full descriptive notes are printed on the reverse.

Scattered through many trade lists, there are stereographs of private collections of mounted birds, insects, bird eggs, and sea shells. Meinerth, Kilburn, J. W. & J. S. Moulton are but a few of many photographers who issued excellent examples.

Underwood assembled a unique educational series of animal views. A complete set of 262 titles was issued about 1908 but smaller selections were available as early as 1903. All major groups of the animal kingdom from protozoa to the anthropoids were illustrated. Complete sets are seldom seen because they were sold almost exclusively to schools and public libraries where the cards were exposed to wear and tear.

The Underwood negatives were purchased by Keystone but only a few of them were used. The 100 card Keystone animal set is composed of views from Underwood, White and Keystone negatives.

Keystone published a "Song Birds" set, 100 cards, beautifully hand tinted. Seventy-five additional bird titles were available untinted only. These are excellent examples of true nature photography, not of mounted specimens. Fine tinted sets were distributed between 1923 and 1930.

In 1902, R. Y. Young issued a "Natural History Series" (50? titles) now very rare. Some of the subjects are life-like mounted museum groups, such as "a tiger cat with a captured deer."

There are many other types of stereographs of zoological interest. Specimens of seashells and corals, alone or placed in still life arrangements, were photographed by Fenton, T. R. Williams, Sedgfield, Soule and other masters, especially during the 1850's and 60's.

Museum displays were frequently photographed, especially in the British Museum and the Smithsonian Institution. C. S. Cudlip issued a remarkable view of "The Bone Hall" (skeletons) of the Smithsonian (1872).

Nearly all travel sets and regional series include examples of indigenous animals, sometimes in natural habitat but more often confined in local zoos. A few examples selected from the great variety of animals in nature are:

- birds and sea lions of the Farallone Islands, California by Watkins
- penguins of South Africa and Antarctica, especially those by Keystone
- herds of bison (1865-1905), many photographers
- beaver dams, many photographers

Note: domesticated and economically useful animals have been excluded from this summary.

See also: HUNTING, LIBRARIES & MUSEUMS

Photo News 9:26-27, 1865; *Phila. Phot.* 2:66, 1865.
Photo News 10:78-79, 89-91, 1866.

A CHECK LIST OF NORTH AMERICAN STEREOGRAPHERS

The following geographic list of photographers or publishers who issued stereographs represents fewer than half of the known names. It is believed that all photographers who produced large series or numbers of titles are included. To insure broad geographic coverage, minor photographers who operated in thinly populated areas are frequently included.

For states like New York, Pennsylvania and Massachusetts, less than a third of the stereographers are given. Only the more important names in the larger cities are mentioned.

For southern and western states about ninety percent of the names known to me are included.

Initials rather than full first names are used. When no initial is given, the imprint or logo has none. Many photographers inconsistently spelled their names (Jeffers, Jeffres, Jeffries). I have chosen the spelling found in the most common imprint.

Not all partnerships are included. For example, John Shaw operated in Boston as Shaw & Co., Shaw & Chamberlain, Shaw & Lord, and Shaw & Rideout.

Those wishing to check the approximate dates of operation are referred to the general index of photographers.

Undoubtedly the selection given here is colored by personal preference and many names of interest to local historians have been excluded.

ALABAMA

Lakin, J. H.	Montgomery
Reed, W. A.	Mobile
Sandoz, A.	Mobile
Tresslar, S. P.	Montgomery
Voyle, J.	Tuscaloosa
Wild, J. W. F.	Demopolis

ARIZONA

Buehman, H.	Tucson
Kolb Brothers	Grand Canyon
Mitchell, D. H.	Prescott
Mitchell & Baer	Prescott
Rothrock, G. H.	Phoenix, Prescott

ARKANSAS

Balch & Clary	Hot Springs
Bankes, T. W.	Little Rock
Barker, A. W.	Eureka Springs
Callahan, D.	Eureka Springs
Clary	Hot Springs
Dawson, R. W.	Little Rock
Diehl, H. P.	Little Rock
Fyler, J. F.	Eureka Springs
Fyler & Chandlee	Eureka Springs
Hartley, J.	Dardanelle
Kennedy, J. F.	Hot Springs
Malone, C.	Princeton
Maxwell	Batesville
Pye & Shinn	Pine Bluff
Tibbs, N. J.	Eureka Springs
White	DeVall's Bluff

CALIFORNIA

Appleton, D. E. & Co.	San Francisco
Baldwin	Santa Cruz
Bell, W. A.	Hollister
Bieder, M.	Los Angeles
Bonine, E. A.	Pasadena
Bouquet, G. F.	San Francisco
Brayton, J. G.	Napa City
Brewster, J. C.	San Buenaventura
Cook, J. J.	San Francisco
Cramer, C. L.	San Francisco
Crawford, G. L.	Georgetown
Dowe, L.	Petaluma, San Francisco
Downing, J. H.	Healdsburg
Durgan, F.	Sacramento
Edouart & Cobb	San Francisco
Ellis, L. S.	Los Angeles
Everett, A. J.	Lakeport
Fagerstein, G.	Yosemite
Fessenden, C. P.	San Diego
Flach, G. A.	Alameda
Flagler & Durose	San Francisco
Foss, O.	San Francisco
Foss & Hickox	San Francisco
Frese, A.	Los Angeles
Frost, E. S.	Pasadena
Gentile	Gold Run
Godfrey, W. N.	Los Angeles
Golsch, A. C.	Los Angeles
Graves, S. F.	Howland Flat
Halsey & Coffin	Dutch Flats
Hart, A. A.	Sacramento
Hawes, A. L.	San Jose
Haworth & McCollin	San Francisco
Hayward, E. J.	Santa Barbara
Hayward & Muzzall	Santa Barbara
Hazeltine, M. M.	Stockton, Yosemite
Heering, J. H.	San Jose
Heller, L.	Yreka
Holm	San Luis Obispo
Houseworth, T.	San Francisco
Howland	San Jose
Ingersoll, W. B.	Oakland
James, C. W.	Pasadena
Johnson, C.	Los Angeles
Johnson, G. H.	Sacramento
Judkins, D. R.	Mendocino
Kusel	Oroville
Lange & Newth	San Francisco
LaRue, E. C.	Pasadena
Lawrence & Houseworth	San Francisco
Lewis, W. S.	Los Angeles
Mains & Shippy	Sucker Flat
Muybridge, E.	San Francisco
Nesemann, E.	Marysville
Newth, E. W.	San Francisco
Nicholas, Norton & Co.	Los Angeles
Norton, T. G.	Pasadena
Ormsby, E. D.	Stockton
Parker & Parker	San Diego
Payne, H. T.	Los Angeles
Percival, O. C.	Nevada City
Perkins, A. J.	Vallejo
Phillips, T. M.	Los Angeles, San Francisco
Pickett & Everett	Amador City
Price, Andrew	Geyser Springs
Rea	Santa Barbara
Reese, M. A.	Santa Cruz
Reilly, J. J.	Stockton
Reilly & Ormsby	Stockton
Reilly & Spooner	Stockton
Rile, H. F.	Santa Monica
Rogers, F. H.	Los Angeles
Rose, G. L.	Pasadena
Ross & Ormsby	Petaluma
Rulofson, W. H.	San Francisco
Sarver, M.	Santa Barbara
Schoene, H.	Santa Clara
Scripture, J. C.	Big Trees

Sellech, S.	San Francisco
Shew, W.	San Francisco
Smith, J. G.	Vallejo
Smith, W. S.	San Francisco
Sourisseau	San Jose
Spooner, J. P.	Stockton
Stanton, T. E.	Los Angeles
Stinson, L. J.	Marysville
Sutterley Brothers	Napa City
Taber, I. W.	San Francisco
Taylor, J.	San Francisco
Todd, J. A.	Sacramento
Tuttle, W. N.	Santa Barbara
Varela, A. C.	Los Angeles
Walker & Fagerstein	Stockton
Watkins, C. E.	San Francisco
Wood	Marysville

COLORADO

Baldwin, S. C.	Cripple Creek
Barnhouse & Wheeler	Lake City
Boston, J. A.	Canon City
Brandt, E.	Colorado Springs
Brisbois, A. & M. L.	Leadville
Chain & Hardy	Denver
Chamberlain, W. G.	Denver
Chase & Wolcott	Trinidad
Collier, J.	Central City, Denver
Cunningham & Co.	Colorado Springs
Dean, F. E.	Gunnison
Duhem & Bro.	Denver
Emery, C. E.	Silver Cliff
Faul, Henry	Central City, Denver
Galbreath, H.	Manitou
Gillingham, C. L.	Colorado Springs
Goodman, C.	Bonanza, Pueblo
Groves, R.	Pueblo
Gurnsey, B. H.	Colorado Springs
Hawkins, B. E.	Denver
Headley, E. B.	Colorado Springs
Hine, T.	Manitou
Hook, W. E.	Colorado Springs
Jackson, W. H.	Denver
Knight, H.	Colorado Springs
Kuykendall, F.	Maysville, Silver Cliff
Luke & Wheeler	Leadville
Martin, A.	Georgetown
Martin & Peers	Central City
McKenney, A. S.	Black Hawk, Central City
Mellen, G. E.	Gunnison
Nast, C. A.	Denver
Nast & Martin	Central City
Nims, F. A.	Colorado Springs
Perry & Bohm	Colorado Springs, Denver
Pollen, C. A.	Colorado Springs
Reed & McKenny	Central City, Denver
Rudy & Clinton	Cascade Canon
Shipler, J. W.	Denver
Stormer, H. W.	Manitou
Talbot, C. W.	Canon City
Talbot, N. H.	Evans
Tangen, E.	Boulder
Thurlow, J.	Manitou
Weitfle, C.	Central City
Wilder, E. A.	Durango
Williams & McDonald	Denver
Wilson, J. G.	Colorado Springs

CONNECTICUT

Adt, A. A.	Waterbury
Allderidge, W.	New Britain
Ayer, E.	Norwich
Barber, A. S.	Willimantic
Beers, W. A.	New Haven
Blakeslee, E. H.	Norwalk
Bolles & Frisbie	New London
Buel, V.	Norwalk
Bundy, J. K.	New Haven
Bundy	Middletown
Bundy & Williams	New Haven
Burrows & Bundy	Middletown
Burwell, F. H.	New Haven
Burwell & Homan	New Haven
Camp, D. S.	Hartford
Crawford	Stamford
Delamater, R. S.	Hartford
Delius, W.	Waterbury
DeSilva, A. M.	New Haven
Doughty, T. M.	Winstead
Douglass, W. F.	New London
Durgan	Norwich
Eckhardt, J. H.	Hartford
Flint, B. W.	New Haven
French, D.	West Meriden
Gorham, L. C.	Westport
Grannis, G. W.	Waterbury
Green, J. F.	Meriden
Guild, H. H.	Milton
Hendricks, W.	Stamford
Hennigar, G. W.	Middletown
Hill, C. G.	Wallingford
Homan, C.	New Haven
Jennings, W. H.	Norwich
Jordan, J. L. & H. A.	New London
Kenyon, F. P.	New London
Laighton Bros.	Norwich
Langley, J.	Norwalk
Lewis	New Britain
Lombard, J. H.	Putnam
McIntosh, A.	Middletown
Meafoy, E. W.	Winstead
Morgan, H. W.	New London
Northrup, S. C.	New Britain
Page, W. F.	Middletown
Parsons, E. W.	Hartford
Peck, H. S.	New Haven
Phelps, G. C.	New Haven
Prescott & White	Hartford
Reeves, W.	New London
Ripley, J. C.	Norwich
Rogers, H. J.	Hartford
Safford, M.	Norwich
Sheldon, K. T.	West Winstead
Taylor, J. C.	Hartford
Thomas, G. S.	New Haven
Udell, H. D.	Hartford
Waite, T.	Hartford
Webster, E. Z.	Norwich
Weeks, J.	Norwich
Wells & Collins	New Haven
White, I.	Hartford
Whitney, E. T.	Norwalk, Stamford
Whitney & Beckwith	Norwalk
Wilcox, G. W.	Stafford Springs
Worden, N. R.	New Britain

DELAWARE

Chapman, H. C.	Milford
Curry, W. H.	Wilmington
Garrett, C. A. & T. P.	Wilmington
Garrett, E. & M.	Wilmington
Holmes, D. R.	Milford
Holmes, J. R.	Milford
James & Webb	Wilmington
Maybin, J. A.	Wilmington
Moser, J. W.	Smyrna
Sexton, T. E.	Wilmington
Torbert, J. E.	Wilmington

DISTRICT OF COLUMBIA, Washington

Bates, N. E.	Johnson, N. G.
Bell, W. & Bro.	Morris, C. E.
Brady, M.	Ogilvie, W.
Bryant & Smith	Pullman, E. J.
Corkhill, W. H.	Rice, M. D. & M. P.
Clindenst	Schindler, A. Z.
Cudlip, C. S.	Siebert, A.
Dillon, L. C.	Smillie, T. W.
Gardner, A.	Smith, W. M.
Gardner, J. J.	Vanorsdell, C. M.
Holmes, D. R.	Wakely, G. D.
Holmes & Jarvis	Walker, L. E.
Jackson, W. H.	Wallach, J.
Jarvis, J. F.	Weaver, H. E.

FLORIDA

Alvord, Kellogg & Campbell	Jacksonville
Brownson, N.	Fernandina

Colby, C. H.	Ocala
Cooley, S. A.	Jacksonville
Cushing, W. H.	St. Augustine
Duganne & Callison	Gainesville
Engle & Furlong	Fernandina
Field, A. S.	Lake City
Field, J. C.	Tampa
Gardner, M. M & W. H.	Orange
Grant, A. G.	Jacksonville, Ocala
Haas, I.	Green Cove
Hunton, F. N.	Jacksonville
Leach, W.	St. Augustine
Mackey, J. E.	Jacksonville
Mangold, J. G.	Palatka
Mears, J. P.	Palatka
Mitchell & DeWall	Jacksonville
Ober Bros.	Fernandina
Pierron, G.	St. Augustine
Pine, F. B.	St. Johns River
Shear, S.	Cocoa
Turton, G. W.	Pensacola
Upton	Jacksonville
Upton & Bolles	Jacksonville
Walker, J. A.	Pensacola
Watson	Jacksonville
White, A. D.	Jacksonville
Whitney, N. L.	Lake Eustis
Wood & Bickel	Jacksonville

GEORGIA

Berry, Kelley & Chadwick	Augusta
Bowers & Spears	Atlanta
Brown & Haygood	Macon
Coonley, J. H.	Savannah
Deane, H. L.	Griffin
Fulghan, J. M.	Sandersville
Gardner, M. M. & W. H.	Atlanta
Greene, M. G.	Columbus
Grice, G. W.	Barnesville
Havens, O.	Savannah
Kuhn, F.	Atlanta
Land, W. J.	Columbus
Leidloff, H.	Atlanta
Motes, C. W.	Atlanta, Athens
Palmer, J. A.	Savannah
Pelot & Cole	Augusta
Pugh, J.	Macon
Reckling, W.	Rome
Riddle, A.	Macon
Ryan, D. T.	Savannah
Schaub, J. L.	Atlanta, La Grange, Macon
Smith & Motes	Atlanta
Stoddart & Co.	Atlanta
Tanner, D. F.	Augusta
Warren, C. J.	Rome
Williams, G. T.	Columbus
Wilson, J. N.	Savannah

HAWAII

Chase, H. L.	Honolulu
Dickson, M.	Honolulu
King, J. W.	Honolulu
Montano, O. O.	Honolulu

IDAHO

Brasel, J.	Muskogee
Hedum & Bishop	Silver City
Tandy, H.C.	Idaho City
Thrasher, I. T.	Lewiston

ILLINOIS

Abbott, J. H.	Chicago
Adams, J. M.	Elgin
Allen, A.	Dunton
Alschuler, S. D.	Chicago
Armour, A. H.	Chicago
Bacon, G.	Pekin
Baer, F.	Highland
Barker & Buckley	Galesburg
Barnard, G. N.	Chicago
Barnes, J.	Rockford
Barr, D. P.	Effingham
Battersby, J.	Chicago
Beers, H. W.	Chicago
Berry, Kellèy & Chadwick	Chicago
Bettz, J. W.	Centralia
Bierer, E. H.	Rockford
Bill, J. O.	Chicago
Bisbee, L.	Chicago
Blackridge, C. F.	Lincoln
Bowman, W. E.	Ottawa
Brand, E. L.	Chicago
Burke, J. J.	Sterling
Burleigh, G. N.	Taylorsville
Calvert & King	Sterling
Carbutt, J.	Chicago
Chase, J. W.	Chicago
Chiverton, A.	Dixon
Clark, F.	Belvidere
Clark Bros.	Rockford
Clement, E. L.	Chicago
Codman	Jacksonville
Cole, H. H.	Peoria
Coles	Pekin
Copelin, A.	Chicago
Copelin & Hine	Chicago
Copelin & Melander	Chicago
Crater & Bill	Chicago
Crawford, J. H.	Morris
Cribfeld, A. R.	Lincoln
Cutter, W.	Galva
Dean, C. W.	Chicago
Denison, H. H.	Elgin
Dowe, L.	Sycamore
Duboce, M.	Springfield
Edgerly, M. L.	Peru
Emerson & Stott	Chicago
Emery, J. M.	Galva
Emery, R.	Napoleon
Fassett, S. M.	Chicago
Fay, W. D.	Joliet
Foster, J. C.	Monmouth
Fox, J.	Chicago
Gale & Curtis	Quincy
Gates, R. R.	Chicago
Gayford, A. B.	Rock Island
German, C. S.	Springfield
Gibbs, L. E.	Ottawa
Giles, W.	Aurora
Gray, B.	Bloomington
Greene, C. M.	Wilmington
Greene, P. B.	Chicago
Hall, A.	Chicago
Hall, A. B.	Chatsworth
Hamill, E. C.	Monmouth
Hart & Anderson	Rockford
Hartley, E. F.	Chicago
Heister, H. T.	Marseilles
Hesler, A.	Chicago, Evanston
Higgins, P. B.	Chicago
Hine, T.	Chicago
Hotchkiss, E.	Kankakee
Immke, H. W.	Princeton
James, J. E.	Galena
Johnson, T. S.	Crete, Pullman
Johnston, W.	Abingdon
Joslin, A. J.	Gilman
Joslin & Phillips	Danville
Kendig, C.	Naperville
Keyes & Chiverton	Dixon
Lapham, K. M.	Decatur
Levey, W. H.	Woodstock
Long & Smith	Quincy
Lovejoy & Foster	Chicago
Masters, W. H.	Princeton
Matthewson, T. C.	Tremont
McMillen, Z. P.	Galesburg
Melander & Bro.	Chicago
Melander & Henderson	Aurora
Miller & Tankersley	Bloomington
Miltz & Saur	Peoria
Moses, G. & A.	Quincy
Murr, C.	Joliet
Naughton, T.	Champaign
Norton & Johnson	Kewanee

Nute, C. N.	Bloomington
Obst, C. L.	Pittsfield
Parker, T.	Springfield
Payne, C. I.	Springfield
Pease	Clinton
Pierce, F. W.	Galena
Pittman, J. A. W.	Carthage, Springfield
Pratt, D. C.	Aurora
Rabal, S.	Evanston
Rawson, D. W. S.	Ottawa, Peru
Reed, Mrs. W. A.	Quincy
Rice & Thompson	Chicago
Robinson, N. A.	Hillsboro
Rocher, H.	Chicago
Sawyer, Jesse	Peoria
Sawyer, S. W.	Chicago
Shaw, J. W.	Chicago
Sherman, G. K.	Elgin
Sherman, O. G.	Marengo
Shreves & Corwin	Bushnell
Sittler & Lunney	Shelbyville
Stewart, J. C.	Carlinsville
Stoddard, J. A.	Chicago
Tandy, W.	Jacksonville
Taylor, G. W.	Sycamore
Thomas, J. J.	Mt. Carmel
Tinsley, J. W. & T. R.	Chicago
Townsend, A. C.	Springfield
Tresslar, S. P.	Dwight
Wasson, C. L.	Decatur
Westermann, O.	Pekin
Wheeler, W. S.	Chicago
Wilson, S. B.	Washington
Winsor, C. A.	Hennepin
Wyckes, J. W.	Quincy

INDIANA

Apple, G. W.	Indianapolis
Brooke, W. R.	Bristol
Bryant, J. W.	Laporte
Bulla Bros.	South Bend
Calvert, J. P.	Mooresville
Charles, D. R.	Lafayette
Clark, D. R.	Indianapolis
Cowey, W. T.	Brookville
Craycraft, A. B.	Vincennes
Curtis, C. F.	Argos
Ennis & Haller	Attica
Ford, F. B.	Kendallville
Gorgas & Mulvey	Madison
Hains, Ben	New Albany
Heichert, H. O.	Frankford
Heldon, J.	Elkhart
Hissong, G. W.	Lagrange
Hodges, J.	Newburgh
Hoff, W. L.	Lagrange
Husher, J. W.	Terra Haute
Indiana College of Photography	Wabash
Kenyon, W.	Crawfordville
Maxwell & Estel	Richmond
Milice, H. C.	Warsaw
Miller, H.	Indianapolis
Mitchell, G.	Greenfield
Mote Bros.	Richmond
Neely, L. W.	Muncie
Pease, C. H.	Goshen
Reid, J. S.	Orange
Salter, W. H.	Indianapolis
Savage, A. J.	Vincennes
Scott, J. M.	Vincennes
Sittler, G. W.	Shelbyville
Stewart	French Creek
Swain, W. A.	Richmond
Thorne, J. R.	Madison
Tomlinson, M.	Plainfield
Townsend, W.	Richmond
Wallin, C. E.	Ft. Wayne
Wolever, A. W.	Delphi
Wolfe, M.	Richmond
Wright, D. H.	Terra Haute

IOWA

Adams, A. W.	Decorah
Addis, A. S.	Dubuque
Armstrong, C. M.	Leon
Atkinson, C. A.	Davenport
Baker, W.	Marshalltown
Baldwin	Des Moines
Barber, E.	Waterloo
Barke	Council Bluffs
Barnett, L. M. G.	Davenport
Belveal, E. S.	Ottumwa
Bilbrough, J. E.	Dubuque
Buser	Cedar Rapids
Chatterton, H. D.	Centerville, Villisca
Cook, I. N.	Davenport
Cook, J. C.	Webster City
Cornell, C. V. D.	Waterloo
Cottrel	Dunlap
Coyle, F. A.	Monticello
DeLong, W. W.	Sioux City
Elliott, W. H.	Marshalltown
Evans, J. G.	Muscatine
Everett & Co.	Des Moines
Fellows, E. G.	Vinton
Fosnot & Hunter	Keosauqua
Freeborn, L. H.	Des Moines
Fry	Villisca
Gardner, R. G.	Maquoketa
Gurnsey & Illingworth	Sioux City
Hamilton, J. H.	Sioux City
Hamilton & Hoyt	Sioux City
Harwood & Mooney	Charles City
Hoyt, B. F.	Manchester
Johnson, P.	Rockford
Jones, C. E.	Davenport
King, J. P.	Waterloo
Leisenring	Ft. Dodge
Libby, E. P.	Keokuk
Manville, W. A.	Marshalltown
Martin, J. P.	Boone, Tama City
Mather, H. S.	Cedar Lake
McManus, C. C.	Nevada
Montfort & Hill	Burlington
Morrison, M.	Ames
Moxley, A. F.	Boone
Mueller, I.	Council Bluffs
Newton, J. J.	Council Bluffs
Olmstead, P. A.	Davenport
Palmer	Lansing
Peterson & Idso	Story City
Phillips, J.	Ft. Madison
Pinckney, J. W.	Sioux City
Rich, J. E.	Charles City
Root, S.	Dubuque
Schooley, Mrs. L. A.	Indianola
Shear, S. R.	Ossian
Shepard, F.	Iowa Falls
Stark, M. W.	Sioux City
Staunton, E. A.	Davenport
Tewkesbury, R. W.	Farmington
Townsend, T. W.	Iowa City
Warner, P. H.	Hopkinton
Weatherly, C. L. & J. A.	Iowa City
Wilson, J. W.	Cherokee

KANSAS

Beck, H.	Winfield
Conklin & Kleckner	Atchison
Corwin, E. H.	Ottawa
Fordice, W. H.	Council Grove
French	Lawrence
Henry, E. E.	Leavenworth
Hickox, R. A.	Emporia
Hopkins & Holcomb	Salina
Kleckner, M. A.	Osborne
Knight, J. L.	Topeka
Leonard & Martin	Topeka
Luke, W. O.	Abilene
Masters, C. H.	Atchison
Merrill, S.	Ft. Riley
Newcomb, N. W.	Marysville
Riddle, J. R.	Topeka
Robinson	Kansas City
Tresslar, F. P & S. P.	St. Scott
Trott, A. P.	Junction City
Underwood & Underwood	Ottawa

Walker	Kansas City
Weeks, J. H.	Lawrence
Werts, J. C.	Chanute
Whitaker, G. C.	Leavenworth

KENTUCKY

Ammon, C.	Maysville
Barr, D. P.	Paducah
Carpenter, W. J.	Lexington
Carpenter & Mullen	Lexington
Elrod Bros.	Lexington
Escott, J. V.	Louisville
Fox, E. H.	Danville
Gurlitz, H.	Sparta
Johns, W. E.	Lexington
Klauber, E.	Louisville
Mullen, J.	Lexington
Rose, P. H.	Paris
Stowe, H. D.	Louisville
Thum, M.	Louisville
Washburn, L. S.	Louisville
Webster, J. B.	Louisville
Wybrant	Louisville

LOUISIANA

Anderson, S. A.	New Orleans
Blessing, S. T.	New Orleans
Constant, A.	New Orleans
Constant & Moses	New Orleans
Cook	New Orleans
Davis Bros.	Hammond
Edwards, J. D.	New Orleans
Johnson, E. P.	New Orleans
Lilienthal, T.	New Orleans
McPherson, W. D.	New Orleans
Miller, H.	New Orleans
Moses, L.	New Orleans
Mugnier, G. F.	New Orleans

MAINE

Abbot, L. L.	Rumford
Adams, H.	Brunswick
Allen, A. H.	South Thomaston, Union
Armbrust, J. P.	Mt. Desert, Vinal Haven, Rockland
Averill, M. L.	Oldtown
Bailey, H.	Augusta
Barnes, G. W.	Brunswick
Berry, E. M.	Bridgton
Bixby & Buck	Skowhegan
Bonney, A. D.	Lewiston, Portland
Bowen, G. O.	Houlton
Bradley, B.	Bar Harbor
Brown, G. E.	Portland
Brown, R.	Rockland
Browne, B. P.	Bath
Bryson, J.	Houlton
Burnham, J. U. P.	Bethel, Norway
Burnham	South Paris
Butler, G. W.	Gorham
Carleton, C. G.	Waterville
Carleton S. L.	Portland
Carleton, W. W.	Saco
Carr, A. B.	Oldtown
Chase, S. J.	Foxcroft
Coffin, E. O.	Winthrop
Cole, B. F.	Biddeford
Collins, G. E.	Portland
Collins, G. F.	Bucksport
Conant, C. B.	Lewiston, Portland
Conant Bros.	Lewiston
Crockett, F. H.	Rockland
Cunningham, F. W.	Bucksport, South Liberty
Dakin, C. L.	Bangor
Dean, W. P.	Lincoln
Dill, H. P.	Phillips
Dinsmore, D. C.	Dover
Dole, A. K.	Bangor
Douglas & Cook	Lewiston
Dupee & Co.	Portland
Durgan, J. O.	Old Orchard Beach, Portland
Emery, E.	Bar Harbor
Farmer, S.	Phillips
Farrar, A. B.	Bangor
Fernald, E. C.	Thomaston
Friend, C. W.	Biddeford
Gannett & Morse	Augusta
Gooding, C. G.	Old Orchard Beach
Grant, M. H.	Calais
Green, J. A. & Son	Buckfield
Green, W. A.	Bethel
Green, W. H.	Paris
Gurney, C. S.	Mechanic Falls
Hale, F. F.	Portland
Hall, E. W.	Caribou
Hammond, C. E.	Winthrop
Hammond, I. L.	Lewiston
Hanson & Kimball	Augusta
Hardy, F. W. & J. P.	Bangor
Hatch, A.	Bath
Hearn	Old Orchard Beach, Portland
Heath & Smith	Portland
Hendee, J. S.	Augusta
Herrick, F. J.	Castine
Higgins, J. C.	Bath
Hill, J. M.	Rumford
Hinds, A. L.	Benton
Hobart, C. O.	Skowhegan
Hogan, J. W.	Brookfield
Holt, C. O.	Canton
Johnson, H. G.	Bethel
Jones, O. M.	Boothbay
Joy, B. F.	Ellsworth
Kilgore, H. L.	Belfast
King, M. F.	Portland
Lamson, J. H.	Portland
Lane, A. H.	Lincoln, Waldoboro
Lane, J. W.	Farmington, Waldoboro
Lane, W. E.	Vinal Haven
Lane	Camden
Larocque, F.	Lewiston
Lawrence, G. C.	Damariscotta
Libbey, C. E.	Calais
Lloyd	Round Lake
Locke, E. P.	Kingfield
Loring	Eastport
Lynd, A.	Perry
McArdle, W. C.	South Paris
McFadden, J. A.	Bath
McKenney, A. M.	Portland
McKenney, E. H.	Biddeford
Marston, C. L.	Bangor
Merrill, G. D.	Farmington
Merrill, I. W.	Farmington
Merrill, S.	Norway
Mills, H. A.	Camden
Mitchell, J. S.	Old Orchard Beach
Monroe, F. F.	Lewiston
Moore, O. M.	Phillips
Moore, O. O.	Waterville
Morrill, F. A.	Augusta
Morrill, F. H.	New Sharon
Morse, A. F.	Hallowell
Morse, L.	Thomaston
Morse, S. R.	Livermore Falls
Morse & Tuttle	Thomaston
Noble, E. A.	Waldoboro
Osgood, G. S.	Blue Hill
Osgood, Z. B.	Damariscotta
Osgood	Ellsworth
Paul, C. A.	Skowhegan
Peables, W. W.	Livermore Falls
Peck, J. M.	Portland
Philpot, F. C.	Limerick, Springvale
Pierce, O. J.	Waterville
Pierce, W.	Brunswick
Quimby, R.	Foxcroft
Robinson, H. W.	Skowhegan
Robinson, H. N.	Dixfield
Rowe, A. J.	Norway
Sanderson, C. S.	Lewiston
Sawtelle, E. E.	Biddeford
Sawyer, S. W.	Bangor
Scales, M. S.	Waterville
Senter, E. B.	Auburn
Shackford, A. W.	Farmington
Simmons, A. R.	Gardiner
Starbird, E. K.	Brunswick

Starbird, E. R.	Farmington
Stevens	Lewiston
Storer & Reed	Brunswick
Trask, M. G.	Bangor
Trask & Dole	Bangor
Tuttle, W. C.	Belfast
Tuttle	Thomaston
Tyler, A. D.	Biddeford
Vose, E.	Machias
Vose, S. S. & Son	Skowhegan, Waterville
Vose	Canton
Vose & Paul	Skowhegan
Wasgatt, L.	Cherryfield
Webber, H. L.	Saco, Old Orchard Beach
Webster, A. G.	Bucksport
Weston, E. R.	East Corinth
Weston, F. C.	Bangor
Wheeldon, G. R.	South Orrington, Winterport
Whittemore, A. J.	Old Orchard Beach
Work, W.	Brunswick
Wormell, E. S.	Portland
Worthley, W. E. G.	Lewiston
Wright, E. N.	Belfast
Wright & Dole	Belfast

MARYLAND

Balch Bros.	Baltimore
Bendann Bros.	Baltimore
Bishop Bros.	Cumberland
Broadbent, S.	Wilmington
Busey, N. H.	Baltimore
Butler, S.	Baltimore
Byerly, J. P.	Frederick
Chase, W. M.	Baltimore
Chase & Bachrach	Baltimore
Crawford, R. C.	Chesterton
Cummins, J.	Baltimore
Darnell, C. H.	Cumberland
Fischer Bros.	Baltimore
Fox, E. G.	Baltimore
Garwood, C.	Baltimore
Hallwig & Co.	Baltimore
Holyland, L.	Baltimore
Israel & Co.	Baltimore
Jones, H.	Baltimore
Lodore, B. F.	Elkton
Marken	Frederick
McLaughlin, G. B.	Cumberland
Millholland, J. A.	Mt. Savage
Pollock, H.	Baltimore
Pridgeon, J.	Baltimore
Recher, E. M.	Hagerstown
Rhoderick, G. C.	Middleton
Robinson, G. W.	Baltimore
Robinson, M. L.	Baltimore
Stewart, C. H.	Baltimore
Van Wagner & Dyer	Baltimore
Walzl, John	Baltimore
Walzl, Richard	Baltimore
Wilkes, D. J.	Baltimore

MASSACHUSETTS

Adams, S. F.	New Bedford
Albee, M. H.	Marlboro
Alden, A. E. & A. J.	Springfield
Alden, A. J.	Pittsfield
Alexander, D. C.	Arlington
Alger, F.	Winchendon
Allen, E. L.	Boston
Allen, W. T.	Leominster
Allen & Rowell	Boston
Anderson, A. W.	Haverhill
Baker, L.	Boston
Barnum, D.	Boston
Barritt	Hyde Park
Barton	Greenfield
Barton, G. L. D.	Boston
Bass, E. A.	Rockland
Batchelder & Black	Boston
Bates, A. A.	Whitinsville
Bates, J.	Boston
Bates, J. C.	Haverhill
Battelle, W.	Taunton
Baxter, O. F.	Chelsea
Bean, L. G.	Lowell
Beckford, C. A.	Salem
Beckwith, E. W.	Plymouth
Bemis, C. E.	Holliston
Berg, E.	Worcester
Best	Boston
Bierstadt Bros.	New Bedford
Black, J. W.	Waltham
Blair & Sons	Worcester
Bowers, W. T.	Lynn
Boynton, O. A.	Boston
Bradford, O. E.	Boston
Bradford & Barton	Greenfield
Bridges, C. L.	Rock Bottom
Brownell, A. C.	Fall River
Bryant, G. S.	Boston
Buchholtz, H.	Springfield
Buel & Seaver	Pittsfield
Burnham, T. R.	Boston
Burrell, D. T.	Bridgewater, Brockton
Burt, A.	Springfield
Burt, H. M.	Northampton
Bushby & Hart	Lynn
Butterfield, D. W.	Boston, Cambridge
Carlisle	Fall River
Carter, M. T.	Worcester
Caswell, J. H.	Holyoke
Chamberlain, J. N.	Southbridge
Chamberlin, E.	Arlington, Ayer
Chandler, M.	Marshfield
Childs, A. A.	Boston
Childs, R. H.	Taunton
Churchill, L. O.	Lowell
Chute, R. J.	Lynn, Melrose
Clapp, E. H.	Springfield
Clark, F.	Pittsfield
Clark, G. W.	Boston
Clough	Beverly
Clough, A. F.	Springfield
Coffrin, W.	Claremont
Colby, J. R.	Boston
Coleman, M. O. T.	Westfield
Collins, I. A.	Leominster
Cook, L. W.	Boston, Weymouth
Cook, O. H.	Danvers
Cook & Friend	Gloucester
Coombs, P.	Newburyport
Connors, S. S.	Westfield
Copeland, C. F.	Brockton
Cowee	West Gardner
Critcherson, G. P.	Leominster, Worcester
Crittenden, J. H.	Fall River
Crockett, F. H.	Rockland
Cross, A. B.	Salem
Currier & Jones	Amesbury, Salisbury
Dame, L.	Newburyport
Danforth, C. H.	Cambridge
Daniels, A. E.	Warren
Davenport, S. T. & S. R.	West Upton
Davis, E. G.	Leominster
Davis, F.	Worcester
Davis, H. J.	Greenfield
Davis, N. S.	Somerville
Day, E.	Waltham
Dewey, R. H.	Pittsfield
Douglas, R.	Lowell
Dunshee, E. P.	Boston
Dyer & Co.	Lawrence
Emery, W. H.	Athol
Evans & Soule	Boston
Fairbanks, J. B.	Natick
Farrar, C. H. J.	Jamaica Plain
Fitton, W. H.	Worcester
Fogg, C. G.	Salem
Folsom, A. H.	Roxbury, Boston
Foss, E. J.	Boston
Fowler, F. W.	Salisbury
Freeman, C. H.	Westboro
Freeman, G. W.	Charlestown
Freeman, J.	Nantucket
Friend, H.	Goucester
Frost, S. F.	Boston
Fuller, G. E.	Lynn
Gardner, W. B.	Somerset, Sherborn

Gates, T.	Westboro, Somerville
Gay, E. R.	Fall River
Gifford, N.	New Bedford
Gilchrest, G. E.	Lowell
Goldsmith & Lazelle	Springfield
Goss, E. L.	Wakefield
Gott, C.	Fitchburg
Goulart, M.	New Bedford
Gould, F. H.	Woburn
Graves, M. H.	Marblehead
Green, G. D.	Holyoke
Guy Bros.	Salem
Hall, H. A.	Lowell
Hall, J.	Great Barrington
Hamor, A. B.	Lawrence
Harriman, W. H.	Georgetown
Hatch, S. R.	Milford
Hatstat, B. F.	Boston
Hawes, J. J.	Boston
Heard, J. H.	Boston
Hemold	Clinton
Heywood, J.	Boston
Hill, J. B.	Beverly
Hills, E. R.	Brookline
Hoag Bros.	Springfield
Hosmer, A. W.	Concord
Houghton & Knowlton	Northampton
Howard, A.	Winchester
Howard, L. B.	Brockton
Howard, S. W. S.	Marshfield, West Bridgewater
Howes, B. B.	Marblehead
Hurd & Smith	North Adams
Hurd & Ward	North Adams
Ide, D. T.	Attleboro
Ireland, G. H.	Springfield
James, E. L.	Southampton
Jaynes, E. L.	Spencer
Jenkins, H.	Barre
Jones, G. H.	Ipswich
Jones & Stiff	Salem
Kidder, G. R.	Watertown
Kimball & Gould	Haverhill
King, H. B.	Taunton
King, T.	Cambridge
Knowlton Bros.	Northampton
Knox, E.	East Boston
Knox, H.	Chicopee
Knox, O. C.	Athol
Latto, J. C.	South Boston
Lawrence, F.	Worcester
Lawrence, J. D.	Northampton
Leck, G. H.	Lawrence
Lefavour, T. S.	Salem
Lefavour & Clough	Beverly
Leland, E. J.	Worcester
Lesure, H. A.	Orange
Lewis, R. B.	Hudson
Lewis, T.	Cambridgeport
Lock & Robbins	Plymouth
Lombard	West Medford
Loomis, G. H.	Boston
Lord, R. E.	Boston
Lovell, J. C.	Amherst
Lowe, F. L.	East Cambridge
Lufkin & Hamor	Lawrence
Marshall, A.	Boston
Marshall, W. I.	Fitchburg
Maxham, L. M.	Taunton
McIntosh, H. P.	Newburyport
Meinerth, C.	Newburyport
Mealey, W. W.	Lawrence
Merrill, J. & Sons	Lowell
Merriman, E. D. & L.	Greenfield
Miller, R. A.	Boston
Mitchell, D. S.	Boston
Moore, F. J.	Westfield
Moore, G. W.	Athol
Morley, E. A.	East Lee
Morrill, E. L.	Lowell
Moseley, R. E.	Haverhill, Newburyport
Moulton, J. C.	Fitchburg
Moulton, J. W. & J. S.	Salem
Nickerson, G. H.	Provincetown
Notman & Campbell	Boston
Nye, W. B.	New Bedford
Ollis, H.	Winchendon
Ormsby & Silsbee	Boston
Osborn, D. C.	Princeton, Sudbury
Packard, H. T.	East Bridgewater
Parlow, L. F.	New Bedford
Patch, J. K.	Shelburne Falls
Peabody, E. N.	Salem
Peebles, O. M.	Athol
Perkins, E. R.	Salem
Perrigo, O. M.	Medfield
Pollock, C.	Boston
Pond, F. L.	Foxboro
Popkins, B. F.	Greenfield
Prescott, D. K.	Boston
Prescott, W. A.	Methuen
Price, E. C.	Westfield
Pritchard, T. P.	Salem
Proctor, G. K.	Salem
Proctor Bros.	Gloucester
Pusey, W. E.	South Adams
Putnam, A. H.	Ayer
Putnam, G. T.	Barre
Putnam, T.	Middleborough
Ramsdell, H. M.	North Adams
Rand, H. M.	Bridgewater
Rand & Latto	Milton Lower Falls, South Boston
Rankin, A. K.	Taunton
Ransom, H.	Sharon
Reed, D. T. & S. C.	Newburyport
Reed, H. J.	Worcester
Reed, S. C.	Georgetown
Richardson, C. F.	Wakefield
Richardson, L. A.	Leominster
Richardson & Son	Marlboro
Robbins, W. S.	Plymouth
Roberts, R. L.	Canton
Robinson, H. N.	Reading
Rogers, J. S. E.	Gloucester
Rogers & North	Springfield
Rohrbach, S.	Millburg
Rollins, E. G.	Gloucester
Rowell, E.	Boston
Sanborn, N. C.	Lowell
Sargent, B. & B. F.	Chelsea
Seaver, C.	Boston, Grantville, West Newton
Shaw, J.	Middleborough
Shaw & Lord	Boston
Shiloh, C. D.	Malden
Shute, C. H. & Son	Edgartown
Skinner, F. A.	Plymouth
Smith, D.	Athol
Smith, D. K.	Lowell
Smith, H. G.	Boston
Smith, H. W.	New Bedford
Sonrel, A.	Boston
Soule, J. P.	Boston
Southworth, A. S.	Charleston
Southworth & Hawes	Boston
Spear, J. H.	Springfield
Spencer, D. H.	Hudson
Spooner, D. B.	Springfield
Staniford, G. E.	Salem
Stiff, C. W.	Danvers
Strand, L. G.	Worcester
Swain, F. C.	Malden
Sweet, J. L.	Clinton
Sweetser, C. A.	Springfield
Sylvester, S. H.	Middleborough
Taber, C.	New Bedford
Talbot, H. N.	North Easton
Taylor & Preston	Salem
Thompson, E.	East Abington
Thompson, W. C.	Amesburg, Salisbury
Thompson & Tyler	Rockland
Tirrell, G. W.	East Weymouth, Nantasket
Towle, S.	Lowell
Townsend, C. H.	Southbridge
Turner, A. M.	South Abington, Brockton
Tuttle, C. B.	Lynn
Van Patten & Tice	Great Barrington
Vickery, D. A.	Haverhill

Waite, E. O.	Bolton, Worcester
Warner, H. D.	Worcester
Warner, M. P.	Holyoke
Warren, H. F.	Waltham
Webster, W. T.	Lynn
Wheeler & Barton	Boston
Whitcomb, I. A.	Lawrence
White, T. E. M.	New Bedford
Wilkinson, O. R.	Medford
Williams, J. H.	South Scituate
Willis & Fisher	Milford
Wires, W. M.	Lynn
Woodward & Son	Taunton

MICHIGAN

Allen, R. L.	Detroit
Andrew & Carson	Hillsdale
Armstrong, W. A.	Saginaw
Arnold & Willyoung	Detroit
Bailey & Whitesides	Marquette
Baldwin, S. C.	Grand Rapids, Kalamazoo
Ball, A. P.	Eaton Rapids
Bardwell, J.	Detroit
Barrows, J. C.	Mendon
Bean, L. W.	Plainwell
Bigelow, L. G.	Detroit
Bingham, H. L.	Kalamazoo
Black, L.	Detroit
Boozer, H. W.	Grand Rapids, Ionia
Brubaker, C. B.	Houghton
Brubaker & Whitesides	Marquette
Brummitt, W. H.	Pontiac
Cadwallader, J.	Detroit
Cain, W. C.	Alpena
Carpenter	Adrian
Childs, F. F.	Houghton, Marquette
Earl & Hawley	Detroit
Emery, A. G.	Marquette
Faulkner, M. M.	Niles
Fenton & Wendell	Mackinac
Foley	Mackinac
Goodridge Bros.	East Saginaw
Greenwood, J. P.	Adrian
Grelling, G.	Detroit
Hall, B. C.	Lansing
Harmer & Verner	Bay City
Hiler, M.	Lowell
Hoag, J. M.	Adrian
Hook, W. E.	Marquette
Huler, E. P.	Sturgis
Jenney, J. A.	Flint
Johnston, T. H.	Detroit
Laricheleere, E. L.	Escanaba
Lawson, N. B.	Muskegon
Moulton, L.	Muskegon
Myers, W. W.	Iona
Rose, J. A.	Hillsdale
Schellhaus, Mrs. L. W.	Ada
Schoff	Ann Arbor
Scotford, J. H.	Lansing
Sessions, I. R.	Olivet
Sheehan	Ann Arbor
Spencer, H. S.	Petosky
Tripp & Schellhaus	Coldwater
Van Slyke	Mason
Walcott	Coldwater
Walter	Cascade
Watson, J. E.	Detroit
Webster	Constantine
Whalen, A. J.	Northville
Wheeler, L. F.	Tecumseh
White, W. S.	Kalamazoo
Whitesides	Marquette
Willyoung, J.	Detroit

MINNESOTA

Austin, J.	Fergus Falls
Ayers, E.	Dodge Center
Beal	Minneapolis
Bingham, F. V.	Medford, Northfield
Brown, W. H.	Red Wing
Brownell, J.	St. Paul
Burnham, A. F.	Faribault
Burritt & Pease	St. Paul
Butler, W. E.	Minneapolis
Caswell & Davy	Duluth
Chesley, G. W.	Owatonna
Cook, J. C.	Rochester
Elmer & Tenney	Winana
Everitt, F. F.	Mankato
Farr, H. R.	Minneapolis
Fearon, R. N.	Minneapolis
Floyd & Power	Minneapolis
Fouch, J. H.	Excelsior
Gaylord, P. B.	Duluth
Gaylord & Thompson	Duluth
Hardy, J.	Fergus Falls
Harvey, E.	Minneapolis
Haynes, F. J.	Morehead, St. Paul
Hillman, W. J.	Cannon Falls
Hoard & Tenney	Winona
Hudson, C. H.	St. Paul
Huntington & Bartram	Minneapolis
Illingworth, W. H.	St. Paul
Illingworth & McLeish	St. Paul
Jacoby, W. H.	Minneapolis
Johnson, C. F.	Duluth
Loomis, F. E.	Stillwater
Martin	St. Paul
McLeish & Cressy	St. Paul
More & Hager	Blue Earth City
Nowack, M.	Minneapolis
Park Bros.	Rochester
Schlattman Bros.	St. Paul
Sinclair, J.	Stillwater
Steele, R. E.	St. Paul
Stiff, C. W.	St. Paul
Stohlmann, G.	St. Paul
Sumner, I. E.	Northfield
Tenney, C. A.	Winona
Thomas, J. E.	Fergus Falls
Thomas, W.	Owatonna
Trenham, N. J.	Alexandria
Upton, B. F.	Minneapolis
Washburn & Bennett	Red Wing
Webb, D. W.	Minneapolis
Whitney, J. E.	St. Paul
Whitney & Zimmerman	St. Paul
Wiggins, S. T.	Winona
Zimmermann, C. A.	St. Paul

MISSISSIPPI

Blanks, A. L.	Vicksburg
Burke, J. J.	Canton
Cory, H. C.	Holly Springs
Gurney	Natchez
Hammersley, C.	Aberdeen
Herrick, H. J.	Vicksburg
Herrick & Dirr	Vicksburg
Hughes & Lakin	Natchez
Kutted, E. V.	Raymond
Lowd, W. Q.	Jackson
Norman, H. C.	Natchez
Pierce	Water Valley
Shinn, H. A.	Meriden

MISSOURI

Babbitt & Shannon	Kansas City
Benecke, R.	St. Louis
Boehl & Koenig	St. Louis
Bower, M. B.	Kansas City
Bower Bros.	West Kansas City
Bushnell, E. P.	Jefferson
Cooper, B. S.	Waverly
Cramer, Gross & Co.	St. Louis
Crosby, G. L.	Hannibal
Faulhaber, G. L.	Sedalia
Fitzgibbon, J. H.	St. Louis
Fox, A. J.	St. Louis
Frazer, Mrs.	St. Genevieve
Goebel, R.	St. Charles
Graham, E. D.	Mexico
Guerin, F. W.	St. Louis
Hallwig, G. O.	St. Louis
Hammersley, C.	St. Louis
Hicks, J. T.	Liberty

Hoelke & Benecke	St. Louis
Johnson, W. S.	Springfield
Judd, W. S.	Carthage
Kramer & Gross	St. Louis
Macurdy, J. C.	Boonville
McLaughlin, T. C.	Breckenridge
Mitchell, T. L.	St. Louis
Outley, J. J.	St. Louis
Ploetz, J.	Kansas City
Rino, O.	St. Louis
Schlater, P.	Kansas City
Scholten, J. A.	St. Louis
Thomas, Frank	Columbia
Thomson	Kansas City
Tilford, W. H.	St. Louis
Uhlman & Rippel	St. Joseph
Wilkinson, J. W.	Ironton
Williams & Thomas	Kansas City
Winter, F.	Kansas City

MONTANA

Beal & Ayres	Big Timber
Belveal, E. S.	Butte
Brewster, J. C.	Helena
Bundy, O. C.	Helena, Virginia City
Douglas, M.	Helena
Forsythe, N. A.	Butte
Huffman, L. A.	Miles City
Rutter, T. H.	Deer Ledge City
Train, E. H.	Helena

NEBRASKA

Cross, W. R.	Niobrara, Norfolk
Eaton, E. L.	Omaha
Great Western Photo. Co.	Omaha
Heyn	Omaha
Jackson, W. H.	Omaha
Jackson Bros.	Omaha
Mitchell, McGowan & Co.	Omaha
Russell, A. J.	Omaha
Smith (Small?), A. M.	Nebraska City
Trivelpiece, R. M.	Gibbon
Wakeley, G. D.	Omaha

NEVADA

Beals, A. J.	Gold Hill
Bennete, J. J.	Pioche
Noe	Virginia City
Sutterley Bros.	Virginia City
Tandy, H. C.	Winnemucca

NEW HAMPSHIRE

Aiken, J. B.	Franklin
Aldrich, G. H.	Littleton
Allen, W. F.	East Jaffrey
Archambault	Suncook
Bagley, E. T.	Lebanon
Batchelder, J.	Andover
Bliven, R. H.	Wolfeboro
Bly, H. O.	Hanover
Bonney, A. D.	Monroe
Bott, H.	Walpole
Bradbury, W. J.	Wilton
Brigham, E. T.	Dover
Brown, H. J.	Newport
Bugbee, F. E.	Wilton
Burns, C. K.	Manchester
Cady, W. J.	Hinsdale
Carr, B.	Concord
Chapin, W. P.	Walpole
Chase, E. L.	Keene
Cheney, C. B.	Oxford
Clark & Lindsay	Laconia
Clough, A. F.	Oxford
Clough, A. H.	Warren
Clough & Kimball	Concord
Colby, L. W.	Manchester
Copeland, O. H.	New Market
Copp, E. J.	Nashua
Couch, C. M.	Concord
Culver, W. W.	Lebanon
Currier, H. J.	New London
Daggett, M. L.	Manchester
Davis Bros.	Portsmouth
Drew, A. P.	Dover
Ellinwood, J. G.	Manchester
Fifield, H. S.	Lincoln
Follansbee, E. R.	East Canaan
Foster, B. F.	Milford
French & Sawyer	Keene
Furnald, D. O.	Manchester
Gardner, C. C.	Bristol, Great Falls
Gerould, E. P.	Charleston
Gleason, W. B.	Whitefield
Glenton, E.	Nashua
Goss, F. H.	Milford
Gould, E. P.	Concord
Greene, M. V. D.	Nashua
Gregory, A. W.	Portsmouth
Hamilton, S. C.	Nashua
Harriman, M. C.	Warner
Hartford, G. W. C.	Rochester
Hibbard, C. B.	Lisbon
Hoag, A. B.	Center Sandwich
Hobbs, W. H.	Exeter
Hodge, E. B.	Plymouth
Keniston, J. F.	Milford
Kilburn Bros.	Littleton
Kilburn, B. W.	Littleton
Kimball, H. A.	Concord
Kimball, W. G. C.	Concord
Kimball & Childs	Manchester
Lamprey, M. S.	Farmington, Fisherville
Lawrence, C. A.	Nashua
Lewis, C. E.	Dover, Wolfeboro
Lindsay, L. F.	Laconia
Lovejoy, C. A.	Nashua
Lovejoy, E.	Milford
Marshall, C. C.	Fisherville
McClary, C. F.	Hillsborough Bridge
McIntyre, H. C.	Concord
Meinerth, C.	Portsmouth
Miller & Wilson	Lancaster
Moon, T. C.	Laconia
Moore, H. P.	Concord
Morrison	Haverhill
Morse, S. M.	Nashua
Moulton, F. J.	Plymouth, Tilton
Moulton, J. S.	Amherst
Munger, A.	Hampton
Newell, L. V.	Portsmouth
Osgood, H. W.	Pittsfield
Parker, J.	Newport
Pattee, H. M.	Claremont, Enfield
Pease, W. H.	North Conway
Philpot, F. C.	Great Falls
Pollard	Haverhill
Poor, B. H.	Franklin
Pressey, W. M.	Plymouth
Quint, S. D.	Manchester
Rice, D. S.	East Jaffrey
Robbins, F.	Keene
Robinson, J. B.	Exeter
Scripture, G. H.	Peterborough
Sherwood, J. A.	Littleton
Simon, D. A.	Manchester
Stark, A. D.	Manchester
Stevens, G. E.	Claremont, North Weare
Swaine, S.	Rochester
Tebbetts & Lindsay	Laconia
Thomas, T. C.	Alton Bay
Ward, E. D.	Lake Village
Webster, G. A.	Dover
Weller, F. G.	Littleton
White, F.	Lancaster
Whittemore, A. J.	Rochester
Wilkins, J.	Suncook
Young, E. J.	Compton Village

NEW JERSEY

Aitken, W.	Millvale
Alexander & Stevens	Morristown
Astle, D.	Vineland
Campbell, A. S.	Elizabeth
Carvalho, D. N.	Red Bank
Cheeseman, J. F. & L. R.	Trenton
Clark, D.	New Brunswick

Cook, H.	Sandy Hook
Costello	Jersey City
Crane, T. F.	Newark
Doremus, J. P.	Paterson
Eaton, W. C.	Newark
Edwards, C. E.	Bridgton
Ellinger, J. R.	Lambertville
Emmell, H. G.	Morristown
Fritz, F. Z.	Lambertville
Good, J.	Trenton
Green, J. T.	Jersey City
Gubelman, T.	Newark
Hill, W. H.	Elizabeth
Johnson, L. D.	Vineland
Kelley	Somerville
Lacey, E. G.	Dover
Lane, C.	Long Branch, Red Bank
Lee	Danville
Letts, J. M.	Bordenton
Lockwood, F. C.	Freehold
McCall, G. H.	Salem
Morse, S. R.	Atlantic City
Moses, M.	Trenton
Pach Bros.	Long Branch
Phillips, H.	Atlantic City
Piard, V.	Jersey City
Poe, R.	Hackensack
Price, F. H.	Elizabeth
Reeve, J. C.	Lambertville
Reid, J.	Paterson
Robinson, C. C.	Newark
Roth, J.	Freehold
Royle, V.	Paterson
Scott, J. C.	New Brunswick
Seeler, E. E.	Trenton
Shear, S.	Asbury Park
Sims, A.	Camden
Smith, J. E.	Bordenton
Stauffer, W. H.	Asbury Park, Trenton
Sunderlin, J. C.	Flemington
Sunderlin, Mary	Flemington
Swain, W. M.	Mt. Holly
Thorn, G.	Plainfield
Vandergrift, J. A.	Burlington
Warren, G. K.	Princeton
Weitfle, C.	Dover
Willard, O. H.	Cape May

NEW MEXICO

Addis, A. S.	Silver City
Bennett, H.	Santa Fe
Bennett & Brown	Santa Fe
Bliss, W. P.	Santa Fe
Brown, N.	Santa Fe
Carter	Albuquerque
Hiester, H. T.	Santa Fe
Henry Bros.	Santa Fe
Irvine & McKenzie	Santa Fe
Wittich, Ben	Albuquerque
Wittich & Russell	Albuquerque

NEW YORK

Abbott, A. A.	Utica
Abbott, R. R.	Union Springs
Akehurst	Utica
Alden Bros.	New York, Saratoga
Allen, J. H.	Union
Allerton	Port Jervis
Alley, A. H.	Moravia
Alman, L.	Lake Mohapae
Anthony, E. & H. T.	New York
Appleton, D.	New York
Armstrong, J. E.	Mt. Morris
Arnold, A.	Greenwich
Arnold, C. R.	Massena
Arnold, T. J.	Saratoga
Auchmoody	Rondout
Austen, J.	Oswego
Averill, A. K.	Plattsburgh
Avery, H. S.	Morris
Avery, R. S.	Pulaski
Babbitt, P. D.	Niagara Falls
Bacon, F. W.	Rochester
Baker, W. J.	Buffalo, Utica
Baldwin, G. W.	Keeseville
Barker, G.	Niagara Falls
Barnard, G. N.	Oswego, Syracuse
Barnett, T.	Niagara Falls
Barnum, D.	Cortland
Beard & Mead	Waverly
Beckel Bros.	Lockport
Beecher, L. G.	Olean
Beer & Co.	New York
Bellewyn, G. W.	Cobbleskill
Bickelmann, C. O.	Tannersville
Bierstadt, C.	Niagara Falls
Bill, C. K.	New York
Bliss, H. L.	Buffalo
Bookhout Bros.	New York
Bowdish, N. S.	Richfield Springs
Brill, J.	New York
Buell, C. W.	Warsaw
Burgess, N. G.	Brooklyn
Burritt, J. C.	Ithaca
Carmon, C.	Andes
Carnell, C. V. & Mrs.	Waterloo
Carriel, W.	Cuba
Carter, G. W.	Lowville
Champ, W. M.	Geneseo
Clapper, J. M.	Troy
Clark	Oneida
Clarke, O. B.	Brookville
Clench, F. B.	Lockport
Cobb, G. M.	Binghamton
Collins, E. M.	Oswego
Comstock, A. B.	Waverly
Conkey, G. W.	Glens Falls
Cook, E. W.	Albany
Cooley, A. A.	Cooperstown
Cooper, C. S.	Clyde
Copeland, G. T.	Gloversville
Cornell, C. S.	Stamford
Cornell, C. L. & N. L.	Randolph
Crane, J. S.	Cohoes
Crane & Baldwin	Ogdensburg
Crocker, M.	Perry
Crowell, F. S.	Kokosing
Crowell, R. W.	Byersville
Crum, R. D.	Watkins Glen
Curtis, G. E.	Niagara Falls
Daft, L.	Troy
Davie, C. L.	Bolivar
Dow, J. M.	Ogdensburg
Drier	New York
Drury, A. K.	LeRoy
Dunshee Bros.	Rochester
Eagles, J. D.	Glenora, Ithaca
Eales, F. A.	Rochester
Edsall, F.	Goshen
Edwards, T.	Cortland
Elton, G.	Palmyra
Emerson, E.	Troy
Epler	Saratoga
Ernsberger & Ray	Auburn
Estabrook, E. M.	New York
Evans, E. D.	Corning
Evans, O. B.	Buffalo, Niagara Falls
Everett, L. C.	Troy
Farrington, M.	Delhi
Fay & Farmer	Malone
Ferris, C.	Malone
Fillmore, L. H.	Ticonderoga, Whitehall
Finley & Sons	Canandaigua
Fisher, A. J.	New York
Flagg, C. F.	Ovid
Flanders, W. C.	Lansingburgh
Folsom, E. S.	Katonah
Folsom Bros.	Brewster
Forshew, F.	Hudson
Fowler & Minor	Waterville
Fox & Gates	Rochester
Frear, W.	Ithaca
Fredericks, C. D.	New York
Fronti	New York
Gardner, W. M.	Cooperstown
Gates, M. E.	Rochester
Gates, W. D.	Havana
Gates Bros.	Watkins Glen

Gates & Malette	Syracuse
Gaylord, M.	Medina
Gelderd, W. P.	Port Chester
Gibbard, C. G.	Auburn
Gilman	Canajoharie
Glosser, H.	New York
Godfrey & Noble	Dansville
Goldbacher, E.	New York
Gorham, L. B.	Mt. Kisco
Griswold, V. M.	Pecksville
Gurney, J. & Son	New York
Haas, P.	New York
Haines & Elliott	Albany
Hall, W. L.	Trumansburg
Hall Bros.	Brooklyn
Hamilton, H.	Peersville
Hammond	Greenport
Harris, E. P.	Skaneateles
Hart, A. P.	Elmira
Hart, C. S.	Watertown
Havens	Sing Sing
Heinz, J.	Albany
Hensel, L.	Port Jervis
Hewitt, F. E.	Nunda
Hine, B.	Walton
Hoard & Upham	Jamestown
Holbrook, W. H.	Watertown
Holmes, W. H.	New York
Holt & Gray	New York
Hope, J. D.	Watkins
Hopkins, A. C.	Palmyra
Hopkins, G. P.	Albion
Hotchkiss, A. E.	Norwich
Hovey, E. P. & J. S.	Rome
Hoyer, C. E.	Staten Island
Hoyer, H.	New York
Hurd, L. F.	Greenwich
Irish, G. S.	Glens Falls, Lake George
Irvine, J. A.	Albany
Irving, J.	Troy
James, W. E.	Brooklyn
Jaynes, A. D.	Corning
Jaynes, G. M.	Batavia
Johnson, A. A.	Cazenovia
Johnson, E. M.	Crown Point
Jordan, J. L. & H. A.	Syracuse
Joy, H. N.	Ovid
Judd, M. E.	Syracuse
Kent, J. H.	Brockport, Rochester
Kesslar, J. J.	Marathon
Kinney, B. C.	Salem
Knight, W. M.	Buffalo
Knight & Eales	Batavia
Kuester & Wyer	Yonkers
Langdon, C. E.	Batavia
Larkin, J. E.	Elmira
Lazier, H.	Syracuse
Letts, L. M.	Dundee
Lewis, A.	Lake Mahopec
Lewis, E.	Kingston
Lindsly, H. R.	Auburn
Lloyd	Waterford
Lloyd, J. H.	Cohoes
Lockwood	New York
Loeffler, J.	Tompkinville
Lovejoy, C. L.	Rome
Marsh, C. M.	Havana
Masterson, E. P.	Port Jervis
Mather & Lyons	Cazenovia
Maynard	White Plains
McDonnald & Sterry	Albany, Saratoga
McIntyre, A. C.	Alexandria Bay
McKernon, P. H.	Saratoga
McLeish & Evans	Corning
McPherson, J.	Niagara Falls
Mead & Beard	Waverly
Meade Bros.	Albany
Meinerth Bros.	Cohoes
Merriman, M. L.	Copenhagen
Mills, J. C.	Pen Yan
Monroe, G. H. & M. H.	Rochester
Monroe, M. H.	Alexandria Bay
Moore, J. R.	Jamestown, Trenton Falls
Morand, A.	Brooklyn

Morris, S. H.	Auburn
Morse & Fronti	New York
Mould, W. & Son	Keeseville
Munday & Williams	Utica
Nims, W.	Ft. Edward
North, A. M.	Afton, Oneonta
North, G. H.	Canandaigua
North, W. C.	Utica
Oakley, A. N.	Rochester
Oliver, F. W.	Oswego
O'Neill, H.	New York
Ormsby, J.	Plattsburgh
Orr & Sons	Glens Falls
Pach, G. W.	New York
Palmer, C. A.	Newburgh
Parker, H. R.	Sherburne
Paterson, U. H.	Binghamton
Paul & Curtis	New York
Pearsall, A.	Brooklyn
Pease, C. H.	Schuylerville
Pease, J. L.	Oneida
Peck, F. B.	Dodleville
Plimpton	Lockport
Pollock, G. E. & W. E.	New York
Pond, C. L.	Buffalo
Pringle, C.	Freedom
Ranger, W. V.	Syracuse
Ranger & Elton	Palmyra
Ranger & Frazee	Syracuse
Ravell, C. H.	Lyons
Ready, J.	Boonville
Record & Epler	Saratoga
Reilly, J. J.	Niagara Falls
Richardson & Clark	Oneida
Rider, J. A.	Hornellsville, Wellesville
Roberts, J. B.	Clyde, Rochester
Roche, T. C.	New York
Rockwood, G. G.	New York
Rogers, S.	Tarrytown
Rood & Emerson	New York
Ropes, H.	New York
Rutherford, W.	Bath
Sanderson, I. H.	Rochester
Sarony, N.	New York
Saunders, I.	Alfred Center, Friendship
Schira, L. J.	Niagara Falls
Schoonmaker & Hill	Troy
Scofield, C. H.	Utica
Sedgwick, S. J.	Newton, Queens
Seely, W. T.	Elmira
Seward, H. W.	Utica
Sherwood, C. C.	Peekskill
Simon, A. W.	Buffalo
Singhi, W. G.	Binghamton
Sipperly, W. H.	Mechanicsville, Saratoga, Schuylersville
Slee Brothers	Poughkeepsie
Smith, A. H.	Lima
Smith, W. G.	Cooperstown
Spencer, S.	Ithaca
Spencer, W. F.	Baldwin
Stacey, C. A.	Lockport
Stacy, G.	New York
Stoddard, S. R.	Glens Falls
Sunderlin, J. R.	Ft. Edward
Sutton, W. L.	Hornellsville
Tall & Summers	Waterloo
Tallman, C. W.	Batavia
Thomalen, E. A.	Saratoga
Thompson, J.	Niagara Falls
Tice, A. W.	Ellenville
Tomlinson, C.	Elmira, Pen Yan
Tooker, T. D.	Avon
Tousley, H. S.	Keeseville
Towne, W. H.	Lansingburgh
Tripp, H.	Schenectedy
Trowbridge & Jennings	Auburn
Tubbs, G. L.	Geneva
Tubbs, S. E.	Auburn
Tucker, W. M.	Little Falls
Tutbill & Teed	Moravia

Upson, J. T.	Buffalo
Vail, J. C. & L. P.	Palmyra
Vail, J. P.	Geneva
Van Aken, E. M.	Elmira, Lowville
Van Wagner, I. M.	Nyack
Veeder, A.	Albany
Waite, W. M.	Troy
Wales, H. R.	Rome
Walker, L. E.	Warsaw
Walker, S. L.	Poughkeepsie
Webster, G. R.	Rochester
Webster & Albee	Rochester
Weil, P. E.	New York
Weld, J. A.	Oneonta
Weld & Avery	Pen Yan
Wells, H. M.	Cambridge
Wendt Bros.	Albany
Wentworth, S. M.	Cherry Valley
Whitaker, R. B.	Liberty
Whitney Beckwith & Paradise	New York
Wildey, O. H.	Homer, Skaneateles
Williamson, C. H.	Brooklyn
Wing & Bush	Castile
Woodward, C. W.	Rochester
Wyer, H. S.	Yonkers
Young, C.	Sinclairville
Young, R. Y.	New York
Zahner, M. H.	Niagara Falls

NORTH CAROLINA

Blackmore, J. H.	Mt. Airy
Engle, J. F.	Asheville
Engle & Taylor	Asheville
Harris, T. C.	Oxford
Herff, V.	Raleigh
Heywood, J. D.	New Berne
Lindsey, T. H.	Asheville
Morgan, R.	Morgantown
Robertson, W. T.	Asheville
Sciadin	Sapphire
Taylor, N. W.	Asheville
Van Orsdell, C. M.	Wilmington

NORTH DAKOTA

Barry, D. F.	Bismark
Berg, J.	Grand Forks
Caswell, W.	Grand Forks
Foster, E. H.	Jamestown
Haynes, F. J.	Fargo
Judd, C. L.	Jamestown
Moore, C.	Pembina

OHIO

Adams, J.	Elmore
Alden, A. R.	Oberlin
Alley, E. H.	Toledo
Baker, F. L.	North Star
Ball, J. P.	Cincinnati
Bartlett, G. O.	Fremont
Battels, B. F.	Akron
Beach, G. F.	Seville
Beach, T. A.	Delaware
Beckwith, M. E.	Cleveland
Bendix, O. E.	Akron
Benedict, H.	Put-In-Bay, Seville
Bennett, W. P.	Marietta
Billinghurst, C. J.	McArthur
Blackman Bros.	Napoleon
Blakeslee & Moore	Ashtabula
Bliven, R. H.	Elmore, Toledo
Bowdish, R. F.	Columbia
Brooks, D. H.	Plain City
Bunker, H. P.	Dayton
Cadwallader	Marietta
Carter, F. M.	Granville
Cassedy, A. J.	Wooster
Coddington & Alsbach	Middletown
Cook, C. E.	Seville
Cook, W. H.	Youngstown
Coughlin & Naeff	Conneaut
Courtney & Apple	Middletown
Covell, F. M.	Rock Creek
Crew, E.	Alliance
Crowell, F. S.	Mt. Vernon
Decker, E.	Cleveland
Dickerson, A. F.	Coshocton
Dickinson, W.	New Richmond
Doty, G. W.	Wooster
Douglass, S. W.	Marietta
Edmondson, G. W.	Plymouth
Eggleston, H. L.	Chardon
Elliott, J. M.	Columbia
Emery, R.	Plymouth
Faze, W. A.	Painesville
Fickes, J. C.	Steubenville
Filson, D.	Steubenville
Foljambe, C.	Cleveland
Foltz, W. E.	Akron
Freedle, J. W.	Cleveland
French, C. M.	Garrettsville, Youngstown
Frisbie	Sandusky
Gano & Clark	Springfield
Gaugher, S. P.	Bellevue
Golden, J. A.	Roseville
Gove & Frees	Tiffin
Graffe	Orrville
Greene, J. M.	Cleveland
Griswold, M. M.	Columbia, Lancaster, Tiffin
Grobe, R.	Fremont
Hammond, N. H.	Sandusky
Haring, J. C.	Massilon
Harlan & Carter	Eaton
Hawkins, B. E.	Steubenville
Hibbard, A. K.	Cleveland
Hoeg & Quick	Cincinnati
Hoover, J. H.	Cincinnati
Huling, D. A.	Cleveland
Johnson, J. H.	New Vienna
Johnson & Menzel	Cleveland
Johnston, A. C.	Greentown
Johnston, W. T.	Mansfield
Kellogg, C. H.	Milan
Kile & Warwick	Dayton, Miamisburg
Knowlton, I. N.	Cumberland
Kohl, W. M.	Cincinnati
Krug, S.	Cincinnati
Landy, J.	Cincinnati
Large, G. W.	Yellow Springs
Lauk, I. A.	Zanesville
LeRoy, F. L.	Youngstown
Liebich	Cleveland
Limpert & North	Columbus
Marshall, M. K.	Circleville
Mason, J. S.	Medina
McDonald, G. A.	Coshocton
McIntire, O.	Canton, Youngstown
McLain, J. D.	Logan
Mendenhall, R.	Cleveland
Meyer, J. H.	Cincinnati
Monosmith, D.	Akron
Muhrman, C. H.	Cincinnati
Nason, J. H.	Cleveland
Nason, P. C.	Columbus
Neff, P.	Gambier
North, W. C.	Cleveland
North & Oswald	Cleveland
Oakley, A. L.	Tiffin
Oldroyd, W.	Columbus
Osbourn, J. W.	Alliance
Phelps, H. M.	Morgan
Platt, A. C. & C. W.	Sandusky
Platt, A. C. & H. M.	Oberlin
Poister, F. E.	Kent
Potter, J. C. & Son	Elyria
Potter, W. H.	Mansfield
Price, A.	Cleveland
Rawlins, W. J.	Wooster
Reeves, H.	Newburgh
Reimann, J.	Cincinnati
Reiterman	Findlay
Roberts, L. W.	Urbana
Rockwell, D. W.	Elyria
Rogers, H. F.	Hamilton
Ryder, J. F.	Cleveland
Sawtelle, W. F.	Wellington
Shaw, T.	Chagrin Falls
Shaw & Higgins	Chagrin Falls

Sheets, F.	Wellsville
Shumway, H. L.	Cuyahoga Falls
Simonds, F. A.	Chillicothe
Skeels, L.	Ravenna
Smith, W. A.	Newark
Smith, W. F.	Ravenna
Smith & Courtney	Canton
Starks & Barton	Zanesville
Steffey, J. H.	Mt. Union
Sweeney, T. T.	Cleveland
Teeple, T.	Wooster
Thomas	Dayton
Thompson, W. J.	Columbus
Thornton, Mrs. M. A.	Perrysburg
Thorp, F.	Bucyrus
Tibbals Bros.	Painesville
Townsend, P. A.	Windsor
Treasize, J. Q. A.	Springfield, Zanesville
Trost, G.	Toledo
Udall, H. D.	Garrettsville, Warren
Udell & Andrus	Cleveland
Vail, J. H.	Middletown
Van Loo, L.	Cincinnati
Waldack, C.	Cincinnati
Warfel, A. B.	Cadiz, Canton
Wark, J.	Kent
Weckman, J. P.	Cincinnati
Weston, B. W.	Leetonia
Wiles & Bliven	Fremont
Willis & Sons	Portsmouth
Winder, J. W.	Cincinnati
Wonders, L.	Alliance
Wood, T. E.	Ashtabula
Yeager, F. L.	Cleveland
Zay, W.	Mansfield
Zutterling, P.	Cincinnati

OKLAHOMA

Soule, W. S.	Ft. Sill
Winkler, C.	Ft. Sill

OREGON

Abell, F. G.	Portland
Bennett, N. S.	Medford
Britt, P.	Jacksonville
Buchtel & Stolte	Portland
Crawford, J. G.	Harrisburg
Crawford & Paxton	Albany
Davidson, T. G.	Portland
Dennie, O.	Portland
Frost, B. G.	Portland
Goethe, M. A.	Portland
Greene, T. C.	Portland
Harnish	Albany
Hazeltine, M. M.	Baker City
Innes, L. J.	Hillsboro
Maris, H. E.	Ashland
Mayer & Callaghan	Portland
Meresse	Forest Grove
Montgomery, J. H.	Salem
Patterson, F.	Hood River
Riggs, J. W.	Ashland
Scotford, J. H.	Portland
Smith, Mrs. P. H.	Joseph
Stauff	Arago
Stevens, D. M.	Portland
Templeton, J. H.	Corvallis
Watson	Portland
Wells, J. W.	Ashland
Wrenshall Bros	Bandon

PENNSYLVANIA

Abrams, N. H. & E. K.	Brownsville
Aeberli, F.	Allegheny
Albee, S.	Pittsburgh
Allen, A. M.	Columbia, Pottsville
Arndt, J.	Liverpool
Aumspach, J. S.	Uniontown
Bachman, A. M.	Allentown
Bairstow	Warren
Baker, W. W.	Franklin
Barker, J. F.	Petroleum Center
Bartlett & French	Philadelphia
Bashline, W. M.	Titusville
Beckwith, E. W.	Plymouth
Beckwith, R. H.	Bradford
Beidel, H. F.	Shippensburg
Bell, W.	Philadelphia
Bertolet, J. M.	Reading
Bishop & Sons	Chambersburg
Black, I.	Franklin
Bliss, L. R.	Coudersport
Bonine, A. F.	Wilcox
Bonine, R. K.	Tyrone
Boss, D. W.	Mechanicsburg
Bossermann, J. O.	Hanover
Bostwick, J. H.	Bristol
Bowie, E.	Corry
Bowman, J. L.	Mahonoy City
Boyer, H. S.	Selinsgrove
Bradley & Meacham	Greenville
Bretz, G.	Pottsville
Broadbent, S.	Philadelphia
Broadbent & Phillips	Philadelphia
Brown, J.	Mauch Chunk
Bryner, J.	New Bloomfield
Burnite & Welden	Harrisburg
Busey, N. H.	York
Buttorff, R. H.	York
Cargo, R. M.	Allegheny
Carnall, W. F.	Rochester
Chillman, H. E.	Philadelphia
Choate, J. N.	Carlisle
Clouder, H. T.	Bethlehem
Cobb, G. M.	Montrose
Conger, C. E.	Brookville, Tionesta
Cook, W. H.	Greensburg
Copeland & Fleming	Pithole
Couch, J. T.	Landisburg
Cowey, T. W.	Canonsburg
Crane, C. S.	Chambersburg
Crane, O. D.	Blossburg
Cremer, J.	Philadelphia
Cummings, T. & W.	Lancaster
Cummings & Good	York
Dellinger, S. L.	Marietta
Deming	Oil City
DeMorat, O. B.	Philadelphia
Detlor & Dow	Bradford
Detlor & Waddell	Bradford
Dockweiler, M.	Plymouth
Donald & Kline	Huntingdon
Dubois, S. F.	Doylestown
Eberman, E. & P. G.	Lancaster
Eck, J. L.	Kutztown
Ensminger, S. A.	Manheim
Entrekin, W. G.	Manayunk
Evans, E. D.	Titusville
Evans, W. M.	Houtzdale
Fellows, C. T.	Philadelphia
Fennemore & Keeler	Philadelphia
Fisher, A. J.	Towanda
Fisher, S. R.	Norristown
Froelich, C.	Honesdale
Fry, Owen	Allentown
Garrett & Sons	West Chester
Gerdom, H. E.	Lykens
Gettys, T. R.	Bedford
Gihon & Thompson	Philadelphia
Gilbert & Bacon	Philadelphia
Gill, W. L.	Lancaster
Gillespie, S. M.	Butler, New Castle
Ginter, W. M.	Lewisburg
Goodridge, G. J.	York
Goetschius, J. C.	Titusville
Graves, C. H.	Philadelphia
Graves, J.	Delaware Water Gap
Green, G. D.	Pottsville
Greene, G. M.	Johnstown
Gross, W. H. S.	Allentown
Gutekunst, F.	Philadelphia
Hall, S. S.	Carbondale
Harman, H. J.	York Springs
Harner & Harding	Susquehanna
Harris, W. J.	West Pittston
Hearn, C. W.	Philadelphia
Heermans, E. A.	Scranton
Hemple, A. H.	Philadelphia
Hensel, L.	Hawley
Hile, W.	Greensburg

Hinkle, D.	Germantown
Houghton, J. M.	Lewisburg
Hurn, J. W.	Philadelphia
Jameson, C.	Harrisburg
Jarecki, O.	Erie
Jeffers, J. E.	York
Jewell, F.	Scranton
Johnson, G. A.	Winburn
Johnson, N. G.	Erie
Johnson, T. H.	Scranton
Jones, P. B.	Williamsport
Keagy, J.	Chambersburg
Keeler, F. S.	Philadelphia
Keet, A. G.	Harrisburg
Kern & Gaughler	Ashland
Kleckner, M. A.	Allentown, Bethlehem, Mauch Chunk
Knecht, G. V.	Sellersville
Knecht, R.	Easton
Kneeland, C.	Pittsburgh
Kreiter, A. S.	Lititz
Langenheim Bros.	Philadelphia
Leaman & Lee	Reading
Lemer, L.	Harrisburg
Lesher, H. C.	Carlisle, Chambersburg
Lewis, F. M.	Clarion
Line, H. C.	Carlisle
Lippincott, J. H.	Philadelphia
Little, J. M.	Columbia
Lufkin, C. F.	Titusville
Macurdy, J. C.	Oil City
Mahan, T. T.	Pittsburgh
Martin, A. A.	Johnsonburg
Mather, J. A.	Titusville
McAllister & Bro.	Philadelphia
McClees & Germon	Philadelphia
McClurg & Robinson	Pittsburgh
McCormick, A.	Oxford
McElhore, S. E.	Brookville
McPherson, J. G.	McKeesport
Moll, D. C.	Shippensburg
Monroe, J. D.	Liverpool
Moran, J.	Philadelphia
Moran & Story	Philadelphia
Morse, J. W.	Bellefonte
Moyer, S. B.	Pottstown
Mumper, L.	Gettysburg, Littlestown
Naramore, D. H.	Wellsboro
Neiler, J. P.	Sharon
Newell, R.	Philadelphia
Nice, J. F.	Williamsport
Noss, D. N. & H.	New Brighton
Ogilvie, W.	Wilkes Barre
Patton & Dietrich	Reading
Pentz, B. C.	York
Phillips, H. C.	Philadelphia
Phipps, A. W.	New Castle
Purviance, W. T.	Pittsburgh
Queen, J. W.	Philadelphia
Rambo, W. B. G.	York
Rau, W. H.	Philadelphia
Richards, S. Y.	Carbondale
Richmond, J. E.	Honesdale
Riddle, J. R.	Fairview
Ripple Bros.	Milton, Sunbury
Robbins, F.	Oil City
Roberts & Fellows	Philadelphia
Rogers, S. G. & T. W.	Carmichaels
Roshon, C. S.	Harrisburg, Milton
Rote, S. A.	Ridgeway
Rothwell, S. W.	Washington
Ruehlman, R.	Easton
Rust, T. D.	Meadville
Saurman, T. R.	Norristown
Saylor, B. F.	Lancaster
Saylor, C. A.	Reading
Schadle, C. C.	Kittanning
Schartel, E. H.	Lebanon
Schofield, J.	Frankford
Schreiber & Sons	Philadelphia
Schurch	Scranton
Sheaffer, S. C.	Hanover
Simons, M. P.	Philadelphia
Simpson, F. H.	Scranton
Singley, B. L.	Meadville
Slaughenhaupt, H. T.	Littlestown, York Springs
Smith, J. G.	Wrightsville
Smith, S. B.	Newville
Snell, W.	Chester
Spencer, F. M.	Mansfield
Spieler, W. F.	Philadelphia
Stebbins, A. B.	Blossburg
Stehman, J.	Lancaster
Stroud, W.	Norristown
Stuber, F. L.	Bethlehem
Thomas, M.	Shamokin
Tipton, W. H.	Gettysburg
Trask, A. P.	Philadelphia
Tyson Bros.	Gettysburg
Van Neida, D. S.	Ephrata, York
Wager, S. D.	Erie
Weaver, P. S. & H. E.	Hanover
Weber Bros.	Erie
Wenderoth, F. A.	Philadelphia
Wertz	Allentown
West, J.	Pleasantville, Bradford
Willard, O. T.	Philadelphia
Williams, L. M.	Columbia
Wilson, E. L.	Philadelphia
Wilt Bros.	Franklin
Winner, J. L.	Shickshinny
Wolle, R. N.	Lititz
Wood, G. H.	Towanda
Wright, B. L.	Canton
Yeager, F. M.	Reading
Young & Rogers	Washington
Zellner, J.	Mauch Chunk
Zuve, L. W.	Duke Center

RHODE ISLAND

Alden, A. E. & A. O.	Providence
Aylesworth, J. H.	Apponaug
Baker, L.	Providence
Birtles, F. C.	Woonsocket
Black	Newport
Browne, S. B.	Providence
Carlisle, G. M.	Providence
Clark	Wakefield
Ghirardini, N.	Providence
Goodwin, J. W.	Providence
Griffin, T. J.	Bristol
Hacker, F.	Providence
Ide, D. T.	Pawtucket
Kenyon, M. H.	Ashaway
Kindler, F.	Newport
Langworthy, O.	Ashaway
Liscomb, W. C.	Bristol
Lombard, W. H.	Warwick
Manchester, W. C.	Central Falls
Manchester Bros.	Providence
Moffitt, A. L.	Pawtucket
Palmer, I. & J. H.	Providence
Robbins, F.	Westerly
Scofield, E. A.	Westerly
Suddard, J. F.	Providence
Talcott, J. H.	Woonsocket
Tatro, E. D.	Narragansett
Williams, J. A.	Newport, Portsmouth
Willis & Fisher	Woonsocket

SOUTH CAROLINA

Barnard, G. N.	Charleston
Cook, G. S.	Charleston
Cooley, S. A.	Hilton Head
Haas & Peale	Hilton Head
Newell, A.	Charleston
Palmer, J. A.	Aiken
Quinby & Co.	Charleston
Reckling, W. A.	Columbia
Souder, S. T.	Charleston
Teague, B. H.	Aiken
Van Santen, F.	Charleston
Wearn & Hix	Columbia
Wheeler, P. H.	Greenville, Laurens, Newberry
Wren & Wheeler	Newberry

SOUTH DAKOTA

Anderson, P. G.	Redfield

Bailey, Dix & Mead	Ft. Randall
Bean, L. V.	Sioux Falls
Bowman, O. E.	Montrose
Burr, H. C.	Yankton
Butler, H.	Vermilion
Carli, C. H.	Groton
Craig, J. T.	Scotland
Cross, W. R.	Hot Springs
Delong, W. W.	Yankton
Dunn & Easton	Sioux Falls
Johnson, C. W.	Mitchell
Kelly, R. L.	Pierre
Locke Bros	Canton
Meyer, F.	Alcester
Miller, F. Q.	Groton
Morrow, S. J.	Yankton
Oppenheimer, B.	Vermilion, Viewville
Pollock, A.	Deadwood
Quiggle & Johnson	Rapid City
Rodacker & Blanchard	Deadwood
Rounds, A. A.	Sioux Falls

TENNESSEE

Balch, H. A.	Memphis
Barnes, U. N.	Nashville
Braid	Nashville
Craven, W. E.	Memphis
Day, Y.	Memphis
Giers, C. C.	Nashville
Hansbury, T. E.	Memphis
Hilliard B. F.	Memphis
Hunt, A. T.	Knoxville
Hurt, J. W.	Barnesville
Judd, C. S.	Monteagle, Sewanee, Shelbyville, Tracy City
Larcomb, A.	Nashville
Linn, J. B.	Lookout Mountain
Maire, E. G.	Columbia
McCormac, W. J.	Clarksville
Moyston, W. H.	Memphis
Payne, T. H.	Chattanooga
Poole, R.	Nashville
Schleier, T. M.	Knoxville

TEXAS

Bailey, F. B.	Huntsville
Baker, R.	Austin
Barr & Wright	Houston
Berry, Kelley & Chadwick,	Dallas
Bingham, H. L.	San Antonio
Blessing, J. B. & Bro.	Houston
Brock, A. A.	San Antonio
Bruce, W. M.	Marshall
Corley, D. B.	Abilene
Cumming, M.	Corsicana
dePlanque, L.	Corpus Christi
Doerr, H. A.	San Antonio
Finch, E.	Alvarado, Waxahatchie
Fisher, C. H.	Bryan, Calvert
Freeman A.	Dallas
Hardesty, J.	San Antonio
Hillyer, H. B.	Austin
Krueger & Piper	San Antonio
Lynn	Paris
Marks, H. R.	Austin
Metcalf, W. H.	San Antonio
Olyphant, W. J.	Austin
Parker, F.	El Paso
Rose, P. H.	Galveston
Selkirk, J. H. & J.	Matagora
Sloan, W. W.	Jefferson

UTAH

Ace & Aebisher	Logan
Agramonte	Salt Lake City
Cardon, T. B. & Bros.	Logan
Carter, C. W.	Salt Lake City
Johnson, C. E.	Salt Lake City
King, J. B.	Salt Lake City
Martin, E.	Salt Lake City
Martineau, J. H.	Logan
Monson, F. I.	Salt Lake City
Newcomb	Salt Lake City
Sainsbury & Johnson	Salt Lake City
Savage, C. R.	Salt Lake City
Savage & Ottinger	Salt Lake City
Warner	Ogden

VERMONT

Adams	Bethel
Aldrich, G. H.	St. Johnsbury
Atwood, W. H.	Quetchee
Baldwin, A. A.	Ludlow
Barnes, O. C.	Stowe
Bent, A. M.	Cavendish
Bixby, M. J.	Burlington
Blanchard, A. N.	Barre, Montpelier
Brown, A. V.	Middlebury
Burnham, L. G.	Burlington, Morrisville
Bushey, E. H.	Lyndonville
Cady, J.	Brandon
Cheney, C. R.	Stowe
Cheney & Clapp	Brattleboro
Churchill, L. O.	Montpelier, Waterbury
Churchill & Sullivan	Montpelier
Clifford, D. A.	St. Johnsbury
Cooper, W. S.	Winooski Falls
Crosier, F.	Lake Pleasant, Readsboro
Cross, D. H.	Bennington
Culver, W. W.	White River Junction
Currier, F. F.	Montpelier
Cushing, H.	Woodstock
Dart, C.	Bennington
Davis, G. B.	Burlington
Emery, F. B.	Montpelier
Flagg, J.	Fair Haven
Freeman, C. H.	Montpelier
Gage, F. B.	St. Johnsbury
Gauvin Bros.	Burlington
Goodrich, C.	Plainfield
Goodwin, Mrs. R. H.	St. Johnsbury
Hastings, G. H.	St. Johnsbury
Herrick, C. N.	Brattleboro
Hersey, S. O.	Montpelier
Hills & Bowers	Burlington
Houston, E. T.	Waterbury
Howe, C. L. & N. S.	Brattleboro
Jackman, L. E.	Springfield
Kinney & Bent	Castleton
McIntosh, R. M.	Northfield
Meeker, J. B.	Rutland
Merrill, J. O.	Rutland
Merrill, N. L.	Stowe
Miller, W. H.	Vergennes
Nese, J. S.	Windsor
Nichols, C. W.	Rutland
Ober, E. R.	Waterbury
Osterhout, H.	Bennington
Parker, J.	Morrisville
Powers, J. D.	Springfield
Richardson, T. G.	St. Albens
Robinson, F.	Morrisville
Slayton, H. E.	Montpelier
Smith, C. E.	Bristol
Smith, R. H.	St. Albans
Sparhawk, L. T.	West Randolph
Styles, A. F.	Burlington
Swan, W. H.	Springfield
Taft, F.	Chester
Taft, P. W.	Bellows Falls, Saxton River
Taylor, F.	West Charleston
Thayer, E. L.	Newport
Vose, A. S.	Bethel
Walker, G. H.	Putney
Webster, J. N.	Barton
Wormell & Morse	Burlington

VIRGINIA

Anderson, D. H.	Richmond
Anderson & Ennis	Richmond
Boude & Miley	Lexington
Brooks, F.	Roanoke
Cook	Richmond
Ellyson & Taylor	Richmond
Hall, A. M.	Alexandria
Johnson, T. H.	Norfolk
Larrabee, W. F.	Ft. Monroe
Lee	Richmond
Lumkin, E. S.	Richmond

Maxwell, D. C.	Lynchburg
Plecker, A. H.	Salem
Rees, C. R.	Richmond
Selden & Co.	Richmond
Walter, T.	Norfolk
Wright & Co.	Richmond

WASHINGTON

Alverson	Seattle
Beers, S. W.	Walla Walla
Blosser, J. A.	Shohomish
Moore, G.	Seattle
Peterson & Bro.	Seattle
Smith, L. E.	North Yakima

WEST VIRGINIA

Abell, J. N.	Martinsburg
Brinkmeier, T.	Moundsville
Brown, J.	Wheeling
Higgins, T. H.	Wheeling
Hull, H. B.	Parkersburg
Kirk, G. W.	Huntington
Lawson & Lyon	Parkersburg
Matthews, L. V.	Huntington
Partridge, A. C.	Wheeling
Plummer, F. W.	Wheeling
Prickett, W. S.	Fairmount
Rankin, R. J.	Martinsburg
Shafer, J. P.	Morgantown
Shepard & Lyman	Wheeling

WISCONSIN

Anderson, E. J.	Edgerton
Bangs & Eno	Milwaukee
Barks, J. F.	Janesville
Bennett, H. H.	Kilbourn City
Bugbee, V. H.	Waukesha
Bullock, J.	Geneva Lake
Burnick, E. H.	Palmyra Springs
Butterfield, L. T.	Prairie du Chien
Carmody, J. D.	Madison
Clements, M.	Sheboygan
Curtiss, E. R.	Madison
Dahl, A. B.	Madison
Dillon, J. W.	Fond du Lac
Ely, C.	Oshkosh, Racine
Farr & Goodman	Prairie du Chien
Faulkner, F. D.	Chippewa Falls
Gesell, G.	Alma
Glass, C. F. & H. B	Janesville
Hook, W. E.	Neenah
Jones, N. P.	Madison
Kellogg, W. F.	River Falls
Lamb, W. H.	Glidden
Lamb, W. W.	Medford
Lockwood, W. M. & Mrs.	Ripon
Lockwood	Green Lake
Love, J. W.	Portage City
McCollister, E. R.	Baraboo
McPherson & Roloson	Darien
Medlar, J. B.	Jefferson
Morganeier, J. H.	Sheboygan
Moseley Bros.	Janesville
Mould, M.	Baraboo, Devils Lake
Moulton, L. V.	Beaver Dam
Munger, D. G.	Oconomowoc
Noyes, J. B.	Geneva Lake
Nye, J. C.	Platteville
Ordemann, T.	Menomonie
Paris, J.	Fond du Lac
Perkins, H. B.	Wanpara
Piper, W. S.	Portage City
Richardson Bros.	Sparta
Rundlett, C. W.	Watertown
Sherman, W. H.	Milwaukee
Sunderland, W. F.	Neosho
Taylor, S. M.	Berlin
Thomas	Racine
Thuemmler, P. E.	Milwaukee
Truesdell & Silsbee	Kenosha
Tyler & Bugbee	Waukesha
Van de Wall, W. B.	Lancaster
Whipple, J. P.	White Water
Whitesides, W.	Ashland
Wyckoff, J. H.	Ripon
Zierer, J.	Oostburg, St. Nazianz

WYOMING

Brown, A. A.	Rawlins
Kirkland, C. D.	Cheyenne
Mitchell, D. S.	Cheyenne

CANADA

Aldrich, T. A.	Huntington
Anderson, R. W.	Toronto
Arless, G. C.	Montreal
Barbour, T.	Yarmouth
Biddle, H.	Hamilton
Bruckof & Co.	St. John
Buell, O. B.	Montreal
Chase, W.	Halifax
Chisholm, C. R.	Montreal
Claudet, F. G.	New Westminster
Climo, J. S.	St. John
Cole, A. G.	Brockville
Cooper, W. A.	Toronto
Davis, S.	Niagara Falls
Desmarais, L. E.	Montreal
Dion, C.	Montreal
Douglas, J.	Quebec
Duffin & Caswell	Winnepeg
Ellisson & Co.	Quebec
Erb, I.	St. John
Esson, J.	Preston
Ewing & Co.	Toronto
Fardon, G. R.	Victoria
Farmer, G. T.	Three Rivers
Field, J. H.	Montreal
Forrest & Lozo	Belleville, Toronto
Gall, C.	Hamilton
Gallop, S. H.	St. John
Gorst, T.	Windsor
Gregory, J. B.	Fredericton
Hammond, N. D.	Liverpool
Henderson, A.	Montreal
Henderson, H.	Kingston
Hollister	Niagara Falls
Hood	Yarmouth
Hunter, T.	Galt
Inglis, J.	Montreal
Kilburn, M. P.	Coaticook
Leet, W. R.	Danville
LeForest, L.	Toronto
Lindop, W. E.	St. Thomas
Marshall, W.	Guelph
Maynard, R.	Vancouver
McClure, J.	St. John
McCorkindale, H.	Quebec
Mooers, W. A.	Fredericton
Murdock, W. & J.	Windsor
Notman, W.	Montreal
O'Conner, W.	Toronto
Palmer, E. J.	Toronto
Parks, G. J.	Montreal
Parsons, S. H.	St. Johns (Nfd.)
Peabody, F. H.	Mansonville
Segree & Co.	Fredericton
Sheldon & Davis	Kingston
Simonson, G. F.	St. John
Smith, F. M. B.	Hamilton
Stark, R.	Paris, Woodstock
Stiff Bros.	Ottawa
Talbot	Quebec
Taylor, F.	Coaticook
Taylor, G. T.	Fredericton
Topley	Ottawa
Turner, E. J.	Toronto
Turner, E. R.	Montreal
Vallee, L. P.	Quebec
Willis, J.	Ottawa
Wright, C. H.	Hamilton

A CHECKLIST OF STEREOGRAPHERS CITED

This alphabetic register of stereographers and publishers cited elsewhere in this book serves as an index as well as a checklist. Each name is accompanied by the following information: country in which the photographer maintained his place of business, approximate date of stereo activity, and references to the pages on which the photographer is cited or illustrated. Illustrations are indicated in bold face type.

The date of stereo activity is indicated by decades, 5 = 1850's, 6 = 1860's, 7 = 1870's, 0 = 1900's, 1 = 1910's, etc. If a photographer produced stereo views for only a few years over a period such as 1868-1872, he may be placed in either decade or both, depending upon the importance of his work. The decades given do not indicate his total period of operation. Many photographers who remained in business thirty years, published stereographs only briefly, often only three or four years.

The country indicates the location of the photographer's studio or business. Many photographers settled in countries other than their birth or worked in more than one country.

Similar names which are repeated may or may not refer to the same person, but the identity has not been established.

The country is usually indicated by an abbreviation as follows:

Arg, Argentina	*Hun*, Hungary
Aus, Austria	*Ind*, India
Austl, Australia	*Ire*, Ireland
Az, Azores	*It*, Italy
Belg, Belgium	*Jam*, Jamaica
Berm, Bermuda	*Jap*, Japan
Braz, Brazil	*Jer*, Jerusalem
Bulg, Bulgaria	*Mex*, Mexico
Can, Canada	*Neth*, Netherlands
Chile	*Nor*, Norway
China	*NZ*, New Zealand
Col, Columbia	*Peru*
CR, Costa Rica	*Pol*, Poland
Cuba	*Port*, Portugal
Den, Denmark	*Rus*, Russia
Ecu, Ecuador	*S Af*, South Africa
Egypt	*Swed*, Sweden
**Fr*, France	*Switz*, Switzerland
GB, Great Britain	*Tas*, Tasmania
**Ger*, Germany	*Tun*, Tunisia
Gib, Gibralter	*Tur*, Turkey
Gr, Greece	*Uru*, Uruguay
Guat, Guatemala	*USA*, United States
Haiti	*WI*, West Indies
Haw, Hawaii	

*Fr (Ger), refers to Alsace-Lorraine, before 1870 France, thereafter Germany.

Nearly 4000 photographers have been cited in this book, 3300 of whom operated in the United States and 650 who operated in fifty countries, but mostly in western Europe. Approximately ten names, not specifically cited, are included without page references.

Hundreds of photographers published stereo views of many parts of the world. References to most of these photographers are in the narrative and in the page numbers in this list.

The list is in no sense complete, less than half of the stereographers known to me have been included. Many photographers are known to me through only one or two stereographs. Unless these examples presented some artistic, documentary or technical feature of significance, the name has been passed over. Unquestionably, many of these photographers are fully as important as those whose names appear here.

APPENDIX
AN ESTIMATE OF THE NUMBER OF AMERICAN STEREOGRAPHERS

Several years ago it occurred to me that it should be possible to estimate the number of stereographers in the United States and Canada by comparing a large random sample of carte de visite photographers with my checklist of 6150 stereographers. Since, for all practical purposes, every photographer between 1860 and 1890 produced cartes de visite and this period coincides with the most active period of stereography 1859-1885, it should be a simple matter to determine what percentage published stereographs and derive various other ratios.

Dealers in photographic images scattered throughout the United States provided me with samples ranging from 200 to more than 2000 cartes de visite* from which I was able to compile a checklist of names, locations and dates of operation. A total of 3784 carte de visite photographers who operated before 1890, representing all states except Arizona, New Mexico, Oklahoma, Wyoming and, of course Alaska, comprise the raw data.

Only names and images that could be dated within an accuracy of two years are included in the tabulations which follow. A photographer who operated in more than one decade is counted only once, being placed in the period in which his stereographs—if any—were principally issued.

Breakdown of decades:

	Number of cdv photographers	*Number who produced stereos*	*Percentage*
1860's	1178	304	25.8
1870's	1792	816	45.0
1880's	814	126	15.4
Totals	3784	1246	32.6

My data on Pennsylvania photographers are more extensive than for any other state:

682	235	34.4%

The two percentages, 32.6 and 34.4 are in such close agreement, the ratio is probably reliable.

The over-all ratio for the 1860's is, however, somewhat misleading. The popularity of stereographs increased progressively during the 1860's reaching a maximum in the early 1870's.

Photographers operating 1860-65	309	58	18.7%
Photographers operating 1868-73	1650	723	43.8%

There are also some significant population and geographic relationships:

Photographers operating in:

The 5 largest cities in the U.S.	403	89	22.8%
The 15 largest cities in the U.S.	716	183	25.5%
50 cities, population 12,000-30,000	1252	394	31.4%
100 towns, population 2,500-8,000	709	363	51.2%
50 villages, population 800-1,500	134	71	53.0%

These figures suggest that the smaller the community the more likely the photographer produced stereographs. Furthermore, it is highly probable that a large number of stereographers who operated in small communites remain unrecorded.

To state the reciprocal of the ratio between carte de visite and stereo photographers: if one third of the photographers produced stereographs, then my index of 6150 stereographers indicates that there were approximately 18,000 photographers in the United States. But my index is incomplete.

Comparison of census records (1860, 1870, 1880) and business directories (1860-1885) of twenty Pennsylvania cities and towns, indicates that my file is less than 50% complete.

Incidentally, the census enumerations of these cities and towns (1860 and 1870) do not record 26.3% of the photographers who were *actually operating at the time of compilation*. Furthermore, those photographers who were operating only in intervening years, such as 1865-1868, 1871-1877, were not recorded in any census.

The available business directories do not list 15.5% of the photographers who were actually operating at the time of compilation.

It would appear, therefore, that the total number of photographers who operated in the United States and Canada between 1860 and 1890 exceeds 40,000 and the number of stereographers probably exceeds 12,000.

**Acknowledgments:* I am grateful for the generous cooperation of the following persons who made it possible for me to examine more than 25,000 cartes de visite: Nyal Anderson (Salt Lake City), Sil Bernard (Philadelphia), Dan Deeks (Cambridge, Mass.), Mrs. Bonnie Douglas (Jackson, Cal.), John Hess (North Andover, Mass.), E. Hooper (Ossipee, N.H.), Cliff Krainik (Chicago), Ronald Lieberman (Glen Rock, Pa.), Frederick C. Lightfoot (Greenport, N.Y.), Art Lyon (Hartford, Conn.), Carl Mautz (Portland, Ore.), Robert L. Merriam (Conway, Mass.), Russell Norton (New Haven, Conn.), Kenneth Partymiller (State College, Pa.), Michael Scharfman (Farmingdale, N.Y.), Charles Semich (Chichester, N.H.), Gary and Linda Vroegindewey (Columbia, Mo.), D. C. Wheeler (Short Beach, Conn.), and Stephen White (Los Angeles, Cal.)

Scores of other persons have provided me with smaller samples or loaned cartes from their private collections. Special thanks are due William Frassanito (Gettysburg), Tom Meador (San Angelo, Tex.) and Glenn Skillin (Philadelphia).

BIBLIOGRAPHY: SOURCES OF INFORMATION

Instead of a conventional bibliography, the reader is here provided with a survey of sources of information which should be helpful in researching stereographs and the photographers who published them.

There is a vast and ever-increasing history of photography. Unfortunately, very few books contain extensive information about stereographs. Often, in fact, stereo views are mentioned in passing or ignored completely. Yet many such books provide excellent background and perspective.

Books useful in research fall into six general categories:

1. General histories of photography
2. Biographies of photographers
3. "Picture books" which identify photographers
4. Exhibition catalogues
5. Guide books to sets of stereographs
6. Monographs, especially on subjects that attracted photographers.

Articles in periodical publications vary considerably in reliability and scope. Several photographic historical periodicals, most of which have been established within the past decade, have become indispensable:

Stereo World (National Stereoscopic Association)
Northlight (Photographic Historical Society of America)
Photographica (New York Photographic Historical Society)
Image (International Museum of Photography at George Eastman House)
Journal of the History of Photography (Taylor & Francis, Ltd., London)

The following nineteenth century periodicals contain many articles on stereography, stereographers and specific series of stereographs, especially during the period 1850-1880.

Humphrey's Journal of Photography and Allied Arts and Sciences (= *The Daguerrean Journal*), New York, 1850-1870.
Photographic Art Journal (later, *The Photographic and Fine Art Journal*) New York, 1851-1860.
Photographic News, London, 1858-1908.
Philadelphia Photographer, Philadelphia, 1864-1885, succeeded by
Wilson's Photographic Magazine, Philadelphia, 1889-1914.
Anthony's Bulletin of Photography, New York, 1870-1902.

BOOKS

Andrews, Ralph W.
Picture Gallery Pioneers; First Photographers of the West, 1850-1875.
192 pp. illus., Superior Publishing Co., Seattle, Wash., 1964.

Barnard, George N.
Photographic Views of Sherman's Campaign.
With a New Preface by Beaumont Newhall, 18 pp; 61 pls. Dover Publications, New York, 1977. A reprint of the 1866 edition published by Barnard.

Beck, Tom
George M. Bretz, Photographer in the Mines.
73 pp. illus. University of Baltimore County Library, Baltimore, 1977.

Belous, Russell E. and Weinstein, Robert A.
Will Soule: Indian Photographer at Fort Sill, Oklahoma, 1869-1874.
120 pp. illus. Ward Ritchie Press, Los Angeles, 1969.

Bill, Jay
Victorian Cameraman: Francis Firth's Views of Rural England, 1850-1898.
112 pp. illus. David & Charles, Newton Abbott, 1973.

Brewster, David
The Stereoscope, Its History, Theory and Construction.
235 pp. illus., John Camden Hotten, London, 1870.

Buckland, Gail
Reality Recorded, Early Documentary Photography.
127 pp. illus. New York Graphic Society, Greenwich, Conn., 1974.

Castle, Peter
Collecting and Valuing Old Photographs.
168 pp. illus. Garnstone Press, London, 1973.

Christ, Yvan
L'age d'or de la photographie.
107 pp. illus. Vincent, Freal & Co., Paris, 1965.

Clark, W. S.
Elements of Geography and History . . . Illustrated by Stereoscopic Views.
401 pp. Clark, Lake & Company, Rockford, Ill., 1871.

Coke, Van Deren
The Painter and the Photograph, from Delacroix to Warhol.
2nd ed. 324 pp. illus. University of New Mexico Press, Albuquerque, 1972.

Coke, Van Deren (ed.)
One Hundred Years of Photographic History. Essays in Honor of Beaumont Newhall.
180 pp. illus. University of New Mexico Press, Albuquerque, 1975.

Columbia University Library
A Catalogue of the Epstean Collection on the History and Science of Photography and its Applications, especially to the Graphic Arts.
No pagination. Columbia University Press, New York, 1937.
Helios Reprint edition, Pawlet, Vermont, 1972.

Darrah, William C.
Stereo Views: A History of Stereographs in America and Their Collection.
255 pp. illus. W. C. Darrah, Gettysburg, Penna., 1964.

Delamotte, Philip H.
The Practice of Photography–A Manual for Students and Amateurs.
67 pp. American edition. Photographic Fine Art Journal, New York, 1854.

Ellison, D. J.
Italy through the Stereoscope.
602 pp. Underwood & Underwood, New York, 1903.

Emery, M. S.
Real Children in Many Lands.
212 pp. Underwood & Underwood, New York, 1905.

Epstean, Edward *see*, Columbia University Library

Erwin, Paul F.
Andrew S. Iddings, Explorer: The Story of His Life and Travels.
421 pp. illus. Creative Writers & Publishers, Cincinnati, Ohio, 1967.

Fowler, Don D.
"Photographed All the Best Scenery." Jack Hillers' Diary of the Powell Expedition, 1871-1875.
220 pp. illus. University of Utah Press, Salt Lake City, 1972.

Frassanito, William
Gettysburg: A Journey in Time.
248 pp. illus. Charles Scribner's Sons, New York, 1972.

Gernsheim Helmut
Creative Photography: Aesthetic Trends, 1839 to Modern Times.
258 pp. illus. Bonanza Books, New York, 1972.

Gernsheim, Helmut and Alison
A History of Photography–from the earliest use of the Camera Obscura in the Eleventh Century up to 1914.
359 pp. illus. Oxford University Press, London, 1955.

Gidal, Tim N.
Modern Photojournalism: Origin and Evolution 1910-1933.
96 pp. illus., Macmillan, New York, 1973.

Gilbert, George
Collecting Photographica. The Images and Equipment of the First Hundred Years of Photography.
302 pp. illus. Hawthorn Books, New York, 1976.

Greenhill, Ralph
Early Photography in Canada.
173 pp. illus. Oxford University Press, Toronto, 1965.

Griffith and Griffith Company
Stereoscopic Views and How to Sell Them.
88 pp. 2nd ed. Philadelphia, 1904.

Hannary, John
Roger Fenton of Crimble Hall.
184 pp. illus. David R. Godine, Boston, 1976.

Hanson, Joseph M.
The World War Through the Stereoscope.
593 pp. (1st ed. 1923) 4th ed. Keystone View Company, Meadville, Penna., 1927.

Hart, A., Jr.
The World in the Stereoscope. A Series of Sketches. 2nd ed.
411 pp. Hart & Anderson, New York, 1872.

Hendricks, Gordon
Eadweard Muybridge: The Father of the Motion Picture.
271 pp. illus. Grossman (Viking Press), New York, 1975

Holmes, Burton
A Trip Around the World through the Telebinocular.
593 pp. Keystone View Company, Meadville, Penna., 1930.
[Superseded Holmes, *A Trip Around the World through the Stereoscope*, 289 pp., 1926.]

Homer, Rachel
The legacy of Josiah Johnson Hawes, 19th Century Photographer of Boston.
131 pp. illus. Barre Publishers, Barre, Mass., 1972.

Horan, James D.
Timothy O'Sullivan: America's Forgotten Photographer.
334 pp. illus. Doubleday & Co., Garden City, N.Y., 1966.

Hurlbut, Jesse L.
Traveling in the Holy Land through the Stereoscope.
220 pp. Underwood & Underwood, New York, 1st ed. 1900; 2nd ed. 1905.

Jackson, Clarence S.
Picture Maker of the Old West–William Henry Jackson.
308 pp. illus. Charles Scribner's Sons, New York, 1947.

Jammes, Andre and Sobieszek, Robert
French Primitive Photography.
[No pagination] illus. Aperture, New York, 1969.

Jenkins, Harold F.
Two Points of View: The History of the Parlor Stereoscope.
77 pp. illus. World in Color Productions, Elmira, N.Y., 1957.

Jenkins, Reese V.
Images and Enterprise. Technology and the American Photographic Industry, 1839-1925.
371 pp. illus. Johns Hopkins University, Baltimore, 1975.

Jones, Edgar
Father of Art Photography–O. G. Rejlander, 1813-1875.
112 pp. illus. New York Graphic Society, Greenwich, Conn., 1973.

Jones, John
Wonders of the Stereoscope.
2 vols. 126 pp. illus.+ 48 card reproductions.
Alfred A. Knopf, New York, 1976.

Keystone View Company
Stereoscopic Encyclopedia. Guide to the Keystone "600 Set."
593 pp. Meadville, Pa., 1st ed. 1906; 7th, 1920.

Lothrop, Eaton S., Jr.
A Century of Cameras from the Collection of the International Museum of Photography at George Eastman House.
150 pp. illus. Morgan & Morgan, New York, 1973.

Mangan, Terry W.
Colorado on Glass.
186 pp. illus. Sundance, Ltd., Denver, 1977.

Mathews, Oliver
Early Photographs and Early Photographers. A Survey in Dictionary Form.
198 pp. illus. Reedminster Publishers, London, 1973.

Meredith, Roy
Mr. Lincoln's Cameraman: Mathew B. Brady.
2nd ed. 368 pp. illus. Charles Scribner's Sons, New York, 1946, reprinted Dover Publications, 1974.

Moss, George H., Jr.
Double Exposure: Early Stereographic Views of Historic Monmouth County, New Jersey and their Relationship to Pioneer Photography.
176 pp. illus. Plowshare Press, Seabright, N.J., 1971.

Naef, Weston J. and Wood, James N.
Era of Exploration, The Rise of Landscape Photography in the American West, 1860-1885.
260 pp. illus. New York Graphic Society & Metropolitan Museum of Art, New York, 1975.

Newhall, Beaumont
The History of Photography from 1939 to the Present Day.
256 pp. illus. Museum of Modern Art & Simon & Schuster, New York, 1949.
Rev. ed. Secker & Warburg, London, 1972.

Newhall, Beaumont
The Daguerreotype in America.
176 pp. illus. Duell, Sloan & Pearce, New York, 1961.

Newhall, Beaumont & Edkins, Diana E.
William H. Jackson.
158 pp. illus. Morgan & Morgan, Dobbs Ferry, N.Y., 1974.

Osborne, Albert F.
The Stereograph and The Stereoscope with Special Maps and Books forming a Travel System.
288 pp. illus. Underwood & Underwood, New York, 1909.

Ricalton, James
China through the Stereoscope. A Journey through the Dragon Empire at the Time of the Boxer Rebellion.
358 pp. Underwood & Underwood, New York, 1901.

Robinson, Henry Peach
Pictorial Effect in Photography.
199 pp. illus. Piper & Carter, London, 1869.
Helios reprint ed. Pawlet, Vermont, 1971.

Root, Marcus A.
The Camera and the Pencil, or the Heliographic Art.
456 pp. illus. M. A. Root, Philadelphia, 1864.

Rudisill, Richard
Mirror Image: The Influence of the Daguerreotype on American Society.
276 pp. illus. University of New Mexico Press, Albuquerque, 1971.

Sloane, Howard N. and Lucille L.
A Picture History of American Mining from Pre-Columbian Times to the Present Era.
342 pp. illus. Crown Publishers, New York, 1970.

Snyder, Joel and Munson, Doug
The Documentary Photograph as a Work of Art; American Photographs 1860-1876.
49 pp. illus. David and Alfred Smart Gallery, University of Chicago, 1976.

Taft, Robert
Photography and the American Scene–A Social History, 1839-1889.
546 pp. illus. Macmillan Company, New York, 1938.
Dover reprint edition, New York, 1970.

Thomas, D. B.
The Science Museum Photography Collection.
113 pp. illus. Her Majesty's Stationers Office, London, 1969.

Tilden, Freeman
Following the Frontier with F. J. Haynes–Pioneer Photographer of the Old West.
406 pp. illus. Alfred A. Knopf, New York, 1964.

Towler, John
The Silver Sunbeam.
351 pp. Joseph H. Ladd, New York, 1864.
Reprint ed. Morgan & Morgan, Hastings-on-Hudson, N.Y., 1969.

Turchon, Lesta V. and McLaird, James D.
The Black Hills Expedition of 1875.
[Jenney-Newton Expedition; McGillicudy, photographer; Benecke, publisher].
126 pp. Dakota Wesleyan Press, Mitchell, S.D., 1975.

Vogel, Hermann (translated by Edward Moelling)
Handbook of the Practice and Art of Photography.
356 pp. illus. Benerman & Wilson, Philadelphia, 1871.

Wadsworth, Nelson B.
Through Camera Eyes.
180 pp. illus. Brigham Young University Press, Provo, Utah, 1975.

Ward, John L.
The Criticism of Photography as Art.
Chapters 1 and 2 (pp. 1-43).
78 pp. illus. Univ. Fla. Humanities Mon. 32, Gainesville, Fla., 1970.

Weinstein, Robert A. and Booth, Larry
Collection, Use, and Care of Historical Photographs.
222 pp. illus. American Association for State and Local History, Nashville, 1977.

Welling, William
Collectors' Guide to Nineteenth Century Photographs.
204 pp. illus. Macmillan Company, New York, 1976.

ARTICLES

Bendix, Howard E.
"Glass Stereo Views: A Statistical Review"
Stereo World, **1** (3):2-4, 10, 1974.

Bendix, Howard E.
"Discovered! Early Bierstadt Photographs"
Photographica **6** (8):4, 5; (9):7, 10; (10):7; **7**(1):4, 1974, 1975.

Bill, J
"Francis Bedford, 1816-1894"
Univ. New Mex Art Bull. No. 7:16-21, 1973.

Carter, Kate B.
"The Story of an Old Album," in
Heart throbs of the West, pp. 101-152, illus. Daughters of Utah Pioneers, Salt Lake City, 1947.

Christ, Yvan
"Le Temp des Crinolines a Travers Les Vues Stereoscopiques."
Jardin des Arts no. 92:22-29, 1962.

Dexter, Lorraine
"Gage of St. Johnsbury—Hills and Dales, 1859"
Vermonter **4** (8):23-29, illus., 1966.

Grosscup, Jeffrey P.
"Stereoscopic Eye on the Frontier West" [Fisk Expedition, 1866].
Mont. Mag. Hist. **25** (2):36-50, 1975.

Hannavy, John
"The Rise and Fall of the Victorian Stereoscope."
Photo. Technique **3** (1):43, illus., 1975.

Henisch, B. A. and H. K.
"Robertson of Constantinople"
Image **17** (3):1-11, illus., 1974.

Hughes, C. Jabez
"Art-Photography: Its Scope and Characteristics."
Photo. News **5**:4, 1861.

Laird, John D.
"Hurst's Stereoscopic Studies of Natural History"
Stereo World **3** (2):12, 13, illus., 1976.

Manchester, Ellen
"Alexander Hesler, Chicago Photographer"
Image **6** (1):7-10, illus., 1973.

Newhall, Beaumont
[Joel Emmons Whitney]
Minn. Hist. **34**:28-33, portrait.

Newhall, Nancy
"The caption, The Mutual Relation of Words and Photographs."
Aperture **1** (1):19-23, 1952.

Peterich, Gerda
"Nineteenth Century Architectural Photographs—A Survey of Approaches and Techniques."
Image **7** (10):220-232, 1958.

Peterich, Gerda
"Photography of the Great Exhibition."
Image **7** (3):53-58, illus., 1958.

Sachse, Julius F.
"Philadelphia's Share in the Development of Photography."
Jour. Frank Inst. **135**:271-287, 1893.

Sellers, Coleman
"An Old Photographic Club." [The Amateur Photographic Exchange Club.]
Anthony's Photo. Bull. serially, May-Nov., 1888.
Reprinted serially, *Stereo World.* Vols. **1**, **2**, 1974-1975.

Sobieszek, Robert A.
"A Note on Early Photomontage Images."
Image **15**:(4):19-24, 1972.

Taft, Robert
"A Photographic History of Early Kansas" [Alex Gardner].
Kans. Hist. Quart. **3**:3-14, 1934; **6**:175, 1937.
Reprinted, with list of titles, in *Stereo World* **3** (2):4, 5, 1976.

Turrill, Charles H.
"An Early California Photographer: C. E. Watkins."
News Notes California Librs. **13** (1):29-37, 1918.

CATALOGS AND TRADE LISTS

About 200 photographers' and publishers' catalogs and trade lists have been recorded. Surely many times this number were distributed. A small selection of the more important is given here. Attention is called to the fact that in these sixteen catalogs alone more than 24,000 titles of stereographs are listed.

The limitations of each catalog must be carefully evaluated. It is accurate only at the time of publication. Obviously it cannot include any titles issued after that date. Less obviously, the catalog is seldom complete. Almost every photographer deleted numbers or titles, made substitutions, and made no mention of custom work.

The first three classic catalogs listed are not in alphabetic order. Those which follow are in sequence.

London Stereoscopic Company, New York City, 1860.
50 pp. lists about 2,000 views.

Anthony, E. and H. T.
"New Catalogue of Stereoscopes and Views" New York, ca. 1867
103 pp. lists 2,000 views; many early titles are not included.

Kilburn Brothers,
"Catalogue of Stereoscopic Views" Littleton, N.H., 1875.
44 pp. lists about 2,100 views.

Bennett, H. H. Studio
"Complete Stereograph List of H. H. Bennett." Kilbourn City, Wisc. 1977
[Compiled from Bennett's Catalogue of 1883 and earlier lists.]
Lists about 1,800 titles.

Brown, W. Henry
"Catalogue of Stereoscopic and Large Views of New Mexico." Santa Fe, 1879.
14 pp. Excellent narrative, lists 150 views.

Continent Stereoscopic Company
"Catalogue of Stereoscopic Views"
23 pp. New York, ca. 1877. Lists about 1,000 views.

Gardner, Alexander
"Catalogue of Photographic Incidents of the War." Washington, D.C. September, 1863.
28 pp. Lists about 700 views. Credits each negative to its photographer.

Houseworth, Thomas & Co.
"Catalogue of Photographic Views of Scenery on the Pacific Coast." San Francisco, October, 1869.
76 pp., plus supplement. Lists about 2,000 views.

Negretti & Zambra
"Egypt and Nubia. Descriptive Catalogue of One Hundred Stereoscopic Views . . . by Francis Frith." London, 1858, 18 pp.

Stoddard, S. R.
"Catalogue of Stereographs of New York Scenery."
11 pp. Glens Falls, N.Y., 1877. Lists about 1,600 views.

Soule, John P.
"Catalogue of Stereographs."
27 pp. Boston, Mass., 1867. Lists about 900 views.

Thorne, George W.
"Catalogue and Price List of Photograph Albums and Photographs."
23 pp. New York, 1866. Lists about 900 views.

Tipton, W. H.
"Catalogue of Photographic Views of the Battlefield of Gettysburg."
36 pp. Gettysburg, Pa. 1894. Lists more than 1,600 stereo views. Tipton issued his first catalogue in 1873, the second in 1876.

White, H. C. Company
"Catalogue [no. 6] of Stereographs."
84 pp. North Bennington, Vt. 1905. Lists more than 6,000 titles.

Wilson, Hood and Company
"Annual Illustrated Catalogue."
148 pp. Philadelphia, 1873.
These catalogues include equipment, supplies and photographs.
The series of stereographs handled by Wilson are given on pp. 146-148.

Woodward, C. W.
"Publisher of Stereoscopic Views."
40 pp. Rochester, N.Y., 1876. Lists about 3,000 views.

Ephemeral Sales Catalogues

The auction and sales catalogues issued by dealers in photographica often contain data and illustrations of seldom-seen stereographs. These records provide a continuing flow of new information. Although some catalogues give minimal descriptive notes, others are highly authoritative and scholarly. The earliest useful dealers' catalogues issued in the United States appeared about 1942.

Prices for stereographs remained nearly stable from 1940 to 1965 but since that time, have risen steadily and sharply commensurate with the growing interest in photographica throughout the world.

CHECKLISTS OF PHOTOGRAPHERS

(Chicago) "Chicago Photographers: 1847 through 1900" 80 pp. Chicago Historical Society, 1958.

(Colorado) Harber, Opal
"Photographers and the Colorado Scene 1853-1900." 38 pp. Denver Public Library, 1961.

(Lancaster, Pennsylvania) Heisey, M. Luther
"The Art of Photography in Lancaster." *Lanc. Co. Hist. Soc. Pap.* **51**:93-113, 1947.

(Maine) Darrah, William C.
"A Checklist of Maine Photographers who issued stereographs." 8 pp. *Maine Hist. Soc. Newsletter.* Spec. Suppl., May, 1967.

(Newburyport, Massachusetts) Varrell, William
"Newburyport: Its Pioneer Photographer." *Stereo World* **2** (1):1, 16; (2):2, 15, 16, 1975.

(New Mexico) Rudisill, Richard
"Photographers of the New Mexico Territory, 1854-1912." 74 pp. Museum of New Mexico, 1973.

(Rochester, New York) Fordyce, Robert
"Stereo Photography in Rochester to 1900." 22 pp. privately published, 1977.

(St. Louis, Missouri) van Ravenswaay, Charles
"Pioneer Photographers of St. Louis." *Missouri Hist. Quart.* **10**:48-71, 1953.

(Utah) Wadsworth, Nelson
"Zion's Cameramen: Early Photographers of Utah and the Mormons." *Utah Hist. Quart.* **40**:24-54, 1972.

(Western United States) Mautz, Carl E.
"Checklist of Western Photographers." Rev. ed. 20 pp. privately published, Portland, Ore., 1976.

Comprehensive checklists of photographers of California, Illinois, Massachusetts, Michigan, Ohio, Pennsylvania, Texas and Vermont are in preparation. These should become available within the next four or five years.

SUPPLEMENTARY REFERENCES

Local newspapers: advertisements, obituaries, news items and notices.

City and Business Directories.

Travel Guides, especially
- Appleton's (USA) 1852-1885
- Baedecker's (Leipzig; American editions published by C. Scribner's) 1859-1930.

United States Decennial Census records.

Gazetteers, especially 1850-1890.

Postal Guides

The gazetteers and postal guides are helpful in locating towns that have disappeared, changed names, or have been absorbed by larger metropolitan cities, etc.

SUBJECT INDEX

Numerals in boldface refer to illustration numbers.
Page numbers197-212 refer to the lists of North American stereographers arranged by States.